P9-BIN-491

Alberta, 1954 – 1979
A Provincial Bibliography

Compiled by

Gloria M. Strathern

The University of Alberta
Department of Printing Services
Edmonton
1982

© Gloria M. Strathern 1981

Published in honour of Alberta's 75th Anniversary

Strathern, Gloria Margaret
Alberta, 1954-1979: a provincial bibliography

Includes indexes

ISBN 0-88864-949-X

REF.
Z1392.A32S89 015.7123

Printed in Canada

31,832

CAMROSE LUTHERAN COLLEGE
Library

Contents

Foreword vii
Introduction ix
Note on Methodology xi
Bibliographies Cited xiii
List of Library Location Symbols xv

Alberta Bibliography

General Works

Bibliography 1
General Works 1
Bibliography of Alberta 1
Libraries and Librarianship 2
Publishing and Journalism 6

Humanities

Religion 9
General Works 9
History of Religion 19
Church Histories 32
Linguistics 53
General Works 53
Indian Languages 56
Slavic Languages 60
Literature 62
General Works 62
Anthologies 66
Fiction 71
Poetry 98
Drama 116
Humour 123

Fine Arts 125
General Works 125
Exhibition Catalogues 128

Performing Arts 141
General Works 141
Magic and Conjuring 141

Music 155
General Works 155
Music Scores 156

Social Sciences

Education 165
General Works 165
School History 171
Higher Education 181

Recreation 184

Sociology 196
General Works 196
Social Relations 201
Social Issues 203
Social Organizations 213
Minority Groups 216

Anthropology and Archaeology 235

Folklore and Legends 244

Economics 246
General Works 246
Business, Industry and Labour 256
Oil and Gas Industries 269

Communication and Transportation 276

Politics 282
National and International Politics 282
Provincial Politics 287
Local and Municipal Politics 294

Law 296
General Works 296
Law Enforcement 299

Geography 302
General Works 302
Description and Travel 313
Gazetteers and Atlases 320
Guide Books 321

History 325
Genealogy and Family History 325
General History 329
Military History. 331
Western Canadian History 333
Alberta History 339
Local History 343

Sciences

Natural History 401

Environment 404

Health Sciences. 406

Agriculture. 410
General Works 410
Farm and Ranch Life 420

Indexes

Author Index 429

Title Index 593

Subject Index 673

Series Index 733

Foreword

Gloria M. Strathern's proposal to prepare an updated bibliography of Alberta books was an ambitious undertaking – one, I am happy to say, that received full support from Alberta's 75th Anniversary Commission.

Any bibliography is an exacting and challenging task. The end product becomes a vital tool for students, researcers, teachers, historians, librarians – indeed almost all sectors of the public. It must provide a scholarly and reliable source of information on all sorts of literary subjects and their authors which, in turn, reveals so much about the heart, mind and soul of a people.

Gloria Strathern's work is, without question, a much-needed complement to the classic reference in its field – Bruce B. Peel's *Bibliography of the Prairie Provinces to 1953*. I commend her and those who labored with her to make this bibliography what it surely is: an enduring and important addition to the cultural stature of this province.

Mary J. LeMessurier
Minister
Alberta Culture

Introduction

This bibliography is published with the aid of a 75th Anniversary grant from the Alberta 75th Anniversary Commission established by the Government of Alberta to commemorate the seventy-fifth year of the Province and is dedicated to the citizens of the Province. The purpose of the bibliography is to document the history and progress of the Province from 1954 to 1979. The work attempts to provide a guide to books, pamphlets, and theses relating to Alberta, by Albertans, both native-born and adopted residents, or published by Alberta regional presses.

Excluded are serial publications, scientific, technical and specialized professional materials. Government publications are not included. They are comprehensively treated in Joseph Forsyth's *Government publications relating to Alberta: A bibliography of publications of the Government of Alberta from 1905 - 1968, and the Government of Canada relating to the province of Alberta from 1867 - 1968,* and in the ongoing *Publications Catalogue* of the Alberta Government Services Public Affairs Bureau.

This bibliography is intended to complement, not duplicate existing works. Bruce B. Peel's classic *Bibliography of the Prairie Provinces to 1953* pioneered the study of publications relating to the Canadian Prairies. Since Peel, bibliographies of Manitoba and Saskatchewan have been published, as have bibliographies of special topics.

As far as could be determined, all identified authors with significant associations with Alberta have been included. Because Alberta is a young province with a mobile population, it has been difficult to identify all items qualifying for inclusion. Alberta-born authors whose entire careers were unrelated to the province are excluded. Writers whose careers were associated with the province in part only, are included only with respect to those aspects relevant to Alberta. Inevitably, some subjective judgements were required.

The association of Alberta with the province of Saskatchewan has been particularly close. Hence, a number of publications eligible for inclusion in this work also appear in Ved Arora's *Saskatchewan Bibliography,* either because they were published in that province or the authors had associations with both provinces. Publications of Alberta regional presses, including those on non-Alberta subjects are included as part of the provincial record. However, Hurtig Publishers and the University of Alberta Press are regarded respectively as a national and a scholarly press. Therefore only Alberta-related items from these publishers are included. All relevant identified masters and doctoral theses in the field have been included.

Within the humanities and social sciences, the bibliography attempts to list popular and scholarly works comprehensively, with the exclusion of technical and specialized professional publications. Works written for children are included, but not school textbooks, with certain exceptions. At the request of scholars and librarians, Ann Anderson's Cree-language texts are included, while other items not clearly identified as textbooks are also included.

Although scientific publications are outside the scope of the bibliography, popular and general works and histories of organizations are provided. The importance of agricultural activities in the province, necessitated the inclusion of agricultural histories and general studies, and accounts of farm and ranch life.

It remains to thank those who have assisted in this undertaking. I am particularly grateful to the staffs on the libraries visited and to Jana Lamont and Ron Senda of the University of Alberta's Computing Services Division; Mr. Michael P. Hades and Mr. Gary Botting, Father G. Durocher for checking all French language material; Mr. B. B. Peel and Professor N. Parker-Jervis of the Western Canadian Publications Project for advice and encouragement. To graduate assistants Catherine Wang, Harriet Judge, Fern Russell and Kathleen Bowman, and the many others who have provided assistance, especially the Alberta 75th Anniversary Commission. Alberta Culture and the Faculty of Library Science, I acknowledge my indebtedness. For any errors and omissions in the work, I accept responsibility and welcome notification of errors, and additions.

Gloria M Strathern
Faculty of Library Science
University of Alberta
July, 1981

Note on Methodology

The major part of this work, including data entry for items into the computer file, has been undertaken as time permitted while the compiler was employed in teaching duties in the Faculty of Library Science at the University of Alberta. Preliminary work on the bibliography was begun in 1978, with the aid of a graduate assistant funded by the Western Canadian Publications Project and the Humanities and Social Sciences Research Fund of the University of Alberta. An item-by-item search of Canadiana from 1954 to date produced a basic working file.

A list of Alberta authors compiled by the Alberta Culture Library and responses to a questionnaire distributed through the *Alberta Authors Bulletin* provided a basic authority file. Further names were obtained from the examination of library collections and a wide range of reference sources. This file was expanded by visits to major collections in Edmonton and Calgary.

This information was entered into a computer file, using SPIRES (The Stanford Public Information Retrieval System) and the University of Alberta Amdahl Computer. Considerable modification of the computer program was necessary. Limitations in the system, such as a lack of square brackets and semi-colons, and cost constraints made necessary some compromises with regards to citations.

Since the computer program could not process cyrillic characters, Ukrainian publications are listed in English, where alternate titles are provided; otherwise they are transliterated. Wherever possible a copy of each item was examined, to verify citations and clarify conflicting information. The location of copies examined has been supplied and a reference to a bibliographical authority, where available, as a further source of information.

In 1979, the compiler was granted study leave from the University to work on the project. A grant from the Alberta 75th Anniversary Commission was received in June 1980, to assist with compilation and publication.

It was originally anticipated that the bibliography would contain several hundred items, arranged alphabetically with subject, title, and series indexes. When the file grew to several thousand items, a classified arrangement, derived from the ninth edition of Eugene P. Sheehy's *Guide to Reference Books,* was developed and an author index added. Chronological and publishers indexes are available from the computer system. They have not been included in the published volume, for reason of cost.

Production of the bibliography by computer was chosen, so that a compatible basis for further bibliographies would be created. The computer file of the bibliography will be retained. The file can be searched and print-outs of the chronological and publishers indexes can be made available at cost on request.

Bibliographies Cited with Citation Used

Artibise — Artibise, Alan F. J. *Western Canada Since 1870 A select bibliography and guide.* Vancouver: University of British Columbia Press, 1978.

Brown — Brown, Barbara, ed. *Canadian business and economics. A guide to sources of information.* Ottawa: Canadian Library Association, 1976.

CBIP — *Canadian books in print.* Toronto: University of Toronto Press, 1973-1979.

Canplains — Canadian Plains Research Centre. *Canplains research inventory.* Regina: Canadian Plains Research Centre, 1980.

Canadiana — *Canadiana.* Ottawa: National Library of Canada, 1954-1980.

de Valk — de Valk, Alphonse, *comp. History Collection, Canadian Catholic Church. catalogue. Collection d'histoire l'eglise catholique canadienne.* Saskatoon: St. Thomas More College, 1971-1975.

Dew — Dew, Ian. F. *Bibliography of material relating to southern Alberta published to 1970.* Lethbridge: University of Lethbridge Learning Resources Centre, 1975.

Drake — Drake, Paul B. *Protestantism on the Prairies to 1977. An annotated bibliography of historical and biographical publications.* 1978. Unpublished M.L.S. major project, University of Alberta.

Glenbow — Glenbow-Alberta Institute Library. *Catalogue of the Glenbow Historical Library.* Boston: G. K. Hall, 1973.

Jarman — Jarman, Lynne. *Canadian music. A selected checklist 1950-1973.* Toronto: University of Toronto Press, 1976.

NUC — National Union Catalog. *A cumulative author list representing Library of Congress printed cards and titles reported by other American Libraries.* Washington: Library of Congress, 1956-1976.

P.N.L.A.	*P.N.L.A. Quarterly. Official organ of the Pacific Northwest Library Association.* Seattle, v.18-43 (1953-1978).
Peel	Peel, *Bruce B. A bibliography of the prairie provinces to 1953 with biographical index.* 2nd ed. Toronto: University of Toronto Press, 1973.
Ceessa	Krotki, Joanna E. *Local histories of Alberta An annotated bibliography.* Edmonton: Division of East European Studies, University of Alberta, 1980. (Central and East European Ethno-Cultural Groups in Alberta Study Project, 5.)
McLeod	McLeod, Gordon D. *A descriptive bibliography of the Canadian prairie novel, 1871-1970.* Winnipeg: University of Manitoba, 1974l. (Ph.D. Thesis.)
Ukrainica Canadian	*Ukrainica Canadiana.* Winnipeg: Ukrainian Canadiana Committee, 1953-1965. (Ukrainian Free Academy of Science. Series: Bibliography.)
U of A Theses	Univerity of Alberta. Library. Special Collections Division. *University of Alberta Theses.* Edmonton: University of Alberta Library, 1971-1979.

Library Locations and Symbols Used

ACG	Glenbow-Alberta Institute, Calgary
ACML	Camrose Lutheran College
ACP	Calgary Public Library
ACU	University of Calgary
AEA	Alberta Historical Resources, Edmonton
AECSJ	Faculté Saint-Jean, University of Alberta, Edmonton
AECYR	Alberta Culture, Edmonton
AEL	Legislature Library, Edmonton
AENB	North American Baptist College, Edmonton
AEP	Edmonton Public Library
AEU	University of Alberta, Edmonton
ALU	University of Lethbridge
ATP	Prarie Bible Institute, Three Hills
BVAU	University of British Columbia, Vancouver
OONL	National Library of Canada, Ottawa
OWA	University of Windsor
SSM	St. Thomas More College, Saskatoon

The Bibliography of Alberta

Bibliography: General Works

1 **Brooks**, Ian R. Native education in Canada and the United States. A bibliography. Calgary: Office of Educational Development, Indian Students University Program Services, University of Calgary, 1976. 298p.

Compiled with the assistance of A.M. Marshall.

Canadiana, 1977. **ACU**

2 **Cameron**, Jack R. A guide to publishing in education. An annotated international index of selected journals in education. Calgary: Foothills Educational Press, Faculty of Education, University of Calgary, 1977. 113p.

Associate editor: William E Geding.

Canadiana, 1977.

3 **Der-Houssikian**, Haig. A bibliography of African linguistics. Edmonton: Linguistic Research, 1972. xxx, 96p. (Current inquiry into language and linguistics, 7)

Canadiana, 1975.

4 An environmental bibliography for reference sources of information and films. Calgary: Calgary Eco Centre, 1971. 19p.

Canadiana, 1975.

5 Glenbow-Alberta Institute. Archives. Royal Canadian Mounted Police. A bibliography of resource material. Calgary: Glenbow-Alberta Institute, 1972. 102p. (Glenbow archives series, 5)

Canadiana, 1974.

6 **Knill**, William Douglas. A classification of theses in education completed at the University of Alberta, 1929-1966. 3rd. rev. ed. Edmonton: University of Alberta, 1966. 5, 67p.

Glenbow. **ACG**

7 **O'Leary**, Timothy J. A preliminary bibliography of the archaeology of Western Canada. Compiled by Timothy J. O'Leary for the Glenbow Foundation. Calgary: Glenbow Foundation, 1960. 23 leaves.

Reproduced from typewritten copy.

Glenbow. **ACG**

Bibliography of Alberta

8 **Dew**, Ian F. Bibliography of material relating to southern Alberta published to 1970. Lethbridge: Learning Resources Centre, University of Lethbridge, 1975. vii, 407 leaves.

Canadiana, 1976. **ACG**

9 **Gill**, Dhara S. A bibliography of socio-economic studies on rural Alberta, Canada. Monticello, Ill.: Council of Planning Librarians, 1977. 206p.

The Bibliography of Alberta

(Council of Planning Librarians. Exchange bibliography, 1260, 1261, 1262)

AEL

10 **Koester**, Charles B. A bibliography of selected theses on (sic) the Library of the University of Alberta relating to Western Canada, 1915-1965. Compiled for Western Canadian Research Project. Edmonton: Western Canadian Research Project, 1965. 21 leaves.

Duplicated.

Canadiana, 1968.

11 **Livermore**, Ronald P. Bibliography of primary sources for classroom study of the history of Alberta. Ottawa: National Library of Canada, 1971. x, 298 leaves. (Canadian theses on microfilm, 10194)

Thesis (M.Ed.), University of Calgary, 1971.
Microfilm of typescript.

Canadiana, 1972.

12 **Peel**, Bruce Braden. A bibliography of the Prairie Provinces to 1953. Toronto: University of Toronto Press, 1956. xix, 680p.

Published in co-operation with the Saskatchewan Golden Jubilee Committee and the University of Saskatchewan.
Also, 2d ed., 1973, University of Toronto Press. 780p.

Canadiana, 1956. **AEU**

13 Schick-Swanson Library and Information Consultants. Pollution in Alberta. A bibliography. Edmonton: Schick-Swanson Library and Information Consultants, 1974. 31p.

Duplicated.

Canadiana, 1975. **AEU**

Libraries and Librarianship

14 **Coburn**, Morton. A survey of seven recently constructed public library buildings in the United States and Canada. Edmonton: Edmonton Public Library, 1963. 93 leaves.

Duplicated.

Canadiana, 1964.

15 **Duke**, William Richard. The Parkland Regional Library. Edmonton: University of Alberta, 1966. xi, 141 leaves.

Thesis (M.Ed.), University of Alberta, 1966.
Typescript.
An evaluation of a combined public and school regional library system.

Canadian theses. **AEU**

16 Edmonton Public Library Performance measurement indicators. Edmonton: Edmonton Public Library, 1978. 12 leaves.

Canadiana 1979. **AECYR**

17 Edmonton Public Library. Summary of salary survey of the professional staff in twenty-six Canadian public and university libraries, June, 1962. Edmonton: Edmonton Public Library, 1962. 12 leaves. ill.

Canadiana, 1965. **AEU**

18 Edmonton Public Library. User survey. Edmonton: Edmonton Public Library, 1976. 49, 1p.

Duplicated. **AECYR**

19 **Ferguson**, Marjorie Ruth. Periodicals in Alberta high schools. Ottawa: National Library of Canada, 1977. ix, 94 leaves. (Canadian theses on microfiche, 34034)

Thesis (M.A.), University of Calgary, 1977.
Microfiche of typescript. **OONL**

20 **Gaver**, Mary Virginia. A survey of educational media services of Calgary public schools, conducted on behalf of the Calgary School Board. Edmonton: School of Library Science, University of Alberta, 1971. iii, 137 leaves.

Canadiana, 1972. **AEU**

21 **Gorosh**, Esther. Calgary's 'temple of knowledge'. A history of the Public Library. Calgary: Century Calgary Publications, 1975. 119p. ill.

Also published as part of *At your service, Part one*, which was issued as v.5 of the Century Calgary Historical Series.

Canadiana, 1977.

22 **Hendricks**, Larry John. The Edmonton Public Library Government Information Division, an element in community development. Ottawa: National Library of Canada, 1977. ix, 75 leaves. (Canadian theses on microfiche, 31980)

Thesis (M.A.), University of Alberta, 1977.
Microfiche of typescript.

Canadiana, 1978. **AEU**

23 **Kamra**, Ardis Daphne. An evaluation of the fiction collections in the elementary school libraries of an Alberta school district. Edmonton: University of Alberta, 1969. xi, 128 leaves.

Thesis (M.Ed.), University of Alberta, 1969.
Typescript.

Canadian theses. **AEU**

24 Library management. Gertrude Pomahac, ed. Calgary: Library Association of Alberta, 1969. viii. 51p. (Library Association of Alberta. Occasional papers, 1)

Papers presented at a workshop sponsored by the Library Association of Alberta, March 15, 1969, at Red Deer.

Canadiana, 1970. **AEU**

25 **Newsom**, Harry E. Guidelines for the development of public library services in Manitoba. Edmonton: University of Alberta, 1974. v, 29, 16 leaves.

Canadiana, 1975.

26 **Newsom**, Harry E. Library service in Alberta. A preliminary report. s.l.: s.n., 1955. 49p.

Duplicated. **AEU**

27 **Newsom**, Harry E. Recommended guidelines for the development of the Parkland Regional Library. By Harry E. Newsom and John Wright. Edmonton: University of Alberta, 1971. 22 leaves.

Duplicated. **AEU**

28 **Norrie**, D.H. WesCan/INFORM. The Western Canada Bibliographic Information Centre. Report for the Canada West Foundation. By D.H. Norrie and O. Standera. Calgary: s.n., 1975. vii, 103p. ill.

Duplicated.
A proposal.

Canadiana, 1976. **AECYR**

29 Northern Alberta Library Development Services. Northern Alberta Library Development Services, 1977-1979. s.l.: Northern Alberta Library Development Services, 1979. 8p. ill.

Cover title.

Canadiana, 1980.

30 **Peel**, Bruce Braden. History of the Library. Edmonton: University of Alberta, 1965. 17p. ill.

Produced for the official opening of the Donald Ewing Cameron Library.

Canadiana, 1965.

31 **Peel**, Bruce Braden. The history of the University of Alberta Library, 1909-1979. Edmonton: University of Alberta Library, 1979. 34p. ill.

Cover title *The University of Alberta Library, 1909-1979.* **AEU**

32 **Peel**, Bruce Braden. Librarianship in Canada, 1946 to 1967. Essays in honour of Elizabeth Homer Morton. Le bibliothécariat au Canada de 1946 à 1967. Hommages à Elizabeth Homer Morton. Victoria, B.C.: Morriss Printing for the Canadian Library Association, 1968. 205p.

AEU

33 **Peel**, Bruce Braden. Survey of Canadian academic libraries conducted between January 29 and May 1, 1967. A partial pictorial record. Edmonton: University of Alberta, 1967. 37 leaves (chiefly ill.).

Limited ed. of 22 numbered copies.
Cover title *Downs survey pictorial record.*

Canadiana, 1968. **AEU**

34 **Pomahac**, Gertrude. Education for librarianship. Papers presented at a workshop sponsored jointly by the School of Library Science, University of Alberta, the Library Association of Alberta (and) the School Library Council. Edited by Gertrude Pomahac. Edmonton: University of Alberta, School of Library Science, 1970. 63p.

Contents: Reed, S.R. Introduction. Issues, decisions and continuing debate. Rothstein, S. The history of American library education, 1870-1970. Hutchings, F.G.B. Research and library education Land, R.B. Pre-service education, content and methodology. Newsom, H.E. Continuing education for librarians. Biographies of speakers Registrants

Canadiana, 1971. **AEU**

35 **Prevey**, Patricia. A study of the holdings of Canadian award-winning novels in Alberta high school media centres. Ottawa: National Library of Canada, 1978. ix, 136 leaves. (Canadian theses on microfiche, 37316)

Thesis (M.Ed.), University of Calgary, 1978.
Microfiche of typescript.

Canadiana, 1979. **OONL**

36 **Reid**, Helen Audrey. An investigation of the role of the school librarian in Alberta. Edmonton: University of Alberta, 1971. x, 208 leaves.

Thesis (M.Ed.), University of Alberta, 1971.

Typescript. **AEU**

37 **Shelton**, Francis Drake. A survey of library facilities in Alberta schools. Ottawa: National Library of Canada, 1971. xv, 165 leaves. ill. (Canadian theses on microfilm, 8898)

Thesis (M.Ed.), University of Calgary, 1971.
Microfilm of typescript.

Canadiana, 1972. **OONL**

38 **Siska**, George Edward. A survey of centralized library services in Alberta schools and library utilization in senior high schools. Edmonton: University of Alberta, 1967. xix, 269 leaves.

Thesis (M.Ed.), University of Alberta, 1967.
Typescript.
An examination of the status of Alberta school libraries in 1964.

Canadian theses. **AEU**

39 **Smyth**, Donald Ross. A storage and retrieval system for the abstracts of theses in education completed at the University of Alberta. Edmonton: University of Alberta, 1970. ix, 247 leaves.

Thesis (M.Ed.), University of Alberta, 1970.

Typescript. **AEU**

40 University of Alberta. Department of Extension. Advisory Committee on Learning Resources. The development of a Learning Resources Centre as a base for the expansion of continuing education in Alberta. A report.

Edmonton: University of Alberta, Department of Extension, 1973. iv, 31 leaves. maps.

Chairman, Duncan D. Campbell.

Canadiana, 1976. **AEU**

41 University of Alberta. Faculty of Library Science. Class of 1972. Frog 'n all. Edmonton: School of Library Science, University of Alberta, 1972. 52p. ill.

Produced by the Thomas Frognall Dibdin Memorial Society.

Canadiana, 1974. **AEU**

42 Western Library Associations Regional Conference, 1st, Calgary, 1964. Proceedings. s.l.: s.n., 1964. 58 (i.e. 68) leaves.

Conference held May 20-22, 1964 with theme *Crisis in education - its meaning for libraries*.

Glenbow. **ACG**

43 **Wiedrick**, Laurence George. Student use of school libraries in Edmonton open area elementary schools. Ann Arbor, Mich.: University Microfilms, 1973. xii, 243p. ill.

Thesis (Ed.D.), University of Oregon, 1973.
Microfilm of typescript.

Canadiana, 1974.

Publishing and Journalism

44 Calgary Herald. The inside story. Calgary: Calgary Herald, 1959. 48p. ill.

Cover title.
Pictorial account of publishing the *Herald*.

Glenbow. **ACG**

45 **D'Albertanson**, Leonard. The story of Alberta Division, Canadian Weekly Newspapers Association. Compiled by Leonard D'Albertanson with the assistance of the officers and members of Alberta Division, C.W.N.A. Wainwright: Wainwright Star-Chronicle, 1955. 110p. ill.

Drawings by Hal Martin.
Cover title *The printed word, 1904-1955*.

Canadiana, 1960. **AEA**

46 **DeGrâce**, Eloi. L'Ouest canadien, historique et index. Edmonton: Eloi DeGrâce, 1979. 23p.

Cover title. Duplicated. **AEA**

47 **Dickson**, Lovat. The house of words. London: Macmillan, 1963. 304p. ill.

Autobiographical.

Glenbow. **ACG**

48 **Edwards**, Bob. The best of Bob Edwards. Edited by Hugh A. Dempsey. Edmonton: Hurtig, 1975. 271p.

Canadiana, 1975. **AEA**

49 **Edwards**, Bob. The wit and wisdom of Bob Edwards. Edited by Hugh Dempsey. A number of drawings by David Shaw. Edmonton: Hurtig, 1976. 124p. ill.

Canadiana, 1977. **AEA**

50 **Faulknor**, Cliff. Pen and plow. Winnipeg: Public Press, 1976. 152p. ill.

Accounts of prairie development, 1882-1893, through the eyes of Western journalists.

ACG

51 **Ferguson**, Ted. Kit Coleman, Queen of Hearts. Toronto: Doubleday Canada, 1978. 182p. ill.

Sub-title on dust jacket *Canada's pioneer woman journalist*. **AECYR**

52 **Kennedy**, Fred. Alberta was my beat. Memoirs of a western newspaperman. Calgary: Albertan, 1975. 392p. ill.

Canadiana, 197. **AEA**

53 **MacEwan**, John Walter Grant. Eye Opener Bob. The story of Bob Edwards. Saskatoon: Western Producer Book Service, 1974. 207p.

First published Edmonton, Institute of Applied Arts, 1957.

Canadiana, 1975.

54 **Mackenzie**, John. Country editor. Relating sixty-seven years of newspaper life on a Scottish island and the Canadian prairie, 1901-1968. Rothesay, Scotland: Bute Newspapers, 1968. 72p. ill.

Glenbow. **ACG**

55 **Menzies**, A.F. Two dollars per year. Grande Prairie: A.F. Menzies, 1963. 177p. ill.

From the author's weekly column *The fifth column*, in the *Herald-Tribune*, Grande Prairie. Each article ends with the words "two dollars per year".

Glenbow. **ACG**

56 **Morrison**, J. Charles. A study of environmental press at the University of Calgary. Ottawa: National Library of Canada, 1975. ix, 80 leaves. ill. (Canadian theses on microfiche, 25042)

Thesis (M.A.), University of Calgary, 1975.
Microfiche of typecript.
A study of the impact of the university environment on undergraduate students.

Canadiana, 1977.

57 **Nimchuk**, Ivan. Nove slovo. Pershi ukrains'kyi populiarnyi shchodennyk u L'vovi, 1812-1914. Edmonton: Printed by the Ukrainian News, 1954. 35p. (Catholic action library, 16)

English subtitle *The first popular Ukrainian daily paper*.

Ukrainica Canadiana, 1954. **AEU**

58 **Peel**, Bruce Braden. Early printing in the Red River Settlement, 1859-1870 and its effect on the Riel Rebellion. Winnipeg: Peguis Publishers, 1974. 56p. ill.

Canadiana, 1975. **ACG**

59 **Peel**, Bruce Braden. Rossville Mission Press. The invention of the Cree syllable characters and the first printing in Rupert's Land. Montreal: Osiris, 1974. 47p. ill.

Limited edition of 200 copies. **AEU**

60 **Pomahac**, Gertrude. Publishing in Canada. Edited by G. Pomahac and M. Richeson. Edmonton: School of Library Science, University of Alberta, 1972. 97p.

Proceedings of an Institute on publishing in Canada.

Canadiana, 1972.

61 **Roche**, Douglas J. It's a new world. Edited by Douglas J. Roche. Edmonton: Western Catholic Reporter, 1970. 222p. ill.

On cover: Best articles from 5 years of the Western Catholic Reporter. **AEA**

62 **Steele**, Charles Frank. Prairie editor. The life and times of Buchanan of Lethbridge. Foreword by Arthur R. Ford. Toronto: Ryerson Press, 1961. 196p. ill.

Glenbow. **ACG**

63 **Stout**, Clarence Howard. Backtrack on old trails. Memoirs of an international life of 91 years, 79 in Alberta. Calgary: L. Stout, 1973. 429p. ill.

Reminiscences of homesteading at Conjuring Lake and a career as a newspaper man.
Limited edition of 200 copies.
Duplicated.

Canadiana, 1975. **AEA**

64 **Webber**, Frank. The publish it yourself author. Edmonton: F. Webber, 1960. 43p, 4p.

Cover title. Duplicated. **AEU**

Religion: General Works

65 Calgary Aquinas studies. Toronto: Pontifical Institute of Mediaeval Studies, 1978. 174p.

Papers presented at the Aquinas Septicentennial Conference held at the University of Calgary in October, 1974.
Edited by Anthony Parel.

CBIP, 1979. **AEU**

66 **Camp**, Fred V. Two wheelchairs and a family of three. Three Hills: Prairie Press, 1978. 99p.

An autobiography.

CBIP, 1979. **ATP**

67 **Choiquier**, Alain. Born again. What it really means. Beaverlodge: Horizon House, 1977. 56p.

Translation of *Un seul chemin*, 1973, Operation Mobilisation France.

P.N.L.A., 1979. **ATP**

68 **Clark**, Molly. The taming of Molly. Beaverlodge: Horizon House, 1976. 91p. (Horizon books)

A religious autobiography.

Canadiana, 1977. **ATP**

69 **Coward**, Harold. Mystics and scholars. The Calgary Conference on Mysticism. Edited by Harold Coward and Terence Penelhum. Toronto: Canadian Corp. for Studies in Religion, 1977. viii, 118p.

Essays on eastern, western, and North American Indian mysticism.

P.N.L.A., 1979.

70 **Cunningham**, Rosemary. When the arrow flies. Three Hills: Prairie Bible Institute, 1966. 147p. ill.

Cover sub-title *Missionary triumphs in Brazil's jungle depths.*

Canadiana, 1967. **ATP**

71 **Darby**, George. Is there anything wrong?. Three Hills: Evangelical Missionary Fellowship, 1961. 107p.

Sermons preached in Calvary Memorial Church, Navarre. Minn.

Canadiana, 1961. **OONL**

72 **Dempsey**, Hugh Aylmer. Blackfoot ghost dance. Calgary: Glenbow-Alberta Institute, 1968. 19p. ill. (Glenbow-Alberta Institute. Occasional paper, 3)

Glenbow. **ACG**

73 **Dempsey**, Hugh Aylmer. A Blackfoot winter count. Calgary: Glenbow Foundation, 1964. 20p. ill. (Glenbow Foundation. Occasional paper, 1)

Glenbow. **ACG**

74 **Dewdney**, Selwyn. The sacred scrolls of the southern Ojibway. Toronto: Published for the Glenbow-Alberta Institute by University of Toronto Press, 1975. viii, 199p. ill.

Canadiana, 1975. **AEU**

75 **Douglas**, Alban Hector. Seventy Bible lessons. Three Hills: Evangelical Missionary Fellowship, 1960. 144p.

Lessons given at the Thursday Night Bible Class at the Youth Gospel Center, Philippines, 1958-1959, and other messages given in Manila area at that time.

Canadiana, 1961. **OONL**

76 **Elliott**, W. Harold. Patchwork pictures. Three Hills: Prairie Bible Institute, 1978. 118p.

CBIP, 1979.

77 **Epp**, Margaret. Into all the world. The story of the missionary outreach of Prairie Bible Institute. Foreword by Rev. L.E. Maxwell. Three Hills: Prairie Press, 1973. 406p. ill.

Canadiana, 1974. **ACU**

78 Eternal pathways. Religious readings. Edmonton: Ukrainian News, 1954. 123p.

Text in Ukrainian.

Ukrainica Canadiana 1954.

79 **Foster**, Kenneth Neill. The happen stance. Beaverlodge: Horizon House, 1977. 159p.

Canadiana, 1977. **ATP**

80 **Fox**, Charles Armstrong. Exploring Paul's Epistles. Reprint edition. Three Hills: Prairie Bible Institute, 1968. 176p.

CBIP, 1979. **ATP**

81 **Friesen**, John W. Religion for people. An alternative. Calgary: Bell Books, 1972. xvi, 142p.

Canadiana, 1975. **AEU**

82 **Goldstein**, Vincent-Marie. Paschal meal. Prepared by Vincent-Marie Goldstein. Edmonton: Hermitage Editions, 1965. 32p.

Also issued in a French language edition.

Canadiana, 1975. **OONL**

83 **Goode**, Chrissie. This is thine. Calgary: Chrissie Goode, 1979. 121p.

Autobiographical anecdotes, and religious experiences. **AECYR**

84 **Harper**, Donald Calvin. Secularization and religion in Alberta. Edmonton: University of Alberta, 1970. xiv, 202 leaves.

Thesis (M.A.), University of Alberta, 1970.
Typescript.

Canadian theses. **AEU**

85 **Harvey**, Richard H. 70 years of miracles. Beaverlodge: Horizon House, 1977. 185p.

Canadiana, 1977. **ATP**

86 **Henderson**, Joseph Frank. Passover celebration. With commentary and notes for Christians. Edmonton: J.F. Henderson, 1977. vi, 53p. music.

Cover title.

Canadiana, 1978. **OONL**

87 **Hiebert**, Henry. Evolution. Its collapse in view? Beaverlodge: Horizon House, 1979. 176p.

88 **Hopkins**, Evan H. Broken bread. A companion to Daily light. With an introduction to the life and ministry of Evans H. Hopkins, by Ted. S. Rendall, Principal, Prairie Bible Institute, Alberta, Canada. Three Hills: Prairie Press, 1973. 1v. (unpaged)

CBIP, 1979.

89 **Horsefield**, R.B. A Cree Bible dictionary. Edited and translated for the Crees, by the Ven. R.B. Horsefield. Toronto: Missionary Society of the Anglican Church of Canada, 1961. (4), 267p.

Title in Cree and English. Text in Cree.
Based largely on Peloubet's and Hasting's dictionaries of the Bible.

Glenbow. **ACG**

90 **Hungry Wolf**, Adolf. Good medicine thoughts. Fort MacLeod: Good Medicine Books, 1972. 32p. ill. (Good medicine books, 6)

Canadiana, 1973. **AEA**

91 Hutterite Brethren. Handbook for sermons on Bible. Compiled by J.B. Wipf. Cayley: Macmillan Colony, 1963. 92p.

Supplied title.
Text in German. Reproduced from handwritten copy.
Contents: 1. Das alte Testament (p.1-44) 2. Das neue Testament(p.44-92).

Glenbow. **ACG**

92 **Jacob**, Edmond. Modern Israel in biblical perspective. Camrose: Camrose Lutheran College Press, 1958. 19p.

Translation of *Israel dans la perspective biblique*. Translator, J. Robert Jacobson.

Canadiana, 1975. **OONL**

93 **Janz**, Leo. The Janz team story. Beaverlodge: Horizon House Publishers, 1977. 111p. (Horizon Books)

An account of an evangelical ministry in Europe and America, led by the author.

Canadiana, 1979. **ACP**

94 Joint International Symposium of Elders and Scholars, Edmonton, 1977. Native religious traditions. Edited by Earle H. Waugh and K. Dad Prithipaul. Waterloo: Wilfred Laurier University Press for the Canadian Corporation for Studies in Religion, 1979 (S R supplements, 8)

Proceedings of the Symposium held in Edmonton, September 15-17, 1977.

Canadiana, 1979. **OONL**

95 **Jones**, Brian K. Something to think about. Lethbridge: Radio Station CJOC, 1971. 106p.

Radio scripts of the late Rev. B.K. Jones of McKillop United Church, Lethbridge. Published by CJOC and the Lethbridge Herald.

96 **Jowett**, John Henry. The school of Calvary. Or, Sharing His suffering. Reprint ed. Three Hills: Prairie Bible Institute, 1969. 69p.

Reprinted from 1911 edition, London, James Clark. **ATP**

97 **Last**, Edward. Handgathered fruit. 4th. ed. Three Hills: Prairie Book Room, 1963. 108p. ill.

Reprinted from Scottish edition, 1928, Stirling, Drummond Tract Depot.

CBIP, 1979. **ATP**

98 **Lester**, Geoffrey Austin. The distribution of religious groups in Alberta, 1961. Edmonton: University of Alberta, 1966. xi, 150 leaves.

Thesis (M.A.), University of Alberta, 1966.
Typescript.

Canadian theses. **AEU**

99 **Lingas**, Helen (Fotos). My centennial torch for world peace. Edmonton: Printed by Commercial Printers for Helen Lingas, 1967. 144p.

A collection of homilies written by Helen Lingas.
Also, 2d. ed., 1968.

Glenbow. **ACG**

100 **MacLellan**, James Alexander. Sermons, addresses, editorial and other writings. Edmonton: Ukrainian News Publishers, 1972. 2v.

The author was chaplain to St. Joseph's Convent, Edmonton.
Vol. 1. printed by Ritter's, Edmonton.

Canadiana, 1975. **AEU**

101 **Martin**, Hugh. The abiding presence. Three Hills: Prairie Bible Institute, 1977. 248p.

2nd printing.

CBIP, 1979. **ATP**

102 **Maxwell**, Leslie Earl. Abandoned to Christ. Three Hills: Prairie Press, 1971. 248p.

First published in 1955, Grand Rapids, Mich., Eerdmans.

CBIP, 1979. **ATP**

103 **Maxwell**, Leslie Earl. Crowded to Christ. Three Hills: Prairie Press, 1974. 354p.

First Canadian edition. First published in 1950, Grand Rapids, Mich., Eerdmans. 2d ed. 1959, paperback ed. 1968.

CBIP, 1979. **ATP**

104 **Maxwell**, Leslie Earl. The Holy Spirit in missions. Three Hills: Prairie Bible Institute, n.d. 30p.

A message delivered at the Student Missions Fellowship Conference, Toronto, December, 1946. **ATP**

105 **Maxwell**, Leslie Earl. The Pentecostal baptism. A biblical analysis and appraisal. Three Hills: Prairie Bible Institute, 1971. 16p.

Cover title.

106 **Maxwell**, Leslie Earl. Prairie pillars. Three Hills: Prairie Bible Institute, 1971. 117p.

On evangelistic work.

Canadiana, 1973. **ATP**

107 **Maxwell**, Leslie Earl. World missions total war. Three Hills: Prairie Press, 1977. 167p.

CBIP, 1979. **ATP**

108 **McCrossan**, T.J. Speaking with other tongues. Sign or gift, which? Mass market ed. Beaverlodge: Horizon House, 1977. 68p.

On spine: Tongues, sign or gift?.
First published 1927, Seattle, Washington, T.J. McCrossan, also published 1977, Hamsburg, Pa., Christian Publications.

Canadiana, 1978. **OONL**

109 **McOuat**, James Earl. Bible history & prophecies. Beaverlodge: E. McOuat, 1973. 119p.

Canadiana, 1975. **OONL**

110 **Mills**, Eric. Help for husbands (and wives). Nine unusual accounts. Edited by Eric Mills. Beaverlodge: Horizon House, 1977. 92p.

A sequel to *Preachers, priests and critters.*
Accounts of Christian experiences.

CBIP, 1979. **ATP**

111 **Mills**, Eric. Preachers, priests and critters and other unusual accounts. Beaverlodge: Horizon House, 1975. 93p.

Ten accounts of Christian experiences presented at summer camps.
Also published in 1978 under title *The Shepherd's psalm and other true accounts.* **ATP**

112 **Moore**, E. Barry. Crisis at 9:25. Beaverlodge: Horizon House, 1978. 95p.

Reprint of 1974 edition, London, Ont., Crusade Evangelism International.
On religious crises and conversion experiences.

CBIP, 1979.

113 **Morley**, Frank Selkirk. Personal peace and power. Calgary: Albertan, 1956. 109p.

Collection of editorials first published in *The Albertan.*

Canadiana, 1962. **OONL**

114 **Morley**, Frank Selkirk. A way of life. Calgary: F. Morley, 1958. 36p.

Canadiana, 1962. **OONL**

115 **Morley**, Frank Selkirk. Why a Presbyterian Church. Calgary: F. Morley, 1955. 40, 4p. tables.

Canadiana, 1962. **OONL**

116 **Murray**, Andrew. Abide in Christ. Three Hills: Prairie Bible Institute, 1960. 191p.

3rd printing 1975, 4th printing 1979.
Originally published 1882, London, J. Nesbet.
Meditations on fellowship with Christ.

CBIP, 1979. **ATP**

117 **Murray**, Andrew. Like Christ. Three Hills: Prairie Press, 1973. 235p.

Originally published 1889, London, J. Nesbet.
Meditations.

CBIP, 1979.

118 **Murray**, Andrew. Working for God. Three Hills: Prairie Bible Institute, 1965. 150p.

A sequel to *Waiting on God.*
Originally published 1901, New York, F.H. Revell. **ATP**

119 National Spiritual Assembly of the Baha'is of Canada. Oki! Nitsitapee. A message to the Blackfoot Indians. Translated by Hugh and Pauline Dempsey. Toronto: Baha'i Publishing Committee, 1955. 11p.

In Blackfoot and English.

Glenbow. **ACG**

120 **O'Reilly**, Paul J. Keep them in Thy name. Priests. Facts and figures about priests and those along the way. Edmonton: s.n., 1961. 92p.

Devotional literature.

de Valk, 1975. **SSM**

121 **Patterson**, Marney. Alive and free. Beaverlodge: Horizon House, 1979. 160p.

Account of personal salvation and evangelism.

CBIP, 1979. **ATP**

122 **Patterson**, Marney. Dare to share. Communicating the good news. Beaverlodge: Horizon House, 1977. 124p.

Canadiana, 1978. **ATP**

123 **Percy**, Douglas Cecil. Man with the heart of a Viking. Beaverlodge: Horizon House, 1976. 147p.

Account of missionary activity in remote areas of North America.

CBIP, 1979.

124 **Pierson**, Arthur Tappan. Godly self-control. Rev. ed. Three Hills: Prairie Bible Institute, 1958. 133p.

First published London, Marshall, Morgan & Scott.

CBIP, 1979. **ATP**

125 **Popowich**, John Damascene D. Child of God. Prayerbook. Mundare: Basilian Fathers, 1956. 164p. ill.

Text in Ukrainian.
Ukrainian title *Bozha dytnya*.

Ukrainica Canadiana, 1957.

126 Prairie Bible Institute. Behold your God. Meditations on our great God. Three Hills: Prairie Bible Institute, 1960. 1v.

A Bible correspondence course.

127 Prairie Bible Institute. Bread enough. Meditations on our great salvation. A salvation course for Christians. Three Hills: Prairie Bible Institute, 1963. 120p.

A correspondence course.

Canadiana, 1963. **OONL**

128 Prairie Bible Institute. Christian harmony. Cheerful co-operation in the work of the Gospel. Devotional studies in the Epistle to the Philippians. Three Hills: Prairie Bible Institute, 1962. 119p.

A Bible correspondence course.

Canadiana, 1962. **OONL**

129 Prairie Bible Institute. Energized to evangelize. Studies in the Book of the Acts. Three Hills: Prairie Bible Institute, 1967. 120p.

A Bible correspondence course.

Canadiana, 1968. **ATP**

130 Prairie Bible Institute. Feed my lambs. A study of Peter and his first letter. Three Hills: Prairie Press, 1964. 128p. ill.

A Bible correspondence course.

Canadiana, 1964. **ATP**

131 Prairie Bible Institute. Full faith. A study of the general Epistle of St. James. Three Hills: Prairie Bible Institute, 1959. 111p.

A Bible correspondence course. **ATP**

132 Prairie Bible Institute. Love's letter. A survey of the letter to Philemon and a summary of the lessons that are pictures. Three Hills: Prairie Bible Institute, 1967. 46p. ill.

A Bible correspondence course.

Canadiana, 1970. **OONL**

133 Prairie Bible Institute. New Testament survey series. Three Hills: Prairie Press, 1963. 4v.

A Bible correspondence course.

Canadiana, 1964. **ATP**

134 Prairie Bible Institute. Sound doctrine. A survey of theological definitions. Three Hills: Prairie Bible Institute, 1960. 56p.

A Bible correspondence course.

Canadiana, 1969. **ATP**

135 Prairie Bible Institute. Spirit-filled saints. A study of Ephesians. Three Hills: Prairie Bible Institute, 1959. 123p.

A Bible correspondence course.

Canadiana, 1960. **OONL**

136 Prairie Bible Institute. Suffering saints. A study of Saint Peter's first Epistle. Three Hills: Prairie Bible Institute, 1958. 79p.

A Bible correspondence course.

Canadiana, 1960. **OONL**

137 Prairie Bible Institute. Unclouded communion. A study of John's first Epistle. Three Hills: Prairie Press, 1960. 117p.

A Bible correspondence course.

Canadiana, 1960. **ATP**

138 **Rendall**, Ted Seator. In God's school. Scriptural studies dealing with various disciplines employed by God in the training of His children. Foreword by Dr. Alan Redpath. Three Hills: Prairie Press, 1971. 191p.

CBIP, 1979. **ATP**

139 **Rendall**, Ted Seator. Jeremiah, prophet of crisis. Topical studies for today of the basic themes of the prophecy of Jeremiah. Three Hills: Prairie Press, 1979. 311p. ill.

CBIP, 1979. **ATP**

140 **Rendall**, Ted Seator. Living the abundant life. Expository studies in the life and ministry of Elisha the Prophet. Three Hills: Prairie Press, 1969. 348p. ill.

Studies first published in the *Prairie Overcomer*.
3rd printing, 1977, with title *Elisha, prophet of abundant life*.

Canadiana, 1970. **ATP**

141 **Rendall**, Ted Seator. Nehemiah. Laws of leadership. Three Hills: Prairie Press, 1979. (1v.)

CBIP, 1979. **ATP**

142 **Roche**, Douglas J. The Catholic revolution. Toronto: Musson Book, 1968. xxiii, 325p. **AEU**

143 **Roche**, Douglas J. Man to Man. A frank talk between a layman and a bishop. By Douglas J. Roche and Bishop Remi De Roo. Edited and with an introduction by Gary MacEoin. Milwaukee: Bruce Publishing, 1969. 240p.

On modern Catholicism.

Canadiana, 1970. **ACP**

144 **Rogers**, Walter Bob. The role of religion in social and economic development. Edmonton: Department of Agricultural Economics, University of Alberta, 1967. 14 leaves. (University of Alberta. Department of Agricultural Economics and Rural Sociology. Special report, 4)

Presented at the Symposium on Stimulants to Social and Economic Development in Slow Growing Regions, Banff, 1966. **AEU**

145 **Schaeffer**, Claude E. Blackfoot shaking tent. Calgary: Glenbow-Alberta Institute, 1969. 38p. ill. (Glenbow-Alberta Institute. Occasional paper, 5)

Glenbow. **ACG**

146 **Scholefield**, Billy. No rocking chair for me! By Billy Scholefield, as told to Juanita C. Snyder. Three Hills: Prairie Bible Institute, 1971. 88p.

Autobiography of a California evangelist.

CBIP, 1979. **ATP**

147 **Sheppard**, Art. We proved God. A living testimony that God is alive today. By Art and Greta Sheppard. Calgary: Sheppard Evangelistic Campaign, 1962. (1v.)

ACP

148 **Shrier**, Clarence. I don't know what your God can do, but my God can do anything. Beaverlodge: Horizon House, 1975. 93p.

On spine: My God can do anything.

Canadiana, 1975. **OONL**

149 **Skwarok**, Josephat. The Eastern Catholic Churches. A compilation of writings, articles, essays, and related themes. Edmonton: E.S.S.D., Religious Department, 1971. 1v.

Duplicated.
Prepared for use in high schools. **AECSJ**

150 **Spicer**, John. Christ today. A series of reflections for adult groups. Edmonton: Archdiocese of Edmonton, 1969. 80p. ill.

de Valk, 1973. **SSM**

151 **Spicer**, John. God's people today. A series of reflections for adult groups. Edmonton: Archdiocese of Edmonton, 1970. 127p. ill.

de Valk, 1973. **SSM**

152 **Sundbo**, Beatrice. Treasures in heaven. Beaverlodge: Horizon House, 1977. 96p.

A Christian mother's reflection on the deaths of her four children.

Canadiana, 1978. **OONL**

153 **Tjart**, David. An inquiry into the religious value orientations of public and private school students at the grade eight level. Ottawa: National Library of Canada, 1976. viii, 95 leaves. (Canadian theses on microfiche, 30852)

Thesis (M.Ed.), University of Alberta, 1976.
Microfiche of typescript.

U of A theses. **AEU**

154 **Townsend**, Arthur Herbert. Tall tales that are true. By British Columbia storyteller Arthur H. Townsend. Beaverlodge: Horizon House, 1975. 93p.

Christian messages.

CBIP, 1979. **ATP**

155 **Tozer**, Aiden Wilson. That incredible Christian. Beaverlodge: Horizon House, 1977. 137p.

Reprint of the 1964 ed. published by Christian Publications, Harrisburg, Pa.
Most of the chapters of this book appeared as editorials in the *Alliance Witness*.

Canadiana 1978. **ATP**

156 **Truscott**, Graham. Every Christian's ministry. Calgary: Gordon Donaldson Missionary Foundation, 1977. 112p. ill.

Canadiana, 1978.

157 **Tyson**, Basil. U.F.O.s. Satanic terror. Beaverlodge: Horizon House, 1977. 122p.

Canadiana, 1978. **OONL**

158 **Whitesell**, Faris Daniel. Great personal workers. Three Hills: Prairie Press, 1975. 159p.

Reprint of U.S. edition, 1956, Chicago, Moody Bible Institute.

CBIP, 1979. **ATP**

159 **Whitesell**, Faris Daniel. The Proverbs. With scripture illustrations. Three Hills: Prairie Press, n.d. 204p.

160 **Workshop on religion and ethnicity**, University of Calgary, 1977. Religion and ethnicity. Essays. By Harold Barclay et al. Edited by Harold Coward and Leslie Kawamura. Waterloo: Wilfred Laurier University Press, for the Calgary Institute for the Humanities, 1978. ix, 181p. ill.

Workshop held August 8-12, 1977.

Canadiana, 1978. **AEU**

161 **Ziehl**, Gary. Criminal forever!. By Gary Ziehl as told to Merribeth Olson. Beaverlodge: Horizon House, 1979. 110p.

Biography of a convicted criminal who converted to Christianity.

CBIP, 1979.

History of Religion

162 L'Abbé Quirion. Heraut de la charité. Montreal: Editions Bellarmin, 1955. 16p. (Oeuvre des tracts, 412)

Cover title *Brief articles on Abbe Quirion, of St. Paul*.

Written in commemoration. **AECSJ**

163 **Amman**, O.A.M. The Studit monks. By O.A.M. Amman and Ieromonakh Marko. Edmonton: Catholic Action, 1955. 36p. ill. (Catholic action library, 19)

Title in Ukrainian and English. Text in Ukrainian.

Canadiana, 1956. **OONL**

164 **Anderson**, N. R. Oblate Fathers in Calgary. Roman Catholic Church, 1875-1889. Calgary: Century Calgary Publications, 1975. 96p. ill.

Also published as part of *The search for souls*, which was issued as v.4 of the Century Calgary Historical Series.

Canadiana, 1977. **AEA**

165 Anglican Church of Canada. Diocese of Edmonton. Women's Auxiliary Diocesan Board. Fifty golden years, 1914-1964. Edmonton: Diocese of Edmonton, Women's Auxiliary Diocesan Board, 1965. 68p. ill.

Drake. **AEA**

166 Basilian Fathers. Basilian Brothers. Mundare: Basilian Fathers, 1954 24p.

Text in Ukrainian and English.
Vocation booklet.

de Valk, 1971. **SSM**

167 Basilian Fathers. The Basilian priest. Mundare: Basilian Fathers, 1954. 28p.

Text in Ukrainian and English.
Vocation booklet.

de Valk, 1971. **SSM**

168 **Beaugrand**, Helen. Heaven via Little New York. Aldergrove, B.C.: Valcraft Print, 1970. 44p. ill.

Biography of the author's father, R.B. Gibson, a United Church minister in Saskatchewan and the Turner Valley. **AEA**

169 **Bentall**, Shirley Franklyn. Buckboard to brotherhood. The Baptist churches in Calgary. Calgary: Century Calgary Publications, 1975. 120 p. ill.

Also published as part of *The search for souls*, which was issued as v.4 of the Century Calgary Historical Series.

Canadiana, 1977. **AEA**

170 **Bezenar**, Gisèle Laliberté. Le père Albert Lacombe. Arsous-kitsi-parpi. Toronto: Holt, Rinehart and Winston of Canada, 1973. 44p. ill. (Collection joie de lire)

French reader for use in English language elementary schools.

Canadiana, 1974. **OONL**

171 **Bibby**, Reginald Wayne. The secular in the sacred. A study of evangelism as reflected in membership additions to Calgary evangelical churches, 1966-1970. Ottawa: National Library of Canada, 1971. xi, 123 leaves. ill. (Canadian theses on microfilm, 10040)

172 **Breton**, Paul-Emile. Au pays des Peaux-de-Lièvres. J.M. Patrick Kearney, o.m.i., héro ignoré de l'Artique. Edmonton: Editions de l'Ermitage, 1962. 177p. ill.

Also, English translation, with title *Irish hermit of the Arctic. The life of Brother J. Patrick Kearney, o.m.i.* Translated by J.S. Mullany, Edmonton, Editions de l'Ermitage, 1963, 153p. ill. Cover title *Irish of the Arctic*.

Glenbow. **ACG**

173 **Breton**, Paul-Emile. Bishop Vital Grandin, Oblate of Mary Immaculate, first bishop of St. Albert (Alberta), Canada. Edmonton: Editions de L'Ermitage, 1958. 16p.

At head of title: The Servant of God.
Also 1964, 30p.

Glenbow. **ACG**

174 **Breton**, Paul-Emile. Blacksmith of God. Translated by T.M. Dolphin. Edmonton: Editions de l'Ermitage, 1960. 191p. ill.

Rev. by Brother J. Mullany.
Biography of Brother Antoine Kowalczyk, first published 1953 in French, with title *Forgeron de Dieu* (Peel 4339).

Canadiana, 1961. **AEA**

175 **Breton**, Paul-Emile. Le grand chef des prairies. Le père Albert Lacombe, o.m.i., 1827-1916. Edmonton: Editions de l'Ermitage, 1954. 232p. ill.

Also English translation *The big chief of the prairies. The life of Father Lacombe*. Translated by Hugh Dempsey, Montreal, Palm Publishers, 1956. xiv, 145p. ill.

Canadiana, 1955. **AEU**

176 **Breton**, Paul-Emile. Hobbema, une florissante mission indienne de l'ouest. Edmonton: Editions de L'Ermitage, 1962. 62, (1)p. ill.

Also English translation *Hobbema, ongoing mission of central Alberta*. Translated, completed and updated to 1968, by E.O. Drouin, 1969, L'Imprimerie Laflamme. 59p. ill.

Glenbow. **ACG**

177 **Breton**, Paul-Emile. Vital Grandin, o.m.i. La merveilleuse aventure de l'évêque sauvage des prairies et du grand nord. Préface de Daniel Rops. Paris: Librairie Arthème Fayard, 1960. 366p. map (Bibliothéque ecclésie, 58)

AECSJ

178 **Byrne**, Marie Bernice Venini. From the buffalo to the Cross. A history of the Roman Catholic Diocese of Calgary. Calgary: Calgary Archives and Historical Publishers, 1973. vii, 555p. ill.

Printed by D.W. Friesen and Sons, Calgary.

Canadiana, 1974. **AEA**

179 Canadian Lutheran Bible Institue, Camrose. O send out Thy light and Thy truth. The prayer and cornerstone of twenty-five years of Christian Bible Institute. Camrose: Canadian Lutheran Bible Institute, 1957. 24p. ill.

ACML

180 **Carter**, David John. The Anglican Church in Calgary. Church activities, 1878-1974. Calgary: Century Calgary Publications, 1975. 159p. ill.

Also published as part of *The search for souls*, issued as v.4 of the Century Calgary Historical Series.

Drake. **AEU**

181 **Carter**, David John. A history of the Anglican Diocese of Calgary. Vancouver: University of British Columbia, 1968. 105 leaves.

Thesis (B. Th.), University of British Columbia, 1968.
Typescript.

Dew. **ACG**

182 **Carter**, David John. Samuel Trivett, missionary with the Blood Indians. 0r, What's a nice boy like you doing in a place like this? Calgary: D.J. Carter, 1975. 92p. ill.

Printed by Kyle Printing & Stationery. **AEA**

183 **Carter**, David John. Where the wind blows. A history of the Anglican Diocese of Calgary, 1888-1968. Calgary: Anglican Book Room, 1968. 52p. ill.

Cover title.

Canadiana, 1969. **AEU**

184 Church of Jesus Christ of Latter-Day Saints. Lethbridge Stake. A history of the Mormon Church in Canada. Lethbridge: Church of Jesus Christ of Latter-Day Saints Lethbridge Stake, 1968. 301p. ill.

Information from various stakes and missions edited by a committee of the Lethbridge Stake. Chairman, Asael E. Palmer.
A centennial project.

Glenbow. **ACG**

185 **Collett**, W.J. United Church in Calgary. Activities and events, 1875-1970. Calgary: Century Calgary Publications, 1975. 71p. ill.

Also published as part of *The search for souls*, which was issued as v.4 of the Century Calgary Historical Series.

Canadiana, 1977. **AEA**

186 **Conroy**, Marion. Early history and growth in Edmonton Diocese. Edmonton: Catholic Women's League, 1962. 177p.

50th anniversary of the Catholic Women's League.

de Valk, 1971. **SSM**

187 **Crawford**, David. Blue flame in the foothills. Presbyterian activities in the Calgary region. Calgary: Century Calgary Publications, 1975. 88p. ill.

Also published as part of *The search for souls*, which was issued as v.4 of the Century Calgary Historical Series.

Canadiana, 1977. **AEA**

188 **Cunningham**, John. She has done what she could (Mark 14, 8 NASV). A biography of Mother Cunningham, who was Dean of Bible School Women at Prairie Bible Institute from 1955 to 1962. Three Hills: Prairie Press, 1976. 56p. ill.

Canadiana, 1977. **ATP**

189 **Desrochers**, Clément. Docile à l'Esprit-Saint. La bienheureuse Marguerite d'Youville. St. Albert: Soeurs Grises de Montréal, 1961. 14p.

de Valk, 1975. **SSM**

190 **Drouin**, Eméric O'Neil. Echos argentins au Diocèse de Saint-Paul-en-Alberta, 1948-1973. A quarter of a century in the St. Paul Diocese, 1948-1973. Edmonton: Editions de l'Ermitage, 1973. 94p. ill.

Text in French and English.

Canadiana, 1974. **AEU**

191 **Drouin**, Eméric O'Neil. Joyau dans la plaine. Saint-Paul, Alberta, colonie métisse 1896-1909, paroisse blanche 1909-1951. Québec: Editions Ferland, 1968. xiii, 500p.

Le nom de l'auteur sur la p. de t. est corrigé à la main de Emile à Eméric.

Glenbow. **ACG**

192 **Drouin**, Eméric O'Neil. Lac Ste. Anne. Sakahigan. Edmonton: Editions de l'Ermitage, 1973. 96p. ill., maps.

A history of the Roman Catholic Church at Lac Ste. Anne.

Ceessa. **AEA**

193 **Drouin**, Eméric O'Neil. One-armed star from the east. Brother Anthony Kowalczyk, o.m.i., June 4, 1866-July 10, 1947. Edmonton: Editions de l'Ermitage, 1978. 51p. **AEA**

194 Edmonton. Community of Our Lady of Charity. Golden jubilee souvenir of the foundation of the Order of Our Lady of Charity. Edmonton: Community of Our Lady of Charity, 1962. 11p. ill.

At head of title: 1912-1962. **AECSJ**

195 Edmonton. St. Francis Friary. The Franciscans in Edmonton. 50 years, 1901-1959. Edmonton: St. Francis Friary, 1959. 16p. ill.

Cover title. **AEA**

196 **Evenson**, George O. Adventuring for Christ. The story of the Evangelical Lutheran Church of Canada. Calgary: Foothills Lutheran Press, 1974. 301p.

Drake. **AEA**

197 Filles de Jésus. Souvenir du cinquantenaire des Filles de Jésus au Canada. Province de l'ouest canadien (Alberta et Montana). Edmonton: Imprimerie La Survivance, 1954. 136p. ill.

Cover title *Magnificat, 50, 1904-1954*.
Text in French and English.

Glenbow. **ACG**

198 **Forsberg**, Roberta Jean. Chief Mountain. The story of Canon Middleton. Edmonton: Historical Society of Alberta, 1964. 7, vii, 119p. ill.

Issued by the author in Whittier, California.
Middleton was an Anglican missionary to the Blood Indians in southern Alberta, 1909-1949.

Canadiana, 1965. **AEA**

199 **Garnier**, Henri. En mission dans l'ouest canadien. Edmonton: s.n., 1954. (4), 91, (3)p. ill.

Deals primarily with Father Garnier's work in the parishes of Vegreville and Lamoureux.

Glenbow. **ACG**

200 **Getty**, Ian Allison Ludlow. The Church Missionary Society among the Blackfoot Indians of southern Alberta, 1880-1895. Ottawa: National Library of Canada, 1970. 150 leaves. ill. (Canadian theses on microfilm, 08852)

Thesis (M.A.), University of Calgary, 1970.
Microfilm of typescript.

Canadiana, 1972. **ACG**

201 **Giroux**, Alice (Soeur Marie Flore d'Auvergne). Les Soeurs de Sainte-Croix dans l'ouest Canadien. Montreal: Soeurs de Sainte-Croix, 1973. 363p. ill.

Half-title *Cinquante ans au service de l'Eglise et de la jeunesse, 1920-1970*.
Dedicated especially to the Sisters of the Peace River Country. **AECSJ**

202 **Gordon**, Ernest Barron. A book of Protestant saints. Three Hills: Prairie Bible Institute, 1968. 376p.

Reprint edition. First published 1940, Grand Rapids, Mich., Zondervan Pub.
Also published 1946, Chicago, Moody Press.

CBIP, 1977.

203 **Grandin**, Vital Justin. Monseigneur Grandin vous parle. Extraits des plus belles lettres de Monseigneur Vital Grandin, o.m.i., premier évêque de

l'Alberta à sa famille, 1829-1902. Edmonton: Editions de l'Ermitage, 1958. 175p. (Documentaire oblat)

Compiled by P.E. Breton. **AEA**

204 Growth. A history and anthology of the Synod of Alberta of the Presbyterian Church in Canada. Calgary: Presbyterian Church in Canada, Synod of Alberta, 1968. 154, (1), A-Mp. (ill.)

Glenbow. **ACG**

205 **Harris**, Joseph Edwin. The Baptist Union of Western Canada. A centennial history, 1873-1973. Saint John, N.B.: Lingley Printing, 1976. vii, 233p. ill.

CBIP, 1979. **AEA**

206 **Harrison**, Eugene Myers. Giants of the missionary trail. Three Hills: Prairie Press, 1954. 184p.

CBIP, 1979.

207 **Heffren**, Henry Charles. Voices of the pioneers. Camrose: Camrose Canadian, 1971. 60p. ill.

A history of the Church of God in Western Canada by a retired minister.

Drake. **AEA**

208 **Heidmeier**, Boniface. Pioneering in the west. By Father Boniface. Vancouver: Alverna Distributers, 1957. 277p. ill.

Printed by Evergreen Press, Vancouver.
Reminiscences of Franciscan missionary activity northeast of Edmonton.

de Valk, 1972. **AEA**

209 **Hudson**, Arland James. Charles Ora Card, pioneer and colonizer. With foreword by Brigham Y. Card. Cardston: A.J. Hudson, 1963. x, 219p. ill.

Revised and enlarged from his M.A. thesis, Brigham Young University.

Glenbow. **ACG**

210 **Hutchinson**, Gerald M. Memorial booklet written on the occasion of the 100th anniversary celebrations honoring the arrival of the Reverend Thomas Woolsey and the Reverend Henry Bird Steinhauer in September, 1855. Edmonton: United Church of Canada, Alberta Conference, 1955. 23p. ill.

On cover: The roots of the province.
Prepared under the authority of the Archives Committee.

Glenbow. **ACG**

211 **Keller**, Weldon Phillip. Charles Bowen. Paul Bunyan of the Canadian West. Beaverlodge: Horizon House, 1977. 141p. ill.

Original title *Bold under God*, published 1973, Chicago, Moody Bible Institute.
Also published under title *A fond look at a frontier preacher*, 1973, Beaverlodge, Horizon House.

Canadiana, 1977. **ATP**

212 **Keller**, Weldon Phillip. Expendable! With God on the prairies. The ministry of Prairie Bible Institute, Three Hills, Alberta, Canada. Three Hills: Prairie Press, 1966. 224p. ill.

Cover sub-title *The story of the Prairie Bible Institute*.
2d ed., 1972. Paper back ed., 1978.

Drake. **AEU**

213 **Kerr**, James Stolee. As grace is given. Camrose: Camrose Lutheran College, 1961. 1, 47, 9p.

At head of title: Golden anniversary pageant.
Written to commemorate the 50th anniversary of the founding of Camrose Lutheran Colege.

Canadiana, 1962. **OONL**

214 **LaBissoniere**, Jean Placidus. Providence trail blazers. Edmonton: Sisters of Providence, 1978. ix, 135p. ill.

History of the Sisters of Charity of Providence in Alberta. **AEA**

215 **Larden**, Robert A. Our apostolic heritage. Calgary: R.A. Larden, 1971. 192p. ill.

Printed by Kyle Printing and Stationery, Calgary.
History of the Apostolic Church of Pentecost of Canada.

Canadiana, 1974. **AEU**

216 **MacGregor**, James Grierson. Father Lacombe. Edmonton: Hurtig 1975. 350p. ill.

Canadiana, 1975. **AEU**

217 **Maclean**, Raymond Angus. The history of the Roman Catholic Church in Edmonton. Edmonton: University of Alberta, 1958. 166 leaves.

Thesis (M.A.), University of Alberta.
Typescript. **AEU**

218 **Mann**, William Edward. Sect, cult and church in Alberta. Toronto: University of Toronto Press, 1955. xiii, 166p. (Social credit in Alberta, its background and development, 6)

Canadiana, 1956. **AEA**

219 **Maxwell**, Grant. Like a Chinook. The Calgary Inter-faith Community Action Committee. An overview, 1959-1974. Narrated and edited by Grant Maxwell. Calgary: Inter-Church Consultants, 1974. 33p. **ACP**

220 **McCraw**, Louise Harrison. James H. McConkey, a man of God. Three Hills: Prairie Bible Institute, 1965. 211p.

Reprinted.

CBIP, 1979. **ATP**

221 **McCrum**, Elizabeth M. A register of service. The centennial history of the Anglican Diocese of Athabasca. Peace River: Diocese of Athabasca, 1976. 156p. ill.

Printed by Valley Printers.

Canadiana, 1977. **AEA**

222 **McDougall**, John. Opening the great West. Experiences of a missionary in 1875-76. With introduction by J. Ernest Nix. Calgary: Glenbow-Alberta Institute, 1970. 63p. ill. (Glenbow-Alberta Institute. Historical paper, 1)

Edited by Hugh Dempsey.

Glenbow. **ACG**

223 **McDougall**, John. Parsons on the plains. Edited by Thomas Bredin. Don Mills, Ont.: Longmans Canada, 1971. 193p. ill.

Excerpts from three works arranged to form a narrative: *Forest, lake and prairie*, Toronto, Briggs, 1895 *Saddle, sled and snowshoes*, Toronto, Briggs, 1876 *Pathfinding on plain and prairie*, Toronto, Briggs, 1898 (Peel 1413, 1450, 1546).

Canadian, 1972. **AEA**

224 **McDougall**, John. Pathfinding on plain and prairie. Stirring scenes of life in the Canadian North-West. With illustrations by J.E. Laughlin. Toronto: Coles, 1971. 277p. ill. (Coles Canadian collection)

Facsmile reprint of Toronto, Briggs, 1898 edition (Peel 1546).

CBIP, 1979. **AEA**

225 **McGibbon**, Grace D. Bradford. Glimpses of the life and work of the Reverend Richard Bradford, as scholar, school principal, chaplain, priest of the Church of England and S.P.G. missionary. Calgary: Grace D.B. McGibbon, 1970. 215p. ill.

Cover title *The Reverend Richard Bradford*.
Printed by Macleod Letter and Printing Services, Calgary.

Drake. **AEU**

226 **Morris,** John Joseph Harrold. The Presbyterian Church in Edmonton, northern Alberta, and the Klondike, 1881-1925, largely according to official documents. Ottawa: National Library of Canada, 1975. iv, 207 leaves. (Canadian theses on microfiche, 23669)

Thesis (Th.M.), Vancouver School of Theology, 1974.
Microfiche of typescript.

Canadiana, 1976. **AEA**

227 **Newton**, Elise. Elizabeth McDougall, madonna of the Plains. Aldergrove, B.C.: Frontier Publishing, 1978. 64p. ill. (Frontier books, 35)

Printed by Valcraft Printing, Aldergrove.
Biography of the wife of the Rev. George McDougall.

CBIP, 1978. **AEA**

228 **Niedzwiecki**, Stella. Ukrainian Rite Catholic Church. An account of church activities in Calgary. Calgary: Century Calgary Publications, 1975. iv, 63p. ill.

Also published as part of *The search for souls*, which was issued as v.4. of the Century Calgary Historical Series.

Canadiana, 1979. **AEA**

229 **Nix**, James Ernest. John Maclean's mission to the Blood Indians, 1880-1889. Ottawa: National Library of Canada, 1978. xi, 245 12 leaves. ill. (Canadian theses on microfiche, 38310)

Thesis (M.A.), McGill University, 1978.
Microfiche of typescript.

Canadiana, 1980. **OONL**

230 **Nix**, James Ernest. Missions among the buffalo. The labours of the Reverends George M. and John C. McDougall in the Canadian Northwest, 1860-1876. Toronto: Ryerson Press, 1960. viii, 3, 123p. ill.

Canadiana, 1960. **ACG**

231 **Patterson**, Muriel Beaton. Messenger of the Great Spirit. Robert Terrill Rundle. New York: Friendship Press, 1961. 23p. (Frontier books, 4)

Reprint of 1947 edition. 2d printing, 1951. **AEU**

232 **Peake**, Frank Alexander. Anglican beginnings in and about Edmonton. Toronto: Anglican Church of Canada, 1961. 17p. ill. (Canadian Church Historical Society. Off-print, 7)

Caption title.
Contains information about William Newton, first Anglican missionary in Edmonton.

Glenbow. **ACG**

233 **Penton**, M. James. Jehovah's Witnesses in Canada. Champions of freedom of speech and worship. Toronto: Macmillan of Canada, 1976. 88p.

CBIP, 1978. **AEA**

234 **Pierce**, R.J. Reverend John Gough Brick. A northern Alberta pioneer. Toronto: Canadian Church Historical Society, 1956. (1v.) (Canadian Church Historical Society. Offprint, 10)

Reprint from *Alberta Historical Review*, v.4, n.2 (Spring 1956).

Drake. **OONL**

235 **Plett**, Jake. Valley of shadows. Beaverlodge: Horizon House, 1976. 168p. (Horizon Books)

Account of the abduction and murder of his wife in Edmonton and his subsequent religious experiences.

Canadiana, 1976. **AEU**

236 Prairie Bible Institute. With God on the Prairies. Miracle of Prairie Bible Institute. Three Hills: Prairie Bible Institute, 1966. 49p. ill.

Glenbow. **ACG**

237 **Prior**, Kenneth H. The reminiscences of thirty years service in Africa, 1926-1956. By Pearl L. Prior and Kenneth H. Prior. Calgary: Riveredge Foundation, 1970. 479p. in various pagings. ill.

Duplicated.
Reminiscences of United Church missionaries in Africa. **AEU**

238 **Redekopp**, Helen. History of Alberta Mennonite Women in Mission, 1947-1977. Coaldale: Alberta Mennonite Women in Mission, 1977. 128p. ill.

Text in English and German.
Printed by D.W. Friesen & Sons, Altona, Manitoba. **AEA**

239 **Ricker**, Harold Byron. Frontiers and reflections. s.l.: s.n., 1977. 79p. ill.

Autobiography of a United Church minister in central Alberta and the Peace River Country. **AEA**

240 **Rimmer**, Harry. The last of the giants. Three Hills: Prairie Press, 1965. 284p.

CBIP, 1979.

241 **Rundle**, Robert Terrill. The Rundle journals, 1840-1848. Edited by Hugh A. Dempsey. Introduction and notes by Gerald M. Hutchinson. Calgary: Historical Society of Alberta, Alberta Records Publication Board and Glenbow-Alberta Institute, 1977. lxiv, 414p. ill. (Historical Society of Alberta, v.1)

Papers of the first Wesleyan Methodist missionary.

CBIP, 1979. **AEA**

242 **Schwermann**, Albert Henry. The beginnings of Lutheran Church, Canada, covering the years 1941 to 1964. Planning a self-governing church for Canada. Edmonton: Lutheran Church, 1971. 113p. ill.

History of Lutheran Church, Missouri Synod. **AEA**

243 The search for souls. Histories of Calgary churches. Calgary: Century Calgary Publications, 1975. 760p. ill. (Century Calgary historical series, v.4)

Each chapter also published separately.
Contents: Crawford, D. Blue Flame in the Foothills The Anglican Church in Calgary Cherland, C. The Lutheran legacy Bentall, S. Buckboard to brotherhood Collett, W.J. United, Church in Calgary Collett, H.L. First Spiritualist Church Niedzwiecki, Ukrainian rite Catholic Church Anderson, N.R. Oblate Fathers in Calgary. **ACU**

244 **Snyder**, Juanita Carroll. Raise up the foundations. Memories of Maria Marshall (Mrs. Andrew Kirk), by her children. As told to Juanita C. Snyder. Three Hills: Prairie Bible Institute, 1966. 69p. ill.

Reminiscences of the wife of the first Presbyterian missionary to the Grande Prairie area.

Glenbow. **ACG**

245 **Stauffer**, Ezra. History of the Alberta-Saskatchewan Mennonite Conference. Illustrations from original drawings by the author. Ryley: Alberta-Saskatchewan Mennonite Conference, 1960. 1v. (loose-leaf). ill.

Duplicated.

Contains church histories and biographies. **AEA**

246 **Steinig**, Serafina. Cos' ci oddam Panie. Rzecz o Matce Marii Kolumbie Biateckiej, fundatorce kontemplatywno-czynnych siostr Dominikanek w Polsce. Calgary: s.n., 1977. xvi, 788p. ill.

Printed by Excello Print, Calgary.

Canadiana, 1978. **OONL**

247 **Stocken**, Harry William Gibbon. Among the Blackfoot and Sarcee. With an introduction by Georgeen Barrass. Calgary: Glenbow Alberta Institute, 1976. 75p. ill.

Autobiography of an Anglican missionary in southern Alberta.

Canadiana, 1977. **AEA**

248 **Swanson**, Cecil. The days of my sojourning. A reminiscence. Calgary: Glenbow-Alberta Institute, 1977. x, 141p. ill.

Reminiscences of the Ven. C. Swanson, pioneer Anglican clergyman.

Canadiana, 1978. **AEA**

249 Tenth anniversary of St. Basil's Villa, Pigeon Lake, Alberta 1950-1960. Toronto: Basilian Press, 1960. 128p. ill.

Text in Ukrainian and English.
History of a children's summer camp.

de Valk, 1971. **SSM**

250 **Thompson**, Margaret Ellis. The Baptist story in Western Canada. Calgary: Baptist Union of Western Canada, 1974. iv, 528p.

Canadiana, 1976. **AEU**

251 **Thomson**, Dorothy J. Vine of His planting. History of Canadian Nazarene College. Edmonton: Printed by Commercial Printers, 1961. 34p. ill.

Published on the 40th anniversary of the Canadian Nazarene College, Red Deer. **AEA**

252 **Townsend**, Arthur Herbert. Cariboo country saints and shenanigans. Beaverlodge: Horizon House, 1976. 122p.

Reminiscences of a Prince George minister.

Canadiana, 1976. **AEU**

253 **Travis**, John. The Rundle adventure story. Banff: s.n., 1968. (2), 18p. (incl. advts.) ill.

Cover title.
Biography of Robert Rundle, Methodist missionary.

Glenbow. **ACG**

254 **Tuttle**, George M. The story of St. Stephen's, Edmonton. Edmonton: St. Stephen's College, 1970. 16p. ill.

Printed by the University of Alberta Printing Department.

Ceessa. **AEA**

255 Ukrainian Catholic unity, 1906-1966. Ivan Isaiv, Osyp Pryima, Petro Savaryn. Edmonton: Ukrains'kyi narodyni dim, 1966. 544p. ill.

Text in Ukrainian. English spine title.
A history of the Ukrainian Catholic Church in Alberta. **AEU**

256 **Vaughan**, Louisa. The work of faith with power. Miracles in a missionary's life in China. Rev. ed. Three Hills: Prairie Press, 1961. 57, 7p.

Formerly entitled *Answered or unanswered*.
Rev. ed., 1977.

CBIP, 1979. **ATP**

257 **Vitt**, Kurt H. Clement Hoyler, God's pacemaker for Moravians in Canada. Impressions. Edmonton: s.n., 1972. 24p. ill. **AEA**

258 **Weinberger**, A.M. I escaped the holocaust. A.M. Weinberger as told to Muriel Leeson. Beaverlodge: Horizon House, 1978. 91p.

Biography of a Jewish rabbi who escaped from Nazi Germany and converted to Christianity.

CBIP, 1979.

259 What about the Grey Nuns? Edmonton: Hamly, 1958. 15p. ill.

de Valk, 1975. **SSM**

260 **Wilkinson**, Florence Gertrude. The Indians of Alberta hear the Gospel. The story of the development of Indian missions in Alberta under the churches which entered union, 1840-1925. Victoria: University of Victoria, 1963. (1v.)

Thesis (Th.M), Victoria University, 1963.
Typescript.

Canadian theses. **OTV**

Church History

261 Acme. United Church. History of the churches of the Acme area. Acme: Acme United Church, 1975. 1v. (unpaged).

Caption title. Duplicated. **AEA**

262 **Albert**, Diane. History of the Fort Kent parish. Histoire de la paroisse de Fort Kent. 50th anniversary. Fort Kent: Fort Kent Catholic Church, 1972. 20p. ill.

Cover title *Fort Kent, 1922-1972*.
Text in English and French.
Duplicated.

Ceessa. **AEA**

263 **Alexander**, Grace. First Baptist Church 75th anniversary, March 7, 1976. Seventy-five years, 1901-1976. Lethbridge: First Baptist Church, 1976. 104p. ill.

Cover title *First Baptist story*.
Printed by Herald Printers, Lethbridge.

Ceessa. **AEA**

264 Alix. United Church. The winds of change. A history of Alix United Church, including Tees United Church, Haynes United Church. Alix: Alix United Church, 1967. 16p.

Cover title.
Duplicated. **AEA**

265 Armena. Scandia Lutheran Church. Seventy-fifth anniversary, 1901-1976. Armena: Scandia Lutheran Church, 1976. 8p. ill.

Cover title.
Printed by Gospel Contact Press. **ACML**

266 **Armstrong**, C.C. The days of our years. Daysland United Church, 1905-1942. Daysland: Knox United Church, 1975. 11, 6p.

Cover title.
Duplicated.
At top of p.1: A history of Knox United Church, Daysland.
Ms. note in Alberta Provincial Archives copy: By C.C. Armstrong.

Ceessa. **AEA**

267 **Bagnall**, Lucy Lowe. At the seventy-fifth milestone. The story of the First Baptist Church, Calgary, Alberta, 1948-1963. Edited by Shirley Franklyn Bentall. Calgary: First Baptist Church Seventyfifth Anniversary Committee, 1963. 56p. ill.

Published as a supplement to *At the sixtieth milestone*, by L.L. Bagnall, 1948 (Peel 4082).

Ceessa. **AEA**

268 Basilian Fathers. In tribute to the Basilian pioneers, 1902-1963. Mundare: Basilian Fathers, 1960. 120p. ill.

Title page and text in Ukrainian and English.

Ceessa. AEA

269 Basilian Fathers. In tribute to the Basilian pioneers, 1902-1977. Edmonton: Basilian Fathers, 1977. 88p.

Title page and text in Ukrainian and English.
Published on the 75th anniversary of the arrival of the Ukrainian Basilian Fathers in Canada. AEA

270 **Bauer**, Reuben Alexander. One of many. Edmonton: La Survivance Printing, 1965. 188p. ill.

History of the German-Russian congregation of the Hope Evangelical and Reformed Church, Stony Plain.

Glenbow. ACG

271 Bawlf Lutheran, 1902-1972. Camrose: Camrose Booster, 1972. 20p. ill.

Cover title.

Ceessa. AEA

272 Beiseker. Our Lady of Assumption Catholic Parish. Souvenir of the golden jubilee, 1908-1958. Beiseker: Our Lady of Assumption Parish, 1958. 13 leaves.

Cover title. Duplicated. AEA

273 **Bekker**, Janny. 25 years, First Christian Reformed Church, Red Deer. Red Deer: First Christian Reformed Church, 1976. 48p. ill.

On cover: Our church ... 25 years of praise and prayer.

Ceessa. AEA

274 Bellevue. St. Cyril's Catholic Church. Golden anniversary, 1915-1965. Bellevue: St. Cyril's Church, 1965. 28p. ill.

Cover title. AEA

275 Berwyn. Bissell Memorial United Church. Twenty-fifth anniversary. Berwyn: Bissell Memorial United Church, 1961. 13 leaves.

Cover title.

Duplicated. AEA

276 Brightview. Emmaus Lutheran Church. Brief history of Emmaus Lutheran Congregation, Brightview, Alberta, and Zion Lutheran Congregation, Peace Hill, Alberta. Brightview: Emmaus Lutheran and Zion Lutheran Church Anniversary Committee, 1960. 16p. ill.

Caption title.
On cover: Golden jubilee, 1960. AEA

277 Bruderheim. Bethlehem Lutheran Church. Seventy years under God, for God. Bethlehem Lutheran Church, Missouri Synod, 1897-1967. Bruderheim: Bethlehem Lutheran Church, 1967. 16p. ill.

Glenbow.

ACG

278 **Bryan**, Gertrude. Land of the Spirit. Originator of the book plan, Jessie Lillicoe. Spirit River: Spirit River United Church Women's Association, 1971. 56p. ill.

Cover title. Duplicated.
A history of the Church and affiliated groups.

Drake.

AEA

279 **Butler**, Betty. St. Barnabas Church, Medicine Hat, 1884-1974. Medicine Hat: St. Barnabas Anglican Church, 1974. 48p. ill.

Cover title.
At head of title: Ninetieth anniversary.
Editor, Mrs. Betty Butler.

Ceessa.

AEA

280 **Byrne**, J. Paul. St Mary's of the Assumption in the Canadian Rockies Banff, Alberta. Banff: St Mary's of the Assumption Church, n.d. 16p.

de Valk, 1971.

SSM

281 Calgary. Brentview Baptist Church. Dedication of Brentview Baptist Church. Calgary: Brentview Baptist Church, 1971. (12p) ill.

Includes a brief history.

AENB

282 Calgary. Canadian Martyrs Catholic Church. The first ten years, 1967-1977. Calgary: Canadian Martyrs Parish, 1977. 56p. ill.

Cover title *Canadian Martyrs tenth anniversary, 1967-1977*.

AEA

283 Calgary. Canadian Martyrs Catholic Church. History of Canadian Martyrs Church. Calgary: Canadian Martyrs Church, 1969. 36p. ill.

Cover title *Canadian Martyrs Church, Calgary, Alberta*.

AEA

284 Calgary. First Baptist Church. Dedicatory services for the reconstructed organ and the renovated sanctuary. Sunday, May 29, 1966. Calgary: First Baptist Church, 1966. 1v.

The organs of the First Baptist Church (1891-1966), by Stuart Kennedy, p.9-10.

Glenbow.

ACG

285 Calgary. First Lutheran Church. Seventy-fifth anniversary. Calgary: First Lutheran Church, 1975. (18p.) ill.

Cover title. Duplicated.

ACML

286 Calgary. Grace Baptist Church. Grace Baptist Church, 1912-1972. Calgary: Grace Baptist Church, 1972. 15p. ill.

Includes a brief history. **AENB**

287 Calgary. Grace Lutheran Church. Grace for 25 years, 1950-1975. Calgary: Grace Lutheran Church, 1975. 20, 2p. ill.

Cover title. Duplicated.

Caption title *A brief history of Grace Lutheran Congregation, 1950-1975*. **ACML**

288 Calgary. Knox United Church. The eightieth anniversary. A memento to Knox United Church, Calgary, Alberta. Calgary: Knox United Church, 1963. 8p. ill.

Cover title. **AEA**

289 Calgary. Mount Calvary Lutheran Church. 50 years of Grace, 1919-1969. Calgary: Mount Calvary Lutheran Church, 1969. 39p. ill.

Cover title.

Glenbow. **ACML**

290 Calgary. Our Lady of Mercy Croatian Catholic Parish. Croation Catholic Parish Our Lady of Mercy, 1967-1977. Calgary: Croatian Catholic Parish, 1977. 44p. ill.

On cover: Souvenir booklet on the occasion of the tenth anniversary of the Croatian Catholic Parish, Our Lady of Mercy, Calgary, Alberta.

Title page and text in English and Croation. **AEA**

291 Calgary. Our Lady of Perpetual Help Parish. 50 years at the foot of the hill, 1925-1975. Commemorating the 50th anniversary of Our Lady of Perpetual Help Parish. Calgary: Our Lady of Perpetual Help Parish, 1975. 38p. ill.

Cover title. **AECSJ**

292 Calgary. St. Anthony's Catholic Parish. Silver jubilee. Calgary: St. Anthony's Catholic Parish, 1978. 8p. ill.

Cover title. **AEA**

293 Calgary. St. Barnabas' Church. 50th anniversary. St. Barnabas' Anglican Church, Calgary, Alberta, June 11, 1956. Calgary: St. Barnabas' Church, 1956. 12p. ill.

Cover title.

Drake. **ACG**

294 Calgary. St. Barnabas' Church. 60th anniversary. St. Barnabas' Anglican Church, Calgary, Alberta, June 11, 1966. Calgary: St. Barnabas' Church, 1966. 16p. ill.

Cover title.

Drake. **ACG**

295 Calgary. St. Boniface Catholic Church. St. Bonifatius Kirche, 1960-1970, Calgary, Alberta. Calgary: St. Boniface Church, 1970. 10p. ill.

Cover title.
Text in German.

Ceessa. **AEA**

296 Calgary. St. Joseph's Catholic Church. Parish means people. 60, St. Joseph's Parish, 1914-1974. Calgary: St. Joseph's Parish, 1974. 13 leaves. ill.

Duplicated. **AEA**

297 Calgary. St. Martin's Anglican Church. Service of dedication by the Right Rev. G.R. Calvert, D.D., Bishop of Calgary, St. Martin's Day, November 11, 1960, 3.00 p.m. Calgary: St. Martin's Anglican Church, 1960. 9p. ill.

Order of service and historical notes.

Canadiana, 1961. **AEA**

298 Calgary. St. Mary's Cathedral. Souvenir of the consecration of St. Mary's Cathedral, Calgary, Alberta, December 11th, 1957. Calgary: St. Mary's Cathedral, 1957. (27)p. ill.

A history of the Cathedral.

Glenbow. **ACG**

299 Calgary. St. Michael and All Angels' Church. St. Michael and All Angels' Anglican Church, Calgary, anniversary, June 3rd, 1959. Calgary: St. Michael and All Angels' Anglican Church, 1959. 7p. ill.

Canadiana, 1965. **AEA**

300 Calgary. St. Pius the Tenth Catholic Parish. 25th anniversary of St. Pius the Tenth Parish, Calgary. Calgary: St. Pius the Tenth Catholic Parish, 1979. 41p. ill.

Cover title.
Contains history and current activities of the parish. **AEA**

301 Calgary. St. Stephen's Anglican Church. Golden jubilee, 1906-1956. Calgary: St. Stephen's Anglican Church, 1956. 12p. ill.

Drake. **ACG**

302 Calgary. Trinity Evangelical Lutheran Church. A history of Trinity Lutheran Church, the Evangelical Lutheran Church of Canada. Calgary: Trinity Evangelical Lutheran Church, 1974. 12p.

Cover title. Duplicated.
At head of title: 75th anniversary, 1899-1974. **ACML**

303 Calgary. Wesley United Church. Wesley United Church, Calgary, Alberta, fiftieth anniversary, 1906-1956. Calgary: Wesley United Church, 1956. 8p.

Ceessa. **AEA**

304 **Campbell**, Alice A. A brief history of Delburne United Church, 1903 to 1958. Delburne: Delburne United Church, 1978. 6p.

Cover title. Duplicated. **AEA**

305 **Campbell**, Elizabeth. Memories of yesteryear, with Beth Campbell. A short history of Holden United Church. Holden: Holden United Church, 1966. 1v. (unpaged).

Ceessa. **AEA**

306 Camrose. Messiah Lutheran Church. Messiah Lutheran through seventy years, 1901-1971. Commemorating the seventieth anniversary of the Messiah Lutheran Congregation, Camrose, Alberta. Camrose: Messiah Lutheran Church, 1971. 8p.

Includes order of service. **ACML**

307 Camrose. St. Francis Xavier Catholic Church. Souvenir of the dedication and official opening. Camrose: St. Francis Xavier Church, 1963. 24p. ill.

Cover title. **AEA**

308 Carstairs. United Church. The Carstairs United Church, 1906-1956. Fifty years of service. Carstairs: Carstairs United Church, 1956. 11 leaves.

Cover title. Duplicated. **AEA**

309 **Carter**, David John. Calgary's Anglican cathedral. The Cathedral Church of the Redeemer. Calgary: Cathedral Church of the Reedemer, 1973. 63p.

Printed by Kyle Printing & Stationery.

Drake. **AEA**

310 **Charyk**, John Constantine. Hanna First United Church golden anniversary, 1912-1962. A dedication of the new church, October 26th, 1962. Hanna: First United Church, 1962. 25p. ill.

Cover title. **AEU**

311 Claresholm. United Church. A history of Claresholm United Church, 1904-1969. Claresholm: Claresholm United Church, 1969. 16p.

Cover title. Duplicated. **AEA**

312 Coaldale. United Church. History of Coaldale United Church, 1904-1975. Coaldale: Coaldale United Church, 1975. 15 leaves.

Cover title. Typescript.

Ceessa. **AEA**

313 **Collett**, H.L. First Spiritualist Church. A short account of spiritualism in Calgary. Calgary: Century Calgary Publications, 1975. 8p. ill.

Also published as part of *The search for souls*, which was issued as v.4 of the Century Calgary Historical Series.

Canadiana, 1977. **AEA**

314 Cowley. United Church. Foothills U.C.W., 1903-1978. Cowley: United Church, 1978. 15 leaves in various pagings.

Cover title. Duplicated. **AEA**

315 **Davidson**, John M. Crescent Heights United Church. Our sixtieth anniversary, 1908-1968. Calgary: Crescent Heights United Church, 1968. 24p. ill.

Printed by Northwest Printing & Lithographing.

Glenbow. **ACG**

316 Dickson. Bethany Lutheran Congregation. 75th anniversary, Bethany Lutheran Congregation, Dickson, Alberta. Dickson: Bethany Lutheran Congregation, 1979. (12p.) ill.

Cover title.
Printed by the Innisfail Province. **ACML**

317 **Donahue**, Geraldine. Saint Agnes Parish, Edmonton, Alberta, silver anniversary, 1953-1978. Edmonton: Catholic Womens League of Canada, Saint Agnes Parish, 1978. 29p. ill.

Duplicated. **AEA**

318 **Donlevy**, William J. History of St. Agnes Parish. Edmonton: Saint Agnes Parish, 1978. 36p. ill.

On cover: Silver Jubilee, Saint Agnes Parish, Edmonton, Alberta, 1953-1978. **AEA**

319 **Dorward**, Christina. A history of Avonmore United Church from 1908. People of His pasture. Edmonton: Avonmore United Church, 1975. 119, 4p. ill.

AEA

320 **Dowkes**, Margaret. History of St. John's Presbyterian Church, Medicine Hat, Alberta, 1883-1973. Hope Hargrave Michael, adviser and editor. Medicine Hat: St. John's Presbyterian Church Session and Board of Managers, 1973. vii, 134p. ill.

Canadiana, 1973. **AEA**

321 **Drouin**, Eméric O'Neil. Bénédiction des cloches de la paroisse-cathédrale de Saint Paul, Alberta, Dimanche, le 26 juin 1960. Edmonton: St. Paul's Catholic Cathedral, 1960. 65p. ill.

Author identified by Rev. G. Durocher.

de Valk, 1975. **SSM**

322 Drumheller. Knox United Church. Golden anniversary, 1910-1960. Drumheller: Knox United Church, 1960. 24p. ill.

Ceessa. **AEA**

323 Drumheller. St. Anthony's Catholic Parish. 50th anniversary, 1917-1967. Drumheller: St. Anthony's Catholic Parish, 1967. 46p. ill.

Cover title. **AEA**

324 Edmonton. Central Lutheran Church. Fiftieth anniversary, 1910-1960. Edmonton: Central Lutheran Church, 1960. 8p. ill.

Cover title. **AEA**

325 Edmonton. Christ Church. Golden jubilee. Christ Church, Edmonton, Canada, 1900 to 1959. Edmonton: Christ Church, 1959. 20p.

Drake. **AEA**

326 Edmonton. Church of the Good Shepherd. Church of the Good Shepherd 65th anniversary. Edmonton: Church of the Good Shepherd, 1975. 28p. ill.

Cover title. **AEA**

327 Edmonton. Highlands United Church. Highlands United Church, Edmonton, Alberta, 50th anniversary, 1912-1962. Edmonton: Highlands United Church, 1962. 15p. ill.

Cover title.

Ceessa. **AEA**

328 Edmonton. Holy Trinity Church. Holy Trinity church .. 75th anniversary. 75 years of service in Christ's name. Edmonton: Holy Trinity Church, 1968. (12), 86p. ill.

Printed by Pioneer Press.
On cover: 75 years 1893-1968.

Glenbow. **ACG**

329 Edmonton. Immaculate Conception Catholic Parish. Fêtes du 60ième anniversaire, Paroisse de l'Immaculée-Conception. Edmonton: Paroisse de l'Immaculée-Conception, 1966. (8)p.

Caption title.
A program of events.
Includes a 4-page history of the Parish. **AECSJ**

330 Edmonton. Knox United Church. Knox United Church, south Edmonton, diamond jubilee of present building, 1907-1967. A history of our church and its early beginnings dating back to 1891, on the occasion of the 60th anniversary of the dedication of the present edifice, November 1967. Edmonton: Knox United Church, 1967. 86p. ill.

Glenbow. **ACG**

331 Edmonton. McDougall United Church. From drums to drums. Souvenir program. Edmonton: McDougall United Church, 1973. 16p. ill.

Produced by the Centennial Pageant Committee.

Canadiana, 1976. **AEA**

332 Edmonton. McDougall United Church. Ninetieth anniversary of McDougall United Church, Edmonton, Alberta, Sunday, October 22, Monday, October 23. Anniversary speaker, Rev. J.E. Nix. Edmonton: McDougall United Church, 1961. 28p. ill.

Cover title.
At head of title: 1871-1961.
Includes brief history of the church.

Glenbow. **ACG**

333 Edmonton. McDougall United Church. The Pioneers. McDougall Church. Our first 100 years, 1871-1971. Edmonton: McDougall United Church, 1971. 32p. ill.

Cover title.
Printed by Douglas Print.

Canadiana, 1976. **AEA**

334 Edmonton. Moravian Church. The Edmonton Moravian Church 50th anniversary celebration. Edmonton: Edmonton Moravian Church, 1955. 20p. ill.

Cover title.

Ceessa. **AEA**

335 Edmonton. Robertson United Church. Robertson United Church, golden anniversary, 1969. Edmonton: Hamly Press, 1969. 48p. ill.

Glenbow. **ACG**

336 Edmonton. Saint Joachim Church. Album souvenir. Centenaire de la paroisse Saint-Joachim d'Edmonton, 1859-1959. Edmonton: Saint Joachim Parish, 1959. 74p. ill.

Glenbow. **ACG**

337 Edmonton. Saints Constantine and Helen Romanian Orthodox Parish. Anniversary. Edmonton: Saints Constantine and Helen Romanian Orthodox Parish, 1969. 38p. ill.

Canadiana, 1972. **AEU**

338 Edmonton. St. Alphonsus Catholic Parish. Golden jubilee. Edmonton: St. Alphonsus Parish, 1974. 28p.

de Valk, 4. **SSM**

339 Edmonton. St. Andrew's Catholic Parish. St. Andrew's Parish 50. Rejoice. Edmonton: St. Andrew's Catholic Parish, 1977. 44p. ill.

Cover title.
Printed by Reliable Printing, Edmonton.
Commemorating the golden jubilee of St. Andrew's Catholic Parish, 1927-1977, Edmonton, Alberta. **AECSJ**

340 Edmonton. St. Barnabas Anglican Church. St. Barnabas Church. Edmonton: St. Barnabas Church, 1979. 12p.

Duplicated. **AEA**

341 Edmonton. St. Faith's Anglican Church. Fiftieth anniversary, 1910-1960. Edmonton: St. Faith's Anglican Church, 1960. 16p. ill.

Cover title.

Drake. **AEA**

342 Edmonton. St. John the Evangelist Church. Fiftieth anniversary, 1916-1966. St. John the Evangelist Church. Edmonton: Church of St. John the Evangelist, 1966. 14p.

Drake. **AEU**

343 Edmonton. St. John's Evangelical Lutheran Church. St. John's Evangelical Lutheran Church, Western Canadian Synod, organized 1903, dedicated May 28, 1972. Edmonton: St. John's Lutheran Church, 1972. 12p. ill.

Cover title.
A history of the Congregation, 1903-1972.

Ceessa. **AEA**

344 **Edmonton. St. Nicholas**, St. Michael Ukrainian Catholic Church. 75th anniversary, Ukrainian Catholic Parish of St. Nicholas, St. Michael. Edmonton: St. Nicholas, St. Michael Ukrainian Catholic Church, 1975. 17p. ill.

Text in Ukrainian and English.

Ceessa. **AEA**

345 Edmonton. St. Pius X Catholic Parish. The first 25 years, 1954-1979. Edmonton: St. Pius X Parish, 1979. 48p. ill.

Cover title. **AEA**

346 Edmonton. Ste. Anne Parish. 1952-1977, Paroisse Ste-Anne. Edmonton: Paroisse Ste. Anne, 1977. 39, 1p.

Cover title. **AECSJ**

347 Edmonton. Strathcona Baptist Church. Strathcona Baptist Church story. Seventy-five years. Edmonton: Strathcona Baptist Church, 1970. 62p. ill. **AEA**

348 Edmonton. Strathearn United Church. Strathearn United Church, Edmonton, Alberta, 1951-1961. Edmonton: Strathearn United Church, 1961. 12p. ill.

Cover title. **AEA**

349 Edmonton. Trinity Evangelical Lutheran Church. 60th anniversary, Trinity Evangelical Lutheran Church, 1902-1962. Edmonton: Trinity Evangelical Lutheran Church, 1962. 24p. ill.

Cover title.
Text in English and German.
Printed by Speedfast Printers, Edmonton.

Ceessa. **AEA**

350 Edmonton. Wesley United Church. Wesley's 60 years, 1907-1967. A chronicle of its early beginnings as the West End Methodist Sunday School and its development as Wesley United Church, Edmonton. Edmonton: Wesley United Church, 1967. 44p. ill.

Cover title.

Ceessa. **AEA**

351 Edmonton. Westminster United Church. 50th anniversary, 1912-1962. Edmonton: Westminster United Church, 1962. 8p. ill.

Cover title. **AEA**

352 Edson. Sacred Heart Catholic Parish. Sacred Heart Parish, 1912-1972. Edson: Sacred Heart Parish, 1972. 20p. ill.

de Valk, 1975. **AEA**

353 Edson. United Church. Edson United Church history. Edson: Edson United Church, 1971. 16p. ill.

Caption title.
On cover: 1911-1971, Sixtieth anniversary, Edson United Church.
Based on a history compiled by Mr. H.A. Switzer. **AEA**

354 Empress. St. Mary the Virgin Anglican Church. St. Mary the Virgin, 1914-1974, 60th anniversary. Empress: St. Mary the Virgin Parish, 1974. 73p. ill.

Cover title. Duplicated. **ACG**

355 **Erickson**, George. History of the Ranfurly United Church and its congregation. Edited by Mrs. Alvin (Jean) Erickson. Compiled by Mr. George Erickson. Ranfurly: Ranfurly United Church, 1975. 16p.

Duplicated.

Ceessa. **AEA**

356 **Fawcett**, John M. A history of St. Paul's United Church, Coleman, Alberta. Coleman: St. Paul's United Church, 1966. 38p. ill.

On cover: 60th anniversary, 1906-1966.

Ceessa. **AEA**

357 **Fischer**, Emil. St. Matthew's Evangelical Lutheran Church, Spruce Grove, Alberta, seventy-fifth anniversary. Spruce Grove: St. Matthew's Evangelical Lutheran Church, 1966. 32p. ill.

Ceessa. **AEA**

358 **Foran**, C.J. History of St. Anthony's Parish. Edmonton: St. Anthony's Parish, 1955. 23p. ill.

On cover: Golden jubilee, St. Anthony's Parish, Edmonton, Alberta, 1905-1955. Souvenir booklet.

Ceessa. **AEA**

359 Fort Vermilion. St. Luke's Anglican Mission. Unchaga = Peace. The centennial history of St. Luke's Anglican Mission, Ft. Vermilion, Alberta. Fort Vermilion: St. Luke's Centennial Historical Committee, 1977. 61p.

Printed by Valley Printers, Peace River.

Drake. **AEA**

360 **Gagajek**, E.G. St. Benoit Parish 50th anniversary. St. Benoit Church, Pickardville, Alberta, 1929-1979. Pickardville: St. Benoit Parish, 1979. 10, 95, 10p. ill.

Printed by Marcel Handie, Stony Plain. **AEA**

361 **Gehring**, A. 75 years of grace, 1894-1969. Stony Plain: St. Matthew's Evangelical Lutheran Church, 1969. 73p. ill.

Cover title. Duplicated.
At head of title: Diamond jubilee. **AEA**

362 **George**, John E. Mayerthorpe Pastoral Charge history. Edmonton: Sun Printing, 1958. 47p. ill.

At head of title: United Church of Canada. **AEA**

363 **Griffin**, John Peter. These are they. A record of Fort Macleod, one of its first churches. Fort Macleod: Trinity United Church, 1974. 303p.

A history of Trinity United Church which was founded in 1878 as a Methodist Mission. Printed in Calgary.

Ceessa. **AEA**

364 **Hackett**, John. A historical sketch, Lamont United Church, 1892-1956. Lamont: Lamont United Church, 1956. 18p. ill.

Cover title. **AEA**

365 **Hambly**, J.R.Stan. Saddlebags to stained glass. The history of Camrose United Church and its founding congregations. Camrose: Camrose United Church, 1975. 180p. ill.

Printed by Gospel Contact Press, Camrose.

Ceessa. **AEA**

366 **Handford**, Ellen A. History of St. Mark's Church. Innisfail: St. Mark's Anglican Church, 1972. 5p.

Duplicated.

Title at head of text. **AEA**

367 Hayter. Our Savior's Lutheran Church. 60th anniversary. Hayter: Our Savior's Lutheran Church, 1970. 24p. ill.

Cover title. **AEA**

368 **Heinen**, Gerty. Iron Springs Christian Reformed Church, 1949-1974, twenty-fifth anniversary. Iron Springs: Iron Springs Christian Reformed Church, 1974. 93p. ill.

Printed by Herald Printers, Lethbridge.
Edited by Gerty Heinen.
Part of text in Dutch.

Ceessa. **AEA**

369 **Hetherington**, Arthur J. Our Lady of Peace. Calgary: Sacred Heart Catholic Church, 1960. leaves 29-58.

Caption title *Chronicles of the early Church in southern Alberta*.
Issued in 1923 on the twenty-fifth anniversary of the founding of the Catholic Parish of the Sacred Heart, Calgary.

Glenbow. **ACG**

370 Hill Spring. Church of Jesus Christ of Latter-Day Saints. 50 years. Hill Spring Ward, 1910-1960. Hill Spring: Church of Jesus Christ of the Latter-Day Saints, 1960. 18, (1) p. ill.

Cover title. Duplicated.
Prepared by the Laurel class under the direction of Mildred Mendenhall.

Glenbow. **ACG**

371 **Hladyshevsky**, M. Ukrainian Catholic parish, Calgary, Alberta. Souvenir of the golden anniversary, 1912-1962. Edmonton: Ukrainian News Publishers, 1962. 166p. ill.

Title page in Ukrainian. Cover title in English. Text partly English, partly Ukrainian.

Canadiana, 1964. **OONL**

372 **Hohensee**, Richard. Seventy five years by the grace of God. A history of Central Baptist Church. Edmonton: Central Baptist Church, 1975. 40p. ill.

Printed by Ukrainian News Publishers.

Caption title.

On cover: 75th anniversary, 1900-1975. **AEA**

373 **Hurko,** T. 10th anniversary first Ukrainian Catholic Church, Smoky Lake, 1964-1974. Smoky Lake: Sts. Volodymyr and Olga Ukrainian Catholic Church, 1974. 32 leaves. ill.

Cover title. Duplicated.Text mainly in Ukrainian. Title page in English and Ukrainian. **AEA**

374 Irma. Sharon Lutheran Church. Golden anniversary, 1910-1960. Irma: Sharon Lutheran Church, 1960. (16)p. ill.

Cover title.

Includes programs of services. **AEA**

375 Irma. United Church. A history of Irma United Church. Published on the occasion of the golden anniversary. Irma: Irma United Church History Committee, 1960. 32p. ill.

Canadiana, 1962. **AEA**

376 **James**, Jean. St. Peter's Lutheran Church, Scapa, Alberta, 1921-1971. Hanna: s.n., 1971. 24p. ill.

Cover title.
Duplicated.

St. Peter's was abandoned in 1966 and the congregation moved to Hanna. **AEA**

377 **Jones**, William Griffith. Over the years at Zion. Time like an ever rolling sea, 1902-1976. Ponoka: Zion United Church, 1976. 32p. (chiefly ill.)

Cover title.
Printed by Ponoka Herald.
Compiled by W. Griff Jones.
A history of Zion United Church.

Ceessa. **AEA**

378 **Jordon**, Mabel E. The McDougall Memorial United Church, Morley, Alberta. The church of the Mountain Stoneys. A souvenir booklet. s.l.: s.n., 1957. (12)p. ill.

Glenbow. **ACG**

379 Jubilé d'argent. Silver jubilee, Mallaig, 1941-66. Mallaig: Catholic Parish of Mallaig, 1966. 9p. ill.

Duplicated.

Text in French. **AEA**

380 **Kennedy**, D.M. The story of our church, St. Paul's United, Fairview. Edited by E.E. Oliver, F.Johnston. Compiled by Mrs. D.M. Kennedy. Fairview: St. Paul's United Church, 1964. 22p. ill.

Cover title. **AEA**

381 Lac La Biche. St. Catherine's Catholic Church. Fiftieth anniversary of St. Catherine Parish, Lac La Biche, Alberta, 1914-1964. Cinquantenaire de la paroisse Ste. Catherine. Lac La Biche: St. Catherine's Parish, 1964. 32p. ill.

Text in French and English.
Printed by Imprimerie la Survivance, Edmonton.

Ceessa. **AEA**

382 Leduc. First Baptist Church. 75th anniversary, First Baptist Church, Leduc, Alberta, 1894-1969. Leduc: First Baptist Church, 1969. 34p. ill.

Ceessa. **AEA**

383 Leduc. Grace Lutheran Church. Grace Lutheran Church (Gnadenthal), Leduc, Alberta. Seventy-fifth anniversary. Leduc: Grace Lutheran Church, n.d. (24p.) ill.

Cover title.
Text partly in English and partly in German. **ACML**

384 Leduc. St. Peter's Lutheran Church. 75th anniversary, June 8, 1900-1975. Leduc: St. Peter's Lutheran Church, 1975. 35p. ill.

Cover title.

Ceessa. **AEA**

385 **Lefsrud**, Patricia. History of Our Lady of Victory Church, Thorsby. Thorsby: Our Lady of Victory Catholic Church, 1974. various pagings.

Duplicated.
Includes histories of other Roman Catholic Churches of the area. **AEA**

386 Lethbridge. Immanuel Lutheran Church. Immanuel Lutheran Church, 60th anniversary, November 2, 1969. Lethbridge: Immanuel Lutheran Church, 1969. (20)p. ill.

Cover title.

Glenbow. **ACG**

387 Lethbridge. St. Augustine's Anglican Church. In His service, St. Augustine's, Lethbridge, 1886-1976. Lethbridge: Lethbridge Anglican Church, 1976. 1v.

Ceessa. **AEA**

388 Lethbridge. St. Patrick's Catholic Parish. St. Patrick's, Lethbridge. Lethbridge: St. Patrick's Parish, 1979. 36p. ill.

Cover title.
Description of current church activities. **AEA**

389 **Lynch-Staunton**, Betty (Frankish). A short history of the Church of St. John the Evangelist, Pincher Creek, Alta. Pincher Creek: Anglican Church

of Canada, 1954. 12p. ill.

Cover title.

Glenbow. **ACG**

390 Manning. St. James' Catholic Church. Memories. The Catholic Church in the Battleriver District, 1929-1979. s.l.: s.n., 1979. 87p. ill.

Printed by Marian Press, Battleford, Sask.
History of St. Elizabeth's Church in North Star, Sacred Heart Church in Notikewin, and St. James' Church in Manning. **AEA**

391 **McHugh**, Sheila Jane (Haire). Once a mission. A history of St. Joseph's Parish, Coalhurst. Coalhurst: St. Joseph's Parish, 1979. vi, 45p. ill.

Printed by Herald Printers, Lethbridge.

Canadiana, 1979. **AEA**

392 McLennan. Saint John the Baptist Parish. La paroisse de Saint Jean-Baptiste. Cinquantenaire. Saint John the Baptist Parish anniversary. McLennan: Saint John the Baptist Parish, 1978. 72p. ill.

Compiled by a Committee of the Parish Council, Chairman: Jean Marsan.
Text in French and English.
History of the cathedral parish of the Archdiocese of Grouard-McLennan. **AECSJ**

393 Medicine Hat. Christ the King Catholic Parish. Christ the King Parish, Medicine Hat, 1954-1979. Medicine Hat: Christ the King Parish, 1979. 12p. ill.

Cover title. **AEA**

394 Medicine Hat. Fifth Avenue United Church. The ever rolling stream. A history of Fifth Avenue United Church, 1883-1963, the 80th anniversary. Medicine Hat: Fifth Avenue United Church, 1963. 1v. ill.

Duplicated.
Also, *Supplement*, 1973, 1v. (unpaged). **AEA**

395 Medicine Hat. Grace Lutheran Church. 25 years of Grace, 1953-1978. Medicine Hat: Grace Lutheran Church, 1978. 32p. ill.

Cover title. **AEU**

396 Medicine Hat. Westminster United Church. Fortieth anniversary, 1914-1954. A report of the Boards and activities of the Westminster United Church. Medicine Hat: Westminster United Church, 1954. 9p.

Cover title. **AEA**

397 Medicine Hat. Westminster United Church. History of Westminster United Church, Medicine Hat. Medicine Hat: Westminster United Church, 1973. 6 leaves.

Caption title. Duplicated. **ACP**

398 **Miller**, H.J. The story of Sarcee Butte United Church. Sixty six years of service. Sarcee Butte: Sarcee Butte United Church, 1972. 13p. ill.

Cover title. Duplicated. **AEA**

399 **Monckton**, Jean A. All Saints' Anglican Cathedral, 1875-1975. Written and compiled by Jean A. Monckton. Edmonton: All Saints Cathedral Centennial Committee, 1975. 103p. ill.

Printed by Spartan Press.

Drake. **AEA**

400 Namao. United Church. Namao United Church 80th anniversary, May 12, 1963. Namao: Namao United Church, 1963. 7 leaves.

Order of service and brief history. **AEA**

401 **Nelson**, Marie. They gathered at the river. Calgary: Central United Church, 1975. 504p. ill.

A history of Central United Church, published on the occasion of the Calgary centennial and the golden jubilee of the United Church of Canada.
Lithographed by Northwest Printing and Lithographing, Calgary.

Canadiana, 1976.

402 **Nix**, James Ernest. Hillhurst's first sixty years, 1907-1967. Hillhurst United Church Calgary, Alberta. Calgary: Hillhurst United Church, 1967. 1v.

Cover title. Duplicated.

Glenbow. **ACG**

403 **Nychka**, Methodius. Mundare, yesterday and today. Dedication souvenir of the Saints Peter and Paul Ukrainian Catholic Church, Mundare, Alberta, June 29, 1969. Edited by the Basilian Fathers. Mundare: Basilian Fathers, 1969. 232p. ill.

Title page and text in Ukrainian and English.
Text comprises history in Ukrainian by Nychka with English translation by Gregory Siermanchewsky, and a history of organizations by Severian Yakymyshyn in Ukrainian and English. **AEA**

404 **O'Brien**, Julia V. 50 years in the Barrhead United Church. A mini history. Barrhead: House of Print, 1978. 81p. ill.

Written for the occasion of the 50th anniversary of Barrhead United Church.
Preface signed: Julia V. O'Brien. **AEU**

405 **Parlby**, Beatrice Georgina. Parish notes. Written and compiled by B. Parlby, of Alix, Alberta, with the assistance of R. P. T. Gillard and the help of many others. Alix: W.R. Newson, 1961. 49p. ill.

Notes on the Anglican parishes of Alix, Bashaw and Mirror. **AEU**

406 Peace River. St. Paul's United Church. 50th anniversary, 1914-1964. Peace River: St. Paul's United Church, 1964. 16p. ill.

Cover title.

Ceessa. **AEA**

407 **Peyton**, Amy. One body in Christ. A history of Robertson-Wesley United Church. Edmonton: Robertson-Wesley United Church, 1975. 64p. ill.

Cover title.

Canadiana, 1976. **AEA**

408 Pincher Creek United Church. 70th anniversary, 1884-1954. Pincher Creek: Pincher Creek United Church, 1954. 24p. ill.

Edited by W.A. McLeod.

Glenbow. **ACG**

409 Ponoka. United Church. An abbreviated history of the Ponoka United Church of Canada. Ponoka: Ponoka United Church, 1962. 102p. ill.

Cover title. Duplicated.
History to 1946 compiled by the Rev. Ernest Davidge and completed to 1961 by Mr. and Mrs. P. Macdonald, assisted by a committee.

Ceessa. **AEA**

410 Red Deer. Mount Calvary Lutheran Church. 25th anniversary, 1946-1971, Mount Calvary Lutheran Church, Red Deer, Alberta, 1971. Red Deer: Mount Calvary Lutheran Church, 1971. 11p. ill.

Ceessa. **AEA**

411 Rexboro. St. Aidan and St. Hilda Anglican Church. St. Aidan & St. Hilda, 1911-1971. Rexboro: St. Aidan & St. Hilda Anglican Church, 1971. 4p. ill.

Cover title.

Ceessa. **AEA**

412 **Riddle**, Helen. Echoes of a bell. Carstairs: Carstairs United Church History Committee, 1976. 1v. (unpaged.) ill.

Cover title. Duplicated.
A history of Carstairs United Church written by Helen Riddle and Hazel Shaw. **AEA**

413 **Robb**, R.J. Trinity United Church golden jubilee anniversary. Calgary: Trinity United Church, 1963. 8p. ill.

Cover title *The triumph of the spirit*.

Ceessa. **AEA**

414 Rolly View. St. Paul's Lutheran Church. History of St. Paul's Lutheran Church, Rolly View, formerly Rosenthal East, Leduc. Rolly View: St. Paul's

Lutheran Church, 1971. 20p. (chiefly ill.)

On cover: 1896-71, 75th anniversary, St. Paul's Lutheran Church, Rolly View. Caption title.
AEA

415 **Ronaghan**, Allen. A history of St. Saviour's Parish, Vermilion, Alberta, andassociated parishes, 1907-1967. Edmonton: Anglican Church of Canada, 1967. 59p. ill.

Cover title.
Printed by Douglas, Edmonton.

Glenbow. **ACG**

416 **Schulze**, Eric J. The story of New Sarepta Moravians. In commemoration of the semi-centennial of the Moravian Congregation, New Sarepta, Alberta, Canada, 1904-1954. New Sarepta: New Sarepta Moravian Congregation, 1954. 22p. ill.

AEA

417 **Sheehan**, Elizabeth A. And we came after. Grande Prairie: St. Paul's United Church, 1961. 47p. ill.

Cover title.
Life and work of Dr. and Mrs. Alexander Forbes, first Prebyterian missionaries in the Grande Prairie area, and the fifty years since the establishment of the mission church.

Glenbow. **ACG**

418 Spruce Grove. St. Andrew's United Church. An historical sketch of St. Andrew's United Church, Spruce Grove, Alberta, 1920-1970. Rev. ed. Spruce Grove: St. Andrew's United Church, 1975. 23p.

Cover title. Duplicated.

Ceessa. **AEA**

419 St. Isidore. Parish Historical Committee. Album souvenir St. Isidore, 1953-78. Edmonton, Imprimerie la Survivance, 1978. 96p. ill.

On cover: Avec les compliments de la fédération de l'UPA du Saguenay-Lac-St-Jean. History of St. Isidore Catholic Parish.
AECSJ

420 **St. Joseph's Seminary**, Edmonton. St. Joseph's Seminary 50th anniversary, 1927-1977. Edmonton: St. Joseph's Seminary, 1977. 32p. ill.

Cover title.
Printed by Bulletin Commercial Printers.
AEA

421 St. Lina. St. Helene's Catholic Church. Cinquantenaire, Ste. Hélène de Ste-Lina. Golden Jubilee, 1914-1964. St. Lina: Ste. Helene Parish, 1964. 17 leaves. ill.

Cover title. Duplicated.
Text in French, with brief English summary.

A history of the Parish, compiled by Father A.M. Desjardins, cf. Fr. G.E. Durocher, College Saint-Jean. **AEA**

422 St. Vincent. Catholic Church. Cinquantenaire de la paroisse Saint-Vincent, Alberta, 1905-1956. St. Vincent: Saint Vincent Parish, 1956. 45p.

Cover title. Duplicated.

Ceessa. **AEA**

423 Stony Plain. St. Matthew's Evangelical Lutheran Church. St. Matthew's Evangelical Lutheran Church. Anniversary of completion of church plant. Fiftieth anniversary of Christian Day School. Stony Plain: St. Matthew's Evangelical Lutheran Church, 1967. 20p. ill.

ACML

424 Stony Plain. United Church. 50 years. 1925-1975. Stony Plain: Stony Plain United Church, 1975. 9p.

Cover title.

Ceessa. **AEA**

425 **Swanson**, Cecil. The harvest of the years. Marking 50th anniversary celebrations of Christ Church, Elbow Park, Calgary, Alberta. Calgary: Christ Church, 1963. 24p. ill.

Drake. **ACG**

426 Tilley. Bethany Lutheran Church. Bethany Lutheran Church twenty-fifth anniversary, 1930-1955. Tilley: Bethany Lutheran Church, 1955. 1v.

Cover title. **ACML**

427 Trochu. St. John's Lutheran Church. Our journey. A history of St. John's Lutheran Church. Trochu: St. John's Lutheran Church, 1978. 32p.

Duplicated. **AEA**

428 United Church of Canada. Westlock and District Pastoral Charge. The first fifty years. Calgary: Graphic Press (Calgary), 1975. 102p. ill.

Drake. **AEA**

429 Vimy. Our Lady of Victory Catholic Church. Cinquantenaire, golden jubilee, 1920-1970. Vimy: Our Lady of Victory Parish, 1970. 28p. ill.

Duplicated.
Text in French, with English summary.

Ceessa. **AEA**

430 **Vitt**, Kurt H. Bruderfeld Moravian Church 75th anniversary, 1895-1970. Edmonton: Bruderfeld Moravian Church, 1970. 24p. ill.

Ceessa. **AEA**

431 **Vitt**, Kurt H. Heimtal Moravian Church. Edmonton: Heimtal Moravian Church, 1971. 23p. ill.

Cover title. **AEA**

432 Wainwright. Grace Lutheran Church. Commemorating fifty years of Christian service to Wainwright and District by Grace Church, 1908-1958. Wainwright: Grace Church, 1958. 16p. ill.

Cover title. **AEA**

433 **Warren**, R.E. The church in the valley. A history of Clive United Church. Clive: Clive United Church, 1967. 16 leaves.

Cover title. Duplicated.

Ceessa. **AEA**

434 Wetaskiwin. Bethel Lutheran Church. Bethel Lutheran Church, Wetaskiwin, Alberta, 1908-1973. Wetaskiwin: Bethel Lutheran Church, 1973. 11p. ill.

Ceessa. **AEA**

435 Wetaskiwin. Calvary Lutheran Church. Calvary Lutheran Church, 1898-1973, 75th anniversary. Wetaskiwin: Calvary Lutheran Church, 1973. 20p. ill.

Printed by the Wetaskiwin News-Advertiser.

Ceessa. **AEA**

436 Wetaskiwin. First United Church. Anniversary church history, 1893-1973. Wetaskiwin: First United Church, 1973. 80p. ill.

Canadiana, 1974.

437 **Whittle**, F.H. St. James United Church, Edmonton, Alberta, 1854 to 1979. 25 years in action for Jesus Christ. Edmonton: St. James United Church, 1979. 16p. **AEA**

438 **Wilk**, Stephen William. A brief history of the Christian faith in Alberta and in the Airdrie pastoral charge of the United Church of Canada. Edited by Rev. Stephen William Wilk, assisted by Frank Hawkey. Calgary: United Church of Canada, 1962. 109p. ill.

Printed by The Albertan.
Cover title *Pioneers of the faith, north of the Bow River*.

Glenbow. **ACG**

439 **Willing**, Will. Grace Lutheran Church 50th anniversary, 1928-1978. Anniversary booklet. Edited by Will Willing and Rev. W. Ritter. Camrose: Grace Lutheran Church, 1979. 1v. (16p.) ill.

Printed by Gospel Contact Press. **ACML**

440 **Young**, J. A short history of Westminster Prebyterian Church. Chauvin: Westminster Presbyterian Church, 1968. 6 leaves.

Cover title. Duplicated.

Ceessa. **AEA**

Linguistics: General Works

441 **Alexander**, Gerda Isolde. Three German dialects in Barrhead, Alberta. Phonology and interference. Ottawa: National Library of Canada, 1975. x, 108 leaves. ill. (Canadian theses on microfiche, 26693)

Thesis (M.A.), University of Alberta, 1975.
Microfiche of typescript.

Canadiana, 1977. **AEU**

442 **Arbuckle**, John. Phonology of the Volhynian German dialect of the Edmonton area. Edmonton: University of Alberta, 1961. x, 91 leaves.

Thesis (M.A.), University of Alberta, 1961.
Typescript.

Canadian theses. **AEU**

443 **Boucher**, Edith. Exploration du langage des enfants francophones albertains de cinq ans. Ottawa: National Library of Canada, 1973. xi, 67 leaves. (Canadian theses on microfiche, 17460)

Thesis (M.Ed.), University of Alberta, 1973.
Microfiche of typescript.

Canadiana, 1974. **AEU**

444 **Bussière**, Adrien L. Performance linguistique. Français/anglais interference entre l'anglais et le français chez les élèves francophones de septième année en Alberta. Ottawa: National Library of Canada, 1974. xi, 229 leaves. (Canadian theses on microfiche, 23359)

Thesis (M.Ed.), University of Alberta, 1974.
Microfiche of typescript.

U of A Theses. **AEU**

445 Canadian languages in their social context. Edmonton: Linguistic Research, 1973. vii, 191p. ill. (Current inquiry into language and linguistics, 07. Sociolinguistics series, 3)

Essays on sociolinguistics in Canada.

Canadiana, 1974. **AEU**

446 **D'Alquen**, Richard. Phonology of the Galician German dialect of Stony Plain, Alberta. Edmonton: University of Alberta, 1962. vi, 129 leaves.

Thesis (M.A.), University of Alberta, 1962.
Typescript.

Canadian theses. **AEU**

447 **Dogil**, Grzegorz. Autosegmental account of phonological emphasis. Edmonton: Linguistic Research, 1979. 164p. ill. (Current inquiry into language and linguistics, 25. Slavic linguistics, 7)

English and Polish phonology.

Canadiana, 1980. **AEU**

448 **Eberhardt**, Elvire. The Bessarabian German dialect in Medicine Hat, Alberta. Ottawa: National Library of Canada, 1973. xii, 209 leaves. (Canadian theses on microfiche, 17501)

Thesis (Ph.D.), University of Alberta, 1973.
Microfiche of typescript.

U of A Theses. **AEU**

449 Le français parle. Etudes sociolinguistiques. Sous la direction de Pierrette Thibault. Edmonton: Linguistic Research, 1978. xiii, 169pl ill. (Current inquiry into language and linguistics, 30)

Papers presented at a workshop on spoken French held at Université de Montréal in November, 1978. **AEU**

450 **Horn**, George M. Toward a more adequate definition of the notion of transformation. Edmonton: Linguistic Research, 1978. 148p. (Current inquiry into language and linguistics, 24)

Theoretical linguistics on the nature of rules of grammar.

Canadiana, 1979.

451 **Kachur**, Braj B. Current trends in stylistics. Edited by Braj B. Kachuru, Herbert F.W. Stahlke. Edmonton: Linguistic Research, 1972. 286p. (Papers in linguistics. Monograph series, 2)

Essays. **AEU**

452 **Kwofie**, Emmanuel N. Teaching a foreigh (sic) language to the West African student. An examination of the linguistic problem, with special reference to French phonology. Edmonton: Linguistic Research, 1978. 75p. (Current inquiry into language and linguistics, 20)

Problems of teaching foreign languages with special reference to the French language on the Ivory Coast and in Ghana.

Canadiana, 1979. **AEU**

453 Language use in Canada. Edmonton: Linguistic Research, 1976. vii, 198p. (Current inquiry into language and linguistics, 12. Sociolinguistic series, 4)

Special issue of *Papers in Linguistics*, v.9, no.3-4, Fall-Winter, 1976.
Essays on sociolinguistics in Canada. **AEU**

454 **Lightner**, Theodore M. Problems in the theory of phonology. Edmonton: Linguistic Research, 1973. 1v. (Current inquiry into language and linguistics, 06. Slavic linguistics, 1)

Contents: v1. Russian phonology and Turkish phonology.

Canadiana, 1972. **AEU**

455 **Lincoln**, Neville J. Phonology of the Metis French dialect of Saint-Paul, Alberta. Edmonton: University of Alberta, 1963. xi, 92 leaves.

Thesis (M.A.), University of Alberta, 1963.
Typescript.

Canadian theses. **AEU**

456 Linguistic diversity in Canadian society. Edmonton: Linguistic Research, 1971. 307p. ill. (Sociolinguistics series, 1)

Essays on sociolinguistics in Canada.

Glenbow. **ACG**

457 **Patterson**, George William. A comparative study of aspects of the vocalic systems of standard French and the French dialect spoken at Falher, Alberta. Edmonton: University of Alberta, 1969. vi, 134 leaves.

Thesis (M.A.), University of Alberta, 1969.
Typescript.

Canadian theses. **AEU**

458 Readings on language in Canada. Edited by Ronald H. Sutherland. Calgary: Department of Linguistics, University of Calgary, 1972. 68 leaves.

Canadiana, 1976. **OONL**

459 **Sadock**, Jerrold M. Studies presented to Robert B. Lees by his students. Edited by Jerrold M. Sadock and Anthony L. Vanek. Edmonton: Linguistic Research, 1970. xvii, 311p. (Papers in linguistics. Monograph series, 1)

Essays honouring Robert B. Lees, Linguistics Professor at the University of Illinois. **AEU**

460 **Sandilands**, John. Western Canadian dictionary and phrase book. With an introduction by John Orrell. Edmonton: University of Alberta Press, 1977. 51p.

Facsimile of 1913 edition. Includes original title page *Western Canadian dictionary and phrase book, things a newcomer wants to know*.
First edition, 1912, printed by Telegram Job Printers, Winnipeg (Peel 2342). Also, 1913 edition, 52, (1)p. (Peel 2342).
Also, 1913 edition, 52, (1)p. (Peel 2342).

CBIP, 1979. **AEU**

461 **Scharschmidt**, Gunter Herbert. A manual in contrastive linguistics. The structures of Russian and English. Edmonton: s.n., 1966. v. ill.

Contents: 1. Phonemics and morphophonemics. 1966.

Canadiana, 1977. **OONL**

462 **Scotton**, Carol Myers. Choosing a lingua franca in an African capital. Edmonton: Linguistic Research, 1972. 211p. (Sociolinguistics series, 2)

An analysis of language choice, attitudes about language and perception of language choice of others ... based on a sample of the African working population in Kampala.

Canadiana, 1972. **AEU**

463 **Smith**, Ivy. A second language as a communication skill. Calgary: Dome Petroleum, 1968. vi, 46p. ill. (Dome Petroleum Teaching Fellowship, 1968)

Canadiana, 1972. **AEU**

464 Studies in generative phonology. Edmonton: Linguistic Research, 1973. 195p. (Papers in linguistics. Monograph series, 3)

Essays in theoretical linguistics on phonology. **AEU**

465 Studies out in left field. Defamatory essays presented to James D. McCawley on the occasion of his 33rd or 34th birthday. Edited by Arnold M. Zwicky, et al. Edmonton: Linguistic Research, 1971. xvi, 200p. ill. (Current inquiry into language and linguistics, 4)

Humorous essays in linguistics. **AEU**

466 **Szwedek**, A. J. Word order, sentence stress and reference in English and Polish. Edmonton: Linguistic Research, 1976. vii, 154p. (Slavic linguistics, 3)

Canadiana, 1978. **AEU**

467 **Tsiapera**, Maria. Generative studies in historical linguistics. Edmonton: Linguistic Research, 1971. 87p. (Current inquiry into language and linguistics, 2)

Papers presented at a colloquium held at the University of North Carolina in April, 1969. **AEU**

Indian Languages

468 **Anderson**, Anne. The animals of the wilds. Outline drawings of the animals of the wilds. Edmonton: Anne Anderson, 1970. 65p. ill.

Cover title *Wild animals. Pukwachi pisiskowak.*

Canadiana, 1972. **AEU**

469 **Anderson**, Anne. Arrangements of alphabet Cree and syllabic symbols. Edmonton: A. Anderson, 1972. 20p. ill.

Original text and drawings by the author.
Cover title *Alphabet and tones of Cree.*

Canadiana, 1975. **AEU**

470 **Anderson**, Anne. Arrangment (sic) of oral Cree for beginners. Edmonton: A. Anderson, 1970. 15 leaves.

Cover title *Beginners Cree*.

Duplicated. **AEU**

471 **Anderson**, Anne. Awasis book. Original text and drawings by author. Edmonton: A. Anderson, 1972. 3v. ill.

Text in Cree and English.
Contents: 1. Colouring 2. Animates 3. Inanimates.

Canadiana, 1975.

472 **Anderson**, Anne. Coversational Cree. CR 102.4, Advanced Cree. Edmonton: A. Anderson, n.d.

Cover title. Duplicated.
At head of title: Trimester 11. **AEU**

473 **Anderson**, Anne. Cree. A book of verbs and endings. Edmonton: Cree Productions, 1975. 128p.

Cover title. Duplicated. **AEU**

474 **Anderson**, Anne. Cree. Book 1 - Book 3. Edmonton: Anne Anderson, 1970. 3v. ill.

Elementary level text.
Comprises illustrations with Cree name below.

Glenbow. **ACG**

475 **Anderson**, Anne. Cree. Nehiyawewin. Edmonton: Anne Anderson, 1970. 44p.

Cover title. **AEU**

476 **Anderson**, Anne. Cree picture dictionary. Edmonton: Cree Productions, 1975. 1v. ill.

Contents: Bk.1. See it, say it, write it. **AEU**

477 **Anderson**, Anne. Cree reader. Edmonton: A. Anderson, 1975. 48p.

Cover title.

Text in Cree and English. **AEU**

478 **Anderson**, Anne. Cree tenses and explanation. Edmonton: A. Anderson, 1972. 16 leaves. ill.

Text in English and Cree.
Printed by INTC Diversified Industries.
Original text and drawings by author.

Canadiana, 1975. **AEU**

479 **Anderson**, Anne. Cree. Twelve basic lesons. Basic course. Edmonton: A. Anderson, 1975. 108p. ill.

Cover title.

AEU

480 **Anderson**, Anne. Cree vocabulary. Edmonton: A. Anderson, 1970. 123 leaves.

Cover title. Duplicated.

Glenbow.

ACG

481 **Anderson**, Anne. Cree vocabulary for little beginners. Edmonton: A. Anderson, 1974. 36 leaves.

Canadiana, 1975.

482 **Anderson**, Anne. Cree vocabulary, 2nd level. Edmonton: A. Anderson, 1974. 26 leaves.

Text in Cree and English.

Canadiana, 1975.

483 **Anderson**, Anne. Cree. What they do book. Kekway e totahkik. Edmonton: Anne Anderson, 1970. 60 leaves. ill.

Beginning text translating words and simple sentences. To be used with teacher. Title page *Ayamechikewin papetos piseskesak. Tanisi e totahkik tanisi esi taputsichik. Reading of different animals. What they do and their habitats.*
Cover title.

Glenbow.

ACG

484 **Anderson**, Anne. Learning Cree. Edmonton: Anne Anderson, 1971. 2v. ill.

Cover title.

Glenbow.

ACG

485 **Anderson**, Anne. Let's learn Cree. Namoya ayiman. Edmonton: Anne Anderson, 1970. 106p.

Glenbow.

ACG

486 **Anderson**, Anne. Little Cree dictionary. Cree to English. Edmonton: Cree Publications, 1973. 50 leaves.

Cover title *Beginners dictionary. Look for words*.

Canadiana, 1975.

AEU

487 **Anderson**, Anne. Little hunter book. Machesis. Edmonton: Anne Anderson, 1972. 7v. ill.

Text in Cree and English.
Contents: 1. The hunter family 2. Machesis pekiskwew. Little hunter speaks 3. Nohtawe pekiskwew 4. Mary pekiskwew. Mary speaks. 5. Susie pekiskwew. Susie

CAMROSE LUTHERAN COLLEGE
Library

speaks 6. Timmie 5. pekiskwew. Timmie speaks 7. Jeannie pekiskwew. Jeannie speaks.

Canadiana, 1975.

488 **Anderson**, Anne. Little hunter book. Machesis. Edmonton: Anne Anderson, 1970. 1v. (unpaged). ill.

Canadiana, 1972. **ACG**

489 **Anderson**, Anne. Plains Cree dictionary in the ″Y″ dialect. Edited by Anne Anderson. Edmonton: Diversified Industries, 1971. (10) 102p.

Also 1975 edition, 255p..

Glenbow. **ACG**

490 **Anderson**, Anne. Read and write. The Cree language. Nehiyawewin. Ayamichike mena musinahike. Edmonton: A. Anderson, 1972. 153p. ill.

Cover title.
Text in Cree. **AEU**

491 **Anderson**, Anne. Teaching of the Cree language. Basic simplified method. Edmonton: Cree Productions, 1973. 36p.

Canadiana, 1975. **ACU**

492 **Anderson**, Anne. Tim and his friends. Edmonton: A. Anderson, 1973. 19p. ill.

A school reader. Includes some text in Cree. **AEU**

493 **Anderson**, Anne. Tim goes to the farm. Edmonton: A. Anderson, 1973. 32p. ill.

A school reader. Includes some text in Cree.

Canadiana, 1976. **AEU**

494 **Anderson**, Anne. Wapi. Edmonton: IRTC Diversified Industries, 1972. 14p. ill.

Includes some text in Cree.

Canadiana, 1975.

495 **Anderson**, Anne. We print and we read. Grade 1. Edmonton: Anne Anderson, 1973. 27 leaves. ill.

A Cree language text-book.

Canadiana, 1975. **AEU**

496 **Bellam**, Ernest Jay. Studies in Stoney morphology and phonology. Ottawa: National Library of Canada, 1975. vii, 86 leaves. (Canadian theses on microfiche, 24970)

Thesis (M.A.), University of Calgary, 1975.
Microfiche of typescript.

Canadiana, 1976. **OONL**

497 **Carter**, Robin Michael. Chipewyan semantics. Form and meaning in the language and culture of an Athapaskan-speaking people of Canada. Ann Arbor, Mich: University Microfilms, 1975. xi, 232 leaves. ill.

Thesis (Ph.D.), Duke University, 1975.
Microfilm of typescript.

Canadiana, 1978.

498 **Frantz**, Donald Gene. Toward a generative grammar of Blackfoot (with particular attention to selected stem formation processes). Edmonton: University of Alberta, 1970. 262 leaves.

Thesis (Ph.D.), University of Alberta.
Typescript.

Dew. **AEU**

499 **Hunter**, Emily. How to learn to read syllabics. St. Paul: Blue Quills Native Education Council, 1972. 1v.

Canadiana, 1975.

500 **Kinsella**, Norman George. The vowel system of Blackfoot. Ottawa: National Library of Canada, 1972. viii, 47 leaves. (Canadian theses on microfilm, 13891)

Thesis (M.A.), University of Calgary, 1972.
Microfilm of typescript.

Canadiana, 1973.

501 **Summer Institute of Linguistics**, Santa Cruz, Calif. The Blackfoot alphabet, with exercises. Santa Cruz, Calif.: Summer Institute of Linguistics, 1968. 14, 2p. ill.

Prepared for Blackfoot Indian Band, Gleichen, Alberta.

Glenbow. **ACG**

502 **Wolfart**, Hans Christoph. Meet Cree. A practical guide to the Cree language. Edmonton: University of Alberta Press, 1973. 63p. ill.

By H. Christoph Wolfart and Janet F. Carroll.

Canadiana, 1973. **AEA**

503 **Wolfart**, Hans Christoph. An outline of Plains Cree morphology. Ann Arbor, Mich.: University Microfilms, 1969. vii, 282 leaves. maps.

Thesis (Ph.D.), Yale University, 1969.
Microfiche of typescript.

Canadiana, 1974.

Slavic Languages

504 **Carlton**, Terence Roy. The declension of nouns in Ukrainian. A student's reference. Edmonton: Department of Slavic Languages, University of Alberta, 1971. 96p.

Canadiana, 1974. **AEU**

505 **Carlton**, Terence Roy. The numeral in Ukrainian, its forms and uses. Edmonton: Department of Slavic Languages, University of Alberta, 1972. 62p.

Canadiana, 1976. **AEU**

506 **Gauk**, Roma Z. Ukrainian Christian names. A dictionary. Edited by Dr. Yar Slavutych. Edmonton: Orma Publishers, 1961. 31p.

Text in English and Ukrainian. **AEU**

507 **Popowich**, John Damascene D. Grammar of Church Slavonic language in Ukrainian reduction. Mundare: Basilian Fathers, 1958. 62, viii p.

Canadiana, 1964. **AEU**

508 **Royick**, Alexander. Lexical borrowings in Alberta Ukrainian. Edmonton: University of Alberta, 1965. vi, 118 leaves.

Thesis (M.A.), University of Alberta, 1965.
Typescript.

Canadian theses. **AEU**

509 **Sawchuk**, William. Let us learn Ukrainian. Book I. Edmonton: Printed by Northland Print, 1968. vi, 96p. ill.

Canadiana, 1969. **AEU**

510 **Shevolov**, George Y. A historical phonology of the Ukrainian language. Heidelberg: Carl Winter Universitatsverlag, 1979. 809p. (Historical phonology of the Slavic languages, 4)

Published for the Canadian Institute of Ukrainian Studies, Edmonton.

511 **Slavutych**, Yar. Conversational Ukrainian. Edmonton: Gateway Publishers, 1959. 2v.

Authorised for use in the Schools of Alberta: verso title page.
2d rev. ed., 1961, xvi, 608p. 3d enl. ed., 1969, 608p. 4th ed., 1973, 608p. French language edition, *L'ukrainen parle*. Traduit et adapte par Hyrhorij Panczuk, 1968, Louvain, Centre d'etudes ukrainien en Belgique. 2v.

Canadiana, 1962.

512 **Slavutych**, Yar. An introduction to Ukrainian. Edmonton: Slavuta Publishers, 1962. 22p. ill.

Canadiana, 1962. **AEU**

513 **Slavutych**, Yar. Ukrainian for beginners. Edmonton: Slavuta Publishers, 1962. 68p. ill.

5th rev. ed., 1975, 60p.
Note, p4: Authorized for use in the Schools of Alberta.

Canadiana, 1976. **AEU**

514 **Slavutych**, Yar. Ukrainian for children. Edmonton: Slavuta Publishers, n.d. 88p.

Printed by Alberta Printing, Edmonton.
Text in English and Ukrainian.

Ukrainica Canadian, 1962.

515 **Slavutych**, Yar. Ukrainian in pictures. Edmonton: Gateway Publishers, 1965. v. ill.

Canadiana, 1976. AEU

516 **Slavutych**, Yar. Ukrains'ka mova za zorovo-slukhovoiu metodoiu. Montreal: Didier, 1968. vii, 65p.

Sponsored by the Ukrainian Canadian Committee.
At head of title: The Center for Curriculum Development, Inc..
Accompanied by Picture book and Teacher's script.

Canadiana, 1970.

517 **Starchuk**, Orest. The Ukrainian language. Edmonton: O. Starchuk, 1958. 7p.

Text in English.

Ukrainica Canadiana, 1958.

518 **Starchuk**, Orest. The Ukrainian language questionnaire. Edmonton: Department of Slavonic Languages, University of Alberta, 1969. 262p.

Text in English and Ukrainian.
Duplicated.

Ukrainica Canadiana.

519 **Vanek**, Anthony L. Aspects of subject-verb agreement. Edmonton: Linguistic Research, 1977. 287p. (Current inquiry into language and linguistics, 23. Slavic linguistics, 5)

With particular reference to Slavic languages.

Canadiana, 1979. AEU

520 **Vanek**, Anthony L. A Doukhobor Russian lexical & dialectological questionnaire. English version. Compiled by A.L. Vanek and R. Darnell. Edmonton: Linguistic Research, 1971. xxip., 66 leaves. (Working papers in linguistic series, 1)

Canadiana, 1952.

Literature: General Works

521 **Alexander**, Laura E. Kroetsch's tragicomic romance. The out west trilogy. Ottawa: National Library of Canada, 1975. iii, 73 leaves. (Canadian theses on microfiche, 26094)

Thesis (M.A.), McMaster University, 1975.
Microfiche of typescript.

Canadiana, 1977. OONL

522 **Carpenter**, David. Alberta in fiction. Ottawa: National Library of Canada, 1973. v, 292 leaves. (Canadian theses on microfiche, 17471)

Thesis (Ph.D.), University of Alberta, 1973.
Microfiche of typescript.

Canadiana, 1974.

523 Crossing frontiers. Papers in American and Canadian western literature. Edited by Dick Harrison. Edmonton: University of Alberta Press, 1979. 174p.

Papers presented at a conference held at Banff, April, 1978.

Canadiana, 1979. **ACU**

524 **Dahlie**, Hallvard. Strange trafficking and curious merchandise. The state of Canadian fiction. Calgary: Faculty of Humanities, University of Calgary, 1979. 16p.

Cover title.
An inaugural professorial lecture in the Faculty of Humanities, University of Calgary, presented January 16, 1979.

Canadiana 1980. **AEU**

525 **Dueck**, Allan Kornelsen. Rudy Wiebe as storyteller. Vision and art in Wiebe's fiction. Ottawa: National Library of Canada, 1974. viii, 143 leaves. (Canadian theses on microfiche, 21804)

Thesis (M.A.), University of Alberta, 1974.
Microfiche of typescript.

Canadiana, 1975.

526 **Ference**, Ermeline Ann. Literature associated with ranching in southern Alberta. Edmonton: University of Alberta, 1971. ix, 102 leaves.

Thesis (M.A.), University of Alberta, 1971.
Typescript.
Examines the value of regional literature as a source of historical evidence of the ranching industry in Southern Alberta.

Canadian theses. **AEU**

527 **Graham**, Frank Neil. Theme and form in the novels of Edward A. McCourt. Windsor: University of Windsor, 1968. (1v.)

Thesis (M.A.), University of Windsor, 1968.
Typescript.

Canadian theses. **OWA**

528 **Harrison**, Dick. The unnamed country. The struggle for a Canadian prairie fiction. Edmonton: University of Alberta Press, 1977. 250p. ill.

Canadiana, 1978. **ACP**

529 **Honcharenko**, Ahapius. Memoirs. Edmonton: Slavuta Publishers, 1965. 18p. ill.

Title page and text in Ukrainian. English title from verso of title page.
First published, 1894, Kolomyya, M. Pavlyk.

Canadiana, 1965.

530 **LeBlanc**, Victoria. From preacher to prophet. A study of the fiction of Rudy Wiebe. Ottawa: National Library of Canada, 1978. iv, 148 leaves. (Canadian theses on microfiche, 38575)

Thesis (M.A.), Concordia University, 1978.
Microfiche of typescript.

Canadiana, 1980. **OONL**

531 Literature, language and culture. Papers read at the University of Alberta Conference on Literacy. Edited by P. Gallivan and R.J. Merrett. Edmonton: Athabascan Publishing, 1977. 76p.

Contents: 1. Why read 2. The experience of the word 3. The language of culture. Gains and losses 4. So how do we teach them? **AEU**

532 **McCourt**, Edward. The Canadian West in fiction. Rev. and enl. Toronto: Ryerson Press, 1970. 131p. (Ryerson paperbacks, 34)

First published, 1949, Toronto, Ryerson Press (Pub 4162).

CBIP, 1979. **AEU**

533 **McKenzie**, Leroy R. The opening line of Paradise Lost. A new dimension in literary criticism. Lethbridge: New Helicon Press, 1974. 104p.

Canadiana, 1974. **AEU**

534 **Papen**, Jean. Georges Bugnet, homme de lettres canadiennes. Québec: Université Laval, 1967. 289 leaves.

Thesis (Ph.D.), Université Laval, 1967.
Typescript.

535 **Potter**, Bruce. Through the bubble. A study of the theme of identity in the novels of W.O. Mitchell. Ottawa: National Library of Canada, 1977. vi, 139 leaves. (Canadian theses on microfiche, 34230)

Thesis (M.A.), University of Calgary, 1977.
Microfiche of typescript.

Canadiana, 1979.

536 **Prokopiw**, Orysia Love Olia (Ferbey). An introduction to Lesya Ukrainka. Calgary: Olha Bassarab Branch, Ukrainian Womens' Association, 1971. (10)p. ill.

Cover title.
On a distinguished Ukrainain poetess. **AEU**

537 **Schcherbak**, Mykola. The burning wood. The poetry of Yar Slavuytch. By Mykola Schcherbak and W.T. Zyla. London: Ukrainian Publishers, 1969. 40p.

Text in Ukrainian. Added title page in English. **AEU**

538 **Scobie**, Stephen. Leonard Cohen. Vancouver: Douglas and McIntyre, 1978. 192p. (Studies in Canadian literature)

CBIP, 1979. **AEU**

539 **Slavutych**, Yar. Greatness of Taras Shevchenko. Edmonton: Slavuta Publishers, 1962. 11p. ill.

Canadiana, 1962. **AEU**

540 **Slavutych**, Yar. The muse in prison. Eleven sketches of Ukrainian poets killed by Communists and twenty-two translations of their poems. Foreword by Clarence A. Manning. Jersey City, N.J.: Svoboda, 1956. 62p. ill.

AEU

541 **Slavutych**, Yar. Shevchenko's celebration. Edmonton: Soyuz Ukrayinciv Samostiynykiv, 1961. 26p.

Text in Ukrainian.

Ukranica Canadiana, 1961.

542 **Slavutych**, Yar. Shevchenko's greatness. Winnipeg: UVAN, 1961. 30p. (Ukrains'ka vil'na akademiia nauk. Literatura, 7)

Text in Ukrainian. Added title page in English. **AEU**

543 **Slavutych**, Yar. T. Shevchenko's craftsmanship. Edmonton: Slavuta Publishers, 1964. 24p. ill.

Ukrainian title *Shevchenko poetyka*.
Title page and text in Ukrainian. Added title page in English.

Canadiana, 1964. **AEU**

544 **Slavutych**, Yar. Ukrainian literature in Canada. Edmonton: Slavuta Publishers, 1966. 15p.

Text in English. **AEU**

545 **Slavutych**, Yar. Ukrains'ka poeziia v Kanadi. Edmonton: Slavuta, 1976. 103p. ill.

Literary criticism of Ukrainian poetry in Canada. **AEU**

546 **Starchuk**, Orest. A survey of Russian literature of the xviii and xlx centuries. Edmonton: University of Alberta, 1966. 401p.

Text in Russian. Title page in English. **AEU**

547 **Ticehurst**, Judith E. The matter of perception in the fiction of W.O. Mitchell. Ottawa: National Library of Canada, 1974. 94 leaves. (Canadian theses on microfiche, 21728)

Thesis (M.A.), Sir George Williams University, 1974.
Microfiche of typescript.

Canadiana, 1975. **AEU**

548 **Verkruysse**, Patricia Louise. Small legacy of truth. The novels of Nellie McClung. Ottawa: National Library of Canada, 1975. vi, 225 leaves. (Canadian theses on microfiche, 27455)

Thesis (M.A.), University of New Brunswick, 1975.
Microfiche of typescript.

Canadiana, 1977. **OONL**

549 **Whitaker**, Muriel. Children's literature. A guide to criticism. Edmonton: Athabascan Publishing, 1976. 48p. **AEU**

550 **Wood**, Kerry. The Icelandic-Canadian poet, Stephan Gudmundsson Stephansson, 1853-1927. A tribute. Red Deer: Kerry Wood, 1974. 1v. (12p.)

Cover title.
A 4-page biography, with English translations of two poems.

Canadiana, 1975. **AEA**

551 **Zyla**, Wolodymyr T. The poetry of Yar Slavutych. Edmonton: Slavuta Publishers, 1978. 431p. ill.

Ukrainian title *Tvorchist' Iar Slavutycha. Statti i retsenzi*.
Articles and reviews on the poetry of Yar Slavuytch.
Text mainly in Ukrainian, with some text in English, French and German.

Canadiana, 1979. **AEU**

Anthologies

552 Alberta diamond jubilee anthology. John W. Chalmers, Editor-in-chief. Edmonton: Hurtig, 1979. 335p.

Poetry editor, James Moir. Fiction editor, June Bhatia. Non-fiction prose editor, Hugh A. Dempsey.

Canadiana, 1979. **AEP**

553 The Alberta golden jubilee anthology. Editor-in-chief, W.G. Hardy. Illustrated by H.G. Glyde. Toronto: McClelland & Stewart, 1955. 471p. ill.

Published by arrangement with the Edmonton Branch, Canadian Authors Association.

Glenbow. **ACG**

554 Alberta Teachers' Association. English Council. How can a song be blue. An anthology of verse by students of Alberta for Project Pandora. General editor, T.W. Gee. Calgary: English Council of Alberta Teachers' Association, 1973. 130p. ill.

Selections from elementary, junior and senior high school students. **AEU**

555 Alberta Teachers' Association. English Council. An icecream cone feeling in the dark of December. An anthology of writing from the students of Alberta. Edmonton: Alberta Teachers' Association, 1969. 90p. ill. **AEU**

556 Alberta Teachers' Association. English Council. A nickel's worth of wishing. Short stories by high school students of Alberta. Edited by T.W. Gee. Illustrations by Myrna Harvey. Calgary: Alberta Teachers' Association, English Council, 1974. 127p.

Printed by Northwest Printing & Lithographing. **AECYR**

557 Alberta writers speak. Edmonton: Words Unlimited Writers Group, 1957-1969. 5v.

1957 edition entitled *Alberta speaks*.

1. 1957 2.1960 3.1964 4.1967 5.1969.. **AEA**

558 Anagramatix. A collection of experimental writings by the adult students of the University of Alberta Extension Department course. Edited by Bill Meilen, Bill. Edmonton: s.n., 1970. (54p.)

Duplicated. **AEU**

559 An anthology of Ukrainian lyric poetry. Part 1. Up to 1919. Edited by Orest Zilynsky. Oakville, Ont.: Mosaic Press, 1978. 439p.

Text in Ukrainian. Added title page in English.
Published for the Canadian Institute of Ukrainian Studies. **AEU**

560 An anthology of Ukrainian poetry in Canada, 1898-1973. Edited by Yar Slavutych. Edmonton: Slovo, 1975. 159p.

Text in Ukrainian. Added title page in English.

CBIP, 1979. **AEU**

561 Around you. An anthology of southern Albertans' literature. Compiled by Gerry Herbert and others. Lethbridge: Paramount Printers, 1972. 1v. (unpaged).

Duplicated.

An OFY Project. **ACP**

562 Best Mounted Police stories. Edited by Dick Harrison. Graphic design and illustrations by J. Frascara. Edmonton: University of Alberta Press, 1978. 258p. ill.

Canadiana, 1979. **AEU**

563 Chinook arch. A centennial anthology of Alberta writing. Editor-in-chief, John Patrick Gillese. Edmonton: Queen's Printer, 1967. 350p.

Prepared under the auspices of the Edmonton Branch, Canadian Authors Association, and published as a centennial year project by the Government of the Province of Alberta.

Glenbow. **ACG**

564 Creation. Robert Kroetsch, James Bacque, Pierre Gravel. Including the authors' conversations with Margaret Laurence, Milton Wilson, Raymond

Brazeau. Edited by Robert Kroetsch. Toronto: New Press, 1970. 213p.

Consists of excerpts from their works followed by 'critical dialogues'. Includes some text in French.

Glenbow. **ACG**

565 Diversions. Theresa M. Ford, Managing Editor. Edmonton: Alberta Education, 1979. 285p. ill. (Western Canadian literature for youth)

Short stories, essays, and poems devoted to the way that Western Canadians use leisure time, printed as part of the Alberta Heritage Learning Resources Project, 1979. **AEP**

566 Fellfield. Writings from the Banff Centre. Banff: Banff Centre School of Fine Arts, 1974. 73p.

Poetry and fiction by students.

Canadiana, 1975. **AEU**

567 Figures in a ground. Canadian essays on modern literature, collected in honour of Sheila Watson. Edited by Diane Bessai and David Jackel. Saskatoon: Western Producer Prairie Books, 1978. 365p. ill.

Includes *Sheila Watson, a biography*.

Canadiana, 1978. **AEU**

568 Fluid filosofies of future fools. By the pupils of Sherwood Heights Junior High School, Sherwood Park, Alberta, 1968-69. Editors and publishers, A. O'Dwyer and G. Whitney. Sherwood Park: Printed by Professional Printing, 1969. 152p.

Poetry and short stories.

Canadiana, 1970. **AEU**

569 Getting here. Stories. Selected by Rudy Wiebe. Edmonton: NeWest Press, 1977. 119p.

Canadiana, 1977. **AEU**

570 Great Canadian adventure stories. Edited by Muriel Whitaker. Illustrated by Vlasta van Kampen. Edmonton: Hurtig, 1979. 224p. ill.

Juvenile literature.

Canadiana, 1979. **AEP**

571 Great Canadian animal stories. Edited by Muriel Whitaker. Illustrated by Vlasta van Kampen. Edmonton: Hurtig, 1978. 232p. ill.

Juvenile literature.

Canadiana, 1979. **AEU**

572 Harbinger. A gathering of southern Alberta writing. Hugh Anderson, editor. Co-editors, Hugh Anderson, Jannie Edwards, Colin Morton. Calgary: Southern Alberta Young Writers' Group, 1973. (93)p. ill.

Duplicated.
Printed in Medicine Hat by Press One on the Seven Persons Repository Press.
An O.F.Y. Project. **ACG**

573 In jeopardy. Theresa M. Ford, Managing Editor. Edmonton: Alberta Education, 1979. 224p. ill. (Western Canadian literature for youth)
Short stories and poetry about people in dangerous situations, printed as part of the Alberta Heritage Learning Resources Project, 1979. **AEP**

574 Interface. Poems by Jannis Allan Hare, Mark Lowey, James M. Moir, Hector Williamson. Edited by Hector Williamson. Calgary: H. Williamson, 1977. 1v. ill. **ACP**

575 Interface tu. 10 Calgary poets. Edited by Hector Williamson. Calgary: H. Williamson, 1978. 100p. **ACP**

576 Mag pil. A collection of poems and stories by students. Edmonton: University of Alberta, Department of English, 1970. 65p.
Duplicated.
Written by students in creative writing classes. **AEU**

577 The new land. Studies in a literary theme. Essays by Richard Chadbourne et al. Edited by Richard Chadbourne and Hallvard Dahlie. Waterloo, Ont.: Wilfred Laurier University Press for Calgary Institute for the Humanities, 1978. viii, 160p.
CBIP, 1978. **AEU**

578 Panorama. Theresa M. Ford, Managing Editor. Edmonton: Alberta Education, 1979. 271p. ill. (Western Canadian literature for youth)
Short stories and poetry printed as part of Alberta Heritage Learning Resources Project, 1979. **AEP**

579 Road to yesterday. Theresa M. Ford, Managing Editor. Edmonton: Alberta Education, 1979. 310p. ill. (Western Canadian literature for youth)
Poetry and short stories about Western Canadian pioneers, printed as part of the Alberta Heritage Learning Resources Project, 1979. **AEP**

580 A sense of place. Theresa M. Ford, Managing Editor. Edmonton: Alberta Education, 1979. 285p. ill. (Western Canadian literature for youth)
Short stories and poetry, printed as part of the Alberta Heritage Learning Resources Project, 1979. **AEP**

581 Settling matters. Perspectives on the past. Edmonton: Writing for Pleasure Group, 1979. 120p. ill.

Reminiscences, short stories, and poems by the group. Sponsored by the Society for the Retired and Semi-Retired. **AEA**

582 The sound of time. Anthology of Canadian-Hungarian authors. Edited byJohn P. Miska. Lethbridge: Canadian-Hungarian Authors Association, 1974. 208p.

Canadiana, 1974. **AEU**

583 Stories from Western Canada. A selection. Edited by Rudy Wiebe. Toronto: Macmillan of Canada, 1972. xvi, 274p.

Glenbow. **ACG**

584 Strathcona harvest. Edmonton: Strathcona Writing Group, 1973-1976. 3v. ill.

Writings by senior Albertans.
Editions 1973, 1974, 1975-76. **AEU**

585 Transitions. Theresa M. Ford, Managing Editor. Edmonton: Alberta Education, 1979. 295p. ill. (Western Canadian literature for youth)

A collection of poetry and short stories printed as part of Alberta Heritage Learning Resources Project, 1979. **AEP**

586 The Vaplite collection. Edited by George Luckyj. Edmonton: Canadian Institute of Ukrainian Studies, 1977. 260p. (Canadian library in Ukrainian studies)

Prefatory matter in English. Text in Ukrainian.
Also published, 1977, Oakville, Ont., Mosaic, for the Canadian Institute of Ukrainian Studies.
Listings of the Free Academy of Proletarian Literature.

Canadiana 1978. **AEU**

587 **Watson**, Sheila. Sheila Watson, a collection. Toronto: Coach House Press, 1974. 189p. ill. (Open letter, 3rd ser, no1)

Short stories and critical essays.

Canadiana, 1975. **AEU**

588 Western moods. Theresa M. Ford, Managing Editor. Edmonton: Alberta Education, 1979. 296p. ill. (Western Canadian literature for youth)

Poetry and short stories which "capture the diverse moods of Western Canada", printed as part of the Alberta Heritage Learning Resources Project, 1979. **AEP**

589 Western profiles. Theresa M. Ford, Managing Editor. Edmonton: Alberta Education, 1979. 303p. ill. (Western Canadian literature for youth)

Poems and short stories about Western Canadians, printed as part of the Alberta Heritage Learning Resources Project, 1979. **AEP**

590 Who owns the earth? Theresa M. Ford, Managing Editor. Edmonton: Alberta Education, 1979. 287p. ill. (Western Canadian literature for youth)

Short stories and poetry concerned with wise use of resources, printed as part of Alberta Heritage Learning Resources Project, 1979. **AEP**

591 Wild rose country. Stories from Alberta. Edited by David Carpenter. Stories by Rudy Wiebe et al. Ottawa: Oberon Press, 1977. 175p.

CBIP, 1978. **AEU**

592 39 below. The anthology of Greater Edmonton poetry. Edited by Allan Shute and R.G. Fyfe. Edmonton: Tree Frog Press, 1973. 129p. **ACU**

Fiction

593 **Alderson**, Sue Ann. Bonnie McSmithers is at it again! Illustrated by Fiona Garrick. Edmonton: Tree Frog Press, 1979. 48p. ill.

Childrens' literature.

CBIP, 1979. **AEP**

594 **Alderson**, Sue Ann. Bonnie McSmithers you're driving me dithers. Illustrations by Fiona Garrick. Edmonton: Tree Frog Press, 1974. 51p. ill.

Childrens' literature.

CBIP, 1979. **AEU**

595 **Alderson**, Sue Ann. Hurry up, Bonnie. Illustrations by Fiona Garrick. Edmonton: Tree Frog Press, 1977. 43p. ill.

Childrens' literature.

CBIP, 1979. **AEU**

596 **Allan**, Iris Constance (Sommerville). The boy in buckskins. Boyhood of John McDougall. Illustrated by G. La Rue. Edmonton: Institute of Applied Art, 1959. 160p. ill.

Fictionalized biography written for children.
Also published 1978, Saskatoon, Western Producer Prairie Books, (Spectra series) 160p. with sub-title *The early life of John McDougall*.

Glenbow. **ACG**

597 **Allan**, Iris Constance (Sommerville). John Rowand, fur trader. A story of the old northwest. Drawings by Doug Sneyd. Toronto: W.J. Gage, 1963. 205p. ill. (Frontier books, 4)

Fictionalized biography written for children. **AEA**

598 **Allan**, Iris Constance (Sommerville). White Sioux. Major Walsh of the Mounted Police. Sidney, B.C.: Gray's Publishing, 1969. 209p. ill.

Fictionalized biography written for children.
Sub-title on dust jacket *The story of Major Walsh of the Mounted Police*.

Dew. AEU

599 **Allan**, Iris Constance (Sommerville). Wop May, bush pilot. Illustrated by William Wheeler. Toronto: Clarke, Irwin, 1966. 170p. ill.

Fictionalized biography written for children. AEA

600 **Allan**, Iris Constance (Sommerville). Young fur trader. Edmonton: Edmonton Public School Board, n.d. 30p. ill. (Edmonton social studies enterprise series, 4)

Fictionalized biography of John Rowand written for children. AEU

601 **Allan**, Luke, pseud. Blue Pete in the badlands. London: H. Jenkins, 1954. 173p.

Novel set in southern Alberta.

Dew. ACG

602 **Allen**, Ralph. Peace River country. Garden City, N.Y.: Doubleday, 1958. 221p.

Also published 1958, London, Hodder & Stoughton. 191p.

Glenbow. ACG

603 **Anderson**, Anne. The affair at Timber Lake. New York: Dell Publishing, 1972. 176p. (A Dell book)

Canadiana, 1975.

604 **Annett**, Ronald Ross. Especially Babe. With introduction by Rudy Wiebe. Edmonton: Tree Frog Press, 1978. 187p.

Reprint of the 1942 edition published New York and London, Appleton-Century and Toronto, Ryerson.
Originally published in the *Saturday Evening Post*, 1938-1942.
Stories set in Jenner, Alberta, in the 1930s.

Canadiana, 1978. AEU

605 **Bakken**, Edna. Chinook Ridge, 1880-1914. E.A. Mitchner, managing editor, Kevin Majeau, research editor. Edmonton: Alberta Education, 1979. 107, 1p. ill.

Juvenile literature.
Account of life in a fictional Alberta town, printed as part of the Alberta Heritage Learning Resources Project, 1980. AEA

606 **Ballem**, John Bishop. The devil's lighter, a novel. Don Mills, Ont.: General Publishing, 1973. 237p.

A novel of the oil industry.
Also published 1974, Markham, Ontario, Paperjacks. AEU

607 **Ballem**, John Bishop. The dirty scenario, a novel. Don Mills, Ont.: General Publishing, 1974. 256p.

A novel of U.S Canadian power politics during an energy crisis.
Also published 1974, Markham, Ontario, Paperjacks. **AEU**

608 **Ballem**, John Bishop. The Judas conspiracy. Don Mills, Ont.: Musson Books, 1976. 303p.

A novel.
Also published 1978, Markham, Ontario, Paperjacks.
A political novel set in Alberta. **AEU**

609 **Ballem**, John Bishop. The moon pool. Toronto: McClelland and Stewart, 1978. 236p.

A novel set in the Canadian arctic.
Also published 1979, Toronto, McClelland & Stewart (Bantam in the Seal book series).
Canadiana, 1979. **AEU**

610 **Barnhouse**, Dorothy P. The quest of the Golden Gannet. St. John's: Breakwater Books, 1979. 97p. ill.

Juvenile fiction.
Winner of Beaver award. **AEU**

611 **Bellingham**, Brenda. Joanie's magic boots. Edmonton: Tree Frog Press, 1979. 125p.

Childrens' literature.
Canadiana, 1980. **AEP**

612 **Bhatia**, June. The latchkey kid. Don Mills, Ont.: Longmans Canada, 1971. 211p.

ACU

613 **Bhatia**, June. Liverpool Daisy. London: Robert Hale, 1979. 254p.

Winner, 1977 Beaver Award. **AEP**

614 **Bhatia**, June. Minerva's stepchild. By Helen Forrester. Toronto: Bodley Head (Toronto), 1979. 289, 1p.

Fictionalized autobiography. A sequel to *Twopence to cross the Mersey*.
Published in association with Clarke, Irwin. **AEP**

615 **Bhatia**, June. Twopence to cross the Mersey. By Helen Forrester. Toronto: Bodley Head (Canada), 1974. 223p.

Fictionalized reminiscences of childhood in Liverpool during the Depression.
Published in association with Clarke, Irwin. **AECYR**

616 **Bialk**, Elisa. Tizz at the Stampede. Pictures by Hildegard Lehmann. Chicago: Children's Press, 1968. 94p. ill.

Juvenile fiction set at the Calgary Stampede.

Canadiana, 1969. **ACP**

617 **Bialk**, Elisa. Tizz in the Canadian Rockies. Illustrated by Hildegard Lehmann. London: J. Cape in association with Clarke, Irwin, Toronto, 1968. 92p. ill.

Juvenile fiction.

Canadiana, 1969.

618 **Boytim**, Richard H. Fibber's fables. Beaverlodge: Horizon House, 1977. 96p. (Horizon books)

Stories based on Aesop's fables, set in North America, designed to illustrate Christian principles.

Canadiana, 1978. **AEU**

619 **Braithwaite**, Max. The valley of the vanishing birds. General editor, Arthur Hammond. Illustrated by Wendy Hawgood. Boston, Toronto: Little, Brown, 1963. 160p. ill. (The secret circle mysteries, 8)

Juvenile novel set in northern Alberta.

Canadiana, 1963.

620 **Bugnet**, Georges. The forest. Translated by David Carpenter. Montreal: Harvest House, 1976. 168p. (French writers of Canada series)

Original French language edition 1935, with title *La forêt*, Montreal, Editions du Totem, 239p. (Peel 3420).
A novel set in the Peace River Country.

CBIP, 1979. **ACP**

621 **Callaway**, Bernice Ann Marr. Down timberland trail. A tale of Upper Canada. Three Hills: Prairie Bible Institute, 1969. 166p. ill.

Childrens' literature.

Canadiana, 1970. **ACG**

622 **Callaway**, Bernice Ann Marr. Tell us a missionary story. Fifteen missionary stories for young folk. Line drawings by Brian Parlane. Three Hills: Prairie Press, 1976. 130p. ill.

A companion to *Tell us a story*.

Canadiana, 1977. **ATP**

623 **Callaway**, Bernice Ann Marr. Tell us a story. Seventeen read-aloud stories for children. Three Hills: Prairie Press, 1975. 127p. ill.

Canadiana, 1976. **ATP**

624 **Chalmers**, John West. Horseman in scarlet. Sam Steele of the Mounties. Drawings by Lex Bell. Toronto: W.J. Gage, 1961. 164p. ill. (Frontier books, 1)

Juvenile fiction. An historical novel.
Sub-title on dust jacket *The story of Sam Steele of the Mounties*.

Dew. **AEU**

625 **Chetin**, Helen. The lady of the strawberries. Illustrated by Anita Kunz. Toronto: Peter Martin Associates, 1978. 89p. ill.

Juvenile fiction set in Alberta. **ACP**

626 **Clark**, Joan. Girl of the Rockies. Illustrated by Douglas Phillips. Toronto: Ryerson Press, 1968. 142p. ill.

Juvenile fiction.
Printed in Great Britain. **AEu**

627 **Clark**, Joan. The hand of Robin Squires. Illustrations by William Taylor and Mary Cserepy. Toronto: Clarke, Irwin, 1977. 145p. ill.

Juvenile fiction. An adventure story set on Oak Island, Nova Scotia.

CBIP, 1979. **AEU**

628 **Clark**, Joan. Thomasina and the trout tree. Pictures by Ingeborg Hiscox. Montreal: Tundra Books, 1971. 1v. (40p.) ill.

A picture story-book for children.
Published simultaneously New York, Tundra Books. **AEU**

629 **Coleman**, MacDonald. Once upon a childhood. With illustrations by Edwin E. Ash. Red Deer: Kingfisher Press, 1979. 188p. ill.

Autobiographical short stories of childhood in Vanguard, Saskatchewan.

Canadiana, 1979. **AEP**

630 **Coleman**, MacDonald. Once upon a little town. Illustrated by Edwin E. Ash. Red Deer: Kingfisher Press, 1979. 193p. ill.

Autobiographical short stories of Vanguard, Saskatchewan. **AEP**

631 **Cormack**, Barbara (Villy). The house. Toronto: Ryerson Press, 1955. 255p.

A novel set in Alberta.

Glenbow. **ACG**

632 **Cormack**, Barbara (Villy). Westward ho! 1903. Illustrated by Anemone Ruder. Don Mills, Ont.: Burns & MacEachern, 1967. 147p. ill.

Juvenile fiction. An historical novel about the Barr Colonists.

Glenbow. **ACG**

633 **Cosgrove**, Edmund. The terror of the tar sands. Illustrated by Don Morrison. Toronto: Burns & MacEachern, 1968. 135p. ill.

Juvenile fiction set in northern Alberta.

CBIP, 1979, **AEU**

634 **Crichton**, Neil. Rerun. A novel. Don Mills: Musson Book, 1976. 213p.

Also 1977, Markham, Ont., Paper Jacks. (CBIP, 1979). **AEU**

635 **Denbury**, Mabel L. The story of Johnny Doogit. New York: Vantage Press, 1959. 62p. ill.

Juvenile literature. **ACP**

636 **Dibdin**, Michael John. Afterpiece. A novel. Edmonton: University of Alberta, 1970. (3), 329 leaves.

Thesis (M.A.), University of Alberta, 1970.
Typescript.

Canadian theses. **AEU**

637 **Dickson**, Lovat. The ante-room. London: Macmillan Company of Canada, 1959. 270p.

Autobiographical.

Glenbow. **ACG**

638 **Diesel**, Gladys Cynthia Rebecca (Shope). The legend of Owl Hoot Hill. Edmonton: s.n., 1961. 8p.

Canadiana, 1962.

639 **Dragland**, Stan. Peckertracks. A chronicle. Toronto: Coach House Press, 1978. 140p.

A novel of a boy growing up in a small Alberta town.

CBIP, 1979. **ACP**

640 **Dyba**, Kenneth. Lucifer and Lucinda. Vancouver: November House, 1977. 106p.

Juvenile fiction.

Canadiana, 1978. **AEU**

641 **Dyba**, Kenneth. Sister Roxy. Vancouver: November House, 1977. 234p. 46,5

CBIP, 1979. **AEU**

642 **Eggleston**, Magdelana (Raskevich). Mountain shadows. London: William Heinemann, 1955. 254p.

Published simultaneously in Toronto. Also published 1956, New York, Roy.
A novel about Lithuanian settlers and racial frictions in a small Alberta community.

Canadiana, 1958. **AEU**

643 **Eggleston**, Wilfrid. The high plains. Ottawa: Borealis Press, 1975. 267p.

A novel set in southern Alberta.
First published 1938, Toronto, Macmillan of Canada. 267p. (Peel 3619).

CBIP, 1979. **AEU**

644 **Eggleston**, Wilfrid. Prairie symphony. Ottawa: Borealis Press, 1978. 271p.

A novel set in southern Alberta.

Canadiana, 1979. **AEU**

645 **Eichner**, Edith (Orsel). Golden dreams, story and drawings. Edmonton: s.n., 1966. 41p. ill.

Translated from the original German text by G.P. Weih and Albin Shanley.

Canadiana, 1967.

646 **Farran**, Roy. The day after tomorrow. London: Panther Books, 1959. 158, 1p. (A Panther book, 999)

A novel based on the author's wartime experiences in Greece.

Canadiana, 1960. **AEU**

647 **Farran**, Roy. Never had a chance. Toronto: Geoffrey Bles, 1967. 221p.

A novel set in the Rocky Mountains.

Glenbow. **ACG**

648 **Farran**, Roy. The search. London: Collins, 1958. 253p.

A novel set in Alberta.

Canadiana, 1960. **AEU**

649 **Faulknor**, Cliff. The in-betweener. Illustrated by Leonard Shortall. Boston: Little, Brown, 1967. 166p. ill.

Juvenile fiction. An adventure story set in British Columbia. **AEU**

650 **Faulknor**, Cliff. The smoke horse. Illustrated by W.F. Phillipps. Toronto: McClelland & Stewart, 1968. 186p. ill.

Juvenile fiction. A tale of White Bull, a young Piegan Indian brave, set in the Rocky Mountains.
Also reprinted in the Candian favourites edition, 1974.

Dew. **AEU**

651 **Faulknor**, Cliff. West to the cattle country. Toronto: McClelland and Stewart, 1975. 47p. ill.

Juvenile fiction. Story of twelve-year old Bob Brandon's six month stay on an Alberta cattle ranch.
Produced with the co-operation of the Alberta Cattle Commission and Alberta Agriculture. **AEA**

652 **Faulknor**, Cliff. The white calf. The story of Eagle child, the Piegan boy, who found a white calf said to have been sent by the Above Ones. Illustrated by Gerald Tailfeathers. Boston: Little, Brown, 1965. 180p. ill.

Juvenile fiction.

Dew. **ACG**

653 **Faulknor**, Cliff. The white peril. Illustrated by Gerald Tailfeathers. Boston: Little, Brown, 1966. 166p. ill.

Juvenile fiction. A sequel to *The white calf*.

Dew. **AEU**

654 **Fidler**, Vera. Chuckwagon of the Circle B. Illustrated by Douglas Stephens. Toronto: Macmillan Company of Canada, 1957. 174p. ill.

Juvenile fiction. **ACG**

655 **Franko**, Ivan. Fox Mykyta. Ivan Franko's Ukrainian classic. English version by Bohdan Melnyk. Illustrated by William Kurelek. Montreal: Tundra Books, 1978. 148p. ill.

Juvenile fiction.
Original Ukrainian version published in western Ukraine, 1890.

CBIP, 1979. **AEU**

656 **Freeman**, Madeline (Austin). A horse for Running Buffalo. Illustrated by Allan Daniel. Toronto: Van Nostrand Reinhold, 1972. vii, 88p. ill.

Juvenile fiction. Story of a Blackfoot Indian boy in Alberta, with an epilogue on the Blackfoot tribe.

Glenbow. **ACG**

657 **Frey**, Cecelia. Breakaway. Toronto: Macmillan of Canada, 1974. 183p.

A novel of homesteading in Alberta in the 1930s.
A finalist in the Search-for-a-new-Alberta novelist competition.

CBIP, 1979. **AECYR**

658 **Gaal**, Arlene Beverly (Walker). Banff's Christmas wish. Illustrated by Jack Kania. Rutland, B.C.: Valley Review Publishers, 1971. (27)p. ill.

Juvenile fiction.

Canadiana, 1972. **AEU**

659 **Gard**, Robert Edward. Devil Red. Illustrated by Richard W. Lewis. New York: Duell, Sloan and Pearce, 1963. 121p. ill.

Juvenile novel set in Alberta. **AEU**

660 **Gard**, Robert Edward. A horse named Joe. Illustrated by C.W. Anderson. New York: Little, Brown, 1956. 237p. ill.

Juvenile fiction set in Alberta.
Published in association with Duell, Sloan and Pearce.

Canadiana, 1958. **AEU**

661 **Gard**, Robert Edward. Scotty's mare. Illustrated by Aaron Bohrod. New York: Duell, Sloan and Pearce, 1957. vii, 152p. ill.

Juvenile novel set in Alberta.

Canadiana, 1958.

662 **Gedge**, Pauline. Child of the morning. Toronto: Macmillan Company of Canada, 1977. 403p.

An historical novel about Hatshepsut.
Also published, 1977, London, Raven.

Canadiana, 1977. AEU

663 **Gedge**, Pauline. The eagle and the raven. A novel. Toronto: MacMillan of Canada, 1978. 694p.

An historical novel about Boudicea.

Canadiana, 1979. AEU

664 **Gillese**, John Patrick. Kirby's gander. Illustrated by Clarence Tillenius. Toronto: Ryerson Press, 1957. ix, 212p. ill.

Animal stories set in Alberta.

Glenbow. ACG

665 **Godfrey**, Denis. The bridge of fire. London: Jonathan Cape, 1954. 285p.

Novel set in Ceylon during second world war.

Canadiana, 1954. AEU

666 **Godfrey**, Denis. No Englishman need apply. A novel. Toronto: Macmillan of Canada, 1965. 272p.

A novel of university life set in western Canada. ACG

667 **Govier**, Kathleen. Random descent. A novel. Toronto: MacMillan of Canada, 1979. 228p.

Canadiana, 1979. AEU

668 **Gowland**, John Stafford. Sikanaska trail. Illustrated by Christopher Brooker. London: Werner Laurie, 1956. 207p. ill.

Stories by a forest ranger set in the Rocky Mountains. AEU

669 **Hagell**, Edward Frederic. When the grass was free. Toronto: Ryerson Press, 1954. x, 127p. ill.

Fictionalized accounts of cattle ranching in southern Alberta.

Glenbow. ACG

670 **Hall**, Gordon Langley. Peter at the Stampede. Illustrated by Jennifer Kent. London: Lutterworth Press, 1961. 142p. ill.

Juvenile fiction. Story of an Ojibway Indian boy.

Canadiana, 1963. AEU

671 **Hall**, Gordon Langley. Peter Jumping Horse. Illustrated by Jennifer Kent. London: Lutterworth Press, 1959. 144p. ill.

Juvenile fiction.
Also published 1962, New York, Holt, Rinehart and Winston. 141p.

Glenbow. ACG

672 **Hancock**, Ronald Lee. The man sitting in Place Pigalle and other short short stories. Illustrated by the author. Calgary: Chinook Publishers, 1973. v, 57p. ill.

ACG

673 **Hanna**, Nell. Thistle creek. Ottawa: Borealis Press, 1978. 231p.

A novel set in a rural Alberta community in the 1920s.

CBIP, 1978. **ACP**

674 **Hanson**, Eric. Trader Eric and other stories. s.l.: s.n., 1957. 208p.

Text in Hebrew with added title page in English. **AEA**

675 **Hardy**, William George. The bloodied toga. A novel of Julius Caesar. Toronto: Macmillan of Canada, 1979. 510p.

Canadiana, 1979. **AEU**

676 **Hardy**, William George. The city of libertines. Toronto: McClelland and Stewart, 1957. 437p.

Also published 1957, New York, Appleton-Century Crofts. 437p.

Mcleod. **AEP**

677 **Hardy**, William George. The scarlet mantle. A novel of Julius Caesar. Toronto: Macmillan of Canada, 1978. 462p.

CBIP, 1979. **AEU**

678 **Harker**, Herbert. Goldenrod. New York: Random House, 1972. 186p.

A novel about rodeo riders, set in southern Alberta. **AEU**

679 **Harker**, Herbert. Turn again home. New York: Random House, 1977. 245p.

A novel about a Mormon family, set partly in Cardston. **AEP**

680 **Harker**, Randal. Adrift. Toronto: Macmillan of Canada, 1977. 247p.

A finalist in the Search-for-a-new-Alberta novelist contest, 1974. **AEU**

681 **Harlow**, Robert G. A gift of echoes. Toronto: Macmillan of Canada, 1965. 248p.

A novel set in the foothills of the Canadian Rockies.
Also published 1973, Scarborough, Ont., New American Library.

Canadiana, 1967. **AEU**

682 **Harvison**, Clifford W. The Horsemen. Toronto: McClelland and Stewart, 1967. xiv, 271p. ill.

A novel of the R.C.M.P.

Glenbow. **ACG**

683 **Hayes**, John Francis. Bugles in the hills. Illustrated by Fred J. Finley. Toronto: Copp Clark, 1955. 312p.

Historical novel of the Mounties' first days.

Dew. **AEU**

684 **Heming**, Eileen. Ted of the Mounties. London: Lutterworth Press, 1955. 95p.

An adventure story for children set in Alberta. **ACG**

685 **Hendrickson**, Magda. This land is our land. Calgary: Foothills Lutheran Press, 1972. 199p.

Fictionalized account of the Norwegian community of Bardo in the 1890s.

Glenbow. **ACG**

686 **Henry**, Lorena Ann. The adventure of Cynthia and her friends. Red Deer: Red Deer College Press, 1975. (20)p. ill.

Childrens' fiction by a seven-year old author.

Canadiana, 1976. **AEU**

687 **Holt**, Stephen. Stormy. Illustrated by Pers Crowell, New York: Longmans, Green, 1955. 5, 150p. ill.

Story of a boy and his horse, set in Alberta.

Canadiana, 1956.

688 **Hughes**, Monica. Beyond the dark river. Toronto: Thomas Nelson & Sons (Canada), 1979. 152p.

Science fiction set in Alberta.
First published 1979, London, Hamish Hamilton. **ACP**

689 **Hughes**, Monica. Crisis on Conshelf Ten. Toronto: Copp Clark, 1975. 143p.

Fiction.
Also, French translation, 1978, with title *Alerte au plateau dix*, Montreal, Duclot.

Canadiana, 1978. **AEU**

690 **Hughes**, Monica. Earthdark. London: Hamish Hamilton, 1977. 122p.

Juvenile fiction.

Canadiana, 1979.

691 **Hughes**, Monica. The ghost dance caper. London: Hamish Hamilton, 1978. 122p.

Juvenile fiction.

Canadiana 1979. **AEP**

692 **Hughes**, Monica. Gold-fever trail. A Klondike adventure. Illustrated by Patricia Peacock. Edmonton: J.M. LeBel Enterprises, 1974. 92p. ill.

Juvenile fiction.

Canadiana, 1975. **AEU**

693 **Hughes**, Monica. The tomorrow city. London, Ont.: Hamilton, 1978. 137p.

Juvenile literature.
Also French language edition, 1978, *Le cerveau de la ville*, Montreal, Lidec and Paris, Duculot, (Travelling sur le futur, 7)
182p.

Canadiana, 1980.

694 **Jakober**, Marie. The mind gods. A novel of the future. Toronto: Macmillan of Canada, 1976. 165p.

Science fiction.
Finalist in 1974 Search-for-a-new-Alberta-Novelist Competition.

CBIP 1979. **AEU**

695 **Jones**, Leanne M. The book about nothing. Illustrated by Audrey Young Oppel. Red Deer: Red Deer College Press, 1978. (42)p.

Childrens' literature.

Canadiana, 1979.

696 **Jones**, Leanne M. Hanok. Illustrated by Audrey Young Oppel. Red Deer: Red Deer College Press, 1977. 32p. ill.

Juvenile fiction.

CBIP, 1979. **AEU**

697 **Kelland**, Clarence Budington. The case of the nameless corpse. New York: Pyramid Books, 1958. 192p.

This book was published serially under the title *The secret of Shining Brook*.
Detective story set in Alberta oilfields.

Glenbow. **ACG**

698 **Kendal**, Wallis. Just Gin. Illustrated by Ib Ohlsson. Toronto: Macmillan of Canada, 1973. 159p. ill.

Juvenile fiction.

CBIP 1978. **AEU**

699 **King**, Donald Robert. Spitzee Anota. Toronto: Longmans, Green, 1957. 252p.

Tale of southern Alberta in the 1870's.
Sequel to *Sukanabi*.

Glenbow. **ACG**

700 **Kinsella**, W.P. Dance me outside. Ottawa: Oberon Press, 1977. 158p.

Short stories.

CBIP 1979. **ACP**

701 **Kinsella**, W.P. Scars. Stories. Ottawa: Oberon Press, 1978. 154p.
CBIP, 1979. **AEU**

702 **Kiriak**, Illia. Sons of the soil. Toronto: Ryerson Press, 1959. 303p.
First published 1939-45 in three volumes as *Syny zemli*, Edmonton, Institution Press, (Peel 3929).
Reprinted as part of Alberta Heritage Learning Resources Project, 1979 (Alberta literature for senior students and adults).
Fictionalized account of Ukrainian settlers near Shandro.
Macleod. **AEA**

703 **Kreisel**, Henry. The betrayal. Toronto: McClelland and Stewart, 1964. 218p.
Also an edition with introduction by Sidney Warhaft, 1971, Toronto, McClelland and Stewart, x, 218p. (New Canadian library, 77).
Mcleod. **AEU**

704 **Kreisel**, Henry. Klanak islands. Eight short stories. Edited by William C. McConnell and Alice McConnell. Vancouver: Klanak, 1959. (1v.)
CBIP, 1979.

705 **Kreisel**, Henry. The rich man. Markham, Ont.: Simon & Schuster of Canada, 1975. 256p. (Canadian pocket book)
First published 1948, Toronto, McClelland and Stewart, 263p. Published in paperback, 1961, Toronto, McClelland (New Canadian library, 24). 208p.
Canadiana, 1976. **AEU**

706 **Kroetsch**, Robert. Badlands. A novel. Toronto: New Press, 1975. 270p.
Also published 1976, Don Mills, Paperjacks.
Novel set in southern Alberta.
Canadiana, 1975. **AEU**

707 **Kroetsch**, Robert. But we are exiles. A novel New York: St. Martin's Press, 1965. 145p.
First published 1965, Toronto, Macmillan, and New York, St. Martin's Press.
Published 1977, Toronto, Macmillan (Laurentian library, 45).
Novel set in the North West Territories.
Glenbow. **ACG**

708 **Kroetsch**, Robert. Gone Indian. Toronto: New Press, 1973. 158p.
Novel set in Alberta.
Canadiana, 1973. **AEU**

709 **Kroetsch**, Robert. The studhorse man. Toronto: Macmillan, 1969. 168p.
Novel set in Alberta.
Also published 1969, London, Macdonald, and New York, Simon and Shuster.
Glenbow. **ACG**

710 **Kroetsch**, Robert. What the crow said. Don Mills, Ont.: General Publishing, 1978. 218p.

Also published 1979, Markham, Ontario, Paperjacks.

Canadiana, 1979. AEU

711 **Kroetsch**, Robert. The words of my roaring. Toronto: Macmillan of Canada, 1966. 211p.

Novel set in Alberta.

Mcleod. AEU

712 **Kurelek**, William. Lumberjack. Paintings and story by William Kurelek. Montreal: Tundra Books, 1974. (48)p. ill.

Juvenile literature.
Published simultaneously, Boston, Houghton Mifflin, iv. unpaged.
Also published 1975, 1977, London, Collins. 48p.

CBIP 1979. AEU

713 **Kurelek**, William. A prairie boy's summer. Paintings and story by William Kurelek. Montreal: Tundra Books, 1975. (48)p. ill.

Juvenile literature.
Also 1976, London, Collins, (48)p., and 1978, Oslo, Bokklubbens Barn, entitled *Bama pa praeriegavden, tegnet og fortait*.

CBIP, 1979. AEU

714 **Kurelek**, William. A prairie boy's winter. Paintings and story by William Kurelek. Boston: Houghton Mifflin, 1973. (48)p. ill.

Juvenile literature.
Published simultaneously, Montreal, Tundra Books, and 1978, Oslo, Bokklubbens Barn, with title *Barna pa praerien, tegnet og fortait*, and 1978, Cobenhagen, Tlyst, with title *Er praeriedreng*.

CBIP 1979. AEU

715 **Leeder**, Terry. White Forehead of the Cypress Hills. Illustrated by Deborah Drew-Brook. Toronto: Dundurn Press, 1979. 63p. ill. (Frontiers and pioneers)

The story of Sitting Bull and Sergeant James Walsh of the R.C.M.P. retold for juveniles.

Canadiana, 1979. ACP

716 **Loggie**, Margaret. One man in his time. Edmonton: University of Alberta, 1960. 258 leaves.

Thesis (M.A.), University of Alberta, 1960.
Typescript.
Novel set in Peace River district.

Canadian theses. AEU

717 **Longstreth**, Thomas Morris. The Calgary Challengers. Illustrated by William Wheeler. Toronto: Macmillan of Canada, 1962. 165p. ill.

An adventure story for juveniles.

718 **Loverso**, Caterina Edwards. Vases. Six short stories. Ottawa: National Library of Canada, 1973. (ix), 115p. (Canadian theses on microfiche, 17598)

Thesis (M.A.), University of Alberta, 1973.
Microfiche of typescript.

U of a Theses. **AEU**

719 **Maclagan**, David. Adventures into unknowns. Five stories for young readers. Written and illustrated by David Maclagan. Edmonton: Hurtig, 1972. 111p., ill.

Also published 1972, Vermont, Charles E. Tuttle.

CBIP 1979. **AEU**

720 **Maitland**, Hugh. Brad Forrest's Calgary adventure. Toronto: Longmans Canada, 1964. 158p. ill. (Brad Forrest adventure series, 4)

Juvenile fiction set in Calgary vicinity.

Glenbow. **ACG**

721 **Manvers**, Betty. Love among the pines. London: Wright & Brown, 1960. 192p. (Amethyst library)

Novel set in Alberta.

Canadiana, 1963.

722 **Mathers**, Beatrice. Children in the sun. By Beatrice Mathers and Audrey McKim. Illustrated by Geoffrey W. Goss. Toronto: United Church of Canada Board of Information and Stewardship, 1964. 76p. ill.

Juvenile literature.

Canadiana, 1969.

723 **McAlpine**, Jennie. Pamela of Echo Glen. New York: Pageant Press, 1954. 118p.

An historical novel set in the Fort Macleod area.

DEW. **ACG**

724 **McClung**, Nellie Letitia. Clearing in the West. My own story. Toronto: Thomas Allen, 1964. 378p.

First published in 1935, Toronto, Thomas Allen, and New York, Revell (Peel 3456).

CBIP, 1979. **AEA**

725 **McCourt**, Edward. Buckskin brigadier. The story of the Alberta field force. Illustrated by Vernon Mould. Toronto: Macmillan, 1955. vii, 150p. ill. (Great stories of Canada)

Glenbow. **ACG**

726 **McCourt**, Edward. Fasting friar. Toronto: McClelland and Stewart, 1963. 222p.

Also published as *The Ettinger affair*, 1963, London, Macdonald.
Mcleod. **AEU**

727 **McCourt**, Edward. Music at the close. Introduction by Allan Bevan. Toronto: McClelland and Stewart, 1966. 218p.

First published 1947, Toronto, Ryerson.
Mcleod. **AEU**

728 **McCourt**, Edward. Walk through the valley. Toronto: McClelland and Stewart, 1958. 222p.

Mcleod. **AEU**

729 **McCourt**, Edward. The wooden sword. Toronto: McClelland and Stewart, 1956. 255p.

Canadiana, 1956. **AEU**

730 **McHugh**, Drake. Edmonton is burning. Edmonton: Puckrin's Production House, 1979. 177p.

Cover from a painting by Dennis Greer.
A novel of political intrigue. **ACP**

731 **McKim**, Audrey. Andy and the gopher. Illustrated by Ronni Solbert. Toronto: Little, Brown, 1959. 119p. ill.

Childrens' fiction set in Medicine Hat.
Canadiana, 1959. **ACP**

732 **McKim**, Audrey. Lexy for short. Illustrated by Charles Geer. New York: Abingdon Press, 1961. 159p. ill.

Juvenile literature. **OONL**

733 **McKim**, Audrey. That summer with Lexy. Illustrated by Charles Geer. New York: Abingdon Press, 1964. 144p. ill.

Juvenile fiction. A sequel to *Lexy for Short*.
Canadiana, 1964. **ACP**

734 **McKim**, Audrey. Thorny's hideaway. Drawings by Don Lambo. New York: Thomas Nelson & Sons, 1961. 7, 147p. ill.

Juvenile fiction. An adventure story set on an Alberta ranch.
Canadiana, 1961. **ACP**

735 **McKinnon**, Claire Schuler. Nisku. Illustrated by Sue Archibald. Red Deer: Red Deer College Press, 1975. 58p. ill.

Juvenile fiction. Stories about a Cree boy.
Canadiana, 1975. **AEU**

736 **McNamee**, James. My uncle Joe. Illustrated by Lewis Parker. Toronto: Macmillan of Canada, 1962. 63p. ill.

A novel set in Alberta.

Glenbow. **ACG**

737 **McNamee**, James. Them damn Canadians hanged Louis Riel! A novel. Toronto: Macmillan of Canada, 1971. 133p.

Setting for most of novel is Alberta.
Parts of this book previously published under title *My uncle Joe*.

Glenbow. **ACG**

738 **Mitchell**, William Ormond. The black bonspiel of Wullie MacCrimmon. Calgary: Frontiers Unlimited, 1965. 56p. ill. (Chinook books, 1)

Glenbow. **ACG**

739 **Mitchell**, William Ormond. Jake and the kid. Toronto: Macmillan of Canada, 1961. 184p.

Also, 1974, in their Laurentian Library series. 21. **AEU**

740 **Mitchell**, William Ormond. The kite. Toronto: Macmillan, 1962. 210p.

Macleod. **AEU**

741 **Mitchell**, William Ormond. The vanishing point. Toronto: Macmillan of Canada, 1973. 393p.

A novel set in the Rocky Mountains.

Also published 1975, Toronto, Macmillan (Laurentian library, 25). **AEU**

742 **Mitchell**, William Ormond. Who has seen the wind. Toronto: Macmillan of Canada, 1962. 299p. (Laurentian library, 14)

First published 1947, Boston, Little, Brown (Peel 4053) and Toronto, Macmillan.
Published as new edition with illustrations by William Kurelek, 1976, Macmillan.
Edition 1976 reprinted 1978, as part of Alberta Heritage Learning Resources Project, 1979, (Alberta literature for senior students and adults) 301p. **AEU**

743 **Moon**, Bryan R. Fourling. Four short stories. Ottawa: National Library of Canada, 1978. vi, 116 leaves. (Canadian theses on microfiche, 36443)

Thesis (M.A.), University of Alberta, 1978.
Microfiche of typescript.

U of A Theses. **AEU**

744 **Morgan**, Marjorie C. Packy, the little elephant who came to the cold. Illustrations by Harry Savage. Edmonton: J.M. LeBel Enterprises, 1973. 75p. ill.

Childrens' fiction. A story of a baby elephant at the Alberta Game Farm.

CBIP, 1979. **AEU**

745 **Morton**, Colin T. Standing in the street. Edmonton: University of Alberta, 1979. vii, 174 leaves.

Thesis (M.A.), University of Alberta, 1979.
Typescript.
Novel set in a small western Canadian college.

U of A Theses. **AEU**

746 **Murphy**, Emily (Ferguson). Janey Canuck in the West. Introduction, Isabel Bassett, general editor, Clara Thomas. Toronto: McClelland and Stewart, 1975. xiii, 223p. ill. (Heritage books, 2)

Autobiographical sketches, first published, 1910 London, Cassell. 305p. (Peel 2163).
Also published 1917, London, J.M. Dent.
Also published, Windjammerbooks, 9.

Canadiana, 1979. **AEU**

747 **Myers**, C. Vernon. Through hell to Alaska. A novel. New York: Exposition Press, 1955. 264p.

A novel of the oil industry set in northern Canada.

Glenbow. **ACG**

748 **Myles**, Eugenie Louise (Butler). The Emperor of Peace River. Edmonton: Institute of Applied Art, 1965. 310p. ill.

Printed by Co-Op Press, Edmonton.
Fictionalized biography of Sheridan Lawrence, the Emperor of Peace River and his wife Juey.
Also published 1978, Saskatoon, Western Producer Press, (Spectra series), 302p..
Reprinted as part of the Alberta Heritage Learning Resources Project, 1979 (Alberta literature for senior students and adults).

Glenbow. **ACG**

749 **Noble**, Iris (Davis). Megan. New York: J. Messner, 1965. 192p.

Juvenile fiction set in Alberta.

Canadiana, 1965.

750 **O'Hagan**, Howard. The school-marm tree. A novel. Vancouver: Talonbooks, 1977. 245p.

A novel set in Jasper in the 1920s, based on a short story by the author.

CBIP, 1979. **AEU**

751 **O'Hagan**, Howard. Tay John, a novel. New York: Clarkson N. Potter, 1960. 263p.

A novel set in the Athabasca River Valley.
Also, edition with introduction by Patricia Morley, edited by Malcom Ross, 1974, Toronto, McClelland and Stewart, (New Canadian library, 105). 264p.

Canadiana, 1960. **ACG**

752 **O'Hagan**, Howard. The woman who got on at Jasper Station, and other stories. Denver: A. Swallow, 1963. 112p. (A Swallow paperback, 53)

Stories set in the Canadian Rockies.

Glenbow. **ACG**

753 **Paperny**, Myra. The wooden people. Illustrated by Ken Stampnick. Toronto: Little, Brown, 1976. 168p. ill.

Juvenile fiction set in a small Alberta town in 1927.

CBIP, 1979. **AEU**

754 **Parker**, William Wilder McKinley. Belle Anne of Pine Point. Edmonton: Wm. W. Mck. Parker, 1965. 99p. ill.

A novelette, with two poems. **ACG**

755 **Parker**, William Wilder McKinley. Bush homestead girl. Or, Myrtle's blueberry kiss. Edmonton: W.W.M. Parker, 1964. 96p. ill.

A story set in the Lac Ste. Anne area.

Mcleod. **ACG**

756 **Parker**, William Wilder McKinley. Flowing gold. Edmonton W.W.M. Parker, n.d. 60p. ill.

Fictional account of life near Waskatenau. **AEU**

757 **Parker**, William Wilder McKinley. Greener prairie. Edmonton: W.W.M.Parker, 1959. 68p.

Fictional account of life near Brooks.

Mcleod. **AEU**

758 **Parker**, William Wilder McKinley. Lake la Nonne Trail. Or, Pal of the pine woods. Edmonton: W.W.M. Parker, 1973. 18p. ill.

A story set in Glenevis, Lac Ste. Anne County.

Canadiana, 1974. **AEU**

759 **Parker**, William Wilder McKinley. North Star. Joan's grey pony. Edmonton: Wm.W. McK. Parker, 1966. 44p. ill.

Juvenile fiction set in Alberta. **AEA**

760 **Parker**, William Wilder McKinley. Silver Forks. Edmonton: W.W.M. Parker, 1955. 66p. ill.

Juvenile fiction set in the Peace River Country. **AEU**

761 **Percy**, Douglas Cecil. Beyond the tangled mountain. Beaverlodge: Horizon House, 1975. 158p.

First published 1962, Grand Rapids, Mich., Zondervan Publishing House.
A novel set in Africa. A sequel to *Hidden Valley* and *When the bamboo sings*.

Canadiana, 1976.

762 **Pfeifer**, Lillian E. The wolfers. Illustrated by David Craig. Toronto: Burns & MacEachern, 1967. 167p. ill.

An historical novel of the northwest in the days of the whiskey traders.

Dew. **AEU**

763 **Pharis**, Robert L. The golden feather. Illustrated by David Sager. Toronto: Longmans Canada, 1964. 182p. ill.

Juvenile novel set in southern Alberta.

Glenbow. **ACG**

764 **Phelan**, Josephine. The bold heart. The story of Father Lacombe. Illustrated by Jerry Lazare. New York: St. Martin's Press, 1954. 182p. ill. (Great stories of Canada, 10)

Juvenile literature.
Also published by Macmillan, Toronto. Reprinted 1956, 1965.

Glenbow. **ACG**

765 **Phelan**, Josephine. The boy who ran away. Illustrated by Vernon Mould. Toronto: Macmillan, 1954. 152p. ill.

Also published, New York, St. Martin's Press. Reprinted 1956, 1966.
Juvenile fiction. An adventure story set in the Northwest Territories, including Fort Edmonton.

CBIP, 1979. **AEU**

766 **Potrebenko**, Helen. A flight of average persons. Stories and other writings. Vancouver: New Star Books, 1979. 227p.

Canadiana, 1979.

767 **Potrebenko**, Helen. Taxi! A novel. Vancouver: New Star Books, 1975. 168p.

CBIP, 1979. **AEU**

768 **Price**, Monty. How Grandfather Burleson saved Christmas for the children of Calgary. New York: Vantage Press, 1976. 17p. ill.

Juvenile Literature. **ACP**

769 **Primeau**, Marguerite. Dans le muskeg. Montréal: Fides, 1960. 222p. (Collection 'La gerbe d'or')

A novel set in the Peace River district. **AEU**

770 **Reilly**, Helen. Compartment K. Calgary: Random House, 1955. 2, 239, 1p.

Setting a transcontinental train and the Rocky Mountains.

Canadiana, 1957.

771 **Riis**, Sharon. The true story of Ida Johnson. Toronto: Women's Press, 1976. 111p.

A novel set in Alberta.

CBIP, 1979. ACG

772 **Riley**, Louise. The mystery horse. Illustrated by John Merle Smith. New York: Messner, 1950. 200p. ill.

An adventure story set on an Alberta ranch.
Also published 1957, Oxford, Blackwell.

Canadiana, 1958.

773 **Riley**, Louise. Train for Tiger Lily. Illustrated by Christine Price. New York: Viking Press, 1954. 186p. ill.

Juvenile fiction.

CBIP, 1979. AEU

774 **Ringwood**, Gwendolyn Margaret (Pharis). Younger brother. Decorations by E. Harper Johnson. New York: Longmans, Green, 1959. 3, 213p. ill.

Juvenile fiction.

Canadiana, 1961. AEP

775 **Running**, Arnold. Stay but till tomorrow. Toronto: Longmans, Green, 1958. 191p.

A novel set in southern Alberta.
Also published 1959, London, E. Benn.

Dew. AEU

776 **Russell**, Sheila (MacKay). The living earth. Toronto: Longmans, Green, 1954. 317p.

A novel set in Alberta.

Mcleod. AEU

777 **Ryga**, George. Ballad of a stone picker. Toronto: Macmillan of Canada, 1966. 159p.

Revised ed. published 1976, Vancouver, Talonbooks. 142p.

Mcleod. AEU

778 **Ryga**, George. The hungry hills. Toronto: Longmans, 1963. 184p.

Also published 1974, Vancouver, Talonbooks, 184p., and reprinted 1979, as part of Alberta Heritage Learning Resources Project, (Alberta literature for senior students and adults).

Mcleod. AEU

779 **Ryga**, George. Night desk. A novel. Vancouver: Talonbooks, 1976. 123p.

A novel set in Edmonton.

CBIP, 1979. ACU

780 **Schleich**, David John. No sweet land. Ottawa: National Library of Canada, 1973. (6), 348 leaves. (Canadian Theses on microfilm, 15336)

Thesis (M.A.), University of Alberta, 1973.
Microfilm of typescript.

Canadiana, 1974. **OONL**

781 **Shute**, Allan. Double feature. Edmonton: Tree Frog Press, 1973. 18 leaves.

Cover title.

Short story. **AEU**

782 **Shute**, Allan. The rain-orb. Edmonton: A.J. Shute, 1969. (6), 457 leaves.

Thesis (M.A.), University of Alberta, 1969.
Typescript.
Fairytale.

Canadian theses. **AEU**

783 **Sikabonyi**, Laszlo A. Billion barrel oil swindle. A novel. Hicksville, N.Y.: Exposition Press, 1976. 256p. (An Exposition-Banner Book)

ACP

784 **Simon**, Olaf Emil Hugo. Curse of the gods. Calgary: Veritas International Publishing, 1977. 202p.

On cover *A startling report on the silent war*.
A novel of the cold war.

Canadiana, 1977. **AEU**

785 **Sluman**, Norma Pauline (Hardman). Blackfoot Crossing. Toronto: Ryerson Press, 1959. vii, 255p.

A novel set in Blackfoot Crossing, 1874.

Glenbow. **ACG**

786 **Sluman**, Norma Pauline (Hardman). Poundmaker. Toronto: Ryerson Press, 1967. viii, 310p.

Fictionalized biography.

Canadiana, 1968. **AEU**

787 **Smith**, Frank Allan. Corpse in handcuffs. Toronto: Macmillan of Canada, 1969. 176p.

A novel. **ACP**

788 **Smith**, Frank Allan. Defectors are dead men. London: Robert Hale, 1971. 191p.

An espionage story set in London. **AECYR**

789 **Smith**, Frank Allan. The traitor mask. London: Robert Hale, 1971. 191p.

A novel of espionage, set in London. Also published Toronto, Macmillan of Canada.

790 **Smith**, Starr. A place for everyone. Illustrated by Dennis Greer. Edmonton: Puckrin's Production House, 1975. 16p. ill. (You're unique)

Juvenile fiction printed in large type.

Canadiana, 1979.

791 **Smith**, Starr. Teamwork. Illustrated by Dennis Greer. Edmonton: Puckrin's Production House, 1975. 16p. ill. (You're unique)

Juvenile fiction printed in large type.

Canadiana, 1979.

792 **Smith**, Starr. Whatever you do. Illustrated by Dennis Greer. Edmonton: Puckrin's Production House, 1975. 18p. ill. (You're unique)

Juvenile fiction printed in large type.

Canadiana, 1979.

793 **Steele**, Harwood Elmes Robert. The marching call. With a foreword by Major-General Victor W. Odlum. Illustrated by John Merle Smith. Toronto: Thomas Nelson, 1955. 249p. ill.

A novel. Fictionalized biography of Sam Steele.

Dew. **AEU**

794 **Stenson**, Fred. Lonesome hero. Toronto: Macmillan of Canada, 1974. 182p.

AEU

795 **Street**, Arthur George. Cooper's crossing. London: R. Hale, 1962. 223p.

A story of country life in England and southern Alberta from 1880 to 1960.

Glenbow. **ACG**

796 **Stringer**, Arthur John Arbuthnott. The mud lark. New York: Bobbs-Merrill, 1957

A novel set in Alberta.

First published 1932, Indianapolis, Bobbs-Merrill, 331p. (Peel 3317). **ACP**

797 **Summers**, Merna. The skating party. Ottawa: Oberon Press, 1974. 120p.

Short stories. **AEU**

798 **Tap**, Monica. Mr. Brown and his magic mustache. Illustrated by Martha Jablonski-Jones. Edmonton: Tree Frog Press, 1979. 44p. ill.

Childrens' literature. **AEP**

799 **Truss**, Jan. Bird at the window. Toronto: Macmillan of Canada, 1974. 178p.

Edition 1974 reprinted as part of Alberta Heritage Learning Resources Project, 1979 (Alberta literature for senior students and adults). 178p. **AEU**

800 **Truss**, Jan. A very small rebellion. Essay by Jack Chambers, cover and illustrations by Peter Millward. Edmonton: J.M. LeBel Enterprises, 1976. 95p. ill.

Canadiana, 1977. **AEU**

801 **Van Der Mark**, Christine. Honey in the rock. Toronto: McClelland and Stewart, 1966. 224p.

Novel set in rural Alberta in the 1930s.

Mcleod. **AEU**

802 **Van Der Mark**, Christine. In due season. A novel. With a new introduction by Dorothy Livesay, and an afterword by Dorothy Wise, the author's daughter. Vancouver: New Star Books, 1979. iv, 372p.

Novel about a woman homesteading in northern Alberta.
First published 1947, Toronto, Oxford University Press. 363p. (Peel 4071).

CBIP 1979. **AEU**

803 **Van Herk**, Aritha. Judith. A novel. Toronto: McClelland and Stewart-Bantam, 1978. 190p.

Also published 1978, Boston, Little, Brown. 190p..
First published as thesis (M.A., University of Alberta, entitled *When pigs fly*.

Canadiana, 1979. **AEU**

804 **Van Herk**, Aritha. When pigs fly. Ottawa: National Library of Canada, 1978. vi, 192 leaves. (Canadian theses on microfiche, 40342)

Thesis (M.A.), University of Alberta, 1978.
Microfiche of typescript.
Later published with title *Judith*.

U of A Theses. **AEU**

805 **Walker**, Ella May. Fortress north. Illustrated throughout by the author. 2d ed. rev. Montreal: Renouf, 1956. xi, 423p. ill.

First published 1947, Toronto, T. Allen, 419p. (Peel 4073).
A novel set in Edmonton and vicinity, 1795-1943.

Canadiana, 1957. **AEU**

806 **Walker**, Margaret (Macleod). Come down from yonder mountain. Toronto: Longmans Canada. 1962. 277p.

A novel. **ACU**

807 **Warren**, Sara Evangeline (Matheson). Andy the milkman. Ilfracombe, Devon: Arthur Stockwell, 1957. 128p.

A novel set in Prince Edward Island. **ACP**

808 **Watson**, Sheila. The double hook. Toronto: McClelland and Stewart, 1959. 127p.

Also an edition with an intro. by John Grube, 1966, Toronto. McClelland, (New Canadian library, 54). 134p. Also French translation, 1976, with title *Sous l'oeil de coyote*, Montreal, Editions la Presse.

Mcleod. **AEU**

809 **Watson**, Sheila. Four stories. Toronto: Coach House Press, 1979. 62p.

Contents: Brother Oedipus. The black farm. Antigone. The rumble seat.

CBIP, 1979. **AEU**

810 **Webber**, Frank. Code of the rangeland. Edmonton: Franklyn M. Webber, 1959. 236p.

A novel set in Alberta.

Glenbow. **ACG**

811 **Webber**, Frank. The curse of the wolf. Edmonton: F. Webber, 1960. 25p.

A novel set in Watson Lake. **AEU**

812 **Webber**, Frank. Grudge. Edmonton: F. Webber, 1960. 288p.

Cover title.

A novel. **AEU**

813 **Webber**, Frank. Twenty pebbles, and other stories. New York: Pageant Press, 1955. 89p.

Glenbow. **ACG**

814 **Weir**, Joan. Career girl. Edmonton: Tree Frog Press, 1979. 144p.

Juvenile literature.

815 **Whitaker**, Muriel. Pernilla in the perilous forest. Illustrated by Jetske Ironside. Ottawa: Oberon Press, 1979. (20)p.

Juvenile fiction.

CBIP 1979. **AEU**

816 **Wiebe**, Rudy. The blue mountains of China. Toronto: McClelland and Stewart, 1970. 277p.

A novel of Russian Mennonites.
Also published 1970 in United States, Wm.B. Eerdmans Publishing. Also, 1975, with introduction by W.J. Keith, Toronto, McClelland and Stewart (New Canadian library, 108). 227p.

Mcleod. **AEU**

817 **Wiebe**, Rudy. First and vital candle. Toronto: McClelland and Stewart, 1966. 354p.

Mcleod. **AEU**

818 **Wiebe**, Rudy. Peace shall destroy many. Toronto: McClelland and Stewart, 1962. 239p.

A novel set in a Saskatchewan Mennonite community in 1944.
Originally written as an M.A. thesis, University of Alberta, 1960.
Also edition with intro. by J.M. Robinson, 1972, Toronto, McClelland. 239p.

Mcleod.

819 **Wiebe**, Rudy. The scorched wood people. A novel. Toronto: McClelland and Stewart, 1977. 352p.

Edition 1977 reprinted as part of Alberta Heritage Learning Resources Project, 1979. (Alberta literature for senior students and adults).

CBIP, 1979. **AEU**

820 **Wiebe**, Rudy. The temptation of Big Bear. Toronto: McClelland and Stewart. 1973. 415p.

Also published 1976, Toronto, McClelland (New Canadian library, 122). 415p.

Canadiana, 1974.

821 **Wiebe**, Rudy. Where is the voice coming from? Toronto: McClelland and Stewart, 1974. 157p.

A collection of short stories, with the majority concerned with the plight of native peoples in the west.
Sub-title on dust jacket, *Stories by Rudy Wiebe*.

822 **Williams**, Fred C. The fifth horseman. Calgary: Pandarus Books, 1973. 202p. ill.

Sub-title on dust cover *The Depression story of rodriders, riots and relief.*
A novel of the Depression in Saskatchewan.

Canadiana, 1974. **ACG**

823 **Willison**, Gladys A. Land of the Chinook. Stories of early Alberta. Illustrated by Vernon Mould. Toronto: Macmillan of Canada, 1955. 197p. ill.

Juvenile literature.

Glenbow. **ACG**

824 **Wood**, Kerry. Bessie the coo. Illustrated by Marjorie M. Wood. Calgary: McAra Printing, 1977. 26p. ill.

A story of a childhood experience written for children.

Canadiana, 1976. **ACP**

825 **Wood**, Kerry. The boy and the buffalo. Illustrated by Audrey Teather. New York: St. Martin's Press, 1963. 120p. ill. (Buckskin books, 9)

Juvenile fiction, set in Alberta.
Also published 1967, Toronto, Macmillan of Canada (Buckskin books, 9). 120p.

Glenbow. ACG

826 **Wood**, Kerry. The map-maker. The story of David Thompson. Illustrated by William Wheeler. Toronto: Macmillan, 1955. 185p. ill. (Great stories of Canada, 7)

A fictionalized biography written for children.

Glenbow. ACG

827 **Wood**, Kerry. The medicine man. An historical day in the life of a Cree camp. Illustrated by Audrey Teather. Red Deer: Kerry Wood, 1968. v, 91p. ill.

Printed by John D. McAra, Calgary.

Glenbow. ACG

828 **Wood**, Kerry. Mickey the beaver, and other stories. Illustrated by Audrey Teather. Toronto: Macmillan of Canada, 1964. 74p. ill.

Three animal stories for children, set in Red Deer.

Glenbow. ACG

829 **Wood**, Kerry. The Queen's cowboy. Colonel Macleod of the Mounties. Illustrated by Joseph Rosenthal. Toronto: MacMillan, 1960. 157p. ill. (Great stories of Canada, 22)

Juvenile literature.

Glenbow. ACG

830 **Wood**, Kerry. Samson's long ride. Illustrated by Audrey Teather. Toronto: Collins, 1968. 77p. ill.

An historical novel of a Stoney Indian boy, written for children.

Canadiana, 1969. ACP

831 **Wood**, Kerry. Wild winter. Illustrated by Victor Mays. Boston: Houghton Mifflin, 1954. 175p. ill.

A novel set in Alberta.
Also published, 1962, Toronto, Macmillan of Canada. 175p.

Glenbow. ACG

832 **Wood**, Kerry. Willowdale. Illustrated by Illingworth Kerr. Toronto: McClelland & Stewart, 1956. 216p. ill.

A novel set in Alberta.

Glenbow. ACG

833 **Wright**, Laurali Rose (Bunny). Neighbours. A novel. Toronto: Macmillan of Canada, 1979. 257p.

Winner 1977-78 Search-For-A-New-Alberta. Novelist Competition.

CBIP, 1979. ACP

834 **Young**, Delbert A. The ghost ship. Illustrations by William Taylor. Toronto: Clarke Irwin, 1972. 191p. ill.

Juvenile fiction. A 20th century boy finds himself aboard the *Golden Hind*. **AEU**

835 **Young**, Delbert A. The mounties. Toronto: Hodder and Stoughton, 1968. 158p. ill.

Juvenile literature. **AECYR**

Poetry

836 **Adams**, Norman Edgar. Calgary. A poem. Calgary: N.E. Adams, 1958. 1 fold. leaf.

Glenbow. **ACG**

837 **Adams**, Norman Edgar. Calgary's great stampede show. A poem. Calgary: N.E. Adams, 1959. 4p.

Canadiana, 1959.

838 Alberta Wheat Pool Women's Association. Poems. Calgary: Alberta Wheat Pool Women's Association, 1966. 24p.

Cover title.
Poems submitted by members.

Glenbow. **ACG**

839 **Albright**, W.D. Poems of W.D. Albright, 1881-1946. Beaverlodge: Albright Family, n.d. 60p.

Cover title. **AEU**

840 **Alexander**, William Hardy. The book of Catullus of Verona done into English verse by William Hardy Alexander. Calgary: West Canadian Microfilm, 1958. 270p.

Microfilm copy of typescript.
Distributed to universities and libraries by the University of Alberta on the occasion of its Jubilee, 1908-1958.
Text in Latin and English, with brief commentary.

Canadiana, 1958.

841 **Almon**, Bert. The return and other poems. Cerillos, New Mexico: San Marcos Press, 1968. 51p.

Canadiana, 1979. **AEU**

842 **Almon**, Bert. Taking possession. Poems. San Luis Obispo, Calif.: Solo Press, 1976. 19p.

Canadiana, 1978. **AEU**

843 **Bagley**, Ray. The poems of Ray Bagley. Calgary: Ray Bagley, 1969. 102p.
Cover title *Those other days*.
Dew. **AEU**

844 **Baldridge**, Mary Humphrey. The loneliness of the poet/housewife. Fredericton, N.B.: Fiddlehead, 1978. 44p. (Fiddlehead poetry books, 244)
CBIP, 1979. **ACP**

845 **Baldridge**, Mary Humphrey. Slide-images. s.l.: Retort Press, 1969. (20)p. **AEU**

846 **Barbour**, Douglas. He & she &. Ottawa: Golden Dog Press, 1974. 28p. **AEU**

847 **Barbour**, Douglas. Landfall. Montreal: Delta, 1971. (25)p. (Buckbooks) **AEP**

848 **Barbour**, Douglas. A poem as long as the highway. Kingston: Quarry Press, 1971. 1v. (34)p. **AEU**

849 **Barbour**, Douglas. Shorelines. Winnipeg: Turnstone, 1979. 1v.
CBIP, 1979.

850 **Barbour**, Douglas. Songbook. Vancouver: Talonbooks, 1973. (124)p. **AEU**

851 **Barbour**, Douglas. The story so far, 5. Toronto: Coach House, 1978. 1v.
CBIP, 1979.

852 **Barbour**, Douglas. Visions of my grandfather. Ottawa: Golden Dog Press, 1977. 1v. (38)p.
Canadiana, 1977. **AEU**

853 **Barbour**, Douglas. White. Fredericton: Fiddlehead Poetry Books, 1972. 68p. (Fiddlehead poetry books)
Limited edition of 500 copies.
CBIP, 1979. **AEU**

854 **Bates**, Maxwell. Far-away flags. Victoria, B.C.: Maxwell Bates, 1964. 58p. **ACP**

855 **Blodgett**, Edward D. Sounding. Edmonton: Tree Frog Press, 1977. 60p.
P.N.L.A., 1977. **AEU**

856 **Blodgett**, Edward D. Take away the names. Toronto: Coach House Press, 1975. (76)p.

857 **Botting**, Gary. Freckled blue and other poems. Red Deer: Red Deer College Press, 1979. 68p.

AECYR

858 **Botting**, Gary. Lady Godiva on a plaster horse. Red Deer: Red Deer College Press, 1975. 31p.

Canadiana, 1979. **AEU**

859 **Botting**, Gary. Prometheus rebound. A dramatic poem. Edmonton: Harden House, 1972. 52p.

AEU

860 **Botting**, Gary. Streaking. Red Deer: Red Deer College Press, 1974. 70p.

Canadiana, 1974. **ACU**

861 **Breen**, Reg. Three little hills of home. Three Hills: Three Hills Order of Royal Purple No.52, 1967. 126p.

Published as a Centennial project. **ACP**

862 **Bresnahan**, Jessie M. Poems of the Peace River Country and others. Ilfracombe, Devon: A.H. Stockwell, 1960. 71p. ill.

Canadiana, 1961. **AEU**

863 **Bugnet**, Georges. Poèmes. Présentation de Jean-Marcel Duciaume. Edmonton: Editions de l'Eglantier, 1978. 106p.

Limited edition of 1000 copies.
Pp.7-38 comprise an introduction, chronology and bibliography. **AEU**

864 **Burrs**, Mick. Adventures of the midnight janitor. Edmonton: Walking Image Press, 1973. (8)p.

Limited edition of 264 copies.
Poem sequence 1968-1971-1973.

Canadiana, 1980.

865 **Carmichael**, Robert Ralph. The seed-pod book of joy. Poems and drawings by R.R. Carmichael. Edmonton: Tree Frog Press, 1974. 28 leaves. ill.

Canadiana, 1975. **AEU**

866 **Carter**, David John. Prairie profiles. Illustrated by Ted Renshaw. Medicine Lodge Coulee: David J. Carter, 1977. 23p. ill.

Canadiana, 1979. **ACP**

867 **Cassidy**, Elizabeth Catherine L. Grain and chaff. s.l.: E.L. Cassidy, 1972. 95p. ill.

Cover title. Duplicated.

Canadiana, 1972. **ACU**

868 **Catley**, Elaine Maud (Clark). At the end of the road. Latest poems. Calgary: E.M. Catley, 1974. (10) leaves.

Canadiana, 1976. **AEU**

869 **Catley**, Elaine Maud (Clark). Light and other poems. Calgary: E.M. Catley, 1960. 32p.

Glenbow. **ACG**

870 **Chapman**, Evangeline. Poems for children. Original poems for children, written for my own. Illustrated by Carol Chapman, at age ten. Calgary: Pedlar Press, 1978. vi, 42p. ill.

Canadiana, 1979. **AEU**

871 **Chapman**, Evangeline. Poems for people over 25. Original poems. Calgary: Pedlar Press, 1977. v, 70p. ill.

CBIP, 1979. **AEU**

872 **Clever**, Glen. Alberta days. Drawings by Douglas A. Fales. Ottawa: Borealis Press, 1974. 76p. ill.

CBIP, 1979. **AEU**

873 **Coleman**, MacDonald. Requiem and other poems. s.l.: s.n., 1970. 6 leaves.

Canadiana, 1976.

874 **Connelly**, Clifford L. Rollicking rhymes. A collection of poems for your delight and entertainment, by C.L. Connelly, Bard of Blindman Valley. College Heights: College Press, n.d. 47p. ill.

Glenbow. **ACG**

875 **Coulton**, Richard Lee. The sea. Images. Longview: R.L. Coulton, 1973. 16p.

Fourteen original poems and articles, with extracts from other publications on the sea.

AEU

876 **Coulton**, Richard Lee. Sonnets of the space age. Longview: R.L. Coulton, 1972. (11)p. ill.

Mimeographed.

Canadiana. **AEU**

877 **Cullen**, Michael. The curried chicken apocalypse. Poems. Saskatoon: Thistledown Press, 1979. 50p.

Canadiana, 1979. **AEU**

878 **Dagg**, Mel. Songs for my owl. Graphics John Hodges. Calgary: Laughing Rooster, 1971. 56p. ill. **ACU**

879 **Daniel**, Lorne. The hunting hand and other poems. Red Deer: Red Deer College Press, 1973. 93p.

Canadiana, 1974. **AEU**

880 **Daniel**, Lorne. Towards a new compass. Poems. Saskatoon: Thistledown Press, 1978. 58p. ill.

Canadiana, 1978. **ACP**

881 **Deeves**, Fred. Rhymes of reason and dis-reason. New York: Vantage Press, 1966. 66p. **ACP**

882 **Delday**, Eva Pearce. Mirror of life. Brooks: Brooks Bulletin, 1967. 56p.

Dew.

883 **Delday**, Eva Pearce. The special breed. Brooks: Brooks Bulletin, 1969. 68p.

Dew.

884 **Dorcas Ladies Aid**, Monarch. Down the trail of memories. Monarch: Dorcas Ladies' Aid, 1963. 148p. ill.

Cover title.
Poems, with a history of Monarch.

Canadiana, 1965. **AEA**

885 **Duciaume**, Jean-Marcel. Et le verbe s'est fait chair. Poèmes. Gravures, Francine Gravel. Edmonton: Editions de l'Eglantier, 1975. (81)p. ill.

Limited edition of 25 copies. Signed by the author and the artist. **ACU**

886 **Duclos**, Jocelyn-Robert. Gethsemani, a dramatic poem. Edmonton: University of Alberta, 1969. cxii, 142 leaves.

Thesis (M.A.), University of Alberta, 1969.
Typescript.

Canadian theses. **AEU**

887 **Fairbairn**, John Alexander Lowry. Rhymes of a prairie Scot. Calgary: John D. McAra Printing, 1977. 99p. ill.

Canadiana, 1979. **ACP**

888 **Floyd**, Keith. Sandman's land. Edited by Allan Shute. Edmonton: Tree Frog Press, 1976. 39p.

Poems to induce sleep in children. Accompanied by an explanatory text.
First published in the *Children's House Magazine*.

Canadiana, 1977. **AEU**

889 **Freebairn**, Adam L. The mountain heights, and other poems. Pincher Creek: A.L. Freebairn, n.d. 31p. **AEU**

890 **Freebairn**, Adam L. Rhymes from the foothills. Pincher Creek: A.L. Freebairn, n.d. 31p. ill. **AEU**

891 **Freebairn**, Adam L. Rhymes of an old timer. Kootenai Brown, Massacre Butte, Lemon Mine, and others. Pincher Creek: A.L. Freebairn, 1964. 122p. ill.

Printed by J.D. McAra, Calgary.

Glenbow. **ACG**

892 **Friesen**, John W. A preacher's poems. Calgary: John W. Friesen, 1973. x,88p.

Duplicated. **ACG**

893 **Germain**, Claude. Singing your song. Poems and lines. Edmonton: White Pelican Press, 1975. 48p.

Canadiana, 1977. **AEU**

894 **Gom**, Leona. The singletree. Poems. Delta, B.C.: Sono Nis Press, 1976. 79p. **ACP**

895 **Gran**, Kenneth. Atomic feelings. Poems. Drawings by Bob Bowman. Red Deer: Red Deer College, 1973. (39)p. ill.

Cover title.

Canadiana, 1974. **AEU**

896 **Greenwood**, Irene. First lust. Red Deer: Red Deer College Press, 1973. 53p.

Canadiana, 1974. **AEU**

897 **Groves**, Edythe Muriel (McNeill). Funnybones. Comic verse. Strathmore: E.M. Groves, 1969. 68p.

Duplicated. **AEU**

898 **Groves**, Edythe Muriel (McNeill). Poetic reflections. Strathmore: Edythe M. Groves, 1975. 64p.

Canadiana, 1976. **AEU**

899 **Groves**, Edythe Muriel (McNeill). Yarns for spinning thoughts. Poems. Strathmore: Edythe M. Groves, 1966. 50p. **AEU**

900 **Guest**, Wilfred. Poetic fancies. A book of poetry. Beaverlodge: W. Guest, 1978. 89p. ill.

Canadiana, 1979.

901 **Hanson**, Joan. Frames. Red Deer: Red Deer College Press, n.d. 38p.

902 **Haydn**, L. Spices and beauty. Calgary: L. Haydn, 1972. 14p. (Haydn booklet, 1)

Canadiana, 1973.

903 **Helgason**, Elma Pearl (Gudlaugson). In the land where the Peace River flows. Poems. Sexsmith: Elma Helgason, 1963. 108p.

Glenbow. **ACG**

904 **Henry**, Julianne. Interlude of love. A poem story. Red Deer: Red Deer College Press, 1977. (44)p. ill.

Canadiana, 1978. **AEU**

905 **Hill**, Agnes Isabel Aston. Through the years. Ilfracombe, Devon: A.H. Stockwell, 1956. 141p.

Glenbow. **ACG**

906 **Honeyman**, Gertrude Evelyn (Dixon). Poems for old and young. Ladner, B.C.: Ladner Optomist, 1962. (47)p.

Majority of poems written in Alberta.

Glenbow. **ACG**

907 **Hooke**, Alfred John. A tribute to Hon. E.C. Manning on the occasion of his 50th birthday party, September 30th, 1958. Edmonton: Alberta Social Credit League, 1958. (4) p. ill.

Glenbow. **ACG**

908 **Hoover**, Walter B. Eschata. Edmonton: University Alberta, 1962. 1 fold. leaf. **AEU**

909 **Hoover**, Walter B. The Holy City. A 4800 line epic poem consisting of twelve complete cantos. College Heights: College Press, 1962. 120p.

Canadiana, 1962. **AEU**

910 **Horne**, Natalie Ruth. If I call, will someone answer? Edmonton: Central Press Society of Alberta, 1974. xii, 216p.

A New Horizon Project.
Duplicated.
Religious poems.

Canadiana, 1974. **AEU**

911 **Huse**, Peter. Prairie poems. Prince George: Caledonia, 1973. (12)p. ill. (Caledonia writing series)

Limited edition of 185 copies. **ACP**

912 **James**, Ferguson. Tales of the pioneer days. A collection of poems on Hanna and district. Hanna: Hanna Herald, 1964. (73)p.

Second edition published 1965.

Canadiana, 1965. **AEU**

913 **Jones**, William Griffith. Ceiriog capers. A sequel to 'Jingles', 1952. Ponoka: W.G. Jones, 1957. (43)p.

On cover: Poetry by Gutyn Ceiriog.
Mimeographed.

Glenbow. **ACG**

914 **Kenworthy**, Mary. Falling leaves. Poems. Calgary: G.L. Studios, 1974. 57p.

Canadiana, 1974. **AEU**

915 **Kenworthy**, Mary. Gleanings of the years. Rockyford: M. Kenworthy, 1972. 33p.

Duplicated. **AEU**

916 **Kirman**, Joseph M. Saga of Canada. Edmonton: s.n., 1976. 16 leaves.

917 **Kitsco**, John Phillip. Canadian poetry. Tears. Poems. Red Deer: New Press, 1975. 25p. ill.

Reprinted 1977.

Canadiana, 1976. **AEU**

918 **Kitsco**, John Phillip. Looking back. Selected early poems. Edmonton: New Press, 1978. 34p.

Canadiana, 1979. **AEU**

919 **Kluge**, Einhard. The green butterfly and other poems. Red Deer: Red Deer College Press, 1973. 1v. (51)p.

920 **Kroetsch**, Robert. The ledger. London, Ont.: Applegarth Follies, 1975. 26p.

Also, Coldstreamn, Ont., Brick Nairn. 32p..

Canadiana, 1979. **AEU**

921 **Kroetsch**, Robert. The sad Phoenician. Toronto: Coach House Press, 1979. 75p. ill.

Limited edition of 1000 copies.

CBIP 1979. **AEP**

922 **Kroetsch**, Robert. Seed catalogue. Poems. Winnipeg: Turnstone Press, 1977. 75p. ill. (Turnstone Press. Poetry series 1, no.7)

CBIP, 1979. **AEU**

923 **Kroetsch**, Robert. The stone hammer poems, 1960-1975. Lantzville, B.C.: Oolichan Books, 1975. 63p.

Also, 2d. ed., 1976.

CBIP, 1979. **AEU**

924 **Lander**, Tim. Except that you're here. Edmonton: Tree Frog Press, 1971. 1v. (40)p. ill.

AEU

925 **Lander**, Tim. The romantic manifesto for the last ditch. Edmonton: Tree Frog Press, 1972. 18p.

Canadiana, 1974. **AEU**

926 **Lane**, P. Calgary city jail. Drawing by S. Cohen. Vancouver: Very Stone House, 1969. 6p. ill.

Canadiana, 1970.

927 **Latta**, William. Drifting into grey. Linoleum cuts by Michael Adams. Winnipeg: Four Humours, 1977. (20)p. ill.

CBIP, 1979. **ACP**

928 **Latta**, William. Summer's bright blood. Selected poems. Illustrated by Neil Wagner. Saskatoon: Thistledown Press, 1976. 39p.

CBIP, 1979. **AEP**

929 **Lawrence**, Karen A. Nekuia. The Inanna poems. Ottawa: National Library of Canada, 1977. v, 68 leaves. (Canadian theses on microfiche, 32012)

Thesis (M.A.), University of Alberta, 1977.
Microfiche of typescript.
Poems relating to the Sumerian deity Inanna.

U of A Theses. **AEU**

930 **Lee**, Beatrice. "Destiny." Calgary: Beatrice Lee, 1967. 181p. ill.

On spine: Poems and lyrics by Beatrice Lee.

Glenbow. **ACG**

931 **Mandel**, Eli. An idiot joy. Edmonton: Hurtig, 1967. 85p.

Canadiana, 1968. **AEU**

932 **Mandel**, Eli. Stony Plain. Erin, Ontario: Press Porcepic, 1973. 96p.

Canadiana, 1973. **AEP**

933 **Mandel**, Miriam. Lions at her face. Cover by Norman Yates. Edmonton: White Pelican Publications, 1973. 64p.

Canadiana, 1973. **AEU**

934 **Mandel**, Miriam. Station 14. Illustrations by Harry Savage, cover by Norman Yates. Edmonton: NeWest Press, 1977. 39p. ill.
AEU

935 **Manly**, Morse. Oasis. Ukrainian poems. Translated from the Ukrainian by Morse Manly in cooperation with the author. Foreword by J.B. Rudnyckyj. New York: Vantage Press, 1959. 63p.

Title page and text in Ukrainian, with added title page in English.
Ukrainian language edition with title *Oaza*, 5, 1960, Edmonton, Slavuta Publishers, 63p.

Canadiana, 1962.

936 ManWoman. Forever together. Selections from The book of astonishment. The dreams & visions of ManWoman. Edited by Allan Shute. Introduction by William Pasnak. Edmonton: Tree Frog Press, 1973. 62p. ill.

Canadiana, 1974. AEU

937 **Martin**, Millicent Mary. Garden of remembrance. Poems. Rosebud: M.M. Martin, 1971. 50p.

Duplicated.
Printed by Edythe M. Groves, Strathmore.

Glenbow. ACG

938 **Marty**, Sid. Headwaters. Toronto: McClelland and Stewart, 1973. 110p.

CBIP, 1979. AEU

939 **Mathews**, Robin Daniel Middleton. The plink savoir. Edmonton: Robin Mathews, 1962. 41p.

Printed in England by Carey & Claridge.

Canadiana, 1963. AEU

940 **Mathews**, Robin Daniel Middleton. Plus ça change. Edmonton: Pioneer Press, 1964. 22p. (A poetry north publication)

Cover title. AEU

941 **Mazepa**, Bohdan. Flaming accords. Poems. Edmonton: Ukrainian Canadian Writers' Association, 1976. 62p.

Text in Ukrainian. Added title page in English. AEU

942 **Mazepa**, Bohdan. Starlit horizons. Lyrics in the Ukrainian language. Edmonton: Nakl. Pryviateliv autora, 1956. 62p.

Text in Ukrainian. Added title page in English.

Ukrainica Canadiana 1956. AEU

943 **McDonald**, Ruth M. (Gulley). Prairie silhouettes. A chap-book of verse. Illustrated by Donna Graham. Edmonton: R. McDonald, 1960. 1v. (12)p. ill.

Canadiana, 1960. AEU

944 **McIlveen**, Esther. For love of life. Musings. Edmonton: Emmaus Community, 1974. 72p.

Canadiana, 1974.

945 **McNamara**, Eugene. In transit. Calgary: Pennyworth Press, 1975. xiv p.

Canadiana, 1976. **AEU**

946 **McNeil**, W.R. Wanderlust. Poems. Strathmore: W.R. McNeill, N.D. 50p.

Duplicated.

Glenbow. **ACG**

947 **Millar**, Will. Tales to warm your mind. A book of nonsense poems. Cover by Nicoletti, other illustrations by Nancy Brown. Calgary: Antrim Music Publishing, 1971. (28)p. ill.

Cover title.
Made in U.S.A.

Canadiana, 1974. **AEU**

948 **Morrissette**, George. Prairie howl. Foreword by Andrew Sukuaski. Edmonton: NeWest Press, 1977. (20)p. ill.

Limited edition of 225 copies. **ACU**

949 **Mouré**, Erin. Empire, York Street. Toronto: Anansi, 1979. 91p. (House of Anansi poetry series, 38)

CBIP, 1979. **ACP**

950 **Murynka**, Dan. Sorrow and wrath. Ukrainian poems. Edmonton: Koshtom V.N. Dukhniiv, 1966. 93p.

Title page and text in Ukrainian. Added title page in English.

Canadiana, 1967.

951 **Nelson**, Alice E. From my heart. Poems from the Canadian prairies. Foreword by Evangelist Ken Campbell. Three Hills: Prairie Press, 1972. 64p.

Canadiana, 1973. **ACP**

952 **Noble**, Charles. Haywire rainbow. Poems. Erin, Ont.: Press Porcepic, 1978. 80p.

CBIP, 1979. **AEU**

953 **O'Neil**, Dollie Gray. Pot-pourri. Calgary: Northwest Print. and Lithographing, 1961. 39p.

Glenbow. **ACG**

954 **Pariseau**, Guy. L'Envers des jours. Edmonton: Editions de l'Eglantier, 1978. 62p. ill.

Canadiana, 1978.

955 **Pariseau**, Jean. Albertaines images et autres griffonnages. Edmonton: Imprimerie La Survivance, 1978. 95p.

Canadiana, 1979.

956 **Parker**, H. Margaret. Roses of love. Illustrated by Wm. W. Parker. Edmonton: Wm.W. Parker, 1970. (24)p. ill. ACG

957 **Parker**, William Wilder McKinley. Canada's 100 birthday verse. Or, Rhymes from the Northwest, Book IV. Edmonton: William W.M. Parker, 1965. 51p. ill.

Glenbow. ACG

958 **Parker**, William Wilder McKinley. Pansy pie and other poems. A third book of verse. Edmonton: W.W.M. Parker, 1961. 63p. ill.

Canadiana, 1965. ACG

959 **Penner**, Helen (Knelson). Happiness and other poems. High Level: H. Penner, 1972. 40p.

Canadiana, 1973.

960 **Penner**, Helen (Knelson). Night music and other poems. High Level: Helen Penner, 1971. 40p.

Mimeographed.

Canadiana, 1971. AEU

961 **Penner**, Helen (Knelson). Poetry Lane. Strathmore: Printed by E.M.Groves, 1969. 53p.

Mimeographed.

Canadiana, 1969. AEU

962 **Penner**, Helen (Knelson). Teardrops and flowers, and other poems. High Level: Helen Penner, Printed by Country Mimeo Shop, 1970. 39p.

Printed by Country Mimeo Shop, Terre, Indiana.

Canadiana, 1970. AEU

963 **Penner**, Helen (Knelson). Your heart and mine. s.l.: s.n., n.d. 38p.

Cover title *Your heart and mine, and other poems*.

Canadiana, 1980.

964 **Ratner**, Rochelle. The tightrope walker. Calgary: Pennyworth Press, 1976. 28p.

Canadiana, 1978.

965 **Redl-Hlus**, Carolyn D. Earthbound. Ottawa: Borealis Press, 1978. x, 51p.

Canadiana, 1979. AEU

966 **Reed**, Gene. Aunt Gene's ramblings. Poems. Black Diamond: Gene Reed, 1971. 41p.

Duplicated.

Canadiana, 1971. AEU

967 **Reese**, Will. The money tree. Illustrations, Phil Switzer. Edmonton: J. M. LeBel Enterprises, 1977. (32)p. ill.

A picture-storybook poem for young children.

Canadiana 1977. AEU

968 **Reid**, Monty Garson. Book of definition. Ottawa: National Library of Canada, 1978. xiii, 76 leaves (Canadian theses on microfiche, 40291)

Thesis (M.A.), University of Alberta, 1978.
Microfiche of typescript.
Poems based on diaries of author's grandfather.

U of A Theses. AEU

969 **Reid**, Monty Garson. Karst means stone. Edmonton: NeWest Press, 1979. 71p.

Biographical poems.

970 **Richman**, Sharon Lea. Quiet winds. Poems. By Sharon Lea Richman, Paul William Stooshnoff. Cover by Detta Lange. Graphics by Garry Newton and Karen Soby. Calgary: S.L. Richman, P.W. Stooshnoff, n.d. 1v. (66) leaves. ill.

Duplicated.

Glenbow. ACG

971 **Ringrose**, Christopher Xerxes. Western reunion. Poems. Drawings by James F. Lindsay. Edmonton: C.X. Ringrose, 1971. 1v. (26)p. ill.

Limited edition of 500 copies.

Canadiana, 1976. ACG

972 **Rippington**, Dennis J. Let swords slash for freedom! Edmonton: Institute for Applied Art, 1970. 10p.

Cover title.

Canadiana, 1971.

973 **Rustland**, Mary Randine. Treasures. Wainwright: Star-Publications, 1973. 205p. ill.

Canadiana, 1973.

974 **Scobie**, Stephen. Air loom. Toronto: Seripress, 1975. (16) leaves. ill.

Limited edition of one hundred copies, signed by the author, issued in portfolio. **AEU**

975 **Scobie**, Stephen. Airwaves, sealevel, landlock. Toronto: Seripress, 1978. Folder(1 leaf)

Concrete poetry. Limited edition of one hundred copies signed by the author. **AEU**

976 **Scobie**, Stephen. Babylondromat. Poems. Vancouver: Hairy Eagle Press, 1966. 20p.

A limited edition of three hundred copies. **AEU**

977 **Scobie**, Stephen. The birken tree. Edmonton: Tree Frog, 1973. 88p.

AEU

978 **Scobie**, Stephen. In the silence of the year. Vancouver: s.n., 1968. (18) leaves.

Limited edition of one hundred reproduced from typescript.
Also published 1971, Montreal, Delta. Buckbooks. iv. (23)p.. **AEU**

979 **Scobie**, Stephen. One word poems. Vancouver: Lighthouse Press, 1969. (10) leaves. (Gronk, series 4, 8)

Typescript reproduced on cards. **AEU**

980 **Scobie**, Stephen. The rooms we are. Poems, 1970-71. Victoria: Sono Nis Press, 1974. 59p.

CBIP, 1979. **ACP**

981 **Scobie**, Stephen. Stone poems. Vancouver: 1969. (19) leaves.

Reproduced from typewritten copy.
Also published 1974, Vancouver, Talonbooks 41 cards in box.
"Poems about a really great bunch of stones and a few personable pebbles".

CBIP, 1978. **AEU**

982 **Shankovs'kyj**, Ihor. Korotke lito. Poezii. Edmonton: Ukrainian Book Store, 1970. 114p.

Ukrainica Canadiana, 1970. **AEU**

983 **Shevchenko**, Taras Hryhorovych. Haydamaky. Edmonton: Hryhoriy Yopyk, 1954. 88p. ill.

Ukrainica Canadiana, 1954. **AEU**

984 **Shute**, Allan. Multimonster in paradise. A unicycle of poems. Illustrated by Harry Savage. Edmonton: Tree Frog Press, 1974. 55p. ill.

Canadiana, 1975. **AEU**

985 **Skorupskyj**, Volodymyr. Along the way. Ukrainian verses. Edmonton: Printed by Alberta Printing, 1957. 56p.

Text in Ukrainian. Added title page in English. **AEU**

986 **Skorupskyj**, Volodymyr. Asters still blooming. Ukrainian verses. Toronto: s.n., 1972. 56p.

Text in Ukrainian. Added title page in English. **AEU**

987 **Skorupskyj**, Volodymyr. The homeless. Ukrainian poems. Edmonton: Ukrains'ka Strilets'ka Hromada, 1958. 62p.

Text in Ukrainian. Added title page in English.
Printed by Alberta Printing. **AEU**

988 **Skorupskyj**, Volodymyr. My home. Ukranian verse. Edmonton: Alberta Printing, 1954. 96p.

Text in Ukranian.
Added title page in English on verso of title page.
Glenbow. **ACG**

989 **Slavutych**, Yar. Along the Zarorozhian places. Sketches. 2d ed. Edmonton: Slavuta Publishers, 1963. 19p. ill.

Text in Ukrainian.
First edition, 1957, Buenos Aires, Peremoha.
Canadiana, 1963.

990 **Slavutych**, Yar. Collected works, 1938-1978. Edmonton: Slavuta Publishers, 1978. 408p.

Ukrainian title *Zibrani tvory*.
Text in Ukrainian.
Canadiana, 1979. **AEU**

991 **Slavutych**, Yar. The conquerors of Prairies. Ukrainian poems. Edmonton: Slavuta Publishers, 1968. 48p.

Title page and text in Ukrainian, title from title page verso.
Also, 1974, Edmonton, Slavuta. Translated into English by R.H. Morrison. 112p.
Ukrainian text with English translation on opposite page. 112p.
Ukrainian title: Zavoionyky prerii.
Canadiana, 1969. **AEP**

992 **Slavutych**, Yar. L'oiseau de feu. Poemes choisis. Traduit et adapté par Rene Coulet du Gard. Edmonton: Edition des deux mondes et Slavuta Publishers, 1976. 50p.

Translation of *Polum'ianyi ptakh*.

CBIP 1979. **AEU**

993 **Slavutych**, Yar. Majesty (Ukrainian poems). Edmonton: Slavuta Publishers, 1962. 45p.

Title page and text in Ukrainian, with added title page in English.

Canadiana, 1962.

994 **Slavutych**, Yar. Mudroschi mandriv. Ukrainian poems. Edmonton: Slavuta Publishers, 1972. 89p.

Text in Ukrainian. Added title page partly in English, partly in Ukrainian. **AEU**

995 **Slavutych**, Yar. Northern lights. An almanac in Ukrainian. Edmonton: Slavuta Publishers, 1964-1967. 3v. ill.

Title page and text in Ukrainian. Added title page in English.
1. 1964-2. 1965 3. 1967.

Canadiana, 1968.

996 **Slavutych**, Yar. Rozstriliana muza. Syl'vety. Detroit: Vyol-vo Prometey, 1955. 93p. ill.

Canadiana, 1979.

997 **Slavutych**, Yar. Selected poems. Translated into Ukrainian by Yar Slavutych. London: Ukrainian Publishers, 1958. 50p.

Title page and text in Ukranian, with added title page in English.

Canadiana, 1962.

998 **Slavutych**, Yar. Trophies. Ukrainian poems, 1938-1963. Edmonton: Slavuta Publishers, 1963. 320p.

Text in Ukrainian. Added title page partly in English, partly in Ukrainian.
Collected poems from seven earlier volumes, published 1945-1962 and issued at Augsburg, Munich, Frankfurt-am-Main, Buenos Aires and Edmonton.
Printed by Alberta Printing.

CBIP 1979. **AEU**

999 **Smith**, Marion Roberta. Koo-Koo-sint. David Thompson in Western Canada. Design, Susan Archibald. Images, Joseph Reeder. Red Deer: Red Deer College Press, 1976. 63p.

Canadiana 1977. **AEU**

1000 **Smith**, Marion Roberta. Prairie child. Red Deer: Red Deer College Press, 1974. 38p. ill.

Also 2d ed., 1976.

Canadiana, 1974. **ACP**

1001 **Smith**, Marion Roberta. The rubbing rock. Red Deer: Red Deer College Press, 1973. 59 leaves.

Canadiana, 1974. **AEU**

1002 **Smith**, Mary Irene (Doherty). Songs of the Athabasca. Regina: s.n., 1960. 65p. ill.

Canadiana, 1963.

1003 **Snider**, Howard. Namus. Ilfracombe, Devon: Arthur H. Stockwell, 1957. 1v. (unpaged)

ACP

1004 **Snow**, John Vance. Beginnings. Calgary: Printed by John Snow, 1969. 17p.

Cover title.

Canadiana, 1970. **ACP**

1005 **Snow**, John Vance. Count illusions. Calgary: J. Snow, 1971. 32p.

Designed and printed by John Snow.

Canadiana, 1971. **ACG**

1006 **Snyder**, William. The battle hymn of the Dominion and other poems. Red Deer: Red Deer College Press, 1975. 62p.

AEU

1007 **Snyder**, William. Waitress! there's an eye in my soup! Red Deer: Red Deer College Press, 1975. 54p.

AEU

1008 **Stelfox**, Henry. Poems. s.l.: s.n., 1957. 89p.

AEA

1009 **Stelfox**, Henry. When the sawflies mate in summer and other Alberta poems. Edmonton: H. Stelfox, 1968. 112p.

Canadiana, 1969. **AEU**

1010 **Stelfox**, Henry. When the sawfly flies and other poems. s.l.: s.n., n.d. 112p.

AEU

1011 **Stone**, Bertha. Medicine Hat and other verses. Medicine Hat: Modern Press, 1960. 78p.

AEA

1012 **Stump**, Sarain. There is my people sleeping. The ethnic poem-drawings of Sarain Stump. Sidney, B.C.: Gray's Publishing, 1970. (157)p. ill.

Also 2d edition, 1974 (CBIP, 1979). **ACG**

1013 **Suknaski**, Andrew. Leaving. Cover design and photographs by Art Mishimura. Seven Persons: Repository Press, 1974. 78p. ill.

Canadiana, 1974. **AEU**

1014 **Svidzins'kyi**, Volodymyr. Selected poems. Edmonton: Slavuta Publishers, 1961. 63p.

Introduction by Y. Slavutych.
Title page in Ukrainian, with added title page in English.

Canadiana, 1962. **AEU**

1015 **Tansem**, Wallace. The legend of the mighty Peace. Artist, Frankie. Wanham: Idletime Enterprises, n.d. 20p. ill.

Canadiana, 1978.

1016 **Teilfer**, Beatrice. Poems of country living. Strathmore: F.M.Groves, 1967. 36p.

Canadiana, 1969.

1017 **Thorseth**, Jessie Braisher. Thoughts of a passer-by. Calgary: Jessie Braisher Thorseth, 1960. 71p. ill.

Cover title. **ACP**

1018 Three. 3. Charles Noble, J.O. Thompson, Jon Whyte. With an introduction by Eli Mandel. Banff: Summerthought, 1973. 107p.

Canadiana, 1974. **AEU**

1019 **Toth**, Nancy. Pattern without end. Poems, 1965-79. Edmonton: Academic Printing and Publishing, 1979. 1v.

Canadiana, 1980.

1020 **Twa**, Jeanne. Let's play northern pole. Edmonton: Harden House, 1976. 1v. (40 leaves.)

1021 **Uher**, Lorna. Crow's black joy. Edmonton: NeWest Press, 1978. 67p.

Winner of 1978 Saskatchewan Culture and Youth Literary Award. **ACU**

1022 **Waltner-Toews**, David. The earth is one body. Winnipeg: Turnstone Press, 1979. 51p.

CBIP, 1979.

1023 **Warren**, Sara Evangeline (Matheson). Echoes from my song tree. Vauxhall: S.E.M. Warren, 1972. 35 leaves.

Duplicated.
Limited edition of 200 copies.

Canadiana, 1975. **AEU**

1024 **Warren**, Sara Evangeline (Matheson). Prairie panels. Lethbridge: Robins Printing, n.d. 22p. **AEU**

1025 **Warren**, Sara Evangeline (Matheson). Songs of the island. Lethbridge: Robins Printing, n.d. 24p. ill.

Poems of Prince Edward Island. **ACP**

1026 **Watson**, Wilfred. Friday's child. London: Faber and Faber, 1955. 56p.

Canadiana, 1956. **AEU**

1027 **Watson**, Wilfred. I begin with counting. Edmonton: NeWest Press, 1978. 104p.

Canadiana, 1979. **AEU**

1028 **Watson**, Wilfred. The sorrowful Canadians and other poems. Les malheureux. Cover by Norman Yates. Edmonton: White Pelican, 1972. 68p.

Photocopied from the original typescripts. **AEU**

1029 **Wright**, Helen Kerr. Images. Calgary: J. Snow, 1971. 20p.

Designed and printed by John Snow.

Canadiana, 1975. **ACG**

1030 **Yanda**, Doris Elizabeth. Canadian tapestry. Poems. Winnipeg: Trident Press, 1970. 199p.

AEU

1031 **Yanda**, Doris Elizabeth. My thoughts fly to Ukraine. Folklore poetry. Edmonton: Printed by Alberta Printing, 1962. 123p. ill.

Text in Ukrainian. Added title page in English. **AEU**

1032 **Yanda**, Doris Elizabeth. The songs of my heart. Second collection of poetry. By Daria Mohylianka. Edmonton: Printed by Alberta Printing, 1964. 126p. ill.

Text in Ukrainian. Added title page in English. **AEU**

1033 **Yorath**, Mary (Smith). West. Calgary: Privately Printed, 1963. (12)p.

Cover title.

Glenbow. **ACG**

Drama

1034 Adventures in acting. A selection of plays for young players. Edited by Walter H. Kaasa and Gordon Peacock. Edmonton: Institute of Applied Art, 1957. 286p. ill.

Canadiana, 1958. **AEU**

1035 **Baldridge**, Mary Humphrey. Bride of the gorilla. Toronto: Playwrights Co-op, 1974. 17 leaves.

Duplicated.

CBIP, 1978. AEU

1036 **Baldridge**, Mary Humphrey. The Mary Shelley play. Toronto: Playwrights Co-op, 1979. 66p.

Duplicated.

Canadiana, 1979. ACU

1037 **Baldridge**, Mary Humphrey. The photographic moment. Toronto: Playwrights Co-op, 1975. 61, 2p.

Duplicated.
A play about homesteaders near Atlee. AEU

1038 **Baldridge**, Mary Humphrey. The suicide meet. With, Pickle, by Sheila Junor-Moore, The Saga of the elk, by Jim Taylor, What it means to me to be a Canadian, compiled from Calgary school children, grades 6 and 7. Toronto: Playwrights Co-op., 1977. 34p.

Duplicated.
Canadiana, 1978. AEU

1039 **Boston**, Stewart. Counsellor extraordinary. Illustrations by Phillip Silver. Toronto: Simon and Pierre, 1972. 47p.

A play about Francis Bacon, written for the Citadel Theatre.

CBIP, 1978. AEU

1040 **Botting**, Gary. The box beyond. A play. Edmonton: Harden House, 1972. 31p. AEU

1041 **Botting**, Gary. Five short plays. Red Deer: Red Deer College Press, n.d. 4v.

CBIP, 1979.

1042 **Botting**, Gary. Harriot! A play. Edmonton: Harden House, 1972. 34p. AEU

1043 **Botting**, Gary. Perambulance and Pipe dream. Two plays. Edmonton: Harden House, 1972. 51p. AEU

1044 **Campbell**, Paddy. Chinook. Toronto: Playwrights Co-op, 1973. 25 leaves.

Cover title. Duplicated.

Reprinted 1974 (CBIP, 1979). AECYR

1045 **Campbell**, Paddy. Hoarse music. A musical plan. Book and lyrics by Paddy Campbell. Music by Wm. Skolnik. Toronto: 1974. 80p. ill. (Canplay series)

Reprinted 1977 (CBIP, 1979). **ACP**

1046 **Chekhov**, Anton Pavlovich. The seagull. A new translation by David French. Toronto: Playwrights Co-op, 1977. 92p.

On cover: 'Anton Chekov's The Seagull'.
Also published 1978, Don Mills, General Publishing. (Canadiana, 1978).

1047 **Chekhov**, Anton Pavlovich. Uncle Vanya. Scenes from rural life. 1st Theatrebooks ed. A new translation by John Murrell. Toronto: Theatrebooks, 1978. 57p.

Translation of 'Diadia Vania'.

CBIP, 1979. **ACU**

1048 **DeFelice**, James. The elixir. Toronto: Playwrights Co-op, 1973. 41 leaves.

Cover title. Duplicated.

CBIP, 1979. **AECYR**

1049 **DeFelice**, James. Fools and masters. Toronto: Playwrights Co-op, 1975. 32 leaves.

Cover title.

CBIP, 1979. **AEU**

1050 **DeFelice**, James. Take me where the water's warm. A summer comedy in three acts. Toronto: Playwrights Co-op, 1978. 87 leaves.

Cover title. Duplicated.

CBIP, 1979. **AECYR**

1051 **Falk**, Rod. Bummy peepee in the toto. Edmonton: Harden House, 1972. 35p.

A play set in a mental institution ward.

Canadiana, 1972.

1052 **Foord**, Isabelle. The beast in the bag and Wild West circus. Two plays for children. Toronto: Playwrights Co-op, 1977. 32p.

Canadiana, 1978. **AEU**

1053 **Foord**, Isabelle. A dream of sky people. A rock myth for young adults. Toronto: Playwrights Co-op, 1973. 25 leaves.

Cover title. Duplicated. Reprinted 1974. Reprinted 1976 with *Shaman*. **AECYR**

1054 **Foord**, Isabelle. I don't care what it looks like, as long as it's warm. A review for young audiences. Toronto: Playwrights Co-op, 1978. 20p.

Juvenile drama.

CBIP, 1979. **ACU**

1055 **Foord**, Isabelle. Junkyard. A timely fantasy for young people ages nine and over. Toronto: Playwrights Co-op, 1973. 22 leaves.

Juvenile drama.
Cover title. Duplicated. Reprinted 1974.

CBIP, 1979. **AECYR**

1056 **Foord**, Isabelle. Say hi to Owsley. Toronto: Playwrights Co-op, 1975. 25 leaves.

Childrens' drama.

CBIP, 1979. **AEU**

1057 **Foord**, Isabelle. Shaman. Toronto: Playwrights Co-op, 1973. 29 leaves.

Cover title. Duplicated.
Reprinted 1976, with *A Dream of Sky People*. **AECYR**

1058 **Graves**, Warren. Chief Shaking Spear rides again. Or, The taming of the Sioux. Toronto: Playwrights Co-op, 1975. 39 leaves.

Cover title. Duplicated.
A melodrama commissioned by Walterdale Theatre Associates for their 10th annual Klondike Days Melodrama.

CBIP, 1978. **ACP**

1059 **Graves**, Warren. The hand that cradles the rock. 2d ed. Toronto: Playwrights Co-op, 1973. 73 leaves. ill.

A comedy.
Cover title.
First edition published 1972.

CBIP, 1979. **AEU**

1060 **Graves**, Warren. The Mumberley inheritance. Or, His substance frittered. Toronto: Playwrights Co-op, 1971. (73) leaves, in two separate pagings

A melodrama.
Cover title.
Seventh printing, 1977.

CBIP, 1979. **AEU**

1061 **Graves**, Warren. The proper perspective and Who's looking after the Atlantic? Two one-act plays. Toronto: Playwrights Co-op, 1978. 40p.

Cover title *Who's looking after the Atlantic & The proper perspective. Two plays*.

Canadiana, 1978. **AEU**

1062 **Graves**, Warren. Scrooge. A Christmas play based on a story by Charles Dickens. Toronto: Playwrights Co-op, 1979. 47p.

Duplicated.

CBIP, 1979. **AECYR**

1063 **Graves**, Warren. Three plays. Toronto: Playwrights Co-op, 1979. 1v.

Contents: 1. The hand that cradles the rock 2. The Mumberly inheritance 3. Chief Shaking spear rides again

CBIP, 1979.

1064 **Graves**, Warren. Yes, dear. A comedy in one act. Toronto: Samuel French (Canada), 1967. 21, 1p. ill. (Canadian playwrights series)

Won Edmonton Journal Literary Award, 1968. **AEU**

1065 **Hagman**, Mary Wilkinson. Mary and the Holy Thorn. Illustrated by the author. New York: Vantage Press, 1966. 56p. ill.

Canadiana, 1970.

1066 **Hornby**, Richard. The kidnappers, by Richard Hornby, Two pollution sketches, by Nina F. Klaiman. Calgary: Department of Drama, University of Calgary, 1974. 42p. (Drama at Calgary, playscript no.1)

Canadiana, 1976.

1067 **Jones**, Sandra. Ready steady go. A play. Toronto: Playwrights Co-op, 1975. 40 leaves.

Cover title. Duplicated.
Second printing, 1977.

CBIP, 1979. **ACP**

1068 **LeMay**, Bonnie. Boy who has a horse. Toronto: Playwrights Co-op, 1974. 31 leaves.

Cover title. Duplicated.
Reprinted March, 1976.
A play for children about a Sioux boy in Saskatchewan during the time of Sitting Bull's refuge.

CBIP, 1979. **ACP**

1069 **LeMay**, Bonnie. Roundhouse. A comedy. Toronto: Playwrights Co-op, 1977. 91p.

Duplicated.

CBIP, 1979. **AECYR**

1070 **Mitchell**, Ken. Davin, the politician. Introduction by C.B. Koester. Edmonton: NeWest Press, 1979. 122p. (Prairie play series, 2)

Original title *The politician*.
Play about Nicholas Flood Davin, 1840-1901, Regina journalist and politician.

CBIP, 1979. **AEU**

1071 **Mitchell**, William Ormond. The devil's instrument. Toronto: Simon and Pierre, 1973. 31p. ill.

Play about a Hutterite boy, set in Alberta.

CBIP, 1979. **AEU**

1072 **Moher**, Frank. Pause. Toronto: Playwrights Co-op, 1975. 35 leaves.

Cover title. Duplicated.
Reprinted 1977.
A farce set in Banff.
Winner of 1974 Edmonton Journal Play award.

CBIP, 1979. **AEU**

1073 **Osborne**, James. The attic. Ottawa: National Library of Canada, 1973. xx, 93 leaves (Canadian theses on microfiche, 17646)

Thesis (M.A.), University of Alberta, 1973.
Microfiche of typescript.

U of A Theses. **AEU**

1074 **Osborne**, James. By the sea. A play in one act. Toronto: Playwrights Co-op, 1973. 32 leaves.

Cover title. Duplicated. **AEU**

1075 **Pengilly**, Gordon D. Songs of believers. Ottawa: National Library of Canada, 1978. iv, 97 leaves. (Canadian theses on microfiche, 36455)

Thesis (M.F.A.), University of Alberta, 1978.
Microfiche of typescript.

U of A Theses. **AEU**

1076 **Peterson**, Leonard. Almighty Voice. Agincourt, Ont.: Book Society of Canada, 1974. xviii, 64p. ill.

Canadiana, 1974. **AEU**

1077 **Pollock**, Sharon. The Komagata Maru incident. Toronto: Playwrights Co-op, 1978. 47p.

Duplicated. **AECYR**

1078 **Pollock**, Sharon. Walsh. Vancouver: Talonbooks. 1973. 112p.

Also printed 1974 and 1976, Vancouver, Talonbooks, (Talonplays). 116p.

CBIP, 1979. **ACP**

1079 **Pollock**, Sharon. The wreck of the national line. Toronto: Playwrights Co-op, 1979. (1v.)

Childrens' drama.

CBIP, 1979.

1080 **Richman**, Sharon Lea. The faces. A verse play, Edmonton: University of Alberta, 1964. iv, 68 leaves.

Thesis (M.A.), University of Alberta, 1964.
Typescript.

Canadian theses. **AEU**

1081 **Ringwood**, Gwendolyn Margaret (Pharis). Look behind you neighbour. A new Canadian historical musical specially commissioned by the Fiftieth Anniversary Committee of Edson, Alta. Presented in the Edson High School Auditorium, Nov. 2nd, 3rd and 4th. Edson: Edson Leader, 1961. (30)p. ill.

Glenbow. **ACG**

1082 **Ringwood**, Gwendolyn Margaret (Pharis). The rainmaker. Toronto: Playwrights Co-op, 1975. 30 leaves.

Cover title. Duplicated.
Reprinted 1976, 1977.
A play set in Medicine Hat.

CBIP, 1979. **ACYR**

1083 **Ringwood**, Gwendolyn Margaret (Pharis). The sleeping beauty. A new version of the old story, and The golden goose. Two plays for children. Toronto: Playwrights Co-op, 1979. 34p.

Duplicated.

Canadiana, 1979.

1084 **Ringwood**, Gwendolyn Margaret (Pharis). Widger's way. Toronto: Playwrights Co-op, 1976. 76p.

Cover title. Duplicated.

CBIP, 1979. **ACP**

1085 **Ryga**, George. Captives of the faceless drummer. Vancouver: Talonplays, 1971. 78p. (Talonplays)

Also, revised editions, 1972 and 1974.

1086 **Ryga**, George. The ecstasy of Rita Joe. Vancouver: Talonplays, 1970. 90p.

Also published 1970, Talonbooks (Talonplays) 126p., 1971, Toronto, Playwrights Co-op, and 1973, Talonbooks,

122p.

1087 **Ryga**, George. The ecstasy of Rita Joe and other plays. With introduction by Brian Parker. Toronto: New Press, 1971. xxiii, 236p. (New drama, 1)

Contents: 1. Indian. 2. The ecstacy of Rita Joe. 3. Grass and wild strawberries.

Glenbow. **ACG**

1088 **Ryga**, George. Ploughmen of the glacier. A play. Vancouver: Talonbooks, 1977. 79p.

CBIP, 1979. **ACP**

1089 **Ryga**, George. Seven hours to sundown. A play. Vancouver: Talonbooks, 1977. 110p.

CBIP, 1979. **ACP**

1090 **Ryga**, George. Sunrise on Sarah. Vancouver: Talonbooks, 1973. 79p. (Talonplays)

CBIP, 1979. **ACP**

1091 **Smiley**, Charles W. The art of communication. Three plays. Toronto: Playwrights Co-op, 1976. 50p.

Cover title.
Contents: 1. George Johnson is an S.O.B 2. The valedictorian 3. The horticulturist.

Canadiana, 1977. **AEU**

1092 **Truss**, Jan. The judgement of Clifford Sifton. A play. Toronto: Playwrights Co-op, 1979. 34p.

Canadiana, 1979. **AEU**

1093 **Truss**, Jan. Ooomerahgi Oh, and A very small rebellion. Two plays for children. Toronto: Playwrights Co-op, 1978. 45p.

Duplicated. **AEU**

1094 **Wade**, Bryan. This side of the Rockies. Toronto: Playwrights Co-op, 1977. 108p.

CBIP, 1979. **AEU**

1095 **Whyte**, Thomas. Dismissal leading to lustfulness. Toronto: Playwrights Co-op, 1974. 38 leaves.

Cover title. Duplicated.

CBIP, 1979. **AECYR**

1096 **Whyte**, Thomas. Free beer. A play in six scenes. Toronto: Playwrights Co-op, 1972. 26 leaves.

Cover title. Duplicated.

Reprinted 1974. **AEU**

1097 **Wiebe**, Rudy. Far as the eye can see. A play by Rudy Wiebe and Theatre Passe Muraille. Edmonton: NeWest Press, 1977. 125p. ill.

First in a projected NeWest series of plays to be devoted to Canadian drama of the prairies. **AEU**

Humour

1098 Andrasz. A wilderness. Outdoors in northern Alberta. Whitecourt: Whitecourt Publishing, 1970. 1v. (unpaged)

Cover title.
Cartoons of hunting adventures.

Glenbow. **ACG**

1099 **Cameron**, Stew. Let the chaps fall where they may. Calgary: s.n., n.d. (12 leaves, chiefly ill.)

Cartoons.
Cover title. **ACP**

1100 **Cameron**, Stew. Pack horse in the Rockies. Dudes, denims & diamond hitches. Calgary: Western Printing & Lithographing, n.d. (12 leaves, chiefly ill.)

Cartoons.

1101 **Cameron**, Stew. Weep for the Cowboy. s.l.: s.n., 1976. (12 leaves, chiefly ill.)

Cartoons. **AEA**

1102 **Cameron**, Stew. What I saw at the Stampede. Calgary: Cameron Cartoons, 1976. (12 leaves, chiefly ill.)

Cartoons.
Cover title. **AEU**

1103 **Evans**, Art. All our own work. By Evans & Jones. Edmonton: Edmonton Journal, 1962. 48p. ill.

Collection of newspaper columns, by Art Evans, and cartoons, by John Yardley-Jones, previously published in 1962 in the *Edmonton Journal*.

Glenbow. **ACG**

1104 **Evans**, Art. Second offence. By Evans & Jones. Edmonton: Edmonton Journal, 1963. 63p. ill.

A collection of columns and cartoons reprinted from the *Edmonton Journal*.

Glenbow. **ACG**

1105 **Evans**, Art. Up for the third time. A collection of columns and cartoons. Edmonton: Edmonton Journal, 1966. 63p. ill.

Columns by Art Evans. Cartoons by John Yardley-Jones. Reprinted from the *Edmonton Journal*.

Canadiana, 1967. **AEU**

1106 Great golf humor. A collection of stories and articles. Edited by Mervyn J. Huston. Edmonton: Hurtig, 1977. 287p.

Canadiana, 1979. **OONL**

1107 **Huston**, Mervyn J. The great Canadian lover and other commentaries and conceits. Toronto: Musson, 1964. 144p.

Also published 1970, Edmonton, Hurtig. 144p. **AECYR**

1108 **Kipling**, Rudyard. Rudyard Kipling's (Medicine) Hat trick. Medicine Hat: Medicine Hat News, 1965. (8)p.

Glenbow. **ACG**

1109 **Oman**, Mary M. Canadian cornography. Illustrated by Darrell Robinson. Cobalt, Ont.: Highway Book Shop, 1977. 91p. ill.

Reprinted from the *Calgary North Hill News*.
Humorous vignettes, each accompanied by a cartoon.

P.N.L.A., 1979. **AEA**

1110 **Simpkins**, James Nathaniel. Jasper. Toronto: Ryerson Press, 1954. (62)p. ill.

Cartoons previously published in *Maclean's Magazine*.

Glenbow. **ACG**

1111 **Soop**, Everett. Soop takes a bow. Standoff: Indian News Media Society, 1979. 1v. (100p., chiefly ill.)

A selection of cartoons extracted from the *Kainai News*, 1968-1979.

Canadiana, 1980.

1112 **Thomas**, Garnet. Soaring with Yawstring. Illustrated by the author. Edmonton: Puckrin's Production House, n.d. 60p. ill.

Collection of gliding cartoons.

1113 **Turner**, John Davenall. The artful codger. Paintings, verse, cartoons, humorous paintings, sculpture, fables and jottings of John Davenall including writings attributed to Orpheus P. Chilblain. Banff: Peter Whyte Foundation, 1978. 48p. ill.

Canadiana, 1979. **OONL**

Fine Arts: General Works

1114 **Antonelli**, Marylu. Pottery in Alberta. The long tradition. Marylu Antonelli and Jack Forbes. Edmonton: University of Alberta Press, 1978. 189p. ill.

Canadiana, 1978. **AEA**

1115 Beaverlodge Artists. Euphemia MacNaught, Robert C. Guest, Marjorie Hunink. Beaverlodge: Beaverlodge and District Historical Association, 1974. 1v. (8p.)(chiefly ill.)

Cover title.
Reprinted from *Beaverlodge to the Rockies*.
Also, Supplement, 1976, 16p. **AEA**

1116 Calgary Allied Arts Council. An arts council in your community? Calgary: Calgary Allied Arts Council, 1958. 32p. ill.

Information to assist in the organization of an arts council.

Canadiana, 1959. **OONL**

1117 **Collinson**, Helen. A university collects. Edited by Helen Collinson. Edmonton: University of Alberta Press, 1979. 51p. ill.

Canadiana, 1979. **AEU**

1118 **Dempsey**, Hugh Aylmer. Tailfeathers, Indian artist. Calgary: Glenbow-Alberta Institute, 1970. 24p. ill. (Glenbow-Alberta Institute. Art series, 2)

Dew. **AEU**

1119 Edmonton Art Gallery. Printmaking. Edmonton: Edmonton Art Gallery, 1975. 9p. ill.

Canadiana, 1977. **OONL**

1120 Edmonton Art Gallery. Understanding children's art. Edmonton: Edmonton Art Gallery, 1975. 6p. ill.

Canadiana, 1977. **OONL**

1121 **Harmon**, Byron. Great days in the Rockies. The photography of Byron Harmon, 1906-1934. Edited by Carole Harmon and the Peter Whyte Foundation. Toronto: Oxford University Press, 1978. 110p. ill.

With a biography by Bart Robinson and an appreciation by Jon Whyte.

Canadiana, 1978. **AEA**

1122 **Hohn**, Hubert. The Banff purchase. Toronto: J. Wiley, 1979. 1v. (unpaged)

Canadiana, 1979. **OONL**

1123 Janus Museum Consultants Limited. A responsive environment for the growth of cultural resources in the city of Calgary, October, 1969. Guidelines for development. Toronto: s.n., 1969. (5), 37 leaves.

Glenbow. **ACG**

1124 **Kaufman**, Carolyn Reesor. Historic churches of Alberta and the Canadian North West. Edmonton: C.R. Kaufman, 1959. 4, 80p. (chiefly ill.)

Printed by Hambly Press, Edmonton.
A brief text accompanies each illustration.

Glenbow. **ACG**

1125 **Kurelek**, William. Fields. Paintings by William Kurelek. Montreal: Tundra Books of Montreal, 1976. 28p. chiefly ill.

Published simultaneously, Plattsburgh, N.Y, Tundra Books of Northern New York.
Paintings done largely from childhood memories. **AEU**

1126 **Kurelek**, William. Kurelek country. Boston: Houghton Mifflin, 1975. 127p. ill. **AEU**

1127 **Kurelek**, William. Kurelek's Canada. Toronto: Pagurian Press, 1975. 127p. ill. (Canadian Heritage Library)

Paintings and text by William Kurelek. **AEU**

1128 **Kurelek**, William. The last of the Arctic. Toronto: McGraw-Hill Ryerson, 1976. 94p. ill.

Also 1976, Toronto, Pagurian Press. **AEU**

1129 **Kurelek**, William. A northern nativity. Christmas dreams of a prairie boy. Montreal: Tundra Books of Montreal, 1976. 48p. ill.

Published simultaneously Plattsburgh, N.Y., Tundra Books of Northern New York. **AEU**

1130 **Kurelek**, William. O Toronto. Paintings and notes by William Kurelek. Introduction by James Bacque. Toronto: New Press, 1973. 43p. ill. **AEU**

1131 **Kurelek**, William. The passion of Christ according to St. Matthew. Illustrated by William Kurelek. Niagara Falls, Ont.: Niagara Falls Art Gallery and Museum, 1975. 192p. chiefly ill.

Printed in Toronto, Harmony Printing.
Introduction and concluding remarks in English, French, and Ukrainian. **AEU**

1132 **Kurelek**, William. Someone with me. The autobiography of William Kurelek. Ithaca, New York: Center for Improvement of Undergraduate Education, Cornell University, 1973. 523p. ill.

Photocopy of typescript. **AEU**

1133 **Semischen**, Orest. Byzantine churches of Alberta. Edited by Hubert Hohn. Edmonton: Edmonton Art Gallery, 1976. 38 leaves (chiefly ill.)

Photographs by Semischen of country churches. **AEA**

1134 **Spencer**, Keith Robinson. Fond memories. Edmonton: J. & S. Philatelic Publishers, 1979. iv, 78p. (chiefly ill.)

Reproductions of postcards of Edmonton from 1905 onwards.

Canadiana, 1980. **AEA**

1135 **Spiteri**, Ed. Images of a city. Calgary: Spiteri Productions, 1975. 104p. ill.

A collection of photographs published under a grant from the Alberta Dept. of Culture, Youth and Recreation as a Calgary centennial project. **AEA**

1136 Ukrainian Canadiana. Edmonton: Ukrainian Women's Association of Canada, 1976. 95p. ill.

Twelve articles on Ukrainian arts and culture.

Canadiana, 1977. **AEU**

1137 **Voyer**, Sylvain. Edmonton had a beautiful river valley. s.l.: s.n., 1960. 10 leaves.

Limited edition of 80 copies.
Lithographs and sketches, with brief accompanying text.
Title from first line of text. Author's signature on leaf 10. **AEU**

1138 **Williamson**, Moncrieff. Robert Harris, 1849-1919. An unconventional biography. Toronto: McClelland & Stewart, 1970. xvii, 222p. ill.

Glenbow. **ACG**

Exhibition Catalogues

1139 The A B C of sculpture. Edmonton: Edmonton Art Gallery, 1974. 32p.

Canadiana, 1977. **OONL**

1140 Alberta Art Foundation. Selections. Glenbow-Alberta Institute, June 24-September 4, 1977. Calgary: Glenbow-Alberta Institute, 1977. 24p. ill.

Canadiana 1979. **OONL**

1141 Alberta College of Art. Ballachey, Besant, Bienvenue, Clark, Crockett, Gallie, Graff, Hohn, Mable, Roberts, Robertson, Van Wyk on paper. Calgary: Alberta College of Art, 1976. 27p. ill.

Exhibition held at the Alberta College of Art Gallery, Sept. 18-Oct. 5, 1976.

Canadiana, 1977. **OONL**

1142 Alberta College of Art. Playboy illustration. Calgary: Alberta College of Art, 1976. 15p. ill.

Catalogue of an exhibition held at the Alberta College of Art, Nov. 12-28, 1976.

Canadiana, 1977. **OONL**

1143 Alberta Potters' Association. National ceramics exhibition, Calgary, October 29 - December 12, 1976. Presented by Alberta Potters' Association and Glenbow-Alberta Institute with the co-operation of the Canadian Guild of Potters. Calgary: Alberta Potters' Association, 1976. 36p. ill.

Text in English and French.

Canadiana, 1977. **AEU**

1144 Alberta Society of Artists. Calgary Local. Young contemporary Calgary artists exhibition. A juried exhibition organized by the Alberta Society of Artists. Calgary: Alberta College of Art, 1974. 16p. ill.

Canadiana, 1976. **OONL**

1145 **Armstrong**, William. Historical watercolours by William Armstrong. Calgary: Glenbow-Alberta Institute, 1972. folder(6p.) ill.

Canadiana, 1972. **OONL**

1146 **Arnold**, Greg. Greg Arnold. Calgary: Alberta College of Art, 1970. 12p. ill.

Canadiana, 1973. **OONL**

1147 **Ballachey**, Barbara. Barbara Ballachey. Edmonton: Edmonton Art Gallery, 1974. 4p. ill.

Exhibition at the Edmonton Art Gallery, May 26-June 26, 1974. **AEU**

1148 **Borch**, Bert. Bert Borch. Calgary: Alberta College of Art, 1972. 7p. ill.

Catalogue of an exhibition held at the Alberta College of Art, March, 1972.

Canadiana, 1973. **OONL**

1149 **Brasini**, Armando. Armando Brasini. Roma Imperiale. Edmonton: Edmonton Art Gallery, 1978. 56p. ill.

Catalogue of an exhibition of an Italian architect, held at the Edmonton Art Gallery, the Art Gallery of York University, and the Art Gallery of Hamilton, Nov., 1978-Aug., 1979.

Canadiana, 1979. **OONL**

1150 **Bres**, Hendrik. Hendrik Bres, Ann Clarke Darrah, Eva Deiner. Edmonton: Edmonton Art Gallery, 1973. 23p. ill.

Exhibition held at the Edmonton Art Gallery, May 13-June 4, 1973. **AEU**

1151 **Burden**, C. Do you believe in television? Calgary: Alberta College of Art, 1976. 8p. ill.

Exhibition held at the Alberta College of Art, Feb. 18, 1976.

Canadiana, 1977. **OONL**

1152 **Bush**, Jack. Jack Bush, works on paper. An exhibition organized by the Edmonton Art Gallery and the David Mirvish Gallery, Toronto. Edmonton: Edmonton Art Gallery, 1973. 8p. ill.

Canadiana, 1974. **OONL**

1153 **Byrne**, J. The death's head knight. Calgary: Alberta College of Art, 1971. 20p. ill. (A.C.A. Comix, 1)

Published for the Alberta College of Art students' exhibition, 1971.

Canadiana, 1971. **OONL**

1154 **Chalke**, John. John Chalke. Edmonton: Edmonton Art Gallery, 1975. 6p. ill.

Catalogue of an exhibition held May 23-June 17, 1975 at the Edmonton Art Gallery.

Canadiana, 1977. **OONL**

1155 **Chester**, D.T. Chester and Bentham. An exhibition of recent paintings by D.T. Chester and recent sculptures by Douglas Bentham organized by the Edmonton Art Gallery, March 1-April 1, 1973. Edmonton: Edmonton Art Gallery, 1973. 1v. (unpaged).

AEU

1156 **Chien-Shih**, Lin. Lin Chien-Shih. Edmonton: Edmonton Art Gallery, 1975. 1 fold. sheet. ill.

Exhibition held at the Edmonton Art Gallery, March 2-24, 1975.

Canadiana, 1976.

1157 **Deacon**, Peter. Peter Deacon Drawings, Nov. 6- 26. Calgary: Alberta College of Art Gallery, 1975. 8 pieces in envelope. ill.

Canadiana, 1977. **OONL**

1158 **Dempsey**, Hugh Aylmer. Ethnic furniture. Calgary: Glenbow-Alberta Institute, 1970. 20p. ill.

Catalogue of exhibition held March 17-April 19, 1970.

Glenbow. **ACG**

1159 **Dmytruk**, Ihur. Ihur Dmystruck. An exhibition organized by the Edmonton Art Gallery, September 2-October 3, 1971. Edmonton: Edmonton Art Gallery, 1971. 16p. ill.

AEU

1160 Edmonton Art Gallery. Accessions, 1972-1974. Edmonton: Edmonton Art Gallery, 1975. 32p. ill.

Canadiana, 1977. **OONL**

1161 Edmonton Art Gallery. Alberta contemporary drawings. Edmonton: Edmonton Art Gallery, 1973. 27p. (all ill.)

Catalogue of an exhibition held April 6-30, 1973.

Canadiana, 1974. **AEU**

1162 Edmonton Art Gallery. The Alberta Society of Artists, 1975. Edmonton: Edmonton Art Gallery, 1975. 11 pieces in portfolio.

Exhibition held at the Edmonton Art Gallery, May 30-June 29, 1975.

Canadiana, 1977. **OONL**

1163 Edmonton Art Gallery. Alberta world reflections. Edmonton: Edmonton Art Gallery, 1975. 2p.

Canadiana, 1977. **OONL**

1164 Edmonton Art Gallery. Alberta '73. A survey of opportunities organized by the Edmonton Art Gallery and the Alberta Society of Artists. Edmonton: Edmonton Art Gallery, 1973. 12p. ill.

Selected by Michael Steiner.

Canadiana, 1975. **AEU**

1165 Edmonton Art Gallery. All Alberta '69. Edmonton: Edmonton Art Gallery, 1969. 16p. ill.

Exhibition held at the Edmonton Art Gallery, March 13-April 4, 1969 and Calgary Allied Arts Centre, April 25-May 11, 1969.

Canadiana, 1970. **AEU**

1166 Edmonton Art Gallery. Art in Alberta, Paul Kane to the present. Edmonton: Edmonton Art Gallery, 1973. 55p. ill.

Exhibition to commemorate the Fiftieth anniversary of the Gallery, and held at the Gallery, April 6-May 10, 1973 and at the Glenbow-Alberta Institute, July1-August 25, 1973.
Text by Karen Wilkin.

Canadiana, 1975. **AEU**

1167 Edmonton Art Gallery. Baker Lake prints/estampes. Ottawa: Canadian Eskimo Art Council, 1970. 44p. (chiefly ill.)

Catalogue of an exhibition.
Introduction in English, French, and Eskimo.

Canadiana, 1973. **AEU**

1168 Edmonton Art Gallery. Calgary printmakers. Edmonton: Edmonton Art Gallery, 1974. 36p. ill.

Catalogue of an exhibition held April 25-May 26, 1974. **AEU**

1169 Edmonton Art Gallery. Canada x ten. David Bolduc, D.T. Chester, Robert Christie, Ann Clarke Darrah, Harold Feist, K.M. Graham, Paul Hutner, Graham Peacock, Milly Ristvedt, Daniel Solomon. Edmonton: Edmonton Art Gallery, 1973. 32p. ill.

Catalogue of an exhibition, organized by the Edmonton Art Gallery, January, 1974.

Canadiana, 1975. **AEU**

1170 Edmonton Art Gallery. Certain traditions. Recent British and Canadian art. Edmonton: Edmonton Art Gallery, 1978. 107p. ill.

Exhibition organized by the Edmonton Art Gallery with the co-operation of the British Council, as part of the cultural program of the Commonwealth Games held in Edmonton in 1978. **AEU**

1171 Edmonton Art Gallery. Changing visions - the Canadian landscape. A travelling exhibition organized by the Edmonton Art Gallery and the Art Gallery of Ontario. Edmonton: Edmonton Art Gallery, 1976. 59p. ill.

French title *Apercus divers. Le paysage canadian.*
French text by Louis Le Gal.

Canadiana, 1977. **AEU**

1172 Edmonton Art Gallery. The collective unconscious. American and Canadian art, 1940-1950. Edmonton: Edmonton Art Gallery, 1975. 34p. ill.

An exhibition organized by the Edmonton Art Gallery, December 5, 1975- January 18, 1976.
Introduction by Karen Wilkin. **AEU**

1173 Edmonton Art Gallery. Edmonton collects. Edmonton: Edmonton Art Gallery, 1973. (1v.)

An exhibition of paintings from private collections in Edmonton. **AEU**

1174 Edmonton Art Gallery. An exhibition of five recent works by Larry Bell, John McCracken, DeWain Valentine, Ron Cooper, Peter Alexander. Edmonton: Edmonton Art Gallery, 1971. 44p. ill.

Exhibition of 5 artists from Los Angeles.

Canadiana, 1972. **AEU**

1175 Edmonton Art Gallery. Folk art of Pakistan. Edmonton: Edmonton Art Gallery, 1972. 4p. ill.

Catalogue of an exhibition held at the Edmonton Art Gallery, November 12-December 5, 1972. **AEU**

1176 Edmonton Art Gallery. The great Canadian super show of Canadian ideas. The Edmonton Art Gallery. August 17-September 12, 1972. Edmonton: Edmonton Art Gallery, 1972. broadside. **AEU**

1177 Edmonton Art Gallery. The Group of Seven in the Rockies. Organized by the Edmonton Art Gallery with the co-operation of the Peter Whyte Gallery, Bannf. Edmonton: Edmonton Art Gallery, 1974. 14p. ill.

Exhibition held at the Edmonton Art Gallery, April 17-May 19, 1974, the Dunlop Art Gallery, Regina, May 31-June 23, 1974, the Peter Whyte Gallery, Banff, July 1-21, 1974. **AEU**

1178 Edmonton Art Gallery. Impressionist paintings from the collection of Mr. and Mrs. J.A. Scrymgeour and Westbourne International Industries. Edmonton: Edmonton Art Gallery, 1972. 12p. ill.

Canadiana, 1972. **AEU**

1179 Edmonton Art Gallery. Masters of the sixties. Edmonton: Edmonton Art Gallery, 1972. 35p. ill.

Organized by the Art Gallery and the David Mirvish Gallery and exhibited in Edmonton and Winnipeg. **AEU**

1180 Edmonton Art Gallery. Play objects. An exhibition of toys and objects for children, May 18-June 4, 1972. Edmonton: Edmonton Art Gallery, 1972. 8p. ill.

Canadiana, 1972. **OONL**

1181 Edmonton Art Gallery. Sculpture in steel. An exhibition organized by the Edmonton Art Gallery, September 6-October 31, 1974, David Mirvish

Gallery, Toronto, January 11 - February 2, 1975. Edmonton: Edmonton Art Gallery, 1974. (36)p. ill.

Canadiana, 1977. **OONL**

1182 Edmonton Art Gallery. Ten Washington artists. Morris Louis, Kenneth Noland, Gene Davis, Thomas Downing, Howard Mehring, Sam Gilliam, Blaine Larson, Michael Clark, J.L. Knight, Rockne Krebs. Edmonton: Edmonton Art Gallery, 1970. 62p. ill.

Canadiana, 1976. **OONL**

1183 Edmonton Art Gallery. Third anniversary exhibition, April 5 - May 7, 1972. Edmonton: Edmonton Art Gallery, 1972. 24p. ill.

An exhibition of works acquired by the Edmonton Art Gallery since moving to its new building.

Canadiana, 1972. **AEU**

1184 Edmonton Art Gallery. West 71. October 7-31. Edmonton: Edmonton Art Gallery, 1971. 8p. ill.

AEU

1185 Edmonton Art Gallery. Junior Gallery. Plains Indian. Edmonton: Edmonton Art Gallery, 1971. 22p. ill.

Exhibition organized by the Edmonton Art Gallery with the co-operation of the Provincial Museum and Archives of Alberta.

Canadiana, 1974. **OONL**

1186 **Enns**, Maureen. Enns, Evans & Ulrich. Calgary: Glenbow-Alberta Institute, 1978. 16p. ill.

Catalogue of an exhibition held at the Walter J. Phillips Gallery, Banff, May 2-28, 1977, and at other museums.

Canadiana, 1979.

1187 **Fafard**, Joe. Joe Fafard. Ceramic pictures. Calgary: Alberta College of Art, 1972. 8p. ill.

Canadiana, 1973. **OONL**

1188 **Feist**, Harold E. Feist, A.C.A. Gallery, Jan. 25-Feb. 5, 1971. Calgary: Alberta College of Art Gallery, 1971. 1 envelope(9 sheets, chiefly ill.)

Not for public distribution.

Canadiana, 1973. **OONL**

1189 **Fenton**, Terry. Modern painting in Canada. A survey of major movements in twentieth century Canadian art. Terry Fenton and Karen Wilkin. Edmonton: Hurtig and Edmonton Art Gallery, 1978. 134p. (chiefly ill.)

Exhibition organized as part of the cultural program of the Commonwealth Games, Edmonton, 1978.

CBIP, 1979. **AEA**

1190 Focus. Photographic essays. Calgary: Glenbow-Alberta Institute, 1972. 74p. ill. (Glenbow-Alberta Institute. Art Series, 4)

Photographic exhibition catalogue. **ACP**

1191 **Gallie**, Tommie. Tommie Gallie, '75. Edmonton: Edmonton Art Gallery, 1975. 5p. ill.

Canadiana, 1977. **OONL**

1192 Glenbow Foundation. Western landscape as history. An exhibition of 25 water colours from the collection of the Glenbow Foundation, Calgary, circulated by the National Gallery of Canada. Ottawa: Queen's Printer, 1965. 13p. ill.

Title and text in English and French in parallel columns.

Glenbow. **ACG**

1193 Glenbow-Alberta Institute. Birds of prey. An exhibition of wildlife art from the eighteenth century to the present. Calgary: Glenbow-Alberta Institute, 1977. 20 leaves. ill. **AEA**

1194 Glenbow-Alberta Institute. Contemporary Indian artists. Calgary: Glenbow-Alberta Institute, 1972. folder(6p.) ill.

Canadiana, 1973. **OONL**

1195 Glenbow-Alberta Institute. Eskimo prints, Cape Dorset. Calgary: Glenbow-Alberta Institute, 1972. folder(6p.) ill.

Canadiana, 1973. **OONL**

1196 Glenbow-Alberta Institute. Glenbow. Calgary: Glenbow-Alberta Institute, 1969. 20p. ill.

Canadiana, 1970. **OONL**

1197 Glenbow-Alberta Institute. Glenbow art circuit, 1971-1972. Exhibitions circulated by Glenbow-Alberta Institute. Calgary: Glenbow-Alberta Institute, 1972. 16 leaves.

Canadiana, 1973. **OONL**

1198 Glenbow-Alberta Institute. Glenbow past and present. Calgary: Glenbow-Alberta Institute, 1966. 20p. ill.

Cover title. **AEA**

1199 Glenbow-Alberta Institute. Graphics by Walter J. Phillips and Canadian art in three dimensions. Calgary: Glenbow-Alberta Institute, 1968. 19p. ill. (Glenbow-Alberta Institute. Art Gallery. Catalogue, 3)

1200 Glenbow-Alberta Institute. Open studio. Calgary: Glenbow-Alberta Institute, 1975. 6p. ill.

Catalogue of an exhibition.

Canadiana, 1976. **OONL**

1201 Glenbow-Alberta Institute. Portraits of the Indians. Calgary: Glenbow-Alberta Institute, n.d. 8p. ill.

Cover title. **AEA**

1202 Glenbow-Alberta Institute. Various art media and techniques. Calgary: Glenbow-Alberta Art Gallery, 1968. 10p. ill. (Glenbow-Art Gallery Catalogue, 2-1968)

Duplicated.
Catalogue of an exhibition held May 7 to June 2, 1968. **AEA**

1203 Glenbow-Alberta Institute. Western untitled. Catalogue of an exhibition. Selected by Terrence Heath. Calgary: Glenbow Alberta Institute, 1976. 76p. ill.

Exhibition held at the Glenbow Alberta Institute Sept. 22 - Oct. 24, 1976.

Canadiana, 1977. **AEA**

1204 Glenbow-Alberta Institute. W.J. Phillips views Western Canada. Calgary: Glenbow-Alberta Institute, 1972. folder(6p.) ill.

Canadiana, 1973. **OONL**

1205 **Gottlieb**, Adolph. Adolph Gottlieb acrylics on paper. Regina: Norman MacKenzie Art Gallery, 1971. 16p. ill.

Catalogue of an exhibition held at Norman MacKenzie Art Gallery, Regina, Jan. 23-Feb 21, 1971, Edmonton Art Gallery, March 4-28, 1971 and Dunkelman Gallery, Toronto, June 5-19, 1971. **AEU**

1206 **Greene**, Stephen. Stephen Greene. Edmonton: Edmonton Art Gallery, 1972. 13p. ill.

Catalogue of an exhibition held Sept. 7-Oct. 8, 1972 at the Edmonton Art Gallery.

Canadiana, 1972. **AEU**

1207 **Guillet**, Glenn. Glen Guillet. Drawings and sculpture. Edmonton: Edmonton Art Gallery, 1973. 6p. ill.

Catalogue of an exhibition held at the Edmonton Art Gallery, January 7-30, 1973. **AEU**

1208 **Guy**, Pierre. Pierre Guy. Edmonton: Edmonton Art Gallery, 1973. 6p. ill.

Catalogue of an exhibition held at Edmonton Art Gallery, April 29-May 29, 1973.

Canadiana, 1973. **AEU**

1209 **Hall**, John. Its the real thing - Hall. Calgary: A.C.A. Gallery, 1970. 16p. ill.

Catalogue of exhibition of paintings of John Hall, Sept. 28 - Oct. 9, 1970.

Canadiana, 1971. **OONL**

1210 **Hohn**, Hubert. Hubert Hohn documentary photographs. Edmonton: Edmonton Art Gallery, 1975. 6p. ill.

Canadiana, 1977. **OONL**

1211 **Janvier**, Alex. Alex Janvier, Edmonton Art Gallery, June 3-July 3, 1973. Edmonton: Edmonton Art Gallery, 1973. 4p. (ill.)

Canadiana, 1964. **AEU**

1212 **Jenkins**, J. George. Prairie images. Paintings by J. George Jenkins. Calgary: Glenbow-Alberta Art Gallery, 1972. (16)p. ill.

Catalogue for exhibition shown at Glenbow-Alberta Art Gallery, Calgary (Oct, 4-Nov. 5, 1972) and Art Gallery of Greater Victoria (Feb. 15-Mar. 5, 1973). Prepared by Lorne Render.

Glenbow. **ACG**

1213 **Kiyooka**, Henry. Harry Kiyooka, paintings and prints. A.C.A. Gallery, Jan.4-22, 1970. Calgary: Alberta College of Art Gallery, 1971. 1 envelope(9 sheets chiefly ill.)

Not for public distribution.

Canadiana, 1973. **OONL**

1214 **Kiyooka**, Henry. Henry Kiyooka paintings & prints. Calgary: Southern Alberta Institute of Technology, 1970. 13p. ill.

Catalogue of an exhibition held at the Alberta College of Art Gallery, Jan 4-22, 1970.

Canadiana, 1971. **OONL**

1215 **Knowles**, Dorothy. Dorothy Knowles. An exhibition. Organized by the Edmonton Art Gallery. Edmonton: Edmonton Art Gallery, 1973. 12p. ill.

Exhibition held at the Glenbow-Alberta Institute, Calgary, the Dunlop Art Gallery, Regina, The Edmonton Art Gallery and the Beckett Gallery, Hamilton, in 1973. **AEU**

1216 **Kurelek**, William. William Kurelek. A retrospective. Edmonton: Edmonton Art Gallery, 1970. 1v. (unpaged) ill.

Catalogue of exhibition, Sept. 20-Oct. 20, 1970, at the Edmonton Art Gallery in association with the Isaacs Gallery, Toronto. **AEU**

1217 **Kurelek**, William. William Kurelek. The Winnipeg Art Gallery, 1966. Winnipeg: Winnipeg Art Gallery, 1966. 10p. ill.

Cover title.
Catalogue of exhibition, Winnipeg Art Gallery. **AEU**

1218 **Lindoe**, Luke. Lindoe, A.C.A. Gallery, Jan. 25-Feb. 5, 1971. Calgary: Alberta College of Art Gallery, 1971. 1 envelope(9 sheets, chiefly ill.)

Canadiana, 1973. **OONL**

1219 **Lougheed**, Don. "Popguns" Don Lougheed. Calgary: Alberta College of Art, 1972. 7p. ill.

Canadiana, 1973. **OONL**

1220 Memorial University Art Gallery. 13 Calgary painters. St. John's, Nfld.: Memorial University, 1967. 7p.

An Atlantic Provinces Art Exhibition, Sept. 1967-Apr. 1968.

Canadiana, 1972. **OONL**

1221 **Mitchell**, Janet. Janet Mitchell. A retrospective exhibition organized by Glenbow-Alberta Institute as a Festival Calgary event, Glenbow-Alberta Institute, March 2-April 3, 1977. Calgary: Glenbow-Alberta Institute, 1977. 25p. ill.

Canadiana 1979. **OONL**

1222 **Nevitt**, Richard Barrington. The frontier art of R.B. Nevitt, surgeon, North-West Mounted Police, 1874-78. Calgary: Glenbow-Alberta Institute, 1974. 29p. ill.

Catalogue of an exhibition organized to mark the centennial of the North-West Mounted Police in Western Canada. **AEA**

1223 **Nicoll**, Jim. Jim Nicoll, paintings and poetry. Calgary: Glenbow-Alberta Institute, 1977. 34p. ill.

An exhibition catalogue.

Canadiana, 1979. **OONL**

1224 **Nicoll**, Marion. Marion Nicoll. A retrospective, 1959-1971. The Edmonton Art Gallery, May 30 - June 29, 1975, the Glenbow Alberta Institute, Calgary, July 22 - August 17. Edmonton: Edmonton Art Gallery, 1975. 23p. ill.

Organized by the Edmonton Art Gallery.

Canadiana, 1977. **OONL**

1225 **Noland**, Kenneth. Kenneth Noland. March 6 - April 21, 1975. An exhibition. Edmonton: Edmonton Art Gallery, 1975. 11p. ill.

Canadiana, 1977. **OONL**

1226 **Norman Mackenzie Art Gallery**, Regina. Diversity, Canada East. Regina: Norman Mackenzie Art Gallery, 1972. 1 portfolio(22 fold. sheets) ill.

Catalogue of an exhibition held at the Edmonton Art Gallery and at the Norman Mackenzie Art Gallery.

Canadiana, 1973. **AEU**

1227 **O'Neil**, Bruce. Bruce O'Neil. Edmonton: Edmonton Art Gallery, 1975. 1 fold. sheet. ill.

Exhibition held at the Edmonton Art Gallery, March 23-April 18, 1975.

Canadiana, 1977. **OONL**

1228 **Perehudoff**, William W. William Perehudoff. Calgary: Glenbow-Alberta Institute, 1977. 16p. ill.

Canadiana, 1979. **OONL**

1229 **Perehudoff**, William W. William Perehudoff. Edmonton: Edmonton Art Gallery, 1972. 12p. ill.

Catalogue of an exhibition held at the Edmonton Art Gallery, December 14, 1972-January 21, 1973. **AEU**

1230 **Peter Whyte Gallery**, Banff. Beyond exceptional pass. An exhibition, a publication .. the Peter Whyte Foundation, the Peter Whyte Gallery, Banff, Canada, 1978. Banff: Peter Whyte Foundation, 1978. 58p. ill.

Exhibition held at the Peter Whyte Gallery, Banff, August 8-28, 1978.

Canadiana 1979.

1231 **Poons**, Larry. Larry Poons recent paintings. Edmonton: Edmonton Art Gallery, 1974. 19p. ill.

Catalogue of an exhibition held at the Edmonton Art Gallery May 2-30, 1974. **AEU**

1232 **Rauschenburg**, Robert. Robert Rauschenburg - Glass handle. Calgary: Alberta College of Art, 1976. 24p. ill.

Exhibition held at the Alberta College of Art Gallery, Oct. 12-Nov. 7, 1976.

Canadiana, 1977. **OONL**

1233 **Render**, Lorne Edgar. A.C. Leighton. Calgary: Glenbow-Alberta Institute, 1971. 24p. ill. (Glenbow-Alberta Institute. Art series, 3)

Glenbow. **ACG**

1234 **Render**, Lorne Edgar. Glenbow collects. An exhibition. Calgary: Glenbow-Alberta Institute, 1969. iv, 61p. ill. (Glenbow-Alberta Institute. Art series, 1)

Exhibition held Sept. 25-Nov. 2, 1969.

Glenbow. **ACG**

1235 **Render**, Lorne Edgar. The mountains and the sky. Calgary: Glenbow-Alberta Institute and McClelland and Stewart West, 1974. 223p. ill.

Landscape paintings from the Glenbow-Alberta Institute collection.

CBIP, 1979. **AEU**

1236 **Rogers**, Otto. New paintings by Otto Rogers. Calgary: Glenbow-Alberta Institute, 1973. 12p. ill.

Catalogue of an exhibition held at the Glenbow-Alberta Institute, Nov. 1-Dec. 3, 1973, the Dunlop Art Gallery, Regina, Feb 2-24, 1974 and Wallack Galleries, Ottawa, June, 1974.

Cover title *Otto Rogers*. **AEU**

1237 **Russell**, Charles M. Charles M. Russell, 1864-1926. An exhibition organized by the Edmonton Art Gallery, the assistance of grants from the City of Edmonton and the Government of the Province of Alberta. Edmonton: Art Gallery, 1967. (20)p. ill.

Exhibition held in Centennial Library, Edmonton, Aug. 3-26, 1967.
Addenda listing additional exhibits from Glenbow Foundation and Kennedy Galleries, New York, tipped in.

Glenbow. **ACG**

1238 Saskatoon Gallery and Conservatory. 8 Calgary artists. Saskatoon: Saskatoon Gallery and Conservatory, 1976. 18p. ill.

Canadiana, 1976. **OONL**

1239 **Savage**, Harry. 8 cents worth of Canada and a few sense more. Edmonton: Edmonton Art Gallery, 1973. 6p. ill.

Canadiana, 1973. **AEU**

1240 **Sen**, Ranjan. Ranjan Sen. Tommie Gallie. Calgary: Glenbow-Alberta Institute, 1975. 7p. ill.

Catalogue of an exhibition.

Canadiana, 1976. **OONL**

1241 **Sinclair**, Robert. Robert Sinclair. Edmonton: Edmonton Art Gallery, 1973. 4p. ill.

Catalogue of an exhibition held at the Edmonton Art Gallery, December 10, 1972 to January 2, 1973. **AEU**

1242 **Spalding**, Jeffrey J. Silversmithing in Canadian history. Calgary: Glenbow-Alberta Institute, 1979. 71p. (chiefly ill.)

Cover title.

CBIP, 1979. **AEA**

1243 **Taylor**, John Benjamin. J.B. Taylor landscapes. A memorial exhibition, organised by the Edmonton Art Gallery and the University of Alberta Department of Art and Design. Edmonton: Edmonton Art Gallery, 1973. 28p. ill.

Exhibition held in Sept.5-23, Confederation Art Gallery and Museum, Charlottetown and Nov. 22-Dec. 1973, Edmonton Art Gallery.

Canadiana, 1973. **AEU**

1244 **Thorburn**, Archibald. Archibald Thorburn. Paintings from the collection of Glenbow-Alberta Institute, Calgary, and Riveredge Foundation, Calgary. Introduction by Lorne E. Render. Calgary: Glenbow-Alberta Institute, 1974. 20p. ill.

Canadiana, 1974. **AEA**

1245 **Tillim**, Sidney. Sidney Tillim. An exhibition of narrative and history paintings, organized by the Edmonton Art Gallery. Edmonton: Edmonton Art Gallery, 1973. 20p. ill.

Text by Terry Fenton.

Canadiana, 1975. **AEU**

1246 **Turner**, John Davenall. J.D. Turner. Edmonton: Edmonton Art Gallery, 1975. 8p. ill.

Canadiana, 1977. **OONL**

1247 University of Alberta. Inuit games and contests. The Clifford E. Lee Collection of prints. Introduction by George Swinton, text by Helen Collinson. Edmonton: University of Alberta Collections, 1978. 76p. ill.

Canadiana, 1978. **AEU**

1248 **Vassarely**, Victor de. Vassarely. Edmonton: Edmonton Art Gallery, 1969. 1 sheet. ill.

Catalogue of an exhibition held June 12-29, 1969.

Canadiana, 1971. **AEU**

1249 **Whitlock**, An. An Whitlock. Calgary: Alberta College of Art, 1976. 6p. ill.

Exhibition held at the Alberta College of Art, Sept. 18-Oct 5, 1976.

Canadiana, 1977. **OONL**

1250 **Will**, John. John Will, Marvin Jones. Calgary: Glenbow-Alberta Art Gallery, 1976. 12p. ill.

Catalogue of an exhibition shown at the Glenbow, Dalhousie University Art Gallery, University of Lethbridge Art Gallery, and the Edmonton Art Gallery.

Canadiana, 1976. **OONL**

1251 **Williamson**, Moncrieff. Through Canadian eyes. Trends and influences in Canadian art, 1815-1965. Calgary: Glenbow Alberta Institute, 1976. (88)p. ill.

Catalogue of an exhibition, selected by Moncrieff Williamson.
Exhibition held at the Glenbow Alberta Institute, Sept. 22-Oct.24, 1976.

Canadiana, 1977. **AEU**

1252 **Wood**, George. The journey goes on .. George Wood, A.C.A. Gallery, Oct. 69. Calgary: Alberta College of Art Gallery, 1969. 36p. ill.

Catalogue of an exhibition of paintings, chiefly of poems.

Canadiana, 1973. **OONL**

1253 **Yates**, Norman. Norman Yates. Edmonton: Edmonton Art Gallery, 1973. 6p. ill.

Catalogue of an exhibition held at Edmonton Art Gallery, March 25-April 24, 1973.

Canadiana, 1973. **AEU**

Performing Arts: General Works

1254 **Andrews**, Val. A practical guide to ventriloquism. Calgary: M. Hades International, 1977

P.N.L.A., 1979.

1255 **Botting**, Gary. The theatre of protest in America. Edmonton: Harden House, 1972. 32p.

Canadiana, 1972. **AEU**

1256 **Doolittle**, Joyce. A mirror of our dreams. Children and the theatre in Canada. Joyce Doolittle & Zina Barnieh. With a chapter on theatre in Quebec, by Helene Beauchamp. Vancouver: Talonbooks, 1979. 213p. (Theatre for young people)

CBIP 1979. **AECYR**

1257 **Jameson**, Sheilagh S. Chautauga in Canada. By Sheilagh S. Jamieson, in collaboration with Nola B. Erickson. Calgary: Glenbow-Alberta Institute, 1979. vi, 161p. ill.

History of Chautauga, a travelling educational and cultural organization. **AEA**

1258 **Jendyk**, Margaret Faulkes. The creative process of drama and its application to drama in education. Edmonton: Department of Drama, University of Alberta, 1978. 175, 10p.

Duplicated.

Canadiana, 1979. **AEU**

1259 **Sheremeta**, James. A survey of professional entertainment and theatre in Edmonton, Alberta, before 1914. Edmonton: University of Alberta, 1970. xi, 296, lix leaves.

Thesis (M.A.), University of Alberta, 1970.
Typescript.

Canadian theses. **AEU**

1260 **Zirkie**, Larry E. The creative world of puppetry. A guide for students and teachers. Calgary: G.L. Studios, 1974. 105p. ill.

Canadiana, 1975. **OONL**

Magic and Conjuring

1261 Aldini. New concepts in magic. Illustrated by Micky Hades. Calgary: M. Hades Enterprises, 1970. 37 leaves. ill.

Duplicated.
Some articles published in various periodicals.

Canadiana, 1973.

1262 Aldini. Novel concepts with cards. Illustrated by Micky Hades. Calgary: M. Hades Enterprises. 1970. 46 leaves. ill.

Duplicated.
Some articles were previously published in various periodicals.

Canadiana, 1970.

1263 Aldini. Roughingly yours. Calgary: M. Hades Enterprises, 1969. 48 leaves. ill.

Duplicated.

Canadiana, 1977.

1264 **Allesi**, Ron. The magic of Ronal. Calgary: Hades International, 1977. 47p. ill.

P.N.L.A., 1979.

1265 Amazing Maurice. Mentalistic encore. Illustrated by Micky Hades. Calgary: M. Hades Enterprises, 1969. 32 leaves. ill.

Duplicated.

Canadiana, 1977.

1266 Amazing Maurice. Paper bag magic. Calgary: M. Hades Enterprises, 1967. 24 leaves. ill.

Duplicated.

Canadiana, 1977.

1267 Amazing Maurice. Phone book magic. Calgary: M. Hades International, 1974. 31p. ill.

Canadiana, 1977.

1268 **Andrews**, Val. Magic in store. The magic Pitchman's handbook. Calgary: M. Hades International, 1976. 45p. ill.

Canadiana, 1977.

1269 **Armstrong**, Bruce. Encyclopedia of suspensions and levitations. With a chronology by S.H. Sharpe. Illustrated by Sid Lorraine. Calgary: M. Hades International, 1976. 266p. ill.

Cover title *Micky Hades' encyclopedia of suspensions and levitations*.

Canadiana, 1977.

1270 **Bell**, Bob. Inside magic. Illustrated by David Bell. Calgary: M. Hades International, 1979. 52p. ill.

Canadiana, 1980.

1271 **Blake**, George. Comedy magic. 2d ed. Calgary: M. Hades International, 1974. 56 leaves. ill.

Duplicated.
1st ed. published in England.

Canadiana, 1977.

1272 **Blake**, George. Commercial card magic. Calgary: M. Hades Enterprises, 1972. 47 leaves. ill.

Duplicated.

Canadiana, 1977.

1273 **Blake**, George. Forgotten magic. 2d ed. Calgary: M. Hades Enterprises, 1972. 55 leaves. ill.

Duplicated.
On cover: 103 tricks, stunts, gags.
1st ed. published in England.

Canadiana, 1977.

1274 **Blake**, George. Loopy loop. Being a combination of effects with an endless chain and developed around the famous figure eight racecourse trick. Calgary: M. Hades Enterprises, 1972. 23 leaves. ill.

Duplicated.
On cover: A treatise on the endless chain.

Canadiana, 1977.

1275 **Blake**, George. Major magic. Calgary: M. Hades International, 1975. 55 leaves. ill.

Duplicated.

Canadiana, 1977.

1276 **Blake**, George. Master magic. Calgary: M. Hades International, 1975. 40 leaves. ill.

Duplicated.

Canadiana, 1977.

1277 **Blake**, George. More master magic. Calgary: M. Hades International, 1975. leaves 42-77. ill.

Duplicated.
A continuation of his *Master magic*1.

Canadiana, 1977.

1278 **Blake**, George. Take a note. Calgary: M. Hades International, 1975. 53 leaves. ill.

Duplicated.
On cover: All you need to know about effects with borrowed bills!.
"Much of the material ... was published way back in 1955 in the then popular *Magic Magazine* ..." p.2.

Canadiana, 1977.

1279 **Brent**, Lu. Lu Brent's best magic tricks. Calgary: M. Hades Enterprises, 1974. 2v. ill.

Duplicated.

Canadiana 1977.

1280 **Brineger**, Ron. Desperado deals. Edited by Stephen Minch. Illustrated by the author. Calgary: M. Hades International, 1976. 30 leaves. ill.

Canadiana, 1977.

1281 **Chandler**, Harold. Chandu's magic variations. Rev. ed. Illustrated by Micky Hades. Calgary: M. Hades Enterprises, n.d. 34 leaves. ill.

Duplicated.
Originally published in New Zealand as *Let's make magic*.

Canadiana, 1977.

1282 **Dalal**, Sam. Magic with a marked deck. 2d ed. Calgary: M. Hades International, 1976. 13 leaves. ill.

1st ed. published in India.

Canadiana, 1980.

1283 **Dayton**, Ronald J. Ropes with a different twist. Illustrated by the author. Calgary: M. Hades International, 1979. 107p. ill.

Canadiana, 1980.

1284 **DeLawrence**, George. Answers to questions. 7th ed. Calgary: M. Hades Enterprises, 1971. 18 leaves.

Duplicated.
Cover title *Answers for questions*.
Previous editions published in United States by Robert Nelson.

Canadiana, 1977.

1285 Diviner of Destiny. Visions of tomorrow. 2d ed. Calgary: M. Hades Enterprises, 1972. 16 leaves. ill.

Duplicated.
1st ed. published in United States.

Canadiana, 1977.

1286 **Dore**, Theo. Magnetrix. Calgary: M. Hades Enterprises, 1971. 54 leaves. ill.

Duplicated.

Canadiana, 1977.

1287 **Ferris**, Ron. Apparitions, animations, and aces. A series of original card effects. Calgary: M. Hades Enterprises, 1973. 31p. ill.

Duplicated.
Designed by Ron Ferris.

Canadiana, 1977.

1288 Genillusions. Selected from the Genii magazine and released by Bill Larsen jr. Edited by Micky Hades. Calgary: M. Hades International, 1979. 108p. ill.

Canadiana, 1980.

1289 **Ginn**, David. Magic that moves me. Calgary: M. Hades Enterprises, 1971. 77p. ill.

Canadiana, 1977.

1290 **Grant**, Gene. Phantini's lost book of mental secrets. 2d ed. Edited by Kenny Woodward, Jr. Cover drawing by Jack Reilly. Calgary: M. Hades International, 1975. 21p. ill.

1st ed. published in U.S.A., c1955.

Canadiana, 1977.

1291 **Guest**, Leslie P. Lecture domaine. If you can't invent - adapt! Illustrated by Ed Mishell. Calgary: M. Hades Enterprises, 1972. 32p. ill. (A Micky Hades lecture book)

Canadiana, 1977.

1292 **Hades**, Michael P. Bang! 50 great tricks, routines, tips and ideas for the practical magician. Illustrated by Micky Hades. Calgary: M. Hades Enterprises, 1968. 35 leaves. ill.

Duplicated.

Canadiana, 1977.

1293 **Hades**, Michael P. How to make flashes, bangs and puffs of smoke. Edited by Mark Steele. Calgary: M. Hades International, 1979. 61p. ill.

Canadiana, 1980.

1294 **Hades**, Michael P. Magic the way I see it. Looking at the commercial side of doing magic. Calgary: M. Hades Enterprises, 1963. 31 leaves. ill.

Duplicated.

Canadiana, 1977.

1295 **Hades**, Michael P. The make-up of magic. Cover design by Everett Andrews. Calgary: Hades Enterprises, 1962. 72p. ill.

Duplicated.

Canadiana, 1962.

1296 **Hades**, Michael P. The new make-up of magic. Rev. and expanded ed. Illustrated by the author. Calgary: M. Hades International, 1974. 132p. ill.

First edition published in 1962 with title *The make-up of magic*.

Canadiana, 1977.

1297 **Hull**, Burling. The amazing world of mentalism. Edited by Stephen Minch. New Art by Paul Lenti. Calgary: M. Hades International,

On spine: World of Mentalism.

Canadiana, 1977.

1298 **Hull**, Burling. Double double magic with cards. Edited by Micky Hades. Calgary: M. Hades Enterprises, 1972. 21 leaves. ill.

Duplicated.
Incorporating selected material from *Nine great card feats* and *Double magic with cards* by the same author.

Canadiana, 1977.

1299 **Hull**, Burling. Gold medal showmanship for magicians and mentalists. Calgary: M. Hades Enterprises, 1970. 95 leaves.

Duplicated.

Canadiana, 1971.

1300 **Hull**, Burling. The new encyclopedic dictionary of mentalism. A gigantic collection of complete mentalism methods, secrets, instructions, routines, acts, programs, shows. Calgary: M. Hades Enterprises, 1972-1977. 3v. ill.

Cover title *Burling Hull's encyclopedic dictionary of mentalism*.
First ed. published in U.S.A. under title *Dictionary of mentalism*.

Canadiana, 1977.

1301 **Hull**, Burling. Stage illusions for the 1, 2 or 3 performer show. 2d ed. Edited by Micky Hades. Illustrated by Shelby Craigen. Calgary: M. Hades Enterprises, 1972. 39 leaves. ill.

Duplicated.
1st ed. published in U.S.A..

Canadiana, 1977.

1302 **Hutton**, Darryl J.P. The dove worker's handbook. By Darryl J.P. Hutton and Micky Hades. Illustrated by Micky Hades. Calgary: M. Hades Enterprises, 1969. 2v. ill.

Duplicated.
2d. ed. of v.1 published in 1976, v.2 in 1977.

Canadiana, 1977.

1303 **Kumar**, S.K. Vasantha. Illusionseseme. Edited by Bob Bell. Illustrated by V.N.K. Menon. Calgary: M. Hades Enterprises, 1971. 95 leaves.

Duplicated.

Canadiana, 1971.

1304 **Larsen**, William W. Conjuring for children. Calgary: M. Hades Enterprises, 1973. 17 leaves.

Duplicated.

Canadiana, 1977.

1305 **Larsen**, William W. Puppetrix. Calgary: M. Hades International, 1974. 17 leaves.

Duplicated.

Canadiana, 1977.

1306 **Larsen**, William W. Twelve illusionettes. Illustrated by Paul Lenti. Calgary: M. Hades International, 1975. 17 leaves. ill.

Duplicated.

Canadiana, 1977.

1307 **Liebertz**, Arnold. Marvelous mysteries of Marvillo. Edited by Stephen Minch. Illustrated by Shelby Craigen. Calgary: M. Hades International, 1975. 39p. ill.

Canadiana, 1977.

1308 **Lundin**, Lloyd. Magazine magicana. Calgary: M. Hades Enterprises, 1970. 91 leaves.

Duplicated.

Canadiana, 1977.

1309 The magic shelf. Compiled by Micky Hades. Calgary: M. Hades Enterprises, 1969. 2v. ill.

A collection of articles which originally appeared as monthly supplements in the *Hade-E-Gram Magizette*.
Duplicated.

Canadiana, 1977.

1310 Magic Wand Club. The centennial magic book. Calgary: M. Hades Enterprises, 1973. 33 leaves. ill.

Duplicated.

Canadiana, 1977.

1311 **Magus**, Jim. Sex and the single magician. A magician's guide to picking up girls. Illustrated by Dennis Patten. Calgary: M. Hades International, 1974. 26p. ill.

Duplicated.

Canadiana, 1977.

1312 Mental mysteries with cards. Edited by William W. Larsen. Calgary: M. Hades International, 1974. 47 leaves. ill.

Duplicated.

Canadiana, 1977.

1313 **Minch**, Stephen. Any second now. Part two of the professional card technique of Martin A. Nash. Illustrated with 92 photographs of the hands of Martin A. Nash. Calgary: M. Hades International, 1977. p.141-285. ill.

Duplicated.
A continuation of *Ever so sleightly*.

Canadiana, 1977.

1314 **Minch**, Stephen. The book of Thoth. Tarot trickery. Calgary: M. Hades International, 1974. 45p. ill.

Canadiana, 1977.

1315 **Minch**, Stephen. Creation of a magical madman, A theater of the absurd for the close-up performer, related in a left-handed manner. Illustrated by Paul Lent. Calgary: M. Hades International, 1977. 97p. ill.

Canadiana, 1978.

1316 **Minch**, Stephen. Ever so sleightly. The professional card technique of Martin A. Nash. Calgary: M. Hades International, 1971. 134p. ill.

Duplicated.

Canadiana, 1977.

1317 **Minch**, Stephen. Mind and matter. A handbook of parapsychokinetic phenomena. Illustrated by Paul Lenti. Calgary: M. Hades International, 1975. 52p. ill.

Canadiana, 1977.

1318 **Minch**, Stephen. Sleight unseen. Part three of the professional card technique of Martin A. Nash. Calgary: M. Hades International, 1979. pp.293-450. ill.

Continues *Ever so sleightly* and *Any second now*.

Canadiana, 1980.

1319 **Musson**, Clettis V. Forty-four foolers. A treasure chest of magic lore. 44 magical effects for the nite club performer and illusionist using the minimum of merchandise to obtain maximum of mystification. 2d ed. Calgary: M. Hades Enterprises, 1972. 49 leaves. ill.

Duplicated.
1st ed. published in U.S.A.

Canadiana, 1977.

1320 **Narvaez**, Armado. With deck in hand. Selected card effects. Written and illustrated by Armado Narvaez, with assistance from Roger Sherman Calgary: M. Hades International, 1978. 39p. ill.

Canadiana, 1980.

1321 **Nelson**, Robert A. The art of cold reading. Rev. ed. Calgary: M. Hades International, 1971. 46, (3) leaves.

Duplicated.
First published, 1951 in U.S.A.

Canadiana, 1977.

1322 **Nelson**, Robert A. Club and party mentalism. Calgary: M. Hades Enterprises, 1972. 43 leaves.

Duplicated.
First published 1960, in U.S.A.

Canadiana, 1977.

1323 **Nelson**, Robert A. Comedy mentalism. 2d ed. Calgary: M. Hades International, 1975. 3v. ill.

Duplicated.
First published 1962-1969, in U.S.A., v.3 published by M. Hades Enterprises, 1973.

Canadiana, 1977.

1324 **Nelson**, Robert A. A complete course in stage hypnotism. A complete course in pseudo stage hypnotism covering all phases of the hypnotic performance. Rev. ed. Calgary: M. Hades Enterprises, 1971. 30 leaves.

Duplicated.
1st ed. published 1965, in United States.

Canadiana, 1977.

1325 **Nelson**, Robert A. Effective answers to questions. New rev. and enl. deluxe ed. Calgary: M. Hades International, 1975. 48 leaves.

Duplicated.
1st ed. published in U.S.A.

Canadiana, 1977.

1326 **Nelson**, Robert A. The ghost book of dark secrets. 2d ed. Calgary: M. Hades Enterprises, 1972. 29 leaves. ill.

Duplicated.
1st ed. published in U.S.A.

Canadiana, 1977.

1327 **Nelson**, Robert A. Hellstromism. Calgary: M. Hades Enterprises, 1972. 25 leaves. ill.

Duplicated.
First published 1935.

Canadiana, 1977.

1328 **Nelson**, Robert A. How to book your attraction. 2d rev. ed. Calgary: M. Hades International, 1975. 38 leaves.

Duplicated.
1st ed. published in U.S.A.

Canadiana, 1977.

1329 **Nelson**, Robert A. How to read sealed messages. 5th rev. ed. Calgary: M. Hades Enterprises, 1972. 25 leaves. ill.

Duplicated.

Canadiana, 1977.

1330 **Nelson**, Robert A. Manual of publicity and exploitation for the mentalist. Rev. ed. Calgary: M. Hades Enterprises, 1971. 39 leaves.

Duplicated.

Canadiana, 1977.

1331 **Nelson**, Robert A. Mentalism and its presentation. By Robert A. Nelson and Syd Bergson. Calgary: M. Hades Enterprises, 1971. (1v.)

Duplicated.

Canadiana, 1977.

1332 **Nelson**, Robert A. The mentalist's manual. Calgary: M. Hades International, 1977. 36 leaves.

Canadiana, 1980.

1333 **Nelson**, Robert A. Miracles in mentalism and psychic experimentation. 2d ed. Calgary: M. Hades Enterprises, 1972. 60p. ill.

1st ed. published in U.S.A. in 1945.

Canadiana, 1977.

1334 **Nelson**, Robert A. More effective answers to questions. 6th rev. ed. Calgary: M. Hades Enterprises, 1973. 18 leaves.

Duplicated.
Previous editions published in U.S.A.
Supplement to *Effective answers to questions*.

Canadiana, 1977.

1335 **Nelson**, Robert A. The Nelson master course of hypnotism. 2d ed. Calgary: M. Hades Enterprises, 1971. 55 leaves.

"Scientific sleep card" laid in.
Duplicated.
1st ed. published in U.S.A.

Canadiana, 1977.

1336 **Nelson**, Robert A. Projected answers. 2d ed. Calgary: M. Hades Enterprises, 1971. 30 leaves.

Duplicated.
First published 1956 in U.S.A.

Canadiana, 1977.

1337 **Nelson**, Robert A. Secret methods of private readers. Rev. ed. Calgary: M. Hades International, 1975. 37 leaves. ill.

Duplicated.
Cover title *Secret methods of private readers, including the further exploits of Doctor A*.

1st ed. published in U.S.A.

1338 **Nelson**, Robert A. Sensational answers. Calgary: M. Hades International, 1975. 30 leaves.

Duplicated.

Canadiana, 1977.

1339 **Nelson**, Robert A. Sensational effects. Rev. and enl. ed. Calgary: M. Hades International, 1975. 30 leaves.

Duplicated.
1st ed. published in U.S.A.

Canadiana, 1977.

1340 **Nelson**, Robert A. Sensational mentalism. Hades, Michael P Calgary: M. Hades Enterprises, 1972-1977. 4v. ill.

Duplicated.
Parts 1-3 written by R.A. Nelson and others. Part 4 published under title and edited by Michael P Hades.

Canadiana, 1973.

1341 **Nelson**, Robert A. A sequel to The art of cold reading. Calgary: M. Hades Enterprises, 1971. 20 leaves.

Duplicated.

Canadiana, 1977.

1342 **Nelson**, Robert A. Super prediction tricks. By Robert A. Nelson and E.J. Moore. Calgary: M. Hades International, 1975. 41 leaves. ill.

Duplicated.

Canadiana, 1977.

1343 **Nelson**, Robert A. Super-mentality. Rev. and enl. ed. Calgary: M. Hades Enterprises, 1971. 39 leaves. ill.

Duplicated.
First published 1929 in U.S.A.

Canadiana, 1977.

1344 **Nelson**, Robert A. Technique of the private reader. Rev. ed. Calgary: M. Hades Enterprises, 1971. 21 leaves.

Duplicated.
First published in U.S.A.

Canadiana, 1977.

1345 **Nelson**, Robert A. T.V. mentalism. Rev. ed. Calgary: M. Hades Enterprises, 1972. 31 leaves. ill.

Duplicated.
First published in U.S.A.

Canadiana, 1977.

1346 **Novak**, John A. The art of escape. Illustrated by the author. Calgary: M. Hades International, 1979. 4v. ill.

Contents: 1. A modern handcuff act 2. Selected chain escapes 3. Metamorphosis and other essays of escape 4. Escapes from a strait jacket.

Canadiana, 1980.

1347 Pages from a medium's notebook. Calgary: M. Hades Enterprises, 1971. 49p.

Duplicated.

Canadiana, 1977.

1348 **Pomeroy**, John D. Basic make-up for magicians. Calgary: M. Hades Enterprises, 1969. 19 leaves.

Duplicated.

Canadiana, 1977.

1349 **Pomeroy**, John D. Dove, silk and flower magic. Illustrated by Paul Lenti. Calgary: M. Hades International, 1975. 42p. ill.

Canadiana, 1977.

1350 **Pomeroy**, John D. Mentology. Calgary: M. Hades Enterprises, 1973. 41 leaves. ill.

Duplicated.

Canadiana, 1977.

1351 **Potter**, Jack. The master index to magic in print, covering books and magazines in English language published up to and including December, 1964. Edited by Mickey Hades. Calgary: M. Hades Enterprises, 1971. 14 v.

Duplicated.
Much of the material appeared first in the periodicals, *The Budget*, and *The Linking Ring* under title *Potter's bar*.
Kept up to date by revisions and additions.

Canadiana, 1971.

1352 **RaMayne**, Korda. The private medium's secret guide. Rev. ed. Calgary: M. Hades Enterprises, 1971. 59 leaves.

Duplicated.
1st ed. published in U.S.A.

Canadiana, 1977.

1353 **Rice**, Harold R. Exclusive magic. 2d ed. Illustrated by Micky Hades. Calgary: M. Hades Enterprises, 1970. 38 leaves. ill.

Duplicated.
First published 1936 in U.S.A.

Canadiana, 1977.

1354 **Rightmire**, Richard. The master mentalist. The full professional show-script. Edited by Burling 'Volta' Hull. Calgary: M. Hades Enterprises, 1972. 24 leaves.

Canadiana, 1977.

1355 **Robertson**, Robin. Handle with care. Illustrated by Micky Hades. Calgary: M. Hades, 1964. 46 leaves.

Chiefly on card tricks.

Duplicated.

Canadiana, 1965.

1356 **Sanderson**, George P. Right under their noses. Calgary: Micky Hades International, 1977. 85p. ill.

Canadiana, 19878.

1357 **Schatz**, Edward R. Practical contact mind reading. Edited and arranged by Brian M. Hades. Calgary: M. Hades International, 1974. 44p.

Duplicated.

Canadiana, 1977.

1358 **Setterington**, Arthur. Off-beat (sic) mental effects. Illustrated by Paul Lenti. Calgary: M. Hades International, 1975. 28p. ill.

Duplicated.
Cover title *Off beat (sic) mentalism*.

Canadiana, 1977.

1359 **Setterington**, Arthur. Straight line mysteries. Illustrated by Shelby Craigen. Calgary: M. Hades Enterprises, 1972. 48p. ill.

Duplicated.

Canadiana, 1973.

1360 **Setterington**, Arthur. Stranger mysteries. Illustrated by Nelson C. Hehne. Calgary: M. Hades Enterprises, 1967. 20 leaves. ill.

Duplicated.

Canadiana, 1977.

1361 **Sherwood**, John C. The conjurer's calculator. Magic with a pocket computer. Calgary: M. Hades International, 1976. 41p. ill.

Canadiana, 1977.

1362 **Siegel**, Paul J. Doorway to delusion. Calgary: M. Hades Enterprises, 1972. 33p. ill.

Canadiana, 1973.

1363 **Siegel**, Paul J. Mentalism a la mode. Calgary: M. Hades International, 1975. 50p. ill.

Duplicated.

Canadiana, 1977.

1364 **Siegel**, Paul J. Windows to the mind. Illustrated by Al Forgione and Micky Hades. Calgary: M. Hades International, 1968. 33 leaves. ill.

Duplicated.

1365 **Skomp**, Stephen. S'komplimentary mentalism. Illustrated by Paul Lenti. Calgary: M. Hades International, 1975. 28p. ill.

Duplicated.

Canadiana, 1977.

1366 **Stiles**, Kirk. Thimbles with a light touch. Illustrated by the author. Calgary: M. Hades Enterprises, 1971. 33p. ill.

Canadiana, 1977.

1367 **Tan**, Choon Tee. Tan Choon Tee on mentalism. Illustrated by Micky Hades. Calgary: M. Hades, 1962. 42 leaves. ill.

Foreword by Irving M. Lewis.
Duplicated.

Canadiana, 1964.

1368 **Tan**, Choon Tee. 25 experiments in mentalism. Rev. ed. Illustrated by Micky Hades. Calgary: M. Hades Enterprises, 1972. 40 leaves. ill.

Duplicated.
First ed. published in 1963 under title *Tan Choon Tee on mentalism*.

Canadiana, 1977.

1369 **Taylor**, Anthony James Charles. The magic of Allan Lambie. Illustrated by Micky Hades. Calgary: M. Hades Enterprises, 1970. 50 leaves. ill.

Duplicated.

Canadiana, 1971.

1370 **Thornton**, Spencer. Thornton's secrets of mental magic. 3d ed. Edited by Kenny Wood, jr. Calgary: M. Hades International, 1978. 28p. ill.

Earlier editions published in U.S.A.
Cover title *Secrets of mental magic*.

1371 **Trost**, Nick. Cardman's secrets, easy to perform, hard to detect. World's best card miracles. 2d ed. Calgary: M. Hades Enterprises, 1971. 2v. ill.

Duplicated.
1st ed. published in U.S.A.

Canadiana, 1977.

1372 **Trost**, Nick. ESP session with Nick Trost. Calgary: M. Hades Enterprises, 1971. 42 leaves. ill.

Duplicated.
Cover title *Telepathy, mind reading, prediction, 17 tricks, 6 routines*.

Canadiana, 1977.

1373 **Trost**, Nick. Nick Trost's card problems. Advanced card miracles. 2d ed. Calgary: M. Hades Enterprises, 1971. (33) leaves. ill.

Duplicated.
1st ed. published in U.S.A.

Canadiana, 1977.

1374 **Trost**, Nick. Nick's routine with the cups and balls. Calgary: M. Hades Enterprises, 1971. 9 leaves. ill.

Duplicated.
On cover: A classic of magic. Plus a bonus trick Bottoms-up Puzzle.

Canadiana, 1977.

1375 **Trost**, Nick. Nick's table trix. 2d ed. Calgary: M. Hades Enterprises, 1972. 22 leaves. ill.

Duplicated.
1st ed. published in U.S.A.

Canadiana, 1977.

1376 **White**, Joseph M. 5 micro-mental programs. Calgary: M. Hades Enterprises, 1966. 60 leaves.

Duplicated.

Canadiana, 1977.

1377 **Wright**, T. Page. The L. W. card mysteries. 2d ed. By T. Page Wright and William Larsen. Calgary: M. Hades International, 1975. 30p.

1st ed. published in U.S.A.

Canadiana, 1977.

1378 **Yeager**, John. Dots Magic. Calgary: M. Hades International, 1975. 25 leaves. ill.

Duplicated.

Canadiana, 1977.

Music: General Works

1379 **Dansereau**, Grace. Discovering music. A child's introduction to the world of music. Calgary: G. Dansereau, 1975. 47p. ill.

A readiness program ... for private study, groups or classroom, with preschoolers or primary graders.

Canadiana, 1979. **OONL**

1380 **De Bruijn**, Bert. Look and play. Instruction for band instruments. Red Deer: B. de Bruijn, 1976. 20 leaves. ill.

Canadiana, 1977. **OONL**

1381 **Draper**, Norman. Bands by the Bow. A history of band music in Calgary. Calgary: Century Calgary Publications, 1975. 72p. ill.

Also published as part of *Past and present*, which was issued as v.1 of the Century Calgary Historical Series.

Canadiana, 1977. **AEA**

1382 Edmonton Symphony Orchestra comes of age. A short history of the the first twenty-one years. s.l.: Rothmans of Pall Mall Canada, 1973. 27p. ill.

Canadiana, 1976. **AEU**

1383 **Malsbary**, Dwight R. Practical music course in elementary theory and sight-singing. 7th print. rev. Three Hills: Prairie Press, 1958. viii, 136, 2p.

1st ed., 1947. rev. ed., 1968. 3d. ed., 1968.

Canadiana, 1960. **OONL**

1384 **Millar**, Gerald Wesley. The measurement of melody. Exshaw: Millar Publications, 1975. 87p. ill.

Canadiana, 1976. **OONL**

1385 Prairie Bible Institute. Practical accordion course. A course based on hymns and variations. Three Hills: Prairie Bible Institute, 1958. 2, 62p.

2d ed., 1967. 2v.

Canadiana, 1960. **ATP**

Music Scores

1386 **Archer**, Violet. April weather. Waterloo, Ont.: Waterloo Music, 1976. 3p.

Words by Amy Bissett.
Composed for medium voice and piano.

Canadiana, 1977. **AEU**

1387 **Archer**, Violet. Cantata sacra. A sacred meditation based on late mediaeval dialogues. Toronto: 1966. 32p.

For solo voices, flute, clarinet, horn, trumpet, viola, violin, violincello, double bass and piano.
English and Latin words.
Photocopy of ms. **AEU**

1388 **Archer**, Violet. Christmas. Text by Althea Bass. Toronto: Chanteclair Music, 1972. 8p. (Festival Singers choral series, E.I. 1014)

For chorus (SSA), oboe(or alternate instrument), harp or piano.

NUC(Music), 1979. **AEU**

1389 **Archer**, Violet. The daffodils. For medium voice and piano. Words by William Wordsworth. Toronto: Canadian Music Centre, 1972. 7p.

Photocopy of ms. **AEU**

1390 **Archer**, Violet. Divertimento for brass quintet. Toronto: Clark & Cruickshank, 1974. score(31p) and 5 parts.

Composed for horn, 2 trumpets, trombone and tuba.

Canadiana, 1977. **AEU**

1391 **Archer**, Violet. Divertimento for orchestra. Don Mills, Ont.: BMI Canada, 1968. 63p.

NUC(Music), 1968-72. **AEU**

1392 **Archer**, Violet. Fanfare and passacaglia. Toronto: BMI Canada, 1974. 21p.

For orchestra.

NUC(Music), 1963-67. **AEU**

1393 **Archer**, Violet. Four bagatelles. Piano solo. Waterloo, Ont.: Waterloo Music, 1979. 15p.

Cover title.

Canadiana, 1979. **OONL**

1394 **Archer**, Violet. Four Canadian folk-songs. Toronto: Canadian Music Centre, 1958. 6p.

French Canadian folk songs for medium voice and piano.
Photocopy of ms. **AEU**

1395 **Archer**, Violet. Four little studies for piano. Waterloo, Ont.: Waterloo Music, 1964. 3p.

NUC(Music), 1973-77. **AEU**

1396 **Archer**, Violet. Gold sun. A song for contralto and piano. Words by Dorothy Livesay. Music by Violet Archer. Toronto: Canadian Music Centre, n.d. 3p.

Photocopy of ms. **AEU**

1397 **Archer**, Violet. Green rain. A song for mezzo soprano and piano. Words by Dorothy Livesay. Music by Violet Archer. Toronto: Canadian Music Centre, n.d. 5p.

Photocopy of ms. **AEU**

1398 **Archer**, Violet. The gulls. For medium voice and piano. Poem by John Gould Fletcher. Music by Violet Archer. Toronto: Canadian Music Centre, 1955. 3p.

Photocopy of ms. **AEU**

1399 **Archer**, Violet. I will lift mine eyes. A general anthem for S.A.T.B. and organ. Waterloo, Ont.: Waterloo Music, 1969. 11p. (Waterloo sacred choral library)

Commissioned by the Edmonton Centre of the Royal Canadian College of Organists for the Centennial year.
Text from Psalm 121.

Canadiana, 1970. **AEU**

1400 **Archer**, Violet. In just spring. For medium voice & piano. Music by Violet Archer. Text by e.e. cummings. Toronto: Canadian Music Centre, 1977. 4p.

Photocopy of ms. **AEU**

1401 **Archer**, Violet. Introit and choral prayer. Toronto: BMI Canada, 1963. 7p.

For chorus (SATB) and organ. **AEU**

1402 **Archer**, Violet. Irradiations, No.18. A song for mezzo soprano and pianoforte. Poem, John Gould Fletcher. Music, Violet Archer. Toronto: Canadian Music Centre, 1955. 5p.

Photocopy of ms. **AEU**

1403 **Archer**, Violet. A la claire fontaine. S.A. et piano. Arranges par Violet Archer. Scarborough, Ont.: Berandal Music, 1970. 7p.

For chorus and piano. **AEU**

1404 **Archer**, Violet. Landscapes. S.A.T.B. Poems by T.S. Eliot. Waterloo, Ont.: Waterloo Music, 1973. 1v. (Waterloo secular choral library)

NUC(Music), 1973-77. **AEU**

1405 **Archer**, Violet. Life in a prairie shack. An Alberta folk song. Toronto: Canadian Music Centre, 1966. 2p.

Words from *An Englishman in Alberta*, by H.A. McGusty, *Alberta Historical Review*, Winter, 1966.
Melody, *A life on the ocean wave*, a mid-19th century English tune.
For medium voice and piano.

Photocopy of ms.

1406 **Archer**, Violet. The Mater Admirabilis Chapel. Text by Althea Bass. Toronto: Chanteclair Music, 1972. 14p. (Festival Singers choral series, E.I. 1015)

For chorus (SSA), oboe and harp or piano.

Jarman. **AEU**

1407 **Archer**, Violet. Minute music for small hands. For piano. New York: Peer International, 1959. 3p.

Added imprint stamped on cover: Montreal, Southern Music Pub. Co. (Canada).

Canadiana, 1964. **AEU**

1408 **Archer**, Violet. Moon songs. For mezzo contralto and piano. Texts by Vachell (sic) Lindsay. Toronto: Canadian Music Centre, 1976. 17p.

Written, 1944.

Photocopy of ms. **AEU**

1409 **Archer**, Violet. My hands. A song for contralto and piano. Words by Dorothy Livesay. Toronto: Canadian Music Centre, 1972. 2p.

Photocopy of ms. **AEU**

1410 **Archer**, Violet. O Lord, Thou hast searched me and known me. Anthem for S.A.T.B. and organ. Waterloo, Ont.: Waterloo Music, 1969. 11p. (Waterloo sacred choral library)

Text from Psalm 139.

Canadiana, 1970.

1411 **Archer**, Violet. O sing unto the Lord. For soprano, alto and two trumpets. Waterloo, Ont.: Waterloo Music, 1969. 8p. (Waterloo sacred choral library)

Text from Psalm 96. **AEU**

1412 **Archer**, Violet. Plainsong. A cycle for mezzo soprano and piano. Text by Dorothy Livesay. Toronto: Canadian Music Centre, 1977. 13p.

Photocopy of ms.

AEU.

1413 **Archer**, Violet. Prelude and allegro for violin and piano. Toronto: BMI Canada, 1958. 12p.

Jarman. **AEU**

1414 **Archer**, Violet. Psalm 150. Anthem for mixed chorus or boys' and men's voices. Waterloo, Ont.: Waterloo Music, 1965. 6p. (Waterloo sacred choral library)

With organ accompaniment.

NUC(Music), 1973-77.

1415 **Archer**, Violet. Rondo. For piano. New York: Peer International, 1964. 11p. **AEU**

1416 **Archer**, Violet. Separation. A song for alto or baritone. Toronto: Canadian Music Centre, 1976. 1p.

Words from a 10th century Chinese poem.
With accompaniment for piano.

Photocopy of ms. **AEU**

1417 **Archer**, Violet. Sganarelle. A one act comic opera. Toronto: Berandol Music, 1974. 359p. (Canadian composers facsimile series)

Libretto compiled by Violet Archer from Samuel A. Eliot's free translation of Molière's play Sganarelle, based on that by Philip Moeller.
Photo reprint edition. **AEU**

1418 **Archer**, Violet. Shout with joy. An anthem for S A J B choir and organ. Waterloo, Ont.: Waterloo Music, 1977. 11p.

Text, Psalm 100 from the Living Bible.

Canadiana, 1977. **AEU**

1419 **Archer**, Violet. Someone. Poem by Walter De La Mare. Waterloo, Ont.: Waterloo Music, 1976. 2p.

Composed for medium voice and piano.

Canadiana, 1977. **AEU**

1420 **Archer**, Violet. Sonata. For cello and pianoforte. Toronto: Canadian Music Centre, 1972. score(55p.) and part.

Composed, 1956.

Photocopy of ms. **AEU**

1421 **Archer**, Violet. Sonata for alto saxophone and piano. Toronto: Clark & Cruickshank, 1974. score(43p.) and part.

Facsimile of the composer's manuscript.
Commissioned by the Canadian Broadcasting Corporation for performance by Paul Brodie at the World Saxophone Congress at Toronto, August, 1972.

Canadiana, 1975. **AEU**

1422 **Archer**, Violet. Sonatina for organ. Toronto: G.V. Thompson, 1971. 11p.

Jarman. **AEU**

1423 **Archer**, Violet. Sonatina no.3. Piano solo. Waterloo, Ont.: Waterloo Music, 1979. 12p.

Cover title.

Canadiana, 1979. **OONL**

1424 **Archer**, Violet. Storm. A song for medium voice and piano. Poem by Wildah Morris. Music by Violet Archer. Toronto: Canadian Music Centre, 1955. 3p.

Photocopy of ms. **AEU**

1425 **Archer**, Violet. Suite for solo flute. Toronto: Canadian Music Centre, 1976. 16p.

Photocopy of ms. **AEU**

1426 **Archer**, Violet. Sweet Jesu, King of bliss. S.A. version. London, Ont.: Iroquois Press, 1967. 3p. (Iroquois Press sacred series, 6)

Text: Anonymous 13th century English.
S.A.T.B. version also published 1967, London, Ont., Iroquois Press. **AEU**

1427 **Archer**, Violet. Ten folk songs for four hands, for players young and old. Toronto: BMI Canada, 1955. 2v.

For piano.
Book one contains melodies of French origin, typical of Quebec Book two contains four melodies of English origin, sung in Nova Scotia, and a weather incantation of the Copper Eskimo.

Jarman. **AEU**

1428 **Archer**, Violet. Theme and variations for piano. Waterloo, Ont.: Waterloo Music, 1964. 5p.

Canadiana, 1965. **AEU**

1429 **Archer**, Violet. Three duets, for two violins. New York: Peer International, 1960. 7p.

Jarman. **AEU**

1430 **Archer**, Violet. Three folk songs of old Manitoba. Accompaniments by Violet Archer. Toronto: Canadian Music Centre, 1966. 5p.

Melodies taken from *Songs of old Manitoba*, chosen and edited by Margaret Arnett MacLeod.
For medium voice and piano.
Photocopy of ms. **AEU**

1431 **Archer**, Violet. Three French-Canadian folk songs for mixed chorus. English translations by Carolyn Osborne. Choral settings by Violet Archer. Toronto: BMI Canada, 1962. 19p.

At head of title: To the Montreal Bach Choir.
Text in French and English.

Jarman.

1432 **Archer**, Violet. Three miniatures for piano. Waterloo, Ont.: Waterloo Music, 1965. 4p.

NUC(Music), 1963-67. **AEU**

1433 **Archer**, Violet. Three sketches for orchestra. Toronto: BMI Canada, 1966. 41p.

Specially written for the Montreal Junior Symphony Orchestra for its premiere performance in the spring of 1961.

NUC(Music), 1963-67. **AEU**

1434 **Archer**, Violet. Trio no. 2, for piano, violin and cello. Waterloo, Ont.: Waterloo Music, 1977. score (64p.) and 2 parts.

Cover title.
Photocopy of ms.

Canadiana, 1978. **AEU**

1435 **Archer**, Violet. The twenty-third Psalm, for medium voice and piano. Toronto: BMI Canada, 1954. 7p.

Jarman. **AEU**

1436 **Archer**, Violet. Two chorale preludes for organ, with Hammond organ registration. New York: Peer International, 1962. 5p.

Jarman. **AEU**

1437 **Archer**, Violet. Two songs. For soprano voice and B-flat clarinet. Poems by William Blake. Music by Violet Archer. Toronto: Canadian Music Centre, 1958. 5p.

Photocopy of ms.

AEU

1438 **Brown**, Gary William. The goat in the boat, by Uncle Gary. All made possible through the help and assistance of Morris D. Shields. Illustrated by Ilene. Cardston: Local Press, 1967. (1v.)

Canadiana, 1967.

1439 **Coe**, Bob. The blue and gold. Edmonton: Bob Coe, 1964. 4p.

Lyrics by Connie Coe, melody by Bob Coe.
Song for Alberta College.

Canadiana, 1964.

OONL

1440 **Dearing**, Kathleen. Favorite Gospel hymns in all major keys, transcribed for the piano. 3d print. rev. Three Hills: Prairie Press, 1959. 1v.

Canadiana, 1960.

ATP

1441 **Dearing**, Kathleen. From hymnbook to keyboard. Three Hills: Prairie Press, 1957. 5v.

Contents: Book 1. Note reading, tetrachord tunes, interval studies, cord construction and sight reading Book 2. Analytical approach to simple hymn playing Book 3. Hymn improvisation in lyric style featuring scale and arpeggio patterns 4. Hymn improvisation in choral style, featuring creative harmony, chord technic and piano variations Book 5. Amplified tonality, octive technic, chords with octave stretch, broken-chord figuration and modulation.

Canadiana, 1960.

ATP

1442 **Dearing**, Kathleen. Hymn styling for alert adults. Hymn miniatures with creative techniques. Three Hills: Prairie Bible Institute, 1975. 29p.

Cover subtitle *Piano miniatures with creative techniques*.
For piano, some hymns with words.

Canadiana, 1977.

OONL

1443 **Dearing**, Kathleen. Prairie hymn originals from our piano studios. Varied ideas of twelve pianists. Compiled and edited by Kathleen Dearing. Three Hills: Prairie Bible Institute, 1962. 1v.

ATP

1444 **Demarest**, Anne Shannon. Banff panorama, a symphonic suite. Transcribed for orchestra by John Paul. Springfield, Mo.: Ashton Publishing, 1973. 51p.

Originally for piano.

Canadiana, 1974.

OONL

1445 **Grier**, Faye. How about me? Fort Saskatchewan: Faye Grier, 1958. 1 sheet.
For voice and guitar.
Canadiana, 1958. **OONL**

1446 Hutterite Brethren. Gesang-Buchlein. Gesammelt aus den Liedern der Hutterischen Bruder. Mit einen Anhang Schoner Lieder, die Bisher nur in Abschriften Vorhanden Waren, aber sehr wichtig sind. McLeod: Riverside Colony, 1955. 136p.
Glenbow. **ACG**

1447 **Iaremenko**, Serhil. Saskachevanka. Ta inshi pisni. Edmonton: Slavuta Publishers, 1977. 32p.
Canadiana 1979. **OONL**

1448 **Inman**, Lester. Beautiful Red Deer. One step. New Westminster, B.C.: Douds Music Publishers, 1958. 3p.
For voice, piano and guitar.
Canadiana, 1958. **OONL**

1449 **Inman**, Lester. Calgary stampede chuckwagon roundup. New Westminster, B.C.: Douds Music, 1959. 3p.
Words and music by Lester Inman.
For voice, piano and guitar.
Canadiana, 1961. **OONL**

1450 **Irving**, Will. Hymns for piano accordion. Three Hills: Prairie Press, 1958. 4, 24p.
Canadiana, 1960. **OONL**

1451 **Jameson**, George Irwin. The trail riders song. Byemoor: George Jameson, 1963. 2p.
Words and music by George Jameson. For voice and guitar.
Canadiana, 1964. **OONL**

1452 **Jones**, Ormond. Please put the music back. College Heights: 1978. 3p.
Words by Gerry Tetz, music by Ormond Jones. For low voice and piano.
Canadiana, 1979. **OONL**

1453 **Lehner**, Cass. The bride & groom waltz. Words by Lily Lehner. Calgary: C. Lehner, 1973. 3p.
For voice and piano, with chord symbols.
Canadiana, 1974. **OONL**

1454 **MacCrimmon**, Iain. Music for the great highland bagpipe. Edmonton: D.G. Saul, 1975. (v.)

Cover title.

Canadiana, 1979. **OONL**

1455 **Malsbary**, Dwight R. An hour at the piano with well-loved hymns. Concert transcriptions. Rev. ed. Three Hills: Prairie Press, 1956. 47p.

Titles in English and Korean.

Canadiana, 1960. **ATP**

1456 **Olson**, Raymond C. Sacred solos for accordion. Arranged by Raymond C. Olson. Three Hills: Prairie Bible Institute, 1974. 16p. **ATP**

1457 **Parker**, William Wilder McKinley. Young Canada. A song. Toronto: Whaley Royce for the composer, n.d. 3p. **AEU**

1458 Prairie Bible Institute. Prairie hymns that live. Three Hills: Prairie Press, 1954. 106p.

Canadiana, 1960. **ATP**

1459 Prairie Bible Institute. Transcripts for the accordion. Hymn variations in medium grade. Three Hills: Prairie Press, 1956. 2, 50, 1p.

Canadiana, 1960. **OONL**

1460 **Price**, Roy. Ye men of Calgary. Toronto: BMI Canada, 1957. 4p.

Song for voice and piano. Words and music by Roy Price.

Canadiana, 1957. **OONL**

1461 **Rausch**, Paul A. Sacred solos for clarinet and piano. Three Hills: Prairie Bible Institute, 1974. 38p.

Canadiana, 1975. **OONL**

1462 **Rickey**, Catherine Jessie. Jeannie. High River: Jesse Music Publications, 1960. 2p.

For voice, piano and guitar.

Canadiana, 1960. **OONL**

1463 **Sinclare**, Colin. My sister. Calgary: Colin Sinclare, 1964. 3p.

Words and music by Colin Sinclare. For voice, guitar and piano.

Canadiana, 1964. **OONL**

1464 **Snyder**, Robert Carl. Gospel duets for the trumpet, with piano accompaniment. Three Hills: Prairie Bible Institute, 1959. 4, 32p.

Canadiana, 1960. **ATP**

1465 **Snyder**, Robert Carl. Gospel songs for the trumpet trio, with piano accompaniment. Three Hills: Prairie Bible Institute, 1959. 29p.

Score for three trumpets.

Canadiana, 1960. **ATP**

1466 **Snyder**, Robert Carl. Specials for brass, with piano accompaniment. Three Hills: Prairie Bible Institute, 1964. 3v.

Canadiana, 1965. **ATP**

1467 **Stevenson**, Scotty. Alberta. New Westminster, B.C.: Empire Music Publishers, 1955. 2p.

Words and music by Scotty Stevenson. For voice and piano.

Canadiana, 1955. **OONL**

1468 **Weikum**, Edward. Don't call on me. Bloomsbury: Edward Weikum, 1959. 4p.

For voice, piano and guitar.

Canadiana, 1960. **OONL**

1469 **Weikum**, Edward. On the hill. Bloomsbury: Edward Weikum, 1959. 2p.

For voice, piano and guitar.

Canadiana, 1960. **OONL**

Education: General Works

1470 **Alberta Conference on Television and Education**, University of Alberta, 1960. Education through television. A summary of proceedings at the Alberta conference on television and education. Edmonton: Department of Extension, University of Alberta, 1960. 38 leaves.

Duplicated.

Canadiana, 1964.

1471 Alberta School Trustees' Association. Study guide for the Commission of Educational Planning report entitled "A choice of futures". Edmonton: Alberta School Trustees' Association, 1972. iii, 59p.

Canadiana, 1975.

1472 Alberta Teachers' Association. The Cameron Commission - two years after. Edmonton: Alberta Teachers' Association, 1960. iv, 68, 71p. tables. (Alberta Teachers' Association. Series on problems in education, 40)

Report on actions taken by various agencies to implement the report of the Royal Commission on Education in Alberta, 1959.

Canadiana, 1962. **AEU**

1473 Alberta Teachers' Association. Committee on Association Services. Service for the seventies. Report. Edmonton: Alberta Teachers' Association, 1970. iii, 115p. ill.

Canadiana, 1971. **AEU**

1474 **Atherton**, Peter John. Quality education - what price? Edmonton: Alberta Teachers' Association, 1969. v, 57p. (Alberta Teachers' Association. Research monograph, 16)

Canadiana, 1970.

1475 **Bilash**, O. Why bilingual education? The English-Ukrainian bilingual program. Edmonton: Canadian Institute of Ukrainian Studies, 1978. 19p. ill.

Cover title.

Canadiana, 1979.

1476 Bilingualism, biculturalism & education. Proceedings from the Conference at Collége Universitaire Saint-Jean, The University of Alberta. Edited by Stephen T. Carey. Edmonton: University of Alberta, 1974. 260p.

AECSJ

1477 **Boughen**, Robert Arthur. A study of educational finance in Alberta, 1958-1971. Ottawa: National Library of Canada, 1974. x, 115 leaves. (Canadian theses on microfiche, 19197)

Thesis (M.Ed.), University of Manitoba, 1974.
Microfiche of typescript.

Canadiana, 1975.

1478 **Caldwell**, Geoffrey Thomas. Educational values in Alberta. A comparison of the orientations of the Department of Education and interest groups. Ottawa: National Library of Canada, 1968. xii, 141 leaves.

Thesis (M.A.), University of Calgary, 1968.
Microfilm of typescript.

Canadiana, 1968. **ACU**

1479 Calgary Association for Retarded Children. Proposed school for Calgary's retarded children. Calgary: Calgary Association for Retarded Children, 1955. 84p. ill.

Glenbow. **ACG**

1480 Calgary Public School Board. Elementary School Program Commission. Direction for education. Report of the Elementary School Program Commisssion of the Public School Board, Calgary, 1965-1967. Calgary: Calgary Public School Board, 1967. 2v. ill.

Edited by E.G. Calbeck.

Canadiana, 1971. **AEU**

1481 **Cameron**, Donald. Education and government. Address given to the 50th anniversary dinner of the Alberta Association of Municipal Districts. Edmonton: Chieftain Petroleum and Tidal Petroleum Corporation, 1958. 22, 1p. ill.

Canadiana, 1961. **ACG**

1482 **Chapman**, Robin James. The nature and role of Regional Offices of Education in the Province of Alberta. Ottawa: National Library of Canada, 1972. ix, 76, 25 leaves. ill. (Canadian theses on microfilm, 13327)

Thesis (M.Ed.), University of Alberta, 1972.
Microfilm of typescript.

Canadiana, 1973.

1483 **Clarke**, Stanley Charles Tremayne. The Cameron Commission ten years after. s.l.: s.n., 1968. 14 leaves.

Text of a banquet address, April 16, 1968. **AEU**

1484 Collège Universitaire Saint-Jean. Ecole bilingue ou unilingue pour les franco-albertains. Premier rapport descriptif. Directeur et coordonnateur du projet, Dr. Ousmane Silla. Recherche interdisciplinaire menée par un groupe de professeurs et d'étudiants. Edmonton: Collège Universitaire Saint-Jean, 1974. 2v.

Duplicated. Also microfilm edition.
Subventionée par le Secrétariat d'Etat, Ottawa. **AECSJ**

1485 The community school, a focus on living. A report presented to the Edmonton Public School Board. Edmonton: Edmonton Public School Board Extension Services, 1971. iv, 69 leaves.

Canadiana, 1975. **AEU**

1486 **Davies**, Paula Bernice. A political analysis of public participation in educational policy in Alberta. Calgary: National Library of Canada, 1976. viii, 137 leaves. (Canadian theses on microfilm, 28499)

Thesis (M.A.), University of Calgary, 1976.
Microfiche of typescript.

Canadiana, 1977.

1487 **DeGama**, Jerrold William. The response of public school supporters to a proposed bilingual elementary school in the city of Calgary. Ottawa: National Library of Canada, 1971. xiii, 159 leaves. ill. (Canadian theses on microfilm, 10062)

Thesis (M.Ed.), University of Calgary, 1971.
Microfilm of typescript.

1488 **Downey**, Lawrence William Lorne. The small high school in Alberta. A report of an investigation. Edmonton: Alberta School Trustees' Association, 1965. 77p.

Canadiana, 1969. **AEU**

1489 **Giles**, Thomas Edward. Educational administration in Canada. Calgary: Detselig Enterprises, 1974. 240p. ill.

Also, 2d ed., 1978. 248p.

Canadiana, 1979. **AEU**

1490 **Hanson**, Eric John. Financing education in Alberta. A study of provincial-municipal requirements, with special reference to education. Edmonton: Alberta Teachers' Association, 1964. vii, 43p. (Alberta Teachers' Association. Research monograph, 8)

2d. ed., 1966 (Alberta Teachers' Association. Research monograph, 11), 81 p. 3d ed., 1969 (Alberta Teachers' Association. Reseach monograph, 14), 52p. 4th ed., 1972 (Alberta Teachers' Association. Research monograph, 19), 59p. 5th ed., 1976 (Alberta Teachers' Association. Research monograph, 24), 92p.

Canadiana, 1964. **AEU**

1491 **Hardy**, William George. Education in Alberta. Calgary: s.n., 1954. 46p.

Originally published as a series of six articles in the *Calgary Herald*, the *Edmonton Journal*, the *Lethbridge Herald* and the *Medicine Hat News*.

Canadiana, 1955. **ACG**

1492 **Holtslander**, Dale. School districts of Alberta. A listing of all Protestant public schools organized in the Province of Alberta. s.n.: s.l., n.d. 1v. ill.

Duplicated. **AEA**

1493 **Humphreys**, Ramona Cecil Marguerite. Legally blind youth of Alberta. A study of their opinions on some of their formal and informal learning experiences. Ottawa: National Library of Canada, 1972. (1v.) (Canadian theses on microfilm, 11320)

Thesis (M.S.W.), University of Calgary, 1972.
Microfilm of typescript.

Canadiana, 1972. **OONL**

1494 Indian Association of Alberta. Alberta Indian Education Center. Edmonton: Indian Association of Alberta, 1970. 1v.

Duplicated.
Papers relating to the development and programs of the proposed center.

Glenbow. **ACG**

1495 **Jenkins**, David Danner. Realism and Alberta's secondary aims. Ottawa: National Library of Canada, 1967. 95 leaves.

Thesis (M.Ed.), University of Calgary, 1967.
Microfiche of typescript.
On secondary education.

Canadiana, 1968.

1496 **Johnson**, Keith. Indian Association of Alberta. Formative educational concerns. Ottawa: National Library of Canada, 1977. viii, 188 leaves. (Canadian theses on microfiche, 34384)

Thesis (M.Ed.), University of Alberta, 1977.
Microfiche of typescript.

Canadiana, 1979.

1497 **Knill**, William Douglas. Hutterian education. A descriptive study based on the Hutterian colonies within Warner County No. 5, Alberta, Canada. Missoula, Mont.: Montana State University, 1958. 203 leaves.

Thesis (M.A.), Montana State University, 1958.
Typescript. **AEU**

1498 **Macklin**, Irvin Victor. Life is more than meat. Should we have a little spiritual or all secular education in Protestant schools of Canada? Grande Prairie: I.V. Macklin, 1960. 52p.

Glenbow. ACG

1499 **Maerz**, Leslie R. Religious education in Alberta public schools. Ottawa: National Library of Canada, 1974. viii, 110 leaves. (Canadian theses on microfiche, 19805)

Thesis (M.A.), University of Calgary, 1974.
Microfiche of typescript.

Canadiana, 1975.

1500 **Manning**, William George. Toward a breakthrough in education. A systems approach to educational productivity. Edmonton: M & M Systems Research, 1970. 46p.

Canadiana, 1975. AEU

1501 **Miller**, Marjorie. The printed word. The growth of sentences for deaf children. Edmonton: Institute of Applied Art, 1958. x, 51p. ill.

Canadiana, 1961.

1502 **Proudfoot**, Alexander J. Intercultural education. A study of the effects of the employment of native teacher aides as cross culture bridges between Indian students and non-Indian teachers. Calgary: Faculty of Education, University of Calgary, 1971. 108 leaves. ill.

Presented to the Department of Indian Affairs and Northern Development.

Canadiana, 1977.

1503 **Ross**, Leonard W. Educational television. Calgary: Dome Petroleum, 1968. 34p. ill.

Canadiana, 1970.

1504 **Schwartz**, Arthur Mark. Patterns of influence in the collective bargaining system of Alberta Teachers' Association. Ottawa: National Library of Canada, 1971. xvi, 193 leaves. ill.

Thesis (M.Ed.), University of Calgary, 1971.
Microfilm of typescript.

Canadiana, 1972.

1505 **Shapiro**, David. Three aspects of the economics of education in Alberta. Ann Arbor, Mich.: University Microfilms, 1972. iv, 109 leaves. ill.

Thesis (Ph.D.), Princeton University, 1972.
Microfilm of typescript.

Canadiana, 1973.

1506 **Smyth**, John M. New trends in high school administration. Calgary: Dome Petroleum, 1969. 53p. ill. (Dome Petroleum Teaching Fellowship, 1969)

Canadiana, 1973.

1507 **Stringham**, Bryant L. The School Act, 1970. A case study of public policymaking in education. Ottawa: National Library of Canada, 1974. xii, 223 leaves. (Canadian theses on microfiche, 21986)

Thesis (Ph.D.), University of Alberta, 1974.
Microfiche of typecript.

U of A theses. **AEU**

1508 **Switlick**, Lillian. An exploratory study of factors affecting responses of Cree students to literary selections. Ottawa: National Library of Canada, 1974. xiv, 279 leaves. (Canadian theses on microfiche, 21514)

Thesis (M.Ed.), University of Alberta, 1974.
Microfiche of typescript.

Canadiana, 1975. **AEU**

1509 **Targett**, Reginald Bryan. The education of exceptional children in the Calgary public school system, 1965. Ottawa: National Library of Canada, 1971. x, 215 leaves. ill. (Canadian theses on microfilm, 08492)

Thesis (M.Ed), University of Alberta at Calgary, 1965.
Microfilm of typescript.

Canadiana, 1972.

1510 **Thierman**, Lois Mary. Student reflections. Edmonton: La Survivance Press, 1969. xii, 243p.

An account of student and teaching experiences, with essays written as a graduate student.

Canadiana, 1970. **AEU**

1511 **Trussler**, Norma Erdine. Educational programs for Indian adults in southern Alberta. Ottawa: National Library of Canada, 1971. ix, 136 leaves. ill. (Canadian theses on microfilm, 10183)

Thesis (M.Ed.), University of Calgary, 1971.
Microfilm of typescript.

Canadiana, 1972. **OONL**

1512 **Verhagen**, Matthew A. Teachers' evaluation of religious education in the elementary schools of the Calgary Roman Catholic Separate Schools District, No. 1. Ottawa: National Library of Canada, 1974. x, 98 leaves. (Canadian theses on microfiche, 21364)

Thesis (M.A.), University of Calgary, 1974.
Microfiche of typescript.

Canadiana, 1975. **OONL**

1513 **Wilcer**, Armin. A study of the degree of implementation of recommendations pertaining to the control of education made by the Royal Commisssion on Education in Alberta, 1959. Edmonton: University of Alberta, 1959. xiii, 141p.

Thesis (M.Ed.), University of Alberta, 1970.
Typescript.

Canadian theses. **AEU**

1514 **Wilson**, LeRoy John. Perren Baker and the United Farmers of Alberta. Educational principles and policies of an agrarian government. Edmonton: University of Alberta, 1970. vii, 144p.

Thesis (M.Ed.), University of Alberta, 1970.
Typescript.

Canadian theses. **AEU**

1515 **Worth**, Walter H. Before six. A report on the Alberta Childhood Education Study. Edmonton: Alberta School Trustees' Association, 1966. 87p.

Canadiana, 1969.

School History

1516 Alberta Teachers' Association. Athabasca Local. A history of the schools of the county of Athabasca. Edited by George S. Opryshko. Athabasca: Alberta Teachers' Association, Athabasca Local, 1967. 144p. ill.

Cover title *Clover & wild strawberries*.

Glenbow. **ACG**

1517 Alberta Teachers' Association. Red Deer District Local. Schools of the parkland, N.W.T. 1886 - Alberta, 1967. Red Deer: Alberta Teachers' Association, Red Deer District Local, 1967. 326p. ill.

"Centennial project".

Glenbow. **ACG**

1518 **Aoki**, Testsuo. The development of the Lethbridge School District No. 51 to 1960. Edmonton: University of Alberta, 1963. vii, 219 leaves.

Thesis (M.Ed.), University of Alberta, 1963.
Typescript.

Canadian theses. **AEU**

1519 Armena Home and School Association. Dear old golden rule days, 1898-1967. Armena: Armena Home and School Association, 1967. 23 leaves. ill.

Duplicated.

A centennial project of the Armena Home and School Association.
Histories of the schools in the Armena district.

Glenbow. **ACG**

1520 **Barry**, Walter W. Anecdotal history of Calgary Separate Schools. Calgary: s.n., 1967. (5), 92 leaves. ill.

Prepared by Anecdotal History Committee consisting of Walter Barry, Mary Inamasu and Albert Standell.

Glenbow. **ACG**

1521 Calgary. Crescent Heights High School. 50th anniversary, Crescent Heights High School, 1915-1965. Calgary: Crescent Heights High School, 1965. 64p. ill.

Duplicated.
On cover: Golden anniversary.

Canadiana, 1965. **ACG**

1522 Calgary. Glengarry Elementary School. Glengarry golden anniversary, 1920-1970. Calgary: Glengarry Elementary School, 1970. 28p. ill.

Glenbow. **ACG**

1523 Calgary. King Edward School. Grade IX MPH Creative Writing Class of 1968-69. Long live the king. The story of 'King Edward'. Calgary: King Edward School, 1969. 79p. ill.

Glenbow. **ACG**

1524 Calgary. Stanley Jones School. Stanley Jones School anniversary, 1913-1973. R.G. Blummell, Principal and Co-ordinator. Calgary: Stanley Jones School, 1973. 41p.

Duplicated. **ACG**

1525 **Carr**, Kevin James. A historical survey of education in early Blackfoot Indian culture and its implication for Indian schools. Edmonton: University of Alberta, 1968. xiv, 254 leaves.

Thesis (M.Ed.), University of Alberta, 1968.
Typescript.

Canadian theses. **AEU**

1526 **Cashman**, Anthony Walcott. Edmonton's Catholic schools. A success story. Edmonton: Edmonton Roman Catholic Separate School District No.7, 1977. 242p. ill.

Ceessa. **AEA**

1527 **Chalmers**, John West. Education behind the buckskin curtain. A history of native education in Canada. Edmonton: University of Alberta Bookstore, 1974. 351p.

Canadiana, 1976. **ACG**

1528 **Chalmers**, John West. Gladly would he teach. A biography of Milton Ezra LaZerte. Edmonton: Alberta Teachers' Association Educational Trust, 1978. xv, 197p. ill.

Canadiana, 1979. **AEA**

1529 **Chalmers**, John West. Schools of the Foothills Province. The story of public education in Alberta. Illustrations by G. Balbar. Maps by R. Anderson. Toronto: University of Toronto Press, 1967. 489p. ill.

Published for the Alberta Teachers' Association.

Glenbow. **ACG**

1530 **Chalmers**, John West. Teachers of the Foothills Province. The story of the Alberta Teachers' Association. Toronto: University of Toronto Press, 1968. 344p. ill.

Published for the Alberta Teachers' Association.

Glenbow. **ACG**

1531 **Charyk**, John Constantine. The little white schoolhouse. Saskatoon: Western Producer Prairie Books, 1970-1977. 3v. ill.

v.1 reprinted, 1977, as part of the Alberta Heritage Learning Resources Project, 1979, (Alberta literature for senior students.
Pioneer and school life in western Canada.
Contents: v1. The little white school house. 1968 v2. Pulse of the community. 1970 v3. Those bittersweet schooldays. 1977.

Canadiana, 1978. **AEA**

1532 Clear Vista. An historical review. Wetaskiwin: Clear Vista School, 1967. 40 leaves. ill.

Cover title. Duplicated.
A history of Clear Vista and other Wetaskiwin district schools, with photographs of current students. **AEA**

1533 **Cook**, Dean. A history of educational institutions in Mormon communities of southern Alberta, 1954. Edmonton: University of Alberta, 1958. 168 leaves.

Thesis (M.Ed.), University of Alberta, 1958.
Typescript.

Canadian theses. **AEU**

1534 **Cook**, Janet McLaren. Through cloud and sunshine. Lethbridge: Southern Printing, 1975. 96p. ill.

Cover title.
Reminiscences, including school teaching in Hanna, Alberta.

Canadiana, 1976. **AEA**

1535 **Cook**, Maisie Emery. Memories of a pioneer schoolteacher. Edmonton: M.E. Cook, 1968. (4), 42p. ill.

Cover title.

Glenbow. ACG

1536 **Corbett**, Edward Annand. We have with us tonight. Introduction by Leonard Brockington. Toronto: Ryerson Press, 1957. xviii, 222p.

Reminiscences of an educator.

Canadiana, 1958. AEA

1537 **Daniels**, Leroi Allister. The history of education in Calgary. Seattle, Wash: University of Washington, 1954. 215 leaves.

Thesis (M.A.), University of Washington, 1954.
Typescript.

Artibise. AEU

1538 Delta Kappa Gamma Society. Zeta Province. Alpha Chapter. Sketches of women pioneer educators of Edmonton. Edmonton: Zeta Province, Alpha Chapter, Delta Kappa Gamma Society, 1972. 50 leaves.

Duplicated.

Canadiana, 1974. AEA

1539 Edmonton. Ross Sheppard Composite High School. A reunion, 1957-1978. Edmonton: Ross Sheppard Composite High School, 1978. 28p. ill.

Cover title. AEA

1540 Edmonton. Rutherford School. Rutherford school, 1910-1967, centennial open house. Edmonton: Rutherford School, 1967. 15 leaves.

Glenbow. ACG

1541 Edmonton. Spruce Avenue School. A historical publication, Spruce Ave. School, 1918-1978. Edmonton: Spruce Avenue School Reunion Committee, 1978. 1v. (unpaged) ill.

Cover title. Duplicated. AEA

1542 **Fowlie**, Doris. History of Bindloss School District 3603, 1919-1969. Medicine Hat: Val Marshall Printing, 1969. 160p. ill.

Cover title.
Compiled by Doris Fowlie.
Half title *ABC's down through the years*.

Glenbow. ACG

1543 From slate pencil to instant ink. Calgary's public, separate, and private schools. Accounts by Calgary authors. Calgary: Century Calgary Publications, 1975. iv, 168p. ill.

Also published as part of *Young people of all ages*, which was issued as v.3 of the Century Calgary Historical Series.

Canadiana, 1977. AEA

1544 Genesee. St. John's School of Alberta. St. John's of Alberta. The story of a school. Edmonton: Company of the Cross, 1968. 23p. ill.

Ceessa. **AEA**

1545 **Groves**, Cyril. The growth and development of the English Council of the Alberta Teachers' Association. Ottawa: National Library of Canada, 1974. x, 188 leaves. (Canadian theses on microfiche, 21280)

Thesis (M.A.), University of Calgary, 1974.
Microfiche of typescript.

Canadiana, 1975.

1546 **Grywalski**, Stanley. A history of technical-vocational education in the secondary schools of Alberta, 1900-1969. Ann Arbor, Mich.: University Microfilms, 1973. vi, 476p. ill.

Thesis (Ph.D.), University of Oregon, 1973.
Microfilm of typescript.

Canadiana, 1974. **OONL**

1547 **Hochstein**, Lucille Agatha. Roman Catholic separate and public schools in Alberta. Edmonton: University of Alberta, 1954. ix, 170p. ill.

Thesis (M.Ed.), University of Alberta, 1954.
Typescript.
A history of the schools from 1885 to 1953.

Canadian theses. **AEU**

1548 **Hodgson**, Ernest Daniel. The nature and purposes of the public school in Northwest Territories (1885-1905) and Alberta (1905-1963). Edmonton: University of Alberta, 1964. xiii, 403 leaves.

Thesis (Ph.D.), University of Alberta, 1964.
Typescript.

Canadian theses. **AEU**

1549 **Houghton**, John Reginald. The Calgary public school system, 1939-1969. A history of growth and development. Ottawa: National Library of Canada, 1971. x, 221 leaves. ill. (Canadian theses on microfilm, 10090)

Thesis (M.Ed.), University of Calgary, 1971.
Microfilm of typescript.

Canadiana, 1972. **AEU**

1550 **Innes**, Duncan R. Strathcona High School, 1907-1967 in retrospect. Centennial edition. Edmonton: Strathcona High School, 1967. 28p. ill.

Accompanied by a pamphlet of 16 leaves containing lists of cup and trophy winners, scholarships and awards and partial index of prominent alumni.
Printed by Commercial Printers, Edmonton.

Glenbow. **ACG**

1551 **James**, Edward Llewellyn. An historical survey of education in the Strathmore area of Alberta, 1900-1958. Edmonton: University of Alberta, 1963. xvi, 154 leaves.

Thesis (M.Ed.), University of Alberta, 1963.
Typescript.

Canadian theses. **AEU**

1552 **Jones**, David C. Shaping the schools of the Canadian West. Edited by David C. Jones, Nancy M. Sheehan, Robert M. Stamp. Calgary: Detselig Enterprises, 1979. viii, 256p.

Essays on the history of education in Western Canada. **AEU**

1553 **Kezar**, J. Inkwells and school bells. History of Mayerthorpe and area school districts. Mayerthorpe: Mayerthorpe School, 1977. 124, 6p. ill.

Cover title.
Compiled by J. Kezar, A. Miner and R. Barker. Printed by Allied Printing and Publishing, Edmonton. **AEA**

1554 **Kozak**, Kathryn. Education and the Blackfoot, 1870-1900. Edmonton: University of Alberta, 1971. 180 leaves.

Thesis (M.A.), University of Alberta, 1971.
Typescript.

Canadian theses. **AEU**

1555 **LaFleur**, Phyllis Maria Elena. Three Alberta teachers. Lives and thoughts. Ottawa: National Library of Canada, 1977. x, 246 leaves. (Canadian theses on microfiche, 34402)

Thesis (M.Ed.), University of Alberta, 1977.
Microfiche of typescript.
Biographies of Earl W. Buxton, Agnes Lynass and Thomas F. Rieger.

U of A Theses. **AEU**

1556 Lethbridge Junior College. Past, present, and future of the Lethbridge Junior College. Lethbridge: Lethbridge Junior College, 1965. 37 (6)p.

Dew. **AEU**

1557 **Lupul**, Manoly Robert. Relations in education between the state and the Roman Catholic Church in the Canadian Northwest, with special reference to the provisional district of Alberta, from 1880 to 1905. Cambridge, Mass.: Harvard University, 1963. 2v.

Thesis (Ph.D), Harvard University, 1963.
Typescript. **AEU**

1558 **Lupul**, Manoly Robert. The Roman Catholic Church and the north-west school question. A study in church-state relations in western Canada, 1875-1905. Toronto: University of Toronto Press, 1974. 292p.

CBIP, 1979. **AEU**

1559 **Lyseng**, Mary J. The history of educational radio in Alberta. Ottawa: National Library of Canada, 1978. xiv, 383 leaves & 6 audio cassettes. ill. (Canadian theses on microfiche, 36426)

Thesis (M.Ed.), University of Alberta, 1978.
Microfiche of typescript.

Canadiana, 1979. **AEU**

1560 **Martin**, John Julius. The history of Severn Creek School No.852 established June 9th, 1903. Rosebud: John J. Martin, 1974. 20p. ill.

Cover title.
Printed by Big Country News, Drumheller.

Ceessa. **AEA**

1561 **McCall**, Ralph Lewis. A history of the rural high school in Alberta. Edmonton: University of Alberta, 1956. v, 86 leaves.

Thesis (M.Ed.), University of Alberta, 1956.
Typescript.

Canadian theses. **AEU**

1562 **McDougall**, William Dewar. The first forty years of the Education Society of Edmonton, 1927-1967. Edmonton: Education Society of Edmonton, 1967. 71 leaves.

Centennial project of the Education Society of Edmonton. **AEU**

1563 **McKay**, Doreen P. (Hull). Forty years on. The story of Kathryn High School, 1927-1967. Kathryn: Kathyrn High School, 1968. 40, (6) leaves. ill.

Glenbow. **ACG**

1564 **McNally**, George Frederick. G. Fred. The story of G. Fred McNally. Recorded by H.T. Coutts and B.E. Walker. Don Mills, Ont.: J.M. Dent & Sons (Canada), 1964. x, 118p. ill.

Autobiography of an Alberta educator. **AEA**

1565 **Morris**, Anne Elizabeth (Peyton). Alberta school districts in pioneer days. Calgary: A.E. Morris, 1964. 12p.

Cover title.
Reminiscences of teaching in the Cereal, Peyton and Chilmark School Districts.

Glenbow. **ACG**

1566 **Myrehaug**, Donald Melker. M.E. Lazerte. Contributions to teacher education in Alberta. Ottawa: National Library of Canada, 1972. 218 leaves. (Canadian theses on microfilm, 13498)

Thesis (M.Ed.), University of Alberta, 1972.
Microfilm of typescript.

Canadiana, 1973. **AEU**

1567 **Nussbaumer**, Margaret. The Worth Report and developments in Alberta's post-secondary policies and structures, 1968 to 1976. Ottawa: National Library of Canada, 1977. xi, 254 leaves. ill. (Canadian theses on microfiche, 34450)

Thesis (Ph.D.), University of Alberta, 1977.
Microfiche of typescript.

Canadiana, 1979. **AEU**

1568 **Oviatt**, Barrie Connolly. The papers of William Aberhart as Minister of Education, 1935-1943. Edmonton: University of Alberta, 1971. vi, 149 leaves.

Thesis (M.Ed.), University of Alberta, 1971.
Typescript.

Canadian theses. **AEU**

1569 **Oviatt**, Patricia Elaine. The educational contributions of H.C. Newland. Edmonton: University of Alberta, 1970. viii, 187 leaves.

Thesis (M.Ed.), University of Alberta, 1970.
Typescript.

Canadian theses. **AEU**

1570 **Paquette**, Mary Elizabeth. The environment of language. An examination of the work of James Britton in the light of the Alberta high school English curriculum. Ottawa: National Library of Canada, 1972. vii, 101 leaves. (Canadian theses on microfilm, 14021)

Thesis (M.Ed.), University of Calgary, 1972.
Microfilm of typescript.

Canadiana, 1973. **OONL**

1571 **Patterson**, Robert Steven. The establishment of progressive education in Alberta. Ann Arbor, Mich.: University Microfilms, 1968. 4, iv, 189 leaves.

Thesis (Ph.D.), Michigan State University, 1968.
Microfilm of typescript.
Covers the period, 1925-1940.

Canadiana, 1970. **AEU**

1572 **Patterson**, Robert Steven. F.W.G. Haultain and education in the early west. Edmonton: University of Alberta, 1961. ix, 124 leaves.

Thesis (M.Ed.), University of Alberta, 1961.
Typescript.

Canadian theses. **AEU**

1573 **Pengelly**, John R. Mirror, 1913-1966. A short history of the school districts of Ellice, Gadsby Lake, George, Hickling, Lake Bend, Mirror, Nebraska, Ripley, Rutherford, Tees, also of Mirror and the London Daily Mirror. Commemorating the life of Mirror High School, 1913-1966. Calgary: Northwest Printing and Lithography, 1966. 30p. ill.

First published as part of the 1966 *Mirror High School Yearbook*. **AEU**

1574 Prairie Park School District No.1582. Compiled by former Prairie Park students. Sedgewick: Community Press, 1976. 19p. ill.

Cover title. Duplicated.
History of the school from 1906 to 1948. **AEA**

1575 **Race**, Cecil L. Compulsory schooling in Alberta, 1888-1942. Ottawa: National Library of Canada, 1978. xv, 229 leaves (Canadian theses on microfiche, 40286)

Thesis (M.Ed.), University of Alberta, 1978.
Microfiche of typescript.

U of A theses. **AEU**

1576 **Ronaghan**, Allen. Morrison, S.D. No. 1639. A history of Morrison School District. Paradise Valley: A. Ronaghan, 1967. (56) leaves. ill.

Published on the occasion of the 60th anniversary of school opening in November of 1907.

Glenbow. **ACG**

1577 **Rusak**, Stephen Thaddeus. Relations in education between Bishop Legal and the Alberta Liberal government, 1905-1920. Edmonton: University of Alberta, 1966. vi, 113 leaves.

Thesis (M.Ed.), University of Alberta, 1966.
Typescript.

Canadian theses. **AEU**

1578 **Simon**, Frank. History of the Alberta Provincial Institute of Technology and Art. Edmonton: University of Alberta, 1962. xiii, 351 leaves.

Thesis (M.Ed.), University of Alberta, 1962.
Typescript.

Canadian Theses. **AEU**

1579 **Simon**, Maurice. Bridgeland Riverside memories. Calgary: 1977. 1v. ill.

Cover title. Duplicated.
A history of Langevin and St. Angela Schools. **ACP**

1580 **Sinclair**, Virginia. Golden memories of Taber Central School, Taber, Alberta, 1910-1971. Compiled and edited by Mrs. David Sinclair. Taber: Taber School Division, 1971. 86p. ill.

Glenbow. **ACG**

1581 **Somerset**, Bertram. Years of wonder. Ilfracombe, Devon: A.H. Stockwell, 1960. 79p.

Reminiscences of school teaching in rural Alberta in the 1950s.

Glenbow. **ACG**

1582 Southern Alberta Institute of Technology. Sixty years, '16 - '76. Calgary: Southern ALberta Institute of Technology, 1976. 46p. ill.

Compiled by the second-year journalism administration students. **ACP**

1583 **Sparby**, Harry Theodore. A history of the Alberta school system to 1925. Ann Arbor, Mich.: University Microfilms, 1958. 229p. ill.

Thesis (Ph.D), Stanford University, 1958.
Microfilm of typescript.

Canadiana, 1959. **AEU**

1584 **Stamp**, Robert Miles. School days. A century of memories. Calgary: Calgary Board of Education and McClelland and Stewart West, 1978. 160p. ill.

Ceessa. **AEA**

1585 **Sugden**, Thomas Curtis. The consolidated school movement in Alberta, 1913-1963. Edmonton: University of Alberta, 1964. vii, 98 leaves.

Thesis (M.Ed.), University of Alberta, 1964.
Typescript.

Canadian theses. **AEU**

1586 **Thompson**, Ray. The Queen's story, 1906-1967. Being a brief account of some of the happenings at Queen Alexandra School. Edmonton: Queen Alexandra School, 1967. 66p. ill.

Reminiscences and history.

Ceessa. **AEA**

1587 Vegreville. St. Martin's School. 50th Anniversary, 1907-1957. Vegreville: St. Martin's School, 1957. 41p.

de Valk, 1972. **SSM**

1588 **Walker**, Bernal Ernest. Public secondary education in Alberta. Organization and curriculum, 1889-1951. Ann Arbor: University Microfilms, 1955. 312 leaves.

Thesis (Ph.D.), Stanford University, 1955.
Microfilm of typescript.

Canadiana, 1956. **AEU**

1589 **Walker**, Marion Ruth. John Walker Barnett, first general secretary of the Alberta Teachers' Association. Edmonton: University of Alberta, 1969. ix, 143 leaves.

Thesis (M.Ed.), University of Alberta, 1969.
Typescript.

Canadian theses. **AEU**

1590 **Weidenhamer**, T. C. The Alberta School Trustees' Association. The story of trustees and school boards working in association in the province of Alberta. Edmonton: Alberta School Trustees' Association, 1976. 544p. ill.

Spine title *A history of the Alberta School Trustees' Association.*
Printed by Douglas Print.

Canadiana, 1977. **AEU**

Higher Education

1591 **Cameron**, Donald. Campus in the clouds. Toronto: McClelland and Stewart, 1956. xi, 1, 127p. ill.

Account of the development of the Banff School of Fine Arts.

Canadiana, 1957. **AEU**

1592 **Cameron**, Donald. The impossible dream. Calgary: Alcraft Printing and Bulletin Commercial Printers, 1977. 252p. ill.

A personal testament to a life spent in trying to promote adult education in Canada.

ACP

1593 **Campbell**, Duncan Darroch. Those tumultuous years. The goals of the President of the University of Alberta during the decade of the 1960's. Edmonton: University of Alberta, 1977. 67p.

Excerpts from speeches of Walter H. Johns, President of the University of Alberta.

Canadiana, 1979. **AEU**

1594 **Campbell**, Gordon. History of the Alberta community college system, 1957-1969. Ottawa: National Library of Canada, 1972. xii, 373 leaves. ill. (Canadian theses on microfilm, 13837)

Thesis (Ph.D.), University of Calgary, 1972.
Microfilm of typescript.

Canadiana, 1973. **AEU**

1595 Collège Universitaire Saint-Jean. Collège Saint-Jean cinquantième anniversaire, 1911-1961. Edmonton: Collège Saint-Jean, 1961. 80p. (incl. advts.) ill.

AECSJ

1596 **Corbett**, Edward Annand. Henry Marshall Tory. Beloved Canadian. eeWith an introduction by Robert C. Wallace. Toronto: Ryerson Press, 1954. xi, 241p. ill.

Based on personal memoirs, reports, and records kept by Dr. Tory.

Glenbow. **ACG**

1597 **Holmes**, Owen Gordon. Come hell or high water. Lethbridge: Lethbridge Herald, 1972. 141p.

History of the foundation of the University of Lethbridge.

Canadiana, 1974. **AEU**

1598 **Kohut**, Irena. Contribution of Donald H. Cameron to adult education. Ottawa: National Library of Canada, 1977. vii, 78 leaves. (Canadian theses on microfiche, 34204)

Thesis (M.A.), University of Calgary, 1977.
Microfiche of typescript.

Canadiana, 1979. **ACU**

1599 **Lister**, Reginald Charles. My forty-five years on the campus. Edmonton: University of Alberta, 1958. 75p. ill.

Reminiscences of the Superintendent of Residences at the University of Alberta.

Glenbow. **ACG**

1600 **Long**, John Clifford. An historical study of the establishment of college systems in Ontario and Alberta in the 1960's. Ottawa: National Library of Canada, 1972. x, 176 leaves. ill. (Canadian theses on microfilm, 13898)

Thesis (M.Ed.), University of Calgary, 1972.
Microfilm of typescript.
Also published 1972, Edmonton, Alberta Colleges Commission. Research studies in post-secondary education, 20.

Canadiana, 1973.

1601 **Macdonald**, John. The history of the University of Alberta, 1908-1958. Edmonton: University of Alberta, 1958. ix, 102p. ill.

Produced and printed for the University of Alberta by W. J. Gage Limited, Toronto.

Glenbow. **ACG**

1602 **Mann**, George. Alberta normal schools. A descriptive study of their development, 1905 to 1945. Edmonton: University of Alberta, 1961. xix, 309 leaves.

Thesis (M.Ed.), University of Alberta, 1961.
Typescript.

Canadian theses. **AEU**

1603 **Mardon**, Ernest G. The founding faculty. Lethbridge: University of Lethbridge, 1968. 108 leaves.

Duplicated.
Biographical sketches of members of the academic and administrative staff of the University of Lethbridge.

Dew. **AEU**

1604 **Markle**, Alexander George. Genesis of the Lethbridge Public Junior College. Edmonton: University of Alberta, 1965. ix, 106 leaves.

Theses (M. Ed.), University of Alberta, 1965.
Typescript.

Canadian theses. **AEU**

1605 **Marzolf**, Archie Durward. Alexander Cameron Rutherford and his influence on Alberta's educational program. Edmonton: University of Alberta, 1961. x, 152 leaves.

Thesis (M.Ed.), University of Alberta, 1961.
Typescript.

Canadian theses. **AEU**

1606 **McLeod**, Norman Leslie. Calgary College, 1912-1915. A study of an attempt to establish a privately financed university in Alberta. Ottawa: National Library of Canada, 1970. ix, 243 leaves. (Canadian theses on microfilm, 7706)

Thesis (Ph.D), University of Calgary, 1970.
Microfilm of typescript.

Canadiana, 1971. **AEU**

1607 **Motherwell**, Elizabeth. No small plans. An affectionate and incomplete biography of Donald Cameron and his principal creation, the Banff School of Fine Arts. s.l.: s.n., 1971. vii, 145p. ill.

Canadiana, 1974. **AEU**

1608 University of Alberta. A pictorial history of golden jubilee week, Edmonton and Calgary, October 26-November 1, 1958. Edmonton: University of Alberta, 1958. 1v. ill.

AEU

1609 University of Alberta Archives. A guide to the Chancellor's papers. 1890's, 1900-10, Alexander Cameron Rutherford, B.A., B.C.L., LL.D. Edmonton: University of Alberta Archives, 1973. ii, 11 leaves. (University of Alberta. Archives. Manuscript group, 2)

Canadiana, 1976.

1610 University of Alberta Archives. A guide to the President's papers. 1927-36 - Robert Charles Wallace. Edmonton: University of Alberta Archives, 1973. iv, 26 leaves. (University of Alberta. Archives. Manuscript group 3/2)

Canadiana, 1975.

1611 University of Alberta Archives. A guide to the William Pearce papers, series 5, settlement, 1880-1927. Edmonton: University of Alberta, 1976. 27 leaves. (University of Alberta. Archives. Manuscript group, 9/2)

Canadiana, 1977.

1612 University of Alberta Senate. Task Force on the Future of the Extension Function. On the future of the extension function. The report. Edmonton: University of Alberta Senate, 1974. 21 leaves.

Chairman: Dora McCulloch.

Canadiana, 1976.

1613 University of Alberta Senate. Task Force on the State of Women. Report on academic women. Edmonton: University of Alberta Senate, 1975. 2, 69p.

Chairman: June Sheppard.

Canadiana, 1976.

1614 University of Alberta Senate. Task Force on University Entrance Requirements. The problem of quotas. A report. Edmonton: University of Alberta Senate, 1974. 30p.

Chairman: Harold A. MacNeil.
Canadiana, 1975.

1615 University of Alberta. Senate. Task Force on University Entrance Requirements. Report. Edmonton: University of Alberta Senate, 1973. 25p.

Chairman: Harold A. MacNeil.

Canadiana, 1975.

Recreation

1616 Alberta Wilderness Association. The Elbow-Sheep headwaters, a recreational wilderness. Calgary: Alberta Wilderness Association, 1972. 41p. ill.

Cover title *Elbow-Sheep Wilderness, wilderness for Albertans.*

Canadiana, 1974. **AEP**

1617 Alberta Wilderness Association. The western Swan Hills. Alberta's forgotten wilderness. Calgary: Alberta Wilderness Association, 1976. 43p. ill., maps.

Published in association with the Edmonton Chapter of the National and Provincial Parks Association of Canada. **AEA**

1618 Alberta Wilderness Association. Wildlands for recreation. Nine areas on Alberta's east slope. Calgary: Alberta Wilderness Association, 1973. 123p. ill., maps.

On cover: Alberta's eastern slope. **AEA**

1619 Alberta Wilderness Association. The Willmore Wilderness Park. Calgary: Alberta Wilderness Association, 1973. 42p. ill.

AEU

1620 Alberta Youth Hostels Council. Development proposal for the eastern slopes of the Canadian Rockies, Alberta, Canada. Calgary: Alberta Youth Hostels Council, 1973. 48p. ill.

On cover: Proposals for education and recreation.

Canadiana, 1976. **AEP**

1621 Alberta Youth Hostels Council. Four development proposals for the eastern slopes of the Canadian Rockies, northern portion only. Edmonton: Youth Hostels Council, 1973. 34 leaves in various foliations. ill.

Canadiana, 1976.

1622 **Anderson**, David Lawrence. The recreational capability and use of Wabamun Lake and the eastern half of Lesser Slave Lake. Edmonton: University of Alberta, 1967. xx, 184 leaves.

Thesis (M.A.), University of Alberta, 1967.
Typescript.

Canadian theses. AEU

1623 **Anderson**, Ruby Olga. A study of leisure-time interests and activities of first year women at the University of Alberta. Edmonton: University of Alberta, 1959. xvi, 196p.

Thesis (M.Ed.), University of Alberta, 1959.
Typescript.

Canadian theses. AEU

1624 **Asquith**, Keith. Attitudes of selected students at the University of Alberta toward physical activity. Edmonton: University of Alberta, 1971. vi, 58 leaves.

Thesis (M.A.), University of Alberta, 1971.
Typescript.

Canadian theses. AEU

1625 **Barraclough**, Morris. From prairie to park. Green spaces in Calgary. Calgary: Century Calgary Publications, 1975. iv, 135p. ill.

Also published as part of *At your service, Part one*, which was issued as v.5 of the Century Calgary

Historical Series. AEA

1626 **Belanger**, Art J. A half mile of hell. The story of chuckwagon racing. Calgary: Frontier Publishing, 1970. 64p. ill. (Frontier books, 23)

Glenbow. ACG

1627 **Benfield**, Richard William. The recreational use of the hydro-electric power reservoirs of Alberta. Ottawa: National Library of Canada, 1975. xvii, 249 leaves. (Canadian theses on microfiche, 26708)

Thesis (M.A.), University of Alberta, 1975.
Microfiche of typescript.

Canadiana, 1977.

1628 **Bird**, C.D. Five natural areas in the city of Calgary. A report prepared by a Committee of the Field Naturalists' Society. 2d ed. rev. C.D. Bird, Chairman and editor. Calgary: Calgary Field Naturalists' Society, 1973. 1v. (various paging).

Cover title. Duplicated. AEA

1629 **Blackburn**, Cecil R. The development of sports in Alberta, 1900-1918. Ottawa: National Library of Canada, 1974. xiii, 505 leaves. (Canadian theses on microfiche, 20970)

Thesis (M.A.), University of Alberta, 1974.
Microfiche of typescript.

U of A Theses. AEU

1630 **Boothman**, Harry. Discussion notes for a seminar on the management of public parks and recreation services. Calgary: s.n., 1975. 80 leaves.

Lecture notes of a series of seminars presented by the Canadian Parks/Recreation Association in Saskatoon and other Canadian cities during 1975.

Canadiana, 1976.

1631 **Broderick**, Kathleen E. A normative study of track and field events for the Alberta Special Games. Ottawa: National Library of Canada, 1974. ix, 42 leaves. (Canadian theses on microfiche, 20973)

Thesis (M.A.), University of Alberta, 1974.
Microfiche of typescript.

U of A Theses. **AEU**

1632 **Buholzer**, William A. Outdoor recreation planning in Alberta. Appraisal of an information generation process. Vancouver: University of British Columbia, 1973. (1v.)

Thesis (M.A.), University of British Columbia, 1973.
Typescript.

Canplains. **BVAU**

1633 Calgary Golf and Country Club. Calgary Golf and Country Club 75 anniversary. Calgary: Calgary Golf and Country Club, 1972. 29p.

ACU

1634 Calgary Herald. 50th anniversary. Golden jubilee, 1912-1962. Calgary Exhibition and Stampede, July 9-14, 1962. Calgary: Calgary Herald, 1962. 52p. (incl. advts.) ill.

Cover title.
Special issue, July 7, 1962.

Glenbow. **ACG**

1635 Calgary Tourist and Convention Association. Catch them all from Calgary. Type of fish, type of bait, where to go, how to get there. Calgary: Calgary Brewing and Malting Co. Ltd, 1963. 12p. ill.

1964 ed. published by Calgary Beverages Ltd.

Canadiana, 1970. **ACG**

1636 **Campbell**, Charles Scott Henry. A survey of leisure reading in the senior high schools of Alberta. Edmonton: University of Alberta, 1962. xv, 176 leaves.

Thesis (M.Ed.), University of Alberta, 1962.
Typescript.

Canadian theses. **AEU**

1637 **Cheng**, Jacqueline Ruth. Images of Banff and Canmore and the use of Banff National Park by motel visitors. Ottawa: National Library of Canada, 1978. xvi, 221 leaves. ill. (Canadian theses on microfiche, 37260)

Thesis (Ph.D.), University of Calgary, 1978.
Microfiche of typescript.

1638 **Davis**, James Martin. We remember . . . Pete Knight. High River: Jim Davis, 1976. 52, 4p. ill.

Reminiscences of a champion rodeo rider.

Canadiana, 1978. **AEA**

1639 **Deeg**, Bart F. A proposal for a trail planning methodology, a case study. The Great Divide Trail. Ottawa: National Library of Canada, 1976. xi, 188 leaves. ill. (Canadian theses on microfiche, 30507)

Thesis (M.E. Des.), University of Calgary, 1976.
Microfiche of typescript.

Canadiana, 1978. **OONL**

1640 **Dent**, Ivor. Getting the games. Edmonton: Ardent Enterprises, 1977. viii, 270p. ill.

The story of the 1978 Commonwealth Games. **ACP**

1641 **Denton**, Daphne. Natural and recreational features of Sandy Beach. Prepared for Canadian Field Naturalists Society by Daphne Denton (and others). Cover drawing by Peter Karsten. Calgary: Calgary Field Naturalists' Society, 1976. iii, 27 leaves. ill.

Duplicated. **AEA**

1642 **Dooling**, Peter John. An explorative study of factors affecting outdoor recreation demand of the Edmonton adult population, Alberta, Canada. Edmonton: University of Alberta, 1967. xiv, 170 leaves. ill.

Thesis (M.A.), University of Alberta, 1967.
Typescript.
Estimates demand for 12 specific sporting activities, examines relationship between socio-economic variables and sports participation, and charts recreational travel patterns of Edmontonians.

Canadian theses. **AEU**

1643 **Dowling**, Phil. The mountaineers. Famous climbers in Canada. Edmonton: Hurtig, 1979. 258p. ill.

Canadiana, 1979. **ACP**

1644 **Dryden**, Dave. Coaching goaltenders. Edmonton: Douglas Print, 1976. 70p. ill.

Canadiana, 1977.

1645 **Dufresne**, Lawrence W. A study of the incidence, nature and cause of football injuries in the city of Edmonton during 1969. Edmonton: University of Alberta, 1971. ix, 70 leaves.

Thesis (M.A.), University of Alberta, 1971.
Typescript.

Canadian theses. **AEU**

1646 Edmonton Grads. 25 years of basketball championships, 1915-1940. s.l.: s.n., 1975. 20p. ill.

History of Edmonton Commercial Graduates Basketball Club.

Canadiana, 1977. AEU

1647 Edmonton Social Planning Council. An approach to planning river valley trails. Edmonton: Edmonton Social Planning Council, 1975. (68) leaves. ill.

Funded by Alberta Environmental Research Trust. AEU

1648 Edmonton Social Planning Council. Mini-parks for Edmonton. Design consultant and editor Leslie Bella, research assistant George Kelly. Edmonton: Edmonton Social Planning Council, 1975. (104) leaves. ill.

Funded by Alberta Environmental Research Trust. AEU

1649 Edmonton '78. The official pictorial record of the XI Commonwealth games. Le record officiel illustré des XIe jeux du Commonwealth. Editor, Gerald Redmond. Edmonton: Executive Sports Publications, 1978. 1v. (205p.) chiefly ill.

Text in English and French. AEU

1650 **Eley**, Frederic Joseph. Some aspects of wilderness perception in Alberta. Edmonton: University of Alberta, 1972. ii, 120 leaves.

Thesis (M.Sc.), University of Alberta, 1972.
Typescript.

Canadian theses. AEU

1651 **Erdmar**, Kenneth Richard. Recreational activities and perception in the Kananaskis region, Alberta. Analysis of a resource use survey. Ottawa: National Library of Canada, 1978. x, 131 leaves. ill. (Canadian theses on microfiche, 37273)

Thesis (M.Sc.), University of Calgary, 1978.
Microfiche of typescript.

Canadiana, 1979. OONL

1652 **Ewanyk**, Leonard John. Hunter-land owner relations in east central Alberta. A socioeconomic study of a property rights conflict. Ottawa: National Library of Canada, 1976. x, 121 leaves. (Canadian theses on microfiche, 27643)

Thesis (M.Sc.), University of Alberta, 1976.
Microfiche of typescript.

U of A Theses. AEU

1653 **Faulknor**, Cliff. Turn him loose! Herman Linder, Canada's Mr. Rodeo. Saskatoon: Western Producer Prairie Books, 1977. 129p. ill.

AEU

1653 **Faulknor**, Cliff. Turn him loose! Herman Linder, Canada's Mr. Rodeo. Saskatoon: Western Producer Prairie Books, 1977. 129p. ill.

AEU

1654 **Ferry**, Joe. Alberta album of curling. A history of Canada's most popular game. Calgary: Alberta Albums, 1965. (24)p. ill.

Cover title.

Glenbow. **ACG**

1655 **Fisk**, Robert Ritchie. A survey of leisure reading in the junior high schools of Alberta. Edmonton: University of Alberta, 1961. xiii, 193 leaves.

Thesis (M.Ed.), University of Alberta, 1961.
Typescript.

Canadian theses. **AEU**

1656 Foothills Cowboys' Association. The west in action. Rodeo. Edited by Graham Pike. Illustrated by Nick Cantwell. Calgary: Calgary Brewing and Malting Co. Ltd., 1971. 6, 88p. ill.

Printed by Universal Printers. **ACG**

1657 **Foster**, Russell James. Camping perception and camping satisfaction in Alberta Provincial Parks. Ottawa: National Library of Canada, 1977. xix, 181 leaves. (Canadian theses on microfiche, 34341)

Thesis (M.A.), University of Alberta, 1977.
Microfiche of typescript.

U of A Theses. **AEU**

1658 **Fournier**, Lionel Joseph. A survey of recreation components operating in selected areas of Alberta. Edmonton: University of Alberta, 1964. xi, 155 leaves.

Thesis (M.A.), University of Alberta, 1964.
Typescript.
Examines leadership, finances, facilities and programs of existing recreational activities in Alberta, with recommendations for improvements.

Canadiana theses. **AEU**

1659 **Gascoyne**, James John. An analysis of injuries which occurred in physical education, intramural and extramural activites and free play in the Calgary Roman Catholic Separate School District #1 during the 1973-1974 and 1974-1975 school years Ottawa: National Library of Canada, 1978. xv, 171 leaves. (Canadian theses on microfiche, 40157)

Thesis (M.Sc.), University of Alberta, 1978.
Microfiche of typescript.

U of A Theses. **AEU**

1660 **Goodwin**, Lou. Fall madness. A history of senior and professional football in

Calgary, Alberta, 1908-1978. Calgary: Calgary Stampeder Football Club, 1979. 133p.

ACP

1661 Great Divide Trail Association. The Great Divide Trail, Banff to Waterton. It's concept and future. 2d ed. Calgary: Great Divide Trail Association, 1976. 52p. ill.

Cover title.

Canadiana, 1979.

1662 Great moments of the X1 Commonwealth Games. Edmonton: City of Edmonton, 1978. 16p. (chiefly ill.)

Cover title.

Canadiana, 1980.

1663 **Harburn**, Norman Alan. Interpretive unit plan, Peace-Athabasca delta. Ottawa: National Library of Canada, 1976. ix, 138 leaves. (Canadian theses on microfiche, 03009)

Thesis (M.N.R.M.), University of Manitoba, 1976.
Typescript.
Outlines suitable part interpretive programs for recreational land in the Peace-Athabasca area of Wood Buffalo National Park. **OONL**

1664 **Haslam**, I.R. A perceived needs assessment of amateur sport administrators in Alberta. Edmonton: University of Alberta, 1979. xiv, 115 leaves.

Typescript.
Thesis (M.A.), University of Alberta, 1979.
Statistical study of perceived needs (affiliation, autonomy, dominance, nurturance, and order) in relation to personal characteristics, with discussion of implications.
U of A Theses. **AEU**

1665 **Hincks**, A. A viewpoint on hostels. Calgary: A. Hincks, 1971. 9p. ill.
Canadiana, 1971. **OONL**

1666 **Kallen**, Urs. A climbing guide to Yamnuska. s.l.: s.n., 1977. 44p. ill.

Second edition, 1977. **ACP**

1667 **Kennedy**, Fred. Calgary Stampede. The authentic story of the Calgary Exhibition and Stampede, the greatest outdoor show on earth, 1912-1964. Vancouver: West Vancouver Enterprise, 1965. 95p. ill.

AEA

1668 **Klippernstein**, David Henry. Recreational enterprises for farmers in Alberta. The distribution of existing facilities and farmers' attitudes. Ottawa, National Library of Canada, 1973. x, 173 leaves. maps. (Canadian theses on microfilm, 15257)

Thesis (M.A.), University of Alberta, 1973.
Microfilm of typescript.
Examines guest farms and ranches as a potential source of farm income.

Canadiana, 1974. **OONL**

1669 **Kunelius**, Rick. Ski trails in the Canadian Rockies. Banff: Summerthought, 1977. 138p. ill.

ACP

1670 **LeButt**, Paul. The Calgary Stampede. Pictures by Danny Price. Fredericton, N.B.: Brunswick Press, 1967. 20p. ill. (A Beaverbook for young Canadians)

Canadiana, 1976.

1671 **Lore**, Mary S. Historical summary of the Skyline Hikers of the Canadian Rockies, 1933-1970. Calgary: s.n., 1970. (31) leaves.

Cover title *Skyline Hikers, historical summary.*

Glenbow. **ACG**

1672 **Macdonald**, Cathy. The Edmonton Grads, Canada's most most successful team. A history and analysis of their success. Ottawa: National Library of Canada, 1976. viii, 194 leaves. (Canadian theses on microfiche, 33206)

Thesis (M.H.K.), University of Windsor, 1977.
Microfiche of typescript.

Canadiana, 1979.

1673 **Marsh**, John Stuart. Recreation trails in Canada. A comment and bibliography on trail development and use with special reference to the Rocky Mountain national parks and proposed Great Divide trail. Calgary: National and Provincial Parks Association of Canada, 1970. 14 leaves.

Prepared for the National and Provincial Parks Association of Canada, Calgary-Banff Chapter.

Glenbow. **ACG**

1674 **Masyk**, William James. The snowmobile, a recreational technology in Banff National Park, environmental impact and decision making. London, Ont.: Dept. of Geography, University of Western Ontario, 1973. xi, 143p. ill. (Studies in land use history and landscape change. National park series, 5)

Originally presented as an M.A. thesis, University of Calgary, 1972.

Canadiana, 1976. **AEU**

1675 **McColl**, Keith. Outdoors unlimited. Complete fishing guide for Central Alberta. Red Deer: 1964. 28p. (incl. advts.)

Glenbow. **ACG**

1676 **McQuaid**, Jennifer Ann. Trail conditions and management in the Rocky Mountains, Alberta. Ottawa: National Library of Canada, 1973. xi, 105 leaves. (Canadian theses on microfilm, 15276)

Thesis (M.Sc.), University of Alberta, 1973.
Microfilm of typescript.

Canadiana, 1974. **AEU**

1677 **Middleton**, Samuel Henry. Kootenai Brown, adventurer, pioneer, plainsman, park warden, and Waterton Lakes National Park. By Chief Mountain. Lethbridge: Lethbridge Herald, 1954. 64p.

Dew. **AEU**

1678 **Nielsen**, William Adam. The potential for wilderness recreation in a sand dune environment in northeast Alberta. Ottawa: National Library of Canada, 1978. xvii, 210 leaves. (Canadian theses on microfiche, 36448)

Thesis (M.Sc.), University of Alberta, 1978.
Microfiche of typescript.

U of A Theses. **AEU**

1679 **Norbeck**, Carl Sterling. Planning study for a national nature preserve along the South Saskatchewan River, Suffield area, Alberta. Ottawa: National Library of Canada, 1972. x, 122 leaves. ill.

Thesis (M.A.), University of Calgary, 1972.
Microfilm of typescript.

Canadiana, 1972.

1680 Now there was an athlete. Amateur sports in Calgary. Accounts by Calgary authors. Calgary: Century Calgary Publications, 1975. iv, 56p. ill.

Also published as part of *Young people of all ages,* which was issued as v.3 of the Century Calgary Historical Series.

Canadiana, 1979.

1681 **Nowicki**, Julian Joseph. Recreational capability and use of some north-central Alberta lakes. Edmonton: University of Alberta, 1969. xxx, 255 leaves.

Thesis (M.A.), University of Alberta, 1969.
Typescript.

Canadian theses. **AEU**

1682 **Olson**, Patricia Lee. A scenic resource and recreational analysis of the Milk River Canyon, southeast Alberta. Ottawa: National Library of Canada, 1976. xiii, 172 leaves. ill., maps (Canadian theses on microfiche, 30563)

Thesis (M.A.), University of Calgary, 1972.
Microfiche of typescript.

Canadiana, 1978. **AEU**

1683 **Oltmann**, Charlotte Ruth. The Kananaskis Valley hikers' and x-c skiers' guide. Seebe: Ribbon Creek Publishing, 1978. 68p. ill.

ACP

1684 **Paterson**, Lynda Elizabeth. Estimation of extra-market benefits associated with the recreational use of the Clearwater-Rocky Forest in Alberta. Ottawa: National Library of Canada, 1976. x, 98 leaves. (Canadian theses on microfiche, 30790)

Thesis (M.A.), University of Alberta, 1976.
Microfiche of typescript.
An estimate of the demand for recreational use of Clearwater-Rocky Forest and users' willingness to pay.

U of A Theses. **AEU**

1685 **Pattison**, William Stanley. Moose hunting activity in northern Alberta. A case study in wildlife economics. Edmonton: University of Alberta, 1970. ix, 108 leaves.

Thesis (M.Sc.), University of Alberta, 1970.
Typescript.

Canadian theses. **AEU**

1686 **Phillips**, William E. Hunter guiding activity in northern Alberta. Wildlife economics and policy. By William E. Phillips and William S. Pattison. Edmonton: University of Alberta Printing Department, 1972. 36p. (University of Alberta. Department of Agricultural Economics and Rural Sociology. Applied Research Bulletin, 14)

AEU

1687 **Prather**, Robert Allan. Alternative methods of estimating benefits. An economic evaluation of big game hunting in Alberta. Ottawa: National Library of Canada, 1975. xi, 144 leaves. ill. (Canadian theses on microfiche, 21940)

Thesis (M.Sc.), University of Alberta, 1974.
Microfiche of typescript.

Canadiana, 1975. **AEU**

1688 **Proudfoot**, James Alexander. Some aspects of the recreational geography of the North Saskatchewan river valley, Edmonton. Edmonton: University of Alberta, 1965. xvii, 90 leaves. maps.

Thesis (M.A.), University of Alberta, 1965.
Typescript.

Canadian theses. **AEU**

1689 **Redmond**, Gerald. Soccer practice. A guide for adult coaches and young players. Edmonton: J.M. Lebel Enterprises, 1978. 111p. ill.

On cover: Official soccer rules, illustrated for beginners, practice drills for coaches.

AEP.

1690 **Redmond**, Gerald. Soccer! A guide for adult coaches and young players. Edmonton: J.M. Lebel Enterprises, 1978. (1v.)

CBIP, 1979. **ACP**

1691 **Reid**, John Edmund. Sports and games in Alberta before 1900. Edmonton: University of Alberta, 1970. vi, 96 leaves.

Thesis (M.A.), University of Alberta, 1970.
Typescript.

Canadian theses. **AEU**

1692 **Rigby**, Douglas William. Recreation travel patterns of Edmontonians. A sample study. Edmonton: University of Alberta, 1966. xii, 140 leaves. ill.

Thesis (M.A.), University of Alberta, 1966.
Typescript.
Analyzes characteristics of day, weekend, and vacation travel trips of Edmontonians.

Canadian theses. **AEU**

1693 **Roberts**, Richard Henry. Factors involved in the selection of outdoor recreation locations by residents of the municipal district of Foothills. Ottawa: National Library of Canada, 1968. viii, 146 leaves. ill. (Canadian theses on microfilm, 02778)

Thesis (M.A.), University of Calgary, 1968.
Microfilm of typescript.

Canadiana, 1969. **OONL**

1694 **Rump**, Paul Charles. The recreational land use of the Bow, Kananaskis, and Spray Lakes Valleys. Ottawa: National Library of Canada, 1967. viii, 185 leaves. (Canadian theses on microfilm, 01705)

Thesis (M.A.), University of Calgary, 1967.
Microfilm of typescript.

Canadiana, 1968. **OONL**

1695 **Seagel**, Erica Jill. Some aspects of the distribution of snowmobiles in southern Alberta. Ottawa: National Library of Canada, 1972. 210 leaves. (Canadian theses on microfilm, 10162)

Thesis (M.A.), University of Calgary, 1971.
Microfilm of typescript.

Canadiana, 1972.

1696 **Spohr**, Gregory. Selected climbs in the Canmore area. Banff: Alpine Club of Canada, 1976. 37p. ill.

Canadiana, 1977. **ACP**

1697 **Stickel**, Lorna J. A study of depreciative behavior in three underdeveloped highway campgrounds in Jasper National Park, Alberta. Ottawa: National Library of Canada, 1973. xvii, 358 leaves. ill. (Canadian theses on microfilm, 15358)

Thesis (M.Sc.), University of Alberta, 1973.
Microfilm of typescript.

Canadiana, 1974.

1698 **Stremecki**, Edward J. How to read and run a river. Grand Centre: E.J. Stremecki, 1973. 52p. ill.

Canadiana, 1974. **AEU**

1699 **Sullivan**, Brian E. Recreation travel in the Cypress Hills. Ottawa: National Library of Canada, 1969. 135 leaves. (Canadian theses on microfilm, 04051)

Thesis (M.A.), University of Calgary, 1968.
Microfilm of typescript.

Canadiana, 1970. **OONL**

1700 **Tessler**, Ronnie. Crackin' out. A rodeo book. Edmonton: NeWest Press, 1979. 60p. (chiefly ill.)

AEU

1701 **Thorington**, James Munroe. A climber's guide to the Rocky Mountains of Canada. 6th edition. With the collaboration of William Lowell Putnam. New York: American Alpine Club, 1966. 377p. maps.

Title on spine *The Rocky Mountains of Canada*.
Based on first edition of *A climber's guide to the Rocky Mountains* by Howard Palmer and James Thorington, 1921, New YorkAmerican Alpine Club. **AEU**

1702 **Thorsell**, James W. Recreational use in Waterton Lakes National Park. London, Ont.: University of Western Ontario, 1967. 188 leaves.

Thesis (M.A.), University of Western Ontario, 1967.
Typescript.

Dew.

1703 **Touchings**, Dawne. Nature trails in Edmonton. Compiled by Dawne Touchings (and others). Edmonton: Edmonton Anti-Pollution Group, 1972. 32p. ill.

Cover title. Duplicated.
A Local Initiatives Project.
Also issued with the Group's Resources Inventory.
Also, 2d ed. with twig key included.

Canadiana, 1975.

1704 **Walker**, Donovan R. The Commonwealth Games management financial feasibility study. D.R. Walker, H.S. Ragan, J.B. Bell. Edmonton: Associated Engineering Services, 1974. (183) leaves. ill.

Study commissioned by the Edmonton Parks and Recreation Dept.

Canadiana, 1980.

1705 Waskahegan Trail Association. The Waskahegan trail guide book. 2d ed. Edmonton: Waskahegan Trail Association, 1975. 126p. maps.

2d ed., 1975, 126p. fold maps. 3rd ed. 1978, 150p. ill., maps. **AEP**

1706 **Wasylynchuk**, Mary Ann. The development of women's field hockey in Alberta, 1962-1973. Ottawa: National Library of Canada, 1975. ix, 163 leaves. (Canadian theses on microfiche, 26948)

Thesis (M.A.), University of Alberta, 1975.
Microfiche of typescript.

U of A Theses. **AEU**

1707 **Whiting**, Peter Gouinlock. An economic evaluation of recreation in Alberta provincial parks in the South Saskatchewan River basin. Ottawa: National Library of Canada, 1972. x, 124 leaves. (Canadian theses on microfilm, 13627)

Thesis (M.Sc.), University of Alberta, 1972.
Microfilm of typescript.

Canadiana, 1973.

1708 **Wilkie**, David Robert. Fitness and Amateur Sport Act in Alberta. Edmonton: University of Alberta, 1968. ix, 171 leaves. ill.

Thesis (M.A.), University of Alberta, 1968.
Typescript.
Studies the administration of the Fitness and Amateur Sports Act through published materials, personal interviews, and questionnaires.

Canadian theses. **AEU**

1709 **Wong**, Robert Allan Gerald. Conflict between cross-country skiers and snowmobilers in Alberta. Edmonton: University of Alberta, 1979. xvi, 186 leaves.

Thesis (M.A.), University of Alberta, 1979.
Typescript.

U of A Theses. **AEU**

1710 **Wood**, Kerry. A time for fun. A guide to hobbies and handicrafts. Illustrated by Helene R. White. Red Deer: Kerry Wood, 1967. (5), 150p. ill.

Glenbow. **ACG**

Sociology: General Works

1711 Alberta Metis Association. Housing Committee. Housing designs for the Alberta Metis Association, 1973. Edmonton: Alberta Metis Association, 1973. 9 leaves. plans.

Canadiana, 1976.

1712 **Ariza**, Jose Hernan. Community development experiences in the Chipewyan community of Cold Lake, Alberta. Ottawa: National Library of Canada, 1974. ix, 128 leaves. (Canadian theses on microfiche, 21747)

Thesis (M.A.), University of Alberta, 1974.
Microfiche of typescript.

Canadiana, 1975. **AEU**

1713 **Bhajan**, Edward R. Community development programs in Alberta. Analysis of development efforts in five communities. Ottawa: National Library of Canada, 1972. 198 leaves. (Canadian theses on microfilm, 13299)

Thesis (M.A.), University of Alberta, 1971.
Microfilm of typescript.
A review of the Alberta government's programs in Fort McMurray, Fort Chipewyan, Hinton, Slave Lake, and Wabasca, from 1964 to 1969.

Canadiana, 1973.

1714 **Buckmire**, George Edward. Changing rural attitudes. By George E. Buckmire and Walter B. Rogers. Edmonton: University of Alberta, Department of Agricultural Economics, 1967. 25 leaves. (University of Alberta. Department of Agricultural Economics and Rural Sociology. Special report, 8)

Canadiana, 1969. **AEU**

1715 **Burnet**, Jean Robertson. Next-year country. A study of· rural social organization in Alberta. Toronto: University of Toronto Press, 1978. xv, 188p (Social credit in Alberta, its background and development, 3)

1st published 1951 (Peel, 4237).

A study of Hanna and district. **AEU**

1716 The Canadian West. Social change and economic development. Edited by Henry C. Klassen. Calgary: University of Calgary, 1977. 220p.

Papers read at the eighth Western Canadian Studies Conference, University of Calgary, February, 1976.
Contents: 1. Robertson, H. Prairie feudalism. Homesteading in the nineteen-seventies 2. Dahlie, H. Frederick Philip Grove and social change 3. Rasporich, A.W. Utopian ideals and community settlements in Western Canada, 1880-1914 4. Jameson, S.S. Women in the southern Alberta ranch community, 1881-1914 5. Phillips, P. Women in the Manitoba labour market 6. Chalmers, J.W. Schools for our other Indians. Education of Western Canadian Metis children 7. Zentner, H. The study of social change in Western Canada. A contra-Marxist approach 8. Richards, J.H. The status of Saskatchewan vis-a-vis the western interior 9. Epp, A.E. The Lake of the Woods Milling Company-10. Armstrong, C. and Nelles, H.V. Competition vs. convenience. Federal administration of Bow River Waterpowers, 1906-13 13. Bliss, M. The ideology of domination. An eastern big-shot businessman looks at Western Canada.

1Canadiana, 1978. **AEA**

1717 **Card**, Brigham Young. The Canadian Prairie Provinces from 1870 to 1950. A sociological introduction. Toronto: J.W. Dent, 1960. xi, 46p.

Glenbow. **ACG**

1718 **Card**, Brigham Young. The expanding relation. Sociology in prairie universities. Regina: Canadian Plains Studies Centre, 1973. 20p. (Canadian Plains Studies. Occasional paper, 1)

Traces the development of sociology in the Canadian Plains region. **AEU**

1719 **Card**, Brigham Young. Trends and change in Canadian society. Their challenge to Canadian youth. Toronto: Macmillan of Canada, 1968. 206p.

Papers by B.Y. Card and others.
Contents: 1. Canada's changing social scene 2. Canada's changing political and economic realms 3. Change and constance in
Canadian morals and values. **AEU**

1720 Edmonton Social Planning Council. West Edmonton Social Task Force. Citizens' resource catalogue. Edmonton: Edmonton Social Planning Council, 1972. 62 leaves. ill.

Canadiana, 1975.

1721 Handicapped Housing Society of Alberta. Access - housing. Edmonton: Handicapped Housing Society of Alberta, 1974. 59, 121p. ill.

Canadiana, 1975. **AEU**

1722 **Harvey**, John Michael. A community development model illustrated with Hinton, Alberta. Ottawa: National Library of Canada, 1972. viii, 110 leaves. (Canadian theses on microfilm, 13394)

Thesis (M.A.), University of Alberta, 1972.
Microfilm of typescript.

Canadiana, 1973.

1723 **Howard**, Jeff. A house for Harry. Andco Housing in action. Edmonton: Alberta Native Communications Society, 1975. 8p. ill.

Produced for Andco Housing.
Cover title.

Canadiana, 1979.

1724 **Koch**, Agnes Bernice. The interorganizational bases of community power. A case study of Banff. Ottawa: National Library of Canada, 1974. vii, 41 leaves. ill. (Canadian theses on microfiche, 19795)

Thesis (M.A.), University of Calgary, 1974.
Microfiche of typescript.

Canadiana, 1975. **OONL**

1725 **Lai**, Rosita Pek Fong. Community leagues as a community development nuclei. Ottawa: National Library of Canada, 1973. 97 leaves. (Canadian theses on microfiche, 17589)

Thesis (M.A.), University of Alberta, 1973.
Microfiche of transcript.

U of A theses. **AEU**

1726 **Mathewson**, Pamela Ann. The geographical impact of outsiders on the community of Fort Chipewyan, Alberta. Ottawa: National Library of

Canada, 1974. xii, 184 leaves. ill. (Canadian theses on microfiche, 21907)

Thesis (M.A.), University of Alberta, 1974.
Microfiche of typescript.

Canadiana, 1976. **AEU**

1727 **Moore**, Linda Ida. Community development and community education. Process analysis. Ottawa: National Library of Canada, 1978. x, 153 leaves. (Canadian theses on microfiche, 40254)

Thesis (M.A.) University of Alberta, 1978.
Microfiche of typescript.
A study of the G.H. Dawe Community Centre in Red Deer.

U of A theses. **AEU**

1728 **National Conference on Urban Renewal as it affects Chinatown**, Calgary, 1969. National Conference sponsored by the Sien Lok Society of Calgary. Calgary: Sien Lok Society of Calgary, 1969. 102p. ill.

Conference held in Calgary, April 6 & 9, 1969.

Canadiana, 1975.

1729 Perspectives on regions and regionalism and other papers. Edited by B.Y. Card, in collaboration with A.K. Davis and others. Edmonton: University of Alberta Printing Services, 1969. xii, 233p. ill.

Meetings held Dec. 28-30.
Proceedings of the 10th meeting, Western Association of Sociology and Anthropology.

Glenbow. **ACG**

1730 **Poetschke**, Donna Marie Brown. Social class and attitudes in Alberta, 1971. Ottawa: National Library of Canada, 1976. xi, 134 leaves. (Canadian theses on microfiche, 30797)

Thesis (M.A.), University of Alberta, 1976.
Microfiche of typescript.
A study of the relationship between social class and class attitudes in Alberta as manifested in survey responses concerning 1971
political issues.

U of A Theses. **AEU**

1731 **Richards**, Leonard. Community development in Alberta. Ottawa: National Library of Canada, 1974. xiii, 332 leaves. ill. (Canadian theses on microfiche, 27509)

Thesis (Ph.D.), University of Toronto, 1974.
Microfiche of typescript.

Canadiana, 1977. **AEU**

1732 **Ritchie**, Ronald Stuart. A hard look ahead. Address given at 1963 biennial conference, Community Funds and Councils of Canada. Calgary: Imperial Oil Limited, 1965. 22 leaves.

Mimeographed.

Canadiana, 1965. **OONL**

1733 **Sheehan**, Patricia. Social change in the Alberta foothills. Toronto: McCelland and Stewart, 1975. 63p. ill. (The New Canadian Geography Project, regional pattern series)

At head of title: A Canadian Studies Foundation, Canadian Association of Geographers project.
Account of a project by the Federal Agricultural and Rural Development Act (ARDA), on Census Division 14, Central Alberta.

Canadiana, 1977. **AEU**

1734 Stimulants to social development in slow growing regions. Proceedings of a symposium .. held at Banff, Alberta, September 6-9, 1966. Edited by G.R. Winter and W. Rogers. Edmonton: Department of Agricultural Economics, University of Alberta, 1967. 2v. ill.

Produced by cooperation of Alberta Department of Agriculture and the Departments of Agricultural Economics of the University of Alberta and the University of British Columbia.

AEU

1735 Task Force on Social Development. Report from the Task Force on Social Development, an independent citizens study committee. Calgary: Social Planning Council of Calgary, 1972. 62p.

The Task Force was created by the United Fund of Calgary and District and the Social Planning Council of Calgary.

Canadiana, 1972. **AEU**

1736 **Torhjelm**, Gary Douglas. The urban hierarchy in Alberta. Ottawa: National Library of Canada, 1972. xiii, 190 leaves. ill. (Canadian theses on microfilm, 11383)

Thesis (M.A.), University of Calgary, 1972.
Microfilm of typescript.
Analysis of the population distribution of Alberta through central place theory.

Canadiana, 1972. **ACU**

1737 **Turner**, Joan Iris. Edmonton and vicinity rural and urban youth. Differences in evaluations of occupations. Edmonton: University of Alberta, 1978. xi, 132 leaves.

Thesis (M.Sc), University of Alberta, 1978.
Typescript.

U of A Theses. **AEU**

1738 **Ume**, Theo Azuka. Human rights awareness among certain socio-economic groups in Edmonton with implications for community development work. Ottawa: National Library of Canada, 1973. xi, 162 leaves. (Canadian theses on microfiche, 17710)

Thesis (M.A.), University of Alberta, 1973.
Microfiche of typescript.

U of A Theses. **AEU**

1739 **Wensel**, Joan. The Alberta Women's Bureau. A community development approach. Ottawa: National Library of Canada, 1977. xix, 391 leaves. (Canadian theses on microfiche, 32833)

Thesis (M.A.), University of Alberta.
Microfiche of typescript.

Canadiana, 1978. **AEU**

1740 **Westbury**, Marilyn Louise. The financing and implementation of community development programs by the Alberta government. Ottawa: National Library of Canada, 1978. xi, 149 leaves. (Canadian theses on microfiche, 36493)

Thesis (M.A.), University of Alberta, 1978.
Microfiche of typescript.

Canadiana, 1979. **AEU**

1741 **Zentner**, Henry. Prelude to administrative theory. Essays in social structure and social progress. Calgary: Strayer, 1973. xxxii, 205p.

AEU

Social Relations

1742 **Beach**, Judith Emily. Attitudes of clients and counsellors toward the Edmonton Family Court Conciliation Project. Ottawa: National Library of Canada, 1974. ix, 70 leaves. (Canadian theses on microfiche, 21758)

Thesis (M.Ed.), University of Alberta, 1974.
Microfiche of typescript.
Examines the attitudes of clients to the legal and social services of the Project.

Canadiana, 1975. **AEU**

1743 **Benham**, Mary Lile. Nellie McClung. Don Mills, Ont.: Fitzhenry & Whiteside, 1975. 61, 1p. ill. (The Canadians)

Canadiana, 1979. **AEU**

1744 **Callaway**, Bernice Ann Marr. To mothers with love. Three Hills: Prairie Press, 1978. 167p.

A guide to Christian motherhood. **ATP**

1745 **Corbet**, Elise Elliott. Alberta women in the 1920's. An inquiry into four aspects of their lives. Calgary: University of Calgary, 1979. vi, 176 leaves.

Thesis (M.A.), University of Calgary, 1979.
Microfiche of typescript.

Canplains. **ACU**

1746 Edmonton Social Planning Council. Maternity leave in Alberta. Edmonton: Edmonton Social Planning Council, 1975. 9 leaves.

Cover title.
Prepared for Options for Women by the Edmonton Social Planning Council. **AEU**

1747 **Hancock**, Maxine Louise. Living on less and liking it more. Chicago: Moody Press, 1977. 158p.

A guide to simple, inexpensive living based on Christian principles. **ACP**

1748 **Hancock**, Maxine Louise. Love, honor and be free. Chicago: Moody Press, 1975

Sub-title on dust jacket *A Christian woman's response to today's call for liberation.*

A personal philosopy of marriage. **AECYR**

1749 **Hancock**, Maxine Louise. People in process. The preschool years. Toronto: G.R. Welch, 1978. 192p.

Also published, Old Tappan, N.J., F.H. Revell.
On child management.

Canadiana, 1979. **AEU**

1750 **Hjartarson**, Freida Amelia. Survey of child care arrangements in Edmonton. Edmonton: University of Alberta, 1971. ix, 74 leaves.

Examines frequency of use of various child care arrangements, and reasons for choice.
Thesis (M.Ed.), University of Alberta, 1971.
Typescript.

Canadian theses. **AEU**

1751 **Hoole**, Arthur Herbert. The development of a family agency. A historical review of the Calgary Family Bureau. Vancouver: University of British Columbia, 1954. (1v.)

Thesis (M.S.W.), University of British Columbia, 1954.
Typescript.

Canadian theses. **BVAU**

1752 **James**, Donna. Emily Murphy. Don Mills, Ont.: Fitzhenry & Whiteside, 1977. 62p. ill. (The Canadians)

Canadiana, 1977. **AEU**

1753 **Leeder**, Terry. Daughter of the old pioneer. Illustrated by Deborah Drew-Brook. Toronto: Dundurn Press, 1979. 63p. ill. (Frontiers and pioneers)

Juvenile literature.

Canadiana, 1979. **OONL**

1754 **McClung**, Nellie Letitia. In times like these. With an introduction by Veronica Strong-Boag. Toronto: University of Toronto Press, 1972. xxii, 129p. (The social history of Canada)

First published 1915 by D. Appleton, and distributed in Canada by McLeod and Allen.
On dust jacket: The rise of feminism. **AEA**

1755 **Montgomery**, Jason. Family crisis as process. Edmonton: University of Alberta, 1979. 165p.

Cover title.

Canadiana, 1979.

1756 **Morley**, Frank Selkirk. Marriage can be beautiful. Calgary: Albertan, 1956. 42, 1p.

Expansion of a series on Christian marriage originally published in *The Albertan*.

Canadiana, 1962.

1757 **Paterson**, John G. To have or to let go. The challenge of conciliation. An evaluation report on the Edmonton Family Court Conciliation Project for the Department of National Health and Welfare, Welfare Grants Directorate. By John G. Paterson and James C. Hackler. s.l.: s.n., 1974. 184p.

On cover: Evalution report on the Edmonton Family Court Conciliation Project.

Canadiana, 1978.

1758 **Savage**, Candace. Our Nell. A scrapbook biography of Nellie L. McClung. Saskatoon: Western Producer Prairie Books, 1979. 253p. ill.

Canadiana, 1979. **AEA**

1759 **Van Pelt**, Nancy L. Parent education guide. A child management program. Calgary: National Health Education Center, 1972. 121 leaves. ill.

Canadiana, 1973.

1760 **Wright**, Helen Kerr. Nellie McClung and women's rights. Agincourt, Ont.: Book Society of Canada, 1979. 75p. ill. (We built Canada)

Canadiana, 1979. **OONL**

1761 **Alberta Conference on Aging**, 1st, Edmonton, 1967. Growing old effectively. Edmonton: Alberta Council on Aging, 1967. 84p. ill.

Duplicated.
Proceedings of the conference.

Canadiana, 1969. **AEU**

Social Issues

1762 Alberta Funeral Information Serice. Facts about funerals. Calgary: Alberta Funeral Information Service, 1972. 32p.

Published in association with Gunderson Public Relations and distributed as a service to citizens of Alberta.

Canadiana, 1975. **ACG**

1763 Alberta Women's Christian Temperance Union. The story of the years. Alberta W.C.T.U., 1913-1963. Edmonton: Alberta Women's Christian Temperance Union, 1963. 20p.

Cover title.

Glenbow. **ACG**

1764 **Anderson**, Frank Wesley. Bill Miner, train robber. Calgary: Frontiers Unlimited, 1963. 56p. ill. (Frontier books, 7)

Glenbow. **ACG**

1765 **Anderson**, Frank Wesley. The Carbon murders mystery. Calgary: Frontier Publishing, 1973. 40p. ill. (Canadian crime classics)

Canadiana, 1974. **OONL**

1766 **Anderson**, Frank Wesley. A concise history of capital punishment in Canada. Calgary: Frontier Publishing, 1973. 79, 1p. ill.

Cover title *Hanging in Canada*.

Canadiana, 1973. **ACG**

1767 **Anderson**, Frank Wesley. The dark strangler. A study in strange behaviour. Calgary: Frontier Publishing, 1974. iv, 38p. ill. (Canadian crime classics)

Canadiana, 1974. **AEU**

1768 **Anderson**, Frank Wesley. The death of Albert Johnson. Calgary: Frontier Publishing, 1968. 56p. ill. (Frontier books, 16)

Account of the pursuit of the Mad Trapper of Rat River.

Glenbow. **ACG**

1769 **Anderson**, Frank Wesley. A frontier guide to outlaws of Manitoba. Calgary: Frontier Publishing, 1971. 48p. ill. (Frontier books, 26)

Glenbow. **ACG**

1770 **Anderson**, Frank Wesley. Murder on the plains. Calgary: Frontiers Unlimited, 1962. 64p. ill. (Frontier books, 2)

By R.G. Evans, pseud.
At head of title: Western Canada's dramatic crimes.

Glenbow. **ACG**

1771 **Anderson**, Frank Wesley. Pardon my therapy. Calgary: Frontier Publishers, 1971. 56p. ill.

A humorous autobiographical account of social work.

Canadiana, 1971. **AEU**

1772 **Anderson**, Frank Wesley. The rum runners. Calgary: Frontiers Unlimited, 1966. 56p. ill. (Frontier books, 11)

Also printed 1977, c1968.
The story of the prohibition years in Alberta, 1916-1934.

Glenbow. **ACG**

1773 **Anderson**, Jean. An analysis of the Public Assistance Appeal System in Alberta. Ottawa: National Library of Canada, 1973. viii, 169 leaves. (Canadian theses on microfilm, 15538)

Thesis (M.A.), University of Calgary, 1973.
Microfilm of typescript.
An analysis of the Alberta Public Assistance Appeal System, 1970.

Canadiana, 1974.

1774 **Barilko**, Olga Louise. A study of the incidence of juvenile delinquency and its treatment in Edmonton in 1944. Edmonton: University of Alberta, 1956. 105 leaves.

Thesis (M.A.), University of Alberta, 1956.
Typescript.
Surveys occurrence of offenses and methods of treatment preferred by Edmonton Juvenile Court.

Canadian theses. **AEU**

1775 **Berry**, Lois Minerva. The Readiness Centre. A case study. Ottawa: National Library of Canada, 1972. viii, 132 leaves. ill. (Canadian theses on microfilm, 10039)

Thesis (M.S.W.), University of Calgary, 1971.
Microfilm of typescript.
An examination of the role of volunteer workers in preparing culturally-deprived children for admission to elementary school.

Canadiana, 1972. **OONL**

1776 **Birch**, Norman Edward. Citizen participation - Fact or fiction. A study of government and non-government attitudes concerning the volunteer role in the field of corrections and rehabilitation in Alberta. Ottawa: National Library of Canada, 1971. ix, 125 leaves. ill. (Canadian theses on microfilm, 10042)

Thesis (M.S.W.), University of Calgary, 1971.
Microfilm of typescript.

Canadiana, 1972. **OONL**

1777 **Butler**, Rodney Franklin. Perceptions of co-therapy. Experiences and impressions of Alberta social workers. Ottawa: National Library of Canada, 1971. x, 154 leaves. ill. (Canadian theses on microfilm, 10045)

Thesis (M.S.W.), University of Calgary, 1971.
Microfilm of typescript.

Canadiana, 1972. **OONL**

1778 **Cairns**, Phyllis Helen. The Alberta Child Welfare client system and the decision-making process. Ottawa: National Library of Canada, 1970. vi, 92 leaves. ill. (Canadian theses on microfilm, 04614)

Thesis (M.S.W.), University of Calgary, 1969.
Microfilm of typescript.

Canadiana, 1970. **OONL**

1779 Citizens' Commission on a Humane Standard of Living. Report. Edmonton: Edmonton Social Planning Council, 1975. 22 leaves.

Reproduced from typescript. **AEU**

1780 **Cleveland**, Albert Allan. The genesis and early growth of the Alberta Human Resources Research Council. Edmonton: University of Alberta, 1969. 166 leaves.

Thesis (M.Ed.), University of Alberta, 1969.
Typescript.

Canadian theses. **AEU**

1781 Co-West Associates. Identification of social needs in the inner city, Emonton and Calgary. Edmonton: Co-West Associates, 1977. viii, 99 leaves.

Duplicated.
Sponsored by the Office of the Official Opposition, Legislative Assembly of Alberta. **ACP**

1782 **Coulter**, Rebecca. Alberta's Department of Neglected Children, 1909-1929. A case study in child saving. Ottawa: National Library of Canada, 1977. xi, 109 leaves (Canadian theses on microfiche, 34321)

Thesis (M.Ed.), University of Alberta, 1977.
Microfiche of typescript.

Canadiana, 1979. **OONL**

1783 **Dragushan**, Jean L. To be poor in Canada. Edmonton: Edmonton Social Planning Council, 1975. 85p. ill.

Prepared with the co-operation of the Edmonton Public School Board.

Canadiana, 1976. **AEU**

1784 **Dukowski**, James Gerard. Project 72. Programming in a residential treatment facility. Ottawa: National Library of Canada, 1976. viii, 103 leaves. (Canadian theses on microfiche, 30664)

Thesis (M.Ed.), University of Alberta, 1976.
Microfiche of typescript.
Description of a rehabilitative treatment facility for young adults who have manifested behavioral patterns of drug abuse or other forms of social adjustment.

U of A Theses. **AEU**

1785 Edmonton Public School Board. Drug report. Edmonton: Edmonton Public School Board. 1971. 119 leaves in various foliations.

Report of the Drug Survey Committee under the chairmanship of K.M. Grierson.

Canadiana, 1973.

1786 Edmonton Welfare Council. Senior Residents Survey Committee. Edmonton Senior Residents' Survey report. Prepared by Robert L. Jones for the Edmonton Welfare Council. Edmonton: Edmonton Welfare Council, 1964. xvi, 269p. ill.

Glenbow. **ACG**

1787 **Eppel**, Helmut Paul. The duties of the provincial government toward the aging homeowner. Edmonton: University of Alberta, 1971. v, 49 leaves.

Thesis (M.B.A.), University of Alberta, 1971.
Typescript.

Canadian theses. AEU

1788 **Fewster**, Gerald D. The social agency. A model of service delivery. Calgary: William Roper Hull Home, 1977. ix, 120p.

Account of a multi-faceted service program for emotionally disturbed children at the William Roper Hull Home, Calgary.

Canadiana, 1978. AEU

1789 **Glick**, Isaac N. An analysis of the Human Resources Development Authority in Alberta. Ottawa: National Library of Canada, 1972. viii, 140 leaves. ill. (Canadian theses on microfilm, 13190)

Thesis (M.A.), University of Alberta, 1972.
Microfilm of typescript.

Canadiana, 1973. OONL

1790 **Gray**, James Henry. Booze. The impact of whiskey on the prairie west. Toronto: Macmillan of Canada, 1972. 243p. ill.

Printed in Toronto by the Alger Press. AEU

1791 **Hayter**, Jacqueline Green. Residential mobility and the function of seven selected high rises in central Edmonton. Ottawa: National Library of Canada, 1973. xxi, 231 leaves. (Canadian theses on microfiche, 17542)

Thesis (M.A.), University of Alberta, 1973.
Microfiche of typescript.

U of A theses. AEU

1792 **Heckbert**, Douglas Robert. Day parole in Alberta. An examination of selected benefits. Edmonton: University of Alberta, 1976. xviii, 385 leaves.

Thesis (M.A.), University of Alberta, 1976.
Typescript.

U of A Theses. AEU

1793 **Heggie**, Grant Barton. A descriptive analysis of vocational rehabilitation programs for the mentally retarded in Alberta. Edmonton: University of Alberta, 1979. xiv, 288 leaves.

Thesis (M.Ed.), University of Alberta, 1979.
Typescript.
Describes and analyzes services provided to the mentally retarded by 22 vocational rehabilitation agencies in Alberta.

U of A Theses. AEU

1794 **Helmers**, Donna Mary. A study of the developmental program of the Woman's Overnight Shelter, Edmonton, January 23, 1970-May 23, 1973. Edmonton: Edmonton Women's Shelter, 1973. viii, 77, 41p.

On cover: Edmonton Womens Shelter, a unique response to the needs of women.

Canadiana, 1975. **AEU**

1795 **Hetland**, Gary Dennis Layne. Socio-economic change in the Grande Cache region of Alberta. Edmonton: University of Alberta, 1969. xxii, 139 leaves.

Thesis (M.Sc.), University of Alberta, 1969.
Typescript.
A study of the Metis people of the area.

Canadian theses. **AEU**

1796 **Holmes**, Robert James. Social work staff turnover in the Alberta Department of Public Welfare. Ottawa: National Library of Canada, 1969. vi, 75 leaves. ill. (Canadian theses on microfilm, 04644)

Thesis (M.S.W.), University of Calgary, 1969.
Microfilm of typescript.

Canadiana, 1970. **OONL**

1797 **Hunt**, Elnora B. Twenty-five years proud. A history of the Rehabilitation Society of Calgary for the Handicapped. Calgary: Rehabilitation Society of Calgary for the handicapped, 1975. 158 (2)p. ill.

Printed by Inter-Collegiate Press, Winnipeg. **ACYR**

1798 **Jackson**, Norman. Staff perceptions of rehabilitation in the Drumheller Institution. Ottawa: National Library of Canada, 1972. ix, 137 leaves. (Canadian theses on microfilm, 11323)

Thesis (M.S.W.), University of Calgary, 1972.
Microfilm of typescript.

Canadiana, 1972. **OONL**

1799 **Jacques**, Barbara E. A study of social assistance in Alberta. Ottawa: National Library of Canada, 1970. viii, 131 leaves. ill. (Canadian theses on microfilm, 06105)

Thesis (M.A.), University of Calgary, 1970.
Microfilm of typescript.

Canadiana, 1971. **OONL**

1800 John Howard Society of Alberta. The alcoholic offender - whose responsibility? Calgary: Department of Public Health, Division of Alcoholism, 1966. 6p.

Canadiana, 1967. **OONL**

1801 **Johnston**, Cheryl Lynn. Perceptions of the medical social worker's functions in the Calgary General Hospital. Ottawa: National Library of Canada, 1971. 88 leaves. ill. (Canadian theses on microfilm, 08956)

Thesis (M.S.W.), University of Calgary, 1971.
Microfilm of typescript.

Canadiana, 1972. **OONL**

1802 **Kelsey**, John Graham Thornton. Communications in a growing organization. A study of the growth and internal communications of the Alberta Human Resources Research Council from January 1969 to January 1970. Edmonton: University of Alberta, 1971. xv, 163 leaves.

Thesis (M.Ed.), University of Alberta, 1971.
Typescript.

Canadian theses. **AEU**

1803 **Klapstein**, Elsie Louise. A native community counselling team. An analysis of the Alberta Newstart experience. Edmonton: University of Alberta, 1971. x, 142 leaves.

Thesis (M.A.), University of Alberta, 1971.
Typescript.

Canadian theses. **AEU**

1804 **Leinweber**, Robert George. A descriptive study of current and future roles of social service personnel in the province of Alberta. Edmonton: University of Alberta, 1972. xvi, 173 leaves.

Thesis (M.Ed.), University of Alberta, 1972.
Typescript.

Canadian theses. **AEU**

1805 **Lysne**, David Edgar. Welfare in Alberta, 1905-1936. Edmonton: University of Alberta, 1966. vii, 162 leaves.

Thesis (M.A.), University of Alberta, 1966.
Typescript.

Canadian theses. **AEU**

1806 **MacDonald**, D.S. Corrections and penology. Where are we going? Calgary: John Howard Society of Alberta, 1965. 5p.

Canadiana, 1967. **OONL**

1807 **MacDougall**, Alexander Joseph. Alberta alcoholism treatment programs, community development and citizen involvement. Ottawa: National Library of Canada, 1974. x, 163 leaves. (Canadian theses on microfiche, 21059)

Thesis (M.A.), University of Alberta, 1974.
Microfiche of typescript.
Examines citizen involvement in Henwood Rehabilitation Centre, Edmonton Out-Patient Clinic, Alcoholics Anonymous, and the High Level community.

Canadiana, 1975. **AEU**

1808 **McLean**, Robert Irwin. A most effectual remedy. Temperance and prohibition in Alberta, 1875-1915. Calgary: University of Calgary, 1969. 161 leaves.

Thesis (M.A.), University of Calgary, 1969.
Typescript.

Dew. **ACU**

1809 **Murphy**, Emily (Ferguson). The black candle, by Emily Murphy (Janey Canuck). Toronto: Coles, 1973. 405p. ill. (Coles Canadian collection)

Facsimile reprint of Toronto, Allen, 1922 edition.
Introduction by Brian Anthony and Robert Solomon.
An account of the narcotics trade. **AEA**

1810 **Paley**, David Thomas. Person perception skills and the helping relationship. A study of Alberta social service aides. Ottawa: National Library of Canada, 1972. x, 94 leaves. (Canadian theses on microfilm, 13513)

Thesis (Ph.D.), University of Alberta, 1972.
Microfilm of typescript.

Canadiana, 1973. **OONL**

1811 **Parnell**, Missy. Rape of the block. Or, Everyperson's guide to neighbourhood defense. Edmonton: Edmonton Social Planning Council, 1974. 86p. ill.

Written by Missy Parnell, Verna Semotuk, Joan Swain.
A guide to organising opposition to development activities. **AEA**

1812 **Parnell**, Ted. Alternatives to poverty and welfare in Alberta. A response to the Edmonton Social Planning Council. Edmonton: Edmonton Social Planning Council, 1973. 38p. ill.

2d ed. 1973, 38p.
Accompanied by supplement.

Canadiana, 1974. **OONL**

1813 **Pinkman**, Francis Edward. Educational upgrading of prisoners in an Alberta correctional institution, 1969-74. Ottawa: National Library of Canada, 1976. xiii, 207 leaves. ill. (Canadian theses on microfiche, 30582)

Thesis (M.A.), University of Calgary, 1976.
Microfiche of typescript.

Canadiana, 1978.

1814 **Rechner**, Robert Douglas. A regional study of personnel turnover in the Alberta Department of Public Welfare. Ottawa: National Library of Canada, 1970. vii, 75 leaves. (Canadian theses on microfilm, 06138)

Thesis (M.S.W.), University of Calgary, 1970.
Microfilm of typescript.

Canadiana, 1971. **OONL**

1815 **Reid**, Douglas Craig Somers. Corrections needs to be corrected. A paper prepared for the 12th Annual Banff Conference for United Church Men. Calgary: John Howard Society of Alberta, 1966. 11p.

Cover title. **AEU**

1816 **Riediger**, Alfred Jacob. Transient men in Edmonton. A descriptive study. Edmonton: University of Alberta, 1971. xviii, 226 leaves.

Thesis (M.Ed.), University of Alberta, 1971.
Typescript.
Examines health, finance, employment, education, legal involvement, mobility, goals/values, and social involvement characteristics of transient men, with recommendations for improved delivery of services by social agencies.

Canadian theses. **AEU**

1817 **Robbins**, Sidney. The Providence Child Development Centre. Help for Calgary's children in need. Calgary: Century Calgary Publications, 1975. iv, 72p. ill.

Also published as part of *At your service, Part two*, which was issued as v.5. of the Century Calgary

Historical Series. **AEA**

1818 **Robinson**, Robert Thomas. The Temporary Absence Program in Alberta. Ottawa: National Library of Canada, 1977. vii, 128 leaves (Canadian theses on microfiche, 34463)

Thesis (M.A.), University of Alberta, 1977.
Microfiche of typescript.
Examination of the policy of gradual release of inmates to the community.

Canadiana, 1979. **OONL**

1819 **Shone**, Margaret Ann. Confluence of mental health and legal systems in the process for compulsory civil commitment in Alberta. Ottawa: National Library of Canada, 1976. xxviii, 273 leaves. (Canadian theses on microfiche, 32832)

Thesis (LL.M.), University of Alberta, 1976.
Microfiche of typescript.

U of A Theses. **AEU**

1820 **Soderstrom**, Roger William. An analysis of the Edmonton Social Planning Council. Ottawa: National Library of Canada, 1975. vii, 139 leaves (Canadian theses on microfiche, 26921)

Thesis (M.A.), University of Alberta, 1975.
Microfiche of typescript.

Canadiana, 1977. **AEU**

1821 **Stretch**, Dianne Kathryn. From prohibition to government control. The liquor question in Alberta, 1909-1929. Ottawa: National Library of Canada, 1979. viii, 120 leaves. (Canadian theses on microfiche, 40506)

Thesis (M.A.), University of Alberta, 1979.
Microfiche of typescript.

U of A Theses. **AEU**

1822 Symposium. Perception and alcoholism. Papers presented at Symposium held on August 20, 1968 at Henwood In-patient Treatment Centre, Edmonton, Alberta, through the cooperation of the Department of Psychology, the University of Alberta and the Division of Alcoholism, Alberta Department of

Public Health. Edmonton: University of Alberta, Dept. of Psychology, 1970. 54 leaves. ill.

Canadiana, 1977. **AEU**

1823 **Thorner**, Thomas. The not so peaceable kingdom. Crime in southern Alberta. Ottawa: National Library of Canada, 1979. viii, 187 leaves. ill. (Canadian theses on microfiche, 34088)

Thesis (M.A.), University of Calgary, 1977.
Microfiche of typescript.

Canadiana, 1979. **OONL**

1824 **Tombs**, Thomas Poole. Social problems of Edmonton, 1963 survey. Edmonton: Edmonton Diocese Social Service, Church of England 1963. 1v. (various pagings). ill.

Caption title *Social problems of Edmonton. A study of social deprivation and social disorganization*.
Duplicated.
Also 2nd ed., 1964.

Glenbow. **ACG**

1825 **Tombs**, Thomas Poole. Trends in sucidal behavior. A sociological and psychological study, Edmonton, Alberta, Canada, period, 1959-1964. Edmonton: Anglican Church of Canada, Diocese of Edmonton, Council of Social Service, 1965. xiv, 126p. ill.

Duplicated.

Glenbow. **ACG**

1826 **Walker**, Ian. Some effects of continuing to provide subsidies for low income families. Study. Calgary: Social Planning Council of Calgary, 1971. 21 leaves. ill.

Canadiana, 1972.

1827 **Warner**, Neil Morgan. Shoplifters in Bigstore. Ottawa: National Library of Canada, 1979. x, 121 leaves. (Canadian theses on microfiche, 40530)

Thesis (M.A.), University of Alberta, 1979.
Microfiche of typescript.
Examination of demographic and behavioral characteristics of a sample of shoplifters in Edmonton, 1975-1977.

U of A Theses. **AEU**

1828 **Wheatley**, Sheila Kathleen. The effect of an alcoholic treatment program on certain alienation and personality dimensions. Ottawa: National Library of Canada, 1976. ix, 76 leaves. (Canadian theses on microfiche, 27757)

Thesis (M.Ed.), University of Alberta, 1976.
Microfiche of typescript.

U of A Theses. **AEU**

1829 **Willihnganz**, R.C. The 16 hour counselor(!). Calgary: University of Calgary Student Counselling Services, 1972. 41, 51p.

Canadiana, 1976.

1830 **Yuen**, Abraham Chick-To. Generating citizen involvement. Community council. Ottawa: National Library of Canada, 1973. vii, 113 leaves. (Canadian theses on microfiche, 17745)

Thesis (M.A.), University of Alberta, 1973.
Microfiche of typescript.
A study of the Area 13 Co-ordinating Council in the City of Edmonton, 1971-1973.

U of A theses. **AEU**

1831 **Yuen**, Kildy Wing-Han. Preventive social services as community development. Ottawa: National Library of Canada, 1976. xiv, 202 leaves. (Canadian theses on microfiche, 27766)

Thesis (M.A.), University of Alberta, 1976.
Microfiche of typescript.
An analysis of the Preventive Social Services Program in Edmonton.

U of A theses. **AEU**

Social Organizations

1832 **Buckley**, Marjorie White. As it happened. The University Women's Club of Edmonton. The first 60 years. Edmonton: University Women's Club of Edmonton, 1973. 56p. ill.

Canadiana, 1974. **AEU**

1833 **Cormack**, Barbara (Villy). Landmarks. A history of the Girl Guides of Alberta. Edmonton: Girl Guides of Canada, Alberta Council. 1968. 113p. ill.

Glenbow. **ACG**

1834 **Davies**, Marcy. Allison Procter, O.B.E., LL.D. 1880-1964. By Marcy Davies, Patti Meekison, Rose Scott. Edmonton: Junior League of Edmonton, 1977. 19p. ill.

Canadiana, 1978. **AEA**

1835 Edmonton Club. The Edmonton Club. 75 years, 1899-1974. Edmonton: Edmonton Club, 1974. (35), 10p. ill.

A chronicle concerning the Edmonton Club, by Louis D. Hyndman: leaves 1-10.
Limited to club members only.

Canadiana, 1977.

1836 Edmonton. St. John's Institute. 40th anniversary of the St. John's Institute, 1959. Edmonton: Alberta Printing, 1959. 266p. ill.

Text in Ukrainian and English.
The 1959 year book.

Glenbow. **ACG**

1837 **Hand**, Fred J. Bow River Lodge, no.1, Calgary, Alta. A brief history of the Grand Lodge of Alberta, 1905-1955, by M.W. Bro. Sam Harris. Edmonton: Canadian Masonic Research Association, 1955. 14p. ill. (Canadian Masonic Research Association. Papers, 28 & 29)

Cover title.
Read at the fifteenth meeting of the Association at Edmonton, Aug. 31, 1955.

Glenbow. **ACG**

1838 **Janis**, Joana. History of the Ukrainian Women's Association of Canada, St. John's Cathedral Branch, 1926-1976. Edmonton: Ukrainian Women's Association of Canada, St. John's Cathedral Branch, 1979. 298p. ill.

Cover title.
Text in Ukrainian and English.
Book Committee Chairman and Co-ordinating Editor, Joana Janis. **AEA**

1839 **Johnson**, Louise C. First fifty years, Edmonton Y.W.C.A., 1907-1957. Edmonton: Young Women's Christian Association, 1957. 126p. ill.

Canadiana, 1966. **AEA**

1840 **Latham**, Ernest. History of District 37-E, part of Multiple District 37. Calgary: Lions International District 37-4, 1976. 1v. (variously paged). ill.

Duplicated. **ACP**

1841 **MacLellan**, James Alexander. My years in Lionism, 1931-1975. Edmonton: Ukrainian News, 1976. 48p.

AEU

1842 **Minuk**, Syd. 50 golden years, 1924-1974. Edited by Syd and Honour Minuk. Calgary: Kinsmen Club of Calgary, 1974. 50p. ill.

Cover title *Kinsmen chronicle*. **AEA**

1843 **Parker**, Fred. The first fifty years of Perfection Lodge no. 9 (G.R. Alta.) Calgary, 1895-1945. Read before the 37th meeting of the Association held at Calgary, Oct. 11th, 1963. Calgary: Canadian Masonic Research Association, 1963. 6p. (Canadian Masonic Research Association. Papers, 72)

Glenbow. **ACG**

1844 **Peach**, Jack. Sara of the Tenth. Calgary: 1961. (4)p. ill.

Biographical sketch of F. Leslie Sara, a Calgary Boy Scout leader.

Glenbow. **ACG**

1845 Plast Association. 15th anniversary of the Plast Association in Edmonton. Edmonton: Plast Association, 1963. 62p. ill.

Text in Ukrainian.

Ukrainca Canadiana, 1963.

1846 **Puffer**, Frances Anita. Friendship and commitment in a volunteer association, the University Women's Club of Edmonton. Edmonton: University of Alberta, 1966. xi, 91 leaves. ill.

Thesis (M.A.), University of Alberta, 1966.
Typescript.

Canadian theses. **AEU**

1847 Ranchmen's Club. A short history of the Ranchmen's Club. A light-hearted account. Calgary: Ranchmen's Club, 1975. iv, 34p. ill.

A Calgary centennial project.

Canadiana, 1979. **ACP**

1848 Scouting in Calgary. Boy scout groups and activities, 1910-1974. Accounts by Calgary authors. Calgary: Century Calgary Publications, 1975. iv, 176p. ill.

Also published as part of *Young people of all ages*, which was issued as v.3 of the Century Calgary historical series.

Canadiana, 1977. **AEA**

1849 **Spiller**, Edward Vincent. The early history of scouting in Calgary, Alberta. Calgary: Boy Scouts Association (Canada) Calgary District, 1956. (2), 17 (i.e. 34)p.

Duplicated.

Glenbow. **ACG**

1850 **Voitkiv**, Mykhailyna. Ukrainian Catholic Women's League of Canada. Edmonton: Ukrainian Catholic Women's League, 1956. 24p. ill.

Title page in Ukrainian and English. Text in Ukrainian.

Canadiana, 1957.

1851 **Wood**, Cornelia R. The story of the Alberta Women's Institutes, 1909-1955. Compiled by Mrs. Cornelia R. Wood. s.l.:, Alberta Women's Institutes, 1955. 75p. ill.

Revision of A story of Alberta Women's Institutes, compiled by Mrs. Adelaide Montgomery and Mrs. Marion M.S. Rogers, 1937, and a supplement compiled by C.R. Wood, 1949.

Canadiana, 1955. **OONL**

1852 Young people of all ages. Sports, schools and youth groups in Calgary. Account, by Calgary authors. Calgary: Century Calgary Publications, 1975. 496p. ill. (Century Calgary historical series, v.3)

Each chapter also published separately.
Contents: Wooliams, E. Boots, tents and miniskirts From slate pencil to instant ink Scouting in Calgary Now there was an athelete.

Canadiana, 1978.

Minority Groups

1853 Alberta Indian Treaties Commemorative Program. As long as the sun shines, the rivers flow and the grass grows. Edmonton: Edmonton Printers, 1977. 16p. (chiefly ill.)

Cover title.
A visit to the United Kingdom in commemoration of Treaty No.6 and Treaty No.7 centennial years, 1976-1977. **AEA**

1854 **Alberta Native Women's Conference**, 1st, Edmonton, 1968. Report. Toronto: Indian-Eskimo Association, 1968. 3, iv, 4-52p.

Canadiana, 1971. **AEU**

1855 **Alberta Native Women's Conference**, 2d, Edmonton, 1969. Report. Edmonton: Native Women's Society, 1969. 53 leaves.

Cover title.
Theme: Sucess with unity. We are responsible. **AEU**

1856 All Chiefs Conference Committee. Where do we go from here? Report of Indian study tour, April 1968, All Chiefs Conference, Alberta. s.l.: s.n., 1968. 31 leaves.

Glenbow. **ACG**

1857 **Anderson**, Alda M. The Metis people of Canada. A history. By the Alberta Federation of Metis Settlement Associations and Daniel R. and Alda M. Anderson. Edmonton: Alberta Federation of Metis Settlement Associations, 1978. 128p. il1.

School text.
Accompanied by teacher's manual.
Produced with the assistance of Syncrude Educational Services. **AEU**

1858 **Anderson**, Francis Garfield. Personal contact affecting city children's knowledge of and attitudes to Alberta Indians. Ottawa: National Library of Canada, 1969. viii, 113 leaves. ill.

Thesis (M.Ed.), University of Calgary, 1969.
Microfilm of typescript.

Canadiana, 1970.

1859 Association canadienne-française de l'Alberta. Aperçu historique de l'A.C.F.A. Edmonton: Assocation canadienne-française de l'Alberta, 1976. 21p.

Caption title.
Cover title *50 ans d'histoire*. **AEU**

1860 Association canadienne-française de l'Alberta. Les hîritiers de lord Durham. Le plan d'action. Edmonton: Association canadienne-française de l'Alberta, 1977. 34 p.

Extracted from v.2 of the study on the status of French-Canadians outside of Quebec, published under the same title. **AEU**

1861 Association canadienne-française de l'Alberta. Conseil régional de Bonnyville. Bonnyville in question, 1975. Projet réalisé dans le cadre du programme de service communautaire étudiant du Secrétariat d'Etat du Canada. Responsable, Donald Cyr. Bonnyville: Association canadienne-française de l'Alberta, 1976. 145p.

Duplicated. **AECSJ**

1862 **Atwell**, Phyllis Harryette. Kinship and migration among Calgarian residents of Indian origin. Ottawa: National Library of Canada, 1969. vii, 85 leaves. ill. (Canadian theses on microfilm, 04603)

Thesis (M.A.), University of Calgary, 1969.
Microfilm of typescript.

Canadiana, 1970.

1863 **Awid**, Richard. A salute to the Arab pioneers of northern Alberta. Edmonton: Canadian Arab Friendship Association, 1973. 30p. ill.

Includes some text in Arabic.

Canadiana, 1977. **AEA**

1864 **Banff Conference on Central and East European Studies**, 1st, 1977. Proceedings. Edited by Tom M.S. Priestly. Edmonton: Central and East European Studies Society of Alberta, 1977. vii, 523 leaves.

Duplicated.
Organized and sponsored by the Central and East European Studies Society of Alberta, University of Alberta Division of East European Studies, University of Calgary Interdisciplinary Committee on Soviet and East European Studies, The Inter-University Committee on Soviet and East European Studies, and the Group for Central and East European Studies.

1865 **Banff Conference on Central and East European Studies**, 2d, 1978. Second Banff Conference on Central and East European Studies, Banff Springs Hotel, Banff, Alberta, March 2-5, 1978. Compiled .. under the direction of Metro Gulutsan. Edmonton: University of Alberta, 1978. 4v. ill.

Organized by Central and East European Studies Association of Canada, Central and East European Studies Society
of Alberta, and the Division of East European Studies of University of Alberta.

Canadiana, 1980. **AEU**

1866 **Baureiss**, Gunter A. The city and the subcommunity. The Chinese of Calgary. Ottawa: National Library of Canada, 1971. xiii, 192 leaves. ill. (Canadian theses on microfilm, 10037)

Thesis (M.A.), University of Calgary, 1971.
Microfilm of typescript.

Canadiana, 1972. **ACU**

1867 **Boldt**, Edward D. Conformity and deviance. The Hutterites of Alberta. Edmonton: University of Alberta, 1966. vii, 94 leaves.

Thesis (M.A.), University of Alberta, 1966.
Typescript.

Canadian theses. **AEU**

1868 Buffalo Child Long Lance. Long Lance. London: Transworld Publishers, 1956. 236p. (Corgi books, T145)

Autobiography of a Blood Indian chief first published 1928, New York, Cosmopolitan Book Co(Peel 3059).

Canadiana, 1956.

1869 **Calf Robe**, Benjamin Augustine. Siksik∴ A Blackfoot Legacy. With Adolf and Beverly Hungry Wolf. Invermere, B.C.: Good Medicine Books, 1979. xvi, 107p. ill.

1870 **Campbell**, Maria. Halfbreed. Toronto: McClelland and Stewart, 1973. 157p.

Autobiography.
Also published, 1973, New York, Saturday Review Press, 157p.

Canadiana, 1973. **AEU**

1871 **Campbell**, Maria. People of the buffalo. How the Plains Indians lived. Illustrated by Douglas Tait and Shannon Twofeathers. Vancouver: J.J. Douglas, 1976. 47p. ill.

Juvenile literature.

Canadiana, 1977.

1872 **Campbell**, Maria. Riel's people. How the Metis lived. Illustrated by David Maclagan. Vancouver: Douglas & McIntyre, 1978. 47p. ill. (How they lived in Canada)

Written for children.

Canadiana, 1979. **AEU**

1873 Canadian confrontations. Hinterlands vs. metropolis. Canadian Indians and Metis, Farmers, The American empire, The sasquatch, Whither the University, and other papers. Edited by Arthur K. Davis. Edmonton: University of Alberta Printing Services, 1970. vi, 117p.

Proceedings of the 11th meeting of the Western Association of Sociology and Anthropology, Banff, 1969.
Meeting held Dec. 28-30. Also participating, the Liaison committee on Education, Canadian Sociology and Anthropology Association.
Part I includes addresses by Indian and Metis leaders.

Glenbow. **ACG**

1874 **Card**, Brigham Young. Alberta Improvement District 124. A case study. Edmonton: University of Alberta, 1965. 169 leaves.

Duplicated.
First three parts reproduced from *The Metis in Alberta Society*, 1963. Part 4 entitled *I.D. 124 four years later. The continuing transition of Lesser Slave Lake society.*
At head of title: Part IV.
AEU

1875 **Card**, Brigham Young. The Metis in Alberta society, with special reference to social, economic and cultural factors associated with persistently high tuberculosis incidence. By B.Y. Card, G.K. Hirabayashi and C.L. French. Edmonton: University of Alberta, 1963. viii, 414p. ill.

"A report on Project A (1960-63), University of Alberta Committee for Social Research, prepared for the Alberta Tuberculosis Association".
Glenbow.
ACG

1876 **Cardinal**, Douglas. Of the spirit. Edited by George Melnyk. Edmonton: NeWest Press, 1977. 126p.

Essays on Indian culture, learning, and social and spiritual reflections.
ACU

1877 **Cardinal**, Harold. Address by Harold Cardinal, President, Indian Association of Alberta, during presentation by the Indian Chiefs of Alberta to the Prime Minister and the Government of Canada, June 4, 1970. Edmonton: Indian Association of Alberta, 1970. 4, 5p.

Cover title. Duplicated.
5p. comprise statement by P.E. Trudeau at the meeting with the Indian Association of Alberta, and the National Indian Brotherhood.
ACG

1878 **Cardinal**, Harold. The rebirth of Canada's Indians. Edmonton: Hurtig, 1977. 222p.

Canadiana, 1977.
ACG

1879 **Cardinal**, Harold. The unjust society. The tragedy of Canada's Indians. Edmonton: Hurtig, 1969. (173)p.

Also, French translation, 1970, *La tragedie des Indiens du Canada*. Traduit par Raymond Gagne et Jacques Vallee. Montreal, Editions du Jour, 223p.
Glenbow.
ACG

1880 **Cashman**, Anthony Walcott. Abraham Cristall. The story of a simple man. Edmonton: 1963. 34p. ill.

Cover title *Abraham Cristall, 1868-1944*.
Biography of Edmonton's first Jewish resident.
Glenbow.
ACG

1881 **Cooney**, Gregory Joseph. Observations on the development of schism in an Alberta Indian revitalization movement. Ottawa: National Library of Canada, 1972. vii, 76 leaves. ill. (Canadian theses on microfilm, 11298)

Thesis (M.A.), University of Calgary, 1972.
Microfilm of typescript.
Canadiana, 1972.
AEU

1882 **Couture**, Joseph Ernest. Alberta Indian youth. A study in Cree and Blood student conflict. Ottawa: National Library of Canada, 1972. xii, 213, 15 leaves. ill. (Canadian theses on microfilm, 11127)

Thesis (Ph.D.), University of Alberta, 1972.
Microfiche of typescript.

Canadiana, 1972.

1883 **Daniels**, Harry W. We are the new nation. The Metis and national native policy. Ottawa: Native Council of Canada, 1979. 54p.

On cover: We are the new nation, Nous sommes la nouvelle nation.

Canadiana, 1980. **AEU**

1884 **Dawson**, John Brian. Chinese urban communities in southern Alberta, 1885-1925. Ottawa: National Library of Canada, 1976. vi, 162 leaves. (Canadian theses on microfiche, 27638)

Thesis (M.A.), University of Calgary, 1976.
Microfiche of typescript.

Canadiana, 1977. **OONL**

1885 Declaration of Metis and Indian rights. With commentary by Harry W. Daniels. Ottawa: Native Council of Canada, 1979. 1 v. (unpaged) ill.

AEU

1886 **Dempsey**, Hugh Aylmer. Charcoal's world. Saskatoon: Western Producer Prairie Books, 1978. 178p. ill.

Printed by Modern Press, Saskatoon.
A study of the motives of a Kainah Indian who killed one man, and made attempts on the lives of several others in 1896.

Canadiana, 1978. **AEA**

1887 **Dempsey**, Hugh Aylmer. Indian tribes of Alberta. Calgary: Glenbow-Alberta Institute, 1978. 88p. ill.

CBIP, 1979. **AEA**

1888 **Dion**, Joseph Francis. My tribe the Crees. Edited and introduction by Hugh Dempsey. Calgary: Glenbow Museum, 1979. x, 194p. ill.

Canadiana, 1979. **AEA**

1889 **Driben**, Paul. We are Metis. The ethnography of a half-breed community in northern Alberta. Ann Arbor, Mich: University Microfilms, 1975. xi, 156 leaves. ill.

Thesis (Ph.D.), University of Minnesota, 1975.
Microfilm of typescript.

Canadiana, 1978. **OONL**

1890 **Economic**, Social and Human Development Conference, Edmonton, 1970. Conference minutes and papers. Edmonton: Indian Association of Alberta, 1970. (248) leaves.

Typewritten title page and contents list supplied in Glenbow copy.
Papers on development potential for Indian people.

Glenbow. ACG

1891 **Emanuel**, Lydia. Attitudes toward identity in a Ukrainian parish. Ottawa: National Library of Canada, 1975. ix, 181 leaves. (Canadian theses on microfiche, 26752)

Thesis (M.A.), University of Alberta, 1975.
Microfiche of typescript.
Study of a Ukrainian Orthodox Community in Edmonton, 1972/73.

Canadiana, 1977. OONL

1892 **Eskrick**, Muriel Elizabeth. The Norwegian settlers, Eagle Hill and Bergen. Stories of the West County. Sundre: Sundre Round-Up, 1971. 57p. ill.

Cover title.

Glenbow. ACG

1893 **Evans**, Simon M. The dispersal of Hutterite colonies in Alberta, 1918-1971. The spatial expression of cultural identity. Ottawa: National Library of Canada, 1973. x, 220 leaves. ill. (Canadian theses on microfiche, 16974)

Thesis (M.A.), University of Calgary, 1973.
Microfiche of typescript.

Canadiana, 1974. AEU

1894 **Ferguson**, Ted. A white man's country. An exercise in Canadian prejudice. Toronto: Doubleday Canada, 1975. 200p. ill.

An account of the Komagata Maru incident.

CBIP, 1979. AEU

1895 **Fernandez**, Isaias B. The history of Filipinos in Alberta. Barrhead: Printed by Barrhead Printers and Stationers, 1973. 1v. (34p.) ill., maps. AEA

1896 Fine Day. My Cree people. Introduction by Adolf Hungry Wolf. Invermere, B.C.: Good Medicine Books, 1973. 63p. ill. (Good medicine books, 9)

A tribal handbook.

Canadiana, 1975. AEA

1897 **Fisher**, Anthony Dwight. The perception of instrumental values among the young Blood Indians of Alberta. Stanford, Calif.: Stanford University, 1966. 223 leaves.

Thesis (Ph.D.), Stanford University, 1966.
Typescript.

Dew.

1898 **Flint**, David. The Hutterites. A study in prejudice. Toronto: Oxford University Press, 1975. 193p. ill.

Concerned especially with the Pincher Creek Colony. ACG

1899 The forgotten people. Metis and non-status Indian land claims. Edited with an introduction by Harry W. Daniels. Ottawa: Native Council of Canada, 1979. 99p. ill.

Canadiana, 1980.

1900 **Fraser**, William Bernard. The Alberta Indian, his past, his present, his future. Calgary: Friends of the Indians Society, 1959. (1), 27 leaves.

Glenbow. **ACG**

1901 **Friesen**, John W. People, culture and learning. Calgary: Detselig Enterprises, 1977. xix, 255p.

Part one concerns culture and learning from a social science perspective. Part two contains three case studies relative to Canada's Indian people, the Hutterites and the Mennonites.

Canadiana, 1977. **AEU**

1902 **Fry**, Olivia Rose. My heritage from the builders of Canada. New York: Carlton Press, 1967. 183p. ill. (Hearthstone books)

Account of a visit to the Ukraine, and a chapter on a visit to Edmonton. **AEA**

1903 **Gershaw**, Fred William. The Blackfeet Confederacy. Medicine Hat: Modern Press, 1961. 10p.

Cover title.

Glenbow. **ACG**

1904 **Getty**, Wayne Edwin Allen. Perception as an agent of sociocultural change for the Stoney Indians of Alberta. Ottawa: National Library of Canada 1974. x, 166 leaves. (Canadian theses on microfiche, 19778)

Thesis (M.A.), University of Calgary, 1974.
Microfilm of typescript.

Canadiana, 1975. **OONL**

1905 Glenbow-Alberta Institute. Archives. Arnold Lupson photographic collection, Calgary, Alberta, 1926-1947. Calgary: Glenbow-Alberta Institute, 1974. 62p. ill. (Glenbow archives series, 6)

Canadiana, 1975. **ACG**

1906 **Gregoret**, Gene Roy. Narrative for the film, 'The Trout Lake Cree'. Edmonton: University of Alberta, 1970. v, 24 leaves.

Thesis (M.A.), University of Alberta, 1970.
Typescript.

Canadian theses. **AEU**

1907 **Gue**, Leslie Robb. A comparative study of value orientations in an Alberta Indian community. Edmonton: University of Alberta, 1967. xv, 341 leaves.

Thesis (Ph.D.), University of Alberta, 1967.
Typescript.

A study of Cree Indians in the Northland School Division #61.

Canadian theses. **AEU**

1908 **Hanks**, Lucien Mason. Tribe under trust. A study of the Blackfoot reserve of Alberta. By Lucien M. Hanks, Jr. and Jane Richardson Hanks. Photos. by F. Gully. Toronto: University of Toronto, 1971. 206p.ill. (Scholarly reprint series)

First published 1950 (Peel 4202).

NUC 1975.

1909 **Hatt**, Fred Kenneth. Ninety nine years from tomorrow. A report on research and reaction. By Fred K. Hatt, Charles W. Hobart, Judy Hatt. Edmonton: University of Alberta Printing Services, 1971. x, 334p. ill.

Results of a study commissioned by the Alberta Provincial Government on the Metis in northeastern Alberta and some public reactions to publication during the 1967 provincial election campaign.

Canadiana, 1976. **AEU**

1910 **Hatt**, Fred Kenneth. The response to directed social change on an Alberta Metis colony. Ottawa: National Library of Canada, 1969. 290 leaves. ill. (Canadian theses on microfilm, 04937)

Thesis (M.A.), University of Alberta, 1969.
Microfilm of typescript.
A study of relations between the Metis in Kikino, near Lac La Biche, and their relations with the provincial government.

Canadiana, 1970.

1911 **Hawrysh**, Wasyl. My Canada and I. Memoirs and stories of Canadian Ukrainian pioneers. Edmonton: Ukrainian News Publishers, 1974. 349p. ill.

Text in Ukrainian. Added English title page. **AEU**

1912 **Heidebrecht**, Herbert V. Values of Mennonite youth in Alberta. Ottawa: National Library of Canada, 1973. x, 161 leaves. ill. (Canadian theses on microfiche, 16990)

Thesis (M.A.), University of Calgary, 1973.
Microfiche of typescript.

Canadiana, 1974.

1913 **Hoe**, Ban Seng. Structural changes in two Chinese communities in Alberta, Canada. Ann Arbor, Mich.: University Microfilms, 1974. x, 399 leaves. ill.

Thesis (Ph.D.), Vanderbilt University, 1974.
Microfilm of typescript.

Canadiana, 1978. **OONL**

1914 **Horna**, Jarmila L.A. Alberta's pioneers from Eastern Europe. Reminiscences. The story of Anthony (Tonek) Slezina. Edmonton: University of Alberta, Division of East European Studies, and Central and

East European Studies Society of Alberta, 1979. 130p. (Ethno-cultural Groups in Alberta Study Project. Monographs, papers and reports, 3)

Duplicated. **AEA**

1915 **Horsch**, John. The Hutterian Brethren, 1582-1931. A story of martyrdom and loyalty. Cayley: Macmillan Colony, 1977. xxi, 168p.

Reprint of the 1931 edition, published by the Mennonite Historical Society, issued as no.2 in the series Studies in Anabaptist and Mennonite History.

P.N.L.A., 1979. **AEU**

1916 **Hostetler**, John Andrew. The Hutterians in perspective. An address to the Humanities Association of Canada, U. of A., Edmonton, Oct., 1960. Slightly rev. s.l.: John Hostetler, n.d. 24 leaves.

Dew. **AEA**

1917 **Hughes**, Stuart. The Frog Lake massacre. Personal perspectives on ethnic conflict. Edited and with an introduction by Stuart Hughes. Toronto: McClelland and Stewart, 1976. xxix, 364p. ill. (Carleton library, 097)

Published in association with the Institute of Canadian Studies, Carleton University.

AEA

1918 **Hungry Wolf**, Adolf. Blackfoot craftworker's book. Compiled by Adolf and Beverly Hungry Wolf. Invermere, B.C.: Good Medicine Books, 1977. 79p. ill. (Good medicine books, 15)

Cover title.
Caption title *Blackfoot craftwork's book*.
A reference book of traditional costumes and accessories. **AEA**

1919 **Hungry Wolf**, Adolf. Blackfoot people. A tribal handbook. Invermere, B.C.: Good Medicine Books, 1975. 59p. ill. (Good medicine books, 12)

Cover title.

Canadiana, 1975. **AEA**

1920 **Hungry Wolf**, Adolf. The Blood people, a division of the Blackfoot confederacy. An illustrated interpretation of the old ways. New York: Harper & Row, 1977. xiii, 370p. ill. **AEA**

1921 **Hungry Wolf**, Adolf. Charlo's People. The Flathead tribe. Invermere, B.C.: Good Medicine Books, 1974. 64p. ill. (Good medicine books, 10)

A tribal handbook.

Canadiana, 1975. **AEA**

1922 **Hungry Wolf**, Adolf. Good medicine companion issue. Golden, B.C.: Good Medicine Books, 1971. 28p. ill. (Good medicine books, 2)

Cover title.

Includes accounts of the Sun Dance, Ghost Dance and Sacred Tobacco ceremonies. **AEA**

1923 **Hungry Wolf**, Adolf. Good medicine. Traditional dress issue. Knowledge and methods of old time clothing. Golden, B.C.: Good Medicine Books, 1971. 64p. ill. (Good medicine books, 3)

Cover title. **AEA**

1924 **Hungry Wolf**, Adolf. Indian summer. Invermere, B.C.: Good Medicine Books, 1975. 120p. ill. (Good medicine books, 13)

A collection of short articles on Indian life and lore.

Canadiana, 1975. **AEA**

1925 **Hungry Wolf**, Adolf. Teachings of nature. Invermere, B.C.: Good Medicine Books, 1975. 60p. ill. (Good medicine books, 14)

Canadiana, 1975. **AEA**

1926 **Hungry Wolf**, Adolf. Tipi life. Fort Macleod: Good Medicine Books, 1972. 34p. ill. (Good medicine books, 5)

On spine: Good medicine tipi life.
Information on constructing and living in a tipi.

Canadiana, 1973. **AEA**

1927 Hutterite Brethren. The Hutterian Brethren of America. Lethbridge: Hutterite Brethren, 1964. 24p.

Glenbow. **ACG**

1928 Indian Association of Alberta. Indian hunting, fishing and trapping rights today. A booklet prepared for treaty Indians. Edmonton: Indian Association of Alberta, 1974. 19 leaves.

Cover title. Duplicated. **AEU**

1929 Indian Association of Alberta. A proposal concerning the economic and human resources development of the Indian peoples of Alberta. Edmonton: Indian Association of Alberta, 1969. 4, 29 leaves.

Duplicated.
Proposal for an Alberta Indian Development Systems (AIDS) to be supported by the federal and provincial governments and private industry. **ACG**

1930 Indian Chiefs of Alberta. Citizens plus. A presentation by the Indian Chiefs of Alberta to Right Honourable P.E. Trudeau, Prime Minister and the Government of Canada. Edmonton: Indian Association of Alberta, 1970. 100p.

Popularly known as the Red Paper.
A response to the federal white paper of 1969.
Pp.57-100 concern the proposed Alberta Indian Education Centre.

Glenbow. **ACG**

1931 **Jackson**, Wayne Harry. Ethnicity and areal organization among French Canadians in the Peace River district, Alberta. Edmonton: University of Alberta, 1970. x, (129) leaves.

Thesis (M.A.), University of Alberta, 1970.
Typescript.

Canadian theses. **AEU**

1932 **Katyi**, Andr ˆ. Angels on Devil's Island. Translated by Judi Simms. Calgary: Kyle Printing & Stationery, 1977. 105p. ill.

Autobiography of an Hungarian emigrant.

Canadiana, 1979. **AEA**

1933 **Khattab**, Abdelmoneim M. The assimilation of Arab Muslims in Alberta. Edmonton: University of Alberta, 1969. ix, 83 leaves.

Thesis (M.A.), University of Alberta, 1969.
Typescript.

Canadian theses. **AEU**

1934 **Knill**, William Douglas. Cultural transmission in a closed society. The Hutterites. Edmonton: University of Alberta, n.d. 23 leaves.

Glenbow. **ACG**

1935 **Kostash**, Myrna. All of Baba's children. Edmonton: Hurtig, 1977. 414p.

History of Ukrainians in Western Canada.

CBIP, 1979. **AEA**

1936 **Kurelek**, William. Jewish life in Canada. Paintings and commentaries by William Kurelek. A historical essay by Abraham Arnold. Edmonton: Hurtig, 1976. 91p. ill.

Canadiana, 1977. **AEU**

1937 **Laing**, Lory Mair. Population growth patterns among Alberta Hutterites. Ottawa: National Library of Canada, 1975. xi, 84 leaves. (Canadian Theses on microfiche, 24079)

Thesis (M.A.), University of Alberta, 1975.
Microfiche of typescript.

U of A Theses. **AEU**

1938 **Larner**, John W. The Kootenay Plains (Alberta) land question and Canadian Indian policy, 1799-1947. Ann Arbor, Mich.: University Microfilms, 1972. ix, 586 leaves. ill.

Thesis (Ph.D.), West Virginia University, 1972.
Microfilm of typescript.
Contends that the Stoney of southwestern Alberta have a claim to the Bighorn and Kootenay Plains.

Canadiana, 1974. **AEU**

1939 **LaRoque**, Emma. Defeathering the Indian. Agincourt, Ont.: Book Society of Canada, 1975. 82p. ill.

A handbook of native studies originated under the auspices of the Alberta Department of Education. **ACP**

1940 **Laurence**, Margaret Christine. U.S. expatriates in Calgary and their problems. Ottawa: National Library of Canada, 1972. viii, 107 leaves. ill. (Canadian theses on microfilm, 11336)

Thesis (M.S.W.), University of Calgary, 1972.
Microfilm of typescript.

Canadiana, 1972. **OONL**

1941 **Laycock**, Mae. Bridges of friendship. Edmonton: Mae Laycock, 1974. 48p. ill.

An account of the work undertaken for the Ukrainian people by the Methodist, Presbyterian, and United Churches, from 1924 to 1937.

Ceessa. **AEA**

1942 **Lehr**, John Campbell. Mormon settlements in southern Alberta. Edmonton: University of Alberta, 1971. ix, 128 leaves.

Thesis (M.A.), University of Alberta, 1971.
Typescript.

Canadian theses. **AEU**

1943 **Lewis**, Oscar. The effects of white contact upon Blackfoot culture, with special reference to the role of the fur trade. Seattle: University of Washington Press, 1966. vi, 73p. ill. (American Ethnological Society. Monographs, 6)

Reprinted 1966.
Thesis (Ph.D.), Columbia University.

Canadiana, 1974.

1944 **Linder**, A. Dorothy. Ethnic strategies of three minority groups in the city of Calgary. Ottawa: National Library of Canada, 1976. vii, 123 leaves. (Canadian theses on microfiche, 28536)

Thesis (M.A.), University of Calgary, 1976.
Microfiche of typescript.

Canadiana, 1977. **OONL**

1945 **Lusty**, Terrance W.J. Metis social-political movement. Calgary: T. Lusty, 1973. 28p. ill.

Canadiana, 1974. **ACG**

1946 **Lusty**, Terrance W.J. Red paper vs white paper. Calgary: Indian and Metis Historical Club, 1970. 15 leaves

Cover title. Duplicated.

A response to the federal government white paper of 1970.

Glenbow. **ACG**

1947 **Lyon**, Louise C. Culture change and education. A study of Indian and non-Indian views in southern Alberta. By Louise C. Lyon and John Friesen. New York: Associated Educational Services Corporation, 1969. iii, 160p. ill. (Selected academic readings)

Glenbow. **ACG**

1948 **Macdonald**, Elizabeth. Japanese Canadians in Edmonton, 1969. An exploratory search for patterns of assimilation. Edmonton: University of Alberta, 1970. viii, 107 leaves.

Thesis (M.A.), University of Alberta, 1970.
Typescript.

Canadian theses. **AEU**

1949 **MacEwan**, John Walter Grant. Portraits from the plains. Toronto: McGraw-Hill, 1971. 287p. ill.

Biographical sketches of Plains Indians.

Glenbow. **ACG**

1950 **MacGregor**, James Grierson. Vilni zemli (free lands). The Ukranian settlement of Alberta. Toronto: McClelland and Stewart, 1969. ix, 274p.

Glenbow. **ACG**

1951 **Mackay**, Donald Stewart. The cultural ecology of the Chipewyan. Ottawa: National Library of Canada, 1978. viii, 227 (i.e. 265) leaves. ill. (Canadian theses on microfiche, 38452)

Thesis (M.A.), Simon Fraser University, 1978.
Microfiche of typescript.

Canadiana, 1980. **OONL**

1952 **Mackie**, Marlene Marie. The accuracy of folk knowledge concerning Alberta Indians, Hutterites, and Ukrainians. An available data stereotype validation technique. Ottawa: National Library of Canada, 1971. xviii, 493 leaves. ill. (Canadian theses on microfilm, 08101)

Thesis (M.A.), University of Alberta, 1971.
Microfilm of typescript.

Canadiana, 1972. **OONL**

1953 **Mackie**, Marlene Marie. The defector from the Hutterite Colony. A pilot study. Calgary: University of Calgary, 1965. vi, 167 leaves. ill. (Canadian theses on microfilm, 08433)

Thesis (M.A.), University of Alberta at Calgary, 1965.
Microfilm of typescript.

Dew. **ACU**

1954 **MacRury**, Katherine Anne. The occupational adjustment of Vietnamese refugees in Edmonton, Canada. Edmonton: University of Alberta, 1979. xiv, 104 leaves.

Thesis (M.Ed.), University of Alberta, 1979.
Typescript.

U of A Theses. **AEU**

1955 **Mann**, George Adolf. Functional autonomy among English school teachers in the Hutterite colonies of southern Alberta. A study of social control. Ann Arbor, Mich.: University Microfilms, 1974. xx, 404 leaves.

Thesis (Ph.D.), University of Colorado, 1974.
Microfilm of typescript.

Canadiana, 1978. **OONL**

1956 **Marunchak**, Michael Hryhor. Among Ukrainian pioneers of Alberta. Winnipeg: General Library, UKT, 1964. 88p. ill.

Title page and text in Ukrainian. Added title page and introduction in English.

Glenbow. **ACG**

1957 **Matejko**, Joanna. Polish settlers in Alberta. Reminiscences and biographies. Toronto: Polish Alliance Press, 1979. 487p. ill.

Added title page and some text in Polish. **ACP**

1958 Metis Association of Alberta. Metis study tour report, December, 1968. Edmonton: Metis Association of Alberta, 1968. 29 leaves.

Canadiana, 1976.

1959 Metis Association of Alberta. Origins of the Alberta Metis. Land claims research project, 1978-79. Edmonton: Metis Association of Alberta, 1979. viii, 485p. maps.

Duplicated. **AEA**

1960 Metis Association of Alberta. A proposal for progress. Position paper. Edmonton: Metis Association of Alberta, 1973. 55 leaves.

Cover title.
Paper submitted to Hon. Peter Lougheed. **AEU**

1961 **Middleton**, Samuel Henry. Kainai chieftainship. History, evolution and culture of the Blood Indians. Origin of the sun-dance. With foreword by Viscount Alexander of Tunis. Lethbridge: Lethbridge Herald, 1954. 178p. ill.

On spine: Blackfoot confederacy, ancient and modern.
On cover: Indian chiefs.
Written at the official request of Head Chief Shot-On-Both-Sides and the Council of the Blood Indians.

Glenbow. **ACG**

1962 **Milloy**, John Sheridan. The Plains Cree. A preliminary trade and military chronology, 1670-1870. Ottawa: Carleton University, 1972. 356 leaves.

Thesis (M.A.), Carleton University, 1972.
Typescript.

Canadian theses, 1972/73-1974/75.

1963 **Mohr**, Hilda (Berg). The great pioneers who cleared and broke the virgin land of Josephburg, 1867-1967. Josephburg: H. Mohr, 1967. 62p.

Cover title *Josephburg heritage, 1867-1967*.
Galicians settled in Josephburg from 1888 onwards. An account of the pioneers and their descendants, with a brief history of the community.

Dew. **ACG**

1964 **Morah**, Benson Chukwuma. The assimilation of Ugandan Asians in Calgary. Ottawa: National Library of Canada, 1974. xi, 164 leaves. (Canadian theses on microfiche, 19810)

Thesis (M.A.), University of Calgary, 1974.
Microfilm of typescript.

Canadiana, 1975. **OONL**

1965 **Mountain Horse**, Mike. My people the Bloods. Editing and introduction by Hugh A. Demspey. Calgary: Glenbow-Alberta Institute and Blood Tribal Council, 1979. xi, 146p. ill.

Account of customs, daily life, war exploits and legends of the tribe.

Canadiana, 1979. **AEA**

1966 **Munroe**, Scott William. Warriors of the rock. Basic social structure of the mountain bands of Stoney Indians at Morley, Alberta. Ottawa: National Library of Canada, 1970. vii, 92 leaves. ill. (Canadian theses on microfilm, 04037)

Thesis (M.A.), University of Calgary, 1969.
Microfilm of typescript.

Canadiana, 1970. **OONL**

1967 One century later. Western Canadian reserve Indians since Treaty 7. Edited by Ian A.L. Getty and Donald B. Smith. Vancouver: University of British Columbia Press, 1978. xvi, 153p. ill.

Contents: 1. Snow, J. Treaty Seven centennial. Celebration or commemoration?-2. Ray, A.J. Fur trade history as an aspect of native history.

Canadiana, 1979. **AEU**

1968 **Palmer**, Howard. History of minority groups in southern Alberta since 1940. s.n.: s.l., 1968. 170 leaves.

Reproduced from typescript.
"University Scholar Project".

Dew. **ALU**

1969 **Palmer**, Howard. Land of the second chance. A history of ethnic groups in southern Alberta. Lethbridge: Lethbridge Herald, 1972. 287p.

Canadiana, 1972. **ACG**

1970 **Palmer**, Howard. Nativism and ethnic tolerance in Alberta, 1920-1972. Ottawa: National Library of Canada, 1973. xiii, 464 leaves. (Canadian theses on microfiche, 17136)

Thesis (Ph.D.), York University, 1973.
Microfilm of typescript.

Canadiana, 1974. **OONL**

1971 **Palmer**, Howard. Responses to foreign immigration. Nativism and ethnic tolerance in Alberta, 1880-1920. Edmonton: University of Alberta, 1971. viii, 291, xv leaves.

Thesis (M.A.), University of Alberta, 1971.
Typescript.

Canadian theses. **AEU**

1972 **Parnell**, Ted. Disposable native. Edmonton: Alberta Human Rights and Civil Liberties Association, 1976. 216p. ill.

Examines the underlying processes of native-white conflict in Alberta. **AEA**

1973 Persistence and change. A study of Ukrainians in Alberta. By C.W. Hobart, W.E. Kalbach, J.T. Borhek, and A.P. Jacoby. s.l.: s.n., n.d. (Canadian centennial series)

Sponsored by the Ukrainian Canadian Research Foundation.
Separate chapters deal with immigration, history, settlement patterns, acculturation, education, and other topics. **AEU**

1974 **Pidruchney**, Anna. From old lands to new. The first Ukrainian Canadians. Vegreville: Anna Pidruchney, 1977. 18p. ill.

Canadiana, 1979. **AEA**

1975 **Pike**, Wentworth E. Eskimos in Alaska. Three Hills: Prairie Bible Institute, 1967. 47p. ill.

Glenbow. **ACG**

1976 **Poetschke**, Thomas R. Reasons for immigration and ethnic identity. An exploratory study of German immigrants in Edmonton, Alberta. Ottawa: National Library of Canada, 1978. ix, 112 leaves. (Canadian theses on microfiche, 36460)

Thesis (M.A.), University of Alberta, 1978.
Microfiche of typescript.

U of A Theses. **AEU**

1977 Polish Alliance of Calgary. 30th anniversary of Polish Alliance in Calgary, 1931-1961. Calgary: Nak. Zwiazku Polakow w Calgary, 1961. 48p. ill.

Text in English and Polish. **AEA**

1978 **Potrebenko**, Helen. No streets of gold. A social history of Ukrainians in Alberta. Vancouver: New Star Books, 1977. 311p. ill.

Canadiana, 1978. **AEA**

1979 **Price**, Richard. Indian land claims in Alberta. Politics and policy-making, 1968-77. Edmonton: University of Alberta, 1977. xi, 309 leaves.

Thesis (M.A.), University of Alberta, 1977.
Typescript.

U of A Theses. **AEU**

1980 **Price**, Richard. The spirit of the Alberta Indian treaties. Edited by Richard Price. Toronto: Institute for Research on Public Policy, 1979. 202p. ill.

A collection of essays and interviews.
Contents: Pt.1. The treaty-making process. Pt.2. Alberta interpretations of the treaties. **AEA**

1981 **Prokopiw**, Orysia Love Olia (Ferbey). The Ukrainians. An outline history. Calgary: Centennial Ukrainian Committee, 1967. 40p. ill.

Canadiana, 1969.

1982 **Pyne**, Garry H. The pre-reserve Blackfoot, cultural persistence and change. Ottawa: National Library of Canada, 1970. iii. 73 leaves.

Thesis (M.A.), Simon Fraser University, 1970.
Microfilm of thesis.

Canadiana, 1971. **OONL**

1983 **Rees-Powell**, Alan Thomas. Differentials in the integration process of Dutch and Italian immigrants in Edmonton. Edmonton: University of Alberta, 1964. xv, 208 leaves.

Thesis (M.A.), University of Alberta, 1964.
Typescript.

Canadian theses. **AEU**

1984 Roots. The ethnic history of Edmonton. Reprinted from the popular series of articles. Edmonton: Edmonton Journal, 1976. 28p. ill. **AEU**

1985 **Ryan**, Joan. Wall of words. The betrayal of the urban Indian. Toronto: Peter Martin Associates, 1978. 117p.

An account of Indian people in Calgary, the work of CUTIA (the Calgary Urban Treaty Indian Alliance) and the death of Nelson Small Legs, Jr. **ACP**

1986 **Sawatzky**, Aron. The Mennonites of Alberta and their assimilation. Edmonton: University of Alberta, 1964. vi, 287 leaves.

Thesis (M.A.), University of Alberta, 1964.
Typescript.

Canadian theses. **AEU**

1987 **Scott-Brown**, Joan M. Stoney ethnobotany. An indication of cultural change amongst Stoney women of Morley, Alberta. Ottawa: National Library of Canada, 1977. x, 194 leaves. maps. (Canadian theses on microfiche, 34081)

Thesis (M.A.), University of Calgary, 1977.
Microfiche of typescript.

OONL

1988 **Seidel**, Rolf Christian. The Hutterite ways. Illustrations by D.J. Greer. St. Albert: Production House, 1973. 13 leaves. ill.

Written for children.

AEA

1989 **Seminar on Cultural Differences**, University of Alberta, 1963. Insights into cultural differences. A compilation of study material from a seminar on cultural differences for the instruction of people working with ethnic groups in the Edmonton area. Edmonton: Edmonton Welfare Council, 1963. 79p. (i.e. 95p.) ill.

Seminar held in Edmonton, June 13-15, 1963.
Sponsored by the Edmonton Welfare Council in co-operation with the Canadian Citizenship Branch.
Editor, J. Motyl.
Comprises two papers by Benjamin Schlesinger and papers given in a panel presentation.

Glenbow.

ACG

1990 **Sharp**, Henry Stephen. The kinship system of the Black Lake Chipewyan. Ann Arbor, Mich.: University Microfilms, 1973. xiii, 310 leaves. ill.

Thesis (Ph.D.), Duke University, 1973.
Microfilm of typescript.

Canadiana, 1978.

OONL

1991 **Skeels**, Lydia Lowndes Maury. Location of the Indian tribes at first white contact in Alberta, Canada. Ottawa: National Library of Canada, 1968. viii, 113 leaves. (Canadian theses on microfilm, 02779)

Thesis (M.A.), University of Calgary, 1968.
Microfilm of typescript.

Canadiana, 1969.

OONL

1992 **Slavutych**, Yar. Collected papers on Ukrainian settlers in Western Canada. Compiled and edited by Yar Slavutych. Edmonton: Shevchenko Scientific Society in Canada, Western Canadian Branch, 1973. 2v.

In Ukrainian, with added English title-page.

ACP

1993 **Snider**, Howard Mervin. Variables affecting immigrant adjustment. A study of Italians in Edmonton. Edmonton: University of Alberta, 1966. xi, 160 leaves. ill.

Thesis (M.A.), University of Alberta, 1966.
Typescript.

Canadian theses.

AEU

1994 **Snow**, John. These mountains are our sacred places. The story of the Stoney Indians. Toronto: Samuel Stevens, 1977. 186p. ill.

Also, paperback edition, 1977, Toronto, Stevens, with sub-title *The story of the Stoney people*.

Canadiana, 1977. **AEA**

1995 **Spiteri**, Ed. Hutterites. The Hutterite Diamond Jubilee. Text by Hugh Dempsey. Calgary: Glenbow-Alberta Institute, 1978. 34 leaves (chiefly ill.)

Photographs by Spiteri.
Text in English and French.

CBIP., 1979. **AEA**

1996 **Stechishin**, Julius William. Istoriia poselennia ukraintsiv u Kanadi. Edmonton: Vyd. Soluzu ukraintsiv samostiinykiv, 1975. 351p. ill.

Canadiana, 1977.

1997 **Stibbe**, Hugo L.P. The distribution of ethnic groups in Alberta, according to the 1961 census. Edmonton: University of Alberta, 1966. ix, 134 leaves. ill.

Thesis (M.Sc.), University of Alberta, 1966.
Typescript.

Dew. **ACU**

1998 Swyripa. Frances. Ukrainian Canadians. A survey of their portrayal in English-language works. Edmonton: University of Alberta Press, 1978. xiii, 169p. (Alberta Library in Ukrainian-Canadian Studies)

Published for the Canadian Institute of Ukrainian Studies.

CBIP, 1979. **AEA**

1999 **Teal**, Greg. Urban anthropology and the problems of the formation of social classes. With reference to Korean immigrants in Edmonton. Ottawa: National Library of Canada, 1979. viii, 127 leaves. (Canadian theses on microfiche, 40511)

Thesis (M.A.), University of Alberta, 1979.
Microfiche of typescript. **AEU**

2000 Ukrainian Canadians, multiculturalism and separatism. An assessment. Edited by Manoly R. Lupul. Edmonton: University of Alberta Press for the Canadian Institute of Ukrainian Studies, 1978. 177p. (Alberta library in Ukrainian-Canadian Studies)

Proceedings of a conference sponsored by the Canadian Institute of Ukrainian Studies, University of Alberta, Edmonton, September 9-11, 1977.

Canadiana, 1978. **AEU**

2001 The Ukrainian pioneers in Alberta, Canada. Joseph M. Lazarenko, Editor-in-Chief. Edmonton: Ukrainian Pioneers Association in Edmonton, 1970. 384p. ill. .

Printed by Alberta Printing.

Glenbow. **ACG**

2002 Ukrainian Pioneers' Association of Alberta. Ukrainians in Alberta. Edmonton: Ukrainian Pioneers' Association of Alberta, 1975. 564p. ill.

Consists chiefly of biographies.
Printed by the Ukrainian News Publishers.

Canadiana, 1976. **AEU**

2003 **Watt**, Carol Luanne. The role of a change agent as a factor in resource development in a reserve community. Ottawa: National Library of Canada, 1973. xiv, 148 leaves. (Canadian theses on microfiche, 17722)

Thesis (M.A.), University of Alberta, 1973.
Microfiche of typescript.

U of A theses. **AEU**

2004 **Wear**, Robert Dalattin. Nomads versus cultivators. A cultural analysis of the Western World. Edmonton: Ethnic Song Publications, 1977. 276p.

Canadiana, 1977.

2005 **Wuttunee**, William I.C. Ruffled feathers. Indians in Canadian society. Calgary: Bell Books, 1971. vii, 174p.

Printed and bound in Japan.
A criticism of the reservation system and the treaty mentality.

Glenbow. **ACG**

2006 **Yedlin**, Tova. Alberta's pioneers from Eastern Europe. Reminiscences. Tova Yedlin and Joanna Matejko, editors. Edmonton: University of Alberta, Division of East European Studies, 1976. 70p. (Central and East European Ethno-Cultural Groups in Alberta Study Project. Monographs, papers and reports, 1)

Duplicated.
Series numbered retroactively. **AEA**

2007 **Zentner**, Henry. The Indian identity crisis. Inquiries into the problems and prospects of societal development among native peoples. Calgary: Strayer Publications, 1973. xxii, 121p.

Six essays, five previously published in journals or conference proceedings.

Canadiana, 1973. **AEU**

Anthropology Archaeology

2008 Aboriginal man and environments on the plateau of northwest America. Editors: Arnoud H. Stryd, Rachel A. Smith. Calgary: Students' Press, 1971. 261p. ill., maps.

Cover title.
Papers from the third Annual Conference of the University of Calgary Archaeological Association, November, 1970. **AEU**

2009 **Anderson**, James Maxwell. Ancient Hispanic inscriptions. Calgary: University of Calgary, 1975. 90p. ill., maps. (University of Calgary. Department of Archaeology. Occasional papers, 3)

2010 Archaeological Society of Alberta. Archaeology in Alberta. Sponsored by the Society, University of Alberta, Glenbow Foundation and Research Council of Alberta. Edmonton: Archaeological Society of Alberta, 1962. 24p. ill.

Presented by the Society in Convocation Hall, University of Alberta, Feb.5-10, 1962.

Glenbow. **ACG**

2011 Archaeological Society of Alberta. Lethbridge Centre. Grassy Lake and Suitor sites. Lethbridge: Archaeological Society of Alberta, Lethbridge Centre, 1978. 25p. ill. (Archaeological Society of Alberta. Lethbridge Centre. Project, 17-18)

Cover title.

Canadiana, 1979.

2012 Archaeological Society of Alberta. Lethbridge Centre. Police Coulee. A pictorial record of prehistoric and historic artifacts, petroglyphs & pictographs. Lethbridge: Archaeological Society of Alberta, Lethbridge Centre, 1973. 15 leaves. ill. (Archaeological Society of Alberta. Lethbridge Centre. Project, 11)

Duplicated.

Canadiana, 1974. **AEU**

2013 Archaeological Society of Alberta. Lethbridge Centre. A report on Blood Indian chief tipi circle and the Stevens Rock at Foremost, Alberta. Lethbridge: Archaeological Society of Alberta, Lethbridge Centre, 1973. 18 leaves. ill. (Archaeological Society of Alberta. Lethbridge Centre. Project, 09-10)

Duplicated.
Caption title *Indian Battle Coulee. A record of artifacts from the last inter-tribal battle*.

Canadiana, 1975. **AEA**

2014 Archaeological Society of Alberta. Lethbridge Centre. Reports on the last Indian battle and the Lindy campsite, the Sundial Butte cairn site, the Gergel campsite, the Burmis Boulder paving site. Lethbridge: Archaeological Society of Alberta, Lethbridge Centre, 1976. 40p. ill. (Archaeological Society of Alberta. Lethbridge Centre. Project, 08, 13-16)

Cover title. Duplicated.
Also, Anderson, Henry R. *Inventory of artifacts from the last Indian battle of 187(mid-October) at Belly River*, 1978. 16p. ill., maps. Supplementary report.

Canadiana. 1976. **AEA**

2015 **Bower**, Carolyn Jane. Petrographic studies of north western plains ceramics. Calgary: University of Calgary, 1973. ix, 159 leaves,

Thesis (M.A.), University of Calgary, 1973.
Typescript.
Pottery from the Morkin site was used as a base for comparison of sherds in Alberta, Saskatchewan, and Montana. **AEA**

2016 **Brumley**, John Harry. The Cactus Flower site and the McKean complex in Alberta. Ottawa: National Library of Canada, 1975. xvii, 262 leaves. ill. (Canadian theses on microfiche, 24978)

Thesis (M.A.), University of Calgary, 1975.
Microfiche of typescript.

Canadiana, 1977.

2017 **Brumley**, John Harry. Suffield archaeological project, 1972. Preliminary report. Medicine Hat: J.H. Brumley, 1973. vi, 136 leaves. ill.

Canadiana, 1975.

2018 **Brumley**, Laurie Ann. The Narrows site in Waterton Lakes National Park, Alberta. Ottawa: National Library of Canada, 1971. xiii, 316(i.e. 332) leaves. ill. (Canadian theses on microfilm, 08841)

Thesis (M.A.), University of Calgary, 1971.
Microfilm of typescript.

Canadiana 1972. **OONL**

2019 **Byrne**, William John. The archaeology and prehistory of southern Alberta as reflected by ceramics. Late prehistoric and protohistoric cultural developments. Ann Arbor, Mich.: University Microfilms, 1973. viii, 231, i-v, 232-605, 1-viii, 606-728 leaves. ill.

Thesis (Ph.D.), Yale University.
Microfilm of typescript.

Canadiana, 1974.

2020 **Calder**, James M. The Majorville cairn and medicine wheel site, Alberta. Ottawa: National Library of Canada, 1975. xiv, 297 leaves. ill. (Canadian theses on microfiche, 24983)

Thesis (M.A.), University of Calgary, 1975.
Microfiche of typescript.

Canadiana, 1977.

2021 **Christensen**, Ole Arne. Banff prehistory. Prehistoric subsistence and settlement in Banff National eses on microfilm, 08841) c studies of north western plains ceramics. Calgary: University of ndian n, Park, Alberta. Ottawa: National Library of Canada, 1971. x, 279 leaves. ill. (Canadian theses on microfilm, 11297)

Thesis (M.A.), University of Calgary, 1972.
Microfilm of typescript.

Canadiana, 1972.

2022 **Conference on Canadian Archaeology Abroad**, University of Calgary, 1973. Papers from Conference on Canadian Archaeology Abroad, held at the University of Calgary, November 23, 24, 25, 1973. Edited by P.L. Shinnie, John H. Robertson, Francois J. Kense. Calgary: University of Calgary Archaeological Association, 1976. i, 286p. ill.

On cover: Canadian archaeology abroad.
Includes some text in French.
Held under the auspices of the Archaeological Association and the Department of Archaeology.

Canadiana, 1978. **OONL**

2023 **Coulton**, Richard Lee. A guide to the historic sites of the Gull Lake region of Alberta. Bentley: R.L. Coulton, 1975. 10p. ill., maps. (Coulton, R.L. Miscellaneous memoirs, 4)

Cover title. Duplicated.

Canadiana, 1976. **AEU**

2024 **Davis**, R.P. Stephen. The Wiser-Stephens 1 site - 40CF81. Ottawa: National Library of Canada, 1976. xi, 209 leaves. ill. (Canadian theses on microfiche, 28495)

Thesis (M.A.), University of Calgary, 1976.
Microfiche of typescript.

Canadiana, 1977. **OONL**

2025 **Dempsey**, Hugh Aylmer. A history of Writing-On-Stone. Calgary: H.A. Dempsey, 1973. 150 leaves.

Duplicated.

Ceessa. **AEA**

2026 Diffusion and migration, their roles in cultural development. Editors, P.G. Duke et al. Calgary: University of Calgary Archaeological Association, 1978. 275p. ill.

Proceedings of the 10th annual conference of the University of Calgary Archaeological Association. **AEU**

2027 Early man and environments in northwest North America. Edited by R.A. Smith and J.W. Smith. Calgary: Students' Press, 1970. 136p. ill.

Proceedings of the 2nd annual Paleo-environmental Workshop of the University of Calgary Archaeological Association.

Dew. **ACG**

2028 Early man in America. From a circum-Pacific perspective. Edited by Alan Lyle Bryan. Edmonton: Archaeological Researches International, 1978. viii, 327p. ill. (University of Alberta. Department of Anthropology. Occasional paper, 1)

Organized as a symposium at the Thirteenth Pacific Science Congress in Vancouver in August 1975.

Canadiana, 1979.

2029 **Elliott**, William John. Hivernant archaeology in the Cypress Hills. Ottawa: National Library of Canada, 1971. xii, 285 leaves. ill. (Canadian theses on microfilm, 09171)

Thesis (M.A.), University of Calgary, 1971.
Microfilm of typescript.

Canadiana, 1972. **OONL**

2030 **Forbis**, Richard George. Cluny, an ancient fortified village in Alberta. Calgary: University of Calgary, Department of Archaeology, 1977. vii, 81p. ill. (University of Calgary. Department of Archaeology. Occasional papers, 4)

P.N.L.A., 1979. **AEU**

2031 Fort Edmonton. The reconstruction story, 1969-1974. L'histoire de la reconstruction. Compilers, B. Werner, P. Hawker. Edmonton: Fort Edmonton Historical Foundation, 1974. 24p. (chiefly ill.)

Cover title.
Text in English and French.
A joint project of Edmonton Parks and Recreation and Fort Edmonton Historical Foundation. **AEA**

2032 **Fromhold**, Joachim. An illustrated guide to projectile points for the Alberta region. Calgary: Department of Archaeology, University of Calgary, 1972. 50 leaves. ill.

Duplicated.

Canadiana, 1973. **ACG**

2033 **Getty**, Ronald M. The Many Snakes Burial (DgOv-12). A primary inhumation from southern Alberta. Lethbridge: Printed by Unileth Press, 1971. 43 leaves, ill.

Glenbow. **ACG**

2034 **Graspointer**, Andreas. Some aspects and problems of the archaeology along the Milk River in southeast Alberta. Calgary: University of Calgary, 1977. xii, 186 leaves. ill., maps.

Thesis (M.A.), University of Calgary.
Typescript. **AEA**

2035 **Hess**, E. Laraine. Osteology and odontology of the Sharphead burial site. Ottawa: National Library of Canada, 1978. xi, 139 leaves. (Canadian theses on microfiche, 40179)

Thesis (M.A.), University of Alberta, 1978.
Microfiche of typescript.

U of A theses. **AEU**

2036 **Hillerud**, John M. The Duffield site and its fossil bison, Alberta, Canada. Omaha: University of Nebraska, 1966. 198 leaves. ill.

Thesis (M.Sc.), University of Nebraska, 1966.
Typescript. **AEA**

2037 Historical archaeology in northwestern North America. Edited by Ronald M. Getty, Knut R. Fladmark. Calgary: University of Calgary Archaeological Association, 1973. 248p. ill.

Proceedings of the 4th annual conference of the University of Calgary Archaeological Association. **AEU**

2038 **Humphreys**, James Trowe. Record in stone. Calgary: Archaeological Society of Alberta, 1967. (8)p. ill.

On cover: Projectile points common to Alberta.

Glenbow. **ACG**

2039 **Ives**, John W. A spatial analysis of artifact distribution on a boreal forest archaeological site. Ottawa: National Library of Canada, 1977. xiii, 162 leaves. (Canadian theses on microfiche, 34373)

Thesis (M.A.), University of Alberta, 1977.
Microfiche of typescript.

U of A Theses. **AEU**

2040 **King**, Donald Robert. Alberta archaeology. A handbook for amateurs. High River: D.R. King, 1968. 12, 140p. ill.
Glenbow. **ACG**

2041 **Lahren**, Larry A. Northwestern plains archaeology. An illustrated guide. By Larry H. Lahren and Harley R. Sorrells. Calgary: Anthropologos Researches International, 1970. 56p. ill.
Glenbow. **ACG**

2042 **Light**, Douglas W. Tattooing practices of the Cree Indians. Calgary: Glenbow-Alberta Institute, 1972. 23p. ill. (Glenbow-Alberta Institute. Occasional paper, 6)
Glenbow. **ACG**

2043 **Losey**, Timothy Campbell. Archaeology of the Cormie Ranch Site, an interim report. Edmonton: Archaeological Society of Alberta, 1972. 25, 3 leaves of plates. ill. (Archaeological Society of Alberta. Newsletter, 28)
Canadiana, 1975. **AEU**

2044 **Losey**, Timothy Campbell. The prehistoric cultural ecology of the western prairie-forest transition zone, Alberta, Canada. Ottawa: National Library of Canada, 1978. xiii, 206 leaves. (Canadian theses on microfiche, 36422)

Thesis (Ph.D.), University of Alberta, 1978.
Microfiche of typescript.

U of A Theses. AEU

2045 **McCullough**, Edward J. Historical resources impact assessment, western portion of Syncrude lease no.17, Alberta. Edmonton: Syncrude Canada, 1978. iii, 38p. ill. (Syncrude Canada. Environmental research monograph, 1978-2)

Edited by B.O.K. Reeves.

Canadiana, 1979. AEU

2046 **McCullough**, Edward J. Prehistoric cultural dynamics of the Lac La Biche region. Ottawa: National Library of Canada, 1978. 241 leaves. ill. (Canadian theses on microfiche, 37297)

Thesis (M.A.), University of Calgary, 1978.
Microfiche of typescript.

Canadiana, 1979. OONL

2047 **McCullough**, Karen Margrethe. Modified deer phalanges at the Draper site. Ottawa: National Library of Canada, 1978. ix, 135 leaves. ill. (Canadian theses on microfiche, 37298)

Thesis (M.A.), University of Calgary, 1978.
Microfiche of typescript.

Canadiana, 1979. OONL

2048 **Nicks**, Gertrude Cecilia. The archaeology of two Hudson's Bay Company posts. Buckingham House (1792-1800) and Edmonton House III (1810-1813). Edmonton: University of Alberta, 1969. ix, 290 leaves.

Thesis (M.A.), University of Alberta, 1969.
Typescript.

Canadian theses. AEU

2049 Post-pleistocene man and his environment on the northern plains. Edited by R.G. Forbis and others. Calgary: Student's Press, 1969. 220p.

Proceedings of the 1st annual Paleo-environmental workshop of the University of Calgary Archaeological Association. AEU

2050 **Potvin**, Annette. The Sun Dance liturgy of the Blackfoot Indian. Ottawa: University of Ottawa, 1966. 171 leaves.

Thesis (M.A.), University of Ottawa, 1966.
Typescript.

Dew. ALU

2051 Problems in the prehistory of the North American subarctic. The Athapaskan question. Editors, J.W. Helmer, S. Van Dyke, F.J. Kense. Calgary: University of Calgary Archaeological Association, 1977. 223, 42p. ill.

Spine title *The Athabaskan question*.
Proceedings of the 9th annual conference of the Association.

Canadiana, 1979.

2052 **Quigg**, J. Michael. The Belly River. Prehistoric population dynamics in northwestern plains transitional zone. Ottawa: National Library of Canada, 1973. xii, 169 leaves. ill. (Canadian theses on microfiche, 17045)

Thesis (M.A.), University of Calgary, 1973.
Microfiche of typescript.

Canadiana, 1974. **OONL**

2053 **Raymond**, J. Scott. Cumancaya. A Peruvian ceramic tradition. J. Scott Raymond, Warren R. DeBoer, Peter G. Roe. Calgary: University of Calgary, 1975. 143p. ill., maps. (University of Calgary. Department of Archaeology. Occasional papers, 2)

2054 **Raymond**, J. Scott. Primitive art and technology. Edited by J.S. Raymond, B. Loveseth, C. Arnold, G. Reardon. Calgary: Archaeological Association, Department of Archaeology, University of Calgary, 1975. 181p. ill.

Papers from a symposium on Primitive Technology and Art, held in Calgary, 1974, the seventh annual conference of the University of Calgary Archaeological Association. **AEA**

2055 **Reeves**, Brian O.K. An archaeological resource inventory of Waterton Lakes National Park and preliminary archaeological report for 1971. Calgary: s.n., 1971. 1v. ill.

Glenbow. **ACG**

2056 **Reeves**, Brian O.K. Culture changes on the northern plains, 1000 B.C. to 1000 A.D. Ottawa: National Library of Canada, 1970. (1v.) (Canadian theses on microfilm, 06862)

Thesis (Ph.D.), University of Calgary, 1970.
Microfilm of typescript.

Dew. **ACU**

2057 **Reeves**, Brian O.K. The Kenney Site. A stratified campsite in southwestern Alberta. Ottawa: National Library of Canada, 1966. (1v.) (Canadian theses on microfilm, 08435)

Thesis (M.A.), University of Calgary, 1966.
Microfilm of typescript.

Dew. **ACU**

2058 **Solecki**, Ralph S. Archaeological reconnaissance north of the Brooks range in northeastern Alaska. Ralph S. Solecki, Bert Salwen, Jerome Jacobson. Appendices by William F. Farrand, Isabella Drew. Calgary: Department of Archaeology, University of Calgary, 1973. vi, 105p. ill., maps. (University of Calgary. Department of Archaeology. Occasional papers, 1)

2059 **Spencer**, J.A. Crystal Spring Indian camp site. Lethbridge: Archaeological Society of Alberta, Lethbridge Centre, 1966. iv, 35p. ill.

Cover title. Duplicated.
Account of collecting and documenting artifacts.

Glenbow. **ACG**

2060 **Stump**, Sarain. American Indian graphic symbols and their adaptation in art. Saskatoon: Saskatchewan Indian Cultural College, 1973. 10 leaves (chiefly ill.)

A booklet of symbols used by Plains Indians to record events. **AEU**

2061 Syncrude Canada Ltd. The Beaver Creek site. A prehistoric stone quarry on Syncrude Lease #22. Edmonton: Syncrude Canada, 1974. v, 113p. ill. (Syncrude Canada. Environmental research monograph, 1974-2)

Study carried out by Timothy Losey and Cort Sims.

Canadiana, 1976. **AEA**

2062 Syncrude Canada Ltd. Syncrude Lease no. 17. An archaeological survey. Edmonton: Syncrude Canada, 1973. 98 (3) leaves. ill. (Syncrude Canada. Environmental research monograph, 1973-4)

Canadiana, 1977.

2063 **Taylor**, Ernest Fraser. Archaeology of the Peace Hills area of central Alberta, Canada. Edmonton: University of Alberta, 1969. ix, 168 leaves.

Thesis (M.A.), University of Alberta, 1969.
Typescript.

Canadian theses. **AEU**

2064 **Thomson**, Hugh Ross. An introduction to the prehistory of the Peace River country. Ottawa: National Library of Canada, 1973. ix, 114p. (Canadian theses on microfiche, 17709)

Thesis (M.A.), University of Alberta, 1973.
Microfiche of typescript.

U of A Theses. **AEU**

2065 **Wilson**, Robert Nathaniel. Ethnological notes on Blackfoot and Blood Indians. Edited by Philip H. Godsell. s.l.: R.N. Wilson, 1958. 2v.

Duplicated.

Dew. **ACG**

2066 **Wormington**, Hannah Marie. An introduction to the archaeology of Alberta, Canada. By H.M. Wormington and Richard G. Forbis. Denver, Colo.: Denver Museum of Natural History, 1965. xviii, 248p. ill. (Denver Museum of Natural History. Proceedings, no. 11)

Appendix: Prehistoric pottery from southeastern Alberta by James B. Griffin.

Glenbow. **ACG**

2067 **Wright**, Bruce William. A proxemic analysis of the Iroquoian settlement pattern. Calgary: Western Publishers, 1979. v, 87p. maps. **AEA**

Folklore and Legends

2068 **Anderson**, Anne. Legends of Wesakecha. Edmonton: A. Anderson, 1973. 44p.

Illustrated with drawings by students at Ermineskin School, Hobbema, Alberta.

Canadiana, 1975. **AEU**

2069 **Anderson**, Anne. The lore of the wilds. Edmonton: Cree Productions, 1976. 39 leaves. ill.

Cover title.

Indian legends. **AEU**

2070 **Brass**, Eleanor. Medicine Boy and other Cree tales. Illustrations by Henry Nanooch. Calgary: Glenbow-Alberta Institute, 1978. (79p.) ill.

Canadiana, 1979. **AEA**

2071 **Campbell**, Maria. Little Cree Badger and the Fire Spirit. Illustrated by David Maclagan. Toronto: McClelland and Stewart, 1977. 32p. ill.

Canadiana, 1977. **AEA**

2072 **Deegan**, Jim. Timberline tales. Folklore in verse of the Canadian Rockies. Jim Deegan, John Porter. Banff: The Peter Whyte Foundation, 1977. (53)p. ill.

Canadiana, 1978. **ACP**

2073 **Fraser**, Frances Jane (Williams). The bear who stole the chinook and other stories. Illustrated by Lewis Parker. Toronto: Macmillan, 1959. 4, 72p. ill.

Legends and folk tales of the Blackfoot Indians.

Canadiana, 1960. **AEU**

2074 **Fraser**, Frances Jane (Williams). The wind along the River. Illustrated by Lewis Parker. Toronto: Macmillan of Canada, 1968. 83p. ill.

Blackfoot legends.

Dew. **AEU**

2075 **Gard**, Robert Edward. Johnny Chinook. Tall tales and true from the Canadian west. Illustrated by Walter Philipps. Edmonton: Hurtig, 1967. xix, 360p. ill.

Alberta folk tales.
First published, 1945, London, Longmans, Green, (Peel 3916).

Canadiana, 1968. **AEA**

2076 **Hungry Wolf**, Adolf. Good medicine. Life in harmony with nature. Golden, B.C.: Good Medicine Books, 1970. 32p. ill. (Good medicine books, 1)

Cover title.
Brief articles on Indian lore.

AEA

2077 **Hungry Wolf**, Adolf. The good medicine book. New York: Warner Paperback Library, 1973. 473p. ill.

Cover title *The good medicine book. The wisdom of the Old Ones, their legends, crafts and sacred ways*, by a Son of the Blackfoot Tribe.

Canadiana, 1974.

AEA

2078 **Hungry Wolf**, Adolf. Good medicine in Glacier National Park. Inspirational photos and stories from the days of the Blackfoot people. Golden, B.C.: Good Medicine Books, 1971. 32p. ill. (Good medicine books, 4)

Cover title.

AEA

2079 **Hungry Wolf**, Adolf. Legends told by the old people. Invermere, B.C.: Good Medicine Books, 1972. 61p. (Good medicine books, 7)

Cover title.

Canadiana, 1975.

AEA

2080 **Hungry Wolf**, Adolf. The spirit at Hidden Valley. A good medicine story. Illustrated by F.N. Wilson. Fort Macleod: Good Medicine Books, 1972. 90p. ill. (Good medicine books, 8)

Canadiana, 1975.

AEA

2081 **Lukoms'ka**, Ol'ha. Nashym naymenshum. Edmonton: Ukrainian Women's Association of Canada, 1956. 33p.

Duplicated.
Children's folk tales and nursery rhymes.

Ukrainica Canadiana, 1956.

2082 **Sanderson**, James Francis. Indian tales of the Canadian prairies. Illustrated by W.B. Fraser. Calgary: Historical Society of Alberta, 1965. 15, (1)p. ill.

Tales of Blackfoot, Cree, Ojibway, Gros Ventres and Young Dog Indians.

Glenbow.

ACG

2083 Tales tall and true. Theresa M. Ford, Managing Editor. Edmonton: Alberta Education, 1979. 272p. ill. (Western Canadian literature for youth)

Collection of true stories, tall tales, and legends of Western Canadian origin, printed as part of the Alberta Heritage Learning Resources Project, 1979. **AEP**

Economics: General Works

2084 **Abell**, Angus Sinclair. Rural municipal government in Alberta, taxation and finance. Ottawa: National Library of Canada, 1976. iii, 154, xiviii leaves. (Canadian theses on microfiche, 25449)

Thesis (M.A.), University of Toronto, 1940.
Microfiche of typescript.

Canadiana, 1976. **OONL**

2085 **Adams**, Trenton Peter. Economic change in the Grande Cache region of Alberta. Edmonton: University of Alberta, 1969. vii, 79 leaves.

Thesis (M.Sc.), University of Alberta, 1969.
Typescript.

Canadian theses. **AEU**

2086 **Ajao**, Adenihun Olanrewaju. The role of government and business in Alberta's export trade. Some implications for regional economic development in the 1970's. Ottawa: National Library of Canada, 1977. xi, 155 leaves. (Canadian theses on microfiche, 34141)

Thesis (M.A.), University of Calgary, 1977.
Microfiche of typescript.

Canadiana, 1979. **OONL**

2087 Alberta Chamber of Commerce. Progress report no. 2 on actions resulting from resolutions. The Alberta Chamber of Commerce Manpower Conference, October 6-8, 1974, Jasper Park Lodge. Edmonton: Alberta Chamber of Commerce, 1976. 11p.

Canadiana, 1980.

2088 **Alberta Chamber of Commerce Manpower Conference**, Jasper, 1974. Proceedings of the Alberta Chamber of Commerce Manpower Conference held in Jasper, October 6-8, 1974. Editors, J.D. Harder, Murray Skinner. Edmonton: Alberta Chamber of Commerce, 1974. 149p. ill.

Sponsored by the Alberta Chamber of Commerce, the Government of Alberta, the Government of Canada, and the Alberta Federation of Labour.

Canadiana, 1980.

2089 Alberta Indian Development Systems Limited. Lesser Slave Lake study. Edmonton: A.I.D.S., n.d. 672p. ill.

Cover title. **AEU**

2090 **Bancroft**, Donald Asa. Equalization of assessments in Alberta. The principles, authorities and methods. Edmonton: University of Alberta, 1961. v, 154 leaves.

Thesis (M.A.), University of Alberta, 1961.
Typescript.

Canadian theses. **AEU**

2091 **Banff Policies Conference on Canadian Economic Survival**, Banff, 1963. Background papers and proceedings. Banff: Banff School of Advanced Management, 1963. 7v. ill.

Second Banff conference on Canadian business policies, sponsored by the Banff School of Advanced Management.

Canadiana, 1964.

2092 **Bohlin**, Karl Magnus. The spatial and economic impact of recreational expenditures and sales in the Pigeon Lake area of Alberta. Ottawa: National Library of Canada, 1975. xii, 210 leaves. (Canadian theses on microfiche, 23990)

Thesis (M.A.), University of Alberta, 1975.
Microfiche of typescript.

U of A Theses. AEU

2093 **Campbell**, Neil MacDougal. A case study in economic development. The Bonnyville and Red Deer farming communities. Edmonton: University of Alberta, 1966. viii, 67p.

Thesis (B.Sc.), University of Alberta, 1966.
Typescript.

Canadian theses. AEU

2094 Canada West Foundation. Federal expenditures in the Western Region. References to processing of raw materials in Western Canada at the Western Economic Opportunities Conference, June, 1973 and the National Energy Conference, January, 1974. Calgary: Canada West Foundation, 1974. 20 leaves.

Canadiana, 1977. AEP

2095 Canada West Foundation. Follow-up on the Western Economic Opportunities Conference. Calgary: Canada West Foundation, 1974. 23 leaves.

Canadiana, 1977. AEP

2096 Canada West Foundation. A report on exports and imports through British Columbia, 1972, with special reference to the Pacific Rim countries of Asia and Oceania. Calgary: Canada West Foundation, 1974. 21 leaves.

AEU

2097 Canada West Foundation. A report on the National Energy Conference, Ottawa, January 22-23, 1974. Calgary: Canada West Foundation, 1974. 20 leaves. (Canada West Foundation. Publication, 73-74/03)

AEU

2098 Canada West Foundation. A report on the Western Economic Opportunities Conference. Calgary: Canada West Foundation, 1973. 23p.

Canadiana, 1977.

2099 **Carney**, Tom. Alberta, profile of development. A political-economic report. Vancouver: D. Miller, 1975. 12p.

Canadiana, 1977.

2100 **Changing Frontier Conference**, Peace River, 1965. Addresses. Peace River: Peace River Chamber of Commerce, 1965. 75p. ill.

Sponsored by the Chamber of Commerce and the Northern Alberta Development Council.
Papers on economic and industrial topics.

Canadiana, 1970. **AEU**

2101 Citizens Research Institute of Canada. Local government financing in Alberta, including an appraisal of provincial-municipal financial relationships. A report prepared for the Union of Alberta Municipalities. Calgary: Albertan, 1954. 43p.

Canadiana, 1957. **AEU**

2102 **Conference on Economic and Social Trends in Western Canada**, Calgary, 1978. Proceedings. Calgary: s.n., 1978. 120p.

Jointly sponsored by the Economic Society of Alberta, Calgary Branch, and Statistics Canada.

2103 **Conference on Productivity in the Canadian Economy**, Calgary, 1978. Proceedings. Edited by Don Seastone and George Linder. Calgary: University of Calgary, Department of Economics and Faculty of Continuing Education, 1978. vi, 64p.

Canadiana, 1979. **AEU**

2104 **Conference on the Alberta Challenge**, Jasper, 1978. Report and proceedings. Balanced Growth Or?, Jasper Park Lodge, Jasper, Alberta, October 1978. Sponsored by Alberta Chamber of Commerce et al. s.l.: s.n., 1978. 147p. ill.

Canadiana 1979.

2105 **Darroch**, G.V. The problem of resource development of the Blackfoot Reserve of southern Alberta. London, Ont.: University of Western Ontario, 1963. 1v.

Thesis (B.A.), University of Western Ontario.
Typescript.

Dew. **OLU**

2106 **Darychuk**, Gregory Michael. The financial implications of international trade participation by Alberta secondary industries. Edmonton: University of Alberta, 1971. (v), 64, (iii) leaves.

Thesis (M.B.A.), University of Alberta, 1971.
Typescript.

Canadian theses. **AEU**

2107 **Davis**, Edgar Hawkins. An economic system for Canada. 2d print. Calgary: Systems Investment, 1976. vii, 274p. ill.

Canadiana, 1979.

2108 **Donald**, J.T. & Co. (1956) Co. Alberta, province of opportunity. A survey of the resources and facilities offered to industry by the province of Alberta, of its present industrialization, and of future probable growth and industrial opportunities in the province. Calgary: Calgary Power Ltd., 1958. 6, 321p. ill.

Prepared by the Economic and Market Research Department, J.T. Donald & Co., Montreal.

Glenbow. **ACG**

2109 **Donaldson**, Ross Murray. The economic base of Camrose. Edmonton: University of Alberta, 1965. xv, 102 leaves.

Thesis (M.A.), University of Alberta, 1965.
Typescript.

Canadian theses. **AEU**

2110 **Earmme**, Seung Young. A water use projection model for the North Saskatchewan River Basin, Alberta, 1980-1985. An input-output approach. Edmonton: University of Alberta, 1979. xiv, 277 leaves.

Thesis (Ph.D.), University of Alberta, 1979.
Typescript.

U of A Theses. **AEU**

2111 Energy use in Canada in comparison with other countries. Calgary: Canadian Energy Research Institute, 1979. viii, 91p. ill. (Canadian Energy Research Institute. Study, 8)

Canadiana, 1980.

2112 **England**, Raymond Edward. A partial study of the resource potential of the Stony Indian reservation. Ottawa: National Library of Canada, 1966. x, 147 leaves. ill. (Canadian theses on microfiche, 08455)

Thesis (M.A.), University of Alberta at Calgary, 1966.
Microfiche of transcript.

Canadiana, 1972. **OONL**

2113 **Fletcher**, Thomas H. Management alternatives in residential water supply. Perception and choice in Alberta. Ottawa: National Library of Canada, 1976. xxi, 226 leaves. (Canadian theses on microfiche, 30676)

Thesis (M.A.), University of Alberta, 1976.
Microfiche of transcript.

U of A Theses. **AEU**

2114 **Frank**, James G. Wages and salaries in the public sector. The Alberta case. Ottawa: National Library of Canada, 1972. xii, 180 leaves. (Canadian theses on microfilm, 13857)

Thesis (M.A.), University of Calgary, 1972.
Microfilm of typescript.

Canadiana, 1973. **OONL**

2115 **Hancock**, Al E. The road to monetary reform. Raymond: Insight Publishing, 1978. 18p.

Canadiana, 1978.

2116 **Hancock**, Al E. Social Credit. A plan for Alberta. Lethbridge: Insight Publishing, 1973. 39p.

On monetary policy.

Canadiana, 1974. **AEU**

2117 **Hanson**, Eric John. A financial history of Alberta, 1905-1950. Rochester, N.Y.: University of Rochester Press, 1954. 17 cards. (Nineteenth century American literature)

Based on his Ph.D. thesis, Rochester University, 1952, University of Rochester Canadian Studies series, 2, xxvi, 741p.

Canadiana, 1955.

2118 **Hanson**, Eric John. The post-Leduc growth of the Edmonton economy. A study sponsored by the Edmonton Chamber of Commerce for presentation to the Royal Commission on Corporate Concentration. Edmonton: E.J. Hanson, 1976. 94p. ill.

Canadiana, 1977.

2119 **Hanson**, Eric John. The potential unification of the Edmonton Metropolitan area. A fiscal study of annexation and amalgamation. Edmonton: University of Alberta, 1968. xvi, 231p. ill.

2120 **Hanson**, Eric John. Some basic concepts in regional income analysis. Edmonton: University of Alberta, 1958. 27 leaves. **AEU**

2121 **Hanus**, Frantisek. Economic analysis of demand and supply of water in Alberta municipalities. Ottawa: National Library of Canada, 1974. xi, 150 leaves. (Canadian theses on microfiche, 21024)

Thesis (M.Sc.), University of Alberta, 1974.
Microfiche of transcript.

U of A Theses. **AEU**

2122 **Herscovitich**, Gail. Industrial water use in Edmonton. Edmonton: University of Alberta, 1969. xvi, 126 leaves.

Thesis (M.A.), University of Alberta, 1969.
Typescript.
Examination of quality and quantity of industrial water demands.

Canadian theses.

2123 Hickling-Johnston Limited. Alberta growth. An economic study for R. Angus Alberta Limited. Toronto: Hickling-Johnston Limited, 1968. ii, 36 leaves. ill.

Updates their study for R. Angus Alberta Limited of 1967.

Canadiana, 1972. **AEU**

2124 Hickling-Johnston Limited. Economic study, town of Fort Saskatchewan, Alberta. Toronto: Hickling-Johnston Limited, 1970. ii, 41 leaves. ill.

Canadiana, 1972.

2125 The impact of foreign investment on Canadian society. A symposium. Calgary: University of Calgary, 1972. 2, 51 leaves.

Sponsored by Calgary Committee for an Independent Canada and Division of Continuing Education, University of Calgary.
Cover title *A Symposium on the impact of foreign investment on Canadian society*.

Canadiana, 1977.

2126 **Kellow**, Richard Lawrence. A study of residential water use in Calgary. Edmonton: University of Alberta, 1970. xi, 176 leaves.

Thesis (M.Sc.), University of Alberta, 1970.
Typescript.
Examines factors, including pricing method, that influence household water consumption.

Canadian theses. **AEU**

2127 **Keys**, Charles L. Spatial reorganization in a central place system. An Albertan case. Ottawa: National Library of Canada, 1975. xiv, 263 leaves. (Canadian theses on microfiche, 24073)

Thesis (Ph.D.), University of Alberta, 1975.
Microfiche of typescript.
Deals with the growth and decline of trade centres in Central Alberta.

U of A Theses. **AEU**

2128 **Knapp**, John L. The economics of industrial water use in Alberta. Quantitive and qualitative assessment. Ottawa: National Library of Canada, 1973. xvi, 205 leaves. (Canadian theses on microfiche, 17576)

Thesis (M.A.), University of Alberta, 1973.
Microfiche of typescript.

U of A Theses. **AEU**

2129 **Koszec**, Paul Caesar. An economic evaluation of the Alberta Estate Tax Rebate Act. Edmonton: University of Alberta, 1969. vii, 101 leaves.

Thesis (M.A.), University of Alberta, 1969.
Typescript.

Canadian theses. **AEU**

2130 **LaPointe**, Louis Henry. Children's participation in the marketplace in selected jurisdictions of Alberta. Ottawa: National Library of Canada, 1977. xv, 112 leaves. (Canadian theses on microfiche, 34051)

Thesis (M.A.), University of Calgary, 1977.
Microfiche of typescript.

Canadiana, 1979.

2131 **MacLeod**, H.L. Properties, investors and taxes. A study of Calgary real estate investment, municipal finances and property tax arrears, 1911-1919. Ottawa: National Library of Canada, 1977. xi, 206 leaves. (Canadian theses on microfiche, 34054)

Thesis (M.A.), University of Calgary, 1977.
Typescript.

Canadiana, 1979. **OONL**

2132 **Martin**, John. Geographic inequalities in property tax levels. A study of the urban municipalities in the Edmonton Regional Planning District. Edmonton: University of Alberta, 1971. xl, 197 leaves.

Thesis (M.A.), University of Alberta, 1971.
Typescript.

Canadian theses. **AEU**

2133 **Mary**, H.W. The influence of aircraft noise annoyance on single-family house prices. A case study of Edmonton's Industrial Airport. Edmonton: University of Alberta, 1975. xiii, 142 leaves.

Thesis (M.), University of Alberta, 1975.
Typescript.

U of A Theses.

2134 **Mellor**, Ian Kenneth. An evaluation of the multiplier effect at Slave Lake and in its tributory area since the establishment of the Lesser Slave Lake Special Incentives Area. Ottawa: National Library of Canada, 1975. xii, 135 leaves. (Canadian theses on microfiche, 24097)

Thesis (M.A.), University of Alberta, 1975.
Microfiche of typescript.

U of A Theses. **AEU**

2135 **Mukasa**, James M. Rural residential subdivision, Parkland County, Alberta. An analysis of the interrelations between environmental factors, location, and land values, as influenced by the process of real estate development. Ottawa: National Library of Canada, 1976. xii, 131 leaves. (Canadian theses on microfiche, 30774)

Thesis (M.A.), University of Alberta, 1976.
Microfiche of typescript.

U of A theses. **AEU**

2136 National Northern Development Conference. Proceedings. Edmonton: National Northern Development Conference, 1958. v. ill.

1st-4th, 1958-67, sponsored jointly by Alberta and Northwest Chamber of Mines and Resources, and the Edmonton Chamber of Commerce.
Contents: 1. 1957-2. Canada's new role in resource development, 1961 3. Canada's northland and world markets, 1964 conference 4. Man and the North, 1967 conference 5. Oil and northern development, 1970 conference 6. Mining and Canada's north, 1973 conference 7. Energy and northern development, 1976 conference

Canadiana. AEU

2137 **National Technical Conference**, 2d, Calgary, 1973. Alberta's role in meeting Canada's energy requirements. Calgary: McDaniel Consultants (1965), 1973. 6 leaves.

On cover: Paper presented at the Second National Technical Conference of the Canadian Gas Association in Calgary, Alberta, 17-19 October, 1973.

Canadiana, 1978.

2138 Northern Alberta Development Council. Report on certain industrial and other factors related to the economy of the central Peace River district, Alberta. Edmonton: Northern Alberta Development Council, 1965. 48p.

Survey conducted by R.N. Harvey.

Brown.

2139 Northern Alberta Development Council. Report on the land, industries and related factors in the Peace River Country, Alberta. Edmonton: Northern Alberta Development Council, 1968. 92p. maps.

Expansion of 1965 report by R.N. Harvey.

2140 **Norton**, Deryk George. Provincial grants to Alberta municipalities. Review assessment and alternative unconditional grant formulae. Edmonton: University of Alberta, 1979. xii, 219 leaves.

Thesis (M.A.), University of Alberta, 1979.
Typescript.

U of A Theses. AEU

2141 **O'Brien**, Allison Douglas. A retail sales tax for Alberta. An economic evaluation of alternative structures. Edmonton: University of Alberta, 1969. vii, 135 leaves.

Thesis (M.A.), University of Alberta, 1969.
Typescript.

Canadian theses. AEU

2142 **One Prairie Province Conference**, Lethbridge, 1970. Proceedings. A question for Canada. Proceedings of a conference to study the feasibility of One Prairie Province, May 10th to 13th, 1970, and selected papers. Edited by David K. Elton. Lethbridge: Lethbridge Herald, 1970. 455p. ill.

Conference co-sponsored by the University of Lethbridge and the Lethbridge Herald.

Glenbow. ACG

2143 **Otter**, Andy Albert den. Sir Alexander T. Galt and the northwest. A case study of entrepreneurialism on the frontier. Edmonton: University of Alberta, 1975. x, 337 leaves.

Thesis (Ph.D.), Alberta, 1975.
Typescript.
Concerned particularly with Galt's activities as a promoter of southern Alberta, including railways, coal mining and irrigation. **AEU**

2144 **Pratt**, Lawrence. The state and province building. Alberta's development strategy, 1971-1976. Edmonton: University of Alberta, Department of Political Science, 1976. 40 leaves. (University of Alberta. Department of Political Science. Occasional papers, 5)

Examines the need to diversify the provincial economy before oil and natural gas reserves are depleted. **AEL**

2145 **Reid**, Bradford Guy. Aircraft noise and residential property values. Hedonic estimates of the costs of aircraft noise in the city of Edmonton. Ottawa: National Library of Canada, 1977. x, 138 leaves. (Canadian theses on microfiche, 34457)

Thesis (M.A.), University of Alberta, 1977.
Microfiche of typescript.

U of A Theses. **AEU**

2146 **Resources Conference of the Northwest Region**, 1st, Grande Prairie, 1960. Transactions of the first Resources Conference of the Northwest Region. Grande Prairie: Grande Prairie Chamber of Commerce, 1960. vii, 141 leaves.

Edited by E.T. Clegg.

Canadiana, 1963.

2147 **Rogers**, Walter Bob. World population and distribution of food. Edmonton: University of Alberta, Department of Agricultural Economics, 1967. 20 leaves. (University of Alberta. Department of Agricultural Economics. Special report, 5)

Canadiana, 1969. **AEU**

2148 **Schultz**, Wolfgang Martin. The people and resources of northeastern Alberta. Economic development potentials and problems of Census Division 12. Edmonton: Department of Agricultural Economics,University of Alberta, 1966. vii, 84p. ill. (University of Alberta. Department of Agricultural Economics. Research bulletin, 2)

Duplicated.
Also Rev. ed., 1967, viii, 89 leaves.

Glenbow. **ACG**

2149 **Smith**, Graham. Boycott against Alberta. Study of freight rates, sales tax and capital, holding back Alberta's development. Calgary: Albertan,

1956. 32p.

Reprinted from a series of articles in *The Albertan*, by Graham Smith, staff reporter.

Glenbow. **ACG**

2150 **Sponchia**, Carl Raymond. Public accounting in Lethbridge. An industry study. Edmonton: University of Alberta, 1972. x, 204 leaves.

Thesis (M.B.A.), University of Alberta, 1972.
Typescript.
Investigation of the economic aspects of public accounting in Lethbridge.

Canadian theses.

2151 **Tomyn**, William. Alberta, bastion of freedom. An address. Edmonton: Alberta Social Credit Board, 1960. 30p.

Glenbow. **ACG**

2152 **Tyre**, Robert. Lethbridge, the action city. Lethbridge: Lethbridge Economic Development Dept., 1972. 11p. ill.

Reprinted from *Trade and Commerce Magazine*, October, 1971.

Canadiana, 1974. **ACG**

2153 **Webster**, Douglas Richard. The incidence impact of a regional development program based on employment creation. The Lesser Slave Lake, Alberta case. Ann Arbor, Mich.: University Microfilms, 1977. vi, 207 leaves. ill.

Thesis (Ph.D.), University of California, 1977.
Microfilm of typescript.

Canadiana, 1979.

2154 **Williams**, Allan Geoffrey. Commuter expenditure patterns in the Edmonton region. An examination of a spread effect from a spontaneous growth centre. Ottawa: National Library of Canada, 1978. xviii, 245 leaves. (Canadian theses on microfiche, 40352)

Thesis (M.A.), University of Alberta, 1978.
Microfiche of typescript.
Examination of spending patterns of inhabitants of Edmonton's satellite communities.

U of A Theses. **AEU**

2155 **Wilson**, Leonard Samuel. Some factors relating to the attraction of manufacturing industries to the province of Alberta. Edmonton: University of Alberta, 1971. viii, 131 leaves.

Thesis (M.A.), University of Alberta, 1971.
Typescript.

Canadian theses. **AEU**

2156 Work and leisure in Canada. Edited by S.M.A. Hameed and D. Cullen. Edmonton: University of Alberta, Faculty of Business Administration and Commerce, 1972. 6 leaves, 142p.

Canadiana, 1974. **AEU**

2157 **Woychuk**, John Kenneth. Tax-exempt property. City of Edmonton, 1970. Ottawa: National Library of Canada, 1972. xiv, 173 leaves. ill. (Canadian theses on microfilm, 13633)

Thesis (M.A.), University of Alberta, 1972.
Microfilm of typescript.

Canadiana, 1973.

Business, Industry and Labour

2158 Alberta Coal Mining Industry Commission. Alberta's coal industry, 1919. Edited and with an introduction by David Jay Bercuson. Calgary: Historical Society of Alberta, Alberta Records Publication Board, 1979. xx, 264p. (Historical Society of Alberta, v.2)

Edited transcript of the hearings of the Alberta Coal Mining Industry Commisssion of 1919.

Canadiana, 1979. **AEA**

2159 **Anderson**, James. Change in a central place system. Trade centres and rural service in central Alberta. Edmonton: University of Alberta, 1967. xi, 196 leaves.

Thesis (M.A.), University of Alberta, 1967.
Typescript.
Deals with the decline of economy of small centres, growth of economy in large centres.

Canadian theses. **AEU**

2160 **Askin**, William R. Labor unrest in Edmonton and district and its coverage by the Edmonton press, 1918-1919. Ottawa: National Library of Canada, 1973. xi, 244 leaves. (Canadian theses on microfilm, 15180)

Thesis (M.A.), University of Alberta, 1973.
Microfilm of typescript.

Canadiana, 1974. **AEU**

2161 **Bailey**, Robert. Medalta. A study for the rehabilitation and reuse of the Medalta Potteries, Medicine Hat, Alberta. By Robert Bailey, Keith Wagland, Harold Kalman. Toronto: Bailey Consulting Resources, 1978. 112p. ill.

AEA

2162 **Baker**, Horace S. The Alberta butter industry. An analysis of location and efficiency. Edmonton: University of Alberta, 1967. ix, 80 leaves. tables, map.

Thesis (M.Sc.), University of Alberta, 1967.
Typescript.

Canadian theses. **AEU**

2163 **Beere**, Reginald Henry. Some aspects of business education in Canada with particular reference to Alberta. Edmonton: University of Alberta, 1961. xi, 245 leaves.

Thesis (M.Ed.), University of Alberta, 1961.
Typescript.

Canadian theses. AEU

2164 **Bercuson**, David Jay. Fools and wise men. The rise and fall of the One Big Union. Toronto: McGraw-Hill Ryerson, 1978. xvii, 300p. ill.

CBIP, 1979. AEU

2165 **Berg**, Barbara Jean. Operation of Program 5 in Alberta. Edmonton: University of Alberta, 1966. xv, 194 leaves. tables.

Thesis (M.B.A.), University of Alberta, 1966.
Typescript.
Evaluation of success of Program 5 in training the unemployed.

Canadian theses. AEU

2166 **Brese**, William Gerald. An analysis of the sulphur industry in Alberta. Edmonton: University of Alberta, 1961. 140 leaves.

Thesis (M.A.), University of Alberta, 1961.
Typescript.

Canadian theses. AEU

2167 **Bullen**, Anne J. McLean. An examination of economic factors affecting the location and operation of the beef packing industry in Canada, with particular reference to Alberta. Ottawa: National Library of Canada, 1972. xi, 172 leaves. ill. (Canadian theses on microfilm, 13318)

Thesis (M.Sc.), University of Alberta, 1972.
Microfilm of typescript.

Canadiana, 1973. AEU

2168 Burns and Elliott. Calgary, Alberta, Canada. Her industries and resources. Compiled and edited by Burns and Elliott. Calgary: Glenbow-Alberta Institute, 1974. 91, 3p. ill. (incl. advts.)

Facsimile reprint of the 1885 edition published in Calgary by Burns and Elliott. AEA

2169 Calgary, metropolitan structure and influence. Edited by Brenton M. Barr. Victoria, B.C.: University of Victoria, Department of Geography, 1975. 271p. ill. (Western geographical series, 11)

Contents: 1. Barr, B.M. The importance of regional inter-industry linkages to Calgary's manufacturing firms 2. McEwen, A. & Barr, B.M. Some aspects of Calgary's role in the intra-industry linkages of Southern Alberta 3. Zieber, G.H Calgary as an oil administrative and oil operations centre 4. Davies, W.K.D. & Gyuse, T.T. Changes in the central place system around Calgary, 1951-1971 5. Smith, P.J. & Harasym, D.G. Planning for retail services in new residential areas since 1944 6. Johnson, D.B. Food store-dwelling linkages in selected areas of Calgary 7. Davies, W.K.D. A multivariate description of Calgary's community areas. AEU

2170 Calgary Power Ltd. Power for progress, thermal and hydro plants. Calgary: Calgary Power Ltd., 1971. 20p. ill.

A promotional booklet. **AEA**

2171 Calgary Power Ltd. Some facts about Calgary Power Ltd. Calgary: Calgary Power Ltd., 1967. (2), 22p. ill.

Glenbow. **ACG**

2172 Canada West Foundation. Western Canada. Location of operating mines, processing plants and metallurgical works, 1974. Calgary: Canada West Foundation, 1975. 31p.

Prepared in co-operation with the Department of Regional Economic Expansion.

Canadiana, 1977. **ACU**

2173 Canada West Foundation. Western Canada. Location of processing of materials of agricultural origin. Calgary: Canada West Foundation, 1975. 2v.

Prepared in co-operation with the Department of Regional Economic Expansion.
Contents: 1. Meat, poultry and dairy plants, 1972. 2. Flour, animal feeds and vegetable oil mills, 1972.

Canadiana, 1977. **ACU**

2174 **Caragata**, Warren. Alberta labour. A heritage untold. Toronto: J. Lorimer, 1979. x, 162p. ill.

A history of organized labour.

Canadiana, 1979. **AEU**

2175 **Cashman**, Anthony Walcott. Edmonton Exhibition, the first hundred years. Edmonton: Edmonton Exhibition Association, 1979. 160p. ill. **AEA**

2176 **Cauvin**, Dennis Mederic. Measurement of a forest's contribution to the economy of Alberta. Ann Arbor, Mich.: University Microfilms, 1972. vi, 207 leaves. ill.

Thesis (Ph.D.), University of Washington, 1972.
Microfilm of typescript.

Canadiana, 1974. **OONL**

2177 **Cerny**, Hana. Manpower requirements in the food service industry with implications for vocational education in Alberta. Ottawa: National Library of Canada, 1976. x, 135 leaves. ill. (Canadian theses on microfiche, 27628)

Thesis (M.Ed.), University of Alberta, 1976.
Microfiche of typescript.

Canadiana, 1977. **AEU**

2178 **Comfort**, Darlene Joy. Pass the McMurray salt please! The Alberta Salt Company as remembered by three Fort McMurray pioneers. Fort McMurray: Fort McMurray Public Library, 1975. 8, 35p. ill.

Canadiana, 1977. **AEA**

2179 **Cook**, Norman Alan. Perceptual variations of retailing in Edmonton. Ottawa: National Library of Canada, 1972. xxxiii, 278 leaves. ill. (Canadian theses on microfilm, 13334)

Thesis (Ph.D.), University of Alberta, 1972.
Microfilm of typescript.

Canadiana, 1973. **AEU**

2180 **Copeland**, James Hubert. A study of broiler marketing in Alberta. Ottawa: National Library of Canada, 1974. xi, 79 leaves. (Canadian theses on microfiche, 21792)

Thesis (M.Sc.), University of Alberta, 1974.
Microfiche of typescript.

Canadiana, 1975. **AEU**

2181 **Crowston**, Michael Anthony. The growth of the metal industries in Edmonton. Edmonton: University of Alberta, 1971. xii, 127 leaves.

Thesis (M.A.), University of Alberta, 1971.
Typescript.

Canadian theses. **AEU**

2182 **Dawson**, James Lawrence. A location analysis for hog assembly centres in Alberta. Edmonton: University of Alberta, 1971. viii, 93, xv leaves.

Thesis (M.Sc.), University of Alberta, 1971.
Typescript.

Canadian theses. **AEU**

2183 **Dawson**, Oliver Glenn. Production efficiency in Alberta beef feedlots. Edmonton: University of Alberta, 1970. viii, 150 leaves.

Thesis (M.Sc.), University of Alberta, 1970.
Typescript.

Canadian theses. **AEU**

2184 Dominion Cartridge Company. Dominion Cartridge Company-Canadian Industries Limited shotshells, 1886-1954. An illustrated handbook. Edmonton: Dominion Cartridge Company, 1967. 32p. ill.

Glenbow. **ACG**

2185 **Dubois**, N. Warren. Northland Utilities Limited. Edmonton: Alberta Power Limited, 1972. 96p.

On cover: Memoirs of an engineer.
Limited edition. **AEA**

2186 **Dyer**, Arthur Cecil. Occupational organization in real estate. The Calgary Real Estate Board and the Alberta Real Estate Association. Ottawa: National Library of Canada, 1977. ix, 139 leaves. ill. (Canadian theses on microfiche, 34166)

Thesis (M.A.), University of Calgary, 1977.
Microfiche of typescript.

Canadiana, 1979. **OONL**

2187 **Ellison**, Anthony P. The effect of rising energy costs on Canadian industries. Calgary: Canadian Energy Research Institute, 1979. viii, 62p. (Canadian Energy Research Institute. Study, 3)

Canadiana, 1979. **AEU**

2188 **Faminow**, Merle Douglas. Beef procurement by Edmonton restaurants. Ottawa: National Library of Canada, 1977. xi, 131 leaves. (Canadian theses on microfiche, 31970)

Thesis (M.Sc.), University of Alberta, 1977.
Microfiche of typescript.

U of A Theses. **AEU**

2189 **Famure**, Oluwole Dada. An economic analysis of institutional buying patterns for meats in Edmonton and surroundings. Ottawa: National Library of Canada, 1978. xvii, 272 leaves. (Canadian theses on microfiche, 40141)

Thesis (Ph.D.), University of Alberta, 1978.
Microfiche of typescript.

U of A Theses. **AEU**

2190 Fort Macleod Chamber of Commerce. Our local industry in Fort Macleod. Fort Macleod: Fort Macleod Chamber of Commerce, 1963. 13, (1)p. ill.

Glenbow. **ACG**

2191 **Geldart**, Howard George. Marketing of wood chips from Alberta sawmills. Ottawa: National Library of Canada, 1978. xi, 102 leaves. (Canadian theses on microfiche, 40159)

Thesis (M.Sc.), University of Alberta, 1978.
Microfiche of typescript.

U of A Theses. **AEU**

2192 **Gilham**, Dwayne Milton. The consumer spatial behavior of Edmonton's inner city residents, 1977. Edmonton: University of Alberta, 1979. xiii, 169 leaves.

Thesis (M.A.), University of Alberta, 1979.
Typescript.
Examines the underlying determinants of the purchase decisions of low income consumers.

U of A theses.

2193 **Gossage**, S.M. Address by S.M. Gossage. Chairman, Metric Commission to the Canadian Gas Association, Calgary, 18 October, 1973. s.l.: s.n. 1973. 10 leaves.

Duplicated.
On metric conversion.

Canadiana, 1976.

2194 Grande Prairie Chamber of Commerce. Grande Prairie trade dollars. Grande Prairie: Grande Prairie Chamber of Commerce, 1977. 33 leaves. ill. (Historical heritage series)

Chiefly photocopies of coin designs and related material.

P.N.L.A., 1979. **AEA**

2195 **Haney**, Harry Damon. Feeder cattle marketing in southern Alberta. Ottawa: National Library of Canada, 1974. xii, 207 leaves. ill. (Canadian theses on microfiche, 21830)

Thesis (M.Sc.), University of Alberta, 1974.
Microfiche of typescript.

Canadiana, 1976. **AEU**

2196 **Haythorne**, Donald Francis. The characteristics of Edmonton welfare recipients in relation to employability and labour force classification. Edmonton: University of Alberta, 1967. vii, 84 leaves.

Thesis (M.A.), University of Alberta, 1967.
Typescript.

Canadian theses. **AEU**

2197 International Brotherhood of Teamsters, Chauffeurs, Warehousemen and Helpers of America. Local 987. Struggles and progress of Teamsters Local 987, Calgary, Alberta, 1910-1955. Calgary: International Brotherhood of Teamsters, Chauffeurs, Warehousemen and Helpers of America, Local 987, 1955. 54 leaves.

Compiler and editor: R. Scott.

Glenbow. **ACG**

2198 **Irving**, Harold A. Regional impact of an Alberta steel plant. Ottawa: National Library of Canada, 1977. vii, 154 leaves. (Canadian theses on microfiche, 34043)

Thesis (M.A.), University of Calgary, 1977.
Microfiche of typescript.

Canadiana, 1979.

2199 **Ivory**, John. Effect of increased wellhead petroleum prices on some Alberta industries. Ottawa: National Library of Canada, 1973. xiii, 337 leaves. (Canadian theses on microfiche, 17562)

Thesis (M.Sc.), University of Alberta, 1973.
Microfiche of typescript.

Canadiana, 1974. **AEU**

2200 **Jasperse**, Frank R. Seasonal variations in employment. The service industries of Alberta. Ottawa: National Library of Canada, 1977. xii, 144 leaves. (Canadian theses on microfiche, 34379)

Thesis (M.A.), University of Alberta, 1977.
Microfiche of typescript.

U of A Theses. **AEU**

2201 **Johnson**, Denis Bruce. A functional comparison of the central retail district with two regional shopping centres in Calgary, Alberta, 1963. Ottawa: National Library of Canada, 1971. ix, 112 leaves. ill. (Canadian theses on microfilm, 08648)

Thesis (M.A.), University of Alberta, 1963.
Microfilm of typescript.

Canadiana, 1972. **AEU**

2202 **Johnson**, Denis Bruce. A study of commercial blight and the function of Whyte Avenue, Edmonton. By Denis B. Johnson and Norah Chowli. Edmonton: University of Alberta, Department of Extension, 1972. vii, 49 leaves. ill.

Canadiana, 1975. **AEU**

2203 Johnstone Walker Ltd. The story of J.W., 1886-1961. 75 years in Edmonton. Edmonton: Johnstone Walker Ltd., 1961. 16p. ill.

Cover title.
A history of the department store. **AEA**

2204 **Karas**, Frank Paul. Labour and coal in the Crowsnest Pass, 1925-1935. Ottawa: National Library of Canada, 1972. ix, 179 leaves. ill. (Canadian theses on microfilm, 13885)

Thesis (M.A.), University of Calgary, 1972.
Microfilm of typescript.

Canadiana, 1973. **AEU**

2205 **Kennedy**, Albert Edward. Bargaining unit determination in Alberta. Recent experience. Ottawa: National Library of Canada, 1978. xviii, 380 leaves. (Canadian theses on microfiche, 36411)

Thesis (M.B.A.), University of Alberta, 1978.
Microfiche of typescript.

U of A Theses. **AEU**

2206 **Kenney**, John. The business career of R. B. Bennett, 1897-1927. Ottawa: National Library of Canada, 1978. iv, 68 leaves. (Canadian theses on microfiche, 38083)

Thesis (M.A.), University of New Brunswick, 1978.
Microfiche of typescript.

Canadiana, 1980. **OONL**

2207 **Khehra**, Gurnam Singh. Structural changes in the Alberta broiler industry. Ottawa: National Library of Canada, 1977. xi, 110 leaves. (Canadian theses on microfiche, 32003)

Thesis (M.Sc.), University of Alberta, 1977.
Microfiche of typescript.

U of A Theses. **AEU**

2208 **LeBlanc**, Darrell Robert. A measure of understanding of certain aspects of Alberta industry. Edmonton: University of Alberta, 1968. xiv, 169 leaves.

Thesis (M.Ed.), University of Alberta, 1968.
Typescript.
Evaluates junior high school students' perceptions of Alberta industry.

Canadian theses. **AEU**

2209 **Lee**, Terence Richard. A manufacturing geography of Edmonton, Alberta. Edmonton: University of Alberta, 1963. xiv, 107 leaves.

Thesis (M.A.), University of Alberta, 1963.
Typescript.

Canadian theses. **AEU**

2210 Lethbridge, city of the year. Lethbridge: Economic Development Department, 1972. 27p ill.

Reprinted from the July, 1972 issue of *Trade and Commerce Magazine*.

Canadiana, 1974. **OONL**

2211 **Lockhart**, William James. Alberta hog market, conduct and performance. Edmonton: University of Alberta, 1967. vii, 67 leaves.

Thesis (M.Sc.), University of Alberta, 1967.
Typescript.

Canadian theses. **AEU**

2212 **Love**, Harold Clyde. Income variation in beef production. A budget study of feeder calf production in southern Alberta, 1946-1965. Edmonton: University of Alberta, Department of Agricultural Economics, 1966. 34 leaves. ill. (University of Alberta. Department of Agricultural Economics and Rural Sociology. Research bulletin, 1) **AEU**

2213 **MacEwan**, John Walter Grant. Pat Burns, cattle king. Saskatoon: Western Producer Prairie Books, 1979. v, 200p. ill.

Canadiana, 1979. **AEA**

2214 **MacGregor**, James Grierson. Edmonton trader. The story of John A. McDougall. Toronto: McClelland & Stewart, 1963. x, 262p. ill. **AEA**

2215 **MacLock**, Robert Bruce. The geography of the forest products industries of northern Alberta. Edmonton: University of Alberta, 1967. x, 118 leaves.

Thesis (M.A.), University of Alberta, 1967.
Typescript.

Canadian theses. **AEU**

2216 **Manning**, Travis Warren. Country livestock auctions and market performance. Edmonton: University of Alberta, Department of Extension, 1966. ii, 36, (2)p. (University of Alberta. Department of Extension. Agricultural Economics. Technical Bulletin, 1)

Glenbow. **ACG**

2217 **Manning**, Travis Warren. Performance of the hog marketing system in Alberta. Edmonton: University of Alberta, Department of Extension, 1967. 26p. ill. (University of Alberta. Department of Agricultural Economics. Research bulletin, 4)

Also: Summary and conclusions. 3p.

Canadiana, 1969. **AEU**

2218 **Martin**, Stephen Paul. Selected aspects of the functional relationship between consumers and commercial ribbons. A case study of Whyte Avenue, Edmonton. Ottawa: National Library of Canada, 1974. xvii, 165 leaves. (Canadian theses on microfiche, 21894)

Thesis (M.A.), University of Alberta, 1974.
Microfiche of typescript.

U of A Theses. **AEU**

2219 **McEwen**, Alice Maude. The industrial reuse of Alberta's deactivated military bases. Ottawa: National Library of Canada, 1976. x, 133 leaves. ill. (Canadian theses on microfiche, 28539)

Thesis (M.A.), University of Calgary, 1976.
Microfiche of typescript.

Canadiana, 1977. **OONL**

2220 **McGeachy**, David Alan. The role of selected Edmonton professionals in the business formation process. Edmonton: University of Alberta, 1971. vii, 91 leaves.

Thesis (M.B.A.), University of Alberta, 1971.
Typescript.
Examines the role of accountants, bankers and lawyers in establishing a small business.

Canadian theses.

2221 **McIntosh**, Curtis Emmanuel. A statistical analysis of cattle prices on terminal and auction markets in Alberta. Edmonton: University of Alberta, 1968. vii, 79 leaves.

Thesis (M.Sc.), University of Alberta, 1968.
Typescript.

Canadian theses. **AEU**

2222 **McMillan**, Charles Joseph. Trade unionism in District 18, 1900-1925. A case study. Edmonton: University of Alberta, 1969. vi, 212 leaves.

Thesis (M.B.A.), University of Alberta, 1969.
Typescript.
History of trade unionism in the coal industry of Western Canada, 1900-1925.

Canadian theses. **AEU**

2223 **Mitchell**, Harold. The spice of life. London: Bodley Head, 1974. 264p. ill.

A biography, including association with the Luscar coal mine.

NUC, 1975. **AEU**

2224 Motor Car Supply Company of Canada Limited. 50th anniversary, 1912-1962. Calgary: Motor Car Supply Company of Canada Ltd, 1962. (24)p. ill.

On cover: 50 years of service.
A history of the company and an article by L.A. Cavanagh, the founder, entitled *Romance of the automobile industry*.

Glenbow. **ACG**

2225 **Mullins**, Gary Edward. The spatial behaviour of Alberta's electricity industry, 1888-1965. The impact of economics of scale. Vancouver: University of British Columbia, 1970. (1v.)

Thesis (M.A.), University of British Columbia, 1970.
Typescript.

Canadian theses. **BVAU**

2226 **Nordegg**, Martin. Pioneering in Canada, 1906-1924. s.l.: Martin Nordegg, 1962. 272 leaves.

Duplicated.
Memoirs of the founder of the Nordegg Coal Mine.

Glenbow. **ACG**

2227 **Nordegg**, Martin. The possibilities of Canada are truly great. Memoirs, 1906-1924. Edited and with an introduction by T.D. Reghr. Toronto: Macmillan of Canada, 1971. xv, 246p. maps.

Nordegg was associated with the Canadian Northern Railway and established the Nordegg Coal Mine. **AEA**

2228 **O'Malley**, Denis Anthony. Regional considerations in pulp. The competitive position of the pulp industry in Alberta. Edmonton: University of Alberta, 1967. xi, 147 leaves.

Thesis (M.B.A.), University of Alberta, 1967.
Typescript.

Canadian theses. **AEU**

2229 **Paproski**, Dennis M. The demand for coal by the electrical generation industry in Alberta. Edmonton: University of Alberta, 1967. viii, 121 leaves. ill.

Thesis (M.A.), University of Alberta, 1967.
Typescipt.

Canadian theses. **AEU**

2230 **Parker**, Lawrence Lee. An examination of pricing practices and procedures in a local house building industry. Edmonton: University of Alberta, 1970. ix, 104 leaves.

Thesis (M.B.A.), University of Alberta, 1970.
Typescript.

Canadian theses. **AEU**

2231 **Peers**, Jeremy James Louden. An analysis of tourist travel to the province of Alberta. Edmonton: University of Alberta, 1969. v, 85 leaves.

Thesis (M.B.A.), University of Alberta, 1969.
Typescript.

Canadian theses. **AEU**

2232 **Peterson**, Dale Douglas. Wholesale trade between Edmonton and selected northern communities. Ottawa: National Library of Canada, 1978. xv, 294 leaves. (Canadian theses on microfiche, 36456)

Thesis (M.A.), University of Alberta, 1978.
Microfiche of typescript.

U of A Theses. **AEU**

2233 **Plunkett**, Richard Ernest. Central business district employment in Edmonton, 1961-1967. Edmonton: University of Alberta, 1972. xvi, 108 leaves.

Thesis (M.A.), University of Alberta, 1972.
Typescript.

Canadian theses. **AEU**

2234 **Ramsay**, Edward A. Apprenticeship discontinuance in three trade areas in the province of Alberta. Ottawa: National Library of Canada, 1974. xv, 199 leaves. (Canadian theses on microfiche, 23365)

Thesis (M.Ed.), University of Alberta, 1974.
Microfiche of typescript.
Study of apprentices who left carpentry, electrical construction and motor mechanics trades.

U of A Theses. **AEU**

2235 **Rendall**, Harold A. The trade areas of Camrose, Wetaskiwin and Ponoka. Edmonton: University of Alberta, 1962. xiv, 107 leaves.

Thesis (M.A.), University of Alberta, 1962.
Typescript.
Delimits the trade areas of the three towns and examines factors influencing size/shape of trade areas.

Canadian theses. **AEU**

2236 **Riley**, Daniel Edward. The Lost Lemon Mine. By Dan Riley, Tom Primrose, and Hugh Dempsey. Calgary: Frontiers Unlimited, 1963. 40p. ill. (Frontier books, 4)

Glenbow. **ACG**

2237 **Ross**, David Philips. The causes of labour disputes in Alberta, 1955-1962. An analysis of collective bargaining criteria. Edmonton: University of Alberta, 1964. xii, 151 leaves.

Thesis (M.A.), University of Alberta, 1964.
Typescript.

Canadian theses. **AEU**

2238 **Seale**, Ronald Gordon. Some geographical aspects of the coal industry in Alberta. Edmonton: University of Alberta, 1966. xxvi, 278 leaves. ill.

Thesis (M.A.), University of Alberta, 1966.
Typescript.

Canadian theses. **AEU**

2239 **Sproule**, Albert Frederick. The role of Patrick Burns in the development of Western Canada. Edmonton: University of Alberta, 1962. v, 250 leaves.

Thesis (M.A.), University of Alberta, 1962.
Typescript.

Canadian theses. **AEU**

2240 **Taraska**, Elizabeth Ann. The Calgary craft union movement, 1900-1920. Ottawa: National Library of Canada, 1975. vi, 99 leaves. map (Canadian theses on microfiche, 23790)

Thesis (M.A.), University of Calgary, 1975.
Microfiche of typescript.

Canadiana, 1976.

2241 **Telmer**, Frederick Harold. An analysis of the iron and steel industry in Alberta. Edmonton: University of Alberta, 1964. 110 leaves.

Thesis (M.A.), University of Alberta, 1964.
Typescript.

Canadian theses. **AEU**

2242 Three or four day work week. Editors, S.M.A. Hameed, G.S. Paul. Edmonton: University of Alberta, Faculty of Business Administration, 1974. xiii, 226p. ill.

Compiled chiefly from papers presented at a conference held at the University of Alberta, June, 1973.

Canadiana, 1975.

2243 **Trace**, Harry Douglas. An examination of some factors associated with the decline of the coal industry in Alberta. Edmonton: University of Alberta, 1958. 107 leaves.

Thesis (M.A.), University of Alberta, 1958.
Typescript.

Canadian theses. AEU

2244 **Uhryn**, Michael. Interest groups and the Alberta Labour Act. Ottawa: National Library of Canada, 1972. x, 168 leaves. (Canadian theses on microfilm, 13609)

Thesis (M.A.), University of Alberta, 1972.
Microfilm of typescript.

Canadiana, 1973. AEU

2245 **Van Deurzen**, Anthony. An analysis of Alberta's beef cattle industry problems. Ottawa: National Library of Canada, 1973. xiii, 72 leaves. ill. (Canadian theses on microfiche, 17713)

Thesis (M.Sc.), University of Alberta, 1973.
Typescript.
Microfiche of typescript.

Canadiana, 1974. AEU

2246 **Ward**, Edward Neville. Residential water use in the Hardisty district, Edmonton, Alberta. Edmonton: University of Alberta, 1971. xi, 123 leaves.

Thesis (M.A.), University of Alberta, 1971.
Typescript.

Canadian theses. AEU

2247 Western Retail Lumbermen's Association. 75 years. Calgary: Western Retail Lumbermen's Association, 1965. (17)p. ill.

Cover title.

Glenbow. ACG

2248 **Westervelt**, Anne Carol Forrester. Farmers' markets. Retail practices and consumer opinions. Ottawa: National Library of Canada, 1978. xii, 123 leaves. (Canadian theses on microfiche, 36494)

Thesis (M.Sc.), University of Alberta, 1978.
Microfiche of typescript.

U of A theses. AEU

2249 **Woo**, Helen Mun-Ying. Population-store relationships over time in north-west Calgary, 1949-1968. Ottawa: National Library of Canada, 1969. x, 128 leaves. ill. (Canadian theses on microfilm, 04710)

Thesis (M.A.), University of Calgary, 1969.
Microfilm of typescript.

Canadiana, 1970.

2250 **Wood**, Kerry. A lifetime of service. George Moon. Red Deer: Red Deer Advocate, 1966. 16p. ill.

Cover title.

Biography of a Red Deer restaurant owner.

Glenbow. ACG

Oil and Gas Industries

2251 **Beach**, Floyd K. Alberta's petroleum paternity. Gardenvale, Quebec: National Business Publications, 1956. 42p. ill.

Cover title.
Reprinted from *Canadian oil and gas industry*. ACG

2252 **Bregha**, François. Bob Blair's pipline. The business and politics of northern energy development projects. Toronto: J. Lorimer, 1979. 220p. ill.

Canadiana, 1979. AEU

2253 **British American Oil Company**, Ltd. BA welcomes you to the new Pincher Creek Gas processing and sulphur plant, October 15th, 1958. s.l., British American Oil Co. Ltd., 1958. (12)p. ill.

Includes historical information.
cover title. ACP

2254 Canadian Petroleum Association. A brief history of the petroleum industry in Canada. Calgary: Canadian Petroleum Association, Public Affairs Department, 1979. (6)p. ill. (Focus on energy, 1)

Canadiana, 1980.

2255 Canadian Petroleum Association. The origins of oil and gas. Calgary: Canadian Petroleum Association, Public Affairs Department, 1979. (6)p. ill. (Focus on energy, 2)

Canadiana, 1980.

2256 Canadian Petroleum Association. Alberta Division. Oil and gas in Alberta. Calgary: Canadian Petroleum Association, Alberta Division, 1960. 23p. ill. AEU

2257 Canadian Western Natural Gas Company Ltd. Canadian Western Natural Gas Company Limited, 1912-1972. Calgary: Canadian Western Natural Gas Company Ltd., 1972. 24p. ill.

Cover title.
Caption title *Our sixtieth year*.

Glenbow. ACG

2258 Canadian Western Natural Gas Company Ltd. Half a century of Service, 1912-1962. Calgary: Canadian Western Natural Gas Company Ltd., 1962. 32p. ill.

Glenbow. ACG

2259 **Celmainis**, Andrew. Examination of the petroleum industry in Alberta. Some aspects of competition in the motor gasoline market. Edmonton:

University of Alberta, 1967. ix, 200 leaves.
Thesis (M.A.), University of Alberta, 1967.
Typescript.

Canadian theses. AEU

2260 **Cloakey**, George H. Problems affecting Canadian participation in the development of the oil and gas resources of Canada. Calgary: s.n., 1961. 7 leaves. ill.

Canadiana, 1965. OONL

2261 **Conder**, John E.H. The disposition of crown petroleum and natural gas rights in Alberta. Edmonton: University of Alberta, 1963. vii, 104 leaves.
Thesis (M.A.), University of Alberta, 1963.
Typescript.

Canadian theses. AEU

2262 **Curtis**, Paul James. Some aspects of industrial linkages in Edmonton's oil industry, with special reference to the tertiary sector. Edmonton: University of Alberta, 1972. xii, 154 leaves.
Thesis (M.A.), University of Alberta, 1972.
Typescript.
Examines agglomeration of secondary and tertiary sectors of the oil industry, and the external economies associated with agglomeration.

Canadian theses. AEU

2263 **De Mille**, George. Oil in Canada West, the early years. Calgary: Northwest Printing and Lithographing, 1970. viii, 269p. ill.

Glenbow. ACG

2264 **Demke**, Gordon J. Supply of natural gas in Alberta. Ottawa: National Library of Canada, 1974. vii, 63 leaves. (Canadian theses on microfiche, 19763)
Thesis (M.A.), University of Calgary, 1974.
Microfiche of typescript.

Canadiana, 1975. OONL

2265 **Edwards**, Michael William. Alberta short run crude oil supply, 1972. Ottawa: National Library of Canada, 1974. 64 leaves. (Canadian theses on microfiche, 19768)
Thesis (M.A.), University of Calgary, 1974.
Microfiche of typescript.

Canadiana, 1975. OONL

2266 **Fitzgerald**, John Joseph. Black gold with grit. Sidney, B.C.: Gray's Publishing, 1978. xvi, 264p. ill.
Sub-title on dust jacket *The Alberta oil sands*.

Canadiana, 1979. ACP

2267 **Foster**, Peter. The blue-eyed sheiks. The Canadian oil establishment. Toronto: Collins, 1979. 320p.

Canadiana, 1979. **AEA**

2268 **Freeman**, James Morton. Biggest sellout in history. Foreign ownership of Alberta's oil and gas industry and the oil sands Edmonton: Alberta New Democratic Party, 1966. 112p.

Glenbow. **ACG**

2269 **Freeman**, James Morton. The case history of Alberta's oil. Economic capitalism. s.l.: s.n., n.d. 73 leaves.

Caption title.
Edited version of his *Biggest sellout in history. Foreign ownership of Alberta's oil and gas industry and the oil sands.* **AEU**

2270 **Govier**, George W. Alberta's oil sands in the energy supply picture. s.l.: s.n., 1973. 22, (11)p. ill.

On cover: Presented at the Canadian Gas Association, Operating Section, Second National Technical Conference, October 18, 1973, Calgary Inn, Calgary, Alberta.
Canadiana, 1978.

2271 The great Canadian oil patch. Toronto: Maclean Hunter, 1970. 355p. ill.

CBIP, 1979. **ACG**

2272 Great Canadian Oil Sands Ltd. Miracle on the Athabasca. Edmonton: Great Canadian Oil Sands Ltd., 1965. 12p. ill., maps.

Caption title *Athabasca, land of promise.*
A promotional booklet.

AEA

2273 **Hanson**, Eric John. Dynamic decade. The evolution and effects of the oil industry in Alberta. Toronto: McClelland & Stewart, 1958. 314p. ill.

Glenbow. **ACG**

2274 **Hillborn**, James D., ed. Dusters and gushers. The Canadian oil and gas industry. By outstanding authorities in the petroleum and related industries. Toronto: Pitt Publishing Co, 1968. 278p. ill.

Series of articles about the exploration, development, and production of petroleum supplies, as well as prominent individuals and companies.

Brown. **AEU**

2275 **House**, John Douglas. The last of the free enterprisers. The oilmen of Calgary. Ottawa: Institute of Canadian Studies, Carleton University, 1979. ix,229p. ill. (Carleton library, 122)

Also published Toronto, Macmillan of Canada.

Canadiana, 1980. **AEU**

2276 Imperial Oil Ltd. A visit to the Leduc oilfield and gas conservation project. Calgary: Imperial Oil Ltd., 1956. 7p. ill.

Glenbow. **ACG**

2277 Imperial Oil Ltd. Wildcat one thirty four. The oil discovery that has given Canada new horizons is ten years old. Calgary Imperial Oil Ltd., 1957. 1v. ill.

Cover title.
Review of the industry on the tenth anniversary of the Leduc strike.

Glenbow. **ACG**

2278 Independent Task Force on the Development of Canada's Petroleum and Mineral Resources. Canada's resources and the national interest. Report by an Independent Task Force on the Development of Canada's Petroleum and Mineral Resources. Initiated by the Canada West Foundation. Calgary: Canada West Foundation, 1977. 1v. and 4v. appendices.

Appendices: A. Taxation of non-renewable resources B. Canada's oil and gas resources C. Canada's Mineral resources D. An oil and natural gas energy plan for Canada, 1977-1985. **AEU**

2279 Independent Task Force on the Development of Canada's Petroleum and Mineral Resources. Canada's resources and the national interest. A report by an Independent Task Force on the Development of Canada's Mining and Petroleum Resources. A summary. Initiated by the Canada West Foundation. Calgary: Canada West Foundation, 1977. 44p. ill.

Summarizes the recommendations of the full report of the Task Force. **AEU**

2280 **Janke**, John William. Environmental economic issues in the sour gas processing industry in Alberta. Ottawa: National Library of Canada, 1974. x, 119 leaves. (Canadian theses on microfiche, 21854)

Thesis (M.A.), University of Alberta, 1974.
Microfiche of typescript.
Examination of the costs of environmental regulations in processing sour gas.

U of A Theses. **AEU**

2281 **Kjellberg**, Sten Oscar. The Canadian petroleum industry, achievements and prospects. Written in collaboration with J.P. Lounsbury. Calgary: Toronto-Dominion Bank, Oil and Gas Dept., 1958. 59p. ill.

2d ed. 1960, 3d ed. 1962 by J.P. Lounsbury, 4th ed. 1964.

Canadiana, 1965.

2282 **Koch**, Edward Leo. Home Oil Calgary. Oil exploration and production. A sample study of an oil producing area, an inductive approach. General editor, Evelyn Moore. Toronto: Holt, Rinehart and Winston, 1971. iii, 60p. ill. (People and places in Canada)

Written for use in social studies in elementary grades.

Canadiana, 1971. **ACP**

2283 LaBorde Simat Ltd. A perspective on the energy resources of Western Canada. Calgary: Canada West Foundation, 1974. iv, 16p. graphs.

Canadiana, 1977.

AEP

2284 **Laxer**, James. The big tough expensive job. Imperial Oil and the Canadian economy. Edited by James Laxer and Anne Martin. Erin, Ont: Press Porcepic, 1976. 256p. ill.

Distributed by Musson Book.

Canadiana, 1977.

AEU

2285 **Lounsbury**, John Patton. The Canadian petroleum industry. The next five years. Calgary: Toronto-Dominion Bank, 1958. (1v.)

2d ed. 1960 entitled *The Canadian petroleum industry, achievements and prospects*. 3d ed. 1962 entitled *The Canadian petroleum industry, the next five years*. 34p.

AEU

2286 **Massey**, D.L. An oil well near Edmonton. s.l.: Ginn and Company, 1969. 24p. ill. (Ginn Studies in Canadian History. Teacher's manual)

AEA

2287 **Maxwell**, Judith. Developing new energy sources. The Syncrude case. Montreal: C.D. Howe Research Institute, 1975. 29p. (HRI observation series, 10)

AEU

2288 **McFayden**, Hector J. Field pricing of natural gas in Alberta, 1955-1971. Ottawa: National Library of Canada, 1972. 7, 63 leaves. ill. (Canadian theses on microfilm, 13903)

Thesis (M.A.), University of Calgary, 1972.
Microfilm of typescript.

Canadiana, 1973.

OONL

2289 **McGechie**, David Henry. Economic approaches to environmental management of the Alberta tar sands. Ottawa: National Library of Canada, 1976. x, 121 leaves. ill. (Canadian theses on microfiche, 27695)

Thesis (M.A.), University of Alberta, 1976.
Microfiche of typescript.

Canadiana, 1977.

AEU

2290 **Minchin**, D. Howard. Cost reduction programs of a natural gas distribution firm. Edmonton: University of Alberta, 1956. v, 65 leaves.

Thesis (M.A.), University of Alberta, 1956.
Typescript.
Examination of means to produce lower operating costs in a gas distribution firm.

Canadian theses.

AEU

2291 **Moynham**, Gordon John. Natural gas exploration and development in Alberta. Edmonton: University of Alberta, 1971. viii, 140 leaves.

Thesis (M.A.), University of Alberta, 1971.
Typescript.

Canadian theses. AEU

2292 **Nickle**, Carl Oloff. A man, a company and an industry in Western Canada. Anglo-American Exploration Ltd. New York: Newcomen Society of North America, 1956. 24p. ill. (Newcommen address)

An address given at Toronto. AEU

2293 Petroleum Resource Communication Foundation. Our petroleum challenge. The new era. Calgary: Petroleum Resources Communication Foundation, 1979. 64p. ill.

Cover title.

Canadiana, 1979. AEU

2294 **Pieuk**, Clare L. Development costs of Alberta crude oil, 1972-1972. Ottawa: National Library of Canada, 1973. 71 leaves. (Canadian theses on microfiche, 19814)

Thesis (M.A.), University of Calgary, 1974.
Microfiche of typescript.

Canadiana, 1975. ACU

2295 **Pratt**, Lawrence. The tar sands. Syncrude and the politics of oil. Edmonton: Hurtig, 1976. 197p. ill.

Canadiana, 1976. ACG

2296 **Presber**, Wayne Orlyn. The economics of conventional crude oil enhanced recovery schemes, province of Alberta. Ottawa: National Library of Canada, 1975. x, 76 leaves. ill. (Canadian theses on microfiche, 25049)

Thesis (M.A.), University of Calgary, 1975.
Microfiche of typescript.

Canadiana, 1976. OONL

2297 **Quicin**, George David. Growth of the Alberta petroleum producing industry. 1947-1952. An income-expenditure analysis. Edmonton: University of Alberta, 1958. xiv, 153 leaves.

Thesis (M.A.), University of Alberta, 1958.
Typescript.
Analyzes sources of income and expenditures of the Alberta petroleum producing industry.

Canadian theses. AEU

2298 **Reid**, Crowther & Partners Limited. Report on the impact of a proposed synthetic crude oil project on Fort McMurray for Syncrude Canada Ltd. s.l.: Reid, Crowther and Partners Ltd., 1973. 83 leaves. ill.

AEU

2299 **Richards**, John. Prairie capitalism. Power and influence in the new

West. Written by John Richards and Larry Pratt. Toronto: McClelland and Stewart, 1979. x, 340p. (Canada in transition series)

Canadiana, 1979.

AEA

2300 **Sharma**, Hari Dutt. Income contribution of the petroleum industry to the province of Alberta for the period 1964-1976, and public policy. Ottawa: National Library of Canada, 1979. x, 106 leaves. (Canadian theses on microfiche, 40495)

Thesis (M.B.A.), University of Alberta 1979.
Microfiche of typescript.

U of A Theses.

AEU

2301 Shell Oil Company of Canada Ltd. The Jumping Pound story. An account of natural gas and sulphur in Alberta. Toronto: 1957. 15p. ill.

Cover title.

ALP

2302 **Sievwright**, Eric Colville. The effect of petroleum development on the Alberta economy, 1947-1957. Montreal: McGill University, 1961. xx, 352 leaves. diagrs.

Thesis (Ph.D.), McGill University, 1961.
Typescript.

Canadian theses.

2303 **Slatter**, E.J. Eric Lafferty Harvie. The oil chapter. s.l.: s.n.: 1974. 124 leaves.

Duplicated.
Edition of seven copies.

AEU

2304 **Smith**, Philip. The treasure-seekers. The men who built Home Oil. Toronto: Macmillan of Canada, 1978. ix, 310p. ill.

Canadiana, 1979.

AEA

2305 **Srebrnik**, Leokadia. Economic evaluation of ethylene production in Alberta. A study of the future ethylene producing industry in Canada. Ottawa: National Library of Canada, 1977. 11, 211 leaves. ill. (Canadian theses on microfiche, 35808)

Thesis (M.A.), McGill University, 1977.
Microfiche of typescript.

Canadiana, 1979.

OONL

2306 Syncrude Canada Ltd. The Syncrude story. Edmonton: Syncrude Canada, 1977. 23p. ill.

A promotional booklet.
Also published in a French language edition.

Canadiana, 1979.

AEA

2307 **Thompson**, Stella Margery. Prorationing of oil in Alberta and some economic implications. Edmonton: University of Alberta, 1968. iv, 121 leaves.

Thesis (M.A.), University of Alberta, 1968.
Typescript.
Evaluation of the policy of regulating oil production so as to meet no more than market demand.

Canadian theses. **AEU**

2308 **Twaits**, William Osborn. Energy taxation. Remarks to the Alberta Society of Petroleum Geologists, Calgary, January 22, 1964. Toronto: W.O. Twaits, 1964. 10 leaves.

Mimeographed.

Canadiana, 1964.

2309 **Uhler**, Russell S. Oil and gas finding costs. Calgary: Canadian Energy Research Institute, 1979. viii, 75p. ill. (Canadian Energy Research Institute. Study, 7)

Canadiana, 1980. **AEU**

2310 **Weinrich**, John E. Economic impact of the Canadian gas industry, local, provincial and regional. Calgary: Calgary Chamber of Commerce, 1966. 214 leaves. ill.

Cover title.

Brown. **AEU**

2311 **Willms**, Arthur Henry. Public utility regulation in Alberta. A case study of the natural gas distributing industry. Ottawa: National Library of Canada, 1970. viii, 156 leaves. ill. (Canadian theses on microfilm, 07750)

Thesis (M.A.), University of Calgary, 1970.
Microfilm of typescript.

Canadiana, 1971.

2312 **Wright**, Robert W. An analysis of the liquified petroleum gas industry in Alberta. Edmonton: University of Alberta, 1959. 87 leaves.

Thesis (M.A.), University of Alberta, 1959.
Typescript.
Examination of anticipated market potential liquified petroleum gas.

Canadian theses. **AEU**

2313 **Zieber**, George Henry. Inter- and intra-city location patterns of oil offices for Calgary and Edmonton, 1950-1970. Ottawa: National Library of Canada, 1971. xvi, 265, 328 leaves. ill. (Canadian theses on microfilm, 09662)

Thesis (Ph.D.), University of Alberta, 1971.
Microfilm of typescript.

Canadiana, 1972. **AEU**

Communication & Transportation

2314 Air Museum of Canada. Air Museum of Canada, Calgary, Canada. Calgary: Air Museum of Canada, 1966. 28p. ill.

Glenbow. **ACG**

2315 Amalgamated Transit Union. Division 583. 50th anniversary, Division 583, Amalgamated Transit Union. Calgary: Amalgamated Transit Union, Division 583, 1965. 1v. (38)p. ill.

Cover title.

Glenbow. **ACG**

2316 **Atrill**, V.H. The Great Plains Project looks at new modes of transportation. Don Mills, Ont.: Canadian Gas Association, 1973. 12, 15, 17 leaves. ill.

Presented to the Canadian Gas Association Second Technical Conference, Calgary, October 18, 1973.
Reviews a Boeing design of a large aircraft for the transportation of oil, liquefied natural gas, etc. in the Arctic.

Canadiana, 1977.

2317 **Bain**, Donald Morrison. Canadian Pacific in the Rockies. Calgary: British Railway Modellers of North America, Calgary Group, 1979. 4v. ill.

Canadiana, 1979. **ACP**

2318 **Baker**, Albert TenBroeke. The Crow's Nest Pass agreement in review. An address. Calgary: Alberta Wheat Pool, 1959. 9p.

Address to luncheon meeting of the Calgary Chamber of Commerce on the C.P.R. freight rates.

Canadiana, 1963.

2319 **Bardock**, Edison Frederick. Pupil transportation in Alberta. Ann Arbor, Mich.: University Microfilms, 1975. ix, 177 leaves.

Thesis (Ed.D.), University of Montana, 1975.
Microfilm of typescript.

Canadiana, 1979. **AEU**

2320 **Barris**, Theodore. Fire canoe. Prairie steamboat days revisited. Toronto: McClelland and Stewart, 1977. 304p. ill.

Canadiana, 1978. **AEU**

2321 **Belanger**, Art J. The Calgary-Edmonton, Edmonton-Calgary trail. Calgary: Frontier Publishing, 1973. 56p. ill., map. (Frontier books, 29)

Canadiana. **AEA**

2322 **Bertram**, Robert Gordon. Productivity relationships in Alberta Government Telephones. Edmonton: University of Alberta, 1971. viii, 105 leaves.

Thesis (M.B.A.), University of Alberta, 1971.
Typescript.

Canadian theses. **AEU**

2323 **Bowman**, Ronald Fraser Patrick. Railways in southern Alberta. Lethbridge: Historical Society of Alberta, Whoop-up Country

Chapter, 1973. 40p. ill. (Historical Society of Alberta. Whoop-up Country Chapter. Occasional paper, 4)

Canadiana, 1974. **AEA**

2324 Calgary Brewing and Malting Co. Calgary carriage collection. Calgary: Calgary Brewing and Malting Company, 1973. 56p. ill.

A collection exhibited at the Horseman's Hall of Fame, Calgary Brewing and Malting Co.

Canadiana, 1974. **AEA**

2325 **Campbell**, E.E.B. Edmonton Transit System story, 1903-1978. 75 year history, from radial railway to light rail transit. 2d ed. Edmonton: E.E.B. Campbell, 1978. xxv, 461p. ill.

Duplicated.
Second title page *A 75-year life-story of the City of Edmonton's transit system.* **AEA**

2326 **Cashman**, Anthony Walcott. The Alberta Motor Association. A history. Edmonton: Alberta Motor Association, 1967. 139p. ill.

Glenbow. **ACG**

2327 **Cashman**, Anthony Walcott. A history of motoring in Alberta. Edmonton: Alberta Motor Association, 1976. 159p. ill.

Printed by Spartan Press. **AEA**

2328 **Cashman**, Anthony Walcott. A moving story. Edmonton: Western Cartage & Storage (1962), 1969. 53p. ill.

Story of Western Cartage & Storage Company.

Canadiana, 1970. **AEU**

2329 **Cashman**, Anthony Walcott. Singing wires. The telephone in Alberta. Edmonton: Alberta Government Telephones Commission, 1972. 496p. ill.

AEA

2330 **Cashman**, Anthony Walcott. The telephone man. A story about Archie Hollingshead. With illustrations by Vivian Thierfelder. Edmonton: Alberta Government Telephones, 1977. 32p.

A story, based on fact, of telephone men in the early years.

2331 **Christenson**, Raymond Andrew. The Calgary and Edmonton Railway and the 'Edmonton Bulletin'. Edmonton: University of Alberta, 1967. ix, 292 leaves.

Thesis (M.A.), University of Alberta, 1967.
Typescript.
Study of the Edmonton and Calgary Railway through reports published in the *Edmonton Bulletin.*

Canadian theses.

2332 **Dean**, Basil. Freedom of the air. Ottawa: Canadian Association of Radio and Television Broadcasters, 1955. 12p.

Reply to and comment on the Report on the Massey Commission.
Originally published as articles in the *Calgary Herald*. First published as a pamphlet in 1951. Re-issued 1955 with some revisions.

Canadiana, 1954.

2333 **Ferguson**, William Paul. The snowbird decades. Western Canada's pioneer aviation companies. Vancouver: Butterworth, 1979. 92p. ill.
AEU

2334 **Freigang**, P.F. The story of the Lethbridge Municipal Railway, 1912-1947. Vancouver: Passenger Transport Enterprises, 1970. 10, 2 leaves. ill.

Duplicated.
Cover title *Lethbridge Municipal Railway, 1911-1947*.
AEU

2335 **Godsell**, Philip Henry. Pilots of the purple twilight. The story of Canada's early bush flyers. Toronto: Ryerson Press, 1955. xii, 2, 225p. ill.
Canadiana, 1955.
ACG

2336 **Hansen**, Evelyn M. Where go the boats. Navigation on the Peace, 1792-1952. By Evelyn Hansen for the Friends of the Museum. Peace River: Peace River Centennial Museum, 1977. 38p. ill.
Canadiana, 1978.
AEA

2337 **Hatcher**, Colin Kirk. Stampede city streetcars. The story of the Calgary Municipal Railway. Montreal: Railfare Enterprises, 1975. 88p. ill., maps. (A Railfare book)
Canadiana, 1976.
AEA

2338 **Hungry Wolf**, Adolf. Rails in the Canadian Rockies. Invermere, B.C.: Good Medicine Books, 1979. 368p. ill.
ACG

2339 The immorality of the motor car. Our critical choice. A report on transportation and the future of Edmonton. Edmonton: University of Alberta, Department of Extension, Community Resources Development Division, 1971. 81p. ill.

An information project of the University Practicum in Community Analysis, winter session, 1970-71.
At head of title: The City of Edmonton transportation bylaw #3655 and the future of Edmonton.

Canadiana, 1974.

2340 **Johnston**, Alexander. Boats and barges on the Belly. Lethbridge: Historical Society of Alberta, Lethbridge Branch, 1960. 48p. ill.
Glenbow.
ACG

2341 **Johnston**, Alexander. The CP Rail High Level Bridge at Lethbridge. Lethbridge: Historical Society of Alberta Whoop-Up County Chapter, 1977. 34p. ill., maps. (Historical Society of Alberta. Whoop-Up County Chapter. Occasional paper, 7)

Canadiana, 1979. **AEA**

2342 **Keith**, Ronald A. Bush pilot with a brief case. The happy-go-lucky story of Grant McConachie. Toronto: Doubleday, 1972. 322p. ill.

Also, 1973, Don Mills, Ont., Paperjacks.

Canadiana, 1974. **AEU**

2343 **Lai**, Hermia Kwok-Lee. Evolution of the railway network of Edmonton and its land use effects. Edmonton: University of Alberta, 1967. x, 170 leaves.

Thesis (M.A.), University of Alberta, 1967.
Typescript.

Canadian theses. **AEU**

2344 **Longair**, Margaret Eleanor (Ritchie). The development of transportation in early Calgary, researched by Margaret E. Longair. Prepared for school use by W.N. Holden and M.E. Longair. Calgary: Calgary Public School Board, 1968. 1 portfolio. ill.

Canadiana, 1972.

2345 **MacEwan**, John Walter Grant. The battle for the Bay. Saskatoon: Western Producer Books, 1975. 258p. ill.

Cover title *The story of the Hudson Bay Railroad*.

Canadiana, 1975. **AEA**

2346 **McCallum**, Joe. CKUA and 40 wondrous years of radio. Compiled and edited by Joe McCallum. Edmonton: 1967. 44p. ill.

Cover title.

Glenbow. **ACG**

2347 **McCartney**, Samuel Trevor. Communications in the county of Camrose. Information flow in a rural area. Edmonton: University of Alberta, 1970. xvi, 142 leaves.

Thesis (M.A.), University of Alberta, 1970.
Typescript.
Examines school bus services, postal services, telephone services, newspapers, radio, and television broadcasts as components of the communications network in the County of Camrose.

Canadian theses. **AEU**

2348 **Mohan**, Elizabeth Marilyn. Aspects of intra-urban mobility, Calgary, 1963-68. Ottawa: National Library of Canada, 1971. x, 139 leaves. (Canadian theses on microfilm, 10136)

Thesis (M.A.), University of Calgary, 1971.
Microfilm of typescript.

Canadiana, 1972.

2349 **Myles**, Eugenie Louise (Butler). Airborne from Edmonton. Being the true tale of how Edmonton, a remote frontier city in northwestern Canada, became the Plymouth of a new age of air discoveries and air conquests and air commerce and how the dreams of her pioneer pilots were realized a thousandfold. Toronto: Ryerson Press, 1959. xii, 280p. ill.

Glenbow. ACG

2350 **Peel**, Bruce Braden. Steamboats on the Saskatchewan. Saskatoon: Western Producer Prairie Books, 1972. 238p. ill.

Glenbow. ACG

2351 **Skuba**, Michael. Population density and pupil transportation costs in Alberta. Edmonton: University of Alberta, 1964. xii, 144 leaves.

Thesis (Ph.D.), University of Alberta, 1964.
Typescript.

Canadian theses.

2352 **Smith**, Benjamin George. An activity systems impact analysis of the Edmonton Transit System strike, 1973-1974. Ottawa: National Library of Canada, 1975. x, 131 leaves. (Canadian theses on microfiche, 24132)

Thesis (M.A.), University of Alberta, 1975.
Microfiche of typescript.
Analyses effects of transit strikes on the activities of Edmonton households.

U of A Theses. AEU

2353 **Stacey**, Earl Clifford. The Monkman Pass Highway. A contribution. Beaverlodge: Beaverlodge and District Historical Association, 1974. 44p. ill. (To the builders of the Peace series)

Canadiana, 1977. AEA

2354 **Trnavskis**, Boris. Passenger demand for a 1976 Q S T O L aircraft system in the Calgary-Edmonton corridor. Ottawa: National Library of Canada, 1974. xi, 273 leaves. (Canadian theses on microfiche, 22275)

Thesis (Ph.D.), University of Calgary, 1974.
Microfiche of typescript.

Canadiana, 1976.

2355 University of Alberta. Practicum in Rapid Transit. An immediate alternative to the McKinnon Ravine Freeway. Cost comparison of a LRT alignment for McCauley Plaza, Jasper line. Edmonton: University Practicum in Rapid Transit, Dept. of Extension, University of Alberta, 1974. 24p. ill.

Canadiana, 1977.

2356 University of Alberta. Practicum in Rapid Transit. Light rapid transit. 2d ed. Edmonton: University Practicum in Rapid Transit, 1973. vii, 72p. ill.

Canadiana, 1975.

2357 **Williams**, James Davies. A history of the Edmonton, Dunvegan and British

Columbia railway, 1907-1929. Edmonton: University of Alberta, 1956. vii, 203 leaves.

Thesis (M.A.), University of Alberta, 1956.
Typescript.

Canadian theses.

2358 **Willis**, Geoffrey Allan. Development of transportation in the Peace River region of Alberta and British Columbia, with an evaluation of present day rail and road commodity flow patterns. Edmonton: University of Alberta, 1966. xi, 139 leaves.

Thesis (M.A.), University of Alberta, 1966.
Typescript.

Canadian theses.

National and International Politics

2359 **Barr**, John J. The unfinished revolt. Some views on western independence. Edited by John Barr and Owen Anderson. Toronto: McLelland and Stewart, 1971. 144p.

Contents: Barr, J.J. Beyond bitterness. Anderson, O. The unfinished revolt. Whyte, Jon. Fable of Twain & Abel. Thompson, John. Re-appropriating the culture of the west. Prendergast, Russell. The national policy and the west. Love, James. Alberta in the financial vise. Dolan, Charles E. Confederalism. Towards striking a new balance. Boothroyd, Peter. Independence for whom? **AEA**

2360 **Blackman**, Warren D. The cost of confederation. An analysis of costs to Alberta. By Michael J. Hollinshead and W. Blackman. Calgary: Independent Alberta Association 1974-1975. 2v.

Studies commissioned by the Independent Alberta Association.
Contents: v.1. Economic activity. - v.2. Inter-governmental transfer of funds **ACU**

2361 Canada West Foundation. A realistic perspective of Canadian confederation. Prepared by M. & M. Systems Research Ltd. Calgary: Canada West Foundation,. 1977. v, 125p. (Canada West Foundation. Publication, 76-77/01) **AEU**

2362 **Edwards**, Clifford Gordon. The National Policy as seen by the editors of the Medicine Hat newspapers. A western opinion, 1885-1896. Edmonton: University of Alberta, 1969. iv, 221p.

Thesis (M.A.), University of Alberta, 1969.
Typescript.

Canadian theses. **AEU**

2363 **Elton**, David K. Alternatives. Towards the development of an effective federal system for Canada. A revision of a discussion paper prepared for the Canada West Foundation. By David Elton, F.C. Englemann, Peter McCormick. Calgary: Canada West Foundation, 1978. 99p.

Cover title.
On cover: Canada West Conference on Confederation, Banff National Park, March 27-29, 1978. Congres de l'ouest canadien sur la confederation.
1st ed., March, 1978, amended May, 1978, revised and updated.

Canadiana, 1979.

AEU

2364 **Elton**, David K. Electoral perception of federalism. A descriptive analysis of the Alberta electorate. Ottawa: National Library of Canada, 1973. xv, 390 leaves. ill. (Canadian theses on microfilm, 15217)

Thesis (Ph.D.), University of Alberta, 1973.
Microfiche of typescript.

Canadiana, 1974.

2365 **Engleman**, Frederick Charles. The Co-operative Commonwealth Federation of Canada. A study of membership participation in party policy-making. Ann Arbor, Mich.: University Microfilms, 1968. vi, 262 leaves.

Thesis (Ph.D.), Yale University, 1954.
Microfilm of typescript.

Canadiana, 1970.

2366 **Gordon**, Stanley Bruce. R.B. Bennett, M.L.A., 1897-1905. Ottawa: National Library of Canada, 1975. iv, 194 leaves. (Canadian theses on microfiche, 25012)

Thesis (M.A.), University of Calgary, 1975.
Microfiche of typescript.

Canadiana, 1977.

OONL

2367 **Grondin**, Conde R. The development of political cynicism among a selected sample of adolescents in Alberta. Ottawa: National Library of Canada, 1975. xxviii, 472 leaves. (Canadian theses on microfiche, 24040)

Thesis (Ph.D.), University of Alberta, 1975.
Microfiche of typescript.

U of A Theses.

AEU

2368 **Hart**, John Edward. William Irvine and radical politics in Canada. Ottawa: National Library of Canada, 1972. 3, v, 337 leaves. (Canadian theses on microfilm, 11078)

Thesis (Ph.D.), University of Guelph, 1972.
Microfilm of typescript.

Canadiana, 1972.

OONL

2369 **Hay**, William A. R.B. Bennett and the charge of one-man government. An analysis of his relationship with potential rivals. Ottawa: National Library of Canada, 1974. 183 leaves. (Canadian theses on microfiche, 19737)

Thesis (M.A.), Lakehead University, 1974.
Microfilm of typescript.

Canadian, 1975.

OONL

2370 **Humphreys**, David Llewellyn. Joe Clark. A portrait. Ottawa: Deneau & Greenberg, 1978. 276p. ill.

Also published, 1979, Don Mills, Ont., Totem.

Canadiana, 1979. **AEP**

2371 **Irvine**, William. The farmers in politics. With an introduction by Reginald Whitaker. Toronto: McClelland and Stewart, 1976. xli, 253p. (Carleton library, 114)

First edition 1920(Peel 2715).
p6: A lucid statment of the distinctive ideological position of the farmers, seen from the parties ... left wing.

Canadiana, 1978. **AEU**

2372 **Irvine**, William. Live or die with Russia. Edmonton: W. Irivine, 1958. 143p. ill.

Publication date supplied.
Advocates co-operation with Russia.

Glenbow. **ACG**

2373 **Irvine**, William. The twain shall meet, by Wm. Irvine and others. Edmonton: William Irvine, 1961. 175p. ill.

Cover title in English and Chinese.
Accounts of a visit of six Canadians to China in 1960.

Canadiana, 1960.

2374 The juridicial nature of Canadian federalism. The status of a province. Calgary: Independent Alberta Association, 1975. 84 leaves.

AEL

2375 **MacKinnon**, Frank. The Crown in Canada. Calgary: Glenbow Alberta Institute, 1976. 189p.

Published in association with McClelland and Stewart West.
An examination of the role of the Crown in the Canadian democratic process.

Canadiana, 1976. **ACP**

2376 **Manning**, Ernest Charles. Political realignment. A challenge to thoughtful Canadians. Toronto: McClelland and Stewart, 1967. 94p.

Advocates reorganization of the Progressive Conservative Party as the basis for an improved political system.

Glenbow. **ACG**

2377 **Mardon**, Ernest G. Who's who in federal politics from Alberta. Lethbridge: Ernest G. Mardon, 1972. 109p. maps.

A biographical dictionary of representatives from 1905 to date.

Canadiana, 1973. **AEU**

2378 **Miller**, James A. The Alberta press and the conscription issue in the First World War, 1914-1918. Ottawa: National Library of Canada. 1974. xiv, 238 leaves. (Canadian theses on microfiche, 21068)

Thesis (M.A.), University of Alberta, 1974.
Microfiche of typecript.

Canadiana, 1975.

2379 **Mitchner**, Ernest Alyn. William Pearce and federal government activity in Western Canada, 1882-1904. Edmonton: University of Alberta, 1971. xvi, 336 leaves.

Thesis (Ph.D.), University of Alberta, 1971.

Typescript.

AEU

2380 **Nielson**, G.E. The line that joins. Calgary: G.E.Nielson, 1969. 25p.

Speech, sponsored by Rotary International, delivered to Waterton-Glacier International Conference, June 14, 1969.

Canadiana, 1970.

OONL

2381 **Nolan**, Michael. Joe Clark, the emerging leader. Photographs by Ted Grant. Toronto: Fitzhenry & Whiteside, 1978. 139p. ill.

Canadiana, 1978.

AEP

2382 **Oliver**, Thelma Isabel. Aspects of alienation in Alberta. Ottawa: National Library of Canada, 1974. 13, 316 leaves. ill. (Canadian theses on microfiche, 21560)

Thesis (Ph.D.), York University, 1974.
Microfiche of typescript.
A study of the relationship between political discontent and alienation in Alberta and the impact of both on the Canadian federal system.

Canadiana, 1975.

OONL

2383 **Richardson**, George H.W. The Conservative Party in the provisional district of Alberta, 1887-1905. Ottawa: National Library of Canada, 1977. viii, 194 leaves. (Canadian theses on microfiche, 32056)

Thesis (M.A.), University of Alberta, 1977.
Microfiche of typescript.

U of A Theses.

AEU

2384 **Roberts**, Stanley C. A summary report on the proceedings of Alternatives Canada, a Canada West Conference on Confederation, held at Banff, March 27-29, 1978. Calgary: Canada West Foundation, 1978. 28p.

On cover: Follow-up on Alternatives Canada Conference, Banff, March 27-29, 1978.

Canadiana, 1979.

OONL

2385 **Roche**, Douglas J. The human side of politics. Toronto: Clarke Irwin, 1976. 209p.

Articles on experiences in federal politics.

Canadiana, 1977.

AEU

2386 **Roche**, Douglas J. Justice not charity. A new global ethic for Canada. Toronto: McClelland and Stewart, 1976. 123p.

A view of Canada's role in economic assistance to underdeveloped countries. **AEU**

2387 **Roche**, Douglas J. What development is all about. China, Indonesia, Bangladesh. Toronto: NC Press Limited, 1979. 169 (1)p.

Account of a six-week journey to Asia, with opinions on Canada's foreign aid program.

Canadiana, 1979. **AECYR**

2388 **Scown**, Dennis R. A history and analysis of the 1971 Alberta general election. Ottawa: National Library of Canada, 1973. vii, 178 leaves. (Canadian theses on microfiche, 19824)

Thesis (M.A.), University of Calgary, 1973.
Microfiche of typescript.

Canadiana, 1975.

2389 **Scratch**, John Ronald. The editorial reaction of the Alberta press to the Bennett government, 1930-1935. Edmonton: University of Alberta, 1968. vi, 147 leaves.

Thesis (M.A.), University of Alberta, 1968.
Typescript.

Canadian theses. **AEU**

2390 **Shingadia**, Ashwin. Edmonton Centre. A constituency study, June 1968. Edmonton: University of Alberta, 1969. vi, 201p.

Theses (M.A.), University of Alberta, 1969.
Typescript.

Canadian theses. **AEU**

2391 **Simon**, Olaf Emil Hugo. To hell with Canada. Calgary: Veritas International Publishing, 1976. 120p.

Also, 2d ed., 1977.
A criticism of the political system and corruption in politics.

Canadiana, 1976. **AEU**

2392 **Stewart**, Kenneth Fenwick. R.B. Bennett as M.P., 1910-1917. Ottawa. National Library of Canada, 1971. vi, 617 leaves. (Canadian theses on microfilm, 10630)

Thesis (M.A.), Queen's University, 1971.
Microfilm of typescript.

Canadiana, 1972. **OONL**

2393 **Thomas**, Lewis Herbert. The struggle for responsible government in the North-West Territories, 1870-97. Toronto: University of Toronto Press, 1956. 276p. ill.

Originally presented as a Ph.D. thesis, University of Minnesota, with title *Responsible government in the Canadian North-West Territories, 1870-1897*.

2d ed., 1978, University of Toronto Press and in their series Canadian university paperbacks, 196.

Canadiana, 1978. AEU

2394 **Webber**, Frank. Was it all a dream? Edmonton: F.W. Webber, 1959. 1, 51p.

Description of an economic and political system, the shareholder's state.

Canadiana, 1960. AEU

2395 **Yurko**, William John. On being a Conservative. Selected speeches, 1968-1971. Edmonton: Edmonton Gold Bar Conservative Association, 1976. 1v. (various paging).

AEL

Provincial Politics

2396 Alberta Social Credit League. Do you know? The authentic report of Alberta's progress with Social Credit government. Rev. ed. Edmonton: Alberta Social Credit League, 1967. 52p.

Cover title.

Glenbow. ACG

2397 **Anderson**, Owen Arthur James. The Alberta Social Credit Party. An empirical analysis of membership, characteristics, participation, and opinion. Ottawa: National Library of Canada, 1972. xiii, 428(i.e. 430)leaves. ill. (Canadian theses on microfilm, 01110)

Thesis (Ph.D.), University of Alberta, 1972.
Microfilm of typescript.

Canadiana, 1972.

2398 **Anton**, Gordon A. The Liberal Party in Alberta. An organizational case study. Ottawa: National Library of Canada, 1972. viii, 94 leaves. ill. (Canadian theses on microfilm, 11288)

Thesis (M.A.), University of Calgary, 1972.
Microfilm of typescript.

Canadiana, 1972.

2399 **Barr**, John J. The dynasty. The rise and fall of Social Credit in Alberta. Toronto: McClelland and Stewart, 1974. 248p.

Canadiana, 1975. AEU

2400 **Betke**, Carl Frederick. The United Farmers of Alberta, 1921-1935. The relationship between the agricultural organization and the government of Alberta. Edmonton: University of Alberta, 1971. viii, 187 leaves.

Thesis (M.A.), University of Alberta, 1971.
Typescript.

Canadian theses. AEU

2401 **Boudreau**, Joseph A. Alberta, Aberhart and Social Credit. Toronto: Holt, Rinehart and Winston of Canada, 1975. v, 122p. ill. (Canadian history through the press series)

Compiled byJ.A. Boudreau.

Canadiana, 1975. **ACG**

2402 Canada West Foundation. Canada West Foundation. Some aspects of its evolution, objectives and philosophy. Calgary: Canada West Foundation, 1976. 3p.

Cover title. **AEU**

2403 **Cashman**, Anthony Walcott. Ernest C. Manning. A biographical sketch. Cover by Garry LaRue. Edmonton: Alberta Social Credit League, 1958. 35p. ill.

Glenbow. **ACG**

2404 **Cashman**, Anthony Walcott. The vice-regal cowboy. Life and times of Alberta's J.J. Bowlen. Edmonton: Institute of Applied Art, 1957. 199p. ill.

Glenbow. **ACG**

2405 **Cormack**, Barbara (Villy). Perennials and politics. The life story of Hon. Irene Parlby, LLD. Ardrossan: B.V. Cormack, 1969. 160p. ill.

Printed by Professional Printing, Sherwood Park.

Glenbow. **ACG**

2406 **Elliott**, David Raymond. The dispensational theology and political ideology of William Aberhart. Ottawa: National Library of Canada, 1975. xi, 202 leaves. ill. (Canadian theses on microfiche, 25001)

Thesis (M.A.), University of Calgary, 1975.
Microfiche of typescript.

Canadiana, 1977.

2407 **Embree**, David Grant. The rise of the United Farmers of Alberta. Edmonton: University of Alberta, 1956. 295 leaves.

Thesis (M.A.), University of Alberta.
Microfilm of thesis. **ACG**

2408 **Foster**, Franklin Lloyd. The 1921 Alberta provincial election. A consideration of factors involved with particular attention to overtones of millennialism within the U.F.A. and other reform movements of the period. Ottawa: National Library of Canada, 1977. vi, 171 leaves. (Canadian theses on microfiche, 37509)

Thesis (M.A.), Queen's University, 1978.
Typescript.

Canadiana, 1980. **OONL**

2409 **Georgeson**, Michael R. A one-party dominant system. The case of Alberta. Ottawa: National Library of Canada, 1974. ix, 138 leaves. (Canadian theses on microfiche, 19777)

Thesis (M.A.), University of Calgary, 1974.
Microfiche of typescript.

Canadiana, 1975.

2410 **Gershaw**, Fred William. Political history of Alberta. Medicine Hat: Modern Press, 1962. 8p. ill.

Glenbow. **ACG**

2411 Glenbow-Alberta Institute. Archives. George Gibson Coote papers, 1907-1956. Calgary: Glenbow Archives, 1969. 31p. (Glenbow archives series, 4)

Duplicated. Inventory.
Coote was active in the United Farmers Association and M.P. for Macleod, 1925-1935.

Dew. **AEA**

2412 **Groh**, Dennis Gregory. The political thought of Ernest Manning. Ottawa: National Library of Canada, 1970. iv, 112 leaves. (Canadian theses on microfilm, 07676)

Thesis (M.A.), University of Calgary, 1970.
Microfiche of typescript.

Canadiana, 1971.

2413 **Halmrast**, Leonard C. The shepherd politician. A brief autobiography. s.l.: s.n., 1968. 51p. ill.

AEA

2414 **Hattersley**, Vera. Gran on Social Credit. Edmonton: Alberta Social Credit League, 1962. 87p.

First published as a series of articles in *The Canadian Social Crediter*.

Canadiana, 1962.

2415 **Hill**, Robert C. Social Credit and the press. The early years. 1977. vi, 135 leaves. (Canadian theses on microfiche, 34365)

Thesis (M.A.), University of Alberta, 1977.
Microfiche of typescript.
A study of the relationship between the press and the Party, culminating in the Accurate News and Information Act of 1937.

U of A Theses. **AEU**

2416 **Hooke**, Alfred John. 30 + 5. I know, I was there. Edmonton: Institute of Applied Art, 1971. 265p. ill.

Recollections of Alberta political events and the Social Credit Party.

Glenbow. **ACG**

2417 **Hulmes**, Frederick George. The senior executive and the fifteenth Alberta legislature. A study in the social and political background of membership. Ottawa: National Library of Canada, 1970. xix, 506 leaves, ill. (Canadian theses on microfilm, 06715)

Thesis (Ph.D.), University of Alberta, 1970.
Microfilm of typescript.

Canadiana, 1971. **AEU**

2418 **Hustak**, Allan. Peter Lougheed. A biography. Toronto: McClelland and Stewart, 1979. 251p.

AEU

2419 **Huston**, Mary Louise. The rise of the Social Credit movement in Alberta, 1932-1935. Edmonton: Western Microfilm Limited, 1959. iii, 113 leaves.

Thesis (M.A.), University of Alberta, 1959.
Microfiche of typescript.

Canadiana, 1973.

2420 **Irving**, John Allan. The Social Credit movement in Alberta. Toronto: University of Toronto Press, 1959. 369p. (Social credit in Alberta, its background and development, 10)

Glenbow. **ACG**

2421 **Johnson**, Leroy Peter Vernon. Aberhart of Alberta. Edmonton: Institute of Applied Art, 1970. 252p.

By L.P.V. Johnson and Ola J. MacNutt.

Glenbow. **ACG**

2422 **Johnson**, Myron. The failure of the CCF in Alberta. An accident of history? Ottawa: National Library of Canada, 1974. viii, 148 leaves. (Canadian theses on microfiche, 21861)

Thesis (M.A.), University of Alberta, 1974.
Microfiche of typescript.

Canadiana, 1975. **AEU**

2423 **Kennedy**, Orvis A. Principles and policies of Social Credit. A free individual enterprise movement opposed to socialism and all other forms of statism. 10th ed. Edmonton: Alberta Social Credit League, 1972. 12p.

First edition December 1951.

Artebise. **AEL**

2424 **MacEwan**, John Walter Grant. Poking into politics. Edmonton: Institute of Applied Art, 1966. ix, (3), 192p. ill.

Author was a Calgary City Councillor, a Member of the Alberta Legislature, and Lieutenant-Governor of Alberta.

Glenbow. **ACG**

2425 **Macpherson**, Crawford Brough. Democracy in Alberta. The theory and practice of a quasi-party system. Toronto: University of Toronto Press,

1954. xii, 258p. (Social credit in Alberta, its background and development, 4)

2d. ed., 1962.

Canadiana, 1954.

AEA

2426 **Malliah**, Holavanahally Lingappa. A socio-historical study of the legislators of Alberta, 1905-1967. Ottawa: National Library of Canada, 1970. xiii, 150 leaves. (Canadian theses on microfilm, 06263)

Thesis (Ph.D.), University of Alberta, 1970.
Microfilm of typescript.

Canadiana, 1971.

AEU

2427 **Mallory**, James Russell. Social Credit and the federal power in Canada. Toronto: University of Toronto Press, 1954. xii, 204p. (Social Credit in Alberta, its background and development, 5)

Glenbow.

ACG

2428 **Manning**, Ernest Charles. Choosing the battleground. Edmonton: Alberta Social Credit League, 1970. 10p.

Glenbow.

ACG

2429 **Manning**, Ernest Charles. The problem and the price of survival. Edmonton: Alberta Social Credit League, 1961

Address to business and professional men and women, Edmonton, Oct. 24, 1961.

2430 **Manning**, Ernest Charles. The Social Credit yardstick. Edmonton: Alberta Social Credit League. n.d. (1v.)

Canadiana, 1962.

2431 **Mardiros**, Anthony. William Irvine. The life of a prairie radical. Toronto: James Lorimer, 1979. 298p.

AEA

2432 **McIntosh**, William Andrew. The United Farmers of Alberta, 1909-1920. Ottawa: National Library of Canada, 1971. v, 124 leaves. (Canadian theses on microfiche, 10119)

Thesis (M.A.), University of Calgary, 1971.
Microfiche of typescript.

Canadiana, 1972.

2433 **Nichols**, Herbert Edward. Alberta's fight for freedom. Edmonton: Alberta Social Credit League, 1963. 5 pamphlets.

Compiled from the archives of the Alberta Social Credit League, giving a factual account of how the people of Alberta fought the money monopoly.
Contents: 1. A history. 2. Public and private debt. 3. Soveignty and constitution. 4. The road to reconstruction. 5. For economic democracy.

Glenbow.

ACG

2434 **Nichols**, Herbert Edward. A handbook of Social Credit. Edmonton: Printed by the Hamly Press, 1954. 134p. ill.

On cover: Equity for all. Economic justice.

Canadiana, 1963. **ACG**

2435 **Pashak**, Leonard Barry. The populist characteristics of the early Social Credit movement in Alberta. Ottawa: National Library of Canada, 1972. v, 63 leaves. ill. (Canadian theses on microfilm, 10152)

Thesis (M.A.), University of Calgary, 1971.
Microfilm of typescript.

Canadiana, 1972. **OONL**

2436 **Robert**, George Rene. Political orientations of Calgary children from grade four to eight. Ottawa: National Library of Canada, 1969. ix, 88 leaves. ill.

Canadian theses on microfilm, 4682.
Thesis (M.Ed.), University of Calgary, 1969.
Microfilm of typescript.

Canadiana, 1970.

2437 **Royer**, Lucien. Political validity of Franco-Albertains. A study of the representativeness of l'Association canadienne française de l'Alberta. Lucien Royer, Jacinthe Perreault. Edmonton: Le centre de recherche franco-albertain, 1970. lv. (80, 82 leaves).

Duplicated.
Text in English, with French translation by Nicole Cleriot.

Stocco. **AEU**

2438 **Schultz**, Harold John. William Aberhart and the Social Credit party. A political biography. Ann Arbor, Mich.: University Microfilms, 1960. 488p leaves.

Thesis (Ph.D.), Duke University, 1959.
Microfilm copy.

Canadiana, 1960.

2439 **Serafy**, Meir. Structure and organization of political parties in Alberta. Ottawa: National Library of Canada, 1976. iv, 398 leaves. (Canadian theses on microfiche, 32178)

Thesis (Ph.D.), Carleton University, 1977.
Microfiche of typescript.

Canadiana, 1979.

2440 **Smith**, Mary Marcia. The ideological relationship between the United Farmers and the Cooperative Commonwealth Federation. Ottawa: National Library of Canada, 1967. 95 leaves. (Canadian theses on microfilm, 01423)

Thesis (M.A.), McGill University, 1967.
Microfilm copy of typescript.

Canadiana, 1968. **OONL**

2441 **Smith**, Peter Douglas. The United Farmers of Alberta and the Ginger Group. Independent political action, 1919-1939. Ottawa: National Library of Canada, 1973. viii, 166 leaves. (Canadian theses on microfilm, 15353)

Thesis (Ph.D.), University of Alberta, 1973.
Microfiche of typescript.

Canadiana, 1974.

2442 **Social Credit Co-ordinating Centre**, Mexborough, Eng. Alberta's progress. The record of the world's first Social Credit province. Mexborough, Eng.: Social Credit Co-ordinating Centre, 1954. (8)p.

Cover title.

Glenbow. **ACG**

2443 Society and politics in Alberta. Research papers. Edited by Carlo Caldarola. London: Methuen Publications, 1979. 392p.

Published simultaneously in Canada by Methuen.

Canadiana, 1979. **AEA**

2444 **Swann**, Francis Richard. Progressive Social Credit in Alberta,1935-1940. Ann Arbor, Mich.: University Microfilms, 1971. 277 leaves. ill.

Thesis (Ph.D.), University of Cincinnati, 1971.
Microfilm of typescript.

Canadiana, 1972.

2445 **Thomas**, Lewis Gwynne. The Liberal Party in Alberta. A history of politics in the Province of Alberta, 1905-1921. Toronto: University of Toronto Press, 1959. 230p. (Social Credit in Alberta, its background and development, 8)

Glenbow. **ACG**

2446 **Trogen**, George Gary. Budget reform in Alberta. Ottawa: National Library of Canada, 1975. viii, 113 leaves. ill. (Canadian theses on microfiche, 25078)

Thesis (M.A.), University of Calgary, 1975.
Microfiche of typescript.

Canadiana, 1976. **OONL**

2447 William Aberhart and Social Credit in Alberta. Edited by Lewis H. Thomas. Toronto: Copp Clark Pub. 1977. 175p. (Issues in Canadian history)

Canadiana, 1977. **AEU**

2448 **Willison**, Gladys A. Stars in time. A history of the Alberta Social Credit Women's Auxiliaries. Edmonton: Alberta Social Credit League Women's Auxiliaries, 1973. 72p. ill.

Cover title.
Printed by Bradburn Printers. **AEA**

Local and Municipal Politics

2449 Alberta Association of Municipal Districts and Counties. Story of rural municipal government in Alberta, 1909-1969. Edmonton: Alberta Association of Municipal Districts and Counties, 1970. 352p. ill.

Brief histories of the Association and individual counties and municipal districts.

Glenbow. **AEA**

2450 **Bettison**, David George. The politics of Canadian urban development. By David G. Bettison, J.K. Kennard and Larry Taylor. Edmonton: University of Alberta Press, 1975. x, 337p.

Published for the Human Resources Research Council of Alberta.
v.1 of a 2-volume work on urbanization in Canada. v.2 has title *Urban affairs in Alberta*.

Canadiana, 1975. **AEU**

2451 **Bettison**, David George. Urban affairs in Alberta. Edmonton: Published for the Human Resources Council of Alberta by the University of Alberta Press, 1975. xii, 529p.

v.2 of a 2-volume work on urbanization in Canada. v.1 has title *The politics of Canadian urban development*.

Canadiana, 1976. **ACG**

2452 **Betts**, George Michael. The Edmonton aldermanic election of 1962. Edmonton: University of Alberta, 1963. vii, 279 leaves.

Thesis (M.A.), University of Alberta, 1963.
Typescript.

Canadian theses. **AEU**

2453 **Dale**, Edmund Herbert. The role of successive town and city councils in the evolution of Edmonton, Alberta, 1892 to 1966. Ottawa: National Library of Canada, 1969. xxv, 590 leaves. ill. (Canadian theses on microfilm, 03872)

Thesis (M.A.), University of Calgary, 1970.
Microfilm of typescript.

Canadiana, 1970. **OONL**

2454 **Deane**, Stanley G. A political history of Seba Beach. Edmonton: S.G. Deane, 1978. 25 leaves.

Cover title. Duplicated. **AEA**

2455 **Diemer**, Hendrikus Lourens. Annexation and amalgamation in the territorial expansion of Edmonton and Calgary. Ottawa: National Library of Canada, 1975. xxiv, 455 leaves. (Canadian theses on microfiche, 24010)

Thesis (M.A.), University of Alberta, 1975.
Microfiche of typescript.

U of A theses. **AEU**

2456 **Foran**, Maxwell Laurence. The Calgary Town Council, 1884-1895. A study of local government in a frontier environment. Ottawa: National Library of Canada, 1970. iv, 153 leaves.

Thesis (M.A.), University of Calgary, 1970.
Microfilm of typescript.

Canadiana, 1971.

2457 **Goldenberg**, Helen. Once upon a chinook. Municipal affairs in Calgary. Calgary: Century Calgary Publications, 1975. 95p. ill.

Written by Helen Goldenberg and Elizabeth de Steur.
Also published as part of *Past and present*, which was issued as v.1 of the Century Calgary Historical Series.

Canadiana, 1977. **AEA**

2458 Good morning, Your worship. Mayors of Calgary, 1884-1975. Accounts by Calgary authors. Calgary: Century Calgary Publications, 1975. iv, 127p. ill.

Also published as part of *Past and present*, which was issued as v.1 of the Century Calgary Historical Series.

Canadiana, 1977. **AEA**

2459 **Hanson**, Eric John. Local government in Alberta. Toronto: McClelland & Stewart, 1956. xi, (1), 145p. ill.

Glenbow. **ACG**

2460 History of local government, Lac St. Anne area. Lac St. Anne: County Lac St. Anne No. 28, 1970. 89p. ill.

Lithographed by the Reporter, Stony Plain.
Written by A. McEachern, F. Wiggins and L.D. Travis.

Ceessa. **AEA**

2461 **Hodgson**, Michael Conn. The fiscal development of the city of Edmonton since 1946. Edmonton: University of Alberta, 1965. xv, 226 leaves.

Thesis (M.A.), University of Alberta, 1965.
Typescript.
A study of expansion in population, incomes, current and capital expenditures, revenue and debt of The City of Edmonton.

Canadian theses. **AEU**

2462 **Kenward**, John Kenneth. Political manipulation and rewards in the Crowsnest Pass, southern Alberta. Ottawa: National Library of Canada, 1971. vii, 165 leaves. (Canadian theses on microfilm, 08765)

Thesis (M.A), Simon Fraser University, 1971.
Microfilm of typescript.

Canadiana, 1972.

2463 **Masson**, Jack K. The demise of alphabet parties. The rise of responsible party politics in cities. Edmonton: University of Alberta, 1975. 20p. (University of Alberta. Department of Political Science. Occasional papers, 4)
AEU

2464 **Masson**, Jack K. Edmonton. The unsettled issues of expansion, governmental reform and provincial economic diversification. Edmonton: Jack K. Masson, 1977. 22 leaves.

Duplicated.
Presented at the annual meeting of the Western Political Science Association, Phoenix, Arizona, March 31-April 2, 1977.

Canadiana, 1979. **OONL**

2465 **Masson**, Jack K. Emerging party politics in urban Canada. Jake D. Masson, James D. Anderson. Toronto: McClelland and Stewart, 1972. 212p. **AEU**

2466 **Raisen**, Sandra Kalef. Elmwood Drive. A case study of municipal decision-making. Ottawa: National Library of Canada, 1972. 101 leaves. ill.

Thesis (M.A.), University of Calgary, 1972.
Microfilm of typescript.

Canadiana, 1972. **OONL**

2467 **Ronaghan**, Allen. Earnest-minded men. An account of local government in the County of Vermilion River. Edited by Allen Ronaghan. Kitscoty: County of Vermilion River, 1973. 648p. ill.

Canadiana, 1974. **OONL**

2468 **Suski**, Julien. Edmonton. Short history, general description and area, general statistics, government of the city, organization and achievements of the city administration. 3rd. ed. Edmonton: City of Edmonton, 1965. 82p. ill.

Canadiana, 1966. **AEU**

Law: General Works

2469 **Ballem**, John Bishop. The oil and gas lease in Canada. Toronto: University of Toronto Press, 1973. 336p.

A legal study.

Canadiana, 1973. **AEU**

2470 **Bercuson**, David Jay. Law and society in Canada in historical perspective. Edited by D.J. Bercuson and L.A. Knafla. Calgary: University of Calgary, 1979 (University of Calgary studies in history, 2) **AEU**

2471 **Bronson**, Harold Emery. A review of legislation pertaining to petroleum resources. Government of Alberta, 1930-1957. Edmonton: University of Alberta, 1958. vii, 129p.

Thesis (M.A.), University of Alberta, 1958.
Typescript.

Canadian theses. AEU

2472 **Chivers**, Barrie. Employer/employee rights in Alberta. Vancouver: International Self-counsel Press, 1976. ix, 114p. (Self-counsel Series)

Canadiana, 1977. AEU

2473 **Daniels**, Christine. Many laws. Story, Christine Daniels and Ron Christiansen, with the help of Brian Thompson and others. Illustrations Ron Christiansen. Edmonton: Metis Association of Alberta, 1970. 1v. ill.

On Canadian criminal law and procedure in relation to Indian and Metis people. Republished Edmonton, Hurtig, 1975, with title *The white man's laws*.

Canadiana, 1971. AEU

2474 **Dickson**, Robert Gary. Divorce guide for Alberta. Step-by-step guide to obtaining your own divorce. 2d ed. Vancouver: International Self-Counsel Press, 1978. xi, 87p. (Self-counsel series)

1st ed. by Richard Garrison has title *Alberta divorce guide*. 3d ed., 1979.

Canadiana, 1978. OONL

2475 **Garrison**, Richard. Alberta divorce guide. How to obtain your own divorce. Toronto: Self-Counsel Press, 1973. 97p. (Self-counsel series)

Canadiana, 1977. - AEU

2476 **Goodine**, Barry Keith. The Alberta Fine Option Program. An evaluation. Edmonton: University of Alberta, 1979. x, 106 leaves.

Thesis (M.A.), University of Alberta, 1979.
Typescript.

U of A Theses. AEU

2477 **Gottselig**, Cheryl. Wills and probate procedure, Alberta. Vancouver: International Self-Counsel Press, 1974. 85p. (Self-counsel series)

Cover title *The layman's guide to drafting wills/probate procedure for Alberta*. 2d. ed., 1977 with title *Wills for Alberta*, 106p.

Canadiana, 1975. AEU

2478 **Hagan**, John. Criminal justice in a Canadian province. A study of the sentencing process. Ottawa: National Library of Canada, 1974. xv, 180 leaves. (Canadian theses on microfiche, 21022)

Thesis (Ph.D.), University of Alberta, 1974.
Microfiche of typescript.

U of A theses. AEU

2479 **Hewitt**, Adlyn Miskew. Family laws for Albertans. Rev. by Adlyn Miskew Hewitt. Edmonton: Women of Unifarm, 1974. 44p.

Canadiana, 1975. AEU

2480 Indian Association of Alberta. Indian treaties and the law. An interpretation for laymen. Edited by Gordon Burrell, Robert Young, Richard Price. Edmonton: Indian Association of Alberta, 1975. 58 leaves.

Duplicated.

AEU

2481 **James**, John. Fight that ticket. Alberta guide to traffic court. Vancouver: International Self-Counsel Press, 1974. 70p. ill. (Self-counsel series)

2d ed., 1979. 83p.

Canadiana, 1974.

AEU

2482 **James**, John. Incorporation and business guide for Alberta. How to form your own corporation. Rev. ed. 1977. Vancouver: International Self-Counsel Press, 1977. 173p. (Self-counsel series)

Previous editions, by R.D. Barry Sullivan, published under title *Alberta incorporation guide*.

Canadiana, 1977.

OONL

2483 **Kemp**, Gerald. The legal status of volunteer workers and voluntary organizations. Calgary: Calgary Volunteer Center, 1976. ii, 175p.

Duplicated.
Report prepared for the Center.

AEA

2484 **McBean**, Jean. Marriage and family law in Alberta. Vancouver: International Self-Counsel Press, 1975. x, 178p. (Self-counsel series)

Canadiana, 1976.

AEU

2485 **McInnes**, Ron W. Alberta landlord-tenant relations (residential tenancies). Toronto: Self-Counsel Press, 1973. 68, 21p. ill.

2d ed., 1973, with title *Landlord/tenant relations for Alberta*. 84p. 3d ed., 1965. 148p.

Canadiana, 1974.

AEU

2486 **Monsma**, Georgia Ellen. Information analysis of the Alberta criminal justice system. Edmonton: University of Alberta, 1971. 119p.

Thesis (M.A.), University of Alberta, 1971.
Typescript.

Canadian theses.

AEU

2487 **Niven**, Michael Bryan. Matrimonial property and the conflict of laws in Alberta. Ottawa: National Library of Canada, 1977. xi, 188 leaves. (Canadian theses on microfiche, 34449)

Thesis (LL.M.), University of Alberta, 1977.
Microfiche of typescript.

U of A Theses.

AEU

2488 **Rodney**, James B. Small Claims Court guide for Alberta. How to collect bad debts. 3d ed. North Vancouver, B.C.: International Self-Counsel Press, 1976. 88p. forms. (Self-counsel series)

2d ed. published in 1972 under title *Layman's guide to Small Claims Court*. 89, 3p.

Canadiana, 1977. OONL

2489 **Rout**, James D. Execution against land in Alberta. Ottawa: National Library of Canada, 1976. x, 217 leaves. (Canadian theses on microfiche, 30810)

Thesis (LL.M), University of Alberta, 1976.
Microfiche of typescript.

U of A Theses. AEU

2490 **Spence**, Anthony John. Legal aid. A facet of equality before the law in Alberta. Ottawa: National Library of Canada, 1973. ix, 130 leaves. (Canadian theses on microfiche, 17697)

Thesis (LL.M.), University of Alberta, 1973.
Microfiche of typescript.

U of A theses. AEU

2491 **Stewart**, George C. Alberta real estate buying/selling guide. Vancouver: International Self-Counsel Press, 1973. 167p. (Self-counsel series)

Canadiana, 1978. AEU

2492 **Sullivan**, R.D.Barry. Alberta incorporation guide. How to form your own company. Vancouver: International Self-Counsel Press, 1971. 122 leaves in various foliations. (Self-counsel series)

Also, 2d ed., 1974. 146 leaves.

Canadiana, 1974. OONL

Law Enforcement

2493 **Anderson**, Frank Wesley. Saskatchewan's provincial police. Calgary: Frontier Publishing, 1972. 64p. ill. (Frontier books, 28)

Canadiana, 1973. ACG

2494 **Anderson**, Frank Wesley. Sergeant Harry Morren, Royal North West Mounted Police. Calgary: Frontier Publishing, 1969. 56p. ill., map. (Frontier books, 21)

Glenbow. ACG

2495 **Anderson**, Frank Wesley. Sheriffs and outlaws of Western Canada. Calgary: Frontier Publishing, 1973. 100p. ill. (A frontier publication)

39 short stories reproduced from *Sagas of the Canadian West*..

2496 **Carpenter**, James Harold. The badge and the blotter. A history of the Lethbridge police. Lethbridge: Historical Society of Alberta, Whoop-up Country Chapter, 1975. viii, 175p. ill.

Printed by D.W. Friesen & Sons, Altona, Manitoba.

Canadiana, 1976. AEA

2497 A chronicle of the Canadian West. North-West Mounted Police report for 1875. Calgary: Historical Society of Alberta, 1975. 36p.

Introduction by S.W. Horrall.

Canadiana, 1976. **AEA**

2498 **Dempsey**, Hugh Aylmer. Men in scarlet. Calgary: Historical Society of Alberta, 1974. 230p. ill.

Papers based on presentation made at a Royal Canadian Mounted Police Conference, University of Lethbridge, May 13-15, 1974.

Canadiana, 1979. **OONL**

2499 **Donaghey**, Sam. A history of the City of Edmonton Police Department. Blue, red and gold, 1892-1972. Edmonton: City of Edmonton Police Department, 1972. 12p.

Canadiana, 1977. **AEA**

2500 **Duncan**, Joy. Red serge wives. Editor, Joy Duncan. Illustrator, Sgt. Dale Davies, R.C.M.P. Edmonton: Centennial Book Committee, 1974. 249p. ill.

Collection of reminiscences of R.C.M.P. wives.

Printed by Co-op Press, Edmonton. **AEA**

2501 **Freuchen**, Peter. The legend of Daniel Williams. New York: J. Messner, 1956. 256p.

On dust jacket: The story of a Bible-toting slave who became a legendary outlaw of the far north.

Glenbow. **ACG**

2502 **Garrod**, Stan. Sam Steele. Don Mills, Ont.: Fitzhenry & Whiteside, 1979. 63, 1p. ill. (The Canadians)

Canadiana, 1979. **OONL**

2503 **Gilkes**, Margaret. Calgary's finest. A history of the city police force. By Margaret Gilkes, Margaret Symons. Calgary: Calgary Century Calgary Publications, 1975. iv, 295p. ill.

Also published as part of *At your service, Part two*, which was issued as v.6 of the Century Calgary Historical Series. **AEA**

2504 **Hamilton Junior High School**, Lethbridge. 1874 trek souvenir publication. Compiled by recruits of Trek 73 and 74. Lethbridge: Hamilton Junior High School, 1974. 50p. ill., maps.

Account of 1973 recreation of the 1874 R.C.M.P. march.

Canadiana, 1977. **AEA**

2505 **Long**, Harold G. Fort Macleod. The story of the North West Mounted Police, 1874-1904, Royal North West Mounted Police, 1904-1920, Royal

Canadian Mounted Police, 1920 to the present time. Edited by H.H. Long. Lethbridge: Fort Macleod Historical Association, 1958. 96p. ill.

Glenbow. **ACG**

2506 **Luckhurst**, Margaret. North West Mounted Police. Early history of the R.C.M.P. Lethbridge: R.C.M.P. Veterans Association, Lethbridge Division, 1974. 55p. ill.

Cover title.
On cover: Centennial souvenir, R.C.M.P. 100th anniversary, 1873-73-1973-73.
Printed by Southern Printing. **AEA**

2507 **Macleod**, R.C. The North West Mounted Police, 1873-1919. Ottawa: Canadian Historical Association, 1978. 22p. (Canadian Historical Association. Historical booklet, 310) **AEA**

2508 **Macleod**, R.C. The NWMP and law enforcement, 1873-1905. Toronto: University of Toronto Press, 1976. 218p. **AEA**

2509 **Nevitt**, Richard Barrington. A winter at Fort Macleod. Edited by Hugh A. Dempsey. Calgary: Glenbow-Alberta Institute, 1974. 134p. ill.

Nevitt was the surgeon with the R.C.M.P. at Fort Macleod in the winter of 1874/75.
Published in association with McClelland and Stewart West.

Canadiana, 1974. **OONL**

2510 Orillia Historical Society. A Medonte pioneer and his famous son. Sketches of Captain Elmes Steele and his son Sir Samuel Benfield Steele. Orillia, Ont.: Orillia Historical Society, 1954. 15p.

Published on the occasion of the unveiling of memorial monuments at Orillia and Fair Valley.
Contents: Henderson, Elmes. The naval and pioneer record of Captain Elmes Steele. Wilson,M.E. The Steele family.

Dew. **ACG**

2511 **Parker**, William. William Parker, mounted policeman. Edited by Hugh A. Dempsey. Edmonton: Hurtig, 1973. xviii, 163p. ill.

Letters and reminiscences of an R.C.M.P. officer, 1874-1912. **AEA**

2512 **Pigeon**, D.H. Research paper on the Alberta Provincial Police. By D.H. Pigeon and C.K. Handy. Calgary: Mount Royal College, 1970. 23 (11) leaves. ill.

Duplicated.
Prepared for Police Science 110, Section O5.

Glenbow. **ACG**

2513 **Routledge**, Penelope Dawn. The North-West Mounted Police and their influence on the sporting and social life of the North-West Territories, 1870-1904. Ottawa: National Library of Canada, 1978. x, 107 leaves. ill.

(Canadian theses on microfiche, 36466)

Thesis (M.A.), University of Alberta, 1978.
Microfiche of typescript.

Canadiana, 1979. **AEU**

Geography: General Works

2514 **Anderson**, Ellis Albert Ahl. The landscape of southwestern Alberta. Vancouver: University of British Columbia, 1959. (1v.)

Thesis (M.A.), University of British Columbia, 1959.
Typescript.

Canadian theses.

2515 **Bailly**, Antoine. Aspects de l'histoire et de l'économie de Falher. Edmonton: Collège St Jean, Département de géographie, 1970. 28 leaves. diags. (Cahiers de géographie, 1)

Duplicated. **AECSJ**

2516 **Baine**, Richard Paul. Calgary, an urban study. Toronto: Clarke Irwin, 1973. 128p. ill. (Urban studies series)

For use in schools.

Canadiana, 1974. **AEU**

2517 **Baker**, Alan Maurice. The Red Deer region. Edmonton: University of Alberta, 1962. x, 160 leaves. maps.

Thesis (M.A.), University of Alberta, 1962.
Typescript.

Canadian theses. **AEU**

2518 **Bannon**, Michael Joseph. The evolution of the central area of Edmonton, Alberta, 1946-1966. Edmonton: University of Alberta, 1967. x, 139 leaves. ill.

Thesis (M.A.), University of Alberta, 1967.
Typescript.

Canadian theses. **AEU**

2519 **Bedford**, Elaine. An historical geography of settlement in the North Saskatchewan River Valley, Edmonton. Ottawa: National Library of Canada, 1976. xiii, 202 leaves. (Canadian theses on microfiche, 30613)

Thesis (M.A.), University of Alberta, 1976.
Microfiche of typescript.
Deals with the conflict between industrial, residential and recreational land use.

U of A theses. **AEU**

2520 **Boileau**, Gilles. Evolution démographique de la population canadienne-française de la region de Rivière la Paix. Montréal: Société d'établissement rurale de la Rivière de la Paix, 1959. 27p.

Duplicated.

2521 **Bromling**, Alvin Joseph. Resident participation in rural development. A comparative analysis of the Alberta experience. Edmonton: University of Alberta, 1970. vii, 182 leaves.

Theses (M.A.), University of Alberta, 1970.
Typescript.

Canadian theses. **AEU**

2522 **Brown**, Sheila Ann. The impact of the Great Slave Lake Railway on agricultural land use in the North Peace, Alberta. Edmonton: University of Alberta, 1971. xiii, 139 leaves.

Thesis (M.A.), University of Alberta, 1971.
Typescript.

Canadian theses. **AEU**

2523 **Buckmire**, George Edward. Occupational mobility of farm people in the Bonnyville district, a low-income agricultural area. Edmonton: University of Alberta, 1966. 173 leaves.

Thesis (M.Sc.), University of Alberta, 1966.
Typescript.

Canadian theses. **AEU**

2524 The Canadian national parks, today and tomorrow. Proceedings. Edited by J.G. Nelson and R.C. Scace. Calgary: University of Calgary, 1969. 2v(1027p.). ill. (Studies in land use history and landscape change. National park series, 3)

Proceedings of the conference on the Canadian National Parks, Today and Tomorrow, organized by the National and Provincial Parks Association of Canada and the University of Calgary.

Canadiana, 1971.

2525 Canadian national parks, today and tomorrow, conference 2. Ten years later. Proceedings of the conference. Edited by J.G. Nelson, et al. Waterloo, Ont.: Faculty of Environmental Studies, University of Waterloo, 1979. 2v. (838p.) ill. (Studies in land use history and landscape change, 7)

Sponsored by the Faculty of Environmental Studies, University of Waterloo, National and Provincial Parks Association of Canada, and Parks Canada, Department of Indian and Northern Affairs, Banff, October 8-13, 1978. **AEU**

2526 Canadian parks in perspective. Based on the conference, The Canadian national parks, today and tomorrow, Calgary, October, 1968. Edited by J.G. Nelson, with the assistance of R.C. Scace. Montreal: Harvest House, 1970. 343p. ill.

Conference organized by the National and Provincial Parks Association of Canada and the University of Calgary.

Canadiana, 1970. **AEU**

2527 **Chalmers**, John West. The land of Peter Pond. Edited by John W. Chalmers and the staff of the Boreal Institute for Northern Studies. G.A. Lester, cartographer. Edmonton: Boreal Insitute for Northern Studies, 1974. 131p. ill. (Boreal Institute for Northern Studies. Occasional publications, 12)

Canadiana, 1975. **AEU**

2528 **Crawford**, Margaret Eleanor. A geographic study of the distribution of population change in Alberta, 1931-1961. Edmonton: University of Alberta, 1962. xiii, 122 leaves. ill.

Thesis (M.A.), University of Alberta, 1962.
Typescript.

Canadian theses. **AEU**

2529 **Darby**, Peter A. The integration of southern Alberta with Canada, 1700-1885. An historical geography. Ottawa: National Library of Canada, 1977. ix, 127 leaves. maps. (Canadian theses on microfiche, 34160)

Thesis (M.A.), University of Calgary, 1977.
Microfiche of typescript.

Canadiana, 1979. **OONL**

2530 **Dykstra**, Theodore Lou. The political geography of a border settlement. Edmonton: University of Alberta, 1970. xiii, 195 leaves.

Thesis (M.A.), University of Alberta, 1970.
Typescript.
A study of Lloydminster.

Canadian theses. **AEU**

2531 Edmonton, the emerging metropolitan pattern. Edited by P.J. Smith. Victoria, B.C.: University of Victoria, 1978. 291p. ill. (Western geographical series, 15) **AEU**

2532 **Ehlers**, Eckart. Das nordliche Peace River Country, Alberta, Kanada. Genese und Struktur eines Pionierraumes im borealen Waldland Nordamerikas. Tubingen: Selbstverlag des Geographischen Instituts der Universitat Tubingen, 1965. vii, 246p. ill. (Tubinger Geographische Studien, 18)

Glenbow. **ACG**

2533 **Eliasoph**, Hy. Edmonton's impact on surrounding urban centers. Ottawa: National Library of Canada, 1978. xvi, 206 leaves. ill. (Canadian theses on microfiche, 36372)

Thesis (M.A.), University of Alberta, 1978.
Microfiche of typescript.

Canadiana, 1979. **AEU**

2534 **Ellis**, Maureen Compston. Local migration in east central (Canadian theses on microfilm, 13361) Alberta. Ottawa: National Library of Canada, 1972. xviii, 147 leaves.

Thesis (M.A.), University of Alberta, 1972.
Microfilm of typescript.

Canadiana, 1973. **OONL**

2535 **Fassnacht**, Susan Doris. Hinton, Alberta, 1811-1957. A study of land use and settlement in a resource based community. Calgary: University of Calgary, 1979. ix, 153 leaves. ill.

Thesis (M.A.), University of Calgary, 1979.
Typescript.

Canplains. **ACU**

2536 **Fraser**, Esther Augusta (Michael). Wheeler. Banff: Summerthought, 1978. 164p. ill.

Biography of Arthur Oliver Wheeler, first surveyor and alpinist to enter the Canadian Rockies. **AEA**

2537 **Gahr**, Gary Allen. Sherwood Park. Resident's attitudes toward a dormitory satellite of Edmonton. Edmonton: University of Alberta, 1979. xv, 197 leaves.

Thesis (M.A.), University of Alberta, 1979.
Typescript.

U of A theses. **AEU**

2538 **Garden**, Robert Ray. The planning of new residential areas in Edmonton, 1950-1976. Edmonton: University of Alberta, 1979. xvi, 209 leaves.

Thesis (M.A.), University of Alberta, 1979.
Typescript.

U of A Theses. **AEU**

2539 **Gill**, Alison Margaret. Off-farm employment and mobility in the Goodfare district, Alberta. Edmonton: University of Alberta, 1971. xv, 161p.

Thesis (M.A.), University of Alberta, 1971.
Typescript.

Canadian theses. **AEU**

2540 Glenbow-Alberta Institute. Archives. Lomen Brothers photographic collection, Nome, Alaska, c.1900-1935. Calgary: Glenbow Alberta-Institute, 1968. 62p. ill. (Glenbow archives series, 3)

Canadiana, 1970. **ACG**

2541 **Haigh**, Richard James. Resident characteristics of six urban fringe communities in the Edmonton region. Ottawa: National Library of Canada, 1978. xii, 176 leaves. (Canadian theses on microfiche, 40170)

Thesis (M.Sc.), University of Alberta, 1978.
Microfiche of typescript.

U of A theses. **AEU**

2542 **Hamilton**, Sally Anne. An historical geography of coal mining in the Edmonton area. Edmonton: University of Alberta, 1971. xii, 190 leaves. maps.

Thesis (M.A.), University of Alberta, 1971.
Typescript.

Canadian theses. **AEU**

2543 **Hassbring**, Lena Margareta. A geographic analysis of land use in Edmonton's rural-urban fringe zone. Edmonton: University of Alberta, 1969. xviii, 190 leaves.

Thesis (M.A.), University of Alberta, 1969.
Typescript.

Canadian theses. **AEU**

2544 **Healy**, Mary Darina. Comparative factorial ecology of large Alberta cities, 1961-1971. Ottawa: National Library of Canada, 1976. xiii, 221 leaves. ill., maps. (Canadian theses on microfiche, 30525)

Thesis (M.A.), University of Calgary, 1976.
Microfiche of typescript.

Canadiana, 1978. **OONL**

2545 **Hull**, Virginia Lee. A geographical study of the impact of two ethnic groups on the landscape in central Alberta. Edmonton: University of Alberta, 1965. x, 117 leaves. ill.

Thesis (M.A.), University of Alberta, 1965.
Typescript.

Canadian theses. **AEU**

2546 **Hutchinson**, Robert Alexander. Scenic assessment and landscape protection. The Edmonton-Devon Restricted Development Area. Ottawa: National Library of Canada, 1978. xvi, 139 leaves. (Canadian theses on microfiche, 36405)

Thesis (M.Sc.), University of Alberta, 1978.
Microfiche of typescript.

U of A theses. **AEU**

2547 **Jones**, David. The Crowsnest Pass, a coal mining valley. A sample study of a coal mining valley, an inductive approach. By David Jones and Giles Lemieux. General editor, Evelyn Moore. Toronto: Holt, Rinehart and Winston of Canada, 1971. iii, 52p. ill. (People and places in Canada)

For social studies in elementary grades.

Canadiana, 1970.

2548 **Jones**, Owen Douglas. The historical geography of Edmonton, Alberta. Ottawa: National Library of Canada, 1976. vii, 136 leaves. (Canadian theses on microfiche, 33092)

Thesis (M.A.), University of Toronto, 1976.
Microfiche of typescript.

Canadiana, 1978. **OONL**

2549 **Kerri**, James Ngoziem Nwannukwu. Fort McMurray. One of Canada's resource frontier towns. Ottawa: National Library of Canada, 1970. iii, 109 leaves. ill. (Canadian theses on microfilm, 06808)

Thesis (M.A.), University of Manitoba, 1970.
Microfilm of typescript.

Canadiana, 1971. **OONL**

2550 **King**, Mona F. Some aspects of post-war migration to Edmonton, Alberta. Edmonton: University of Alberta, 1971. viii, 169 leaves.

Thesis (M.A.), University of Alberta, 1971.
Typescript.

Canadian theses. **AEU**

2551 **Lake**, David Wayne. The historical geography of the Coal Branch. Edmonton: University of Alberta, 1967. ix, 170 leaves. ill.

Thesis (M.A.), University of Alberta, 1967.
Typescript.

Canadian theses. **AEU**

2552 **Lamont**, Glenda Rae. Migrants and migration in part of the southwest Peace River region, Alberta. Edmonton: University of Alberta, 1970. xii, 161 leaves.

Thesis (M.A.), University of Alberta, 1970.
Typescript. **AEU**

2553 **Lavender**, David. The Rockies. New York: Harper & Row, 1968. 404p. ill. (A region of America book)

Also, rev. ed., 1973. 433p.

Canadiana, 1969. **AEU**

2554 **MacGregor**, James Grierson. Behold the shining mountains. Being an account of Anthony Henday, 1754-55, the first white man to enter Alberta. Edmonton: Applied Art Products, 1954. 276p. ill.

Canadiana, 1955. **AEU**

2555 **MacIver**, Ian. The land and water resources of the Spring Creek basin. Some problems of settlement on the agricultural frontier in Alberta, Canada. Edmonton: University of Alberta, 1966. xvi, 202 leaves.

Thesis (M.Sc.), University of Alberta, 1966.
Typescript.

Canadian theses. **AEU**

2556 **Mallett**, Robin Barrie. Settlement process and land use change. Lethbridge-Medicine Hat area. Edmonton: University of Alberta, 1971. xvi,

179 leaves.

Thesis (M.A.), University of Alberta, 1971.
Typescript.

Canadian theses. **AEU**

2557 **Manzie**, Alan Andrew. Evaluations of planning conceptions. Planned and actual uses in Mayfair Park, Edmonton. Ottawa: National Library of Canada, 1978. xx, 303 leaves. (Canadian theses on microfiche, 36438)

Thesis (M.A.), University of Alberta, 1978.
Microfiche of typescript.

U of A theses. **AEU**

2558 **Marriott**, Peter John. Migration of people to and within the county of Grande Prairie, Alberta, 1956 to 1967. Edmonton: University of Alberta, 1969. x, 99 leaves.

Thesis (M.A.), University of Alberta, 1969.
Typescript.

Canadian theses. **AEU**

2559 **McCracken**, Kevin William John. Patterns of intra-urban migration in Edmonton and the residential relocation process. Ottawa: National Library of Canada, 1973. xiii, 213 leaves. ill. (Canadian theses on microfilm, 15272)

Thesis (Ph.D.), University of Alberta, 1973.
Typescript.

Canadiana, 1974. **OONL**

2560 **Moncrieff**, Patrick Merlin. Alternative land uses in southwestern Alberta. A study in natural resource economics. Ottawa: National Library of Canada, 1972. x, 134 leaves. ill. (Canadian theses on microfilm, 13487)

Thesis (M.Sc.), University of Alberta, 1972.
Microfilm of typescript.

Canadiana, 1973.

2561 **Moodie**, Donald Wayne. The St. Albert settlement. A study in historical geography. Edmonton: University of Alberta, 1965. xiii, 179 leaves.

Thesis (M.A.), University of Alberta, 1965.
Typescript.

Canadian theses. **AEU**

2562 **Morasch**, Loyde Hudson. Disaggregate modal split model for Calgary. Ottawa: National Library of Canada, 1973. xii, 116 leaves. ill. (Canadian theses on microfilm, 15599)

Thesis (M.Sc.), University of Calgary, 1973.
Microfilm of typescript.

Canadiana, 1974. **OONL**

2563 **Munson**, J. West. Development control vs. zoning. The emergence of land use controls in Alberta. Ottawa: National Library of Canada, 1977. vii, 168 leaves. (Canadian theses on microfiche, 34220)

Thesis (M.A.), University of Calgary, 1977.
Microfiche of typescript.

Canadiana, 1979. **ACU**

2564 **Nandt**, Frank R. An evaluation of relocation in urban renewal. Ottawa: National Library of Canada, 1976. xi, 175 leaves. (Canadian theses on microfiche, 30689)

Thesis (M.A.), University of Alberta, 1976.
Microfiche of typescript.
A study of the effects of the Downtown Redevelopment Project in the city of Lethbridge.

U of A theses. **AEU**

2565 **Naughton**, Patrick William. The reaction of homeowners along the North Saskatchewan Valley in Edmonton to the erosional hazard. Edmonton: University of Alberta, 1972. xii, 158 leaves.

Thesis (M.Sc.), University of Alberta, 1972.
Typescript.

Canadian theses. **AEU**

2566 On the edge of the shield. Fort Chipewyan and its hinterland. John W. Chalmers, editor. G.A. Lester, cartographer. Edmonton: Boreal Institute for Northern Studies, University of Alberta, 1971. 60p. ill. (Boreal Institute for Northern Studies. Occasional publications, 7)

A series of papers first presented over Radio CKUA in 1970.

Canadiana, 1972. **AEA**

2567 **Payne**, Robert John. Children's urban landscapes in Huntington Hills, Calgary. Ottawa: National Library of Canada, 1977. xii, 447 leaves. ill. (Canadian theses on microfiche, 34229)

Thesis (Ph.D.), Uniiversity of Calgary, 1977.
Microfiche of typescript.

Canadiana, 1979. **OONL**

2568 **Peddie**, Richard. Urban parks and planning in Calgary, Alberta. Ottawa: National Library of Canada, 1968. xii, 158 leaves. ill. (Canadian theses on microfilm, 02772)

Thesis (M.A.), University of Calgary, 1968.
Microfilm of typescript.

Canadiana, 1969. **OONL**

2569 **Raby**, Stewart. Water supplies and watershed management in the Oldman River basin, Alberta. Ottawa: National Library of Canada, 1963. viii, 149 leaves. (Canadian theses on microfilm, 10555)

Thesis (M.Sc.), University of Alberta, 1963.
Microfiche of typescript.

Canadiana, 1972. **AEU**

2570 Research studies by Western Canadian geographers. The Edmonton papers. Edited by Brenton M.Barr. Vancouver: Tantalus Research, 1977. 166p. (B.C. geographical series, 24. Occasional papers in geography)

Papers presented at the annual meeting of the Western Division, Canadian Association of Geographers, Edmonton, 1976.

Canadiana, 1977. **AEU**

2571 **Ross**, Carlyle Bonston Albert. A case study of the success of settlement in a southern Peace River district. Edmonton: University of Alberta, 1969. x, 138 leaves.

Thesis (M.Sc.), University of Alberta, 1969.
Typescript.

Canadian theses. **AEU**

2572 **Rust**, Ronald Stuart. An analysis and evaluation of land use in the special areas of Alberta. Edmonton: University of Alberta, 1957. 2v. (418p.) ill.

Thesis (M.A.), University of Alberta, 1957.
Typescript.
Reviews land use in drought areas of east central Alberta, and analyzes the impact of the Special Areas Act, with recommendations for land use changes.

Canadian theses. **AEU**

2573 **Sabine**, Robert Douglas. Pigeon Lake summer cottage shoreland use. Edmonton: University of Alberta, 1969. xlii, 143 leaves. maps.

Thesis (M.Sc.), University of Alberta, 1969.
Typescript.

Canadian theses. **AEU**

2574 **Sadler**, Barry. Conflicts of perception and use in Banff National Park. Edmonton: University of Alberta, 1970. xxii, 155 leaves.

Thesis (M.A.), University of Alberta, 1970.
Typescript.

Canadian theses. **AEU**

2575 **Scace**, Robert Chaston. Banff. A cultural-historical study of land use and management in a national park community to 1945. Calgary: University of Calgary, Department of Geography, 1968. vii leaves, 154p. ill. (Studies in land use history and landscape change. National park series, 2)

J.G. Nelson, Director.
Thesis (M.A.), University of Calgary, 1968.

Glenbow. **ACG**

2576 **Scace**, Robert Chaston. The management and use of a Canadian plains oasis. The Cypress Hills public reserves. Ottawa: National Library of Canada, 1975. xv, 327 leaves. ill. (Canadian theses on microfiche, 21348)

Thesis (Ph.D.), University of Calgary, 1972.
Microfiche of typescript.

Canadiana, 1975. AEU

2577 **Scott**, William Guy. Urban growth management. The development of a program for the Edmonton area. Calgary: National Library of Canada, 1976. ix, 133 leaves. (Canadian theses on microfiche, 28806)

Thesis (M.Sc.), University of British Columbia, 1976.
Microfiche of typescript.

Canadiana, 1977. OONL

2578 **Singh**, Jaswant. Land use changes in the Eastern Irrigation District of Alberta. Edmonton: University of Alberta, 1968. xiv, 122 leaves. ill.

Thesis (M.A.), University of Alberta, 1968.
Typescript.

Dew. AEU

2579 **Smith**, Peter John. The Edmonton-Calgary corridor. P.J. Smith and Denis B. Johnson. Edmonton: Department of Geography, University of Alberta, 1978. xvii, 159p. ill. (University of Alberta studies in geography)

Canadiana, 1979. AEU

2580 **Staite**, M.J. Flood plain management in the Drumheller Valley. Alternative land use policies. Edmonton: University of Alberta, 1979. xviii, 278 leaves.

Thesis (M.A.), University of Alberta, 1979.
Typescript.

U of A theses. AEU

2581 **Stevens**, Grey Philip. A residential subdivision for Calgary, Alberta. Winnipeg: University of Manitoba, 1962. (1v.)

Thesis (M.Sc.), University of Manitoba.
Typescript.

Canadian theses. MWU

2582 **Stokes**, Ernest B. The development and evaluation of an urban growth model for Calgary. Ottawa: National Library of Canada, 1973. xi, 203 leaves. ill. (Canadian theses on microfiche, 17068)

Thesis (M.A.), University of Calgary, 1973.
Microfiche of typescript.

Canadiana, 1974. OONL

2583 **Stone**, Donald Norman George. The process of rural settlement in the Athabasca area, Alberta. Edmonton: University of Alberta, 1970. xv, 189 leaves.

Thesis (M.A.), University of Alberta, 1970.
Typescript.

Canadian theses. AEU

2584 **Takla**, Emile Fawzy. Changes in land use patterns in downtown Calgary, 1953-1969. Ottawa: National Library of Canada, 1971. xii, 160 leaves. ill. (Canadian theses on microfilm, 10177)

Thesis (M.A.), University of Calgary, 1971.
Microfilm of typescript.

Canadiana, 1972. **OONL**

2585 **Thirnbeck**, Alan Roger. An analysis of a group of prairie settlements north east of Calgary. Ottawa: National Library of Canada, 1971. viii, 145 leaves. ill. (Canadian theses on microfilm, 10180)

Thesis (M.A.), University of Calgary, 1971.
Microfilm of typescript.

Canadiana, 1972. **OONL**

2586 **Tomkins**, Doreen Margaret. Alberta, where the mountains meet the plains. Doreen Margaret Tomkins, with George S. Tomkins and Neville V. Scarfe. Toronto: W.J. Gage, 1970. 43p. ill. (Regional studies of Canada)

Written for use in schools.

Glenbow. **ACG**

2587 **Trnavskis**, Boris. Internal accessibility in the Peace River area, Alberta. Ottawa: National Library of Canada, 1971. x, 185 leaves. ill. (Canadian theses on microfilm, 08904)

Thesis (M.A.), University of Calgary, 1971.
Microfilm of typescript.

Canadiana, 1972. **OONL**

2588 Two studies on Fort McMurray. Resident mobility in resource frontier communities. An examination of selected factors, by John S. Matthiasson. Functions of voluntary associations in a resource frontier community. The case of Fort McMurray, Alberta, Canada, by James N. Kerri. Winnipeg: University of Manitoba, Center for Settlement Studies, 1971. vii, 54, vii. 35p. (University of Manitoba. Center for Settlement Studies. Series 2. Research reports, no.6)

Canadiana, 1972. **ACG**

2589 **Udo**, Reuben K. Applied population geography. A survey. Edmonton: International Geographical Union Commission on Population Geography, 1976. 20p.

Canadiana, 1977. **OONL**

2590 **Van Kirk**, Sylvia Marian. The development of national park policy in Canada's national parks, 1885 to 1930. Edmonton: University of Alberta, 1969. ix, 194 leaves.

Thesis (M.A.), University of Alberta, 1969.
Typescript.

Canadian theses. **AEU**

2591 **Ward**, Roland Gerald. Country residential development in the Edmonton area to 1973. A case study of exurban residential growth. Edmonton: University of Alberta, 1977. xviii, 218 leaves.

Thesis (M.A.), University of Alberta, 1977.
Typescript.

U of A theses. **AEU**

2592 **Watson**, Kenneth Frank. Landbanking in Red Deer. Ottawa: National Library of Canada, 1974. xiv, 259 leaves. ill. (Canadian theses on microfiche, 19676)

Thesis (M.A.), University of British Columbia, 1974.
Microfiche of typescript.

Canadiana, 1975. **OONL**

2593 **Whitehead**, Jimmy Carl. Country residential growth in the Calgary region. A study of ex-urbanization. Vancouver: University of British Columbia, 1968. (1v.)

Thesis (M.A.), University of British Columbia, 1968.
Typescript.

Canadian theses.

2594 **Windsor**, Robert Francis. The campus fringe of University of Alberta. Edmonton: University of Alberta, 1964. xi, 157 leaves. map.

Thesis (M.A.), University of Alberta, 1964.
Typescript.

Canadian theses. **AEU**

2595 **Wong**, William Ho-Ching. Migration patterns in west-central Alberta. Ottawa: National Library of Canada, 1979. xii, 187 leaves. (Canadian theses on microfiche, 40536)

Thesis (Ph.D.), University of Alberta, 1979.
Microfiche of typescript.

U of A theses. **AEU**

Description and Travel

2596 **Arscott**, W. Hugh. Down a wet highway. Saskatoon: Western Producer Prairie Books, 1969. 171p. ill.

Account of a trip down the South Saskatchewan River from Red Deer to Saskatoon, 1966.

Glenbow. **ACG**

2597 **Baird**, David McCurdie. Banff National Park. How nature carved its splendor. Rev. ed. Edmonton: Hurtig, 1977. 237p. ill., maps.

Published in co-operation with Parks Canada and the Geological Survey of Canada. 1st ed., 1968, published as Geological Survey of Canada Miscellaneous Report, 13.

Canadiana, 1979. **AEA**

2598 **Baird**, David McCurdie. Jasper National Park. Behind the mountains and the glaciers. 2d rev. ed. Edmonton: Hurtig, 1977. 160p. ill.

Published in co-operation with Parks Canada and the Geological Survey of Canada. 1st edition, 1963, published by Geological Survey of Canada as *Miscellaneous report, 6*.

P.N.L.A., 1979. **AEA**

2599 Banff, Canada, requests. s.l.: Olympic 72 Organization, 1968. 55p. ill.

Cover title.
Printed by Aircraft Printing.
Text in English, French, German and Spanish.
Title on page one: Banff requests the International Olympic Committee to call upon the youth of all countries to assemble in Banff in 1972 to celebrate the XIth Olympic Winter Games. **ACU**

2600 **Barnett**, Donald C. Alberta. A people and a province. By Don C. Barnett and R. Pat Mogen. Editor Sharon Rinkoff. Vancouver: Fitzhenry and Whiteside, 1975. 96p. ill.

Canadiana, 1978. **AEU**

2601 **Bell**, Wade. The North Saskatchewan River book. Toronto: Coach House Press, 1976. 97p.

CBIP, 1979. **AEU**

2602 **Bickersteth**, John Burgon. The land of open doors. Being letters from western Canada, 1911-13. Toronto: University of Toronto Press, 1976. 265p. (30) leaves of plates. ill. (The Social history of Canada, 29)

With a new introduction by the author.
Letters written by a lay Anglican missionary among homesteaders and railroad builders in Alberta.
Reprint of the 1914 edition published by Wells Gardner, Darton, London, and Musson, Toronto (Peel 2443).

Canadiana, 1977. **AEU**

2603 **Boon**, Ivor. Alberta, western treasure chest. By Ivor Boon and Marjorie Boon. Calgary: Western Canada Institute, n.d. 114p. ill.

Juvenile literature. **AEU**

2604 **Brooks**, Bill. Alberta. Editor, John Robert Colombo. Text and photos by Bill Brooks. Willowdale, Ont.: Hounslow Press, 1978. 1v. (unpaged) of photographs.

Printed by Heritage Press.
Cover title *The colour of Alberta*.

Canadiana, 1978. **AEA**

2605 By canoe from Toronto to Fort Edmonton in 1872 among the Iroquois and Ojibways, with a chapter on winter in Canada, by An anonymous traveler. Thirty wood engravings. Toronto: Canadiana House, 1968. 74p. ill.

Limited edition of 100 copies.

Canadiana, 1969. AEU

2606 Calgary applies for the X Olympic Winter Games, 1978. Calgary,: Southam Printing, 1963. (52p.) ill.

Text in English, French and German.
On cover: Banff, Alberta, Canada. ACU

2607 **Coutant**, Frank R. Shangri La. A luxury valley in Alberta's Rocky Mountains. A study in contrasts. s.l.: s.n., 1970. 12p. ill.

Caption title *Sixty years later an Alberta pioneer flies back on velvet*.
A brief reminiscence of pioneering in Edmonton in 1910 and a visit to Jasper Lodge in 1970. ACG

2608 **Czolowski**, Ted. Alberta, the emerging giant. By Ted Czolowski, Elaine Johnson. Vancouver: C and B Publishing, 1975. 96p. (chiefly ill.) AEA

2609 **Gowland**, John Stafford. Return to Canada. London: T. Werner Laurie, 1957. 199p. ill.

Account of a journey across Canada. ACG

2610 **Hadikin**, Wesley Fred. Landscape perception in the Crowsnest Pass area, Alberta. Ottawa: National Library of Canada, 1973. xiv, 160p. ill. (Canadian theses on microfilm, 15244)

Thesis (M.Sc.), University of Alberta, 1973.
Microfilm of typescript.

Canadiana, 1974.

2611 **Helmericks**, Constance. Down the wild river north. Illustrated by Michael Allen Hampshire. Boston: Little, Brown, 1968. x, 501p. ill.

Glenbow. ACG

2612 **Hill**, Alexander Staveley. From home to home. Autumn wanderings in the north-west in the years 1881, 1882, 1883, 1884. Illustrated from sketches by Mrs. Staveley Hill and photos. by Alexander Staveley Hill. New York: Argonaut Press for University Microfilms, 1966. 432p. ill.

Facsimile reprint of 1885 edition (Peel 821).
An account of travels in Canada and ranching at the Oxley Ranch, Alberta. AEA

2613 **Hocking**, Anthony. Alberta. Toronto: McGraw-Hill Ryerson, 1979. 80p. ill. (Canada series)

Canadiana, 1979. AEU

2614 **Holmes**, Rex. The last summer. Memories of the Peace River country. Illustrations by Jean Redfern. Toronto: Baxter Publishing, 1965. 178p. ill.

Reminiscences of the 1930s.

Mcleod. AEU

2615 **Hummena**, Dokiia. Eternal flames of Alberta. Edmonton: P.A. Paush, 1959. 183p.

Title page and text in Ukrainian. Added title page in English.
Account of a visit to Alberta in 1956.

Canadiana, 1965. **OONL**

2616 **Kelly**, Leroy Victor. North with Peace River Jim. With introduction and editing by Hugh A. Dempsey. Calgary: Glenbow-Alberta Institute, 1972. 76p. ill. (Glenbow-Alberta Institute. Historical paper, 2)

Originally published in the *Calgary Herald*, Aug. 13-Oct. 1, 1910.
Account of a visit to the Peace River Country, by a party of journalists, sponsored by James Kennedy Cornwall (Peace River Jim).

Glenbow. **ACG**

2617 **Kirman**, Joseph M. Alberta. Facts for valuing. Don Mills, Ont: Dent, 1979. (1v.) (World discovery program, 1)

Children's literature.

CBIP, 1979. **AEU**

2618 **Kroetsch**, Robert. Alberta. Toronto: Macmillan of Canada, 1968. (12), 231p. ill. (The traveller's Canada)

Glenbow. **ACG**

2619 **Liddell**, Kenneth Eric. Alberta revisited. Toronto: Ryerson Press, 1960. xiv, 234p. ill.

Canadiana, 1960. **AEU**

2620 **Liddell**, Kenneth Eric. I'll take the train. Saskatoon: Western Producer Prairie Books, 1977. 196p. ill. (Prairie books)

1st printed in 1966.
Reminiscences of train journeys and people associated with them.

CBIP, 1979. **ACG**

2621 **Liddell**, Kenneth Eric. Roamin' empire of southern Alberta. Calgary: Frontiers Unlimited, 1963. 64p. ill. (Frontier books, 6)

Cover title *Southern Alberta's roamin' empire*.

Glenbow. **ACG**

2622 **Liddell**, Kenneth Eric. This is Alberta. Toronto: Ryerson Press, 1972. 190p. ill. (Ryerson travel library)

Dew. **AEU**

2623 **Lister**, Phil. Enjoying the Rockies. St. Albert: Puckrin's Production House, 1978. 22p. ill.

Canadiana, 1978. **OONL**

2624 **Long**, Philip Sheridan. Your historical Canadian border route no. 3. Calgary: Bonanza Books, 1974. 1v. (incl.advts.)

Cover title.
Printed by Excello Printing, Calgary.
A guide book.

ACP

2625 **McCourt**, Edward. The road across Canada. Illustrated by John A. Hall. Toronto: Macmillan of Canada, 1965. 199p. ill.

Glenbow.

ACG

2626 **McCourt**, Edward. Saskatchewan. Toronto: Macmillan of Canada, 1968. x, (4), 238p. ill. (The Traveller's Canada)

Glenbow.

ACG

2627 **McCourt**, Edward. The Yukon and the Northwest Territories. New York: St. Martin's Press, 1969. 236p. ill. (Traveller's Canada)

Also published Toronto, Macmillan of Canada.

Canadiana, 1971.

OONL

2628 **McLaurin**, Colin Campbell. Without reservations. Flying around the world. Calgary: 1959. 102p. ill.

Account of a holiday tour.

Glenbow.

ACG

2629 **Morse**, Randy. The mountains of Canada. Introduction by Andy Russell. Edmonton: Hurtig, 1978. 144p. chiefly ill.

CBIP, 1979.

AEA

2630 **Parker**, H. Margaret. Grandma's visit to England & Scotland. Edmonton: Wm. W. Parker, 1900. 12p. ill.

Account of a trip made by Mr. and Mrs. W.W. Parker.

2631 **Petrigo**, Walter. Focus on Calgary. Calgary: Petrigo of Canada, 1964. (78)p.

Photographs by Petrigo, with a 4-page introductory text.

Glenbow.

ACG

2632 **Petrigo**, Walter. Petrigo's Alberta. Calgary: Petrigo of Canada, 1976. 160p. (chiefly ill.)

Photographs by Petrigo, with a 4-page introductory text.

AEU

2633 **Petrigo**, Walter. Petrigo's Calgary. Calgary: McClelland and Stewart West, 1975. 158p. (chiefly ill.)

Photographs by Petrigo, with a 4-page introductory text.

Canadiana, 1976.

AEU

2634 **Reilly**, Pat. Alberta. Norwich, England: Jarrold, 1959. 32p. ill (Cotman color series)

Glenbow. **ACG**

2635 Rocky Mountain skylines. Your view book of the Canadian Rockies, Banff, Jasper, Yoho and Glacier National Parks. Banff: Byron Harmon Photos, 1973. 26p. ill.

Canadiana, 1977. **OONL**

2636 **Romaine**, Edward. This is Alberta in 1963. Calgary: Albertan, 1963. 176p. ill.

Cover title.
Special issue of *The Albertan*, June, 1963.

Glenbow. **AEA**

2637 **Russell**, Andy. The Rockies. Edmonton: Hurtig, 1975. 160p. ill.

Canadiana, 1975. **ACG**

2638 **Shaw**, Charles Aeneas. Tales of a pioneer surveyor. Edited by Raymond Hull. Introduction by Norman Aeneas Shaw. Don Mills, Ont.: Longman Canada, 1970. 167p. ill.

Shaw was Chief Engineer of the survey party that laid the C.P.R. route through the Rocky Mountains.

Glenbow. **ACG**

2639 Shining mountains. The splendour of Banff National Park. West Vancouver, B.C.: Whitecap Books, 1979. 55p. ill.

Canadiana, 1980. **AEU**

2640 **Siemens**, William J. Wo de hombre. Illustrated by Jeanette Heaward. Port Orchard, Wash.: Publishers Printing, 1972. 511, 10p. ill.

Limited edition of 100 copies.
Account of a hunting trip in the Rockies with a Stoney Indian group about 1940. **ACG**

2641 **Simpkins**, Bill. Chinook country. Alberta south. Photographs by Bill Simkins, introduction by Grant MacEwan, foreword by Peter Lougheed. Toronto: Oxford University Press, 1979. 96p. ill.

Canadiana, 1979. **OONL**

2642 **Southesk**, James Carnegie, Earl of. Saskatchewan and the Rocky Mountains. A diary and narrative of travel, sport, and adventure, during a journey through the Hudson's Bay Company's territories, in 1859 and 1860. Edmonton: Hurtig, 1969. 448p.

First edition privately printed Edinburgh, 1874. Published Edinburgh and Toronto, 1875 (Peel 430).

Dew. **AEU**

2643 **Sprague**, Marshall. The great gates. The story of the Rocky Mountain passes. Boston: Little, Brown, 1964. 468p. ill.

Dew. AEU

2644 **Sugino**, Shan. The Rockies. High where the wind is lonely. Photographs by Shin Sugino. Text by Jon Whyte. Toronto: Gage, 1978. (96)p. ill.

Canadiana, 1979. ACP

2645 **Tanaka**, Hiroshi. Asian landscapes, as seen by a Japanese pilgrim. Lethbridge: University of Lethbridge, 1977. (65)p. ill.

Canadiana, 1978. AEU

2646 **Thompson**, Raymond. Wilderness adventures. Lynnwood, Wash.: Raymond Thompson, 1974. 106p.

Duplicated.
Reproduced from items previously published in various newspapers and magazines. Tales of the Athabasca and Peace River districts. AEU

2647 University of Alberta. Archives. A guide to the papers of Louis Auguste Romanet, 1890's, 1900. Edmonton: Archives, University of Alberta, 1975. 77 leaves. (University of Alberta. Archives. Manuscript group, 7)

Duplicated.

Canadiana, 1977. AEU

2648 **Vandersteene**, Roger. Wabasca. Dix ans de vie indienne. Adaptè du neerlandais par Jacques De Deken. Gemmenich, Belgium: Editions O.M.T., 1960. 223p. ill.

Account of Trout and Chipewyan Lakes and the Cree Indians, including traditions.

Glenbow. ACG

2649 **Whillans**, James William. First in the West. The story of Henry Kelsey, discoverer of the Canadian prairies. Edmonton: Applied Art Products, 1955. 175p.

On cover: The travels of Henry Kelsey, 1690-1691. Saskatchewan jubilee edition, 1955.

Canadiana, 1956.

2650 **Whishaw**, Laura. As far as you'll take me. London: Hammond, 1959. 222p.

Account of a hitchhiking trip from Edmonton to Alaska.

Canadiana, 1959. AEA

2651 **Whitely**, Opal Stanley. Opal. Arranged and adapted by Jane Boulton. Don Mills, Ont.: Collier Macmillan Canada, 1976. 183p. ill.

Diary written in 1912 at the age of twelve in an Oregon lumber camp.
First published by the Atlantic Monthly Press, 1920. AEU

2652 **Wiebe**, Rudy. Alberta, a celebration. Stories by Rudy Wiebe. Photographs by Harry Savage. Edited by Tom Radford. Edmonton: Hurtig, 1979. 208p. ill.

Canadiana, 1979. **ACP**

2653 **Wilson**, Thomas Edmund. Trail blazer of the Canadian Rockies. Edited by Hugh A. Dempsey. By Thomas Edmund Wilson as told to W.E. Round. Calgary: Glenbow-Alberta Institute, 1972. 54p. ill. (Glenbow-Alberta Institute. Historical paper, 3)

Introduction by Sue Baptie.
Original title of ms. *The last of the pathfinders*.

Glenbow. **ACG**

Gazetteers and Atlases

2654 **Anderson**, Jacqueline Margaret. A road map study based on the 1974 official Alberta road map. Ottawa: National Library of Canada, 1975. xv, 225, 6 leaves. ill. (Canadian theses on microfiche, 26696)

Thesis (M.Sc.), University of Alberta, 1975.
Microfiche of typescript.

Canadiana, 1977. **OONL**

2655 Atlas of Alberta. Edmonton: University of Alberta Press, 1969. 162p. maps.

Compiled by the Department of Geography, University of Alberta. Produced by the Technical Division, Alberta Department of Lands and Forests and Survey Branch, Alberta Department of Highways. Centennial Project of the Government of Alberta and the University of Alberta.

Published in association with the University of Toronto Press. **AEU**

2656 Canada. Geographic Board. Place-names of Alberta. Toronto: Canadiana House, 1969. 138p. map.

Facsimile reprint of 1928 edition published for the Geographic Board by the Dept. of the Interior (Peel 3062).

Canadiana, 1972.

2657 **Dempsey**, Hugh Aylmer. Indian names for Alberta communities. Calgary: Glenbow-Alberta Institute, 1969. 19p. ill. (Glenbow-Alberta Institute. Occasional paper, 4)

Glenbow. **ACG**

2658 **Holmgren**, Eric Joseph. 2,000 place names of Alberta. By Eric J. Holmgren and Patricia M. Holmgren. Saskatoon: Modern Press, 1972. 210p. ill.

Also, 2d ed., 1974 and 3d ed., 1976 with title *Over 2,000 place names of Alberta*.

Glenbow. **ACG**

2659 Junior atlas of Alberta. Our place on earth and how we live. Edmonton: Curriculum Branch, Alberta Education, 1979. 80p. ill.

Juvenile literature.
Prepared as a cooperative venture between Alberta Education and the University of Alberta Department of Geography, and published as part of the Alberta Heritage Learning Resources Project.

Accompanied by teacher's manual. **AEU**

2660 **Mardon**, Ernest G. Community names of Alberta. Lethbridge: University of Lethbridge, 1973. 223p.

Canadiana, 1974. **ACG**

2661 **Mardon**, Ernest G. The history of place names in southern Alberta. Lethbridge: Canadian Institute of Onomastic Sciences and Ukrainian Free Academy of Sciences, 1972. 23p. (Onomastica, 43)

Paper delivered at the annual meeting of the Institute, Memorial University, May, 1971.

Canadiana, 1972. **ACG**

2662 Sanford Evans Services Ltd. Alberta place guide (and) Alberta population maps. Winnipeg: Sanford Evans Services Ltd., 1963. 2 v.

Population figures are from 1961 census.

Dew. **AEA**

Guidebooks

2663 **Anderson**, Frank Wesley. A frontier guide to mystic Jasper and the Yellowhead Pass. Calgary: Frontier Publishing, 1973. 56p. ill. (Frontier books, 30)

Canadiana, 1974. **AEU**

2664 **Anderson**, Frank Wesley. A frontier guide to the Dewdney Trail. Calgary: Frontier Publications, 1969. 3v. ill. (Frontier books, 19-20, 27)

Contents: 1. Hope to Rock Creek. 2. Rock Creek to Salmo 3. Salmo to Wild Horse.
Canadiana, 1972. **AEA**

2665 **Anderson**, Frank Wesley. A frontier guide to the dynamic Crow's Nest Pass. Aldergrove, B.C.: Frontier Publishing, 1969. 56p. ill. (Frontier books, 5)

AEA

2666 **Buss**, Kingsley Benjamin. Edmonton trails. Edmonton: Whistler Publishing, 1974. 76p. ill.

On Cover: Edmonton trails for all seasons.
A guide book.

Canadiana, 1975. **AEA**

2667 Calgary Olympic Development Association. Banff, Canada, proposed site for 1968 Winter Olympic Games. Calgary: Calgary Olympic Development Association, 1962. 40p. ill.

A promotional booklet.
Lithographed by The Albertan, Calgary. **AEA**

2668 Calgary Real Estate Board. This is Calgary. A pictorial guide. Vancouver: Quest Travelbooks, 1973. 95, 1p. (chiefly ill.) **AEA**

2669 **Chipeniuk**, R.C. Lakes of the Lac La Biche District. Lac La Biche: R.C. Chipeniuk, 1975. 318p. ill., maps.

Printed by D.W. Friesen and Sons, Calgary.
A guide book and history. **AEA**

2670 Devon Chamber of Commerce. Town of Devon, Alberta. An ideal place to live. Devon: Devon Chamber of Commerce, 1964. 8p. ill.

Cover title.
A promotional booklet. **AEA**

2671 A frontier guide to Calgary to Medicine Hat. Calgary: Frontier Publishers, 1970. 53p. ill. (Frontier books, 24)

Canadiana, 1971.

2672 A frontier guide to Calgary-Banff highway. Calgary: Frontier Publishing, 1968. 56p. ill. (Frontier books, 17)

Canadiana, 1969. **ACG**

2673 Frontier guide to enchanted Banff and Lake Louise. Calgary: Frontiers Unlimited, 1965. 64p. ill. (Frontier books, 10)

Glenbow. **ACG**

2674 Frontier guide to the Fraser Canyon 'Valley of death'. Calgary: Frontiers Unlimited, 1968. 56p. ill. (Frontier books, 13)

Glenbow. **ACG**

2675 Frontier guide to the incredible Rogers Pass. Calgary: Frontiers Unlimited, 1968. 56p. ill. map. (Frontier books, 8)

Glenbow. **ACG**

2676 Frontier guide to the romantic Crow's Nest Pass. Calgary: Frontiers Unlimited, 1963. 48p. ill. (Frontier books, 5)

Glenbow. **ACG**

2677 Frontier guide to Waterton, land of leisure. Calgary: Frontiers Unlimited, 1967. 47 (1)p. ill. (Frontier books, 15)

Compiled by Frank Anderson.

Glenbow. **ACG**

2678 **Fryer**, Harold. Ghost towns of Alberta. Langley, B.C.: Stagecoach Publishing, 1976. 200p. ill.

Printed by D.W. Friesen & Sons, Calgary.
Note on dust jacket: The third in our Canadian Ghost Towns Series.
Incorporates F.W. Anderson's *Ghost Town Journals*.

Canadiana, 1977. **AEU**

2679 **Fryer**, Harold. Stops of interest in Alberta. Wild rose country. Aldergrove, B.C.: Frontier Publishing, 1976. 2v. ill. (Frontier books, 33-34)

Canadiana, 1976. **AEU**

2680 Grande Prairie Chamber of Commerce. Grande Prairie today! A guide. Grande Prairie: Grande Prairie Chamber of Commerce, 1978. 24p. ill.

Cover title.

Canadiana, 1979.

2681 **Guiltner**, James Carl. The Peace River country and McKenzie highway to Yellowknife. (John Hart Highway and Alaska Highway, 1867-1967). Historical and tourist guide. Edmonton: James C. Guiltner, 1963. 336p. (incl. advts.) ill.

Cover title.
Spine title *The mighty Peace River country*.

Glenbow. **ACG**

2682 Kidmonton. Every kid's guide to Edmonton. Edited by Kristin Murray and Allan Shute, with Kim McCarthy et al. Edmonton: Tree Frog Press, 1978. 224p. ill.

2683 Lac La Biche Chamber of Commerce. Lac La Biche pow wow and fish derby. Lac La Biche: Lac La Biche Chamber of Commerce, 1965. 64p. (incl. advts.) ill.

Printed by Commercial Printers, Edmonton.
A promotional booklet.
Cover title *Lac La Biche, the pow wow & fish derby town*.

Glenbow. **ACG**

2684 Lethbridge Chamber of Commerce. Fingertip facts about Lethbridge and district. Compiled for the City of Lethbridge and the Economic Development Commission. Lethbridge: Lethbridge Chamber of Commerce, 1968. 26 leaves.

Canadiana, 1970.

2685 Lethbridge Chamber of Commerce. Lethbridge, the big little city. Irrigation capitol of Canada. Lethbridge: Lethbridge Chamber of Commerce, 1976. 32p. ill.

Cover title.

Canadiana, 1980. **OONL**

2686 **Levesque**, Gerard R. The North. Edmonton: Gerard R. Levesque, 1962. 127p. ill.

A handbook for the Yukon and the Northwest Territories.

Glenbow. **ACG**

2687 **Levesque**, Gerard R. Survey of Fairview, located in the heart of the inland empire. Prepared by G.R. Levesque. Fairview: Fairview District Chamber of Commerce, 1962. 20p. ill.

Revised edition, 1963.
Cover title.
A promotional booklet.

Glenbow. **ACG**

2688 **Marsh**, John Stewart. The students' guide to Calgary. Calgary: University of Calgary Graduate Students' Association, 1970. 56p.

Rev. 2d ed.

Canadiana, 1974.

2689 **Patton**, Brian. The Canadian Rockies trail guide. A hiker's manual. Banff, Glacier-Revelstoke, Jasper, Kootenay, Waterton, Yoho. By Brian Patton and Bart Robinson. Banff: Summerthought Publication, 1971. 207p. ill.

Also, rev. ed., Canmore, Devil's Head Press, 1978, 266p.

Glenbow. **ACG**

2690 **Patton**, Brian. Parkways of the Canadian Rockies. An interpretive guide to roads in the mountain parks. Banff: Summerthought, 1975. 192p. ill.

Canadiana, 1976. **ACP**

2691 **Primrose**, Tom. The Cypress Hills. Calgary: Frontier Publishing, 1969. 48p. ill. (Frontier books, 22)

Glenbow. **ACG**

2692 **Scharff**, Robert. Canada's mountain national parks. Banff, Jasper, Glacier, Kootenay, Mount Revelstoke, Waterton Lakes (and) Yoho. By Robert Scharff in association with the Natural and Historic Resources Branch. New York: D. McKay, 1966. 184p.

Dew. **AEU**

2693 **Scharff**, Robert. Glacier National Park and Waterton Lakes National Park. Edited by Robert Scharff, with the co-operation of National Park Service. New York: David McKay, 1967. 184p. ill.

A guide book.

Dew. **AEU**

2694 Southern Alberta Tourist Council. Visit southern Alberta, land of green acres. Lethbridge: Southern Alberta Tourist Council, 1964. (14)p. ill.

A promotional booklet.

Glenbow. **ACG**

2695 **Thomas**, Harriet Hartley. From barnacle to Banff. A story of the rising of the Rockies from the depth of the ocean to the height of a world famous resort. Calgary: John McAra Printing, 1973. 84p. ill., map.

2d ed. 1945. Revised 1958, 1973.
On title page: A tourist's guide to where to go and what to do in Banff, play ground of the Rockies.

Ceessa. **AEA**

2696 **Williams**, Mabel Berta. The Banff-Jasper highway descriptive guide. Illustrated by Mabel Bain. Saskatoon: H.R. Larson Publishing, 1963. ix, 136p. ill.

Rev. ed..
First published 1948. **AEA**

Genealogy and Family History

2697 **Adamson**, Philip Edward. The Adamson saga, 1536-1936. Edmonton: Robarts, 1962. 9, 184, 6p. ill.

Glenbow. **ACG**

2698 **Allan**, Iris Constance (Sommerville). Mother and her family. Memories of a railway town. Cobalt, Ont.: Highway Book Shop, 1977. 77p. ill.

Biography of the Sommerville family in Transcona, Manitoba. **AEU**

2699 **Bérubé**, Roland. Les Bérubés de Beaumont. s.l.: s.n., 1964. 38p.

Privately printed.

2700 **Blackburn**, John Hiram. The Blackburn story. Recollections of the Pennsylvania Blackburns and their descendants. Edmonton: John Blackburn, 1967. 90p. ill.

Glenbow. **ACG**

2701 **Cameron**, William Stuart. Some we have met and stories they have told. Oldtimers of the valley, in the mountains, the prairies. Creston, B.C.: Creston Review, 1967. 154p. ill.,

Cover title. Duplicated.
Pioneer reminiscences, including Alberta. First published in the *Creston Review.* **AEU**

2702 Descendants of Benjamin Bullock III. Compiled by Canadian Branch of Benjamin Bullock III family. Lethbridge: Paramount Printers, 1956. 278p. ill.

Reproduced from typewritten copy.

Glenbow. **ACG**

2703 **Gaetz**, Annie Louise (Siddall). Footprints of the Gaetz family. Descendants of Martin Gaetz. Red Deer: Annie Louise Gaetz, 1961. 35p.

Glenbow. **ACG**

2704 **Giesinger**, Paul. History of the Giesinger (Gisinger) kinship. A chronicle of migration and colonization across more than seven centuries and four continents. Calgary: P. Giesinger, 1976. 248p. ill.

For private circulation only.

2705 **Goertzen**, Peter. Goertzen. Edmonton: P. Goertzen, 1976. 176p. ill.

Printed by D.W. Friesen & Sons, Calgary.
A family history. **AEA**

2706 **Gouldie**, Helen Norma (Schielke). Schielke family tree. Compiled and edited by H. Norma Gouldie. Didsbury: Booster Printing, 1975. 162p. ill.

Duplicated. **AEA**

2707 **Gouldie**, Helen Norma (Schielke). The Willing family. Didsbury: Booster Printing, 1975. 20 leaves. ill.

Duplicated.
Family history. **AEA**

2708 **Green**, Gladys Hope. The Hope family & neighbors of Red Deer Lake, S.D. No.28. Delburne: Printed by Stone's Printing, 1975. 50p. ill.

Compiled by G.H. Green, Hilda Hope Payne, Minnie Hope Nelson and Richard Joseph Hope. **AEA**

2709 **Greene**, Gordon Kay. Daniel Kent Greene, his life & times, 1858-1921. Drawings by Herbert B. Harker. Edmonton: 1960. (3) p., 151, 157, (1) leaves. ill.

Duplicated.
Contents: 1. Biography of Daniel Kent Greene. 2. The progeny of Evan Molbourne Greene.

Glenbow. **ACG**

2710 **Hansen**, Harry Benjamin. The Hansens. A history of the Hansen family from 1863 to 1969. Bentley: Harry B. Hansen, 1969. 103p. **AEA**

2711 **Houston**, John Richard. Numbering the survivors. A history of the Standish family of Ireland, Ontario and Alberta. Edited by George Hancocks. Agincourt, Ont.: Generation Press, 1979. xvi, 314p. ill.

Canadiana, 1980. **OONL**

2712 **Howg**, Carl Magnus. Our Haugs in America. Calgary: C.M. Howg, n.d.

Cover title.
Family history. **AEA**

2713 **Jouan**, Marion L. A lily bloomed. Tomahawk: M. Jouan, 1977. 60p. ill.
Cover title.
Printed by Friesen Printers, Calgary.
Biography of Alexander Maxwell Campbell and history of the family, Saskatchewan pioneers.
Canadiana, 1978. AEU

2714 **Knowlton**, Faye (Pringle). These were the early days. Calgary: Knowlton Realty, 1965. (2), 82p. ill.
A history of the B.F. Young family.
Glenbow. ACG

2715 **MacEwan**, John Walter Grant. And mighty women too. Stories of notable western Canadian women. Saskatoon: Western Producer Prairie Books, 1975. 275p. ill.
Printed by Modern Press.
Canadiana, 1976. AEA

2716 **MacEwan**, John Walter Grant. Fifty mighty men. Illustrated by Wm. W. Perehudoff. Saskatoon: Modern Press, 1958. (7), 342p. ill.
Reprinted 1959, 1963, 1965, 1975.
Glenbow. ACG

2717 The Martin family, Pine Hill-Ridgewood, 1889- . s.l.: s.n., 1964. 10p.
Cover title. AEA

2718 **Melberg**, Karin. Yesterday's children. Fairview, Fairview Post, 1979. 123p. ill.
On cover: Biographies of Peace River pioneers interviewed by Karin Melberg. AECYR

2719 **Miles**, Walter K. My genealogy. Spokane, Wash.: Walter K. Miles, 1979. 2v.
Duplicated.
Limited edition of 100 copies.
v.2 concerns Samuel Henry Harkwood Livingston and his Metis wife, Jane Mary (Howse) Livingston.
NUC 1979. ACP

2720 **Morris**, Anne Elizabeth (Peyton). Jacques Lodges, Calgary, Alberta. Calgary: A.E. Morris, 1964. 52p.
A brief history of Jacques Lodges, with biographies of residents.
Cover title.
Canadiana, 1975. AEU

2721 **Nelson**, Mervin James. The Nelson family. Calgary: M.J. Nelson, 1977. 58p. ill.
Canadiana, 1979. AEA

2722 **O'Donoghue**, Denise. The challenge of life. New York: Vantage Press, 1977. 106p.

Autobiography of a multiple sclerosis victim.

CBIP, 1979-80. **AECYR**

2723 **O'Hagan**, Howard. Wilderness men. Garden City, N.Y.: Doubleday, 1958. 263p.

Nine biographical sketches including Albert Johnson and Almighty Voice.
Also published Vancouver, Talonbooks, 1978. 189p.

Glenbow. **ACG**

2724 **Paradis**, Norma L. (Thomson). The clan McRae. A Canadian ceilidh. Victoria, B.C.: Morriss Printing, 1977. 81, 11p. **AEA**

2725 **Philip**, Catherine Rose. The Crosses of Alberta. Toronto: Maclean-Hunter Publishing, 1965. 1v. (various pagings) ill.

Articles reissued in printed covers from *Chatelaine*, June, July and August 1965, on the Cross family of Alberta, together with their connections with the families of Drever, Pinkham and Macleod.

Glenbow. **ACG**

2726 **Philip**, Catherine Rose. The women of Calgary and district, 1875-1914. Ottawa: National Library of Canada, 1975. viii, 148 leaves. (Canadian theses on microfiche, 25048)

Thesis (M.A.), University of Calgary, 1975.
Microfiche of typescript.

Canadiana, 1976. **OONL**

2727 Pioneer women of Western Canada. Edited by Margo Smith and Carol Pasternak. Toronto: Ontario Institute for Studies in Education, 1978. iv, 134p., ill. (Curriculum series, 32)

Researched and compiled by Men and Women Unlimited, Calgary, Alberta, as part of an Opportunities for Youth Project.

Canadiana, 1978. **AEU**

2728 **Puffer**, Gordon Percival. A giant among pioneers. Edmonton: 1976. 270p. ill.

Printed by Parkland Colorpress, College Heights.
A family history, with emphasis on William Franklin Puffer.

Canadiana, 1977. **AEA**

2729 **Ronaghan**, Allen. All the way over. A handbook of the descendants of James Ronaghan in North America. Islay: A. Ronaghan, 1973. 67 leaves.

Duplicated.

Canadiana, 1974. **AEA**

2730 **Smith**, Patricia Ruth. Dawn to dusk. American ancestry of Andrew F. Cole and Acenith A. Bishop. Red Deer: Patricia R. Smith, 1977. 105p. ill.

Duplicated.
Printed by Royell Reproductions, Red Deer.

AEA

2731 Stony Plain Golden Age Club. Anniversary in gold. Stony Plain, Alberta, 1908-1973. Stony Plain: Stony Plain Golden Age Club, 1973. viii, 147p. of plates.

Photographs of members, with brief biographical notes.
A New Horizons Project.

Ceessa.

AEA

2732 **Thomson**, John H.R. Fourteen generations in North America. Compiled by John H.R. Thomson. Calgary: 1967. (1), a-b, (4), 86 leaves. ill.

Duplicated.

Glenbow.

ACG

2733 **Wiggins**, Frank W. The immigrant, an autobiography. Edmonton: Frank W. Wiggins, 1967. 119p. ill.

Cover title. Duplicated.

Glenbow.

ACG

2734 **Winspear**, Frances George. Out of my mind. Foreword by Walter H. Johns. Victoria, B.C.: Morris Printing, 1969. 167p. illus.

Reminiscences of an Edmonton accountant.

Glenbow.

ACG

General History

2735 **Brice**, Edward. The history of the world, A.D. 1960 to A.D. 2000. Edmonton: Edward Brice, 1960. 249, 4p.

On history and Biblical prophecy.

Canadiana, 1961.

2736 **Coulet du Gard**, René. La France contemporaine, 1900-1976. Edmonton: Slavuta Publishers, 1975. 198p. ill.

Canadiana, 1976.

2737 **Dempsey**, Hugh Aylmer. How to prepare a local history. Calgary: Glenbow-Alberta Institute, 1968. 22p. (Glenbow archives series, 2)

Glenbow.

ACG

2738 **Gwagnin**, Aleksandr. Khronika zemli Rus'koi (Ukrains'koi), de opysano vsi mista, zamky v provintsiiakh do ykh prynalezhnykh. Osyp Mazuvok. Edmonton: s.n., 1969. 1v. (various paging). ill.

A translation of Book 3, *Kronika zemie Ruskiey*, of the Polish edition of the author's *Kronika Sarmacyey europskiey*, which was a revised and enlarged translation of the Latin original *Sarmatiene Europeae description*.
Facsimile of the original Polish edition, Krakow, 1611, on alternate pages. **AEU**

2739 **Hardy**, William George. From sea unto sea. Canada, 1850 to 1910. The road to nationhood. Toronto and New York: Doubleday, 1970. 528p. ill. (Canadian history series, v4)

Distribution limited to schools and school libraries.

Canadiana, 1971. **AECYR**

2740 **Hardy**, William George. The Greek and Roman world. Rev. ed. Toronto: McClelland and Stewart, 1962. 118p.

First edition, 1960, Toronto, Canadian Broadcasting Corporation.
Text of ten radio talks given on C.B.C. University of the Air, 1960.

Canadiana, 1962.

2741 **Hardy**, William George. Origins and ordeals of the western world. Cambridge, Mass.: Schenkman Publishing, 1968. 512p. ill.

Lessons from our heritage in history.

Canadiana, 1970.

2742 **Hardy**, William George. Our heritage from the past. Illustrated by Lewis Parker, maps by Cyril Finch. Toronto: McClelland and Stewart, 1964. 244p. ill.

High school text history of Greek and Roman civilization with brief section on civilization of early man. **AEU**

2743 **MacDonald**, Robert. The romance of Canadian history. Calgary: Ballantrae Foundation, 1971. 3v. ill.

Contents: v1. Years and years ago. A prehistory. 1971 v2. The owners of Eden. The life and past of the native people v3. The unchartered nations. **AEU**

2744 **Nelson**, Marie. The history book handbook. Your complete guide to writing and publishing a history book. Calgary: Nor-Rand Publishing, 1973. 68p. ill.

Canadiana, 1977.

2745 **Ronning**, Chester. A memoir of China in revolution from the Boxer Rebellion to the People's Republic. New York: Pantheon Books, 1974. 306p. ill.

2746 Science, technology and culture in historical perspective. Edited by Louis A. Knafla, Martin S. Staum, T.H.E. Travers. Calgary: University of Calgary, 1976. (6), 261p. ill. (University of Calgary studies in history, 1)

Papers given at the University of Calgary History Colloquium, 1973-74.

Canadiana, 1977.

2747 **Young**, Delbert A. According to Hakluyt. Tales of adventure and exploration. Toronto: Clarke, Irwin. 1973. 197p.

Written for children.

AEU

Military History

2748 **Corbet**, E. Calgary's stone frigate, H.M.C.S. Tecumseh, 1923-1973. Calgary: Century Calgary Publications, 1975. 64p. illus.

Also published as part of *At your service, Part two*, which was issued as v.6 of the Century Calgary Historical Series.

Canadiana, 1978.

AEA

2749 **Cunniffe**, Richard. Scarlet, rifle green, and khaki. The military in Calgary. Calgary: Century Calgary Publications, 1975. 40p. ill.

Also published as part of *At your service, Part one*, which was issued as v.5 of the Century Calgary Historical Series.

Canadiana, 1977.

2750 **Dean**, Basil. The northern approaches. Calgary: Calgary Herald, 1961. 9p. map.

Series of articles on arctic defences reprinted from the *Calgary Herald*.

Canadiana, 1961.

2751 Eighth Recce Association. Sabretache. The memorial journal of the VIII Recce Association. Calgary: Foothill Printers, 1966. 79p. ill.

To commemorate the 25th anniversary of the founding of the 8th Canadian Reconnaissance Regiment (14th Canadian Hussars).
Editor, C.D. Williams.

Glenbow.

ACG

2752 **Farran**, Roy. The history of the Calgary Highlanders, 1921-1954. Calgary: Bryant Press, 1954. 223p. ill.

Glenbow.

ACG

2753 **Fraser**, William Bernard. Always a Strathcona. Calgary: Lord Strathcona's Horse (Royal Canadians), 1976. 252p. ill.

A history.
Printed by Comprint Publishing.

ACP

2754 **Mainprize**, R.B. The roll of honour and nominal roll, Princess Patricias' (sic) Canadian Light Infantry, 1939-1945. Calgary: 1960. 170p. ill.

On spine: P.P.C.L.I., volume IV, 1939-45.
Issued as v.4 of the history of the regiment. Sequel to Hodder-Williams, Ralph. *Princess*

Patricia's Light Infantry, 1914-1919. London, Hodder & Stoughton, 1923. 2v. and, Stevens, G.R. *Princess Patricia's Light Infantry, 1919-1957*. Griesbach, Historical Committee of the Regiment, 1959.

Canadiana, 1971.

2755 **Manarey**, Richard Barrie. The Canadian bayonet. Photographs by Erich Franke. Edmonton: Century Press, 1971. 51p. ill.

Canadiana, 1971.

2756 **Service**, G.T. The Gate. The history of the Fort Garry Horse. Edited by Captain G.T. Service and Captain J.K. Marteinson. Calgary: Fort Garry Horse Regimental History Committee, 1971. 228p. ill.

Canadiana, 1972. **ACG**

2757 **Stevens**, George Roy. A city goes to war. Brampton, Ont.: Charters Publishing, 1964. (9), 431p. ill.

Published for Edmonton Regiment Associates.
History of the Loyal Edmonton Regiment (3PPCLI).

Glenbow. **ACG**

2758 **Stevens**, George Roy. Princess Patricia's Canadian Light Infantry, 1919-1957. Foreword by the Lady Patricia Ramsay and an introd. by Brigadier A. Hamilton Gault. Griesbach: Historical Committee of the Regiment, 1959. 411p. ill.

Issued as v.3 of the history of the regiment. Sequel to Hodder-Williams, R. *Princess Patricia's Light Infantry, 1914-1919*. London: Hodder & Stoughton, 1923. 2v.

Canadiana, 1958. **AEU**

2759 **Stewart**, John Smith. Memoirs of a soldier. Lethbridge: Robins Southern Printing, n.d. 184p. ill.

Edited by Ian Stewart Simpson from taped conversations and diaries and letters kept in the Boer War and the First World War. **AEA**

2760 **Williams**, Jeffery. Princess Patricia's Canadian Light Infantry. London: Leo Cooper, 1972. 110p. ill. (Famous regiments)

Canadiana, 1974. **AEU**

2761 **Zarn**, George. Prairie boys afloat. By the hired hand at Idlewood Farm. High River: George Zarn, 1979. 260p.

Reminiscences of navy life during World War II. **AECYR**

Western Canadian History

2762 **Anderson**, Frank Wesley. The Hope slide story. Calgary: Frontiers Unlimited, 1968. 46p. ill., map. (Frontier books, 12)

Printed by the High River Times.

Glenbow. **ACG**

2763 **Anderson**, Frank Wesley. Regina's terrible tornado. Calgary: Frontiers Unlimited, 1964. 56p. ill. (Frontier books, 9)

Glenbow. **ACG**

2764 **Anderson**, Frank Wesley. Riel's Manitoba uprising. Calgary: Frontier Publishing, 1974. 64p. ill. (Frontier books, 31)

Canadiana, 1974. **ACG**

2765 **Anderson**, Frank Wesley. 1885. The Riel Rebellion. Calgary: Frontiers Unlimited, 1962. 80p. ill. (Frontier books, 3)

Printed by High River Times.
Originally appeared in the *Western Producer* in serial form, 1955.

Glenbow. **ACG**

2766 Calgary Brewing and Malting Co. Proudly Western. An historical series. Calgary: Calgary Brewing and Malting Co., 1960. 11, 1p. ill.

Canadiana, 1960. **ACG**

2767 **Campbell**, Maria. She who knows the truth of Big Bear. History calls him traitor, but history sometimes lies. s.l.: s.n., 1977. 6 leaves.

Caption title.
Reprinted from *Maclean's Magazine*. **AEU**

2768 **Cashman**, Anthony Walcott. An illustrated history of Western Canada. Edmonton: Hurtig, 1971. 272p. ill.

Glenbow. **ACG**

2769 **Cavell**, Edward. Journeys to the far west. Toronto: James Lorimer, 1979. 164p. ill.

CBIP 1979. **AECYR**

2770 **Centennial Conference on the history of the Canadian West**, Banff, 1967. Papers. Edmonton: University of Alberta, 1967. 14v.

Duplicated.
Contents: 1. Morton, W.L. A century of plain and parkland. 2. Knill, W.D. Cultural transmission in a closed society. The Hutterites. 3. Nicks, J. Archaeology and fur trade history. 4. Eccles, W.J. New France and the western frontier. 5. Thomas, L.G. The historiography of the Canadian West, to 1870-71. 6. Roy, R.H. West of the mountains, eand East. 7. Peel, Bruce B. Steamboats on the Saskatchewan.

8. Cousins, W.J. No loyalists in British Columbia. 9. Fisher, A.D. Cultural conflict on the prairies, Indian and white. 10. Bowfield, H. Writing local history. 11. Chalmers, J.W. Social stratification in the fur trade 12. Johnson, D. The use of historical material in writing for mass media. 13. Diving into the past, relic from the rapids. 14. List of delegates.

2771 **Chalmers**, John West. Fur trade governor. George Simpson, 1820-1960. Edmonton: Institute of Applied Art, 1960. 190p. ill.

Glenbow. **ACG**

2772 **Chalmers**, John West. Red River adventure. The story of the Selkirk settlers. Illustrated by Lewis Parker. Toronto: Macmillan, 1956. 158p. ill. (Great stories of Canada, 12)

Juvenile fiction.
Reprinted 1959, 1966. **ACG**

2773 **Chambers**, Brian. Louis Riel. A critical examination of the psychiatric evidence. Ottawa: National Library of Canada, 1976. v, 136 leaves (Canadian theses on microfiche, 30502)

Thesis (M.A.), University of Calgary, 1976.
Microfiche of typescript.

Canadiana, 1978.

2774 **Coleman**, MacDonald. The face of yesterday. The story of Brandon, Manitoba. Illustrated by Peter Parker. Brandon: Brandon Junior Chamber of Commerce, 1957. 106p. ill. **ACG**

2775 **Davidson**, William McCartney. Louis Riel, 1844-1885. A biography. Calgary: Albertan, 1955. (4), 214p. ill.

Foreword dated 1928.
Replaces his *The life and times of Louis Riel*, Calgary, Albertan, 1951 (Peel 2692).

Glenbow. **ACG**

2776 The early west. Edmonton: Historical Society of Alberta, 1957. 36p. ill.

Editor, Hugh A. Dempsey.
Published by the Historical Society of Alberta in commemoration of its golden jubilee.
Contents: 1. Stanley, G. & A.E. Peterson. Massacre at Frog Lake. 2. Dempsey, H.A. A Mountie's diary, 1875. 3. Talbot, P.A. Pioneering on Strawberry Plain. 4. Lacombe, A. Crowfoot, great chief of the Blackfeet. 5. Stanley, G.D. Medical pioneering in Alberta 6. Berrry, G.L. Fort Whoop-Up and the whiskey traders.

Glenbow. **ACG**

2777 **Erasmus**, Peter. Buffalo days and nights. Peter Erasmus, as told to Henry Thompson. Introduction by Irene Spry. Calgary: Glenbow-Alberta Institute, 1976. xxxii, 343p. ill.

Reminiscences of the first half of his life, told at age 87 to Henry Thompson. **AEA**

2778 Essays on Western history. In honour of Lewis Gwynne Thomas. Edited by Lewis H. Thomas. Edmonton: University of Alberta Press, 1976. xi, 217p. map.

AEU

2779 **Fairfield**, David James. Chesterfield House and the Bow River Expedition. Edmonton: University of Alberta, 1970. 177 leaves.

Thesis (M.A.), University of Alberta, 1970.
Typescript.

Canadian theses. AEU

2780 **Flanagan**, Thomas. Louis 'David' Riel. 'Prophet of the new world.'. Toronto: University of Toronto Press, 1979. (xii), 216p.

Biography. AEU

2781 **Fraser**, William Bernard. Big Bear, Indian patriot. Calgary: Historical Society of Alberta, 1966. 15p. ill.

AEU

2782 **Fryer**, Harold. The Frog Lake massacre. Aldergrove, B.C.: Frontier Publishing, 1975. 56p. ill., map. (Frontier books, 32)

Typesetting and layout by Valcraft Printing, Aldergrove. AEA

2783 **Gray**, James Henry. Boomtime. Peopling the Canadian Prairies. Saskatoon: Western Producer Prairie Books, 1979. 148p. ill.

Printed in Saskatoon by Modern Press. AEU

2784 **Gray**, James Henry. The boy from Winnipeg. Illustrated by Myra Lowenthal. Toronto: Macmillan of Canada, 1970. 204p. ill.

Autobiography.
Paperbark ed. published 1977, Toronto, Macmillan (Laurentian Library, 52).

CBIP, 1970. AEU

2785 **Gray**, James Henry. The roar of the twenties. Toronto: Macmillan of Canada, 1975. 358p. ill.

Reprinted as part of Alberta Heritage Learning Resources Project, 1979 (Alberta literature for senior students
and adults). Social history of the Prairie Provinces.

CBIP, 1979. AEU

2786 **Gray**, James Henry. Troublemaker!. A personal history. Toronto: Macmillan of Canada, 1978. 307p. ill.

An historical memoir of the Prairie Provinces, 1935-1955.

Canadiana, 1978. AEU

2787 **Gray**, James Henry. The winter years. The depression on the Prairies. Toronto: Macmillan of Canada, 1966. 220p. ill.

Canadiana, 1967. AEU

2788 **Henry**, Alexander. Travels and adventures in Canada and the Indian territories, between the years 1760 and 1776. Edited with notes, illustrative and biographical by James Bain. Edmonton: Hurtig, 1969. xivi, 374p. ill.

Glenbow. **ACG**

2789 **Howard**, Joseph Kinsey. Strange empire. Louis Riel and the Metis people. Swan ed. Toronto: Swan Publishing, 1965. 480p.

Facsimile reprint of the 1952 edition (Peel 4296).
Also published Toronto, J. Lewis and Samuel, 1974. 601p.

Dew. **AEU**

2790 **Lusty**, Terrance W.J. Louis Riel, humanitarian. Calgary: T. Lusty, 1973. 28p. ill.

Canadiana, 1975. **ACG**

2791 **MacEwan**, John Walter Grant. Cornerstone colony. Selkirk's contribution to the Canadian West. Saskatoon: Western Producer Prairie Books, 1977. 228, 7p. ill.

AEA

2792 **MacEwan**, John Walter Grant. A short history of Western Canada. Toronto: McGraw-Hill Ryerson, 1974. vi, 166p. ill.

First published in 1968 under title *West to the sea.*

Canadiana, 1974. **OONL**

2793 **MacEwan**, John Walter Grant. West to the sea. J.W. Grant MacEwan, Maxwell Foran. Toronto: McGraw-Hill, 1968. ix, 163p. ill.

A history of the four western provinces written for students.

Glenbow. **ACG**

2794 **MacGregor**, James Grierson. Overland by the Yellowhead. Saskatoon: Western Producer Book Service, 1974. 270p. ill.

A history.

AEA

2795 **MacGregor**, James Grierson. Peter Fidler. Canada's forgotten surveyor 1769-1822. Toronto: McClelland and Stewart, 1967. xix, (1), 265p. ill.

Glenbow. **ACG**

2796 **MacGregor**, James Grierson. Senator Hardisty's prairies, 1849-1889. Saskatoon: Western Producer Prairie Books, 1978. 263, 10p. ill.

Canadiana, 1978. **AEA**

2797 **Martin**, John Julius. Westward bound. True stories of early western Canada. A volume in three parts. Edited by Mrs. Edythe M. Groves. Strathmore: Mrs. Edythe M. Groves, 1968. (5), 46p.

Duplicated.
Contents: 1. Westward bound with the early Protestant missionaries. 2. Westward

bound with the Scarlet and Gold (N.W.M.P.). 3 Westward bound in 1880, with Jack, Jenny and Benny.

Glenbow.

ACG

2798 **McCourt**, Edward. Remember Butler. The story of Sir William Butler. London: Routledge & K. Paul, 1967. xii, 276p. ill.

Also published in Toronto by McClelland and Stewart.

Glenbow.

ACG

2799 **McCourt**, Edward. Revolt in the west. The story of the Riel Rebellion. Illustrated by Jack Ferguson. Toronto: MacMillan, 1958. (4), 11-159p. ill. (Great stories of Canada, 17)

Written for teen-agers.

Glenbow.

ACG

2800 **McKee**, Sandra Lynn. Gabriel Dumont, Indian fighter. Calgary: Frontiers Unlimited, 1967. 51p. ill. (Frontier books, 14)

Glenbow.

ACG

2801 **Montizambert**, Nancy. Canada. The story of the Prairie Provinces. Toronto: McGraw-Hill, 1966. 128p. ill. (Story of Canada series)

Designed primarily for young people and new settlers.

Canadiana, 1967.

OONL

2802 **Nicks**, John Stewart. The Pine Island posts, 1786-1794. A study of competition in the fur trade. Ottawa: National Library of Canada, 1975. xi, 236 leaves. (Canadian theses on microfiche, 26864)

Thesis (M.A.), University of Alberta, 1975.
Microfiche of typescript.

U of A Theses.

AEU

2803 Prairie perspectives. Papers of the Western Canadian Studies Conference. Edited with an introd. by David P. Gagan. Prepared by the Dept. of History, University of Calgary. Toronto: Holt, Rinehart and Winston, 1970. v, 95p. ill.

Contents: 1. Gagan, D. Introduction. 2. Stanley, G.F.G. The Western Canadian mystique. 3. Smith, D. Liberals and Conservatives on the Prairies, 1917-1968-4. Rea, J.E. The roots of Prairie society. 5. Stahl, J. Prairie agriculture. A prognosis. 6. Zentner, H. The impending identity crisis among native peoples. 7. Smith, D. Conclusion.

Glenbow.

ACG

2804 Prairie perspectives, 2. Selected papers of the Western Canadian Studies Conferences, 1970. Prepared by the Department of History, University of Calgary. Edited with an introd. by A.W. Rasporich, H.C. Klassen. Toronto: Holt, Rinehart and Winston of Canada, 1973. vii, 211p. illus.

Contents: Morton, W.L. The west and the nation, 1870-1970. Careless, J.M.S. Aspects of urban life in the west, 1870-1914. Phillips, P. The National Policy and the development of the Western Canadian Labour Movement.. Nelson, J.G. Animals, fire and landscape in the north-western plains of North America in pre and early European days.. Dunbar, G.S. Isotherms and politics. Perception of the Northwest in the 1850s.. Warkenfin, J. Steppe, desert and empire.. MacEwan, G. Struggles, triumphs and heartaches with western wheat.. Proudfoot, B. Agricultural settlement in Alberta north of Edmonton. Seldon, J. Postwar migration and the Canadian West. An economic analysis. Dempsey, H.A. Local history as source materials for Western Canadian studies. Thomas, L.H. British visitors' perceptions of the West, 1885-1914. Mandel, Eli. Romance and realism in Western Canadian fiction.

Canadiana, 1973. **AEU**

2805 **Riel**, Louis. The diaries of Louis Riel. Edited by Thomas Flanagan. Edmonton: Hurtig, 1976. 187p.

An English translation of Riel's diaries.

Canadiana, 1977. **ACG**

2806 The settlement of the West. Edited by Howard Palmer. Calgary: University of Calgary, 1977. 271p. ill.

Printed by Comprint Publishing.
Papers presented at an inter-disciplinary conference, sponsored by The University of Calgary History Department, March, 1975.
Contents: 1. Flanagan, T. Louis Riel. Insanity and prophecy 2. Thomas L.H. A judicial murder. The trial of Louis Riel-3. Hall, D.J. Clifford Sifton. Immigration and settlement policy, 1896-1905-4. Troper, H. Public versus private land promotion. The Western Canadian Immigration Association 5. Dahlie, J. Scandinavian experiences on the prairies, 1890-1920 6. Eggleston, W. The old homestead. Romance and reality 7. Kerr, D. Wholesale trade on the Canadian plains in the late nineteenth century 8. Carpenter, D.C. Patrified mummies and mummified daddies 9. McGinnis, D. Farm labour in transition 10. Anderson, A.B. Farm labour in transition. 11. Wright, R.W. and Mansell, R.L. The role of migration in Alberta's economic development, 1975-1985.

Canadiana, 1978. **AEU**

2807 The twenties in western Canada. S.M. Trofimenkoff. Ottawa: National Museum of Man, 1972. 259p. (Mercury series. History series. Paper, no. 1)

Papers of the 11th Western Canadian studies conference, 1972.
Contents: 1. Ricou, L.R. From king to interloper. Man on the prairies in Canadian fiction, 1920-1929. 2. Bercuson D.J. Western labour radicalism and the One Big Union. 3.Macperson, I. The Co-Operative Union of Canada and the prairies, 1919-1929. 4. Page, D.M. The development of a western Canadian Peace Movement. 5. Griezic, F.J.K. The Honourable Thomas Alexander Crerar. 6. Flanagan, T. Political geography and the United Farmers of Alberta. 7. Thompson, J.H. The voice of moderation. The defeat of prohibition in Manitoba. 8. Calderwood, W. Pulpit, press and political reactions to the Ku Klux Klan in Saskatchewan. 9. Huel, R. French language education in Saskatchewan. 10. Roy, P.E. The oriental menace in British Columbia.

Artebise. **AEU**

2808 University of Alberta. Archives. A guide to the William Pearce papers, series 6, surveys, 1878-1928. Edmonton: Archives, University of Alberta,

1976. 30 leaves. (University of Alberta. Archives. Manuscript group, 9/2)

Canadiana, 1977.

AEU

2809 Western perspectives 1. Edited with an introd. by David Jay Bercuson. Prepared by the Department of History, University of Calgary. Toronto: Holt, Rinehart and Winston of Canada, 1974. vii, 115p. maps.

Papers of the Western Canadian Studies Conference, 1973.
Contents: 1. Rea, J.E. Images of the West. 2. Artebise, A.F.J. Winnipeg and the city planning movement, 1910-1915. 4. Weir, T. Winnipeg. A city in the making. 5. Taylor, J.H. Urban social organization and urban discontent, the 1930s. 6. Archer, C.I. The transient presence. A reappraisal of the Spanish attitudes towards the northwest coast in the eighteenth century. 7. Pierce, R.A. Russia and British Columbia to 1867. 8. Avakumovic, I. The Communist party of Canada and the prairie farmer: The interwar years. 9. Abella, I. Communism and anti-Communism in the British Columbia labour movement, 1940-1948. 10. Smith, D. E. Liberalism in Saskatchewan. 11. Coleman, I. Reflections of a social historian.

Canadiana, 1974.

AEU

Alberta History

2810 **Anderson**, Frank Wesley. Almighty Voice. Calgary: Frontier Publishing, 1971. 47p. ill. (Frontier books, 25)

Glenbow.

ACG

2811 **Anderson**, Frank Wesley. Canada's worst mine disaster. Calgary: Frontier Publishing, 1969. 48p. ill. (Frontier books, 18)

Cover title *Hillcrest, 1914. Canada's worst mine disaster.*
Also published with illustrated cover and cover title *Hillcrest Mine Disaster.*

Glenbow.

ACG

2812 **Asante-Kwatia**, David Christian. The influence of irrigation and the railroad on the settlement of southern Alberta. Ottawa: National Library of Canada, 1977. xi, 150 leaves. (Canadian theses on microfiche, 31933)

Thesis (M.Sc.), University of Alberta, 1977.
Microfiche of typescript.

U of A theses.

AEU

2813 **Barnett**, Donald C. Poundmaker. Don Mills, Ont.: Fitzhenry & Whiteside, 1976. 61, 1p. ill. (The Canadians)

Also, French translation by George Burns, 1978, Longueuil, Quebec, Editions Julienne.

Canadiana, 1977.

AEA

2814 **Bohnec**, Ruth. Pages from the past. E.A. Mitchner, Managing Editor, Barbara Jensen, Research Editor. Edmonton: Alberta Education, 1979. 120p. ill.

Juvenile literature.
Printed as part of the Alberta Heritage Learning Resources Project, 1980. **AEP**

2815 Calgary Power Ltd. Alberta, land of freedom and opportunity. Calgary: Calgary Power Ltd., 1965. 15p. ill.

Cover title.
At head of title: Diamond jubilee, 1905-1965.
A comic book history.

Glenbow. **ACG**

2816 Calgary Power Ltd. Our Alberta heritage. Calgary: Calgary Power Ltd., 1967. 1v. (loose-leaf). ill.

"These vignettes of Alberta originally appeared in our radio series 'Our Alberta Heritage'. The people at Calgary Power are pleased to make them available to all Albertans. These concise accounts of Alberta people and places back up our belief that Canada's most colorful and enterprising province is - Our Alberta".

Glenbow. **ACG**

2817 **Cameron**, William Bleasdell. Blood red the sun. Edmonton: Hurtig, 1977. 225p.

First edition, Toronto, Ryerson Press, published in 1926 under title *The war trail of Big Bear* (Peel 2957).
Contains two added chapters.

Canadiana, 1977.

2818 **Cashman**, Anthony Walcott. A picture history of Alberta. Edmonton: Hurtig, 1979. 214p. ill.

Canadiana, 1979. **AEA**

2819 **Chumak**, Sebastian Z. The spirit of Alberta. An illustrated heritage. Editor in Chief, Sebastian Z. Chumak. Edmonton: Alberta Heritage Foundation, 1978. 239p. ill.

Essays on notable people, places, objects and events.

CBIP, 1979. **AEP**

2820 **Coull**, Adrienne. Souvenirs. E.A. Mitchner, Managing Editor. Edmonton: Alberta Education, 1979. 96p. ill.

Juvenile literature.
Printed as part of Alberta Heritage Learning Resources Project, 1980. **AEL**

2821 **Dempsey**, Hugh Aylmer. Crowfoot, Chief of the Blackfeet. Edmonton: Hurtig, 1972. xix, 226p. ill.

Also published, 1972, Norman, University of Oklahoma Press. 226p. (Civilization of the American Indian series, v.122).

Canadiana, 1973. **AEA**

2822 **Dempsey**, Hugh Aylmer. Jerry Potts, plainsman. Calgary: Glenbow Foundation, 1966. 23p. ill. (Glenbow-Alberta Institute. Occasional paper, 2)

Glenbow. **ACG**

2823 **Fisher**, John. Our heritage. A series of historical sketches of Alberta. Lethbridge: Sicks' Breweries Ltd., 1955. 52p.

Cover title.

Glenbow.

ACG

2824 The formation of Alberta. A documentary history. Edited by Douglas R. Owram. General editor, R.C. Macleod. Calgary: Historical Society of Alberta, Alberta Records Publication Board, 1979. lx, 403p. (Historical Society of Alberta, v.3)

ACG

2825 **Fraser**, Esther Augusta (Michael). The Canadian Rockies. Early travels and explorations. Edmonton: Hurtig, 1969. xvi, 252p. ill.

Glenbow.

ACG

2826 **Fryer**, Harold. Alberta, the pioneer years. Langley, B.C.: Stagecoach Publishing, 1977. 192p. ill.

A collection of articles.
Printed by D.W. Friesen & sons, Altona, Manitoba.

Canadiana, 1978.

AEA

2827 **Hacker**, Carlotta. Crowfoot. Don Mills, Ont.: Fitzhenry and Whiteside, 1977. 63, 1p. ill.

A biography.
Also, French translation by Jean-Pierre Fournier, 1978, Longueil, Quebec, Editions Julienne.

Canadiana, 1979.

AEA

2828 **Hamilton**, Jacques. Our Alberta heritage. Illustrated by Tom Nelson. Calgary: Calgary Power Ltd., 1975. 5v.

Re-issued in one volume, 1977.
A 60th anniversary project.
Series two, v.4-5 illustrated by Diane Bersea.
Contents: 1. People. 2. Places. 3. Progress. 4. Mountainmen. 5. New Pioneers.

Canadiana, 1972.

AEU

2829 **Hope**, Adrian. The story of Chief Medicine Hat. As told to Grade III. Edmonton: 1962. 11p. ill.

Transcribed from a tape-recording made in the Edmonton University School, November, 1962.

Glenbow.

ACG

2830 **Johnson**, Alice Margaret. Saskatchewan journals and correspondence. Edmonton House, 1795-1800, Chesterfield House, 1800-1802. Edited with an introduction by Alice M. Johnson. London: Hudson's Bay Record Society, 1967. cii, 368p. map. (Hudson's Bay Record Society. Publication, v.26)

Ceessa.

AEA

2831 **Johnston**, Alexander. The battle at Belly River. Stories of the last great Indian battle. Lethbridge: Historical Society of Alberta, Lethbridge Branch, 1966. (3), 22, (6)p. ill.

Glenbow. **ACG**

2832 **Karklins**, Karlis. Nottingham House. The Hudson's Bay Company in Athabasca, 1802-1806. Moscow: University of Idaho, 1979. 423 leaves. ill., maps.

Thesis (M.A.), University of Idaho, 1979.
Typescript. **AEA**

2833 **Long**, Philip Sheridan. Jerry Potts, scout, frontiersman and hero. Calgary: Bonanza Books, 1974. 219p. ill. **ACG**

2834 **Luxton**, Eleanor Georgina. The golden link. An address to the Southern Alberta Pioneer and Old Timers Association. Calgary: Calgary Power Ltd. 1956. 4p.

Cover title. **AEU**

2835 **Macdonald**, R.H. Grant MacEwan. No ordinary man. Saskatoon: Western Producer Prairie Books, 1979. (8) 273p. ill.

Title on dust cover *Grant MacEwan, no ordinary man. A biography*.

CBIP, 1979. **AEA**

2836 **MacEwan**, John Walter Grant. Sitting Bull. The years in Canada. Edmonton: Hurtig, 1973. 221p. ill.

Canadiana, 1974.

2837 **MacEwan**, John Walter Grant. Tatanga Mani, Walking Buffalo of the Stonies. Edmonton: Hurtig, 1969. 208p. ill.

Glenbow. **ACG**

2838 **MacGregor**, James Grierson. A history of Alberta. Edmonton: Hurtig Publishers, 1972. 335p. ill.

Reprinted, 1977.

Canadiana, 1973.

2839 **MacGregor**, James Grierson. John Rowand, czar of the prairies. Saskatoon: Western Producer Prairie Books, 1978. 8, 184, 6p. ill. **AEA**

2840 **Macklin**, Irvin Victor. They've turned their back to the Bible. Grande Prairie: I.V.Macklin, 1955. 67p.

A personal view of economic, political and religious events in Alberta over the last 40 years.

Drake. **ACG**

2841 **Rodney**, William. Kootenai Brown, his life and times, 1839-1916. Sidney, B.C.: Gray's Publishing, 1969. 251p.

Dew.

ACG

2842 **Sharp**, Paul Frederick. Whoop-up country. The Canadian-American West, 1865-1885. With drawings by Charles M. Russell. Minneapolis: University of Minnesota Press, 1955. xix, 347p. ill.

Also published 1960, by the Historical Society of Montana. And 1973, by the University of Oklahoma.

Canadiana, 1974.

ACG

2843 **Wood**, Kerry. The great chief, Maskepetoon, warrior of the Crees. Illustrated by John A. Hall. Toronto: Macmillan, 1957. 160p. ill. (Great stories of Canada, 14)

Juvenile biography.

Glenbow.

ACG

2844 **Zaslow**, Morris. Alberta's story. Toronto: Grolier Society of Canada, 1955. 12p. ill.

Cover title *A salute to Alberta*.

Canadiana. 1955.

Local History

2845 Acadia Women's Institute. A history of the Huxley area. A centennial project in honour of our pioneers. Huxley: Acadia Women's Institute, 1967. 203p. ill.

On cover: Back over the trail.
Centennial Committee: Chairman, Bessie Vanover, Treasurer, Eira Silver, Secretary, Violet Silver.

Glenbow.

ACG

2846 Acme and District Historical Society. Acme memories. Acme: Acme and District Historical Society, 1978. vi, 542p. ill.

Printed by Friesen Printers, Calgary.

Canadiana, 1980.

AEA

2847 Alberta's County of Mountain View. Didsbury: Mountain View County No.17, 1965. 40p. ill.

Cover title *Alberta's County of Mountain View. Rustic beauty*.
Edited by C.H. Emard.
Printed by Commercial Printers, Edmonton.

Glenbow.

ACG

2848 **Alcorn**, Phyllis Maureen (Gravistin). In the bend of the Battle. A history of Alliance and district. Edited by Phyllis M. Alcorn. Sketches by Ruth Peacock. Alliance: Alliance Lions Club, 1976. 639p. ill.

Printed by Inter Collegiate Press, Winnipeg.

Canadiana, 1977. **AEU**

2849 **Allen**, W.G.P. The trail through the Pembina Valley, 1790-1912. s.l.: 46,5W.G.P. Allen, n.d. 302 leaves, maps. **AEU**

2850 **Allisson**, Rhonda. Victoria Park. Calgary's urban centre moves west of the Elbow. Calgary: Century Calgary Publications, 1975. iv, 56p. ill.

Also issued as part of *Communities of Calgary*, which was issued as v.2 of the Century Calgary Historical Series.

Canadiana, 1978. **AEA**

2851 **Almberg**, Ruby. Echoes along the Ribstone. s.l.: Grassland Pioneers Historical Society, 1978. 1064p. ill.

Editor: Ruby Almberg.
Holmes Printing.
History of the Czar-Hughenden area.

Ceessa. **AEA**

2852 **Anderson**, Elbe. Pictorial album of Veteran, Loyalist and Hemaruka. A companion to: Where the prairie meets the hills. Editors, Elbe and Angus Anderson. Veteran: Veteran Historical Society, 1979. 272p. (chiefly ill.)

Printed by Friesen Printers, Calgary.
Sequel to *Where the prairie meets the hills*, 1977, Veteran, Veteran Regional History.

AEA

2853 **Anderson**, Elbe. Where the prairie meets the hills. Veteran, Loyalist and Hemaruka districts. Veteran: Veteran Regional History, 1977. 432p. ill.

Printed by Friesen Printers, Calgary.
Edited by Elbe and Angus Anderson and Shirley Vetter.
Sequel *Pictorial album of Veteran, Loyalist and Hemaruka*, 1979, Veteran, Veteran Historical Society.

P.N.L.A., 1979. **AEU**

2854 **Anderson**, Frank Wesley. The Frank Slide story. Calgary: Frontiers Unlimited, 1961. (4) 60p. ill., map. (Frontier books, 1)

Printed by the High River Times.

Glenbow. **ACG**

2855 **Anderson**, Frank Wesley. Ghost towns journal. Calgary: Frontier Publishing, 1968. 2v. ill. (Frontier books, 39-40)

Cover titles.
Reprinted 1978.
Contents: v.1. The dead and dying ghost towns of southwest Alberta. v.2. The dead and dying ghost towns of south-east Alberta.

Ceessa. **AEA**

2856 **Appleby**, Edna (Hill). Canmore, the story of an era. Canmore: E. Appleby, 1975. 163p. ill.

Printed by D.W. Friesen & Sons Ltd., Calgary.

Canadiana, 1975.

AEA

2857 Arrowwood Farm Women's Union. The Arrowwood story (Mistsa-Katpiskoo). In the shadow of the Buffalo Hills. High River: Farm Women's Union of Alberta, Arrowwood Local, 1964. 130p. ill.

Cover title.

Glenbow.

ACG

2858 **Ashton**, Ada. Crestomere-Sylvan Heights heritage. College Heights: Crestomere-Sylvan Heights Book Committee, 1969. 449p. ill.

Printed by College Press, College Heights.
Written by Ada Ashton, assisted by Blanche Hoar and Jean Tilgen.
History of the area between Ponoka and Rimbey.

Glenbow.

ACG

2859 At your service, part one. Calgary's library, Parks Department, military, medical services and Fire Department. Accounts by Calgary authors. Calgary: Century Calgary Publications, 1975. 519p. ill. (Century Calgary historical series, v.5)

Each chapter also published separately.
Contents: Gorosh, E. Calgary's Temple of Knowledge. Barraclough, M. From prairie to park. Cunniffe, D. Scarlet rifle green andkhaki. Hardwick, E. The science, the art and the spirit. Kubota, C. Sirens and cinders.

Canadiana, 1977.

AEA

2860 At your service, part two. Calgary's police force, navy base, post office, transit system and private service groups. Calgary: Century Calgary Publications, 1975. 576p. ill. (Century Calgary historical series, v.6)

Each chapter also published separately.
Contents: Gilkes, M., Calgary's Finest-Corbet, E., Calgary's stone frigate- Applegate, M., Moving the Mail and Moving the people-Browarny, L. A friend in need-Robbins, S. Providence Child Development Centre

Canadiana, 1978.

OONL

2861 **Baergen**, William Peter. The fur trade at Lesser Slave Lake, 1815-1831. Edmonton: University of Alberta, 1967. viii, 209 leaves. ill.

Thesis (M.A.), University of Alberta, 1967.
Typescript.

Canadian theses.

2862 **Ballhorn**, Dora. Community history. Wetaskiwin: Angus Ridge Women's Institute, 1961. 114p. ill.

History committee, Dora Ballhorn, Freda Nelles.
History of the area southeast of Wetaskiwin.

Glenbow.

ACG

2863 Bancroft Women's Institute. The heritage of Bancroft. Calgary: Bancroft Women's Institute, 1961. 257p. ill.

Printed by J.D. McAra, Calgary.

Glenbow. **ACG**

2864 Barons History Book Club. Wheat heart of the West. A history of Barons and district. Barons: Barons History Committee, 1972. vii, 576p. ill.

Printed by D.W. Friesen and Sons, Calgary.

Glenbow. **ACG**

2865 Barrhead and District Historical Society. Trails Northwest. A history of the district of Barrhead, Alberta, 1867-1967. Barrhead: Barrhead and District Historical Society, 1967. (6), 305p. ill.

Glenbow. **ACG**

2866 **Barrhead Elementary School. Grade IVA**, 1966/67. The pioneer days of Barrhead. Barrhead: Barrhead Elementary School, 1967. (7) leaves

Mimeographed.

Glenbow. **ACG**

2867 Barrhead History Book Committee. The golden years. Barrhead: Barrhead History Book Committee, 1978. 499p. ill.

Spine title: Barrhead.
Sponsored by the Barrhead and District Chamber of Commerce.

Canadiana, 1979. **AEU**

2868 **Barritt**, Vera Rennetta. To the future, your heritage, Ripley. 1883, 1903-1963. Ripley: 1964. 64p. (incl advts.). ill.

Glenbow. **ACG**

2869 Bassano History Book Club. Best in the west by a damsite, 1900-1940. Bassano: Bassano History Book Club, 1974. viii, 607p. ill.

Printed by D.W. Friesen & Sons Ltd., Calgary.
A project of the Bassano Kinette Club.

Ceessa. **AEA**

2870 **Batchelor**, Bruce Edward. The agrarian frontier near Red Deer and Lacombe, Alberta, 1884-1914. Ottawa: National Library of Canada, 1978. 2v. ill. (Canadian theses on microfiche, 38424)

Thesis (Ph.D.), Simon Fraser University, 1978.
Microfiche of typescript.

Canadiana, 1980. **OONL**

2871 **Bates**, Jane Eliza Woolf. Founding of Cardston and vicinity. Pioneer problems. Compiled by Zina Woolf Hickman. s.l.: William L. Woolf, 1960. 214p. ill.

Cover title.
Also, 2d ed., 1974.

Glenbow. **ACG**

2872 Battle Bend Circle. Battle Bend pioneers. Battle Bend: Battle Bend Circle, 1962. 42p. ill.

Duplicated.

Ceessa.

AEA

2873 **Battle**, Lester. The Delia Craigmyle saga. Delia: Delia and District Historical Society, 1970. 1v. ill.

Preface signed: Lester Battle.
Printed by Southern Printing Co., Lethbridge.

Glenbow.

ACG

2874 **Beaupré**, Marie Cimon. Leurs rêves, nos mémoires. Région Peavine Creek. Edmonton: Bulletin Commercial, 1979. 516p. ill. (map in pocket)

Cover title.
Half-title *Histoire de la région Donnelly-Falher et biographies des pionniers.*

Printed by Bulletin Commercial, Edmonton.

AEA

2875 Beaver Mines Women's Institute. History. Fifty years, 1920-1970, Beaver Mines Women's Institute. Beaver Mines: Beaver Mines Women's Institute, 1970. 28 leaves.

Glenbow.

ACG

2876 Beddington Farm Women's Union. The Nose Creek story from 1792. As prepared and written by members of the community. Beddington: Farm Women's Union of Alberta, Beddington Local, 1961. 5, 156p. ill.

Printed by John D. McAra, Calgary.

Canadiana, 1962.

AEA

2877 **Bell**, Margaret Cravath. The history of Cravath Corners, 1910-1926. Brooks: Brooks Bulletin, 1963. (8)p. ill.

Cover title.
Reprinted from the *Brooks Bulletin*.

Glenbow.

ACG

2878 **Bell**, Margaret Cravath. The Hussar heritage. Hussar: Hussar United Church Ladies' Aid, 1964. 198p. ill.

Cover title.
Also, Rev. ed., 1978. 223p.

Glenbow.

ACG

2879 **Bennett**, Mary. Reflections. A history of Elk Point and district. Edited by Mary Bennett. Compiled by the Elk Point and District Historical Society. Elk Point: Elk Point and District Historical Society, 1977. 457p. ill.

Also, 1977 supplement, Winnipeg, Intercollegiate Press, 1978. 195p. ill.
Printed by Inter-Collegiate Press, Winnipeg.

Ceessa.

AEA

2880 **Bent**, S.A. Bow Island, 1912-1962, 50th anniversary. The story of the beginning. Bow Island: Bow Island Jubilee Committee, 1962. 15p.

Cover title. Duplicated.

Glenbow. **ACG**

2881 **Bert**, Phyllis. Stories of the pioneers of the west country. Celebrating the 50th jubilee of the founding of Rocky Mountain House, Alberta. Rocky Mountain House: Rocky Mountain House Jubilee Committee, 1962. 56, (14)p. ill.

Historian: Mrs. Phyll Bert.

Glenbow. **ACG**

2882 **Bérubé**, Roland. Lamoureux. The church, 1877-1967, the pioneers, 1872-1967. 2d ed. Edmonton: French Language Services, 1967. 47p.

A Canadian centennial Project.

Duplicated. **ACU**

2883 **Bezanson**, A. Maynard. Sodbusters invade the Peace. Toronto: Ryerson Press, 1954. 200p.

Also published 1954, New York, Bouregy & Curl. Printed by Ryerson Press, Toronto. Autobiographical account of settlement at Big Smoky.

Glenbow, Ceesa. **ACG**

2884 **Bickley**, Ruby Viola. Ridgewood community, Red Deer, Alberta, 1889-1967. Ridgewood: Ridgewood Women's Institute, 1967. 112, (2)p. ill.

Cover title.
Printed by Fletcher Printing, Red Deer.
Greater part of the work, 1889-1957, compiled by Mrs. Bickley and completed up to centennial year by the Centennial Committee of Ridgewood Women's Institute.
History of the area southwest of Red Deer.

Glenbow. **ACG**

2885 Bindloss Pioneer Committee. Golden memories, 1912-1963. Bindloss: Bindloss Pioneer Committee, 1963. 254p. ill.

Printed by Val Marshall Printing, Medicine Hat.

Glenbow. **ACG**

2886 **Blackburn**, John Hiram. Land of promise. Edited and with an introduction by John Archer. Toronto: Macmillan of Canada, 1970. xiii, 238p. ill.

Reminiscences of farming at Tofield in the 1910s and the Vegreville district, 1917-1930.

Glenbow. **ACG**

2887 Blairmore Lion's Club. The story of Blairmore, Alberta, 1911-1961. Editorial Board: William Jallep, Eric Price, Vern Decoux. Blairmore: Blairmore Lion's Club, 1962. 124p. ill.

Printed by Lethbridge Herald. **AEA**

2888 **Blower**, James. Gold rush. A pictorial look at the part Edmonton played in the gold era of the 1890s. Foreword by the Honourable Grant MacEwan. Toronto: Ryerson Press, McGraw-Hill Co. of Canada, 1971. 199p. (chiefly ill.) (Canadian heritage library)

Glenbow. **ACG**

2889 **Blue**, F. Rosyth memoirs, 1906-1965. Hardisty: Farm Women's Union of Alberta, Rosyth Local, 1967. 1v. ill.

Peace Hills Printers, Wetaskiwin.
Compiled by Mrs. F. Blue and Mrs. H. Burpee.

Glenbow. **ACG**

2890 **Blue**, F. Wind, willows and prairie-wool. A centennial project. Naco: Farm Women's Union of Alberta, Naco Local, 1967. 1v. ill.

Cover title. Duplicated.
Compilers, Mrs. F. Blue and Mrs. H. Burpee.
History of the communities of Sedalia, Naco and Little Gem.

Glenbow. **ACG**

2891 **Blumell**, James E. This is our land. A centennial history. Cessford: New Cessford School, 1967. 2v. ill., maps.

Duplicated.
The centennial project for English 10 and 20, 1966/67.
A history of Big Stone, Cessford, Finnegan, Hudson Bay Camp, Pollockville, Sunnynook and Wardlow.

Ceessa. **AEA**

2892 **Boileau**, Gilles. Les canadiens français de la région de Saint-Paul. Montréal: Société canadienne d'établissement rural, 1900. 69 leaves. maps, diag.

Duplicated. Produced under a grant from the Quebec Ministry of Cultural Affairs. **AECST**

2893 **Bolinger**, Ralphene. The Gleichen call. A history of Gleichen and surrounding areas, 1877 to 1968. Gleichen: Gleichen United Church Women, 1968. 376p. ill.

Also, 2d ed., 1969.
Published in co-operation with the Gleichen Lions Club.
Editors: Ralphene Bollinger, Audrey Kilcup, Opal McMillan, Ellay Hayes.

Glenbow, Ceesa. **ACG**

2894 **Boote**, Walter H.S. Ogden whistle. A history of Millican, Ogden Flats, Maryland, Valleyfield, Bonnybrook, South Hill, Cepeear, Lynnwood,

Lynwood Ridge, River Glen, Crestwood, C.P.R. Ogden Shops. Calgary: Ogden Area History Committee, 1975. 157p. ill.

Chairman: Walter Boote.
Printed by D.W. Friesen & Sons, Calgary.
A Century Calgary centennial publication.

Canadiana, 1976. **AEA**

2895 **Borgstede**, Arlene. St. Albert, a pictorial history. Compiled and edited by Arlene Borgstede. St. Albert: St. Albert Historical Society, 1978. 79p. (chiefly ill.)

Canadiana, 1980. **AEA**

2896 **Bowman**, Gladys. Garrington Post Office, 1907. Sundre: Sundre Round-Up, 1969. (37)p. ill.

Cover title. At head of title: Canada.

Glenbow. **ACG**

2897 **Braithwaite**, C.R. Early settlers of the Shady Nook district and the close surrounding area. s.l.: C.R. Braithwaite, 1967. (1), 9 leaves.

Duplicated.
History of the area south west of Red Deer.

Glenbow. **ACG**

2898 **Brewster**, F.O. They came west. Pat's tales of the early days. Banff: F.O. Brewster, 1979. 62p. ill.

A sequel to his *Weathered wood*, 1977. **AEA**

2899 **Brewster**, F.O. Weathered wood. Anecdotes and history of the Banff-Sunshine area. Banff: F.O. Brewster, 1977. 64p. ill.

Printed by Banff Cragg and Canyon.
Edited and designed by Jon Whyte.

P.N.L.A., 1979. **AEA**

2900 **Brown**, Harriet C. Beavertales. A history of Ryley and district. Ryley: Royal Canadian Legion no.192, Ryley Branch, Ladies Auxiliary, 1978. 331p. ill.

Printed by Friesen Printers, Calgary.

Canadiana, 1979. **AEA**

2901 **Buckley**, Evelyn. Chaps and chinooks. A history west of Calgary. Calgary: Foothills Historical Society, 1976. 2v. ill.

Lithographed by Northwest Printing and Lithographing.
A history of the Brushy Creek, Jumping Pound, Springbank and Pirmez Creek districts west of Calgary. **AEA**

2902 Buffalo Coulee Home and School Association Centennial Committee. Buffalo Coulee progress (1902-1967). Buffalo Coulee: Buffalo

Coulee Home and School Association Centennial Committee, 1967. 120p. ill.

Printed by Meridian Printing, Lloydminster.
Written and published by the Association on behalf of the County of Minburn No.27, in commemoration of the Centennial of Canadian Confederation.
History of the area between Vermilion and Wainwright.

Glenbow. ACG

2903 Buford 4-H Horticultural and Clothing Clubs. Pioneer reflections. Buford: 4-H Horticultural and Clothing Clubs, 1967. 71, (1) p. ill.

Duplicated.

Glenbow. ACG

2904 **Buk**, Nickolas. The history of Two Hills, including the Lanuke District. Two Hills: N. Buk and S. Urchak, 1979. 84p. ill.

Compiled by Nickolas Buk and Stephen Urchak. AEA

2905 **Burles**, Mary-Jo. Cowley. 60 years a village, 1906-1966. Cowley: s.n., 1966. 15p. ill.

Cover title.
Co-authors, Mary-Jo Burles and Marjorie Haugen.
Sponsored by Cowley Lions Club and the Village of Cowley on the occasion of Cowley's Diamond Jubilee.

Glenbow. ACG

2906 Burnt Lake History Society. Along the Burnt Lake Trail. A history of Shady Nook, Burnt Lake, Centerville, Pine Hill, Marianne, Kuusamo and Evarts. Red Deer: Burnt Lake History Society, 1977. 752p. ill., maps.

Printed by Friesen Printers, Calgary.
History of the area south west of Red Deer.

Canadiana, 1978. AEA

2907 **Butterwick**, Alyce. Shortgrass country. A history of Foremost and Nemiskam. Foremost: Foremost Historical Society, 1975. vii, 688p. ill.

Printed by D.W. Friesen and Sons, Calgary.

Canadiana, 1976. AEA

2908 Calahoo trails. A history of Calahoo, Granger, Speldhurst, Noyes Crossing, East Bibly, Green Willo, 1842-1955. Editor: Mrs. K. Dalheim, co-editor, Mrs. M. Kerr. Calahoo: Calahoo Women's Institute, 1955. 313p. ill.

Printed by Inter-Collegiate Press, Winnipeg.

Canadiana, 1979. AEA

2909 **Calder School Reunion Association**, Edmonton. Early history of Calder School and district. Edmonton: Calder School Reunion Association, 1977. 42p. ill.

Cover title.
History of the Calder district of Edmonton.

Ceessa. **AEA**

2910 Calgary Centennial Committee. A year to remember. A report on the celebrations in Calgary to mark the centenary of Canadian Confederation - 1967. Calgary: Calgary Centennial Committee, 1968. (4), 75 leaves. ill.

Glenbow. **ACG**

2911 Calgary Herald. 75th anniversary, 1883-1958. Calgary: Calgary Herald, 1958. (92)p. (incl. advts.) ill.

Cover title.
Special edition of Sept. 6, 1958.

Glenbow. **ACG**

2912 Calgary Power Ltd. Heritage Park memories. Calgary: Calgary Power Ltd., 1966. (26)p. (chiefly ill.)

Cover title.
Foreword by Grant MacEwan.

Glenbow. **ACG**

2913 **Cameron**, Margaret Hunter. Dog Pound, 1880-1920. Didsbury: Didsbury Booster, 1971. 38p. ill.

Compiled by Margaret Cameron and Pearl R. Stone.

Glenbow. **ACG**

2914 **Campbell**, Alice A. Milk River country. Milk River: Milk River Old Timers Association, 1959. 439p. ill.

Printed by Lethbridge Herald.

Glenbow. **ACG**

2915 **Campbell**, Isabel M. Grande Prairie, capitol (sic) of the Peace. Grande Prairie: Isabel M. Campbell, 1968. 146p. ill.

Cover title.

Glenbow. **ACG**

2916 **Campbell**, Isabel M. Pioneers of the Peace. Editor, Isabel M. Campbell. Artist, Robert C. Guest. Grande Prairie: Grande Prairie and District Old Timers' Association, 1975. 428p. ill.

Printed by D.W. Friesen & Sons, Calgary.

Canadiana, 1976. **AEU**

2917 **Campbell**, Jessie J. Chatter chips from Beaver Dam Creek. Castor and her neighbours, 1909-1974. Castor: J. Campbell, 1975. 637p. ill.

Printed by Parkland Color Press, College Heights.
Sponsored by Castor Old Timers Association.

Ceessa. **AEA**

2918 **Campbell**, Marie J. Still God's country. The early history of Byemoor and area. Byemoor: Byemoor History Committee, 1975. 249p. ill.

Editor: Marie J. Campbell.
Printed by D.W. Friesen and Sons, Calgary.

Canadiana, 1975. **AEA**

2919 **Campbell**, Robert Eldon. I would do it again. Reminiscences of the Rockies. Foreword by T.U. "Tommy" Primrose. Toronto: Ryerson Press, 1959. ix, (1), 204p. ill.

Glenbow. **ACG**

2920 Camrose Canadian. The golden trail. Edited by the staff of the Camrose Canadian. Camrose: Lions Club of Camrose, 1955. 136p. ill.

A history of Camrose and area.
Cover title.

Glenbow. **ACG**

2921 Cardston Diamond Jubilee Committee. Cardston diamond jubilee, 1887-1962, jubilee souvenir. Cardston: Cardston Diamond Jubilee Committee, 1962. 54, (2)p. ill.

Glenbow. **ACG**

2922 Carmangay and District History Book Committee. Bridging the years, Carmangay and district. Carmangay: Carmangay and District History Book Committee, 1968. 475p. ill.

Sponsored by the Carmangay and District Home and School Association.
Printed by Southern Printing, Lethbridge.

Glenbow. **ACG**

2923 **Carron**, Selma. Golden memories, Warburg and district. Warburg: Warburg and District Historical Society, 1977. 524p. ill.

Editor, Selma Carron, assistant editor, Winfield Scott.
Printed by Friesen Printers, Calgary. **AEA**

2924 Carseland and Cheadle Historical Book Committee. Trails to the Bow. Carseland and Cheadle chronicles. Carseland: Carseland and Cheadle Historical Book Committee, 1971. vi, 533p. ill.

Printed by D.W. Friesen & Sons, Calgary.

Glenbow. **ACG**

2925 Carstairs Centennial History Committee. Prairie trails. Pioneer history of Carstairs and District. Carstairs: Carstairs Centennial History Committee, 1967. 218, (1)p. ill.

Cover title.
Duplicated.
Printed by the Didsbury Booster, Didsbury.

Glenbow. **ACG**

2926 **Cashman**, Anthony Walcott. The best Edmonton stories. Edmonton: Hurtig, 1976. 207p.

Forty of these stories previously appeared in the author's *The Edmonton story* and *More Edmonton stories*.

Canadiana, 1977. **AEA**

2927 **Cashman**, Anthony Walcott. The Edmonton story. The life and times of Edmonton, Alberta. Edmonton: Institute of Applied Art, 1956. 279, (5)p. ill.

Glenbow. **ACG**

2928 **Cashman**, Anthony Walcott. More Edmonton stories. The life and times of Edmonton, Alberta. Edmonton: Institute of Applied Art, 1958. 261p. ill.

Glenbow. **ACG**

2929 Castor Fiftieth Anniversary Committee. Celebrate with Castor, 1910-1960. Castor: Castor Fiftieth Anniversary Committee, 1960. 8p. ill.

Cover title.
Program of official events with brief historical notes.

Glenbow. **ACG**

2930 Cayley Women's Institute. Under the Chinook Arch. A history of Cayley and surrounding areas. Calgary: Cayley Women's Institute, 1967. 346p. ill.

Published on behalf of Foothills Municipal District No.31.

Glenbow. **ACG**

2931 Cereal Women's Institute. Down Cereal's memory trails, 1910-1967. Cereal: Cereal Women's Institute, 1968-1977. 2v. ill.

v.1. 1968 v.2. 1977.
V.2 printed by Derkson Printers, Manitoba.

Glenbow. **ACG**

2932 **Chévigny**, Delamen (Plamondon). Jubilé d'or. Plamondon golden jubilee, 1908-1958. s.l.: s.n., 1958. 4, 21, 7, 1p. ill.

Cover title. Duplicated.
Text in English and French.
Chiefly a history of Plamondon. **AEA**

2933 **Chadwick**, Donna. Candelight years. Drumheller: Innisfail and District Historical Society, 1974. 501p. ill.

Printed by D.W. Friesen & Sons, Calgary.

Ceessa. **ACG**

2934 **Charuk**, Myrtle. The history of Willingdon, 1928-1978. St. Paul: L.H. Drouin, St. Paul Journal, 1978. 116p. ill.

Ceessa. **AEA**

2935 Chauvin Rebekah Lodge #120. Singing rails and tales. Chauvin: Chauvin Rebekah Lodge #120, 1975. 54p. ill.

Duplicated.
History of Chauvin and district.

Ceessa. **AEA**

2936 **Cheek**, Orville. Buried treasures. The history of Elnora, Pine-Lake and Huxley. Chief editor, Orville Cheek, editor, Mrs. William Wagstaff, assistant editor, Mrs. Charles Hodgkinson. Elnora: Elnora History Committee, 1972. 324p. ill.

Cover title.
Printed by D.W. Friesen & Sons, Calgary.

Canadiana, 1973. **AEA**

2937 Chestermere Historical Society. The changing scene. A supplement to Saddles, sleighs and sadirons, 1972-1978. Chestermere: Chestermere Historical Society, 1978. 113p. ill.

Lithographed by Northwest Printing & Lithographing Ltd.
Supplement to *Saddles, sleighs and sadirons*, by Marie Nelson, 1971.
History of the Conrich-Delacour area. **AEA**

2938 **Chevraux**, Sharleen M. The ten dollar bets. A history of Killam and district. Sharleen M. Chevraux, editor and chairman. Killam: Killam Town Council, 1967. 141p. ill.

Printed by Inter-Collegiate Press, Winnipeg.
A centennial project.

Ceessa. **AEA**

2939 **Chubb**, Jean (Hall). Leaves of yesteryear. A history of the Bon Accord district and the biographies of the men and women who pioneered the area. Compiled in 1967-69 by Jean Chubb and Hilda Milligan. Bon Accord: Bon Accord F.W.U.A. (local 502), 1969. x, 239p. ill.

Printed by Co-op Press, Edmonton.

Glenbow. **ACG**

2940 Claresholm History Book Club. Where the wheatlands meet the range. Claresholm: Claresholm History Book Club, 1974. 549p. ill.

Printed by D.W. Friesen & Sons, Calgary.

Canadiana, 1975. **AEU**

2941 **Clark**, Edith J. (Lawrence). Trails of Tail Creek country. Erskine: E.J. Clarke, 1968. (12), 416p. ill.

Cover title.

History of the area from Buffalo Lake to the Red Deer River including the Tail Creek settlement.

Glenbow. **ACG**

2942 **Clarke**, Elizabeth. Blueberry Mountain history. s.l.: s.n., 1975. 29p. ill.

Cover title.
An Opportunities for Youth Summer Project, 1974.
Compilers, Elizabeth Clarke, Andrew Clarke, Mary Clarke and Patty Agrey.

Ceessa. **AEA**

2943 Cleverville Pioneer Club History Book Committee. Cleverville, Champion, 1905 to 1970. A history of Champion and area. Champion: Champion History Committee, 1972. iii, 738p. ill.

Printed by D.W. Friesen and Sons, Calgary.

Glenbow. **ACG**

2944 Coaldale Jubilee Committee. Coaldale, the gem of the West. Coaldale: J.J. Loewen, 1955. 40, (1)p. ill.

"To commemorate 50 years of growth and progress in Coaldale and district".
Booklet Committee: D.R. Baldwin, Mrs. W.J. Baldry, Henry Daine.

Glenbow. **ACG**

2945 Cochrane and Area Historical Society. Big Hill country. Cochrane and area. Cochrane: Cochrane and Area Historical Society, 1977. 804p. ill.

Printed by D.W. Friesen and Sons, Calgary.

Candiana, 1977. **AEA**

2946 **Collins**, Ruth Johanna (Ignatius). Winnifred. Our trails, trials and memories. Maleb: s.n., 1965. 187, ii p. ill.

Cover title. Duplicated.

Glenbow. **ACG**

2947 **Comfort**, Darlene Joy. Meeting place of many waters. A history of Fort McMurray. Fort McMurray: Comfort Enterprises, 1974. 2v. ill.

Duplicated.
Contents: 1. The fur trade era. 2. Ribbon of water and steamboats north.

Ceessa. **AEA**

2948 Comité 50 de Girouxville. Album souvenir, 1928-1978. Girouxville: Comité 50 de Girouxville, 1978. 48p. (incl. advts.) ill.

Cover title *Girouxville, 1928-1978*. **AECS**

2949 Communities of Calgary. From scattered towns to a major city. Accounts by Calgary authors. Calgary: Century Calgary Publications, 1975. 424p. ill. (Century Calgary historical series, v.2)

Each chapter also published separately.
Contents: Communities six. Hub of three hamlets. Comier, R. Inglewood and

Ramsay. Allison, R. Victoria Park. Nielsen, D.B.
Bowness country homes and amusements west of Calgary

Canadiana, 1977. **OONL**

2950 Communities six. Calgary grows to the northeast and southwest. Accounts by Calgary authors. Calgary: Century Calgary Publications, 1975. iii, 72p. ill.

Also published as part of *Communities of Calgary*, which was issued as v.2 of the Century Calgary Historical Series.

Canadiana, 1977. **AEA**

2951 Conquerville Women's Institute. Conquerville, a growing community. Maleb: Conquerville Women's Institute, 1965. (4), 180, (1)p. ill.

A history sponsored by Conquerville Women's Institute to commemorate the 50th year.
Edited by Margaret Dragland.
Cover title. Duplicated.

Glenbow. **ACG**

2952 Coronation Board of Trade. Coronation. Coronation: Coronation Board of Trade, 1955. (2), 26p. ill.

Printed by Review Printers.
Published on the occasion of Alberta's golden jubilee, 1905 to 1955.

Glenbow. **ACG**

2953 Coronation Book Committee. In the beginning. A history of Coronation, Throne, Federal and Fleet Districts. Coronation: Coronation T & C Golden Age Club, 1979. 556p. ill.

Printed by Friesen Printers. **AEA**

2954 Coronation Old-Timers' Centennial Book Committee. Shadows of the Neutrals. Edited by residents of Brownfield, Silver Heights, Talbot and Bulwark. Coronation: Coronation Old-Timers Centennial Book Committee, 1967. (4), 214p. ill.

Printed by College Press, College Heights.
With this is bound, as issued, the Committee's *Open memory's door*, 1967. Edited by Blanche Adcock & others. (6), 74p. ill..
Sequel, *Lengthening shadows of the Neutrals*, 1979, Brownfield, New Dawn Seniors Club.

Glenbow. **ACG**

2955 **Coulton**, Betty. The great lone land. Consort's fifty years of progress, 1912-1962. Consort: s.n., 1962. 89p. ill.

Cover title.
Title page, *Consort's fifty years of progress, 1912-1962*.
Compilers: Betty Coulton, A. Hadwin, J. George, M. McCarthy.

Glenbow. **ACG**

2956 Crossfield History Committee. Prairie sod and goldenrod. Crossfield: Crossfield History Committee, 1977. 359p. ill.

Printed by Friesen Printers, Calgary.

Ceessa. AEA

2957 Crowsnest Pass Historical Society. Crowsnest and its people. Coleman: Crowsnest Pass Historical Society, 1979. xii, 914p. ill.

Printed by Friesen Printers, Calgary. AEA

2958 Cumberland memories. Cumberland: Cumberland School Reunion Book Committee, 1978. 160p. ill.

Duplicated.
Cover title.
History of the area west of Delburne. AEA

2959 **Cunniffe**, Richard. Calgary - in sandstone. Calgary: Historical Society of Alberta, Calgary Branch, 1969. 29p. ill.

Glenbow. ACG

2960 **Dahlgren**, Dorothy. Tales of the tarsands. Fort McMurray: Bernard Jean Publishing, 1975. 87p.

Stories, originally written for radio, of settlers in the Fort McMurray area. ACP

2961 Dalemead Indus History Committee. Tales from two townships. The story of Dalemead, Indus and Shepard. Dalemead: Dalemead Community Club, 1968. 336p. ill.

A centennial project.

Glenbow. ACG

2962 Dalum History Book Committee. The history of Dalum, commemorating its 50th anniversary, May 5, 1968. Drumheller: Big Country News, 1968. (2), 226p. ill.

1969 supplement (p.227-230) entitled *Some important firsts*, tipped in.
Sponsored by the Bethlehem Lutheran Church.

Glenbow. ACG

2963 **Dawe**, Robert Wellington. The development of the Red Deer community in relation to the development of western Canada. Edmonton: University of Alberta, 1954. x, 289 leaves.

Thesis (M.A.), University of Alberta, 1954.
Typescript.
Also published 1954 under title *History of Red Deer*, Red Deer, Kiwanis Club of Red Deer.

Canadian theses. AEU

2964 **Dawe**, Robert Wellington. History of Red Deer, Alberta. Red Deer: Kiwanis Club of Red Deer, 1954. 82p. ill.

Written as an M.A. Thesis, University of Alberta, 1954, under title *The development of the Red Deer community in relation to the development of western Canada*.

Glenbow. **ACG**

2965 **Dawson**, Carl Addington. The settlement of the Peace River Country. A study of a pioneer area. By C.A. Dawson. Assisted by R.W. Murchie. Millwood, N.Y.: Kraus Reprint, 1974. xi, 284p. ill.

Reprint of the 1934 edition published by Macmillan of Canada, Toronto, as v.6 of the series Canadian frontiers of settlement (Peel 3377).

Canadiana, 1979. **OONL**

2966 De Winton and District Historical Committee. Sodbusting to subdivision. De Winton: De Winton and District Historical Committee, 1978. 587p. ill.

Printed by Friesen Printers, Calgary. **AEA**

2967 **Delday**, Eva Pearce. Brooks. Between the Red Deer and the Bow. Edited by Pearl Thomas. Brooks: E. Delday, 1975. viii, 291p. ill.

Written by Eva Delday, Historian for the Brooks and District Historical Society.
Printed by D.W. Friesen and Sons, Calgary.
Spine title *Brooks, beautiful, bountiful*.

Canadiana, 1975. **AEA**

2968 **Demorest**, Evelyn. Golden memoirs, 1912-1963. Medicine Hat: Printed by Val Marshall Printing, 1963. 254p. ill., map.

History of the Medicine Hat area.
Pioneer committee: Evelyn Demorest, Ingrid Sturm, Doris Fowlie.

Ceessa. **AEA**

2969 **Denney**, C.D. The Athabasca Landing Trail. Edmonton: C.D. Denney, 1970. 7 leaves. ill., map.

Printed by Echo Printing, Athabasca. **AEA**

2970 **Devore**, Roy W. The history of Walterdale. Edmonton: s.n., 1956. iii, 17p. ill.

History of a former subdivision of Edmonton, founded by John Walter.

Glenbow. **ACG**

2971 The Dickson story. Translated by Hans and Myrtle Hansen. s.l.: s.n., n.d. 60 leaves.

Duplicated.
Published in Danish, 1948. This translation includes extracts from the *Bethany Lutheran Church and Home*, and some articles from former residents. **AEA**

2972 Dinton Women's Institute. Gladys and Dinton through the years. A history of the Gladys and Dinton Districts and the biographies of the men and women who pioneered the area. Compiled 1963 and 1964 by the Dinton and Gladys Women's Institutes. Dinton: Dinton Women's Institute, 1965. 325p. ill.

Printed by Northwest Printing & Lithographing,Calgary.
History of the area northeast of High River.

Glenbow. **ACG**

2973 **Dodd**, Edward J. Remember when. The history of Trochu and district. Trochu: Trochu History Book Committee, 1976. 432p. ill.

Chairman and editor: Ned Dodd.
Printed by D.W. Friesen and Sons, Calgary.

Ceessa. **AEA**

2974 Donalda Jubilee Committee. Fifty years on the coulee rim. A factual history of Donalda and district, prepared for Donalda's fiftieth anniversary, 1963. Donalda: Donalda Jubilee Committee, 1963. 152p. ill.

Cover title.

Glenbow. **ACG**

2975 **Doolan**, Jean. The last best west. A history of the village and district of New Brigden, Alberta. Edited by Myrtle Herron and Adella Code. Cover by Doris Heatherington, maps by B.W. Hornett and John Wilson. Compiled by New Brigden Community Club. New Brigden: New Brigden Community Club, 1955. 30p. map.

Glenbow. **ACG**

2976 **Dorcas Ladies Aid**, Eagle Hill. The Eagle calls. History of Eagle Hill. Eagle Hill: Dorcas Ladies Aid, 1975. 424p. ill.

Printed by Carstairs and District Community Press.

Ceessa. **AEA**

2977 **Doty**, Arlynn. Roads to Pipestone. Pipestone: Pipestone Community Club, 1970. 1v. (unpaged) ill.

Cover title.
Editor: Arlynn Doty.
History of the area east of Pigeon Lake.

Glenbow. **ACG**

2978 **Dougan**, Harvey. The English colony. Nightingale and District. Nightingale: Nightingale Women's Institute, 1979. 439p. ill.

Printed by Macleod Printing and Mailing. **AEA**

2979 **Douglas**, Helen Frances. Echoes of Willow Creek. Compiled by Helen Douglas and Vilda Ohler, assisted by Maud Ramage. Granum: Willow Creek Historical Society, 1965. 104p. ill.

Printed by the Lethbridge Herald.
Primarily a history of the Society.

Glenbow.

ACG

2980 **Douglas**, Helen Frances. Golden kernels of Granum. The story of the early settlers of Granum. s.l.: s.n., 1955. 79p.

Glenbow.

ACG

2981 **Dragland**, Margaret (Hansen). The Piegan country. Editor and publisher, Alfred Bakstad, artist and writer. Margaret Dragland. Maleb: Margaret Dragland, 1966. (5), 196p. ill.

Cover title. Duplicated.
Includes a brief history of southeastern Alberta.
Printed by Val Marshall's Printing, Medicine Hat.

Glenbow.

ACG

2982 Drayton Valley High School. The history of Drayton Valley. Drayton Valley: Know Your Neighbour Project, 1971. (3), 20 leaves. ill.

Cover title. Duplicated.
Prepared by D.V.H.S. students for the Know Your Neighbour project.

Glenbow.

ACG

2983 **Dreger**, A.F. A most diversified character. Edmonton: A.F.Dreger, 1971. 146p. ill.

Reminiscences. Written by A.F. Dreger, a pioneer of the Edmonton district, after the age of 84.

AEA

2984 **Drouin**, Eméric O'Neil. Habitat St. Paul, 1976-1980. St. Paul: St. Paul Journal, 1976. 80p. ill.

Text partly in French.
A history and description of social and cultural conditions of St. Paul.

Canadiana, 1977.

2985 **Drouin**, Lucien Henri. History of St. Paul, Alberta, 1909-1959. St. Paul: St. Paul Journal, 1960. 232p. (incl. advts.). ill.

In French and English, continuously paged.
French supplement edited by Bishop Philippe Lussier.

Glenbow.

ACG

2986 Drumheller East Farmer Women's Union. Memories of Verdant Valley, Cassel Hill, Livingston, Rainbow. Drumheller: Farmers Union of Alberta, Drumheller East Centennial Committee, 1966. 500p. ill.

Contents: 1. Clipsham, Muriel G. Verdant Valley, Part I. 2. Adic, Adelaide Green. Verdant Valley, Part 2. 3. Gaschnitz, Eleanor Chambers. Cassel Hill. 4. Howard, Alice Bell. Rainbow.

Glenbow.

ACG

2987 Drybelt pioneers of Sundial, Enchant (and) Retlaw. s.l.: Book Committees of Sundial, Enchant and Retlaw, 1967. (4), 330p. ill.

Printed by Southern Printing, Lethbridge.
Cover title.

Glenbow. **ACG**

2988 **Dubuc**, Denis. Jean-Côté, histoire et généalogie d'une paroisse du nord albertain. Falher: D. Dubuc, 1973. ix, 69p.

Cover title.
Text in French and English.

Canadiana, 1976. **AEA**

2989 **Durie**, Elizabeth. Park Grove echoes. Park Grove: Park Grove Community Centre, 1979. 190p. ill.

Duplicated.
History of the area northwest of Vegreville. **AEA**

2990 Eagle Valley Book Club. Wagon trails plowed under. A history of Eagle Valley, Sundre East and Sangro. Sundre: Eagle Valley Book Club, 1977. 289p. ill.

Canadiana, 1979. **AEA**

2991 East prairie metis, 1939-1979. 40 years of determination. Edmonton: Federation of Metis Settlements, 1979. vi, 100p. ill.

Canadiana, 1980. **OONL**

2992 Eastburg Farm Women's Union. Eastburg. Eastburg: Farm Women's Union of Alberta, Eastburg Local, 1963. 1v. (unpaged). ill.

Duplicated.
History of an area between Westlock and Barrhead. **AEA**

2993 Eastway Ladies' Social Club. Trails to highways. Vulcan: Eastway Ladies' Social Club, 1972. vi, 458p. ill.

A history of the Buffalo Hills area, north of Vulcan.

Canadiana, 1973. **AEA**

2994 Eckville and District Historical Society. Homesteads and happiness. Eckville: Eckville and District Historical Society, 1979. 1065p. ill., maps.

Printed by Friesen Printers, Calgary. **AEA**

2995 Edgerton and District Historical Society. Winds of change. Edgerton: Edgerton and District Historical Society, 1976. 781p. ill.

Canadiana 1977. **AEA**

2996 Edson Leader. Edson flashback. Excerpts from Old Time articles published in the Edson Leader during the town's 60th anniversary year. In collaboration with Mrs. Margaret Ahlf. Edson: Edson Leader, 1971. 1v. ill.

Glenbow. ACG

2997 **Edstrom**, Sylvia. Memoirs of the Edberg pioneers. Gathered and compiled by Sylvia Edstrom and Florence Lundstrom. s.l.: s.n., 1955. 121p. ill.

Printed by Douglas Printing, Edmonton.

Glenbow. ACG

2998 Empress Golden Jubilee Committee. Golden jubilee, Empress, 1914-1964. Empress: Empress Golden Jubilee Committee, 1964. 95, (20)p. ill.

Cover title.
Printed by Val Marshall Printing, Medicine Hat.

Glenbow. ACG

2999 **Eskrick**, Muriel Elizabeth. Portrait of a pioneer. Stories of the west country. Sundre: Sundre Round-Up, 1969. 85p. ill.

History of the Sundre area.

Glenbow. ACG

3000 **Eskrick**, Muriel Elizabeth. The road to Ya Ha Tinda. A story of pioneers. Sundre: Sundre Round-Up, 1960. 20p.

Cover title.
2d ed. 1969.
History of the Sundre area.

Glenbow. ACG

3001 Falher Jubilee Committee. Jubilé de Falher. Jubilee, 1919-1979. Falher: s.l., 1979. (40)p.

Text in French and English. AECSJ

3002 **Farnalls**, Paul L. Memoirs of life in Alberta. Edmonton: Commercial Printers, 1960. 46p. ill.

Reminiscences of pioneering in the Lacombe district, and political life in Alberta.
Contents: 1. Early experiences of pioneering in Alberta. 2. Some organizations important in the development of the country and the writer's interest in them.

Glenbow. ACG

3003 Fencelines and Furrows History Book Society. Fencelines and Furrows. Blackie: Fencelines and Furrows History Book Society, 1969. 568p. ill.

Lithographed by Northwest Printing & Lithographing, Calgary.
Also 2d ed., 1971. 576p.

Glenbow. ACG

3004 Ferguson Flats Ladies' Club. Reminiscing in Ferguson Flats, 1900-1974. Ferguson Flats: Ferguson Flats Ladies' Club, 1975. 1v. ill.

History of the area east of Elk Point.

Ceessa. AEU

3005 **Filipenko**, Laura. From the Bigknife to the Battle, Gadsby and area. Gadsby: Gadsby Pioneers Association, 1979. x, 582p. ill.

Editor, Laura Filipenko.
Printed by Friesen Printers, Calgary.

Canadiana, 1980. AEA

3006 **Finlay**, Charles M. History of Mannville and district. Mannville: Mannville Old Timers' Association, 1961. 158p. ill.

Edited by Charles M. Finlay.
Printed by Douglas Printing, Edmonton.

Glenbow. ACG

3007 **Finstad**, Helen. Prairie footprints. A history of the community in southern Alberta known as Pendant d'Oreille. Pendant d'Oreille: Pendant d'Oreille Lutheran Church Women, 1970. 265p. ill.

Editor: Helen Finstad.
Printed by Val Marshall Printing (1969), Medicine Hat.

Glenbow. ACG

3008 **Fitzgerald**, Walter P. The wheels of time. A history of Rivière Qui Barre. Rivière Qui Barre: Rivière Qui Barre Book Committee, 1978. 12, 375p. ill.

Cover title.
Editor: Walter P. Fitzgerald.

Ceessa. AEA

3009 **Flauret**, Louis. Okotoks. 50th anniversary celebrations, 6 Sept. 54. Okotoks: Town of Okotoks, 1954. 9 leaves.

Cover title. Duplicated.

Dew. AEU

3010 **Florkewich**, Violet. Hills of Hope. Compiled by Hills of Hope Historical Committee. Spruce Grove: Carvel Unifarm, 1976. 533p. ill.

Editing: Mrs. Violet Florkewich, John Hrasko, Allan Olson.
Printed by D.W. Friesen & Sons, Calgary.
History of the Wabamun Lake area.

Canadiana, 1977. AEA

3011 **Foran**, Maxwell Laurence. Calgary. An illustrated history. Photos assembled by Edward Cavell. Toronto: James Lorimer, 1978. 293p., illus. (History of Canadian cities)

Also published in a French language edition.
Published in collaboration with the National Museum of Man.

Canadiana, 1979. AEA

3012 Fort Edmonton Historical Association. Edmonton, the way it was. Edmonton: Fort Edmonton Historical Foundation, 1977. 158p. (chiefly ill.)

Also issued in a deluxe edition, limited to 500 copies.

Canadiana, 1979. AEA

3013 Fort Macleod History Book Committee. Fort Macleod - Our colourful past. A history of the town of Fort Macleod from 1874 to 1924. Fort Macleod: Fort Macleod History Book Committee, 1977. 531p. ill.

Canadiana, 1978. AEA

3014 **Fortier**, Hilaire J. Lamoureux, ses débuts, ses pionniers. The history, the pioneers. Alberta golden jubilee, 1905-1955. Lamoureux: Lamoureux Jubilee Committee, 1955. (4), 46 leaves.

Cover title. Duplicated.
Text in French and English.
Editor, H.J. Fortier.

Glenbow. ACG

3015 **Fowler**, Mrs. Gordon. The Big Valley story. Golden memories, 1914-1964. Stettler: Stettler Independent, 1964. 112p. ill.

Cover title.
Compiled by Mrs. Gordon Fowler.

Glenbow. ACG

3016 **Fowlie**, Helen Elizabeth (Holt). Social Plains School District golden jubilee booklet, 1913-1963. Bindloss: Social Plains Women's Institute, 1963. (75)p. ill.

Cover title.

Glenbow. ACG

3017 **Fraser**, William Bernard. Calgary. Calgary: Alberta Teachers' Assocation, Calgary Public Schools Local, 1967. (8), 134p. ill.

Published by Holt, Rinehart and Winston of Canada.
Published in commemoration of Canada's Centennial year.

Glenbow. ACG

3018 Freedom and Naples Farm Women's Union. The history of the Freedom and Naples communities. Freedom: Farm Women's Union of Alberta, Freedom and Naples Local, 1963. 123p. ill.

Glenbow. ACG

3019 Freeway west. Falun: Falun Historical Society, 1974. 1072p. ill.

Editors, Gordon R. and Mrs. Gladys Erickson.
History of County of Wetaskwin No.10.

Canadiana 1977. AEA

3020 Frog Lake Community Club. Land of red and white. Heinsburg: Frog Lake Community Club Book Committee, 1977. 440p. ill.

Printed by Inter-Collegiate Press, Winnipeg.

Canadiana, 1978. **AEA**

3021 From frontier days in Leduc and District. 65 years of progress, 1891-1956. Leduc: Leduc Town Council, 1957. 184p. ill.

Jubilee Booklet Committee, Mrs. Frances McInnis, Ivan Maclaren, W.A. Bell. Editor-in-chief, C.H. Stout.
Printed by Representative Publishing. **AEA**

3022 Frontier Calgary, town, city and region, 1875-1914. Edited by Anthony W. Rasporich and Henry C. Klassen. Calgary: McClelland and Stewart West, 1975. xii, 306p. ill.

Papers presented at a Conference held to mark the Calgary Centennial.

Canadiana, 1976. **AEA**

3023 Frontier days. 50 golden years. Bonnyville: Bonnyville Tribune, 1957. 34p. (incl. advts.) ill.

Caption title.
A supplement to the *Bonnyville Tribune*, August 2, 1957. **AECSJ**

3024 **Gaetz**, Annie Louise (Siddall). The park country. A history of Red Deer and district. Rev. ed. Red Deer: 1960. ix, 1, 173p.

Printed by Evergreen Press, Vancouver.
First edition, 1948 (Peel 4095).

Canadiana, 1961. **AEA**

3025 **Gershaw**, Fred William. Highlights of Medicine Hat and district. Medicine Hat: s.l., n.d. 13p. ill.

Canadiana, 1963. **OONL**

3026 **Gershaw**, Fred William. Medicine Hat. Early days in southern Alberta. Medicine Hat: s.n., 1954. 70p. ill.

Glenbow. **ACG**

3027 **Gershaw**, Fred William. Sammis, the Medicine Hat. Medicine Hat: Val Marshall Printing, 1967. 240p. ill.

A history of Medicine Hat.

Glenbow. **ACG**

3028 **Gershaw**, Fred William. The short grass area. A brief history of southern Alberta. s.l., s.n.: 1956. 123p. ill.

Glenbow. **ACG**

3029 **Gest**, Lillian. History of Moraine Lake in the Canadian Rockies, east of Lake Louise, Alberta. s.l.: s.n., 1970. 39p. ill., map.

Ceessa. **AEA**

3030 **Gest**, Lillian. History of Mount Assiniboine in the Canadian Rockies. Banff: L. Gest, 1979. 60p. ill.

Printed by Banff Craig & Canyon.

AEA

3031 **Gibson**, Jean. The old house. A history of The Spruces, a stopping house and farm home. Red Deer: Fletcher Print, 1975. 21p. ill.

Cover title.
The Spruces was moved to Innisfail in 1972.

Canadiana 1977.

AEA

3032 **Gilpin**, John Frederick. The city of Strathcona, 1891-1912. We see just ahead the glory of the sun in his might. Ottawa: National Library of Canada, 1979. vii, 169 leaves. (Canadian theses on microfiche, 36384)

Thesis (M.A.), University of Alberta.
Microfiche of typescript.
A history of Strathcona, before amalgamation with Edmonton.

Canadiana, 1979.

AEU

3033 **Girard**, Arthur J. Plamondon homecoming 73. An historical booklet and a community birthday calendar. Co-ordinator, Arthur J. Girard. s.l.: s.n., 1973. 1v.

Duplicated.
Caption title.
On cover: Chronological, genealogical, historical calendar of Plamondon, Alberta, 65th anniversary, 1973, July 1-8.

Ceessa.

AEA

3034 Girl Guides of Canada. Calgary area. Camp Mockingbird. Calgary: Girl Guides of Canada, 1964. 22 leaves.

Caption title.
Collection of articles on the history of the Calgary area.

Canadiana, 1965.

OONL

3035 Glendale Women's Institute. Taming the prairie wool. A history of the districts of Glendale, Westminster and Bearspaw, west of Calgary. Glendale: Glendale Women's Institute, 1965. 190p. ill.

Glenbow.

ACG

3036 Golden jubilee, Round Hill, Alberta, 1905-1955. s.l.: s.n., 1955. (16)p. ill.

Glenbow.

ACG

3037 The good land of Alberta. Carbon district, crop, coal and cattle centre, 1895-1962. Carbon: s.n., 1962. 24p. (incl. advts.) ill.

Glenbow.

ACG

3038 **Gore**, Lily Grace (Graham). M.D. of Kneehill, 1904-1967. Kneehill: Municipal District of Kneehill Council, 1968. 328p. ill.

Published as a Centennial Project.

Glenbow. **ACG**

3039 **Grahn**, Laurie. Village of Hay Lakes 50th anniversary, 1928-1978. s.l.: s.n., 1978. 39p.

Duplicated.
Cover title. **AEA**

3040 **Grant**, John W. Vignettes of old south Calgary. Growing up in the early days. Calgary: Century Calgary Publications, 1975. iv, 47p. ill.

Also published as part of *Past and present*, which was issued as v.1 of the Century Calgary historical series.

Ceessa. **AEA**

3041 Granum History Committee. Leavings by trail. Granum: Granum HistoryCommittee, 1977. 557p. ill.

Canadiana, 1979. **AEU**

3042 **Gratz**, Humphrey. Footprints on Mi-Chig-Wun. Memoirs of Sunnyslope pioneers. Sunnyslope: Sunnyslope History Book Committee, 1973. 608p. ill.

Canadiana, 1975. **AEU**

3043 **Green**, Margaret V. The 49ers. Stories of the early settlers. Kitscoty: Thomasville Community Club, 1967. (5), 46p.

Duplicated.
A centennial project of the Thomasville Community Club.
On cover: Homestead stories of Twp 49-2 & 49-3-W4.
History of the area southwest of Lloydminster.

Glenbow. **ACG**

3044 Greenlawn Centennial Committee. In retrospect, 1967. Dewberry: Greenlawn Centennial Committee, 1968. 272p. ill.

Cover title.
Printed by Inter-Collegiate Press, Winnipeg.
A history of the area north of Dewberry.

Glenbow. **ACG**

3045 **Griffith**, Donald. Notes on the Goodridge area. Goodridge: D. Griffith, 1967. 1v. ill.

Duplicated. **AEU**

3046 **Hall**, Cecil T. The golden years of Redcliff. Redcliff: C.T. Hall, 1962. (3), 80, (2)p. ill.

Duplicated.

Glenbow. **ACG**

3047 **Hambly**, J.R.Stan. The Battle River country. An historical sketch of Duhamel and district. New Norway: Duhamel Historical Society, 1974. 374p. ill.

Editor: J.R. Stan Hambly.
Printed by D.W. Friesen & Sons, Calgary.
History of the area north of New Norway.

Canadiana, 1975.

3048 Hand Hills Book Committee. Hand Hills heritage. Hand Hills: Hand Hills Book Committee, 1968. iii, 579p. ill.

Printed by College Press, College Heights.

Glenbow. **ACG**

3049 Hanna Jubilee Committee. Pioneer days of Hanna and district. 50th anniversary ed., Aug. 7, 1962. Hanna: Hanna Jubilee Committee, 1962. 92p. (incl. advts.) ill.

Printed by the Hanna Herald,.
Cover title.

Glenbow. **ACG**

3050 **Hansen**, Evelyn M. Brick's Hill, Berwyn and beyond. Berwyn: Berwyn Centennial Committee, 1968. iii, 282p, (12)p. ill.

Subtitle on cover *A history of Berwyn and district*.
Editor, E.M. Hansen.
Printed by Commercial Printers, Edmonton.

Ceessa, Glenbow. **ACG**

3051 **Hardin**, Samuel H. History of greater Vegreville. Vegreville: S. Hardin, 1969. 253(i.e. 279)p. ill.

Duplicated.

Glenbow. **ACG**

3052 **Harrison**, Irene. Lure of the homestead. Ohaton: Ohaton Community Book Club, 1977. 388p. ill.

Printed by Friesen Printers, Calgary.
Edited by Irene Harrison.

Canadiana, 1978. **AEA**

3053 **Hart**, Edward John. Diamond hitch. The early outfitters and guides of Banff and Jasper. Banff: Summerthought, 1979. 160p. ill., maps.

Canadiana, 1979. **AEA**

3054 **Hart**, Edward John. The history of the french-speaking community of Edmonton, 1795-1935. Edmonton: University of Alberta, 1971. viii, 216 leaves.

Thesis (M.A.), University of Alberta, 1971.
Typescript.

Canadian theses. **AGU**

3055 Harvest of memories. Lethbrige: Majestic-Farrell Lake Women's Institute, 1968. (4), 367p. ill.

Cover title.
Printed by Southern Printing.

Glenbow. **ACG**

3056 **Hayhurst**, William. A brief history of the Rocky Mountains. Jasper: William Hayhurst, 1957. 15p. ill.

Canadiana, 1957. **OONL**

3057 Hays 25th Book Committee. From sod to silver. Lethbridge: Herald Printers, 1977. 247p. ill.

On cover: Hays, 1952-1977.

Canadiana, 1978. **AEA**

3058 Heaton Moor and Brookland Book Committee. Seventy years gone by. History of Heaton Moor and Brookland. s.l.: Brookland Research Society, 1979. 97 (2)p. ill.

Cover title.
History of the area south east of Barrhead. **AEA**

3059 **Hedley**, Ralph. East of Beaver Hills. A history of Lamont, its people and their achievements, 1892-1955. Lamont: R. Hedley, 1955. 78 leaves.

Duplicated. **AEA**

3060 **Heinsen**, Annie. Grub-axe to grain. Spruce View: Spruce View School Area Historical Society, 1973. 289p. ill.

Leader: Mrs. Fred. Heinsen.
Printed by D.W. Frisen & Sons, Calgary.

Canadiana, 1974. **AEA**

3061 Hesketh Pope Lease Historical Committee. Memories, yours and mine. A history of Beveridge Lake, East View, Garrett, Hesketh, Humbolt, Kirby, Lenox, Marne, Webbs school districts. Hesketh: Hesketh Pope Lease Historical Society, 1972. vii, 663p. ill.

Printed by D.W. Friesen & Sons, Calgary.
History of the area east of Drumheller.

Glenbow. **ACG**

3062 **Hewitt**, Dorcas Alma. The Fort Pitt trail. Mostly tales of pioneer days. Compiled by Dorcas Alma Hewitt. Lloydminster, 1968. 302p. ill.

History of settlement in the Lloydminster area. **AEA**

3063 **Hicken**, John Orvin. Events leading to the settlement of the communities of Cardston, Magrath, Stirling and Raymond, Alberta. Logan: Utah State University, 1968. 130 leaves.

Thesis (M.Sc.), Utah State University, 1968.
Typescript.

Dew.

3064 **Hicken**, John Orvin. Raymond, 1901-1967. Compiled by J. Orvin Hicken assisted by Kay B Redd and John L. Evans. Raymond: Raymond Chamber of Commerce, 1967. 700p. ill.

Cover title *Roundup*.
Printed by the Lethbridge Herald.

Canadiana, 1968. **AEA**

3065 High Prairie Farm Women's Union Centennial Book Committee. Pioneers who blazed the trail. High Prairie: Farm Women's Union of Alberta, High Prairie Local 204, 1967. 320p. ill.

Cover title *A history of High Prairie and District*.
Lithographed by South Peace News (High Prairie).

Glenbow. **ACG**

3066 High River Pioneers' and Old Timers' Association. Leaves from the medicine tree. A history of the area influenced by the tree, and biographies of pioneers and old timers who came under its spell prior to 1900. Lethbridge: High River Pioneers' and Old Timers' Association, 1960. 528p. ill.

Printed by The Lethbridge Herald.

Glenbow. **ACG**

3067 **Higinbotham**, David. When the west was young. Lethbridge: Hamilton Trek, 1978. 328p. ill.

Experiences in the Macleod-Lethbridge district.
First published Toronto, Ryerson, 1933 (Peel 3337).
Reprinted, with an introduction by Norman Lindsay Higinbotham. **ACP**

3068 Hilda Town and Country Ladies Club. Hilda's golden heritage. Hilda: Hilda Town and Country Ladies Club, 1974. 305p. ill.

Canadiana, 1975. **OONL**

3069 Hill Spring Cultural Society. Hill Spring and its people. Hill Spring: Hill Spring Cultural Society, 1975. 406p. ill., map.

Printed by D.W. Friesen and Sons, Calgary.

Ceessa. **AEA**

3070 Hills of Home Historical Committee. The hills of home. Milk River: Hills of Home Historical Committee, 1975. 220p. ill., maps.

Printed by Southern Printing, Lethbridge.
Includes histories of St. Kilda, Knapper, Aden and Pinhorn.

Ceessa. **AEA**

3071 Hines Creek High school. History of Hines Creek, 1867-1967. Centennial ed. Hines Creek: Hines Creek High School, 1967. (16)p. ill.

Printed by Inter-Collegiate Press, Manitoba.
Caption title *The overall summary of the history of Hines Creek*.
No title page. Title taken from dedication.

Glenbow. **ACG**

3072 History of Lomond and district. Lethbridge: Southern Printing, 1966. 371p. ill. **AEA**

3073 **Hogg**, Archie L. Tails and trails, 1900-1972. Compiled and edited by East Longview Historical Society. Longview: Tails and Trails History Book Society, 1973. 432p. ill.

Cover sub-title *A history of Longview and surrounding area*.
Archie L. Hogg, President of the Work Committee.
Lithographed by North West Printing & Lithographing Ltd.

Ceessa. **AEA**

3074 **Holmgren**, Eric Joseph. Isaac M. Barr and the Britannia Colony. Edmonton: University of Alberta, 1964. 174 leaves.

Thesis (M.A.), University of Alberta, 1964.
Typescript.

Canadian theses. **AEU**

3075 **Howe**, Helen D. Seventy-five years along the Red Deer River. Calgary: D.W. Friesen, 1971. viii, 375p. ill.

A history of the Red Deer Valley in eastern Alberta.

Glenbow. **ACG**

3076 Hub of three hamlets. Community cooperation east of Calgary. Calgary: Century Calgary Publications, 1975. (1v.)

Also issued as part of *Communities of Calgary*, issued as v.2 of Century Calgary Historical Series.

3077 **Huddlestun**, Frederick Molden. A history of the settlement and building up of the area in S.W. Alberta bordering Waterton Park on the north, from 1889. Pincher Creek: F.M. Huddlestun, 1969. (1) 118p.

Cover title. Duplicated.

Glenbow. **ACG**

3078 **Hughes**, John. A history of Athabina. Athabina: J. Hughes, 1962. 11 leaves.

Duplicated.
Produced for the Athabina Athletic Association Homecoming, August 5, 1962.
History of the area between the Athabasca and Pembina Rivers. **AEA**

3079 **Hugo**, Pauline. Memoirs of the Ghost Pine homesteaders. Three Hills: Ghost Pine Community Group, 1954. 196p. ill.

Printer's note: Mrs. Pauline Hugo, continuity.

Printed by Capital Printers.
History of the area east of Three Hills.

Glenbow.

ACG

3080 **Hyrnchuk**, Audrey. Memories, Redwater and district. Redwater: Redwater Pioneers Club, 1972. v, 227p. ill.

Printed by D.W. Friesen & Sons, Calgary.
Compiled and edited by Mrs. Audrey Hrynchuck and Mrs. Jean Klufas.

Glenbow.

ACG

3081 I remember Peace River, Alberta and adjacent districts. Peace River: Women's Institute of Peace River, 1976. 2v. ill.

Contents: 1. 1800's-1913. Edited by Yvette T.M. Mahé.-2. 1914-1916. Editor, Katharine E.E. Hoskin.

Canadiana, 1975.

AEA

3082 Inglewood and Ramsay. Cradle of Calgary. Calgary: Century Calgary Publications, 1975. (1v.)

Also issued as part of *Communities of Calgary*, issued as v.2 of the Century Calgary Historical Series.

3083 Innisfail and District Historical Society. Innisfail, 75 years a town, 1903-1978. Innisfail: Innisfail and District Historical Society, 1978. 76p. ill.

Ceessa.

AEA

3084 **Jackknife**, Albina. Elizabeth Metis Settlement. A local history. Elizabeth: Elizabeth Metis Settlement Association, 1977. vi, 61p. ill., map.

Cover title.
Albina Jackknife, Director of History Book.
Printed by Friesen Printers, Altona, Manitoba.

Ceessa.

AEA

3085 **Jackson**, Joyce. Luscar come back. s.l.: s.n., 1978. 103p. ill.

Cover title. Duplicated.

AEA

3086 **James**, Jean. Hanna North. Edited by Jean James. Hanna: Hanna North Book Club, 1978. 882p. ill.

Printed by Robins Southern Printing, Lethbridge.
Cover title *Hanna North. A rural history, 1908-1978*.

Canadiana, 1979.

AEA

3087 **James**, Jean. This was Endiang. Endiang: J. James, 1969. 122p. ill.

Printed by Modern Press, Saskatoon.

Canadiana, 1971.

AEA

3088 **Jankunis**, Frank J. Southern Alberta. A regional perspective. Dr. F.Jankunis, editor. Illustrations by G.S. Young. Lethbridge: University of Lethbridge, 1972. 123p. ill.

A collection of essays on the geography, natural history, settlement and history of southern Alberta.

Glenbow. **ACG**

3089 **Jensen**, Ethel. Tributaries of the Blindman. College Heights: Parkland Colourpress, 1974. 1002p. ill., map.

Signed on inserted slip, Ethel Jensen, Ken Smithson.
History of ten school districts now served by the centralized Bluffton School.
Produced by a Book Committee originating with the Great Two Day Springdale Homecoming Picnic of 1972.

Ceessa. **AEA**

3090 **Jenson**, Bodil Jelhof. The county of Mountain View, Alberta. A study in community development, 1890-1925. Edmonton: University of Alberta, 1972. x, 203 leaves.

Thesis (M.A.), University of Alberta, 1972.
Typescript.

Canadian theses. **AEU**

3091 **John Wilson Elementary School**, Innisfail. A look at yesterday. Innisfail: John Wilson Elementary School, 1974. 45p.(chiefly ill.)

Cover title. Duplicated.

Ceessa. **AEA**

3092 **Johnson**, G. Rudolph. The Northfield settlement, 1913-1969. By Mr. and Mrs. G.R. Johnston. Grande Prairie: Menzies Printers, 1969. 78p. ill.

The Northfield settlement is now part of the district of La Glace.

Glenbow. **ACG**

3093 **Johnson**, Leroy Peter Vernon. Strictly for posterity. Edmonton: L.P.V. Johnson, 1974. viii, 229p. ill.

Account of pioneering in Stavely, Alberta. **AEA**

3094 **Jorgenson**, Robert D. The squatters. Westlock: R.D. Jorgenson, 1966. 8p.

Cover title.
History of early settlement in the Westlock and Barrhead Districts. **AEA**

3095 **Jouan**, Marion L. Tomahawk trails. Tomahawk: Tomahawk Trail Book Club, 1974. viii, 612p. ill.

Printed by D.W. Friesen and Sons, Calgary.
Editor-in-chief: Marion Jouan.

Canadiana, 1975. **AEU**

3096 K.I.K. Historical Committee. K.I.K. country. Keoma: K.I.K. Historical Committee, 1974. viii, 743p. ill.

A history of the Kathyrn, Irricana and Keoma communities.

Canadiana, 1975.

AEA

3097 **Kasa**, Gaylerde. Trails and trials. Meeting Creek: Meeting Creek School, 1969. 43p. ill.

Duplicated.
Editor in Chief, Gaylerde Kasa, assistant editor, Ronnie Bjorge.

AEA

3098 **Kilgour**, Betty. As the years go by. Three Hills: Three Hills Rural Community Group, 1970. 630p. ill.

Editor: Betty Kilgour.
History of Three Hills and District.
Printed by D.W. Friesen and Sons, Calgary.

Glenbow.

ACG

3099 Kinette Club of Didsbury. Echoes of an era. Compiled by the Kinette Club of Didsbury. Didsbury: Didsbury Booster, 1969. 230p. ill.

Subtitle on cover *History of Didsbury and district.*

Glenbow.

ACG

3100 **Kitchen**, Melba. Buffalo trails and tales. Compiled by the ladies of the Gilt Edge Booster Club. Wainwright: Gilt Edge Ladies Booster Club, 1973. 483p. ill.

Mrs. Melba Kitchen, editor.
A history of the Municipal District of Wainright.

Canadiana, 1974.

AEA

3101 **Klein**, Mary. Ten dollars and a dream. Dixonville: L.I.F.E. History Committee, 1977. 286p. ill.

Editor: Mary Klein, Associate editor, Margaret I. Sorenson.
Printed by Friesen Printers, Calgary.
History of Beaton Creek, Brissen, Craven Lake, Dixonville, Golden Ridge. Grayling Creek, Hasell and Silver Hills.

Canadiana, 1978.

AEA

3102 **Kubota**, Carol. Sirens and cinders. A history of the Calgary Fire Department. Calgary: Century Calgary e Kinette Club of Didsbury. Didsbury: Didsbury Booster, 8p. des of Canada, 1964. 22 leaves. Women's nor anff Publications, 1975. 63p. ill.

Also published as part of *At your service, Part one*, which was issued as v.5 of the Century Calgary Historical Series.

Canadiana, 1977.

ACG

3103 Lac La Biche Heritage Society. Lac La Biche yesterday and today. Lac La Biche: Lac La Biche Heritage Society, 1975. 198p. ill. maps.

Printed by D.W. Friesen & Sons, Calgary.

Canadiana, 1975. **AEA**

3104 Lac Ste. Anne Historical Society. Archives Committee. West of the fifth. A history of Lac Ste. Anne Municipality. Edmonton: Institute of Applied Art, 1959. vii, 233p. ill.

Glenbow. **ACG**

3105 Lacombe and District Board of Trade. The Lacombe story, our heritage. One hundred years of progress. Lacombe: Lacombe Globe, 1967. 48p. ill.

A centennial project.

Glenbow. **ACG**

3106 Lacombe Rural History Club. Wagon trails to hard top. History of Lacombe and area. Lacombe: Lacombe Rural History Club, 1972. vii, 906p. ill.

Printed by D.W. Friesen & Sons, Calgary.

Glenbow. **ACG**

3107 Lamerton Historical Society. Land of the lakes. A story of the settlement and development of the country west of Buffalo Lake. Lamerton: Lamerton Historical Society, 1974. 544p. ill.

Ceessa. **AEA**

3108 The Langdon legend. Langdon: Langdon Women's Institute, 1966. 155p. ill.

Cover title.
Printed by Times Press, Calgary.

Dew. **AEU**

3109 The lantern years. Buffalo Park to Neutral Hills. Hughenden: Hughenden Women's Institute, 1967. 301p. ill.

Printed by Intercollegiate Press, Winnipeg.
Editorial committee: Mary Burpee and others.

Glenbow. **ACG**

3110 **Larson**, Lena. Pioneer round-up. A history of Albritt, Demmitt, Goodfare, Hythe, Lymburn, Valhalla. Hythe: Pioneer History Society of Hythe and Area, 1972. v, 800p. ill.

Canadiana, 1973. **AEU**

3111 **Law**, D.B. History of the Glenwood District. Glenwood: Glenwood Village Council, 1969. 7p.

Dew.

3112 **Leggett**, Viola (Shanks). Gem golden jubilee, 1914-1964. Gem: Gem Ladies Club, 1964. 56p. ill.

Cover title.
Compiled by Viola Leggett and Edna George.
Printed by the Brooks Bulletin.

Canadiana, 1969.

AEA

3113 Lethbridge Herald. Alberta's golden jubilee. Lethbridge: Lethbridge Herald, 1955. 68p.(chiefly ill.)

Cover title.
Half title *50 years a province*.
History of Lethbridge and Lethbridge organizations.

AEU

3114 Lethbridge Herald. Alberta's golden jubilee edition, 1905-1955. Lethbridge: Lethbridge Herald, 1955. 32p.(incl. advts.) ill.

Special edition of June 25, 1955.

ACG

3115 Lethbridge Herald. Alberta's golden jubilee edition, 1905-1955. Lethbridge: Lethbridge Herald, 1955. (96)p. (incl. advts.) ill.

Special edition of June 25, 1955.

ACG

3116 Lethbridge Herald. Cardston 75th anniversary, 1887-1962. Lethbridge: Lethbridge Herald, 1962. 48p.(incl. advts.) ill.

In 2 sections, each with 24 numbered pages.
Special edition of June 23, 1962.

Glenbow.

ACG

3117 Lethbridge Herald. Golden anniversary and progress edition, 1907-1957. Lethbridge: Lethbridge Herald, 1957. 256p.(incl. advts.)

Dew.

ACG

3118 Lewisville pioneers. Wetaskiwin: Peace Hills Printers, 1967. 111, (1)p. ill.

History and biography of the Battle Lake, Rose Briar, and Star School Districts.

Glenbow.

ACG

3119 **Loiselle**, Lorraine. They came, they saw, they lived. Ils sont venus, ils ont vu, ils y vécurent. s.l.: s.n., 1973. 38, 47p.

By Lorraine Loiselle, Joanne Gagnon, Myriam Laberge.
Duplicated.
Text in English and French.
History of Smoky River District.

Ceessa.

AEA

3120 Lomond Book Committee. History of Lomond and district. Lomond: Lomond Book Committee, 1966. 371p. ill.

Printed by Southern Printing, Lethbridge.

Dew.

AEU

3121 Lougheed Women's Institute. Verdant valleys in and around Lougheed. Lougheed: Lougheed Women's Institute, 1972. viii, 488p. ill.

Printed by D.W. Friesen & Sons, Calgary.

Glenbow. **ACG**

3122 **Luxton**, Eleanor Georgina. Banff, Canada's first national park. A history and a memory of Rocky Mountains Park. Banff: Summerthought, 1975. x, 157p. ill. **AEA**

3123 **Lyalta**, Ardenode, Dalroy Historical Society. Along the fireguard trail. A history of Lyalta-Ardenode-Dalroy Districts. Lyalta: Lyalta, Ardenode, Dalroy Historical Committee, 1979. 343p. ill.

Printed by Friesen Printers, Calgary. **AECYR**

3124 **Lynes**, Edith M. Brief history of Foremost, 1913-1963. Golden jubilee Foremost. Foremost: Foremost Jubilee Committee, 1963. 43p.

Cover title. Duplicated. **ACG**

3125 **Lynn**, Esther. Derbytown echoes. A history of Rockwood, Lobley, Eagle Point, James River. Youngstown: Derbytown Book Club, 1975. 217p. ill., maps.

Printed by D.W. Friesen & Sons, Calgary.
History of the area north of Sundre.

Canadiana, 1975. **AEA**

3126 M.I.P. History Book Committee. Spurs and shovels along the Royal Line. Patricia: M.I.P. History Book Committee, 1979. 448p. ill.

Printed by Friesen Printers, Calgary.
History of the Millicent, Iddlesleigh and Patricia areas. **AEA**

3127 **MacDonald**, George Heath. Edmonton, fort - house - factory. Edmonton: Douglas Printing, 1959. 236p. ill.

Glenbow. **ACG**

3128 **MacDonald**, George Heath. Fort Augustus-Edmonton. Northwest trails and traffic. Edmonton: Douglas Printing, 1954. (21), 28-255p. ill.

Glenbow. **ACG**

3129 **MacEwan**, John Walter Grant. Calgary cavalcade from fort to fortune. Edmonton: Institute of Applied Art, 1958. x, 246p. ill.

Glenbow. **ACG**

3130 **MacGregor**, James Grierson. The Battle River Valley. Saskatoon: Western Producer Prairie Books, 1976. 174p. ill.

Canadiana, 1977. **AEU**

3131 **MacGregor**, James Grierson. Edmonton. A history. Edmonton: Hurtig, 1967. 326p. ill.

Partly subsidized by the Edmonton Civic Centennial Committee.
Facsimile of first issue of *The Bulletin* in pocket.
Also, 2d ed., 1975, 340p.

Glenbow.

ACG

3132 **MacGregor**, James Grierson. The Klondike rush through Edmonton, 1897-1898. Toronto: McClelland and Stewart, 1970. xvi, 274p. ill.

Glenbow.

ACG

3133 **MacGregor**, James Grierson. Pack saddles to Tête Jaune Cache. Toronto: McClelland and Stewart, 1962. 256p.

New ed. published 1973, Edmonton, Hurtig. 256p.
The opening up of northern Alberta, through the eyes of James Shand-Harvey.

Glenbow.

ACG

3134 **MacGregor**, James Grierson. Paddle wheels to bucket-wheels on the Athabasca. Toronto: McClelland and Stewart, 1974. xii, 190p. ill.

Canadiana, 1975.

AEU

3135 **MacLean**, Hec. Waterhole and the land north of the Peace. Edited by Hec MacLean. Fairview: Waterhole Old Timers Association, 1970. 304p. ill.

Glenbow.

ACG

3136 **Macleod Sketch Club**, Fort Macleod. Story of Macleod. Fort Macleod: Macleod Sketch Club, 1955. 28p. ill.

Printed by Kellaway Print., Calgary.

Glenbow.

ACG

3137 Magrath and District History Association. Irrigation builders. Magrath: Magrath and District History Association, 1974. 545p. ill.

Printed by Southern Printing, Lethbridge.

Canadiana, 1977.

AEA

3138 **Maloff**, Greta. Recollections of the homestead trails, 1900-1978. Bearberry: Bearberry Wapitana Society, 1978. 579p. ill.

Printed by Sundre Round-up.
Cover title *Recollections of homestead trails. History of Bearberry and Sunberry Valleys.*
History of the area west of Sundre.

AEA

3139 Mannville and District Old Timers' Association. Trails to Mannville. Mannville: Mannville and District Old Timers' Association, 1976. 138p. ill.

Canadiana, 1977.

OONL

3140 **Mansell**, Erica. Wheels to Woodville. s.l.: s.n., 1978. 190p. ill.

Edited by Erica Mansell and Lorraine Fowler.
History of the Woodville School District, midway between In nisfree and Viking.

Ceessa. **AEA**

3141 **Martin**, Isabel. Forests to grainfields. Compiled by the History Book Committee. Berrymoor: Berrymoor-Carnwood Historical Society, 1977. 394p. ill.

Editor, Mrs. Isabel Martin.
Printed by Friesen Printers, Calgary.
The Berrymoor-Carnwood Historical Society comprised the Berrymoor 3Bs Club and the Carnwood Country Club Society.
Covers Aliske, Berrymoor, Breton, Buck Creek, Carnwood, Funnell, Lindale, New Moose Hill, North End and Onion Creek.

Canadiana, 1979. **AEA**

3142 **Martin**, John Julius. The Dinosaur Valley, Drumheller, Alberta. Rosebud: John J. Martin, 1971. 54p. ill., maps.

Ceessa. **AEA**

3143 **Martin**, John Julius. The prairie hub. A challenge to thoughtful Canadians. An outline history of early western events. From the Hand Hills to the Buffalo Hills. Edited by Mrs. Edythe M. Groves. Strathmore: Strathmore Standard, 1967. (17), 243, (4) p. ill.

History of Gleichen and District.

Glenbow. **ACG**

3144 **Martin**, John Julius. The Rosebud trail. Edited by Betty-Rose Jenkins. 1963. 187p. ill.

History of the Rosebud Creek district of Alberta.

Glenbow. **ACG**

3145 **Maruschak**, Pauline. A glimpse into the past. Hay Lakes and District. Compiled by Pauline Maruschak. Hay Lakes: Hay Lakes Municipal Library Board, 1967. 63p.

Ceessa. **AEA**

3146 Marwayne Chamber of Commerce. Our golden years, Marwayne, Alberta, 1926-1976. Marwayne: Marwayne Chamber of Commerce, 1976. 61p. ill.

AEA

3147 Marwayne Farm Women's Union. Pioneering the parklands. Marwayne: Farm Women's Union of Alberta, Marwayne Local, 1967. 208p. ill.

Printed by Inter-Collegiate Press, Winnipeg.

Glenbow. **ACG**

3148 **Masters**, Kathy. Beautiful fields. Bashaw: Bashaw History Committee, 1975. 200p. ill.

Printed by D.W. Friesen and Sons, Calgary.
Compiled by Kathy Masters, Marilyn Masters, Deb Williams, Sandra Schultz, Lois Hameister.

Canadiana, 1975.

AEA

3149 **Maw**, Margaret. Meet southern Alberta. Stories by Margaret Maw. Edited by W.E. Ross. Calgary: Southern Alberta Pioneers and Old Timers Association, 1954. 116p. ill.

Printed by John D. McAra.
Published in aid of the association's Memorial Building Fund.

Glenbow.

ACG

3150 **McCall**, Ralph Lewis. The Acme story, 1910-1960. Acme: Sentinel, 1960. (5) 421p. ill.

Cover title.

Glenbow.

ACG

3151 **McCarty**, Richard Frances. Fort Assiniboine, Alberta, 1823-1914. Fur trade post to settled district. Ottawa: National Library of Canada, 1976. x, 278 leaves. (Canadian theses on microfiche, 30752)

Thesis (M.A.), University of Alberta, 1976.
Microfiche of typescript.

U of A Theses.

AEU

3152 **McCarty**, Tom. As we remember Big Valley. Big Valley: T. McCarty, 1974. 196p. ill.

Cover title.
Printed by D.W. Friesen & Sons, Calgary.

Canadiana, 1975.

AEA

3153 **McKechnie**, Christine. Homestead memories. Compiled by the Lloydminster Quota Club under the direction of Miss Christine McKechnie. Saskatoon: Freeman Publishing, 1967. 115p.

Reminiscences of pioneers in the Lloydminster area.

Canadiana, 1968.

AEA

3154 **McNeill**, Leishman. The Calgary Herald's tales of the old town. 2d. ed. Calgary: Calgary Herald, 1966. (6), 102p. ill.

Reprinted from a series of articles written for the *Calgary Herald* during Calgary's 75th anniversary celebrations.
1st ed. 1951, with title *Tales of the old town* (Peel 4253).

Glenbow.

ACG

3155 **McRoberts**, Mrs. Dick. The times of Irma. A history of Irma & district. Mrs. Dick McRoberts, editor. Irma: Irma 60th Anniversary Committee, 1972. 118p. ill.

Printed by the Wainwright Star Chronicle.

Canadiana, 1977.

AEA

3156 Mecca Glen Centennial Committee. Mecca Glen memories. Ponoka: Mecca Glen Centennial Committee, 1968. 326p. ill.

Edited by the residents of Asker, Water Glen, Concord, Eureka, Climax, Magic, Calumet, Schultz, Ellice and Rutherford.

Glenbow. **ACG**

3157 **Meeres**, E.L. The homesteads that nurtured a city. The history of Red Deer, 1880-1905. Red Deer: Fletcher Printing, 1978. iv, 287p. ill.

Cover title.

Canadiana, 1979. **AEA**

3158 Memories of Fairgrove district. Fairgrove: Community Press, 1977. 106p. ill.

Duplicated.
Introduction by Mrs. Ben Weber.

Ceessa. **AEA**

3159 **Merriken**, Ellenor (Ranghild). The Nose Hills country. Federalsburg, Md.: Ellenor Merriken, 1960. 4, 133, 1p.

Printed in Canada.
Reminiscences of a Norwegian pioneer family from the 1910s to the 1930s.

Glenbow. **ACG**

3160 **Michael**, Hope Hargrave. 90 years at Elkwater Lake, Cypress Hills, Alberta. An interesting account of the early days in the Elkwater area, written in 1948. Medicine Hat: Medicine Hat Historical and Museum Foundation, 1972. 36p.

Glenbow. **ACG**

3161 Millarville Historical Society. Foothills echoes. Millarville: Millarville Historical Society, 1979. viii, 571p. ill.

Printed by Friesen Printers, Calgary.
Sequel to *Our Foothills*, Millarville, Kew, Priddis and Bragg Creek Historical Society, 1975.
History of the Millarville and Kew districts. **AEA**

3162 **Millarville**, Kew, Priddis and Bragg Creek Historical Society. Our foothills. Sarcee Indian Reserve, Bow-Crow Forest, Sheep Run. Calgary: Millarville, Kew, Priddis and Bragg Creek Historical Society, 1975. 486p. ill.

Printed by D.W. Friesen & Sons, Calgary.

Canadiana, 1976. **AEU**

3163 Millet and District Historical Society. Tales and trails of Millet. Millet: Millet and District Historical Society, 1978. 2v. ill.

Ceessa. **AEA**

3164 Milo and District Historical Society. Snake Valley. A history of Lake McGregor and area. Milo: Milo and District Historical Society, 1973. iv,

610p. ill.

Printed by D.W. Friesen & Sons, Calgary.

Canadiana, 1974.

AEA

3165 **Moore**, Winnie. Across the Smoky. Debolt: Debolt and District Pioneer Museum Society, 1978. 357p. ill.

Editors: Winnie and Fran Moore.
A history of Debolt and district.
Printed by Friesen Printers, Calgary.

Canadiana, 1979.

AEA

3166 Morrin and District History Book Committee. Blooming prairie. A history of Morrin and district. Morrin: Morrin and District History Book Committee, 1970. 639p. ill.

Printed by D.W. Friesen & Sons, Altona, Manitoba.

Glenbow.

ACG

3167 **Morrow**, James William. Early history of Medicine Hat country. Medicine Hat: Medicine Hat Historical Society, 1964. 67p. ill.

First published, 1923, in *The News*, Medicine Hat, also separately (Peel 2861). Revised and reprinted 1974, 95, 11p.

Canadiana, 1964.

AECYR

3168 Munson Women's Institute. Munson and district. Munson: Munson Centennial Book Committee, 1967. vii, (1), 564p. ill.

Glenbow.

ACG

3169 **Murdoch**, Olive K. They builded better than they knew. The history of the building of the Northern Alberta Pioneers' and Oldtimers' Association memorial log cabin. Edmonton: Northern Alberta Pioneers' and Oldtimers' Association, 1959. 12p.

Cover title.

Glenbow.

ACG

3170 Nanton and District Historical Society. Mosquito Creek roundup. Nanton: Nanton and District Historical Society, 1976. 610p. ill.

Printed by D.W. Friesen & Sons, Calgary.
1st printing 1975, 2d printing 1976.

AEA

3171 **Nelson**, Ethel. Wild flowers and buffalo bones. A parade of pioneers. This story focuses on Lucerne School District No. 2934, established, 1913. Edmonton: Chalmers Women's Institute, 1972. vi, 109p. ill.

Duplicated.

Ceessa.

AEA

3172 **Nelson**, Marie. Saddles, sleighs and sadirons. Chestermere: Chestermere Historical Society, 1971. 645p. ill.

A history of the Conrich-Delacour area.
Also, supplement, 1978, with title *The changing scene*.

Glenbow. ACG

3173 New Dawn Seniors Club. Lengthening shadows of the Neutrals. Brownfield: New Dawn Seniors Club, 1979. 526p. ill.

Printed by Friesen Printers, Calgary.
A sequel to *Shadows of the Neutrals*, Coronation. Old-Timers Association, 1967. AEA

3174 New Norway Community Club. Memory opens the door. New Norway: New Norway Community Club, 1972. 258p. ill.

Cover title.

Ceessa. AEA

3175 **Nicholson**, Harold. Heart of gold. Fairview, 1928-1978. Edited by T. Dale Roberts. Fairview: Fairview Town Council, 1978. iv, 228p. ill.

Printed by Bulletin-Commercial, Edmonton.
Published as the jubilee project of the Fairview Town Council.

Ceessa. AEA

3176 **Nielsen**, Dorothy. Bowness Golden Jubilee, 1911-1961. Fifty years of growth. Bowness: Bowness Historical Committee of the Golden Jubilee, 1961. 44p. ill.

Editor: Mrs. Charles V. Nielsen.
Cover title *Golden Jubilee, Bowness, 1911-1961*.
Printed by Burnand Printing.
Also reproduction with title *Bowness, country homes and amusements west of Calgary*, 1975, Calgary, Century Calgary Publications.
Also published as part of *Communities of Calgary*, issued as v.2. of the Century Calgary Historical Series.

Glenbow. ACG

3177 **Nobleford**, Monarch History Book Club. Sons of wind and soil. Nobleford: Nobleford, Monarch History Book Club, 1976. 415p. ill.

A history of the Nobleford, Monarch and Kipp area.
Printed by D.W. Friesen and Sons, Calgary.

Canadiana 1977. AEA

3178 **Noel**, Oliver. A pictorial history of St. Paul and district. Prepared by Oliver Noel and family. St. Lina: Oliver Noel, 1979. 256p.

Cover title *Saint Paul des Métis 1909 to St. Paul, 1979*.
Printed by Inter-Collegiate Press, Winnipeg. AEA

3179 North Lone Pine Women's Institute. Bucking poles and butter churns. History of Lone Pine and district. Didsbury: North Lone Pine Women's

Institute, 1972. 432p. ill.

Printed by Carstairs News, Carstairs.
A history of the area between Didsbury and Three Hills.

Canadiana, 1974. **AEA**

3180 Olds Old Timers Association. See Olds first. A history of Olds and surrounding district. Olds: Olds Old Timers Association, 1968. 271p. ill.

Glenbow. **ACG**

3181 **Olecko**, Doreen. Sagitawah saga. The story of Whitecourt. Whitecourt: The Town of Whitecourt, 1976. 148p. ill.

Printed by D.W. Friesen & Sons, Calgary.

Canadiana 1977. **AEA**

3182 **Oltmann**, Charlotte Ruth. The valley of rumours. The Kananaskis. Seebe: Ribbon Creek Publishing, 1976. 141p. ill.

3183 **Ondrik**, Alice. Etzikom, 1915-1975. Etzikom: s.n., 1975. 11p.

Cover title *Etzikom, 1915-1975, diamond jubilee.*
Duplicated.

Ceessa. **AEA**

3184 Opportunities for Youth Project. A history of Stony Plain, Alberta. Stony Plain: s.n., 1971. (46) leaves. ill.

Know Your Neighbour Project.

Glenbow. **ACG**

3185 **Otter**, Andy Albert den. A social history of the Alberta Coal Branch. Edmonton: University of Alberta, 1967. xvii, 221 leaves, ill.

Thesis (M.A.), University of Alberta, 1967.
Typescript.

Canadian theses. **AEU**

3186 Our bend in the Peace. The story of Royce and Lubeck. Hines Creek: Lubeck Merrymakers Society, 1979. viii, 347p. ill.

Printed by Friesen Printers, Calgary.
History of the area west of Hines Creek. **AEA**

3187 **Parker**, James McPherson. The fur trade of Fort Chipewyan on Lake Athabaska, 1778-1835. Edmonton: University of Alberta, 1967. x, 214 leaves. ill.

Thesis (M.A.), University of Alberta, 1967.
Typescript.

Canadian theses. **AEU**

3188 **Parlby**, Beatrice Georgina. Pioneers and progress. Alix: Alix-Clive History Club, 1974. viii, 880p. ill.

Printed by D.W. Friesen & Sons, Calgary.

Canadiana, 1975.

3189 Past and present. People, places and events in Calgary. Accounts by Calgary authors. Calgary: Century Calgary Publications, 1975. 391p. ill. (Century Calgary historical series, v.1)

Each chapter also published separately.
Contents: Draper, N. Bands by the Bow. Good morning, Your Worship. Goldenberg, H. Once upon a Chinook. Reminiscences. Grant, J.W. Vignettes of old south Calgary.

Canadiana, 1977. **OONL**

3190 **Patterson**, Arthur B. Smoky River to Grande Prairie. Editor, Arthur B. Patterson. Grande Prairie: Golden Years Club of Bezanson, 1978. vi, 578p. ill.

Printed and bound by Friesen Printers, Calgary.
History of Bezanson, Crystal Creek, East Kleskun, Fitzimmons, Five Mile, Kleskun Hill, Kleskun Lake, Lindsay, Somme, Tranquility andTwilight.

Canadiana, 1979. **AEA**

3191 **Patterson**, E.R. The early history of the town of Claresholm. s.l.: s.n., 1969. 42 leaves.

Dew. **ALU**

3192 **Pawlowske**, Kathy. Treasured memories, Gwynne and district. Gwynne: Gwynne Historical Society, 1977. 632p. ill.

Printed by Co-op Press, Edmonton.

Ceessa. **AEA**

3193 **Peach**, Jack. Peach preserves. Calgary: Sandstone Publishing, 1978. 1v. ill.

Reminiscences of Calgary.
Illustrated by Willis Magee. **ACU**

3194 **Peat**, Annie Laurie Stafford. Nineteenth century Lethbridge. Lethbridge: Historical Society of Alberta, Whoop-up Country Chapter, 1978. 52p. (Historical Society of Alberta. Whoop-up Country Chapter. Occasional paper, 8)

Edited by G.E. Orchard.

Canadiana, 1979. **AEA**

3195 **Phillips**, Grace A. Tales of Tofield. Tofield: Tofield Historical Society, 1969. 355p. ill.

Edited by Grace A. Phillips.
Printed by Leduc Representatives, Lynyard Publishers.

Canadiana, 1971. **ACG**

3196 Pincher Creek and District Historical Society. Pincher Papers, 1. By Albert Colclough and Fred H. Schofield. Pincher Creek: Pincher Creek and District Historical Society, 1974. 56, 10p.

Cover title. Duplicated.
Reminiscences of two Pincher Creek pioneers.

Ceessa.

AEA

3197 Pincher Creek Historical Society. Prairie grass to mountain pass. History of the pioneers of Pincher Creek and district. Pincher Creek: Pincher Creek Historical Society, 1974. viii, 867p. ill.

Printed by D.W. Friesen & Sons, Calgary.

Canadiana, 1975.

AEA

3198 Pincher Creek Old Timers Association. Pincher Creek Old Timers souvenir album, 1878-1958. Pincher Creek: Pincher Creek Old Timers Association, 1958. 69p. (chiefly ill.)

Cover title *Memories*.
Also, *The new memories book. The Old Timers souvenir album, 1878-1958. Reprinted and enlarged and including several of Mr. A.L.Freebairn's poems*, 1975. 96p. ill.

Canadiana, 1962.

AEA

3199 Pioneer heritage of Kirriemuir, Altario and Compeer. Wheatsheaf: Wheatsheaf Women's Institute, 1971. 1129p. ill.

Cover title.

Ceessa.

AEA

3200 **Playle**, Marguerite. The hills of home. Drumheller Valley. Drumheller: Drumheller Valley History Association, 1973. viii, 624p. ill.

Printed by D.W. Friesen & Sons, Calgary.

Canadiana, 1974.

AEA

3201 Ponoka and District Historical Society. Ponoka panorama. Ponoka: Ponoka and District Historical Society, 1973. 961p. ill.

Printed by Parkland Colorpress, College Heights.

Canadiana 1977.

AEA

3202 The Ponoka book. Published as a tribute to the pioneers who opened up the district and to commemorate the town's fiftieth anniversary, 1904-1954. Ponoka: 1954. 1, 93p. ill.

Cover title *Ponoka 50th anniversary, 1904-1954*.

Canadiana, 1961.

AEA

3203 **Pottage**, Bessie Fern. As the wheel turns. A history of Merna and district. Mrs. Steve (Bessie) Pottage, editor. Sedgewick: Community Press, 1971. 118p. ill.

Glenbow.

ACG

3204 Provost Chamber of Commerce. The Provost story. Provost: Provost News Print, 1967. 29p. ill.

Cover title.
At head of title: Provost, the friendly town.
Text signed George S. Holmes.
A promotional handbook.

Ceessa. **AEA**

3205 Provost Promotions and Publications Ltd. Calgary 100. 100 year history of Calgary. Calgary: Provost, 1975. 224p. (incl. advts.) ill. (A Provost publication)

Cover title. **AECSJ**

3206 **Prud'homme**, Essie. Yesteryears of the Hays Municipality. 1967 centennial project of the County of Red Deer No. 23. Hays: County of Red Deer No.23, 1967. v, 118p. ill.

Editors: Tom Murray, Ray Heard.

Glenbow. **ACG**

3207 Readymade Historical Society. Readymade and district. Lethbridge: Readymade Women of Unifarm, 1977. 385p. ill.

Printed by Southern Printing, Lethbridge.
A history of the area south east of Coaldale. **AEA**

3208 **Ream**, Peter Tennant. The Fort on the Saskatchewan. A history of Fort Saskatchewan, specially prepared for the 70th anniversary of First United Church. Edmonton: Douglas Print, 1957. 7, 155p. ill.

Also, 1962, *Appendix to The Fort on the Saskatchewan*. Prepared in conjunction with the 75th anniversary of the First United Church, Fort Saskatchewan, Fort Saskatchewan, First United Church, 1962. 18 leaves. ill. Cover title. Duplicated. Also 2d ed., Fort Saskatchewan, Fort Saskatchewan Historical Society, 1974. xii, 591p. ill. Also 2d ed. Fort Saskatchewan, Fort Saskatchewan Historical Society, 1974. xii, 591p. ill. **AEA**

3209 Red Deer East Historical Society. Mingling memories. Red Deer: Red Deer East Historical Society, 1979. vii, 1067p. ill.

Printed by Friesen Printers, Calgary.
A history of the area south and east of Red Deer.

Canadiana, 1980. **AEA**

3210 **Reid**, Gordon. Around the Lower Peace. High Level: Lower Peace Publishing, 1978. 84p. ill.

Printed by D.W. Friesen and Sons, Calgary.

Canadiana, 1979. **AEA**

3211 **Reid**, Gordon. Frontier notes. High Level: Gordon Reid, 1976. 69p. ill.
Canadiana, 1976. **AEA**

3212 **Reid**, Gordon. Notes of the north. High Level: Notes of the North, 1977. 71p. ill.

Printed by D.W. Friesen and Sons, Calgary.

Canadiana, 1978. **AEA**

3213 Reminiscences. Life in Calgary then and now. Violet Cawthorn, Lois Cummings, Elsie Kneeshaw, Mary Middlemass. Calgary: Century Calgary Publications, 1975. 47p. ill.

Also published as part of *Past and present*, which was issued as v.1 of the Century Calgary Historical Series.

Canadiana, 1977. **AEA**

3214 **Repp**, Isobel. Bowtell tales to 1976. Stories in word and picture. Bowtell: Bowtell Community Association, 1976. 160p. ill.

Cover title.
Compiled and researched by Isobel Repp and Margaret Scott.
Sponsored by the Bowtell Community Association.
Lithographed by the Lloydminster Times Publishing.
Includes a history of Borradaile.

Canadiana, 1977. **AEA**

3215 **Reynolds**, A. Bert. Siding 16. An early history of Wetaskiwin to 1930, from materials gathered by Mrs. Daisy Lucas and others. Wetaskiwin: Wetaskiwin R.C.M.P. Centennial Committee, 1975. ix, 304p. ill.

Printed by Wetaskiwin Times and Bulletin Commercial Printers.

Canadiana, 1976. **AEA**

3216 Ricinus-Caroline History Committee. In the shade of the mountains. A history of the following school districts, Chedderville, Clear Creek, Crammond, Crooked Creek, Dovercourt, Hazeldell (North), Caroline, Pineview, Ricinus, Shilo, South Fork, Wooler. Caroline: Ricinus-Caroline History Committee, 1979. 392p. ill.

Printed by Friesen Printers, Calgary. **AECYR**

3217 Rivercourse Sewing Circle. Rivercourse centennial. Rivercourse: Rivercourse Sewing Circle, 1967. (1), 53 leaves. ill.

Cover title. Duplicated.

Glenbow. **ACG**

3218 **Robinson**, Bart. Banff Springs. The history of a hotel. Banff: Summerthought, 1973. 115, 3p. ill.

Canadiana, 1973. **ACG**

3219 Rocky Mountain House Reunion Historical Society. The days before yesterday. History of Rocky Mountain House district. Edited by Freeda Fleming, assistant editor, Angie Edgerton. Rocky Mountain House: Rocky Mountain House Reunion Historical Society, 1977. xi, 709p. ill.

Spine title *The days before yesterday, 1799-1977*.

Canadiana, 1980. AEA

3220 **Roen**, Hazel Bessie. The grass roots of Dorothy, 1895-1970. Compiled and edited by Hazel B. Roen. Dorothy: Dorothy Community, 1971. viii, 355p. ill.

Lithographed by Northwest Printing, Calgary.

Glenbow. ACG

3221 **Rogers**, Edith Blanche (Cox). History made in Edmonton. Edmonton: Edith Rogers, 1975. 176p. ill.

Written primarily for the students of Edith Rogers School, Edmonton. Recollections of schools and settlers in the Edmonton area.

Ceessa. AEA

3222 **Ronaghan**, Allen. There'll always be an Islay. Islay: Morrison Museum Association, 1977. vii, 411p. ill.

Cover title.
Edited by Allen Ronaghan.

Canadiana, 1979. AEA

3223 Rosemary, land of promise. Rosemary: Rosemary Historical Society, 1977. 404p. ill.

Printed by Friesen Printers, 1977.

Canadiana, 1977. AEA

3224 **Ross**, Mary Francis (Antoniuk). Oh! The Coal Branch. A chronicle of the Alberta Coal Branch, by Toni Ross. Edmonton: 1976. 340p. ill.

Printed by D.W. Friesen and Sons, Calgary. AEA

3225 **Rowe**, Jean I. A history of the people of Michichi. Michichi: Michichi Book Committee, 1970. viii, 487p. ill.

Printed by D.W. Friesen and Sons, Calgary.
Editor: Jean I. Rowe.

Glenbow. ACG

3226 Rumsey Centennial Book Committee. Pioneer days. Scollard, Rumsey, Rowley. Stettler: Rumsey Centennial Book Committee, 1967. 128p. ill.

Cover title.
Printed by Stettler Independent.

Glenbow. ACG

3227 Rush Centre Women's Institute. Esther community history. Hanna: Rush Centre Women's Institute, 1962. 46p. ill.

Printed by the Hanna Herald.

Glenbow. ACG

3228 **Rutledge**, Elaine. A treasury of memories. A story of the Monitor and Pemukan Districts in Alberta, Canada. Co-edited by Elaine Rutledge and Marina Liknes. Monitor: L.A.C.C., 1975. 682p. ill.

Printed by Intercollegiate Press, Winnipeg.

Canadiana, 1977.

AEA

3229 **Sanderson**, Mary M. Historical panorama of Alix and district. s.l.: s.n., 1967. 54p. ill.

Cover title.
Duplicated by Northwest Printing & Lithographing, Calgary.
Compiled by Mary M. Sanderson from newspaper clippings, booklets, etc.

Ceessa.

AEA

3230 Scandia Historical Committee. Scandia since seventeen. Scandia: Scandia Historical Committee, 1978. 340p. ill.

Canadiana, 1979.

3231 Scenic Heights Farmers' Union. The Big Horn School District. Compiled and written by the Scenic Heights Farmers' Union of Alberta, Local no.144, the original settlers of the Big Horn School District and Malcolm A. Menzies. s.l.: Farmers' Union of Alberta, Local No. 144, 1967. 1v. (62p.) ill.

AEU

3232 **Schissel**, Wendy. Beiseker's golden heritage. Beiseker: Beiseker Historical Society, 1977. 525p. ill.

Printed by Friesen Printers, Calgary.
Editors: Wendy and Ben Schissel and Lynn Harty.
The book covers sixteen school districts.

Canadiana, 1978.

AEA

3233 **Schutz**, Fred. Pas-ka-poo. An early history of Rimbey and the Upper Blindman Valley. Compiled and written by Fred Schutz, with editing assistance from Jack Parry. Rimbey: Rimbey Record, 1962. ix, 196p. ill.

Canadiana, 1964.

AEA

3234 **Scriven**, Mary (Johnson). Homesteading in the Consul district. Medicine Hat: Mary Scriven, 1961. 62, (1) leaves. ill.

Cover title. Duplicated.
Preface signed, Mary and Ralph Scriven.

Glenbow.

ACG

3235 Senior Citizen's Club of Provost. Early furrows. A story of our early pioneers in Provost, Hayter, Bodo and surrounding districts. Provost: Senior Citizen's Club of Provost, 1977. vi, 600, viii p. ill.

Printed by Holmes Printing.

Ceessa.

AEA

3236 Settlers along the Bow. A history of Rainier, Bow City. Bow City: Rainier-Bow City History Book Club, 1975. 296p. ill.

Printed by D.W. Friesen & Sons, Calgary.

Canadiana, 1976. **AEA**

3237 **Shaw**, Keith. Chief Mountain country. A history of Cardston and district. Cardston: Cardston and District Historical Society, 1978. 536p. ill.

Printed by Friesen Printers, Calgary.

Canadiana, 1979. **AEA**

3238 Sheep River Historical Society. In the light of the flares. History of Turner Valley oilfields. Turner Valley: Sheep River Historical Society, 1979. 758p. ill.

Printed by Friesen Printers, Calgary. **AEA**

3239 **Shepherd**, George. West of yesterday. Edited with a commentary by John H. Archer. Toronto: McClelland and Stewart, 1965. 157p.

History of the Cypress Hills.

Dew. **AEU**

3240 **Sheppard**, Bert. Spitzee days. Calgary: J.D. McAra, 1971. 280p. ill.

A history of the High River country and its settlers.
Illustrations by Rich Roenisch.

Glenbow. **ACG**

3241 **Shiels**, Bob. Calgary. Calgary: Calgary Herald, 1974. 208p. illus.

Cover title *Calgary ... a not too solemn look at Calgary's first 100 years.*

Canadiana, 1975. **AEA**

3242 Short Grass Historical Society. Long shadows. A history of shortgrass country. Bow Island: Short Grass Historical Society, 1974. 333p. ill.

Printed by Commentator Publishing.
A history of the Milk River, south of Foremost.

Ceessa. **AEA**

3243 Sibbald Women's Institute. Sibbald community history, 1910-1962. Sibbald: Sibbald Women's Institute, 1962. 63p. ill.

Printed by the Hanna Herald.

Glenbow. **ACG**

3244 **Soby**, Trudy. Be it ever so humble. Calgary: Century Calgary Publications, 1975. 55p. ill.

Photographs and sketches of Calgary houses, with brief text.

Canadiana, 1977. **AEU**

3245 **Soby**, Trudy. A walk through old Calgary. Calgary: Century Calgary Publications, 1975. 48p. ill.

Photographs and sketches, with brief text.

Canadiana, 1977. **AEU**

3246 Some did, some didn't win their $10.00 bet with the government. History of Iddlesleigh, Rainy Hills. Calgary: Albertan, 1961. 48p. ill.

Cover title.

Glenbow. **ACG**

3247 **Sorgard**, Marie. Coyote Flats. Coyote Flats: Coyote Flats Historical Society, 1967-1976. 2v. ill.

Marie Sorgard, editor and co-ordinator.
Printed by Southern Printing, Lethbridge.
v.1 sub-titled *Historical Review, 1905-1965*, v.2 subtitled *50 years of progress*. V.1 published 1967, reprinted 1976.
Includes Turin, Gold Ridge, Iron Springs, Battersea, Barrhill, Bulmer, Circle, Picture Butte, Granite Falls and Shaughnessy Districts.

Canadiana 1977. **AEA**

3248 **Speers**, Bertha M. A cameo of the west. A story of the pioneers of present Namao School District no.24. Namao: Namao U.C.W. and the Namao F.U.A., Local No. 539, 1969. 363p. ill.

A revised and enlarged edition of *The Cameo* published by the Namao U.F.W.A., Local 61 in 1936 (Peel 3525).
Also, Supplement, n.d. 7p.

Glenbow. **ACG**

3249 **Speight**, Anne. Prairie echoes, Metiskow, Cadogan, Cairns. Precious memories of the former Hillcrest Municipality. Cadogan: Hillcrest Heritage Society, 1976. 567p. ill.

Editor: Anne Speight.
Printed by Friesen Printers, Calgary. **AEA**

3250 **St. André**, Lucie. Histoire de Girouxville. Girouxville history, v.1, 1911-1930. Girouxville: Société Historique de Girouxville, 1976. 144p. ill.

Printed by D.W. Friesen & Sons, Calgary.
Text in English and French.
Editors: Lucie St. André and Edith Lorrain.

Canadiana 1977. **AEA**

3251 St. Lina History Book Committee. St. Lina and surrounding area. St. Lina: St. Lina History Book Committee, 1978. x, 310p. ill.

Printed by Friesen Printers, Calgary.

Ceessa. **AEA**

3252 St. Paul. Ecole Racette. Projet centenaire, Grade 10. St. Paul: Ecole Racette, 1967. 1v. (27p)

Cover title. Duplicated.
Histories of settlements in the St. Paul area. **AEU**

3253 **Stacey**, Earl Clifford. Beaverlodge to the Rockies. Editor, E.C. Stacey, Associate editors, Madelon Truax, Percy Hunter, Evelyn Stacy. Beaverlodge: Beaverlodge and District Historical Association, 1974. 576p. ill.

Printed by D.W. Friesen and Sons, Calgary.
Also, *Supplement*, 1976. 348p.

Canadiana 1975, 1977. **AEA**

3254 **Stainton**, Irene Hackett. Along the Victoria trail. Lamont and districts. Edited by Irene Hackett Stainton and Elizabeth Course Carlsson. Edmonton: Lamont and District Historian, 1978. 402p. ill.

Printed by Friesen Printers, Calgary.

Canadiana, 1979. **AEA**

3255 Standard Community. Golden jubilee celebration, June 19th, 1960. Standard: Standard Community, 1960. (20) leaves. ill.

Cover title. Duplicated.

Glenbow. **ACG**

3256 Standard Historical Book Society. From Danaview to Standard. Standard: Standard Historical Book Society, 1979. 381p. ill.

Printed by Friesen Printers, Calgary. **AECYR**

3257 Stavely Historical Book Society. The butte stands guard. Stavely: Stavely Historical Book Society, 1976. 431p. ill.

Printed by D.W. Friesen and Sons, Calgary.

Canadiana, 1977. **AEA**

3258 **Stone**, Pearl R. People and places by Pearl. Cremona: P.R. Stone, 1978. (iv), 157p. ill.

Cover title.
Printed by Contemporary Graphics, Didsbury.

Canadiana, 1980. **AEU**

3259 Stories of old St. Albert. First hand accounts of St. Albert's past. St. Albert: Bridging the Gap Opportunities for Youth, 1974. 1v.

Duplicated. **AEA**

3260 Strathcona Historical Group. Strathcona, the asset of heritage. A plan for the future. A proposal. Edmonton: Strathcona Historical Group, 1973. 143, 54p. ill.

Canadiana, 1975.

3261 **Stubbs**, Hugh. The early devisers. Vermillion: Forestburg Historical Society, 1977. xvi, 240p. ill.

Printed by Vermillion Standard.
Editor: Hugh Stubbs.
A history of the communities of Hastings, Coulee, Duxbury and Forestburg.

Ceessa. **AEA**

3262 Sunshine Women's Institute. The history of the border country of Coutts. Lethbridge: Southern Printing, 1965. 2v. ill.

Contents: 1. 1890-1957. Compiled by the Women's Institute of Coutts. 2. 1959-1965.

Glenbow. **ACG**

3263 **Sveen**, Evelyn. The golden years. Barrhead: Barrhead History Book Committee, 1978. 499p. ill.

Sponsored by the Barrhead and District Chamber of Commerce.
Editor: Evelyn Sveen.
Printed by Friesen Printers, Calgary.

Ceessa. **AEA**

3264 Taber Booklet Committee. Golden jubilee, commemorating fifty years of picture history of Taber, Alberta, 1905-1955. Taber: Taber City Council, 1955. 204p. (incl. advts.) ill.

Canadiana, 1959. **AEA**

3265 Taber Historical Committee. From tank 77 to Taber today. A history of Taber, its district and its people. Taber: Taber Historical Committee, 1977. 617p. ill.

Canadiana, 1979.

3266 **Tardif**, Emile. Centenaire de Saint-Albert. Saint Albert centennial. 1861-1961. Edmonton: Printed by La Survivance Printing, 1961. 94, (2)p. (incl. advts.) ill.

Text in French and English.

Glenbow. **ACG**

3267 **Tardif**, Emile. Saint Albert. Edmonton: La Survivance Printing Limited, 1961. 79p. ill.

A history of Saint Albert, with emphasis on the old mission.
Also issued in a French Language edition.

Glenbow. **ACG**

3268 **Teviotdale**, Agnes Kathleen (Wilson). Vast prospects and splendid songs. Harry Wilson, Strathcona pioneer of 1892. Edmonton: A.K. Teviotdale, 1972. 39p. ill.

A biography.

Canadiana, 1973. **AEA**

3269 **Théroux**, Théodore. Impressions de voyage et histoire de St. Joseph de Végreville. Mémoire. Vegreville: s.n., 1972

Diary kept during the first year of settlement, 1894, published 1933 (Peel 3358). Translation by Mrs. G. Bourget and Mrs. J. Hantiuk, Vegreville.

Duplicated. **AEA**

3270 **Thibault**, Margaret Fraser. The Teepee Creek terror. Editor, Margaret Fraser Thibault, associate editor and compiler, Jean Fraser Rycroft. Artists, Clara Gliege et al. Teepee Creek: Teepee Creek Stampede Historical Society, 1978. 162p. ill.

Printed by D.W. Friesen & Sons, Calgary.

Canadiana, 1979. **AEA**

3271 **Thibodeau**, Ruth. The Moyerton story, "cradled 'twixt hills." s.l.: s.n., 1970. 52p. ill.

Chairman of Editorial Committee: Ruth Thibodeau.
Moyerton is now part of the Paradise Valley district.

Glenbow. **ACG**

3272 **Thomas**, Jack. Silver sage. Bow Island: Bow Island Lions Club, 1972. 703p. ill.

Spine title *Bow Island, 1900 to 1920*.
Compiled by Jack Thomas, based on research of Clarence Gatz.
Includes material from Winnifred, Conquerville and Burdett areas.

Ceessa. **AEA**

3273 **Thompson**, Jean. Pioneer days. Millet: Millet School, 1963. 46p.

Cover title. Duplicated.
Reminiscences of Millet residents collected by Grade 7, 1961, and edited by Mrs. Jean Thompson.

Ceessa. **AEA**

3274 **Thompson**, Ruby G. Lea (Trench). Pioneers of Athabasca. Edited by Raymond Thompson. Alderwood Manor, Wash.: Raymond Thompson, 1967. 58p. ill.

Cover title. Duplicated.
Account of pioneering at Edson in 1920.

Ceessa. **AEA**

3275 Tofield Jubilee Committee. A concise history of Tofield and district. Tofield: Tofield Jubilee Committee, 1955. 29p. ill.

Ceessa. **AEA**

3276 **Toverud**, Mrs. Alf. Let us not forget. A history of Viking and district. Prepared by Mrs. Alf. Toverud and Mrs. Harold Gares. Viking: Viking Historical Society, 1968. 115p. ill.

Printed by College Press, College Heights. **AEA**

3277 Trail blazers. Compiled and published by the Conroy Club, Winfield, Alberta and the Yeoford Ladies Club. Winfield: Conroy Club, 1973. 448p. ill.

Printed by L & W Printing.
History of the western part of the County of Wetaskiwin.

Canadiana, 1977. **AEA**

3278 **Treacy**, Robert M. Sandstone brick and wood. A collection of Calgary pioneer homes and histories. Calgary: Lawson Graphics Western, 1975. 54p. ill.

A Calgary centennial project. **ACP**

3279 **Turnbull**, Elizabeth. The pathfinders. A history of Onoway, Bilby, Brookdale, Glenford, Goldthorpe, Heatherdown, Hillcrest, Nakamun, Rich Valley, Speldhurst, Stettin and Sturgeon River. Compiled by the Onoway and District Historical Society. Onoway: Onoway Women's Institute, 1978. 693p. ill.

Editor, Elizabeth Turnbull, co-editor, Edith Payne.
Published by Inter-Collegiate Press, Winnipeg. **AEA**

3280 **Tymchuk**, Lee. Early Calgary friends. Stories of the past Written by Lee Tymchuk. Illustrated by Barbara Ballachey. Lettering by Sandra Duncan. Calgary: City of Calgary, 1978. 40p. ill.

On title page: Fort Calgary.
Juvenile literature.
Contents: 1. Bull's Head 2. Father Doucet 3. Inspector Brisebois 4. Sam Livingston. **ACP**

3281 **Ulliac**, Arvine (Plamondon). Cinquantenaire de l'arrivée des pionniers à Gourin, 11 avril, 1914. s.l.: s.n., 1964. 28p. ill.

Caption title *1914-1916, en souvenir de Monsieur et Madame Joseph Ulliac. D'un Gourin à l'autre*.
A history of the Ulliac family and Gourin, a post office, west of Lac La Biche.

Ceessa. **AEA**

3282 Vauxhall and Districts Book Committee. Where waters flow. Vauxhall: Vauxhall and Districts Book Committee, 1969. 364p. ill.

Printed by Val Marshall Print, Medicine Hat.

Glenbow. **ACG**

3283 Vermilion Oldtimers' Association. Vermilion memories. Calgary: Vermilion Oldtimers' Association, 1967. 200p. ill.

Compiled as centennial project.
Lithographed by Kyle Printing, Calgary.

Glenbow. **ACG**

3284 Veteran Jubilee Publicity Committee. Memoirs of Veteran. Veteran: Veteran Jubilee Publicity Committee, 1969. iv, 90p.

Cover title. Duplicated. **ACG**

3285 Vulcan and District Historical Society. Wheat country. A history of Vulcan and district. Vulcan: Vulcan and District Historical Society, 1973. 990p. ill.

Printed by D.W. Friesen & Sons, Calgary.

Canadiana, 1974. **AEA**

3286 **Walton**, Robert N. Lone Butte north. Hanna: Lone Butte Book Club, 1974. 384p. ill.

On cover: A history of Bull Pound, Earltown, Eden, Fraserton, Golden Hill, Lake Rose, Lone Butte, Normandale, Olive, Red Rose.
Printed by D.W. Friesen & Sons, Calgary.

Canadiana, 1975. **AEU**

3287 Wandering River Women's Institute. Wandering River history book, 1968. Westlock: Wandering River Women's Institute, 1968. 1v. (66p.). ill.

Cover title.
Duplicated.
Printed by Greig Printing, Westlock.

Ceessa. **AEA**

3288 **Ward**, Tom. Cowtown. An album of early Calgary. Calgary: City of Calgary Electric System, 1975. 496p. ill.

Published in association with McClelland and Stewart West.

Canadiana, 1976. **ACG**

3289 Warner Old Timers' Association. Warner pioneers. Lethbridge: Lethbridge Herald, 1962. 304p. ill.

Glenbow. **ACG**

3290 Waskatenau School. Waskatenau, 1867-1967. A centennial project by the teachers and pupils of the Waskatenau School. Waskatenau: County of Smoky Lake No.13, 1967. 1v. ill.

Cover title *A century of progress, 1867-1967. An historical study of the Waskatenau, Smoky Lake-Warspite, Vilna and Spedden school communities*.
Printed by Modern Press, Edmonton.

Ceessa. **AEA**

3291 **Watson**, George. Lethbridge. Alberta's Golden Jubilee. Lethbridge: Lethbridge Booklet Committee, 1955. (68)p. ill.

Cover title.

Glenbow. **ACG**

3292 **Watson**, George. Through the looking glass. Lethbridge, 1867-1975. Lethbridge: Lethbridge School District No. 51 and Alberta

Historical Society, Fort Whoop-Up Chapter, 1975. 14p. ill.

Cover title.
Compiled by George Watson and Audrey Baines (Chiswick).
A history of the naming of Lethbridge streets.

AEA

3293 **Weber**, Manasseh. Such was life. Illustrated by the author. Calgary: Times Press, 1956. 72p. ill.

Cover title.
A rhymed history of Didsbury.

Glenbow.

ACG

3294 West of the 4th Historians Book Committee. West of the fourth. Lloydminster: West of the Fourth Historians, 1979. viii, 633p. ill.

Cover title *West of the 4th*.
Subtitle on spine *Lloydminster area south*.

AEA

3295 Westerdale Willing Workers History Committee. A trail grows dim. Calgary: Westerdale Willing Workers, 1967. (11), 173, (7)p. ill.

Printed by John D. McAra, Calgary.
A centennial project.
A history of Dogpound Valley.

Glenbow.

ACG

3296 **Wetton**, Cecilia. The promised land. The story of the Barr Colonists. Lloydminster: Lloydminster Times, 1979. 72p. ill.

First published in 1953 (Peel 4368).

AECYR

3297 Whitla Community Clubs. Tribute to Whitla pioneers. Medicine Hat: Val Marshall Printing (1969) Ltd., 1969. 200p. ill.

Cover title.
Compiled by Isabel Olsen, Alice Verhaest, Cecil Smith and Frank Gechter.

Glenbow.

ACG

3298 **Wiedeman**, Joyce. Saga of Schuler stalwarts. Joyce Wiedeman, editor, Gladys Knodel, assistant editor. Schuler: Schuler History Committee, 1973. iv, 256p. ill.

Cover title.
Printed by Val Marshall Printing(1969), Lethbridge.

Canadiana, 1977.

AEA

3299 **Wilk**, Stephen William. One day's journey. Airdrie: Community Improvement Club, 1963. vii, 429p. ill.

A history of the Airdrie district.
Supplement *Some rules and aids to guide you in writing your personal history project*, p.403-416.

Glenbow.

ACG

3300 **Williams**, Vicky. Calgary, then and now. Vancouver: Bodima Books, 1978. 124p. (chiefly ill.) (A Bodima Book)

AEU

3301 **Willsie**, Merle. White Creek echoes. Innisfail: Innisfail Booster, 1967. (2), 55p. ill.

Cover title. Duplicated.
A history of the area west of Bowden.

Glenbow. **ACG**

3302 **Wilson**, Dora. Cherished memories. Ardrossan: Ardrossan Women of Unifarm, 1972. viii, 712p. ill.

Covers the former rural areas of Wye, Baker, Uncas, Garden, Deville, Douglas, Bremner, Agricola, Ardrossan, Salisbury, Brookville, Ypres Valley, East Clover Bar, North Cooking Lake, Clover Bar.

Glenbow. **ACG**

3303 Winterburn Women's Institute. Memory trails to Winterburn. Winterburn: Winterburn Women's Institute, 1977. 197, 6p. ill.

Cover title.

Ceessa. **AEA**

3304 **Wood**, Kerry. A corner of Canada. A personalized history of the Red Deer country. A Canadian centennial project. Red Deer: Kerry Wood, 1966. 168p. ill.

Printed by John D. McAra, Calgary.

Glenbow. **ACG**

3305 **Wood**, Kerry. A letter from Red Deer. Red Deer: K. Wood, 1954. 1 sheet.

Canadiana, 1955. **OONL**

3306 **Wood**, Kerry. Red Deer. A love story. Red Deer: K. Wood, 1975. 62p. ill.

Printed by Advocate Printers, Red Deer.
Local history and biography.

Ceessa. **AEU**

3307 Youngstown and district pioneers. Youngstown: Youngstown Women's Institute, 1962. 75, (1)p. ill.

Glenbow. **ACG**

3308 Zella Women's Institute. Zella remembers from oil lamps to oil wells. Zella: Zella Women's Institute, 1978. 299p. ill.

Cover title. Duplicated.
A history of the area west of Didsbury. **AEA**

Natural History

3309 **Allison**, Patricia. Seasons. Spring. Edmonton: Puckrin's Production House, 1977. 10, 38 leaves. ill.

Cover title.
Natural history elementary school text.

Canadiana, 1978. **OONL**

3310 **Allison**, Patricia. Seasons. Fall. Edmonton: Puckrin's Production House, 1977. 10, 54 leaves. ill.

Cover title.
A natural history elementary school text.

P.N.L.A., 1979. **OONL**

3311 **Allison**, Patricia. Seasons. Summer. Edmonton: Puckrin's Production House, 1977. 10, 41p. ill.

Cover title.
A natural history elementary school text.

P.N.L.A., 1979. **OONL**

3312 **Blacklock**, Les. The high west. Text by Andy Russell. New York: Viking Press, 1974. 141p. ill. (A studio book)

Paperback ed. published in 1976, Toronto, Macmillan.
Encounters with wildlife in the Rocky Mountains.

CBIP, 1979. **AEU**

3313 **Blood**, Donald Arthur. Rocky Mountain wildlife. Text, Don Blood. Photography, Tom W. Hall and others. Illustrations, Susan Im Baumgarten. Saanichton, B.C.: Hancock House, 1976. 129, 3p. ill.

A popular, extensively illustrated treatment.

CBIP, 1979. **AEA**

3314 Bow Valley Naturalists. Vermilion Lakes, Banff National Park. An introductory study. Banff: Bow Valley Naturalists, 1978. iii, 68p. ill.

Canadiana, 1979. **ACP**

3315 **Brown**, Annora. Old man's garden. Illustrated by the author Toronto: Dent, 1954. viii, 268p.

Botany, with some history and reminiscences of the prairies.
Also published by Gray's Publishing, Sidney, B.C., 1970. 268p.

Dew. **ACU**

3316 **Cormack**, Robert George Hall. Wild flowers of Alberta. Edmonton: Hurtig, 1977. 415p. ill.

First published, 1967, Edmonton, Queen's Printer.

Canadiana, 1977. **ACP**

3317 **Gowland**, John Stafford. Smoke over Sikanaska. Illustrated by Spencer Roberts. London: Werner Laurie, 1955. 191p.

Autobiography of a Rocky Mountain forest ranger.
Sub-title on dust jacket *The story of a forest ranger*.
Also published, 1955, New York, Ives.
Also, 1959, Winnipeg, Harlequin Books.

Canadiana, 1958. **AEU**

3318 **Griffiths**, Deidre. Island forest year. Elk Island National Park. Written and illustrated by Deidre Griffiths. Edmonton: University of Alberta Press, 1979. x, 257p. ill.

Diary of a naturalist.

Canadiana, 1979. **AEA**

3319 **Hampson**, Cy. Into the woods beyond. Toronto: Macmillan of Canada, 1971. 118p. ill.

Popular accounts of Alberta animals by a biologist.

CBIP, 1979. **AECYR**

3320 **Hardy**, William George. Alberta, a natural history. Editor-in-chief, W.G. Hardy. Edmonton: Hurtig, 1967. vii, 343p. ill.

Glenbow. **ACG**

3321 **Lister**, Robert. The birds and birders of Beaverhills Lake. Edmonton: Edmonton Bird Club, 1979. 264p. ill.

AEA

3322 **Marty**, Sid. Men for the mountains. Toronto: McClelland & Stewart, 1978. 270p. ill.

Account of life as a Parks Canada ranger in the Rocky Mountains.

Canadiana, 1978. **AEU**

3323 The nature of things. Compiled by Wendy Spratt. E.A. Mitchner, managing editor. Edmonton: Alberta Education, 1979. 96p. ill.

Childrens' literature.
Printed as part of the Alberta Heritage Learning Resources Project, 1980. **AEU**

3324 **Noble**, Lyle Barry. Man and grizzly bear in Banff National Park, Alberta. Ottawa: National Library of Canada, 1972. viii, 119 leaves. ill. (Canadian theses on microfilm, 13933)

Thesis (M.A.), University of Calgary, 1972.
Microfilm of typescript.

Canadiana, 1973. **AEU**

3325 **Oeming**, Al. A visit to Al Oeming's Alberta Game Farm. Ardrossan: Alberta Game Farm, 1964. 64p. ill.

Canadiana, 1969. **OONL**

3326 **Russell**, Andy. Alpine Canada. Photography by J.A. Kraulis. Edmonton: Hurtig, 1979. 143p. ill.

Canadiana, 1979. **ACP**

3327 **Russell**, Andy. Andy Russell's adventures with wild animals. With illustrations by Harry Savage. Edmonton: Hurtig, 1977. 183p. ill.

Also published, New York, Knopf, 1978. 178p. (A Borzoi book).

Canadiana, 1979. **AEA**

3328 **Russell**, Andy. Grizzly country. New York: Knopf, 1967. 302p. ill.

Also published, 1970, London, Jarrold. Paperback ed., 1979, Mississauga, Ballantine.

Dew. **ALU**

3329 **Russell**, Andy. Horns in the high country. New York: Knopf, 1973. xv, 259p. ill.

Paperback ed., 1979, Mississauga, Ballantine.

Canadiana, 1974. **OONL**

3330 **Russell**, Andy. Trails of a wilderness wanderer. New York: Knopf, 1970. 297p. ill.

Autobiography of an Alberta sometime cowboy, rancher, trapper, guide and wild life photographer.
Also published, 1979, New York, Ballantine Books. 241p.

Dew. **AEU**

3331 **Salt**, Walter Ray. The birds of Alberta. With their ranges in Saskatchewan & Manitoba. Rev. ed. W. Ray Salt & Jim. R. Salt. Edmonton: Hurtig, 1976. 498p. ill.

1st ed., 1958, and 2d rev. ed., 1966, published by the Alberta Department of Industry and Development.

Canadiana, 1977. **ACG**

3332 **Schalkwyk**, Helene M.E. Mushrooms of the Edmonton area, edible and poisonous. Edmonton: Helene M.E. Schalkwyk, 1975. 32p. ill.

Cover title.

Canadiana, 1975. **AEU**

3333 **Smeeton**, Miles. Moose magic. Drawings by P.F. Wright. Toronto: Collins & Harvill, 1974. 191p. ill.

Account of a game farm near Cochrane.

CBIP, 1979. **AECYR**

3334 **Spencer**, Richard Bruce. A study of the wildlife on four selected Edmonton ravines and of the recreation uses and preferences of city ravines. Ottawa: National Library of Canada, 1976. xvii, 183 leaves. (Canadian theses on microfiche, 30834)

Thesis (M.Sc.), University of Alberta, 1976.

Microfiche of typescript.

U of A Theses. **AEU**

3335 **Wood**, Kerry. The creek. Illustrated by Marjorie and Kerry Wood. Red Deer: Kerry Wood, 1970. 34p. ill.

Juvenile literature.

Glenbow. **ACG**

Environment

3336 **Anderson**, Robert William. The influence of professional, institutional and biographical factors on the attitudes of forest resource managers in Alberta. Ottawa: National Library of Canada, 1973. xi, 188 leaves. (Canadian theses on microfilm, 15178)

Thesis (M.Sc.), University of Alberta, 1973.
Microfilm of typescript.

Canadiana, 1974. **AEU**

3337 **Brown**, Gordon L. Environmental impact assessment of a sour gas processing development in the Brazeau region of Alberta. Ottawa: National Library of Canada, 1977. ix, 118, 28 leaves. ill. (Canadian theses on microfiche, 35828)

Thesis (M.N.R.N.), University of Manitoba, 1977.
Microfiche of typescript.

Canadiana, 1979. **OONL**

3338 EcoScalgary. Study on pollution. Calgary: EcoScalgary, 1971. 1v. (various paging) maps.

Cover title *Pollution in Calgary*. **AEA**

3339 Edmonton Anti-Pollution Group. The nature, extent and sources of environmental knowledge and opinions in Edmonton. Edmonton: Edmonton Anti-pollution Group, 1972. 124p.

Written by Drake Hocking, Raymond Pong, and Charles Hodgson.
On cover: Environmental knowledge and opinion, Edmonton.
"A report on Project #431-302, Local Initiatives Program".

Canadiana, 1977. **OONL**

3340 Edmonton Anti-Pollution Group. Resources inventory and guide to environmental studies. Edmonton: Edmonton Anti-Pollution Group, 1972. 1v. ill., maps.

On cover: Sources and resources.
Published under the Local Initiatives Program.
Contents: 1. Sources and resources. 2. Fong, Raymond, comp. Annotated bibliography. 3. Miller, Joyce, comp. Resource material sources and environment organizations. 4. Valgardson, Donna & Ann Stewart. Environmental education. 5. Touchings, Dawne, comp. Nature trails in Edmonton. 2d ed. **AEA**

3341 **Edward**, Barry Francis. A resource planning study of the wildlife of Cypress Hills Provincial Park, Alberta. Ottawa: National Library of Canada, 1975. ix, 137 leaves. ill. (Canadian theses on microfiche, 23729)

Thesis (M.Sc.), University of Calgary, 1975.
Microfiche of typescript.

Canadiana, 1976.

OONL

3342 **Edwards**, Felicity Nan. A touch of gas. An ecological enquiry into the effects of the gas processing industry on a community in northwest central Alberta. Ottawa: National Library of Canada, 1977. xii, 154 leaves (Canadian theses on microfiche, 34167)

Thesis (M.Sc.), University of Calgary, 1977.
Microfiche of typescript.

Canadiana, 1979.

OONL

3343 **MacEwan**, John Walter Grant. Entrusted to my care. Saskatoon: Modern Press, 1966. (7), 269p. ill.

On the conservation of wildlife and natural resources.

Glenbow.

ACG

3344 **Nelson**, James Gordon. The last refuge. Montreal: Harvest House, 1973. 230p. ill. (Environment series)

A history of land use from the earliest missionary contacts, focussing on the Cypress Hills area of Alberta and Saskatchewan.

Canadiana, 1974.

AEU

3345 **Pollution Workshop**, Banff, 1970. Proceedings. Montreal: Canada Council of Resource Ministers, 1971. x, 53, 55, x p.

Text in English and French, each with special title page and separate paging.
Cover title: Pollution.
Intergovernmental workshop on environment management.

Canadiana, 1974.

AEU

3346 **Snipe**, James Holloway. The ecological and economic impact of water resource development in southern Alberta. The case of fish and wildlife. Edmonton: University of Alberta, 1970. viii, 86 leaves.

Thesis (M.Sc.), University of Alberta, 1970.
Typescript.

Canadian theses.

AEU

3347 **Van Camp**, Jack. Planning for urban wildlife. A method and its application to Fish Creek Provincial Park, Alberta. Ottawa: National Library of Canada, 1976. vi, 148 leaves. ill. (Canadian theses on microfiche, 30588)

Thesis (M.E.Des.), University of Calgary, 1976.
Microfiche of typescript.

Canadiana, 1976.

OONL

Health Sciences

3348 **Anderson**, A.J. The golden anniversary of the Alberta Pharmaceutical Association, 1911-1961. Edmonton: Alberta Pharmaceutical Association, 1961. 47, 1p. ill.

Compiled and written by Professor A.J. Anderson.
Printed by Hambly Press, Edmonton.

Canadiana, 1961. **AEA**

3349 **Browarny**, Lavonne. A friend in need. St. John Ambulance in Calgary. Calgary: Century Calgary Publications, 1975. 96p. ill.

Also published as part of *At your service, Part two*, which was issued as v.6 of the Century Calgary Historical Series.

Canadiana, 1979. **AEA**

3350 Calgary General Hospital. Calgary General Hospital, 1890-1955. Sixty-five years of community service. Calgary: Calgary General Hospital, 1956. 11, 57p. ill.

Cover title.
Caption title *Case history of the Calgary General Hospital, 1890-1955*.

Canadiana, 1956. **ACG**

3351 Calgary General Hospital Alumnae Association. 25 years of alumnae life. The birth of an idea, the fulfilment of a dream, the realization of a wonderful Association, 1936-1961. Calgary: Calgary General Hospital Alumnae Association, 1961. 97p. ill.

Cover title. **ACP**

3352 Canadian Red Cross Society. Alberta Northwest Territories Division. Calgary Branch. Calgary Branch, Alberta Northwest Territories Division, The Canadian Red Cross Society. A historical account of its development and status at 1976. Calgary: Canadian Red Cross Society, Alberta-Northwest Territories Division, Calgary Branch, 1976. 52 leaves.

A loose leaf publication. **ACP**

3353 **Cashman**, Anthony Walcott. Heritage of service. The history of nursing in Alberta. Edmonton: The Alberta Association of Registered Nurses, 1966. (5), 340p. ill.

Glenbow. **ACG**

3354 **Chatenay**, Henri Paul. Echoes of silence. The chronicles of William Graham Mainprize, M.D., 1911-1974. With introductions by E.W. Barootes, M.D. and W.D. MacRae, M.D. Edmonton: H.P. Chatenay, 1978. 125p. ill.

75th anniversary edition, First Baptist Church and Town of Midale, Saskatchewan, 1903-1978.
Printed by Alberta Handicapped Forum.

Canadiana, 1979. **AEU**

3355 **Colley**, Kate (Brighty). While rivers flow. Stories of early Alberta. Drawings by Margaret Manuel Elwell. Saskatoon: Prairie Books, Western Producer, 1970. 148p. ill.

First appeared as a serial in the *Western Producer*.
Sub-title on dust jacket, *An account of pioneer nursing adventures in Alberta*.

Glenbow.

ACG

3356 **Collins**, Paul Victor. The public health policies of the United Farmers of Alberta government, 1921-1935. Ottawa: National Library of Canada, 1969. viii, 143 leaves. (Canadian theses on microfilm, 05309)

Thesis (M.A.), University of Western Ontario, 1969.
Microfilm of typescript.

Canadiana, 1970.

OONL

3357 **Copeland**, Donalda Murray (McKillop). Remember, nurse. As told to Eugenie Louise Myles. By Donalda McKillop Copeland. Toronto: Ryerson Press, 1960. (4), 250p. ill.

Published 1964, London, Souvenir Press, with title *Nurse among the Eskimos*.
Reminiscences of nursing in the Arctic.

Glenbow.

ACG

3358 **Cormack**, Barbara (Villy). The Red Cross Lady (Mary H. Conquest M.B.E.) Edmonton: Institute of Applied Art, 1960. 92p. ill.

Glenbow.

ACG

3359 **De Groot**, Pieter. The Alberta community health self-study outline. A community development approach to health care planning. Ottawa: National Library of Canada, 1977. viii, 263 leaves (Canadian theses on microfiche, 31977)

Thesis (M.A.), University of Alberta, 1977.
Microfiche of typescript.

Canadiana, 1978.

AEU

3360 **Dorward**, Christina. Below the flight path. A history of the Royal Alexandra Hospital and School of Nursing. Edmonton: Royal Alexandra Hospital, 1968. 152p. ill.

Printed by Commercial Printers, Edmonton.
Written by Christina Dorward and Olive Tookey.

Ceessa.

AEA

3361 Edmonton Dental Nurses and Assistants Association. One hundred years of dentistry. Edmonton: Edmonton Dental Nurses and Assistants Association, 1967. 47 leaves.

Duplicated.
In commemoration of Canada's centennial year.

AEU

3362 **Gahagan**, Alvine (Cyr). Yes, father. Pioneer nursing in Alberta. Manchester, N.H.: Hammer Publications, 1979. vi, 186p. ill., map.

An autobiography.

AEA

3363 **Galt School of Nursing**, Lethbridge. Golden jubilee, 1910-1960. Lethbridge: Galt School of Nursing, 1960. 52p. ill.

Cover title.
Editor: Mrs. Marjorie Chapman (MacDonald).

Glenbow. **ACG**

3364 Ganton and Watson Red Cross Auxiliary. We thy servants, 1939-1967. s.l.: Ganton and Watson Red Cross Auxiliary, 1967. 37p. ill.

Glenbow. **ACG**

3365 Lethbridge Municipal Hospital. Night and day. Lethbridge: Lethbridge Municipal Hospital Student Body, 1960. 35, (1)p. ill.

Glenbow. **ACG**

3366 **Love**, Florence A. (McDonald). The Lamont Public Hospital School of Nursing, 1912-1914. The Archer Memorial Hospital of Lamont School of Nursing, 1951-1962. Lamont: Archer Memorial Hospital of Lamont Alumnae Association, 1962. 86p. ill.

Cover title *The lamp is golden. Lamont and its nurses, 1912-1962*.

Ceessa. **AEA**

3367 **McFadden**, Isobel. The indomitable Savage. Dr. Margaret Savage. Toronto: United Church of Canada, Board of Information and Stewardship, 1963. 40p.

Glenbow. **ACG**

3368 **McGugan**, Angus Cecil. The first fifty years. A history of the University of Alberta Hospital, 1914-1964. Edmonton: University of Alberta Hospital, 1964. vii, 88p. ill.

Canadiana, 1965. **AEA**

3369 **McLeod**, Scott H. Nova Scotia farm boy to Alberta M.D. Calgary: S.H. McLeod, 1968. 110p. ill.

Reminiscences of an Alberta physician.

Glenbow. **ACG**

3370 **Prime**, Michael George Ray. The maximand of the hospital. A study of the factors governing the allocative behaviour of public general hospitals in the province of Alberta, 1952-1968. Ottawa: National Library of Canada, 1974. viii, 157 leaves. ill. (Canadian theses on microfiche, 22500)

Thesis (M.A.), Queen's University, 1974.
Microfiche of typescript.

Canadiana, 1976. **OONL**

3371 **Rehwinkel**, Bessie Lee (Efner). Dr. Bessie. The life story and romance of a pioneer lady doctor on our western and the Canadian frontier. As told by herself and here presented in a running narrative by her husband. St. Louis, Mo.: Concordia Pub. House, 1963. 171p.

Bessie Efner, physician, married A. Rehwinkel, Lutheran minister at Pincher Creek, and Edmonton, 1912-1914.

Dew.

AEU

3372 **Repka**, William. Howard Lowrie, M.D., physician, humanitarian. Toronto: Progress Books, 1977. 108p. (Portraits of Canadians in struggle series)

CBIP, 1979.

3373 **Ronaghan**, Allen. The hospital on the hill, 1912-1962. Islay: Municipal Hospital Board Historical Committee, 1962. 163p. ill.

History of Islay Municipal Hospital.
Committee members: A. Ronaghan, author, J.W. Shaw, Marie M. Carey.
Also, Jubilee edition, 1972. 20p. ill. *A supplement*.

Glenbow.

ACG

3374 **Rothwell**, Alfred. Love and good sense. The first half-century of the Salvation Army Grace Hospital, Calgary, 1926-1976. Calgary: Grace Hospital, 1976. 79p. ill.

Canadiana, 1977.

ACP

3375 The science, the art and the spirit. Hospitals, medicine and nursing in Calgary. Evelyn Hardwick, Eileen Jameson, Eleanor Tregillus. Calgary: Century Calgary Publications, 1975. vii, 160, 2p. ill.

Also published as part of *At your service, Part one*, which was issued as v.6 of the Century Calgary Historical Series.

Ceessa.

AEA

3376 **Scott**, John William. The history of the Faculty of Medicine of the University of Alberta, 1913-1963. Edmonton: University of Alberta, 1963. ix, 43p.

Glenbow.

ACG

3377 Sisters of Charity of Our Lady of Evron. 60th anniversary, St. Louis Hospital, Bonnyville, Alberta. Bonnyville: St. Louis Hospital, 1979. 1v. (20p.)

Cover title.
Caption title *60 years of service to Bonnyville district*.

AEA

3378 Sisters of Charity of St. Vincent de Paul of Halifax. 50th anniversary, Immaculata Hospital, Westlock, Alberta. Westlock: Immaculata Hospital, 1977. 20p. ill.

Cover title.

AEA

3379 **St. Joseph's General Hospital**, Vegreville. Memories. Vegreville: St. Joseph's General Hospital Alumnae, 1971. 66p. (chiefly ill.)

Editor, Lynn Gillman.
Historical notes and photographs published on the occasion of the closing of the nursing school. **AEA**

3380 **St. Mary's Hospital**, Camrose. St. Mary's Hospital, Camrose, Alberta, 50th anniversary, 1924-1974. Camrose: Sisters of Providence, 1974. 56p. ill.

Cover title.

Ceessa. **AEA**

3381 **Stewart**, David. Planning the use of available resources in upgrading the health of registered Indians in Alberta. Toronto: University of Toronto, 1967

Thesis (M.Sc.), University of Toronto, 1967.
Typescript.

Canadian theses. **OONL**

3382 **Stewart**, Irene. These were our yesterdays. A history of district nursing in Alberta. Compiled and edited by Irene Stewart. Calgary: Irene Stewart, 1979. 298p. ill.

Printed by D.W. Friesen and Sons, Altona, Manitoba. **AEA**

3383 **Tunney**, Evelyn. Sisters of Service, Edson, Alberta, 1926-1976. 50 years of service, St. John's Hospital. Compiled and photos selected by Evelyn Tunney. Edson: Sisters of Service, 1976. 28p. ill.

Macdonald Dowrie, printer.

Canadiana, 1977. **AEA**

3384 **Wilson**, Betty. To teach this art. The history of the Schools of Nursing at the University of Alberta, 1924-1974. Edmonton: Hallamshire Publishers, 1977. 191p. ill.

ACP

Agriculture: General Works

3385
Ahimbisibwe, Josiah Karibondo-Karabashensheire. An economic output and pricing policy for service co-operatives. A case study of Alberta co-operative seed cleaning plants. Ottawa: National Library of Canada, 1978. xii, 92 leaves. (Canadian theses on microfiche, 36341)

Thesis (M.Sc.), University of Alberta, 1978.
Microfiche of typescript.

U of A Theses. **AEU**

3386 Alberta Beekeepers Association. Kids! Honey fun with Berta bee. Winterburn: Alberta Beekeepers Association, 1972. 4p. ill.

Canadiana, 1973.

3387 Alberta Hereford Association. Jubilee brochure. Alberta herefords, 1905-1955. Calgary: Alberta Hereford Association, 1955. 96p. ill.

Cover title.
Title on p.1 *Fifty years of progress in the breeding of registered herefords, 1905-1955. Advertisements of registered breeding farms*, p.62-91.

Glenbow.

ACG

3388 Alberta Wheat Pool. Grain varieties in Alberta, summarized by Alberta Wheat Pool for Alberta's School students. Calgary: Alberta Wheat Pool, 1973. 16p. ill.

Cover title.

ACP

3389 Alberta Wheat Pool. History, ownership & government of Alberta Wheat Pool. Calgary: Alberta Wheat Pool, 1969. 17p.

Cover title.
At head of title: Committeemen's handbook.

ACP

3390 Alberta Wheat Pool. Students' story of co-operation. 3rd printing. Calgary: Alberta Wheat Pool, 1966. 26p. ill.

Cover title.
Printed for the Wheat Pool by Ryle Printing Limited, Calgary.
Written for use in schools.

AEA

3391 Alberta Women's Institutes. Alberta Women's Institutes, 1909-1954. The world at our door. s.l.: Alberta Women's Institutes, 1954. 6p.

Canadiana, 1955.

OONL

3392 Alberta Women's Institutes. We take pleasure in introducing you to Alberta Women's Institutes. Edmonton: Alberta Women's Institutes, 1960. 1 fold. leaf.

Printed by Reliable Printing.

Glenbow.

ACG

3393 **Andrew**, David Anderson. The Hereford in Canada, 1860-1968. Calgary: Canadian Hereford Association, 1962. xx, 552p. ill.

Glenbow.

ACG

3394 **Beattie**, Allen W. Trails grown over. Calgary: Alberta Wheat Pool, 1972. 32p. (chiefly ill.)

Cover title.
Note on rear cover: Presented to members of the Alberta Wheat Pool commemorating fifty years of service and progress by this pioneer cooperative, 1973.
Lithographed by Kyle Printing and Stationery.

Canadiana, 1975.

AEA

3395 **Bell**, N. Fred. My fifteen years with 4-H clubs. s.l.: s.n., 1972. 88p. ill.

Duplicated.
Dedicated to the 60th anniversary of the movement.

3396 **Birdsall**, J. Everett. Sixty years of service, 1917-18 to 1977-78. A brief history of the Olds College Alumni Association. Olds: Olds College Alumni Association, 1978. 128p. ill.

Printed by D.W. Friesen, Altona, Manitoba. **AEA**

3397 **Bishop**, J.T. Alberta hail research a major agricultural disaster. Farmers are the pawns of bureaucratic politics. Three Hills: J.T. Bishop, 1970. 9p. ill.

Cover title.
Caption title *A review of the weather modification situation in Alberta*. **AEU**

3398 **Boylen**, Diana M. Farm land tenure in Alberta. Attitudinal and socio-economic variables. Ottawa: National Library of Canada, 1976. xvii, 194 leaves. ill. (Canadian theses on microfiche, 30626)

Thesis (M.A.), University of Alberta, 1976.
Microfiche of typescript.

Canadiana, 1979. **AEU**

3399 East Central Irrigation Association. Red Deer irrigation development. Hanna: 1954. 28p. ill.

Glenbow. **ACG**

3400 **Eastern Irrigation District**, Brooks. The history of the Eastern Irrigation District. 25th anniversary, May 1st, 1950, Brooks, Alta. Brooks: Eastern Irrigation District, 1960. 64p. ill.

Glenbow. **ACG**

3401 Farm & Ranch Management Consultants Ltd. Tradition and transition. Extension education for the farm unit in a changing society.A study of all agricultural extension services in Alberta with new directions charted to 1980. Calgary: Farm & Ranch Management Consultants Ltd., 1970. 1v. (various paging).

Prepared for the Alberta Provincial Government.

Canadiana, 1972.

3402 **Faulknor**, Cliff. The romance of beef. Calgary: Canadian Hereford Association, 1967. (20)p. ill.

Glenbow. **ACG**

3403 **Forbes**, L. Mackenzie. An analysis of the relationship between sale values of public grazing leases and sale values of comparable private range lands in southern Alberta. Logan: Utah State University, 1965. 58 leaves.

Thesis (M.Sc.), Utah State University, 1965.
Typescript.

Dew.

3404 **Fraser**, Frances Jane (Williams). The Milo-Queenstown U.F.W.A. and F.W.U.A. 50 golden years, 1917-1967. Vulcan: Farm Women's Union of

Alberta, Milo and Queenstown Local, 1967. (3), 9, (1)p. ill.
Cover title.
Glenbow.
ACG

3405 **Friesen**, Bruno. Farm stored grain on the Prairies, a cost study. A study prepared for the Grains Group. Calgary: Alberta Wheat Pool, 1971. 33 leaves. ill,
Canadiana, 1975.
OONL

3406 **Garrow**, Patrick. The status and anticipated manpower requirements by selected sectors of the agricultural industry in Alberta. A case study. Ottawa: National Library of Canada, 1970. xvii, 340 leaves. ill.
Thesis (Ph.D.), University of Calgary, 1970.
Microfilm of typescript.
Canadiana, 1971.
AEU

3407 Glenbow-Alberta Institute. Archives. Western Stock Growers' Association papers, 1896-1963. Calgary: Glenbow Foundation, 1968. 9p. (Glenbow archives series, 1)
Canadiana, 1970.
ACG

3408 **Glenn**, John Elmer. The role of government legislation, policy and agency activity in irrigation development. The Cypress Hills area, 1888-1968. Ottawa: National Library of Canada, 1968. xv, 258 leaves. ill. (Canadian theses on microfilm, 04021)
Thesis (M.A.), University of Calgary, 1969.
Microfilm of typescript.
Dew.
ALU

3409 **Gould**, Ed. Ranching. Ranching in Western Canada. Saanichton, B.C.: Hancock House, 1978. 165, 3p. ill.
An extensively illustrated history.
Canadiana, 1979.
AEA

3410 Grande Prairie Women's Institute. History of the Grande Prairie Women's Institute. Grande Prairie: Grande Prairie Women's Institute, 1973. 60 leaves.
Cover title. Duplicated.
AEA

3411 **Gray**, James Henry. Men against the desert. Saskatoon: Western Producer Prairie Books, 1967. xiv, 250p. ill.
An account of the conquest of the desert in the Palliser Triangle in the 1930's.
Canadiana, 1968.
AEU

3412 **Holloway**, J. H. A history of the Alberta Land Surveyors Association. Edmonton: Alberta Land Surveyors Association, 1964. 88p. ill.
Glenbow.
ACG

3413 **Horner**, Donald George. Income distribution in Alberta agriculture. Ottawa: National Library of Canada, 1975. xi, 192 leaves. ill. (Canadian theses on microfiche, 24056)

Thesis (M.A.), University of Alberta, 1975.
Microfiche of typescript.

Canadiana, 1975. **AEU**

3414 **Johnston**, Alexander. Cowboy politics. The Western Stock Growers' Association and its predecessors. Calgary: Western Stock Growers' Association, 1971. (48)p. ill.

Glenbow. **ACG**

3415 **Kelly**, Leroy Victor. The range men. The story of the ranchers and Indians of Alberta. With a new introduction by Michael Ginsberg. New York: Argonaut Press, 1965. 468p. ill.

Reprint of the first edition, 1913 (Peel 2404).

Glenbow. **ACG**

3416 The ladies present. Farm women's week. Thirtieth anniversary, 1930-1960. Olds: Olds School of Agriculture, 1960. (19) leaves. ill.

Duplicated.

Glenbow. **ACG**

3417 **Long**, Philip Sheridan. The great Canadian range. Toronto: Ryerson Press, 1963. 178p.

Also, 2d ed., 1970, Vancouver, Cypress, and 3d ed., 1974, Calgary, Bonanza Books.
Ranching life and stories from southern Alberta and southeast Saskatchewan.

Dew. **AEU**

3418 **Love**, Britten Innis. Veterinarians of the North-West Territories and Alberta. The story of the veterinary profession in this area, 1860-1955. Edmonton: Alberta Veterinary Medical Association, 1965. 126p. ill.

The Centennial project of the Alberta Veterinary Medical Association.

Glenbow. **ACG**

3419 **Love**, Harold Clyde. Crop production risk in Alberta. Variations in yield, price, and gross income per acre for barley, oats and wheat, 1946-66, by census division. Edmonton: University of Alberta, Department of Agricultural Economics, 1968. v, 54p. ill. (University of Alberta. Department of Agricultural Economics and Rural Sociology. Research bulletin, 5)

AEU

3420 **MacEwan**, John Walter Grant. Between the Red and the Rockies. Toronto: University of Toronto Press, 1963. 300p. ill.

Popular history of prairie agriculture.
First published 1952, Toronto, University of Toronto Press. (Peel 4309) Reprinted 1953, 1956.

Also published 1979, Saskatoon, Western Producer Prairie Books, (Spectra books). Edition 1979 reprinted as part of Alberta Heritage Learning Resources, Project, 1979. (Alberta literature for senior students and adults).

CBIP, 1979.

AEL

3421 **MacEwan**, John Walter Grant. Blazing the old cattle trail. Illustrated by Wm. W. Perehudoff. Saskatoon: Modern Press, 1962. 248p. ill. (Prairie books)

Stories of cattle drives in Western Canada.
Originally published in weekly installments in the *Western Producer*.
Reprinted, 1975, Western Producer Books.

Glenbow.

ACG

3422 **MacEwan**, John Walter Grant. Harvest of bread. Saskatoon: Prairie Books, 1969. 180p. ill.

A history of wheat farming in western Canada.

Glenbow.

ACG

3423 **MacEwan**, John Walter Grant. Hoofprints and hitching posts. Illustrated by Wm. W. Perehudoff. Saskatoon: Modern Press, 1964. (5), 249p. ill.

Glenbow.

ACG

3424 **MacEwan**, John Walter Grant. John Ware's cow country. Edmonton: Institute of Applied Art, 1960. 261p. ill.

Reprinted, 1965, 1973.
John Ware, a negro ex-slave, ranched in the High River district.
Reprinted, 1974, Western Producer Prairie Books. Paperback ed., 1976.

Glenbow.

ACG

3425 **MacEwan**, John Walter Grant. Memory meadows. Horse stories from Canada's past. Saskatoon: Western Producer Prairie Books, 1976. 212p. ill.

AEA

3426 **MacEwan**, John Walter Grant. Power for prairie plows. Saskatoon: Western Producer Prairie Books, 1971. 115p. ill.

Glenbow.

ACG

3427 **MacEwan**, John Walter Grant. The rhyming horseman of the Qu'Appelle. Captain Stanley Harrison. Saskatchewan: Western Producer Prairie Books, 1978. 219p. ill.

CBIP, 1979.

AEU

3428 **Mazurok**, Osyp. Al'bom Ukrain'skoi molochars'kö Kooperatsii. "Maslosoiuz", 1902-1942. Edmonton: Hurtok Maslosoyuznykiv, 1962. 16p. (chiefly ill.)

Ukrainica Canadiana 1962.

AEU

3429 **McCallum**, D. Hall. The golden anniversary of the Alberta Dairymen's Association. Historical notes on Alberta dairying to commemorate the 50th annual meeting. Edmonton: Alberta Dairymen's Association, 1970. 72p. ill.

Cover title.
Editor: D.H. McCallum.
Printed by Co-op Press. **AEA**

3430 **McDougall**, Robert. The Cochrane Ranch, 1881-1894. A local history. Calgary: Robert McDougall, n.d. 33p., 12 leaves. ill.

Duplicated.

Ceessa. **AEA**

3431 **Miller**, Kenneth Frank. Economic efficiency in the utilization and improvement of the publicly owned pastureland of Alberta. Edmonton: University of Alberta, 1970. xi, 137 leaves.

Thesis (M.Sc.), University of Alberta, 1970.
Typescript.

Canadian theses. **AEU**

3432 **Mitchner**, Ernest Alyn. William Pearce, father of Alberta irrigation. Edmonton: University of Alberta, 1966. ix, 154 leaves.

Thesis (M.A.), University of Alberta, 1966.
Typescript.

Canadian theses. **AEU**

3433 **Nesbitt**, Leonard D. Tides in the West. Illustrated by Wm. W. Perehudoff. Saskatoon: Modern Press, 1962. 413, 5p. ill.

1st edition published without attribution, 1936 (Peel 3490).
On cover *A Wheat Pool history*.
A history of the Alberta Wheat Pool.

Glenbow. **ACG**

3434 **Ola**, Timothy. Agricultural policy in Alberta. A study on some aspects of consistency in policy. Ottawa: National Library of Canada, 1975. xii, 175 leaves. (Canadian theses on microfiche, 24107)

Thesis (M.Sc.) University of Alberta, 1975.
Microfiche of typescript.

U of A Theses. **AEU**

3435 Olds School of Agriculture. Golden echoes, 1913-1963. Winnipeg: Intercollegiate Press, 1963. 121p. ill,

Cover title.

Glenbow. **ACG**

3436 **Otter**, Andy Albert den. Irrigation in southern Alberta, 1882-1901. Lethbridge: Alberta Historical Society, Whoop-up Country

Chapter, 1975. 24p. ill. (Historical Society of Alberta. Whoop-up Country Chapter. Occasional paper, 5)

Reprinted from *Great Plains Journal*, v11 no2, 1972.

Canadiana, 1975.

AEA

3437 **Palmer**, Asael E. When the winds came. How the battle against soil drifting was won on the Canadian prairies. Lethbridge: A.S. Palmer, 1968. 57p. ill.

Glenbow.

ACG

3438 **Patching**, Edwin Arthur. Students story of wheat. Calgary: Alberta Wheat Pool, 1954. 35p. ill.

Cover title.
Written for use in schools.
New ed. 1960. 47p.

Glenbow.

ACG

3439 **Peterson**, Ed. Wetaskiwin Co-op. 50 years of progress, 1917-1967. Wetaskiwin: Wetaskiwin Co-operative Association, 1967. 52p. ill.

Glenbow.

ACG

3440 **Pich**, George. Agriculture innovations, county of St. Paul, Alberta. Edmonton: University of Alberta, 1970. xii, 191 leaves.

Thesis (M.A.), University of Alberta, 1970.
Typescript.

Canadian theses.

AEU

3441 **Porter**, Eugene Oliver. Lord Beresford and Lady Flo. El Paso, Texas: Texas Western Press, University of Texas at El Paso, 1970. 44p. ill. (Southwestern studies. Monograph, 25)

Lord Beresford owned the Mexico Ranch on the north side of the Red Deer River, near Steveville.

Glenbow.

ACG

3442 **Priestley**, Norman F. Furrows, faith and fellowship. Edmonton: Alberta Agricultural Centennial Committee, 1967. 317p. ill.

By Norman F. Priestley and Edward B. Swindlehurst.
Sub-title on dust jacket *The history of the farm movement in Alberta, 1905-1966*.
Printed by Co-op Press, Edmonton.

Glenbow.

ACG

3443 **Radke**, Claude Douglas. Administrative decentralization. A case study of the Alberta Department of Agriculture. Ottawa: National Library of Canada, 1972. 198 leaves. (Canadian theses on microfilm, 08388)

Thesis (M.A.), Carleton University, 1971.
Microfilm of typescript.

Canadiana, 1972.

AEU

3444 **Rogers**, Walter Bob. The economic benefits and costs of irrigation in the eastern irrigation district of Alberta. By Walter B. Rogers, Travis W. Manning and Herbert W. Grubb. Edmonton: University of Alberta, Department of Agriculture Economics, 1966. 43 leaves. (University of Alberta. Department of Agricultural Economics and Rural Sociology. Research bulletin, 3)

AEU

3445 **Rogers**, Walter Bob. Effects of farm technology and consequent problems of adjustment, effects of industrialization on agricultural production. By Walter B. Rogers and George S. Buckmire. Edmonton: University of Alberta, Department of Agricultural Economics, 1967. 30 leaves. (University of Alberta. Department of Agricultural Economics. Special report, 6)

Canadiana, 1969.

3446 **Rogers**, Walter Bob. The rural church, the farm family. Edmonton: University of Alberta, Department of Agricultural Economics, 1967. 28 leaves. (University of Alberta. Department of Agricultural Economics and Rural Sociology. Special report, 7)

Contents: 1. The rural church, by W.B.Rogers 2. The farm family, by G.E. Buckmire.

Canadiana, 1969. **AEU**

3447 Royal Bank of Canada. The Royal Bank of Canada, 8th Avenue & Centre Street, Calgary, Alberta. An important part of the history of Alberta and the Royal Bank of Canada. Calgary: Royal Bank of Canada, 1977. 35p. ill.

Cover title.
p16-34 comprise the Brand Board Display in the Bank. **ACP**

3448 **Russell**, Andy. Men of the saddle. Working cowboys of Canada. Toronto: Van Nostrand Reinhold, 1978. 192p. ill.

Text by Andy Rusell, photographs by Ted Grant.

Canadiana, 1978. **AEA**

3449 Sicks' Lethbridge Brewery Ltd. Brands and how to read them. Lethbridge: Sicks' Lethbridge Brewery Ltd., 1962. 11p. ill.

Glenbow. **ACG**

3450 **Stacey**, Earl Clifford. Peace Country heritage. Saskatoon: Western Producer Book Service, 1974. xi, 173p. ill.

Contents: Pt.1. Dr. William Donald Albright Pt.2. Dominion Experimental Station and Research Station, Canada Department of Agriculture (i.e. Beaverlodge Station).

AEA

3451 **Stacey**, Earl Clifford. W.D. Albright. A contribution. Beaverlodge: Beaverlodge and District Historical Association, 1974. 24p. ill. (To the builders of the Peace series)

Printed by D.W. Friesen & Sons, Calgary.

Canadiana 1977. **AEA**

3452 **Storey**, H.C. A review of the work of the Health of Animals Branch in Alberta. Edmonton: Alberta Veterinary Medical Association, 1961. (8)p.

Prepared in January, 1956.

Glenbow. **ACG**

3453 **Susko**, Rudolf. Economics of size on Alberta grain farms. Edmonton: University of Alberta, 1971. ix, 116 leaves.

Thesis (M.Sc.), University of Alberta, 1971.
Typescript.

Canadian theses. **AEU**

3454 **Swindlehurst**, Edward B. 4-H in Alberta, 1917-1967. Edmonton: 4-H and Alberta Department of Youth, 1968. 125p. ill.

Glenbow. **ACG**

3455 **Toma**, Darrell Michael. Alberta Grazing Associations. A study of public resource utilization. Edmonton: University of Alberta, 1979. xi, 156 leaves.

Thesis (M.Sc.), University of Alberta, 1979.
Typescript.

U of A Theses. **AEU**

3456 **Toogood**, J.A. For the record. Alberta Institute of Agrologists, 1947-1968. s.l.: s.n., 1968. 28 leaves.

ACP

3457 **Tracie**, Carl Joseph. Agricultural settlement in the south Peace River area. Edmonton: University of Alberta, 1967. viii, 91 leaves. ill.

Thesis (M.A.), University of Alberta, 1967.
Typescript.

Canadian theses. **AEU**

3458 **Tracie**, Carl Joseph. An analysis of three variables affecting farm location in the process of agricultural settlement. The south Peace River area. Ottawa: National Library of Canada, 1970. x, 155 leaves. ill. (Canadian theses on microfilm, 06243)

Thesis (Ph.D.), University of Alberta, 1970.
Microfilm of typescript.

Canadiana, 1971. **AEU**

3459 University of Alberta. Archives. A guide to the William Pearce papers, series 7, irrigation, 1890-1927. Edmonton: Archives, University of Alberta, 1976. 14 leaves. (University of Alberta. Archives. Manuscript group, 9/2)

Canadiana, 1977. **AEU**

3460 **Wilson**, LeRoy John. The education of the farmer. The educational objectives and activities of the United Farmers of Alberta and the Saskatchewan Grain Growers' Association, 1920-1930. Ottawa: National Library of Canada, 1975. xiii, 271 leaves. (Canadian theses on microfiche, 26956)

Thesis (Ph.D.), University of Alberta, 1975.
Microfiche of typescript.

Canadiana, 1977. **AEU**

Farm & Ranch Life

3461 **Andrews**, Allen. The splendid pauper. Philadelphia: Lippincott, 1968. 255p. ill.

A biography of Moreton Frewen. Includes references to Powder River Cattle Company, which held land in Alberta, and to other Canadian activities of Frewen.

Glenbow. **ACG**

3462 **Ball**, Josiah. Memories of central Alberta. Botha: Joe Ball, 1976. 235p. ill.

Reminiscences of the Botha and Stettler areas.
Duplicated.

Ceessa. **AEA**

3463 **Brandt**, Ernie. A cowboy's memoirs. Black Diamond: Ernie Brandt, 1977. 92p. ill.

Printed by Southern Printing, Lethbridge.
Reminiscences, mostly of New Mexico.

Glenbow. **ACG**

3464 **Breen**, David Henry. The cattle compact. The ranch community in southern Alberta, 1881-1896. Calgary: University of Calgary, 1968. iv, iii, 147 leaves. (Canadian theses on microfilm, 08443)

Thesis (M.A.), University of Calgary, 1969.
Microfilm of typescript.

Dew. **ACG**

3465 **Brickman**, Julius E. Memories of yesterday. s.l.: J.E. Brickman, 1966. 32p.

Translated from the German by Professor E. Link.
Recollections of pioneering in the Forestburg district, with poems and religious themes.

ACP

3466 **Cantlon**, F.M. Oatmeal porridge and green poplar poles. A story of a pioneer family on the prairies in the early years. Sedgewick: Community Press, 1976. 111p. ill.

Reminiscences of homesteading, from the 1920s in southern Manitoba. **AECYR**

3467 **Carpenter**, Jock. Fifty dollar bride. Marie Rose Smith. A chronicle of life in the 19th century. Sidney, B.C.: Gray's Publishing, 1977. 160p. ill.

Biography of the author's grand-mother Marie Rose and her husband, Charley Smith, who settled on the Jughandle Ranch, near Lethbridge. **AEA**

3468 **Carter**, Eva. The history of organized farm women of Alberta. Edmonton: Farm Women's Union of Alberta, 1954. 64p.

Printed by Douglas Print.
A history of the Farm Women's Union of Alberta.
Glenbow.
ACG

3469 **Cayford**, Elmer H. Barefoot days. Illustrated by the author. Saskatoon: Western Producer Book Service, 1974. 137p. ill.

Reminiscences of boyhood, homesteading in the Bow River Valley and Manitou Lake Districts, in the early 1900s.
AEA

3470 **Chevraux**, Sharleen M. From the ground up. E.A. Mitchner, Managing Editor, Robert Pool, Research Editor. Edmonton: Alberta Education, 1979. 108p. ill.

Children's literature.
Printed as part of Alberta Heritage Learning Resources Project, 1980. **AEU**

3471 **Christianson**, Chris J. Early rangemen. Lethbridge: Southern Printing, 1973. 124p. ill.

Illustrated by Jacquiee Lund.
Glenbow.
ACG

3472 **Christianson**, Chris J. My life on the range. Lethbridge: Southern Printing, 1968. (4), 108p. ill.

Glenbow.
ACG

3473 **Cox**, Barbara J. Summer of childhood. s.l.: Cox, 1978. (1v.)

Printed Victoria, B.C., Book Preparation Services.
Reminiscences of pioneering in Peace River District, British Columbia.
Canadiana, 1978.
OONL

3474 **DeLeeuw**, Gary. Alberta foothills. A sample study of life within view of the Canadian Rockies. Rev. ed. General ed., Evelyn Moore. Toronto: Holt, Rinehart and Winston of Canada, 1971. 60p. ill. (People and places in Canada)

For social studies in elementary grades.
Also, French translation with title *Un ranch en Alberta. Etude d'un ranch des montagnes rocheuses canadienne*. 1969. 87p. ill.
Glenbow.
ACG

3475 **Diesel**, Gladys Cynthia Rebecca (Shope). Salute to the past. Edmonton: Commercial Printers, 1957. 188p. ill.

Canadiana, 1962.
OONL

3476 **Eggleston**, Wilfrid. While I still remember. A personal record. Toronto: Ryerson Press, 1968. 329p.

The author emigrated to Canada with his family in 1909, living in Alberta and Saskatchewan.

Glenbow. **ACG**

3477 **Gudlaugson**, Magnus Gudmundur. Three times a pioneer. Edited by Holmfridur Danielson. Winnipeg: 1958. (6), 104p. ill.

Duplicated.
Reminiscences of the Peace River district.

Glenbow. **ACG**

3478 **Gulutsan**, Lena (Hyrhor). Deedo's children. Story of John Hyrhor of Nipawin, Saskatchewan. Edmonton: L. Gulutsan, 1978. vi, 160p. ill.

Duplicated. **AEA**

3479 **Helenius**, Alice Cummings. It's good to remember. Drawings by Tom Dixon. Puyallup, Wash.: Printed by Valley Press, 1977. 190p. ill.

Reminiscences of the author's family, including residence in the Rocky Mountain House area.
Foreword by Dan Brockman, President of the Rocky Mountain House Reunion Society.

AEA

3480 **Hodgson**, John Fraser. Once upon a life time. Saskatoon: Modern Press, Prairie Books Service, 1966. 414p. ill.

Reminiscences of childhood in Swift Current, Saskatchewan, and farming in Alberta by a Coaldale resident.

Dew. **AEA**

3481 **Hodgson**, John Fraser. Wanderings of an expert. Lethbridge: Southern Printing, 1971. 226p. ill.

Reminiscences of farm life and experiences as a serviceman for International Harvester in the Lethbridge area.

Glenbow. **ACG**

3482 **Horvat**, Joseph. In the land of the free. The diary of Joseph Horvat's first forty years in Canada, 1927-1967. Written in thanksgiving in Canada's centennial year. Edmonton: J. Horvat, 1967. 43p. ill.

Cover title.
Duplicated.
Reminiscences of farming at Wildwood, Alberta. **AEA**

3483 **Jackson**, Frank. A candle in the grub box. The story of Frank Jackson. As told to Sheila Douglas. Victoria, B.C.: Shires Books, 1977. v, 144p. ill., map.

Cover title *A candle in the grub box. A struggle for survival in the northern wilderness*.
Pioneering in Southern Alberta and the Peace River Country.

Canadiana, 1978. **AEA**

3484 **Jackson**, Frank. Jam in the bedroll. The continuing story of Frank Jackson. As told to Sheila Douglas. Nanaimo, B.C.: Shires Books, 1979. 151p. ill., map

Cover title *Jam in the bedroll. A sequel to A candle in the grub box.*
Account of pioneering in the Peace River Country during the Depression. **AEA**

3485 **Johnson**, James Foster. The story of a maverick. The memories of James Foster Johnson. s.l.: s.n., 1969. 79 leaves.

Duplicated.
Reminiscences of a Michichi resident. **ACU**

3486 **Lake**, Owen Hayden. Autobiography and people I have met along the highways and byways. s.l.: O.H. Lake, 1976. 50p.

Duplicated.
On cover: Minnie and Owen Lake, pioneers of the Duchess district.
Ceessa. **ELF**

3487 **Lawrence**, Sheridan. Sheridan Lawrence, Emperor of the Peace. As told to his wife, Julia Lawrence. Peace River: S. Lawrence, 1977. viii, 61p. ill.

Cover title.
Limited edition of 100 privately printed copies.
Autobiography of a pioneer settler. **AEA**

3488 **Lodge**, Tom. Beyond the Great Slave Lake. London: Cassell, 1957. 198p. ill.

Account of author's experiences working on a cattle ranch near Pincher Creek and as a commercial fisherman at Great Slave Lake.
Glenbow. **ACG**

3489 **Long**, Philip Sheridan. Dreams, dust and depression. Calgary: Cypress Publishing, 1972. 228p.

Reminiscences of the Depression in Northern Montana.
Glenbow. **ACG**

3490 **Long**, T.B. 70 years a cowboy (a biography). Regina: Western Printers Association, 1959. 62p.

2d rev. ed. with title *Seventy years a cowboy. As told to Philip Sheridan Long*, Saskatoon, Freeman Publishing, 1965. 140p..
Dew. **ACG**

3491 **MacGregor**, James Grierson. North-West of 16. Toronto: McClelland & Stewart, 1958. 224p.

Reminiscences of homesteading in the Eastburg district.
Glenbow. **ACG**

3492 **Magill**, Katherine. Back o' Baffuf. Cobalt, Ont.: Highway Book Shop, 1977. 76p. ill.

Reminiscences of farming in the Vermilion District during the 1940s under the Veterans Land Grant system.

Canadiana, 1978. **AEA**

3493 **McCallum**, William Symington. A Scot in Canada. Adventures on a range, by Anon. Special limited ed. Calgary: Printed by North Hill News, 1963. 77p.

Cover title *Reminiscences of farming life in the Lloydminster area and later life in Calgary*.

Canadiana, 1965. **AEU**

3494 **McKinnon**, John Angus. The Bow River Range, 1898-1974, JY. Calgary: J.A.McKinnon, 1974. 214, 2p. ill.

An autobiography. **ACG**

3495 **McKinnon**, Lachlin. Lachlin McKinnon, pioneer, 1865-1948. s.l.: s.n., 1956. (4), 130p. ill.

Printed by John D. McAra.
Reminiscences of a southern Alberta rancher. Privately published in a limited edition of 500 copies.

Glenbow. **ACG**

3496 **Mitchell**, Frank E. A history of pioneering in the Pakan district. s.l.: s.n., 1973. 62p. ill.

Cover title.
Reminiscences, 1899-1973.

Ceessa. **AEA**

3497 **Mueller**, Walter R. Reminiscing with Walt. As told to Gertrude Bryan. Spirit River: Walter Mueller, 1964. 43, 2p.

AEU

3498 **Parton**, Alfred. The story of my life. New York: Vantage Press, 1966. 48p.

Reminiscences of farming near Morinville.

Glenbow. **ACG**

3499 **Patterson**, Raymond Murray. The Buffalo Head. New York: W. Sloane Associates, 1961. 273p.

Account of Alberta ranch life in the 1930's.
Also, 1972, Toronto, Macmillan. 273p. **AEU**

3500 **Patterson**, Raymond Murray. Far pastures. Sidney, B.C.: Gray's Publishing, 1963. 290p.

Second edition, 1973.
Also printed as part of Alberta Heritage Learning Resources Project, 1979 (Alberta literature for senior students and adults). **AEU**

3501 **Peterson**, Flora (Culp). Life and she. Boston: Christopher, 1960. 166p.

Reflections and psychic experiences of a homesteader in the Brooks district.

Canadiana, 1962.

AEA

3502 **Pettinger**, William. A prairie letter. Selected, annotated & illustrated by David William Pettinger. Berwick, Ont.: Stormont Press, 1969. 23p. ill.

Limited edition of 250 copies.
Reminiscences of Eagle Creek, Saskatchewan, and New Brigden, Alberta.

Glenbow.

ACG

3503 **Reed**, Job. Job Reed's letters. Life in Lethbridge, 1886-1906. Lethbridge: Historical Society of Alberta, Whoop-up Country Chapter, 1979. 50p. ill. (Historical Society of Alberta. Whoop-up Country Chapter. Occasional paper, 9)

ACP

3504 **Roberts**, Sarah Ellen. Of us and the oxen. Saskatoon: Modern Press, 1968. (6), 260p.

A story of homesteading in Alberta, near Talbot, 1906 to 1912. The original manuscript is in the Glenbow Institute. Published in the *Western Producer*, 1966. Also published, 1971, University of Texas Press, with title *Alberta homestead. Chronicle of a pioneer family*, 1971. 272p. (M.K. Brown Range Life Series, 10).
Edited by Lathrop E. Roberts.

Glenbow.

ACG

3505 **Rude**, Selmer J. Life experiences. Camrose: S.J. Rude, 1969. 44p. ill.

Autobiography.

Canadiana, 1970.

OONL

3506 **Russell**, Andy. Trails of a wilderness wanderer. New York: Knopf, 1971. xv, 297p. ill.

Also published in paperback, 1979, Mississauga, Ballantine.

CBIP, 1979.

AEU

3507 **Smith**, Sidney Bailey. Through the years with Sidney B. Smith. 1960. (4), 172p. ill.

Autobiography of an English Mormon who emigrated to southern Alberta in the 1920s.

Glenbow.

ACG

3508 **Spurrell**, William. Adventures in two worlds. I worshipped the old, but thrilled to the new. Memoirs of William Spurell, Sr. Carstairs: Carstairs News, 1974. 142p. ill.

Reminiscences of a Starland resident.

Canadiana 1977.

AEU

3509 **Stelfox**, Henry. Rambling thoughts of a wandering fellow, 1903-1968. Edited by John G. Stelfox. Edmonton: I.D.B. Press, 1972. ix, 235p. ill.

Reminiscences of a Rocky Mountain House farmer, conservationist and Indian agent. Includes considerable information on wild life.

Glenbow. **ACG**

3510 **Stewart**, Norman. Children of the pioneers. Calgary: Foothill Printers, 1962. (1), 106, (1), 12, (1)p. ill.

Cover title.
An account of farming in the Red Deer area from 1884.

Glenbow. **ACG**

3511 **Thomson**, Georgina Helen. Crocus and meadowlark country. Recollections of a happy childhood and youth on a homestead in southern Alberta. Edmonton: Institute of Applied Art, 1963. 277p. ill.

The Thomson family homesteaded near Nanton, in the Parkland District.
Printed by Co-Op Press, Edmonton.

Glenbow. **ACG**

3512 **Warren**, Ernest Herbert Falkland. Seventy south Alberta years. The autobiography of Ernest Herbert Falkland (Bert) Warren, as written by S. Evangeline Warren. Ilfracombe, Devon: A.H. Stockwell, 1960. 255p. ill.

An account of ranching in the Lethbridge area.

Glenbow. **ACG**

3513 **Webber**, Frank. The northwest quarter of thirty-six. Edmonton: Franklyn M. Webber, 1964. (4), 247p.

An account of homesteading in the Boyne Lake District.
On title page: A hand made production, screen printed.

Glenbow. **ACG**

AUTHOR INDEX

AUTHOR INDEX

Abell, Angus Sinclair
Rural municipal government in Alberta, taxation and finance, . . . 2084
Acadia Women's Institute
A history of the Huxley area, ... 2845
Acme and District Historical Society
Acme memories, ... 2846
Acme. United Church
History of the churches of the Acme area, ... 261
Adams, Michael
Drifting into grey, ... 927
Adams, Norman Edgar
Calgary A poem, ... 836
Calgary's great stampede show A poem, ... 837
Adams, Trenton Peter
Economic change in the Grande Cache region of Alberta, ... 2085
Adamson, Philip Edward
The Adamson saga, 1536-1936, ... 2697
Adcock, Blanche
Shadows of the Neutrals, ... 2954
Adic, Adelaide Green
Memories of Verdant Valley, Cassel Hill, Livingston, Rainbow, . . . 2986
Ahimbisibwe, Josiah Karibondo-Karabashensheire
An economic output and pricing policy for service co-operatives, . . 3385
Ahlf, Margaret
Edson flashback, ... 2996
Air Museum of Canada
Air Museum of Canada, Calgary, Canada, ... 2314
Airdrie Community Improvement Club
One day's journey, ... 3299
Ajao, Adenihun Olanrewaju
The role of government and business in Alberta's export trade, . . . 2086
Albert, Diane
History of the Fort Kent parish, ... 262
Alberta Art Foundation
Selections, ... 1140
Alberta Association of Municipal Districts and Counties
Story of rural municipal government in Alberta, 1909-1969, ... 2449
Alberta Association of Registered Nurses
Heritage of service, ... 3353
Alberta Beekeepers Association
Kids! Honey fun with Berta bee, ... 3386
Alberta Chamber of Commerce
Progress report no 2 on actions resulting from resolutions, ... 2087
Report and proceedings, ... 2104
Alberta Chamber of Commerce Manpower Conference, Jasper, 1974
Proceedings of the Alberta Chamber of Commerce Manpower Conference held in Jasper, October 6-8, 1974, ... 2088
Alberta Coal Mining Industry Commission
Alberta's coal industry, 1919, ... 2158

Alberta College of Art
Ballachey, Besant, Bienvenue, Clark, Crockett, Gallie, Graff, Hohn, Mable, Roberts, Robertson, Van Wyk on paper, ... 1141
Bert Borch, ... 1148
The death's head knight, ... 1153
Do you believe in television?, ... 1151
Feist, ACA Gallery, Jan 25-Feb 5, 1971, ... 1188
Greg Arnold, ... 1146
Harry Kiyooka, paintings and prints, ... 1213
Henry Kiyooka paintings & prints, ... 1214
Its the real thing - Hall, ... 1209
Joe Fafard, ... 1187
The journey goes on , ... 1252
Lindoe, ACA Gallery, Jan 25-Feb 5, 1971, ... 1218
Peter Deacon Drawings, Nov 6- 26, ... 1157
Playboy illustration, ... 1142
"Popguns" Don Lougheed, ... 1219
Robert Rauschenburg - Glass handle, ... 1232
An Whitlock, ... 1249
Young contemporary Calgary artists exhibition, ... 1144
Alberta Conference on Aging, 1st, Edmonton, 1967
Growing old effectively, ... 1761
Alberta Conference on Television and Education, University of Alberta, 1960
Education through television, ... 1470
Alberta Federation of Metis Settlement Associations
The Metis people of Canada, ... 1857
Alberta Funeral Information Serice
Facts about funerals, ... 1762
Alberta Hereford Association
Jubilee brochure, ... 3387
Alberta Heritage Foundation
The spirit of Alberta, ... 2819
Alberta Heritage Learning Resources Project
Between the Red and the Rockies, ... 3420
Bird at the window, ...799
Chinook Ridge, 1880-1914, ...605
Diversions, ...565
The Emperor of Peace River, .748
Far pastures, ... 3500
From the ground up, ... 3470
The hungry hills, ...778
In jeopardy, ...573
Junior atlas of Alberta, ... 2659
The little white schoolhouse, ... 1531
The nature of things, ... 3323
Pages from the past, ... 2814
Panorama, ...578
Road to yesterday, ...579
The roar of the twenties, ... 2785
The scorched wood people, ...819

A sense of place, ...580
Sons of the soil, ...702
Souvenirs, ... 2820
Tales tall and true, ... 2083
Transitions, ...585
Western moods, ...588
Western profiles, ...589
Who has seen the wind, ...742
Who owns the earth?, ...590
Alberta Indian Development Systems Limited
Lesser Slave Lake study, ... 2089
Alberta Indian Treaties Commemorative Program
As long as the sun shines, the rivers flow and the grass grows, ... 1853
Alberta Metis Association. Housing Committee
Housing designs for the Alberta Metis Association, 1973, ... 1711
Alberta Motor Association
A history of motoring in Alberta, ... 2327
Alberta Native Communications Society
A house for Harry, ... 1723
Alberta Native Women's Conference, 1st, Edmonton, 1968
Report, ... 1854
Alberta Native Women's Conference, 2d, Edmonton,1969
Report, ... 1855
Alberta Potters' Association
National ceramics exhibition, Calgary,
October 29 - December 12, 1976, ... 1143
Alberta Power Limited
Northland Utilities Limited, ... 2185
Alberta School Trustees' Association
The small high school in Alberta, ... 1488
Study guide for the Commission of Educational Planning
report entitled
"A choice of futures", ... 1471
Alberta Social Credit League
Do you know?, ... 2396
Ernest C Manning, ... 2403
A tribute to Hon EC Manning on the occasion of his
50th birthday party, September 30th, 1958, ...907
Alberta Social Credit League Women's Auxiliaries
Stars in time, ... 2448
Alberta Society of Artists
Alberta '73, ... 1164
Alberta Society of Artists. Calgary Local
Young contemporary Calgary artists exhibition, ... 1144
Alberta Teachers' Association
The Cameron Commission - two years after, ... 1472
Alberta Teachers' Association. Athabasca Local
A history of the schools of the county of Athabasca, ... 1516
Alberta Teachers' Association. Calgary Public Schools Local
Calgary, ... 3017

Alberta Teachers' Association. Committee on Association Services
Service for the seventies, ... 1473
Alberta Teachers' Association. English Council
How can a song be blue, ... 554
An icecream cone feeling in the dark of December, ... 555
A nickel's worth of wishing, ... 556
Alberta Teachers' Association. Red Deer District Local
Schools of the parkland, NWT 1886 - Alberta, 1967, ... 1517
Alberta Veterinary Medicine Association
A review of the work of the Health of Animals Branch in Alberta, . 3452
Alberta Wheat Pool
Farm stored grain on the Prairies, a cost study, ... 3405
Grain varieties in Alberta, summarized by Alberta Wheat Pool for
Alberta's School students, ... 3388
History, ownership & government of Alberta Wheat Pool, ... 3389
Students' story of co-operation, ... 3390
Alberta Wheat Pool Women's Association
Poems, ... 838
Alberta Wilderness Association
The Elbow-Sheep headwaters, a recreational wilderness, ... 1616
The western Swan Hills, ... 1617
Wildlands for recreation, ... 1618
The Willmore Wilderness Park, ... 1619
Alberta Women's Christian Temperance Union
The story of the years, ... 1763
Alberta Women's Institutes
Alberta Women's Institutes, 1909-1954, ... 3391
We take pleasure in introducing you to Alberta Women's Institutes, . 3392
Alberta Youth Hostels Council
Development proposal for the eastern slopes of the
Canadian Rockies, Alberta, Canada, ... 1620
Four development proposals for the eastern slopes of the
Canadian Rockies, northern portion only, ... 1621
Albright, W.D
Poems of WD Albright, 1881-1946, ... 839
Alcorn, Phyllis Maureen (Gravistin)
In the bend of the Battle, ... 2848
Alderson, Sue Ann
Bonnie McSmithers is at it again!, ... 593
Bonnie McSmithers you're driving me dithers, ... 594
Hurry up, Bonnie, ... 595
Aldini
New concepts in magic, ... 1261
Novel concepts with cards, ... 1262
Roughingly yours, ... 1263
Alexander, Gerda Isolde
Three German dialects in Barrhead,
Alberta Phonology and interference, ... 441
Alexander, Grace
First Baptist Church 75th anniversary, March 7, 1976, ... 263

Alexander, Laura E
Kroetsch's tragicomic romance, ... 521
Alexander, William Hardy
The book of Catullus of Verona done into English verse by William Hardy Alexander, ... 840
Alix. United Church
The winds of change, ... 264
Alix-Clive History Club
Pioneers and progress, ... 3188
All Chiefs Conference Committee
Where do we go from here?, ... 1856
Allan, Iris Constance (Sommerville)
The boy in buckskins, ... 596
John Rowand, fur trader, ... 597
Mother and her family, ... 2698
White Sioux, ... 598
Wop May, bush pilot, ... 599
Young fur trader, ... 600
Allan, Luke, pseud.
Blue Pete in the badlands, ... 601
Allen, Ralph
Peace River country, ... 602
Allen, W.G.P
The trail through the Pembina Valley, 1790-1912, ... 2849
Allesi, Ron
The magic of Ronal, ... 1264
Allison, Patricia
Seasons, ... 3309
Seasons Fall, ... 3310
Seasons Summer, ... 3311
Allisson, Rhonda
Victoria Park, ... 2850
Almberg, Ruby
Echoes along the Ribstone,. 2851
Almon, Bert
The return and other poems,. 841
Taking possession, ... 842
Alternatives Canada, a Canada West Conference on Confederation, Banff, 1978. A summary report on the proceedings of Alternatives Canada, a Canada West Conference on Confederation, held at Banff, March 27-29, 1978,. 2384
Amalgamated Transit Union. Division 583
50th anniversary, Division 583, Amalgamated Transit Union, ... 2315
Amazing Maurice
Mentalistic encore, ... 1265
Paper bag magic,. 1266
Phone book magic, ... 1267
Amman, O.A.M.
The Studit monks, ... 163

Amy, William Lacey *see* Allan, Luke, pseud.
Blue Pete in the badlands, ... 601
Anderson, A.J
The golden anniversary of the Alberta Pharmaceutical Association, 1911-1961, ... 3348
Anderson, Alda M
The Metis people of Canada,. . . . 1857
Anderson, Angus
Pictorial album of Veteran, Loyalist and Hemaruka,. . . . 2852
Where the prairie meets the hills, ... 2853
Anderson, Anne
The affair at Timber Lake, ... 603
The animals of the wilds, ... 468
Arrangements of alphabet Cree and syllabic symbols, ... 469
Arrangment (sic) of oral Cree for beginners, ... 470
Awasis book,. . . . 471
Coversational Cree, ... 472
Cree, ... 474
Cree, ... 473
Cree Nehiyawewin, ... 475
Cree picture dictionary, ... 476
Cree reader, ... 477
Cree tenses and explanation, ... 478
Cree Twelve basic lesons, ... 479
Cree vocabulary, ... 480
Cree vocabulary for little beginners,. . . . 481
Cree vocabulary, 2nd level,. . . . 482
Cree What they do book, ... 483
Learning Cree,. . . . 484
Legends of Wesakecha, ... 2068
Let's learn Cree Namoya ayiman,. . . . 485
Little Cree dictionary Cree to English,. . . . 486
Little hunter book Machesis, ... 487
Little hunter book Machesis, ... 488
The lore of the wilds, ... 2069
Plains Cree dictionary in the "Y" dialect, ... 489
Read and write The Cree language, ... 490
Teaching of the Cree language Basic simplified method, ... 491
Tim and his friends, ... 492
Tim goes to the farm, ... 493
Wapi,. . . . 494
We print and we read Grade 1,. . . . 495
Anderson, C.W.
A horse named Joe,. . . . 660
Anderson, Daniel R
The Metis people of Canada,. . . . 1857
Anderson, David Lawrence
The recreational capability and use of Wabamun Lake and the eastern half of Lesser Slave Lake, ... 1622

Anderson, Elbe
Pictorial album of Veteran, Loyalist and Hemaruka,. 2852
Where the prairie meets the hills,. 2853
Anderson, Ellis Albert Ahl
The landscape of southwestern Alberta,. 2514
Anderson, Francis Garfield
Personal contact affecting city children's knowledge of and attitudes to Alberta Indians, ... 1858
Anderson, Frank Wesley
Almighty Voice, ... 2810
Bill Miner, train robber,. 1764
Canada's worst mine disaster, ... 2811
The Carbon murders mystery, ... 1765
A concise history of capital punishment in Canada, ... 1766
The dark strangler, ... 1767
The death of Albert Johnson,. 1768
The Frank Slide story, ... 2854
A frontier guide to mystic Jasper and the Yellowhead Pass,. 2663
A frontier guide to outlaws of Manitoba,. 1769
A frontier guide to the Dewdney Trail, ... 2664
A frontier guide to the dynamic Crow's Nest Pass, ... 2665
Frontier guide to Waterton, land of leisure,. 2677
Ghost towns journal, ... 2855
The Hope slide story, ... 2762
Murder on the plains, ... 1770
Pardon my therapy,. 1771
Regina's terrible tornado, ... 2763
Riel's Manitoba uprising, ... 2764
The rum runners,. 1772
Saskatchewan's provincial police, ... 2493
Sergeant Harry Morren, Royal North West Mounted Police, ... 2494
Sheriffs and outlaws of Western Canada, ... 2495
1885 The Riel Rebellion, ... 2765
Anderson, Henry R
Reports on the last Indian battle and the Lindy campsite, the Sundial Butte cairn site, the Gergel campsite, the Burmis Boulder paving site, 2014
Anderson, Hugh
Harbinger,. 572
Anderson, Jacqueline Margaret
A road map study based on the 1974 official Alberta road map,. . . 2654
Anderson, James
Change in a central place system,. 2159
Anderson, James Maxwell
Ancient Hispanic inscriptions, ... 2009
Anderson, Jean
An analysis of the Public Assistance Appeal System in Alberta, . . . 1773
Anderson, N. R
Oblate Fathers in Calgary,. 164

Anderson, Owen Arthur James
The Alberta Social Credit Party, ... 2397
The unfinished revolt, ... 2359
Anderson, Robert William
The influence of professional, institutional and biographical factors on the attitudes of forest resource managers in Alberta, . . . 3336
Anderson, Ruby Olga
A study of leisure-time interests and activities of first year women at the University of Alberta, ... 1623
Andrasz
A wilderness, ... 1098
Andrew, David Anderson
The Hereford in Canada, 1860-1968, ... 3393
Andrews, Allen
The splendid pauper, ... 3461
Andrews, Val
Magic in store, ... 1268
A practical guide to ventriloquism, ... 1254
Anglican Church of Canada. Diocese of Edmonton. Women's Auxiliary Diocesan Board
Fifty golden years, 1914-1964, ... 165
Angus Ridge Women's Institute
Community history, ... 2863
Annett, Ronald Ross
Especially Babe, ... 604
Anon *see* McCallum, William Symington
A Scot in Canada, ... 3493
Anton, Gordon A
The Liberal Party in Alberta, ... 2398
Antonelli, Marylu
Pottery in Alberta, ... 1114
Antoniuk, Mary Frances *see* Ross, Mary Frances (Antoniuk)
Oh! The Coal Branch, ... 3224
Aoki, Testsuo
The development of the Lethbridge School District No 51 to 1960, . 1518
Appleby, Edna (Hill)
Canmore, the story of an era, ... 2856
Arbuckle, John
Phonology of the Volhynian German dialect of the Edmonton area, . . 442
Archaeological Society of Alberta
Archaeology in Alberta, ... 2010
Archaeological Society of Alberta. Lethbridge Centre
Crystal Spring Indian camp site, ... 2059
Grassy Lake and Suitor sites, ... 2011
Police Coulee, ... 2012
A report on Blood Indian chief tipi circle and the Stevens Rock at Foremost, Alberta, ... 2013
Reports on the last Indian battle and the Lindy campsite, the Sundial Butte cairn site, the Gergel campsite, the Burmis Boulder paving site, 2014

Archer, John H.
Land of promise, ... 2886
West of yesterday, ... 3239
Archer, Violet
April weather, ... 1386
Cantata sacra, ... 1387
Christmas,. 1388
The daffodils, ... 1389
Divertimento for brass quintet, ... 1390
Divertimento for orchestra,. 1391
Fanfare and passacaglia,. 1392
Four bagatelles Piano solo,. 1393
Four Canadian folk-songs, ... 1394
Four little studies for piano, ... 1395
Gold sun, ... 1396
Green rain, ... 1397
The gulls, ... 1398
I will lift mine eyes,. 1399
In just spring, ... 1400
Introit and choral prayer, ... 1401
Irradiations, No18, ... 1402
A la claire fontaine,. 1403
Landscapes, ... 1404
Life in a prairie shack, ... 1405
The Mater Admirabilis Chapel,. 1406
Minute music for small hands For piano,. 1407
Moon songs, ... 1408
My hands,. 1409
O Lord, Thou hast searched me and known me,. 1410
O sing unto the Lord, ... 1411
Plainsong, ... 1412
Prelude and allegro for violin and piano, ... 1413
Psalm 150, ... 1414
Rondo, ... 1415
Separation, ... 1416
Sganarelle, ... 1417
Shout with joy,. 1418
Someone, ... 1419
Sonata, ... 1420
Sonata for alto saxophone and piano, ... 1421
Sonatina for organ, ... 1422
Sonatina no3 Piano solo,. 1423
Storm, ... 1424
Suite for solo flute, ... 1425
Sweet Jesu, King of bliss, ... 1426
Ten folk songs for four hands, for players young and old,. 1427
Theme and variations for piano, ... 1428
Three duets, for two violins, ... 1429
Three folk songs of old Manitoba,. 1430

Three French-Canadian folk songs for mixed chorus, ... 1431
Three miniatures for piano, ... 1432
Three sketches for orchestra, ... 1433
Trio no 2, for piano, violin and cello, ... 1434
The twenty-third Psalm, for medium voice and piano, ... 1435
Two chorale preludes for organ, with Hammond organ registration, . 1436
Two songs, ... 1437
Archibald, Susan
Koo-Koo-sint, ...999
Nisku, ...735
Ardrossan Women of Unifarm
Cherished memories, ... 3302
Ariza, Jose Hernan
Community development experiences in the Chipewyan community of Cold Lake, Alberta, ... 1712
Armena Home and School Association
Dear old golden rule days, 1898-1967, ... 1519
Armena. Scandia Lutheran Church
Seventy-fifth anniversary, 1901-1976, ...265
Armstrong, Bruce
Encyclopedia of suspensions and levitations, ... 1269
Armstrong, C.C.
The days of our years,. 266
Armstrong, William
Historical watercolours by William Armstrong, ... 1145
Arnold, Abraham
Jewish life in Canada,. 1936
Arnold, C.
Primitive art and technology,. 2054
Arnold, Greg
Greg Arnold, ... 1146
Arrowwood Farm Women's Union
The Arrowwood story (Mistsa-Katpiskoo), ... 2857
Arscott, W. Hugh
Down a wet highway, ... 2596
Art Gallery of Greater Victoria
Prairie images, ... 1212
Art Gallery of Ontario
Changing visions - the Canadian landscape, ... 1171
The influence of irrigation and the railroad on the settlement of southern Alberta,. 2812
Ash, Edwin E.
Once upon a childhood, ...629
Once upon a little town, ...630
Ashton, Ada
Crestomere-Sylvan Heights heritage, ... 2858
Askin, William R
Labor unrest in Edmonton and district and its coverage by the Edmonton press, 1918-1919, ... 2160

Asquith, Keith
Attitudes of selected students at the University of Alberta toward physical activity, ... 1624
Association canadienne-française de l'Alberta. Conseil régional de Bonnyville
Bonnyville in question, 1975, ... 1861
Association canadienne-française de l'Alberta
Aperçu historique de l'ACFA, ... 1859
Les héritiers de lord Durham, ... 1860
Athabina Athletic Association Homecoming
A history of Athabina, ... 3078
Atherton, Peter John
Quality education - what price?, ... 1474
Atrill, V.H.
The Great Plains Project looks at new modes of transportation, . . . 2316
Atwell, Phyllis Harryette
Kinship and migration among Calgarian residents of Indian origin, . 1862
Austin, Madeline *see* Freeman, Madeline (Austin)
A horse for Running Buffalo, ... 656
Awid, Richard
A salute to the Arab pioneers of northern Alberta, ... 1863
Bérubé, Roland
Les Bérubés de Beaumont, ... 2699
Lamoureux, ... 2861
Baergen, William Peter
The fur trade at Lesser Slave Lake, 1815-1831, ... 2862
Bagley, Ray
The poems of Ray Bagley, ... 843
Bagnall, Lucy Lowe
At the seventy-fifth milestone, ... 267
Bailey, Robert
Medalta, ... 2161
Bailly, Antoine
Aspects de l'histoire et de l'éconmie de Falher, ... 2515
Bain, Donald Morrison
Canadian Pacific in the Rockies, ... 2317
Bain, James
Travels and adventures in Canada and the Indian territories, between the years 1760 and 1776, ... 2788
Bain, Mabel
The Banff-Jasper highway descriptive guide, ... 2696
Baine, Richard Paul
Calgary, an urban study, ... 2516
Baines, Audrey (Chiswick)
Through the looking glass, ... 3292
Baird, David McCurdie
Banff National Park, ... 2597
Jasper National Park, ... 2598
Baker, Alan Maurice
The Red Deer region, ... 2517

Baker, Albert TenBroeke
The Crow's Nest Pass agreement in review, ... 2318
Baker, Horace S
The Alberta butter industry, ... 2162
Bakken, Edna
Chinook Ridge, 1880-1914, ...605
Bakstad, Alfred
The Piegan country, ... 2981
Baldridge, Mary Humphrey
Bride of the gorilla,. 1035
The loneliness of the poet/housewife, ...844
The Mary Shelley play, ... 1036
The photographic moment,. 1037
Slide-images, ...845
The suicide meet,. 1038
Ball, Josiah
Memories of central Alberta,. 3462
Ballachey, Barbara
Barbara Ballachey, ... 1147
Early Calgary friends,. 3280
Ballem, John Bishop
The devil's lighter, a novel,. 606
The dirty scenario, a novel, ...607
The Judas conspiracy,. 608
The moon pool,. .609
The oil and gas lease in Canada, ... 2469
Ballhorn, Dora
Community history,. 2863
Bancroft, Donald Asa
Equalization of assessments in Alberta, ... 2090
Bancroft Women's Institute
The heritage of Bancroft, ... 2864
Banff Centre School of Fine Arts
Fellfield, ...566
Banff Conference on Central and East European Studies,
1st, 1977 Proceedings,. 1864
Banff Conference on Central and East European Studies, 2d, ... 1978
Second Banff Conference on Central and East European Studies,
Banff Springs Hotel, Banff, Alberta, March 2-5, 1978,. 1865
Banff Policies Conference on Canadian Economic Survival, Banff 1963
Background papers and proceedings,. 2091
Bannon, Michael Joseph
The evolution of the central area of Edmonton, Alberta, 1946-1966, . 2518
Barbour, Douglas
He & she &, ...846
Landfall, ...847
A poem as long as the highway, ...848
Shorelines,. 849
Songbook, ...850
The story so far, 5, ...851

Visions of my grandfather, ... 852
White, ... 853
Barclay, Harold
Religion and ethnicity, ... 160
Bardock, Edison Frederick
Pupil transportation in Alberta, ... 2319
Barilko, Olga Louise
A study of the incidence of juvenile delinquency and its treatment in Edmonton in 1944, ... 1774
Barker, R
Inkwells and school bells, ... 1553
Barnett, Donald C
Alberta, ... 2600
Poundmaker, ... 2813
Barnhouse, Dorothy P
The quest of the Golden Gannet, ... 610
Barnieh, Zina
A mirror of our dreams, ... 1256
Barons History Book Club
Wheat heart of the West, ... 2865
Barr, Brenton M
Calgary, metropolitan structure and influence, ... 2169
Research studies by Western Canadian geographers, ... 2570
Barr, John J
The dynasty, ... 2399
The unfinished revolt, ... 2359
Barraclough, Morris
From prairie to park, ... 1625
Barrhead and District Historical Society
Trails Northwest, ... 2866
Barrhead Elementary School. Grade IVA, 1966/67
The pioneer days of Barrhead, ... 2867
Barrhead History Book Committee
The golden years, ... 3263
The golden years, ... 2868
Barris, Theodore
Fire canoe, ... 2320
Barritt, Vera Rennetta
To the future, your heritage, Ripley 1883, 1903-1963, ... 2869
Barry, Walter W
Anecdotal history of Calgary Separate Schools, ... 1520
Bashaw History Committee
Beautiful fields, ... 3148
Basilian Fathers
Basilian Brothers, ... 166
The Basilian priest, ... 167
In tribute to the Basilian pioneers, 1902-1963, ... 268
In tribute to the Basilian pioneers, 1902-1977, ... 269
Bass, Althea
Christmas, ... 1388

The Mater Admirabilis Chapel,. 1406
Bassano History Book Club
Best in the west by a damsite, 1900-1940, ... 2870
Batchelor, Bruce Edward
The agrarian frontier near Red Deer and Lacombe, Alberta, 1884-1914, ... 2871
Bates, Jane Eliza Woolf
Founding of Cardston and vicinity, ... 2872
Bates, Maxwell
Far-away flags, ... 854
Battle Bend Circle
Battle Bend pioneers, ... 2873
Battle, Lester
The Delia Craigmyle saga,. 2874
Bauer, Reuben Alexander
One of many, ... 270
Baumgarten, Susan Im
Rocky Mountain wildlife, ... 3313
Baureiss, Gunter A
The city and the subcommunity, ... 1866
Beach, Floyd K
Alberta's petroleum paternity, ... 2251
Beach, Judith Emily
Attitudes of clients and counsellors toward the Edmonton Family Court Conciliation Project, ... 1742
Bearberry Wapitana Society
Recollections of the homestead trails, 1900-1978, ... 3138
Beattie, Allen W
Trails grown over, ... 3394
Beaugrand, Helen
Heaven via Little New York,. 168
Beaupré, Marie Cimon
Leurs rêves, nos mémoires,. 2875
Beaver Mines Women's Institute
History,. 2876
Beaverlodge and District Historical Association
Beaverlodge to the Rockies, ... 3253
The Monkman Pass Highway, ... 2353
Beddington Farm Women's Union
The Nose Creek story from 1792,. 2877
Bedford, Elaine
An historical geography of settlement in the North Saskatchewan River Valley, Edmonton,. 2519
Beere, Reginald Henry
Some aspects of business education in Canada with particular reference to Alberta, ... 2163
Beiseker Historical Society
Beiseker's golden heritage, ... 3232
Beiseker. Our Lady of Assumption Catholic Parish
Souvenir of the golden jubilee, 1908-1958, ... 272

Bekker, Janny
25 years, First Christian Reformed Church, Red Deer,. 273
Belanger, Art J
The Calgary-Edmonton, Edmonton-Calgary trail, ... 2321
A half mile of hell, ... 1626
Bell, Bob
Illusionseseme, ... 1303
Inside magic, ... 1270
Bell, David
Inside magic, ... 1270
Bell, J.B
The Commonwealth Games management financial feasibility study, . 1704
Bell, Lex
Horseman in scarlet, ... 624
Bell, Margaret Cravath
The history of Cravath Corners, 1910-1926, ... 2878
The Hussar heritage, ... 2879
Bell, N. Fred
My fifteen years with 4-H clubs, ... 3395
Bell, Wade
The North Saskatchewan River book, ... 2601
Bella, Leslie
Mini-parks for Edmonton, ... 1648
Bellam, Ernest Jay
Studies in Stoney morphology and phonology,. 496
Bellevue. St. Cyril's Catholic Church
Golden anniversary, 1915-1965,. 274
Bellingham, Brenda
Joanie's magic boots, ... 611
Benfield, Richard William
The recreational use of the hydro-electric power reservoirs of Alberta, 1627
Benham, Mary Lile
Nellie McClung, ... 1743
Bennett, Mary
Reflections, ... 2880
Bent, S.A.
Bow Island, 1912-1962, 50th anniversary, ... 2881
Bentall, Shirley Franklyn
At the seventy-fifth milestone, ... 267
Buckboard to brotherhood,. 169
Bentham, Douglas
Chester and Bentham,. 1155
Bercuson, David Jay
Alberta's coal industry, 1919, ... 2158
Fools and wise men, ... 2164
Law and society in Canada in historical perspective, ... 2470
Western perspectives 1, ... 2809
Berg, Barbara Jean
Operation of Program 5 in Alberta, ... 2165

Berg, Hilda *see* Mohr, Hilda (Berg)
The great pioneers who cleared and broke the virgin land of Josephburg, 1867-1967, . . . 1963
Bergson, Syd
Mentalism and its presentation,. . . 1331
Berry, Lois Minerva
The Readiness Centre, . . . 1775
Berrymoor 3Bs Club
Forests to grainfields, . . . 3141
Berrymoor-Carnwood Historical Society
Forests to grainfields, . . . 3141
Bersea, Diane
Our Alberta heritage, . . . 2828
Bert, Phyllis
Stories of the pioneers of the west country, . . . 2882
Bertram, Robert Gordon
Productivity relationships in Alberta Government Telephones,. . . 2322
Berwyn. Bissell Memorial United Church
Twenty-fifth anniversary, . . . 275
Berwyn Centennial Committee
Brick's Hill, Berwyn and beyond, . . . 3050
Bessai, Diane
Figures in a ground, . . . 567
Betke, Carl Frederick
The United Farmers of Alberta, 1921-1935, . . . 2400
Bettison, David George
The politics of Canadian urban development, . . . 2450
Urban affairs in Alberta, . . . 2451
Betts, George Michael
The Edmonton aldermanic election of 1962, . . . 2452
Bezanson, A. Maynard
Sodbusters invade the Peace, . . . 2883
Bezenar, Gisèle Laliberté
Le père Albert Lacombe Arsous-kitsi-parpi, . . . 170
Bhajan, Edward R
Community development programs in Alberta, . . . 1713
Bhatia, June
Alberta diamond jubilee anthology, . . . 552
The latchkey kid,. . . 612
Liverpool Daisy, . . . 613
Minerva's stepchild,. . . 614
Twopence to cross the Mersey, . . . 615
Bialk, Elisa
Tizz at the Stampede,. . . 616
Tizz in the Canadian Rockies, . . . 617
Bibby, Reginald Wayne
The secular in the sacred, . . . 171
Bickersteth, John Burgon
The land of open doors, . . . 2602

Bickley, Ruby Viola
Ridgewood community, Red Deer, Alberta, 1889-1967, ... 2884
Bilash, O.
Why bilingual education?, ... 1475
Bindloss Pioneer Committee
Golden memories, 1912-1963, ... 2885
Birch, Norman Edward
Citizen participation - Fact or fiction, ... 1776
Bird, C.D.
Five natural areas in the city of Calgary,. 1628
Birdsall, J. Everett
Sixty years of service, 1917-18 to 1977-78, ... 3396
Bishop, J.T.
Alberta hail research a major agricultural disaster, ... 3397
Bissett, Amy
April weather, ... 1386
Bjorge, Ronnie
Trails and trials, ... 3097
Blackburn, Cecil R.
The development of sports in Alberta, 1900-1918, ... 1629
Blackburn, John Hiram
The Blackburn story, ... 2700
Land of promise, ... 2886
Blacklock, Les
The high west, ... 3312
Blackman, Warren D.
The cost of confederation, ... 2360
Blairmore Lion's Club
The story of Blairmore, Alberta, 1911-1961, ... 2887
Blake, George
Comedy magic,. 1271
Commercial card magic,. 1272
Forgotten magic, ... 1273
Loopy loop, ... 1274
Major magic, ... 1275
Master magic, ... 1276
More master magic, ... 1277
Take a note, ... 1278
Blake, William
Two songs, ... 1437
Blodgett, Edward D.
Sounding, ...855
Take away the names,. 856
Blood, Donald Arthur
Rocky Mountain wildlife, ... 3313
Blower, James
Gold rush,. 2888
Blue, F.
Rosyth memoirs, 1906-1965, ... 2889
Wind, willows and prairie-wool A centennial project, ... 2890

Blue Quills Native Education Council
How to learn to read syllabics, .499
Blumell, James E
This is our land, ... 2891
Bohlin, Karl Magnus
The spatial and economic impact of recreational expenditures and sales in the Pigeon Lake area of Alberta,. 2092
Bohnec, Ruth
Pages from the past, ... 2814
Bohrod, Aaron
Scotty's mare, ...661
Boileau, Gilles
Les canadiens français de la région de Saint-Paul,. 2892
Evolution démographique de la population canadienne-française de la region de Rivière la Paix, ... 2520
Boldt, Edward D
Conformity and deviance, ... 1867
Bolinger, Ralphene
The Gleichen call, ... 2893
Bon Accord Farm Women's Union
Leaves of yesteryear, ... 2939
Boniface, Father *see* Heidmeier, Boniface
Pioneering in the west, ...208
Boon, Ivor
Alberta, western treasure chest,. 2603
Boon, Marjorie
Alberta, western treasure chest,. 2603
Boote, Walter H.S
Ogden whistle, ... 2894
Boothman, Harry
Discussion notes for a seminar on the management of public parks and recreation services, ... 1630
Borch, Bert
Bert Borch, ... 1148
Boreal Institute for Northern Studies
The land of Peter Pond, ... 2527
Borgstede, Arlene
St Albert, a pictorial history,. 2895
Borhek, J.T
Persistence and change, ... 1973
Boston, Stewart
Counsellor extraordinary, ... 1039
Botting, Gary
The box beyond, ... 1040
Five short plays, ... 1041
Freckled blue and other poems,. .857
Harriot!, ... 1042
Lady Godiva on a plaster horse, .858
Perambulance and Pipe dream,. 1043
Prometheus rebound, ...859

Streaking, ...860
The theatre of protest in America, ... 1255
Boucher, Edith
Exploration du langage des enfants francophones albertains de cinq ans, ...443
Boudreau, Joseph A
Alberta, Aberhart and Social Credit, ... 2401
Boughen, Robert Arthur
A study of educational finance in Alberta, 1958-1971, ... 1477
Boulton, Jane
Opal, ... 2651
Bow Island Jubilee Committee
Bow Island, 1912-1962, 50th anniversary, ... 2881
Bow Island Lions Club
Silver sage, ... 3272
Bow Valley Naturalists
Vermilion Lakes, Banff National Park, ... 3314
Bower, Carolyn Jane
Petrographic studies of north western plains ceramics, ... 2015
Bowman, Bob
Atomic feelings, ...895
Bowman, Gladys
Garrington Post Office, 1907, ... 2896
Bowman, Ronald Fraser Patrick
Railways in southern Alberta, ...232
Bowness Historical Committee of the Golden Jubilee
Bowness Golden Jubilee, 1911-1961,. 3176
Bowtell Community Association
Bowtell tales to 1976, ... 3214
Boylen, Diana M.
Farm land tenure in Alberta,. 3398
Boytim, Richard H.
Fibber's fables,. 618
Braithwaite, C.R.
Early settlers of the Shady Nook district and the close surrounding area,. 2897
Braithwaite, Max
The valley of the vanishing birds, ...619
Brandt, Ernie
A cowboy's memoirs, ... 3463
Brasini, Armando
Armando Brasini,. 1149
Brass, Eleanor
Medicine Boy and other Cree tales, ... 2070
Bredin, Thomas
Parsons on the plains, .223
Breen, David Henry
The cattle compact,. 3464
Breen, Reg
Three little hills of home, ...861

Bregha, François
Bob Blair's pipline, ... 2252
Brent, Lu
Lu Brent's best magic tricks, ... 1279
Bres, Hendrik
Hendrik Bres, Ann Clarke Darrah, Eva Deiner, ... 1150
Brese, William Gerald
An analysis of the sulphur industry in Alberta, ... 2166
Bresnahan, Jessie M.
Poems of the Peace River Country and others, ... 862
Breton, Paul-Emile
Au pays des Peaux-de-Lièvres, ... 172
Bishop Vital Grandin, Oblate of Mary Immaculate, first bishop of St. Albert (Alberta), Canada, ... 173
Blacksmith of God, ... 174
Le grand chef des prairies, ... 175
Hobbema, une florissante mission indienne de l'ouest, ... 176
Monseigneur Grandin vous parle, ... 203
Vital Grandin, omi, ... 177
Brewster, F.O.
They came west, ... 2898
Weathered wood, ... 2899
Brewster, Pat *see* Brewster, F.O.
They came west, ... 2898
Brice, Edward
The history of the world, AD 1960 to AD 2000, ... 2735
Brickman, Julius E.
Memories of yesterday, ... 3465
Bridging the Gap Opportunities for Youth
Stories of old St. Albert, ... 3259
Brightview. Emmaus Lutheran Church
Brief history of Emmaus Lutheran Congregation, Brightview, Alberta, and Zion Lutheran Congregation, Peace Hill, Alberta, ... 276
Brighty, Kate *see* Colley, Kate (Brighty)
While rivers flow, ... 3355
Brineger, Ron
Desperado deals, ... 1280
British American Oil Company, Ltd.
BA welcomes you to the new Pincher Creek Gas processing and sulphur plant, October 15th, 1958, ... 2253
British Railway Modellers of North America. Calgary Group
Canadian Pacific in the Rockies, ... 2317
Broderick, Kathleen E.
A normative study of track and field events for the Alberta Special Games, ... 1631
Bromling, Alvin Joseph
Resident participation in rural development, ... 2521
Bronson, Harold Emery
A review of legislation pertaining to petroleum resources, . . . 2471

Brook, Deborah Drew- *see* Drew-Brook, Deborah
White Forehead of the Cypress Hills, ... 715
Brooker, Christopher
Sikanaska trail, ... 668
Brookland Research Society
Seventy years gone by, ... 3058
Brooks and District Historical Society
Brooks, ... 2967
Brooks, Bill
Alberta,. 2604
Brooks, Ian R
Native education in Canada and the United States, ... 1
Browarny, Lavonne
A friend in need, ... 3349
Brown, Annora
Old man's garden, ... 3315
Brown, Gary William
The goat in the boat, by Uncle Gary, ... 1438
Brown, Gordon L.
Environmental impact assessment of a sour gas processing development in the Brazeau region of Alberta, ... 3337
Brown, Harriet C.
Beavertales, ... 2900
Brown, Joan M. Scott- *see* Scott-Brown, Joan M.
Stoney ethnobotany, ... 1987
Brown, Nancy
Tales to warm your mind, ... 947
Brown, Sheila Ann
The impact of the Great Slave Lake Railway on agricultural land use in the North Peace, Alberta, ... 2522
Bruderheim. Bethlehem Lutheran Church
Seventy years under God, for God, ... 277
Brumley, John Harry
The Cactus Flower site and the McKean complex in Alberta, ... 2016
Suffield archaeological project, 1972 Preliminary report, ... 2017
Brumley, Laurie Ann
The Narrows site in Waterton Lakes National Park, Alberta, ... 2018
Bryan, Alan Lyle
Early man in America, ... 2028
Bryan, Gertrude
Land of the Spirit, ... 278
Reminiscing with Walt, ... 3497
Buckley, Evelyn
Chaps and chinooks, ... 2901
Buckley, Marjorie White
As it happened, ... 1832
Buckmire, George Edward
Changing rural attitudes, ... 1714
Effects of farm technology and consequent problems of adjustment, effects of industrialization on agricultural production, ... 3445

Occupational mobility of farm people in the Bonnyville district, a low-income agricultural area, ... 2523
The rural church, the farm family, ... 3446
Buffalo Child Long Lance
Long Lance, ... 1868
Buffalo Coulee Home and School Association Centennial Committee
Buffalo Coulee progress (1902-1967), ... 2902
Buford 4-H Horticultural and Clothing Clubs
Pioneer reflections, ... 2903
Bugnet, Georges
The forest,. 620
Poèmes, ... 863
Buholzer, William A.
Outdoor recreation planning in Alberta, ... 1632
Buk, Nickolas
The history of Two Hills, including the Lanuke District, ... 2904
Bullen, Anne J. McLean
An examination of economic factors affecting the location and operation of the beef packing industry in Canada, with particular reference to Alberta,. 2167
Bunny, Laurali Rose *see* Wright, Laurali Rose (Bunny)
Neighbours, ... 833
Burden, C.
Do you believe in television?,. 1151
Burles, Mary-Jo
Cowley, ... 2905
Burnet, Jean Robertson
Next-year country, ... 1715
Burns and Elliott
Calgary, Alberta, Canada Her industries and resources, ... 2168
Burnt Lake History Society
Along the Burnt Lake Trail, ... 2906
Burpee, H.
Rosyth memoirs, 1906-1965, ... 2889
Wind, willows and prairie-wool A centennial project, ... 2890
Burpee, Mary
The lantern years, ... 3109
Burrell, Gordon
Indian treaties and the law, ... 2480
Burrs, Mick
Adventures of the midnight janitor, ... 864
Bush, Jack
Jack Bush, works on paper, ... 1152
Buss, Kingsley Benjamin
Edmonton trails, ... 2666
Bussière, Adrien L.
Performance linguistique, ... 444
Butler, Betty
St. Barnabas Church, Medicine Hat, 1884-1974, ... 279

Butler, Eugenie Louise *see* Myles, Eugenie Louise (Butler)
Airborne from Edmonton, ... 2349
Butler, Rodney Franklin
Perceptions of co-therapy, ... 1777
Butterwick, Alyce
Shortgrass country, ... 2907
Byrne, J.
The death's head knight,. 1153
Byrne, J. Paul
St. Mary's of the Assumption in the Canadian Rockies Banff, Alberta, . 280
Byrne, Marie Bernice Venini
From the buffalo to the Cross, ... 178
Byrne, William John
The archaeology and prehistory of southern Alberta as reflected by ceramics Late prehistoric and protohistoric cultural developments, 2019
Cairns, Phyllis Helen
The Alberta Child Welfare client system and the decision-making process,. 1778
Calahoo Women's Institute
Calahoo trails, ... 2908
Caldarola, Carlo
Society and politics in Alberta, ... 2443
Calder, James M.
The Majorville cairn and medicine wheel site, Alberta,. 2020
Calder School Reunion Association, Edmonton
Early history of Calder School and district,. 2909
Caldwell, Geoffrey Thomas
Educational values in Alberta, ... 1478
Calf Robe, Benjamin Augustine
Siksiká, ... 1869
Calgary Allied Arts Centre
All Alberta '69, ... 1165
Calgary Allied Arts Council
An arts council in your community?, ... 1116
Calgary Association for Retarded Children
Proposed school for Calgary's retarded children, ... 1479
Calgary. Brentview Baptist Church
Dedication of Brentview Baptist Church;. 281
Calgary Brewing and Malting Co
Calgary carriage collection, ... 2324
Proudly Western,. 2766
Calgary. Canadian Martyrs Catholic Church
The first ten years, 1967-1977, ... 282
History of Canadian Martyrs Church, ... 283
Calgary Centennial Committee
A year to remember, ... 2910
Calgary Chamber of Commerce
Economic impact of the Canadian gas industry, local, provincial and regional,. 2310

Calgary Conference on Mysticism
Mystics and scholars, ... 69
Calgary. Crescent Heights High School
50th anniversary, Crescent Heights High School, 1915-1965, ... 1521
Calgary Field Naturalists' Society
Five natural areas in the city of Calgary,. 1628
Natural and recreational features of Sandy Beach, ... 1641
Calgary. First Baptist Church
Dedicatory services for the reconstructed organ and the renovated sanctuary Sunday, May 29, 1966,. 284
Calgary. First Lutheran Church
Seventy-fifth anniversary, ... 285
Calgary General Hospital
Calgary General Hospital, 1890-1955, ... 3350
Calgary General Hospital Alumnae Association
25 years of alumnae life,. 3351
Calgary. Glengarry Elementary School
Glengarry golden anniversary, 1920-1970, ... 1522
Calgary Golf and Country Club
Calgary Golf and Country Club 75 anniversary,. 1633
Calgary. Grace Baptist Church
Grace Baptist Church, 1912-1972, ... 286
Calgary. Grace Lutheran Church
Grace for 25 years, 1950-1975, ... 287
Calgary Herald
The Calgary Herald's tales of the old town, ... 3154
The inside story, ... 44
The northern approaches, ... 2750
50th anniversary, ... 1634
75th anniversary, 1883-1958,. 2911
Calgary Institute for the Humanities
The new land, ... 577
Religion and ethnicity, ... 160
Calgary. King Edward School. Grade IX MPH Creative Writing Class of 1968-69 . . . .
Long live the king, ... 1523
Calgary. Knox United Church
The eightieth anniversary, ... 288
Calgary. Mount Calvary Lutheran Church
50 years of Grace, 1919-1969, ... 289
Calgary Olympic Development Association
Banff, Canada, proposed site for 1968 Winter Olympic Games, . . . 2667
Calgary. Our Lady of Mercy Croatian Catholic Parish
Croation Catholic Parish Our Lady of Mercy, 1967-1977, ... 290
Calgary. Our Lady of Perpetual Help Parish
50 years at the foot of the hill, 1925-1975, ... 291
Calgary Power Ltd.
Alberta, land of freedom and opportunity, ... 2815
Alberta, province of opportunity, ... 2108
Heritage Park memories, ... 2912

Our Alberta heritage, . . . 2816
Power for progress, thermal and hydro plants, . . . 2170
Some facts about Calgary Power Ltd., . . . 2171
Calgary Public School Board
A survey of educational media services of Calgary public schools, conducted on behalf of the Calgary School Board, . . . 20
Calgary Public School Board. Elementary School Program Commission
Direction for education, . . . 1480
Calgary Real Estate Board
This is Calgary, . . . 2668
Calgary. St. Anthony's Catholic Parish
Silver jubilee, . . . 292
Calgary. St. Barnabas' Church
50th anniversary, . . . 293
60th anniversary, . . . 294
Calgary. St. Boniface Catholic Church
St. Bonifatius Kirche, 1960-1970, Calgary, Alberta, . . . 295
Calgary. St. Joseph's Catholic Church
Parish means people, . . . 296
Calgary. St. Martin's Anglican Church
Service of dedication by the Right Rev GR Calvert, DD, Bishop of Calgary, St Martin's Day, November 11, 1960, 300 pm, . . . 297
Calgary. St. Mary's Cathedral
Souvenir of the consecration of St Mary's Cathedral, Calgary, Alberta, December 11th, 1957, . . . 298
Calgary. St. Michael and All Angels' Church
St. Michael and All Angels' Anglican Church, Calgary, anniversary, June 3rd, 1959, . . . 299
Calgary. St. Pius the Tenth Catholic Parish
25th anniversary of St Pius the Tenth Parish, Calgary, . . . 300
Calgary. St. Stephen's Anglican Church
Golden jubilee, 1906-1956, . . . 301
Calgary. Stanley Jones School
Stanley Jones School anniversary, 1913-1973, . . . 1524
Calgary Tourist and Convention Association
Catch them all from Calgary, . . . 1635
Calgary. Trinity Evangelical Lutheran Church
A history of Trinity Lutheran Church, the Evangelical Lutheran Church of Canada, . . . 302
Calgary. Wesley United Church
Wesley United Church, Calgary, Alberta, fiftieth anniversary, 1906-1956, . . . 303
Callaway, Bernice Ann Marr
Down timberland trail, . . . 621
Tell us a missionary story, . . . 622
Tell us a story, . . . 623
To mothers with love, . . . 1744
Callbeck, E.G.
Direction for education, . . . 1480

Cameron, Donald
Campus in the clouds, . . . 1591
Education and government, . . . 1481
The impossible dream, . . . 1592
Cameron, Jack R.
A guide to publishing in education, . . . 2
Cameron, Margaret Hunter
Dog Pound, 1880-1920, . . . 2913
Cameron, Stew
Let the chaps fall where they may, . . . 1099
Pack horse in the Rockies, . . . 1100
Weep for the Cowboy, . . . 1101
What I saw at the Stampede, . . . 1102
Cameron, William Bleasdell
Blood red the sun, . . . 2817
Cameron, William Stuart
Some we have met and stories they have told, . . . 2701
Camp, Fred V.
Two wheelchairs and a family of three, . . . 66
Campbell, Alice A.
A brief history of Delburne United Church, 1903 to 1958, . . . 304
Milk River country, . . . 2914
Campbell, Charles Scott Henry
A survey of leisure reading in the senior high schools of Alberta, . . . 1636
Campbell, Duncan Darroch
The development of a Learning Resources Centre as a base for the expansion of continuing education in Alberta, . . . 40
Those tumultuous years, . . . 1593
Campbell, E.E.B.
Edmonton Transit System story, 1903-1978, . . . 2325
Campbell, Elizabeth
Memories of yesteryear, with Beth Campbell, . . . 305
Campbell, Gordon
History of the Alberta community college system, 1957-1969, . . . 1594
Campbell, Isabel M.
Grande Prairie, capitol (sic) of the Peace, . . . 2915
Pioneers of the Peace, . . . 2916
Campbell, Jessie J.
Chatter chips from Beaver Dam Creek, . . . 2917
Campbell, Maria
Halfbreed, . . . 1870
Little Cree Badger and the Fire Spirit, . . . 2071
People of the buffalo, . . . 1871
Riel's people, . . . 1872
She who knows the truth of Big Bear, . . . 2767
Campbell, Marie J.
Still God's country, . . . 2918
Campbell, Neil MacDougal
A case study in economic development, . . . 2093

Campbell, Paddy
Chinook, ... 1044
Hoarse music, ... 1045
Campbell, Robert Eldon
I would do it again, ... 2919
Camrose Canadian
The golden trail, ... 2920
Camrose. Messiah Lutheran Church
Messiah Lutheran through seventy years, 1901-1971, ... 306
Camrose. St. Francis Xavier Catholic Church
Souvenir of the dedication and official opening, ... 307
Canada. Department of Regional Economic Expansion
Western Canada Location of operating mines, processing plants and metallurgical works, 1974, ... 2172
Western Canada Location of processing of materials of agricultural origin, ... 2173
Canada. Geographic Board
Place-names of Alberta, ... 2656
Canada. Statistics Canada
Proceedings, ... 2102
Canada West Conference on Confederation, Banff, ... 1978
Alternatives, ... 2363
A summary report on the proceedings of Alternatives Canada, a Canada West Conference on Confederation, held at Banff, March 27-29, 1978, 2384
Canada West Foundation
Canada West Foundation, ... 2402
Canada's resources and the national interest, ... 2279
Canada's resources and the national interest, ... 2278
Federal expenditures in the Western Region, ... 2094
Follow-up on the Western Economic Opportunities Conference, ... 2095
A realistic perspective of Canadian confederation, ... 2361
A report on exports and imports through British Columbia, 1972, with special reference to the Pacific Rim countries of Asia and Oceania, . 2096
A report on the National Energy Conference, Ottawa, January 22-23, 1974, ... 2097
A report on the Western Economic Opportunities Conference, ... 2098
WesCan/INFORM, ... 28
Western Canada Location of operating mines, processing plants and metallurgical works, 1974, ... 2172
Western Canada Location of processing of materials of agricultural origin, ... 2173
Canadian Association of Geographers. Western Division
Research studies by Western Canadian geographers, ... 2570
Canadian Association of Radio and Television Broadcasters
Freedom of the air, ... 2332
Canadian Eskimo Art Council
Baker Lake prints/estampes, ... 1167
Canadian Gas Association
Alberta's oil sands in the energy supply picture, ... 2270
Alberta's role in meeting Canada's energy requirements, ... 2137

Canadian Hereford Association
The Hereford in Canada, 1860-1968, ... 3393
Canadian Institute of Ukrainian Studies
An anthology of Ukrainian lyric poetry, ... 559
A historical phonology of the Ukrainian language,. 510
Ukrainian Canadians, ... 1998
Ukrainian Canadians, multiculturalism and separatism, ... 2000
Why bilingual education?, ... 1475
Canadian Library Association
Librarianship in Canada, 1946 to 1967, ... 32
Canadian Lutheran Bible Institute, Camrose
O send out Thy light and Thy truth The prayer and cornerstone of twenty-five years of Christian instruction, 1932-1957, ... 179
Canadian Parks/Recreation Association
Discussion notes for a seminar on the management of public parks and recreation services, ... 1630
Canadian Petroleum Association
A brief history of the petroleum industry in Canada,. 2254
The origins of oil and gas, ... 2255
Canadian Petroleum Association. Alberta Division
Oil and gas in Alberta, ... 2256
Canadian Red Cross Society. Alberta Northwest Territories Division.
Calgary Branch. Calgary Branch, Alberta Northwest Territories Division, The Canadian Red Cross Society,. 3352
Canadian Western Natural Gas Company Ltd
Canadian Western Natural Gas Company Limited, 1912-1972, . . . 2257
Half a century of Service, 1912-1962, ... 2258
Canadian-Hungarian Authors' Association
The sound of time, ... 582
Cantlon, F.M.
Oatmeal porridge and green poplar poles, ... 3466
Cantwell, Nick
The west in action, ... 1656
Caragata, Warren
Alberta labour,. 2174
Card, Brigham Young
Alberta Improvement District 124, ... 1874
The Canadian Prairie Provinces from 1870 to 1950, ... 1717
The expanding relation, ... 1718
The Metis in Alberta society, with special reference to social, economic and cultural factors associated with persistently high tuberculosis incidence,. 1875
Perspectives on regions and regionalism and other papers, . . . 1729
Trends and change in Canadian society, ... 1719
Cardinal, Douglas
Of the spirit,. 1876
Cardinal, Harold
Address by Harold Cardinal, President, Indian Association of Alberta, during presentation by the Indian Chiefs of Alberta to the Prime Minister and the Government of Canada, June 4, 1970,. . 1877

The rebirth of Canada's Indians, ... 1878
The unjust society, ... 1879
Cardston and District Historical Society
Chief Mountain country, ... 3237
Cardston Diamond Jubilee Committee
Cardston diamond jubilee, 1887-1962, jubilee souvenir,. 2921
Carey, Marie M.
The hospital on the hill, 1912-1962,. 3373
Carey, Stephen T.
Bilingualism, biculturalism & education,. 1476
Carleton University. Institute of Canadian Studies
The Frog Lake massacre, ... 1917
Carlsson, Elizabeth Course
Along the Victoria trail, ... 3254
Carlton, Terence Roy
The declension of nouns in Ukrainian, ... 504
The numeral in Ukrainian, its forms and uses, ... 505
Carmangay and District History Book Committee
Bridging the years, Carmangay and district, ... 2922
Carmichael, Robert Ralph
The seed-pod book of joy, ... 865
Carney, Tom
Alberta, profile of development,. 2099
Carnwood Country Club Society
Forests to grainfields, ... 3141
Carpenter, David
Alberta in fiction, ... 522
The forest,. 620
Wild rose country, ... 591
Carpenter, James Harold
The badge and the blotter,. 2496
Carpenter, Jock
Fifty dollar bride,. 3467
Carr, Kevin James
A historical survey of education in early Blackfoot Indian culture and its implication for Indian schools, ... 1525
Carron, Selma
Golden memories, Warburg and district, ... 2923
Carseland and Cheadle Historical Book Committee
Trails to the Bow, ... 2924
Carstairs Centennial History Committee.
Prairie trails,. 2925
Carstairs. United Church
The Carstairs United Church, 1906-1956, ... 308
Carter, David John
The Anglican Church in Calgary,. 180
Calgary's Anglican cathedral, ... 309
A history of the Anglican Diocese of Calgary, ... 181
Prairie profiles,. 866
Samuel Trivett, missionary with the Blood Indians, ... 182

Where the wind blows, ... 183
Carter, Eva
The history of organized farm women of Alberta, ... 3468
Carter, Robin Michael
Chipewyan semantics, ... 497
Cashman, Anthony Walcott
Abraham Cristall, ... 1880
The Alberta Motor Association, ... 2326
The best Edmonton stories, ... 2926
Edmonton Exhibition, the first hundred years, ... 2175
The Edmonton story, ... 2927
Edmonton's Catholic schools, ... 1526
Ernest C Manning, ... 2403
Heritage of service, ... 3353
A history of motoring in Alberta, ... 2327
An illustrated history of Western Canada, ... 2768
More Edmonton stories, ... 2928
A moving story, ... 2328
A picture history of Alberta, ... 2818
Singing wires, ... 2329
The telephone man, ... 2330
The vice-regal cowboy, ... 2404
Cassidy, Elizabeth Catherine L.
Grain and chaff, ... 867
Castor Fiftieth Anniversary Committee
Celebrate with Castor, 1910-1960, ... 2929
Catley, Elaine Maud (Clark)
At the end of the road, ... 868
Light and other poems, ... 869
Catullus, Caius Valerius
The book of Catullus of Verona done into English verse by William Hardy Alexander, ... 840
Cauvin, Dennis Mederic
Measurement of a forest's contribution to the economy of Alberta, ... 2176
Cavanagh, L.A.
50th anniversary, 1912-1962, ... 2224
Cavell, Edward
Calgary An illustrated history, ... 3011
Journeys to the far west, ... 2769
Cayford, Elmer H.
Barefoot days, ... 3469
Cayley Women's Institute
Under the Chinook Arch, ... 2930
Ceiriog, Gutyn *see* Jones, William Griffith
Ceiriog capers, ... 913
Celmainis, Andrew
Examination of the petroleum industry in Alberta, ... 2259
Centennial Conference on the history of the Canadian West, Banff, 1967 Papers, ... 2770

Central and East European Studies Society of Alberta
Proceedings,. 1864
Second Banff Conference on Central and East European Studies, Banff Springs Hotel, Banff, Alberta, March 2-5, 1978,. 1865
Cereal Women's Institute
Down Cereal's memory trails, 1910-1967, ... 2931
Cerny, Hana
Manpower requirements in the food service industry with implications for vocational education in Alberta, ... 2177
Cessford. New Cessford School
This is our land, ... 2891
Chévigny, Delamen (Plamondon)
Jubilé d'or, ... 2932
Chacmool *see* University of Calgary Archaeological Association
Papers from Conference on Canadian Archaeology Abroad, held at the University of Calgary, November 23, 24, 25, 1973, ... 2022
Chadbourne, Richard
The new land, ...577
Chadwick, Donna
Candelight years,. 2933
Chalke, John
John Chalke,. 1154
Chalmers, John West
Alberta diamond jubilee anthology, ...552
Education behind the buckskin curtain, ... 1527
Fur trade governor, ... 2771
Gladly would he teach, ... 1528
Horseman in scarlet, ...624
The land of Peter Pond, ... 2527
On the edge of the shield, ... 2566
Red River adventure, ... 2772
Schools of the Foothills Province, ... 1529
Teachers of the Foothills Province, ... 1530
Chalmers Women's Institute
Wild flowers and buffalo bones, ... 3171
Chambers, Brian
Louis Riel, ... 2773
Chambers, Jack
A very small rebellion, .800
Chandler, Harold
Chandu's magic variations,. 1281
Changing Frontier Conference, Peace River, ... 1965
Addresses,. 2100
Chapman, Carol
Poems for children, ...870
Chapman, Evangeline
Poems for children, ...870
Poems for people over 25, ...871
Chapman, Marjorie (MacDonald)
Golden jubilee, 1910-1960,. 3363

Chapman, Robin James
The nature and role of Regional Offices of Education in the Province of Alberta,. 1482
Charuk, Myrtle
The history of Willingdon, 1928-1978,. 2934
Charyk, John Constantine
Hanna First United Church golden anniversary, 1912-1962, ... 310
The little white schoolhouse, ... 1531
Chatenay, Henri Paul
Echoes of silence,. 3354
Chauvin Rebekah Lodge . . . . #120
Singing rails and tales, ... 2935
Cheek, Orville
Buried treasures, ... 2936
Chekhov, Anton Pavlovich
The seagull, ... 1046
Uncle Vanya, ... 1047
Cheng, Jacqueline Ruth
Images of Banff and Canmore and the use of Banff National Park by motel visitors, ... 1637
Chester, D.T.
Chester and Bentham,. 1155
Chestermere Historical Society
The changing scene, ... 2937
Saddles, sleighs and sadirons,. 3172
Chetin, Helen
The lady of the strawberries, ... 625
Chevraux, Sharleen M.
From the ground up, ... 3470
The ten dollar bets, ... 2938
Chief Mountain
Kootenai Brown, adventurer, pioneer, plainsman, park warden, and Waterton Lakes National Park,. 1677
Chien-Shih, Lin
Lin Chien-Shih, ... 1156
Chilblain, Orpheus P. *see* Turner, John Davenall
The artful codger, ... 1113
Chipeniuk, R.C.
Lakes of the Lac La Biche District, ... 2669
Chiswick, Audrey Baines *see* Baines, Audrey (Chiswick)
Through the looking glass, ... 3292
Chivers, Barrie
Employer/employee rights in Alberta,. 2472
Choiquier, Alain
Born again, ... 67
Chowli, Norah
A study of commercial blight and the function of Whyte Avenue, Edmonton,. 2202
Christensen, Ole Arne
Banff prehistory, ... 2021

Christenson, Raymond Andrew
The Calgary and Edmonton Railway and the 'Edmonton Bulletin',. . 2331
Christiansen, Ron
Many laws, ... 2473
Christianson, Chris J.
Early rangemen, ... 3471
My life on the range, ... 3472
Chubb, Jean (Hall)
Leaves of yesteryear, ... 2939
Chumak, Sebastian Z.
The spirit of Alberta, ... 2819
Church of Jesus Christ of Latter-Day Saints. Lethbridge Stake
A history of the Mormon Church in Canada, ... 184
Citizens' Commission on a Humane Standard of Living
Report, ... 1779
Citizens Research Institute of Canada
Local government financing in Alberta, including an appraisal of provincial-municipal financial relationships, ... 2101
Claresholm History Book Club
Where the wheatlands meet the range,. 2940
Claresholm. United Church
A history of Claresholm United Church, 1904-1969,. 311
Clark, Edith J. (Lawrence)
Trails of Tail Creek country, ... 2941
Clark, Elaine Maud *see* Catley, Elaine Maud (Clark)
At the end of the road, ... 868
Clark, Joan
Girl of the Rockies, ... 626
The hand of Robin Squires, ... 627
Thomasina and the trout tree, ... 628
Clark, Molly
The taming of Molly, ... 68
Clarke, Elizabeth
Blueberry Mountain history, ... 2942
Clarke, Stanley Charles Tremayne
The Cameron Commission ten years after, ... 1483
Clegg, E.T.
Transactions of the first Resources Conference of the Northwest Region,. 2146
Cleichen United Church Women
The Gleichen call, ... 2893
Cleriot, Nicole
Political validity of Franco-Albertains,. 2437
Cleveland, Albert Allan
The genesis and early growth of the Alberta Human Resources Research Council, ... 1780
Clever, Glen
Alberta days, ... 872
Cleverville Pioneer Club History Book Committee
Cleverville, Champion, 1905 to 1970, ... 2943

Clipsham, Muriel G.
Memories of Verdant Valley, Cassel Hill, Livingston, Rainbow, ... 2986
Cloakey, George H.
Problems affecting Canadian participation in the development of the oil and gas resources of Canada, ... 2260
Coaldale Jubilee Committee
Coaldale, the gem of the West, ... 2944
Coaldale. United Church
History of Coaldale United Church, 1904-1975,. 312
Coburn, Morton
A survey of seven recently constructed public library buildings in the United States and Canada, ... 14
Cochrane and Area Historical Society
Big Hill country, ... 2945
Coe, Bob
The blue and gold, ... 1439
Cohen, S.
Calgary city jail, ...926
Colclough, Alex
Pincher Papers, 1, ... 3196
Coleman, MacDonald
The face of yesterday,. 2774
Once upon a childhood, ...629
Once upon a little town, ...630
Requiem and other poems,. 873
Collège Universitaire Saint-Jean
Collège Saint-Jean cinquantième anniversaire, 1911-1961, ... 1595
Ecole bilingue ou unilingue pour les franco-albertains, ... 1484
Collett, H.L.
First Spiritualist Church, ...313
Collett, W.J.
United Church in Calgary,. 185
Colley, Kate (Brighty)
While rivers flow,. 3355
Collins, Paul Victor
The public health policies of the United Farmers of Alberta government, 1921-1935, ... 3356
Collins, Ruth Johanna (Ignatius)
Winnifred,. 2946
Collinson, Helen
Inuit games and contests, ... 1247
A university collects, ... 1117
Colombo, John Robert
Alberta,. 2604
Comfort, Darlene Joy
Meeting place of many waters, ... 2947
Pass the McMurray salt please!, ... 2178
Comité 50 de Girouxville
Album souvenir, 1928-1978, ... 2948

Committee for an Independent Canada. Calgary Committee
The impact of foreign investment on Canadian society,. 2125
Conder, John E.H.
The disposition of crown petroleum and natural gas rights in Alberta,. 2261
Conference on Canadian Archaeology Abroad, University of Calgary, 1973
Papers from Conference on Canadian Archaeology Abroad, held at the University of Calgary, November 23, 24, 25, 1973, . . . 2022
Conference on Economic and Social Trends in Western Canada, Calgary, 1978 Proceedings, ... 2102
Conference on Productivity in the Canadian Economy, Calgary, 1978
Proceedings, ... 2103
Conference on the Alberta Challenge, Jasper, ... 1978
Report and proceedings, ... 2104
Conference on the Canadian national parks, today and tomorrow, 1968
The Canadian national parks, today and tomorrow, ... 2524
Canadian parks in perspective, ... 2526
Conference on the Canadian national parks, today and tomorrow, 1978
Canadian national parks, today and tomorrow, conference 2, ... 2525
Connelly, Clifford L.
Rollicking rhymes, ...874
Conquerville Women's Institute
Conquerville, a growing community,. 2951
Conroy Club
Trail blazers, ... 3277
Conroy, Marion
Early history and growth in Edmonton Diocese,. 186
Cook, Dean
A history of educational institutions in Mormon communities of southern Alberta, 1954, ... 1533
Cook, Janet McLaren
Through cloud and sunshine, ... 1534
Cook, Maisie Emery
Memories of a pioneer schoolteacher, ... 1535
Cook, Norman Alan
Perceptual variations of retailing in Edmonton, ... 2179
Cooney, Gregory Joseph
Observations on the development of schism in an Alberta Indian revitalization movement,. 1881
Copeland, Donalda Murray (McKillop)
Remember, nurse, ... 3357
Copeland, James Hubert
A study of broiler marketing in Alberta, ... 2180
Corbet, E.
Calgary's stone frigate, HMCS Tecumseh, 1923-1973,. 2748
Corbet, Elise Elliott
Alberta women in the 1920's, ... 1745
Corbett, Edward Annand
Henry Marshall Tory,. 1596
We have with us tonight, ... 1536

Cormack, Barbara (Villy)
The house, ... 631
Landmarks, ... 1833
Perennials and politics, ... 2405
The Red Cross Lady (Mary H Conquest MBE), ... 3358
Westward ho! 1903, ... 632
Cormack, Robert George Hall
Wild flowers of Alberta, ... 3316
Coronation Board of Trade
Coronation, ... 2952
Coronation Book Committee
In the beginning, ... 2953
Coronation Old-Timers' Centennial Book Committee
Shadows of the Neutrals, ... 2954
Coronation T & C Golden Age Club
In the beginning, ... 2953
Cosgrove, Edmund
The terror of the tar sands, ... 633
Coulet du Gard, René
La France contemporaine, 1900-1976, ... 2736
L'oiseau de feu, ... 992
Coull, Adrienne
Souvenirs, ... 2820
Coulter, Rebecca
Alberta's Department of Neglected Children, 1909-1929
A case study in child saving, ... 1782
Coulton, Betty
The great lone land, ... 2955
Coulton, Richard Lee
A guide to the historic sites of the Gull Lake region of Alberta, ... 2023
The sea, ... 875
Sonnets of the space age, ... 876
Coutant, Frank R.
Shangri La, ... 2607
Coutts, H.T.
G. Fred, ... 1564
Coutts Women's Institute
The history of the border country of Coutts, ... 3262
Couture, Joseph Ernest
Alberta Indian youth, ... 1882
Coward, Harold
Mystics and scholars, ... 69
Religion and ethnicity, ... 160
Co-West Associates
Identification of social needs in the inner city, Emonton and Calgary, 1781
Cowley. United Church
Foothills UCW, 1903-1978, ... 314
Cox, Barbara J
Summer of childhood, ... 3473

Cox, Edith Blanche *see* Rogers, Edith Blanche (Cox)
History made in Edmonton, ... 3221
Craig, David
The wolfers, ...762
Craigen, Shelby
Marvelous mysteries of Marvillo, ... 1307
Stage illusions for the 1, 2 or 3 performer show,. 1301
Crawford, David
Blue flame in the foothills, .187
Crawford, Margaret Eleanor
A geographic study of the distribution of population change in Alberta, 1931-1961, ... 2528
Crestomere-Sylvan Heights Book Committee
Crestomere-Sylvan Heights heritage, ... 2858
Crichton, Neil
Rerun, ...634
Crossfield History Committee
Prairie sod and goldenrod, ... 2956
Crowell, Pers
Stormy, ...687
Crowsnest Pass Historical Society
Crowsnest and its people, ... 2957
Crowston, Michael Anthony
The growth of the metal industries in Edmonton, ... 2181
Cserepy, Mary
The hand of Robin Squires, ...627
Cullen, Dallas
Work and leisure in Canada, ... 2156
Cullen, Michael
The curried chicken apocalypse, ...877
Cummings, Edward Estlin
In just spring, ... 1400
Cunniffe, Richard
Calgary - in sandstone, ... 2959
Scarlet, rifle green, and khaki, ... 2749
Cunningham, John
She has done what she could (Mark 14, 8 NASV), ...188
Cunningham, Rosemary
When the arrow flies, ... 70
Curtis, Paul James
Some aspects of industrial linkages in Edmonton's oil industry, with special reference to the tertiary sector, ... 2262
Cyr, Alvine *see* Gahagan, Alvine (Cyr)
Yes, father, ... 3362
Cyr, Donald
Bonnyville in question, 1975, ... 1861
Czolowski, Ted
Alberta, the emerging giant, ... 2608
Dagg, Mel
Songs for my owl, ...878

Dahlgren, Dorothy
Tales of the tarsands, ... 2960
Dahlie, Hallvard
The new land, ...577
Strange trafficking and curious merchandise, ...524
Dalal, Sam
Magic with a marked deck, ... 1282
D'Albertanson, Leonard
The story of Alberta Division, Canadian Weekly Newspapers Association, ... 45
Dale, Edmund Herbert
The role of successive town and city councils in the evolution of Edmonton, Alberta, 1892 to 1966, ... 2453
Dalemead Indus History Committee
Tales from two townships, ... 2961
Dalheim, K
Calahoo trails, ... 2908
D'Alquen, Richard
Phonology of the Galician German dialect of Stony Plain, Alberta, . .446
Dalum History Book Committee
The history of Dalum, commemorating its 50th anniversary, May 5, 1968, ... 2962
Daniel, Allan
A horse for Running Buffalo, .656
Daniel, Lorne
The hunting hand and other poems, ...879
Towards a new compass,. 880
Daniels, Christine
Many laws, ... 2473
Daniels, Harry W
Declaration of Metis and Indian rights, ... 1885
The forgotten people, ... 1899
We are the new nation, ... 1883
Daniels, Leroi Allister
The history of education in Calgary,. 1537
Danielson, Holmfridur
Three times a pioneer,. 3477
Dansereau, Grace
Discovering music, ... 1379
Darby, George
Is there anything wrong?, ... 71
Darby, Peter A
The integration of southern Alberta with Canada, 1700-1885,. . . . 2529
Darnell, Regna Diebold
Canadian languages in their social context,. 445
Language use in Canada, ...453
Linguistic diversity in Canadian society, ...456
Darrah, Ann Clarke
Hendrik Bres, Ann Clarke Darrah, Eva Deiner,. 1150

Darroch, G.V.
The problem of resource development of the Blackfoot Reserve of southern Alberta,. 2105
Darychuk, Gregory Michael
The financial implications of international trade participation by Alberta secondary industries, ... 2106
Davenall, John *see* Turner, John Davenall
The artful codger, ... 1113
David Mirvish Gallery, Toronto
Jack Bush, works on paper, ... 1152
Masters of the sixties,. 1179
Sculpture in steel, ... 1181
Davidge, Ernest
An abbreviated history of the Ponoka United Church of Canada, . . . 409
Davidson, John M.
Crescent Heights United Church,. 315
Davidson, William McCartney
Louis Riel, 1844-1885, ... 2775
Davies, Dale
Red serge wives, ... 2500
Davies, Marcy
Allison Procter, OBE, LLD 1880-1964, ... 1834
Davies, Paula Bernice
A political analysis of public participation in educational policy in Alberta, ... 1486
Davis, Arthur Keith
Canadian confrontations, ... 1873
Perspectives on regions and regionalism and other papers, ... 1729
Davis, Edgar Hawkins
An economic system for Canada, ... 2107
Davis, James Martin
We remember Pete Knight, ... 1638
Davis, R.P. Stephen
The Wiser-Stephens 1 site - 40CF81, ... 2024
Dawe, Robert Wellington
The development of the Red Deer community in relation to the development of western Canada, ... 2963
History of Red Deer, Alberta, ... 2964
Dawson, Carl Addington
The settlement of the Peace River Country, ... 2965
Dawson, James Lawrence
A location analysis for hog assembly centres in Alberta, ... 2182
Dawson, John Brian
Chinese urban communities in southern Alberta, 1885-1925, ... 1884
Dawson, Oliver Glenn
Production efficiency in Alberta beef feedlots, ... 2183
Dayton, Ronald J.
Ropes with a different twist, ... 1283
De Bruijn, Bert
Look and play,. 1380

De Groot, Pieter
The Alberta community health self-study outline, ... 3359
De La Mare, Walter
Someone, ... 1419
De Mille, George
Oil in Canada West, the early years, ... 2263
De Roo, Remi
Man to Man, ... 143
de Steur, Elizabeth
Once upon a chinook, ... 2457
de Vassarely, Victor, *see* Vassarely, Victor de
Vassarely, ... 1248
De Winton and District Historical Committee
Sodbusting to subdivision, ... 2966
Deacon, Peter
Peter Deacon Drawings, Nov 6- 26, ... 1157
Dean, Basil
Freedom of the air, ... 2332
The northern approaches, ... 2750
Deane, Stanley G.
A political history of Seba Beach, ... 2454
Dearing, Kathleen
Favorite Gospel hymns in all major keys, transcribed for the piano, . 1440
From hymnbook to keyboard, ... 1441
Hymn styling for alert adults, ... 1442
Practical music course in elementary theory and sight-singing, . . . 1383
Prairie hymn originals from our piano studios Varied ideas of twelve pianists, ... 1443
DeBoer, Raymond
Cumancaya, ... 2053
Deeg, Bart F.
A proposal for a trail planning methodology, a case study, ... 1639
Deegan, Jim
Timberline tales, ... 2072
Deeves, Fred
Rhymes of reason and dis-reason, ... 881
DeFelice, James
The elixir, ... 1048
Fools and masters, ... 1049
Take me where the water's warm, ... 1050
DeGama, Jerrold William
The response of public school supporters to a proposed bilingual elementary school in the city of Calgary, ... 1487
DeGrâce, Eloi
Ouest canadien, historique et index, ... 46
Deiner, Eva
Hendrik Bres, Ann Clarke Darrah, Eva Deiner, ... 1150
DeLawrence, George
Answers to questions, ... 1284

Delday, Eva Pearce
Brooks, ... 2967
Mirror of life, ... 882
The special breed, ... 883
DeLeeuw, Gary
Alberta foothills, ... 3474
Delia and District Historical Society
The Delia Craigmyle saga,. 2874
Delta Kappa Gamma Society. Zeta Province. Alpha Chapter
Sketches of women pioneer educators of Edmonton, ... 1538
Demarest, Anne Shannon
Banff panorama, a symphonic suite,. 1444
Demke, Gordon J.
Supply of natural gas in Alberta, ... 2264
Demorest, Evelyn
Golden memoirs, 1912-1963, ... 2968
Dempsey, Hugh Aylmer
Alberta diamond jubilee anthology, ... 552
The best of Bob Edwards, ... 48
Blackfoot ghost dance, ... 72
A Blackfoot winter count, ... 73
Charcoal's world,. 1886
Crowfoot, Chief of the Blackfeet, ... 2821
The early west,. 2776
Ethnic furniture, ... 1158
Le grand chef des prairies,. 175
A history of Writing-On-Stone,. 2025
How to prepare a local history, ... 2737
Hutterites,. 1995
Indian names for Alberta communities, ... 2657
Indian tribes of Alberta,. 1887
Jerry Potts, plainsman, ... 2822
The Lost Lemon Mine, ... 2236
Men in scarlet,. 2498
My people the Bloods,. 1965
My tribe the Crees,. 1888
North with Peace River Jim,. 2616
Oki! Nitsitapee A message to the Blackfoot Indians,. 119
Opening the great West,. 222
The Rundle journals, 1840-1848, ... 241
Tailfeathers, Indian artist, ... 1118
Trail blazer of the Canadian Rockies, ... 2653
William Parker, mounted policeman, ... 2511
A winter at Fort Macleod,. 2509
The wit and wisdom of Bob Edwards, ... 49
Dempsey, Pauline
Oki! Nitsitapee A message to the Blackfoot Indians,. 119
den Otter, Andy Albert *see* Otter, Andy Albert den
A social history of the Alberta Coal Branch, ... 3185

Denbury, Mabel L.
The story of Johnny Doogit, ...635
Denney, C.D.
The Athabasca Landing Trail, ... 2969
Dent, Ivor
Getting the games, ... 1640
Denton, Daphne
Natural and recreational features of Sandy Beach, ... 1641
Der-Houssikian, Haig
A bibliography of African linguistics, ... 3
Desjardins, A.M
Cinquantenaire, Ste Hélène de Ste-Lina,. 421
Desrochers, Clément
Docile à l'Esprit-Saint, ...189
Devon Chamber of Commerce
Town of Devon, Alberta, ... 2670
Devore, Roy W
The history of Walterdale, ... 2970
Dew, Ian F
Bibliography of material relating to southern Alberta published to 1970, . 8
Dewdney, Selwyn
The sacred scrolls of the southern Ojibway,. 74
Dibdin, Michael John
Afterpiece, ...636
Dickens, Charles
Scrooge,. 1062
Dickson. Bethany Lutheran Congregation
75th anniversary, Bethany Lutheran Congregation, Dickson, Alberta, . 316
Dickson, Lovat
The ante-room,. 637
The house of words,. 47
Dickson, Robert Gary
Divorce guide for Alberta, ... 2474
Diemer, Hendrikus Lourens
Annexation and amalgamation in the territorial expansion of Edmonton and Calgary, ... 2455
Diesel, Gladys Cynthia Rebecca (Shope)
The legend of Owl Hoot Hill, ...638
Salute to the past, ... 3475
Dinton Women's Institute.
Gladys and Dinton through the years, ... 2972
Dion, Joseph Francis
My tribe the Crees, ... 1888
Diviner of Destiny
Visions of tomorrow, ... 1285
Dixon, Gertrude Evelyn *see* Honeyman, Gertrude Evelyn (Dixon)
Poems for old and young, .906
Dmytruk, Ihur
Ihur Dmystruck, ... 1159

Dodd, Edward J
Remember when,. 2973
Dogil, Grzegorz
Autosegmental account of phonological emphasis, ...447
Doherty, Mary Irene *see* Smith, Mary Irene (Doherty)
Songs of the Athabasca,. 1002
Dolphin, T.M
Blacksmith of God, ...174
Dominion Cartridge Company
Dominion Cartridge Company-Canadian Industries Limited shotshells, 1886-1954,. 2184
Donaghey, Sam
A history of the City of Edmonton Police Department,. 2499
Donahue, Geraldine
Saint Agnes Parish, Edmonton, Alberta, silver anniversary, 1953-1978, ...317
Donald, J.T. & Co.(1956) Co
Alberta, province of opportunity, ... 2108
Donalda Jubilee Committee
Fifty years on the coulee rim, ... 2974
Donaldson, Ross Murray
The economic base of Camrose,. 2109
Donlevy, William J
History of St Agnes Parish, ...318
Doolan, Jean
The last best west, ... 2975
Dooling, Peter John
An explorative study of factors affecting outdoor recreation demand of the Edmonton adult population, Alberta, Canada, ... 1642
Doolittle, Joyce
A mirror of our dreams,. 1256
Dorcas Ladies Aid, Eagle Hill
The Eagle calls, ... 2976
Dorcas Ladies Aid, Monarch
Down the trail of memories, ...884
Dore, Theo
Magnetrix, ... 1286
Dorward, Christina
Below the flight path,. 3360
A history of Avonmore United Church from 1908, ...319
Doty, Arlynn
Roads to Pipestone,. 2977
Dougan, Harvey
The English colony Nightingale and District, ... 2978
Douglas, Alban Hector
Seventy Bible lessons,. 75
Douglas, Helen Frances
Echoes of Willow Creek,. 2979
Golden kernels of Granum, ... 2980

Douglas, Sheila
A candle in the grub box, ... 3483
Jam in the bedroll, ... 3484
Dowkes, Margaret
History of St John's Presbyterian Church, Medicine Hat, Alberta, 1883-1973, ... 320
Dowling, Phil
The mountaineers, ... 1643
Downey, Lawrence William Lorne
The small high school in Alberta, ... 1488
Dragland, Margaret (Hansen)
Conquerville, a growing community,. 2951
The Piegan country, ... 2981
Dragland, Stan
Peckertracks, ... 639
Dragushan, Jean L
To be poor in Canada, ... 1783
Draper, Norman
Bands by the Bow, ... 1381
Drayton Valley High School
The history of Drayton Valley, ... 2982
Dreger, A.F
A most diversified character,. 2983
Drew-Brook, Deborah
Daughter of the old pioneer, ... 1753
White Forehead of the Cypress Hills, ... 715
Driben, Paul
We are Metis, ... 1889
Drouin, Eméric O'Neil
Bénédiction des cloches de la paroisse-cathédrale de Saint Paul, Alberta, Dimanche, le 26 juin 1960,. 321
Echos argentins au Diocèse de Saint-Paul-en-Alberta, 1948-1973, . . . 190
Habitat St Paul, 1976-1980, ... 2984
Hobbema, une florissante mission indienne de l'ouest, ... 176
Joyau dans la plaine, ... 191
Lac Ste-Anne Sakahigan, ... 192
One-armed star from the east, ... 193
Drouin, Lucien Henri
History of St Paul, Alberta, 1909-1959, ... 2985
Drumheller East Farmer Women's Union
Memories of Verdant Valley, Cassel Hill, Livingston, Rainbow, . . . 2986
Drumheller. Knox United Church
Golden anniversary, 1910-1960,. 322
Drumheller. St. Anthony's Catholic Parish
50th anniversary, 1917-1967,. 323
Drumheller Valley Historical Association
The hills of home Drumheller Valley, ... 3200
Dryden, Dave
Coaching goaltenders,. 1644

Dubois, N. Warren
Northland Utilities Limited, ... 2185
Dubuc, Denis
Jean-Côté, histoire et généalogie d'une paroisse du nord albertain, . . 2988
Duciaume, Jean-Marcel
Et le verbe s'est fait chair, ...885
Poèmes, ...863
Duclos, Jocelyn-Robert
Gethsemani, a dramatic poem, ...886
Dueck, Allan Kornelsen
Rudy Wiebe as storyteller, ...525
Dufresne, Lawrence W
A study of the incidence, nature and cause of football injuries in the city of Edmonton during 1969, ... 1645
Duhamel Historical Society
The Battle River country, ... 3047
Duke, P.G.
Diffusion and migration, their roles in cultural development, ... 2026
Duke, William Richard
The Parkland Regional Library, ... 15
Dukowski, James Gerard
Project 72,. 1784
Duncan, Joy
Red serge wives, ... 2500
Duncan, Sandra
Early Calgary friends,. 3280
Dunkelman Gallery, Toronto
Adolph Gottlieb acrylics on paper, ... 1205
Dunlop Art Gallery, Regina
The Group of Seven in the Rockies, ... 1177
Durie, Elizabeth
Park Grove echoes, ... 2989
Dyba, Kenneth
Lucifer and Lucinda, ...640
Sister Roxy, ...641
Dyer, Arthur Cecil
Occupational organization in real estate, ... 2186
Dykstra, Theodore Lou
The political geography of a border settlement, ... 2530
Eagle Hill. Dorcas Ladies Aid, *see* Dorcas Ladies Aid, Eagle Hill
The Eagle calls, ... 2976
Eagle Valley Book Club
Wagon trails plowed under, ... 2990
Earmme, Seung Young
A water use projection model for the North Saskatchewan River Basin, Alberta, 1980-1985, ... 2110
East Central Irrigation Association
Red Deer irrigation development, ... 3399
East Longview Historical Society
Tails and trails, 1900-1972, ... 3073

Eastburg Farm Women's Union
Eastburg, ... 2992
Easter, Roselynn
Rosemary, land of promise, ... 3223
Eastern Irrigation District, Brooks
The history of the Eastern Irrigation District,. 3400
Eastway Ladies' Social Club
Trails to highways, ... 2993
Eberhardt, Elvire
The Bessarabian German dialect in Medicine Hat, Alberta,. 448
Eckville and District Historical Society
Homesteads and happiness, ... 2994
Economic, Social and Human Development Conference, Edmonton, 1970
Conference minutes and papers, ... 1890
Economic Society of Alberta. Calgary Branch
Proceedings, ... 2102
EcoScalgary
Study on pollution, ... 3338
Edgerton and District Historical Society.
Winds of change,. 2995
Edgerton, Angie
The days before yesterday,. 3219
Edmonton Anti-Pollution Group
The nature, extent and sources of environmental knowledge
and opinions in Edmonton,. 3339
Nature trails in Edmonton, ... 1703
Resources inventory and guide to environmental studies, ... 3340
Edmonton Art Gallery
Accessions, 1972-1974, ... 1160
Adolph Gottlieb acrylics on paper, ... 1205
Alberta contemporary drawings, ... 1161
The Alberta Society of Artists, 1975, ... 1162
Alberta world reflections, ... 1163
Alberta '73, ... 1164
Alex Janvier, Edmonton Art Gallery, June 3-July 3, 1973, ... 1211
All Alberta '69, ... 1165
Armando Brasini,. 1149
Art in Alberta, Paul Kane to the present, ... 1166
Baker Lake prints/estampes, ... 1167
Barbara Ballachey, ... 1147
Bruce O'Neil, ... 1227
Calgary printmakers, ... 1168
Canada x ten, ... 1169
Certain traditions, ... 1170
Changing visions - the Canadian landscape, ... 1171
Charles M Russell, 1864-1926, ... 1237
Chester and Bentham,. 1155
The collective unconscious,. 1172
Diversity, Canada East, ... 1226
Dorothy Knowles, ... 1215

Edmonton collects, ... 1173
An exhibition of five recent works by Larry Bell, John McCracken, DeWain Valentine, Ron Cooper, Peter Alexander,. 1174
Folk art of Pakistan, ... 1175
Glen Guillet,. 1207
The great Canadian super show of Canadian ideas, ... 1176
The Group of Seven in the Rockies, ... 1177
Hendrik Bres, Ann Clarke Darrah, Eva Deiner,. 1150
Hubert Hohn documentary photographs, ... 1210
Ihur Dmystruck, ... 1159
Impressionist paintings from the collection of Mr and Mrs JA Scrymgeour and Westbourne International Industries, . . . 1178
Jack Bush, works on paper, ... 1152
JB Taylor landscapes, ... 1243
JD Turner, ... 1246
John Chalke,. 1154
John Will, Marvin Jones, ... 1250
Kenneth Noland March 6 - April 21, 1975, ... 1225
Larry Poons recent paintings,. 1231
Lin Chien-Shih, ... 1156
Marion Nicoll, ... 1224
Masters of the sixties, ... 1179
Modern painting in Canada, ... 1189
Norman Yates,. 1253
Pierre Guy, ... 1208
Play objects, ... 1180
Printmaking,. 1119
Robert Sinclair, ... 1241
Sculpture in steel, ... 1181
Sidney Tillim, ... 1245
Stephen Greene, ... 1206
Ten Washington artists, ... 1182
Third anniversary exhibition, April 5 - May 7, 1972,. 1183
Tommie Gallie, '75,. 1191
Understanding children's art,. 1120
Vassarely, ... 1248
West 71, ... 1184
William Kurelek,. 1216
William Perehudoff, ... 1229
8 cents worth of Canada and a few sense more, ... 1239

Edmonton Art Gallery. Junior Gallery
Plains Indian, ... 1185

Edmonton Bird Club
The birds and birders of Beaverhills Lake, ... 3321

Edmonton. Central Lutheran Church
Fiftieth anniversary, 1910-1960, ... 324

Edmonton Chamber of Comerce
The post-Leduc growth of the Edmonton economy, ... 2118

Edmonton. Christ Church
Golden jubilee,. 325

Edmonton. Church of the Good Shepherd
Church of the Good Shepherd 65th anniversary, ... 326
Edmonton Club
The Edmonton Club, ... 1835
Edmonton. Community of Our Lady of Charity
Golden jubilee souvenir of the foundation of the
Order of Our Lady of Charity, ... 194
Edmonton Dental Nurses and Assistants Association
One hundred years of dentistry,. 3361
Edmonton. Edith Rogers School
History made in Edmonton, ... 3221
Edmonton Grads
25 years of basketball championships, 1915-1940, ... 1646
Edmonton. Highlands United Church
Highlands United Church, Edmonton, Alberta, 50th anniversary,
1912-1962, ... 327
Edmonton. Holy Trinity Church
Holy Trinity church 75th anniversary, ... 328
Edmonton. Immaculate Conception Catholic Parish
Fêtes du 60ième anniversaire, Paroisse de l'Immaculée-Conception, . . . 329
Edmonton. Knox United Church
Knox United Church, south Edmonton, diamond jubilee of
present building, 1907-1967, ... 330
Edmonton. McDougall United Church
From drums to drums Souvenir program, ... 331
Ninetieth anniversary of McDougall United Church, Edmonton,
Alberta, Sunday, October 22, Monday, October 23 Anniversary
speaker, Rev JE Nix, ... 332
The Pioneers, ... 333
Edmonton. Moravian Church
The Edmonton Moravian Church 50th anniversary celebration, ... 334
Edmonton. Parks and Recreation Department
The Commonwealth Games management financial feasibility study, . 1704
Edmonton Public Library
Performance measurement indicators, ... 16
Summary of salary survey of the professional staff in
twenty-six Canadian public and university libraries, June, 1962, ... 17
User survey, ... 18
Edmonton Public School Board
Drug report, ... 1785
Edmonton Public School Board. Extension Services
The community school, a focus on living,. 1485
Edmonton. Robertson United Church
Robertson United Church, golden anniversary, 1969, ... 335
Edmonton. Ross Sheppard Composite High School
A reunion, 1957-1978,. 1539
Edmonton. Rutherford School
Rutherford school, 1910-1967, centennial open house, ... 1540
Edmonton. Saint Joachim Church
Album souvenir, ... 336

Edmonton. Saints Constantine and Helen Romanian Orthodox Parish
Anniversary, . . . 337
Edmonton Social Planning Council
Alternatives to poverty and welfare in Alberta, . . . 1812
An approach to planning river valley trails, . . . 1647
Maternity leave in Alberta, . . . 1746
Mini-parks for Edmonton, . . . 1648
Rape of the block, . . . 1811
Report, . . . 1779
To be poor in Canada, . . . 1783
Edmonton Social Planning Council. West Edmonton Social TaskForce
Citizens' resource catalogue, . . . 1720
Edmonton. Spruce Avenue School
A historical publication, Spruce Ave School, 1918-1978, . . . 1541
Edmonton. St. Alphonsus Catholic Parish
Golden jubilee, . . . 338
Edmonton. St. Andrew's Catholic Parish
St Andrew's Parish 50, . . . 339
Edmonton. St. Barnabas Anglican Church
St Barnabas Church, . . . 340
Edmonton. St. Faith's Anglican Church
Fiftieth anniversary, 1910-1960, . . . 341
Edmonton. St. Francis Friary
The Franciscans in Edmonton 50 years, 1901-1959, . . . 195
Edmonton. St. John the Evangelist Church
Fiftieth anniversary, 1916-1966, . . . 342
Edmonton. St. John's Evangelical Lutheran Church
St John's Evangelical Lutheran Church, Western Canadian Synod, organized 1903, dedicated May 28, 1972, . . . 343
Edmonton. St. John's Institute
40th anniversary of the St John's Institute, 1959, . . . 1836
Edmonton. St. Nicholas, St. Michael Ukrainian Catholic Church
75th anniversary, Ukrainian Catholic Parish of St Nicholas St Michael, . . . 344
Edmonton. St. Pius X Catholic Parish
The first 25 years, 1954-1979, . . . 345
Edmonton. Ste. Anne Parish
1952-1977, Paroisse Ste-Anne, . . . 346
Edmonton. Strathcona Baptist Church
Strathcona Baptist Church story, . . . 347
Edmonton. Strathearn United Church
Strathearn United Church, Edmonton, Alberta, 1951-1961, . . . 348
Edmonton. Trinity Evangelical Lutheran Church
60th anniversary, Trinity Evangelical Lutheran Church, 1902-1962, . . . 349
Edmonton Welfare Council. Senior Residents Survey Committee.
Edmonton Senior Residents' Survey report, . . . 1786
Edmonton. Wesley United Church
Wesley's 60 years, 1907-1967, . . . 350
Edmonton. Westminster United Church
50th anniversary, 1912-1962, . . . 351

Edson Fiftieth Anniversary Committee
Look behind you neighbour, ... 1081
Edson Leader
Edson flashback, ... 2996
Edson. Sacred Heart Catholic Parish
Sacred Heart Parish, 1912-1972, ... 352
Edson. United Church
Edson United Church history, ... 353
Edstrom, Sylvia
Memoirs of the Edberg pioneers, ... 2997
Edward, Barry Francis
A resource planning study of the wildlife of Cypress Hills Provincial Park, Alberta, ... 3341
Edwards, Bob
The best of Bob Edwards, ... 48
The wit and wisdom of Bob Edwards, ... 49
Edwards, Clifford Gordon
The National Policy as seen by the editors of the Medicine Hat newspapers, ... 2362
Edwards, Felicity Nan
A touch of gas,. 3342
Edwards, June, *see* Bhatia, June
Liverpool Daisy, ... 613
Edwards, Michael William
Alberta short run crude oil supply, 1972,. 2265
Efner, Bessie Lee *see* Rehwinkel, Bessie Lee (Efner)
Dr Bessie, ... 3371
Eggleston, Magdelana (Raskevich)
Mountain shadows, ... 642
Eggleston, Wilfrid
The high plains, ... 643
Prairie symphony, ... 644
While I still remember, ... 3476
Ehlers, Eckart
Das nordliche Peace River Country, Alberta, Kanada, ... 2532
Eichner, Edith (Orsel)
Golden dreams, story and drawings, ... 645
Eighth Recce Association
Sabretache, ... 2751
Eley, Frederic Joseph
Some aspects of wilderness perception in Alberta, ... 1650
Eliasoph, Hy
Edmonton's impact on surrounding urban centers, ... 2533
Eliot, Samuel A
Sganarelle, ... 1417
Eliot, Thomas Stearns
Landscapes, ... 1404
Elizabeth Metis Settlement Association
Elizabeth Metis Settlement, ... 3084

Elk Point and District Historical Society
Reflections, ... 2880
Elliott, David Raymond
The dispensational theology and political ideology of William Aberhart, ... 2406
Elliott, W. Harold
Patchwork pictures, ... 76
Elliott, William John
Hivernant archaeology in the Cypress Hills, ... 2029
Ellis, Maureen Compston
Local migration in east central Alberta, ... 2534
Ellison, Anthony P
The effect of rising energy costs on Canadian industries, ... 2187
Elnora History Committee
Buried treasures, ... 2936
Elton, David K
Alternatives, ... 2363
Electoral perception of federalism, ... 2364
Proceedings, ... 2142
Elwell, Margaret Manuel
While rivers flow,. 3355
Emanuel, Lydia
Attitudes toward identity in a Ukrainian parish,. 1891
Emard, C.H
Alberta's County of Mountain View, ... 2847
Embree, David Grant
The rise of the United Farmers of Alberta, ... 2407
Empress Golden Jubilee Committee
Golden jubilee, Empress, 1914-1964, ... 2998
Empress. St. Mary the Virgin Anglican Church
St Mary the Virgin, 1914-1974, 60th anniversary, ...354
England, Raymond Edward
A partial study of the resource potential of the Stony Indian reservation, ... 2112
Engleman, Frederick Charles
Alternatives, ... 2363
The Co-operative Commonwealth Federation of Canada, ... 2365
Enns, Maureen
Enns, Evans & Ulrich, ... 1186
Epp, Margaret
Into all the world, ... 77
Eppel, Helmut Paul
The duties of the provincial government toward the aging homeowner, ... 1787
Erasmus, Peter
Buffalo days and nights, ... 2777
Erdmar, Kenneth Richard
Recreational activities and perception in the Kananaskis region, Alberta, ... 1651

Erickson, George
History of the Ranfurly United Church and its congregation, ...355
Erickson, Gladys
Freeway west, ... 3019
Erickson, Gordon R
Freeway west, ... 3019
Erickson, Jean
History of the Ranfurly United Church and its congregation, ...355
Erickson, Nola B
Chautauga in Canada, ... 1257
Eskrick, Muriel Elizabeth
The Norwegian settlers, Eagle Hill and Bergen,. 1892
Portrait of a pioneer, ... 2999
The road to Ya Ha Tinda, ... 3000
Evans, Art
All our own work, ... 1103
Second offence, ... 1104
Up for the third time, ... 1105
Evans, John L
Raymond, 1901-1967, ... 3064
Evans, R.G. *see* Anderson, Frank Wesley
Murder on the plains, ... 1770
Evans, Simon M
The dispersal of Hutterite colonies in Alberta, 1918-1971, ... 1893
Evenson, George O
Adventuring for Christ, ...196
Ewanyk, Leonard John
Hunter-land owner relations in east central Alberta, ... 1652
Fafard, Joe
Joe Fafard, ... 1187
Fairbairn, John Alexander Lowry
Pincher Creek Old Timers souvenir album, 1878-1958, ... 3198
Rhymes of a prairie Scot, .887
Fairfield, David James
Chesterfield House and the Bow River Expedition, ... 2779
Fales, Douglas A
Alberta days, ...872
Falher Jubilee Committee
Jubilé de Falher, ... 3001
Falk, Rod
Bummy peepee in the toto, ... 1051
Faminow, Merle Douglas
Beef procurement by Edmonton restaurants, ... 2188
Famure, Oluwole Dada
An economic analysis of institutional buying patterns
for meats in Edmonton and surroundings, ... 2189
Farm & Ranch Management Consultants Ltd.
Tradition and transition, ... 3401
Farnalls, Paul L
Memoirs of life in Alberta, ... 3002

Farran, Roy
The day after tomorrow, ... 646
The history of the Calgary Highlanders, 1921-1954, ... 2752
Never had a chance, ... 647
The search, ... 648
Farrell Lake Women's Institute, *see* Majestic-Farrell Lake Women's Institute
Harvest of memories, ... 3055
Faryna, Natalka
Ukrainian Canadiana, ... 1136
Fassnacht, Susan Doris
Hinton, Alberta, 1811-1957, ... 2535
Faulknor, Cliff
The in-betweener, ... 649
Pen and plow, ... 50
The romance of beef, ... 3402
The smoke horse, ... 650
Turn him loose! Herman Linder, Canada's Mr Rodeo, ... 1653
West to the cattle country, ... 651
The white calf, ... 652
The white peril, ... 653
Fawcett, John M
A history of St Paul's United Church, Coleman, Alberta, ... 356
Federation of Metis Settlements
East prairie metis, 1939-1979, ... 2991
Feist, Harold E
Feist, ACA Gallery, Jan 25-Feb 5, 1971, ... 1188
Fencelines and Furrows History Book Society
Fencelines and Furrows, ... 3003
Fenton, Terry
Modern painting in Canada, ... 1189
Ferbey, Orysia Love Olia *see* Prokopiw, Orysia Love Olia (Ferbey)
The Ukrainians, ... 1981
Ference, Ermeline Ann
Literature associated with ranching in southern Alberta, ... 526
Ferguson Flats Ladies' Club
Reminiscing in Ferguson Flats, 1900-1974, ... 3004
Ferguson, Jack
Revolt in the west, ... 2799
Ferguson, Marjorie Ruth
Periodicals in Alberta high schools, ... 19
Ferguson, Ted
Kit Coleman, Queen of Hearts, ... 51
A white man's country, ... 1894
Ferguson, William Paul
The snowbird decades, ... 2333
Fernandez, Isaias B
The history of Filipinos in Alberta, ... 1895
Ferris, Ron
Apparitions, animations, and aces, ... 1287

Ferry, Joe
Alberta album of curling, ... 1654
Fewster, Gerald D
The social agency, ... 1788
Fidler, Vera
Chuckwagon of the Circle B,. 654
Filipenko, Laura
From the Bigknife to the Battle, Gadsby and area, ... 3005
Filles de Jésus
Souvenir du cinquantenaire des Filles de Jésus au Canada
Province de l'ouest canadien (Alberta et Montana), ...197
Fine Day
My Cree people, ... 1896
Finlay, Charles M
History of Mannville and district,. 3006
Finley, Fred J
Bugles in the hills, ...683
Finstad, Helen
Prairie footprints,. 3007
First United Church, Fort Saskatchewan
The Fort on the Saskatchewan,. 3208
Fischer, Emil
St Matthew's Evangelical Lutheran Church, Spruce Grove,
Alberta, seventy-fifth anniversary,. 357
Fisher, Anthony Dwight
The perception of instrumental values among the young
Blood Indians of Alberta, ... 1897
Fisher, John
Our heritage, ... 2823
Fisk, Robert Ritchie
A survey of leisure reading in the junior high schools of Alberta, . . 1655
Fitzgerald, John Joseph
Black gold with grit, ... 2266
Fitzgerald, Walter P
The wheels of time,. 3008
Fladmark, Knut R
Historical archaeology in northwestern North America, ... 2037
Flanagan, Thomas
The diaries of Louis Riel, ... 2805
Louis 'David' Riel, ... 2780
Flauret, Louis
Okotoks 50th anniversary celebrations, 6 Sept 54, ... 3009
Fleming, Freeda
The days before yesterday,. 3219
Fletcher, John Gould
The gulls, ... 1398
Irradiations, No18, ... 1402
Fletcher, Thomas H
Management alternatives in residential water supply, ... 2113

Flint, David
The Hutterites,. 1898
Florkewich, Violet
Hills of Hope, ... 3010
Floyd, Keith
Sandman's land, ...888
Foord, Isabelle
The beast in the bag and Wild West circus, ... 1052
A dream of sky people, ... 1053
I don't care what it looks like, as long as it's warm, ... 1054
Junkyard, ... 1055
Say hi to Owsley,. 1056
Shaman, ... 1057
Foothills Cowboys' Association
The west in action, ... 1656
Foothills Historical Society
Chaps and chinooks, ... 2901
Foran, C.J
History of St Anthony's Parish,. 358
Foran, Maxwell Laurence
Calgary An illustrated history, ... 3011
The Calgary Town Council, 1884-1895, ... 2456
West to the sea, ... 2793
Forbes, Jack
Pottery in Alberta, ... 1114
Forbes, L. Mackenzie
An analysis of the relationship between sale values of public grazing leases and sale values of comparable private range lands in southern Alberta,. 3403
Forbis, Richard George
Cluny, an ancient fortified village in Alberta,. 2030
Post-pleistocene man and his environment on the northern plains, . . 2049
Ford, Theresa M
Diversions,. 565
In jeopardy, ...573
Panorama,. 578
Road to yesterday, ...579
A sense of place, ...580
Tales tall and true, ... 2083
Transitions, ...585
Western moods, ...588
Western profiles, ...589
Who owns the earth?,. 590
Foremost Historical Society
Shortgrass country, ... 2907
Foremost Jubilee Committee
Brief history of Foremost, 1913-1963, ... 3124
Forestburg Historical Society
The early devisers, ... 3261

Forgione, Al
Windows to the mind, ... 1364
Forrester, Helen *see* Bhatia, June
Twopence to cross the Mersey, ... 615
Forsberg, Roberta Jean
Chief Mountain, ... 198
Fort Edmonton Historical Association
Edmonton, the way it was, ... 3012
Fort Macleod Chamber of Commerce
Our local industry in Fort Macleod, ... 2190
Fort Macleod History Book Committee
Fort Macleod - Our colourful past, ... 3013
Fort McMurray Public Library
Pass the McMurray salt please!, ... 2178
Fort Saskatchewan. First United Church
The Fort on the Saskatchewan, ... 3208
Fort Saskatchewan Historical Society
The Fort on the Saskatchewan, ... 3208
Fort Vermilion. St. Luke's Anglican Mission
Unchaga = Peace, ... 359
Fortier, Hilaire J
Lamoureux, ses débuts, ses pionniers, ... 3014
Foster, Franklin Lloyd
The 1921 Alberta provincial election, ... 2408
Foster, Kenneth Neill
The happen stance, ... 79
Foster, Peter
The blue-eyed sheiks, ... 2267
Foster, Russell James
Camping perception and camping satisfaction in
Alberta Provincial Parks, ... 1657
Fournier, Jean-Pierre
Crowfoot, ... 2827
Fournier, Lionel Joseph
A survey of recreation components operating in selected
areas of Alberta, ... 1658
Fowler, Lorraine
Wheels to Woodville, ... 3140
Fowler, Mrs. Gordon
The Big Valley story, ... 3015
Fowlie, Doris
Golden memoirs, 1912-1963, ... 2968
History of Bindloss School District 3603, 1919-1969, ... 1542
Fowlie, Helen Elizabeth (Holt)
Social Plains School District golden jubilee booklet, 1913-1963, ... 3016
Fox, Charles Armstrong
Exploring Paul's Epistles, ... 80
Frank, James G
Wages and salaries in the public sector, ... 2114

Frog Lake Community Club
Land of red and white, ... 3020
Fromhold, Joachim
An illustrated guide to projectile points for the Alberta region, . . . 2032
Fry, Olivia Rose
My heritage from the builders of Canada, ... 1902
Fryer, Harold
Alberta, the pioneer years, ... 2826
The Frog Lake massacre, ... 2782
Ghost towns of Alberta, ... 2678
Stops of interest in Alberta, ... 2679
Fyfe, R.G.
39 below, ... 592
Gaal, Arlene Beverly (Walker)
Banff's Christmas wish, ... 658
Gadsby Pioneers Association
From the Bigknife to the Battle, Gadsby and area, ... 3005
Gaetz, Annie Louise (Siddall)
Footprints of the Gaetz family, ... 2703
The park country, ... 3024
Gagajek, E.G.
St Benoit Parish 50th anniversary, ... 360
Gagan, David P.
Prairie perspectives, ... 2803
Gagnon, Joanne
They came, they saw, they lived, ... 3119
Gahagan, Alvine (Cyr)
Yes, father, ... 3362
Gahr, Gary Allen
Sherwood Park, ... 2537
Gallie, Tommie
Ranjan Sen Tommie Gallie, ... 1240
Tommie Gallie, '75, ... 1191
Gallivan, P.
Literature, language and culture, ... 531
Galt School of Nursing, Lethbridge
Golden jubilee, 1910-1960, ... 3363
Ganton and Watson Red Cross Auxiliary
We thy servants, 1939-1967, ... 3364
Gard, Robert Edward
Devil Red, ... 659
A horse named Joe, ... 660
Johnny Chinook, ... 2075
Scotty's mare, ... 661
Garden, Robert Ray
The planning of new residential areas in Edmonton, 1950-1976, . . . 2538
Gares, Mrs. Harold
Let us not forget, ... 3276
Garnier, Henri
En mission dans l'ouest canadien, ... 199

Franko, Ivan
Fox Mykyta,. 655
Frantz, Donald Gene
Toward a generative grammar of Blackfoot (with particular attention to selected stem formation processes), ...498
Frascara, J.
Best Mounted Police stories, ...562
Fraser, Esther Augusta (Michael)
The Canadian Rockies Early travels and explorations, ... 2825
Wheeler, ... 2536
Fraser, Frances Jane (Williams)
The bear who stole the chinook and other stories, ... 2073
The Milo-Queenstown UFWA and FWUA, ... 3404
The wind along the River, ... 2074
Fraser, William Bernard
The Alberta Indian, his past, his present, his future, ... 1900
Always a Strathcona, ... 2753
Big Bear, Indian patriot,. 2781
Calgary,. 3017
Indian tales of the Canadian prairies, ... 2082
Freebairn, Adam L.
The mountain heights, and other poems, ...889
Rhymes from the foothills,. 890
Rhymes of an old timer,. .891
Freedom and Naples Farm Women's Union
The history of the Freedom and Naples communities, ... 3018
Freeman, James Morton
Biggest sellout in history, ... 2268
The case history of Alberta's oil, ... 2269
Freeman, Madeline (Austin)
A horse for Running Buffalo, ...656
Freigang, P.F.
The story of the Lethbridge Municipal Railway, 1912-1947, ... 2334
French, C.L.
The Metis in Alberta society, with special reference to social, economic and cultural factors associated with persistently high tuberculosis incidence,. 1875
French, David
The seagull, ... 1046
Freuchen, Peter
The legend of Daniel Williams,. 2501
Frey, Cecelia
Breakaway, ...657
Friesen, Bruno
Farm stored grain on the Prairies, a cost study, ... 3405
Friesen, John W.
Culture change and education, ... 1947
People, culture and learning, ... 1901
A preacher's poems, ...892
Religion for people, ... 81

Garrick, Fiona
Bonnie McSmithers is at it again!, .593
Bonnie McSmithers you're driving me dithers, ...594
Hurry up, Bonnie, ...595
Garrison, Richard
Alberta divorce guide,. 2475
Garrod, Stan
Sam Steele, ... 2502
Garrow, Patrick
The status and anticipated manpower requirements by selected sectors of the agricultural industry in Alberta, ... 3406
Gary, Uncle *see* Brown, Gary William
The goat in the boat, by Uncle Gary, ... 1438
Gaschnitz, Eleanor Chambers
Memories of Verdant Valley, Cassel Hill, Livingston, Rainbow, . . . 2986
Gascoyne, James John
An analysis of injuries which occurred in physical education, intramural and extramural activites and free play in the Calgary Roman Catholic Separate School District #1 during the 1973-1974 and 1974-1975 school years,. 1659
Gatz, Clarence
Silver sage, ... 3272
Gauk, Roma Z.
Ukrainian Christian names A dictionary,. 506
Gaver, Mary Virginia
A survey of educational media services of Calgary public schools, conducted on behalf of the Calgary School Board, ... 20
Gedge, Pauline
Child of the morning, ...662
The eagle and the raven A novel, ...663
Geding, Willliam E.
A guide to publishing in education, ...2
Gee, T.W.
How can a song be blue,. 554
A nickel's worth of wishing, ...556
Geer, Charles
Lexy for short, ...732
That summer with Lexy, ...733
Gehring, A.
75 years of grace, 1894-1969, ...361
Geldart, Howard George
Marketing of wood chips from Alberta sawmills, ... 2191
Gem Ladies Club
Gem golden jubilee, 1914-1964, ... 3112
Genesee. St. John's School of Alberta
St John's of Alberta, ... 1544
Genii (magazine)
Genillusions,. 1288
George, Edna
Gem golden jubilee, 1914-1964, ... 3112

George, John E.
Mayerthorpe Pastoral Charge history, ...362
Georgeson, Michael R
A one-party dominant system, ... 2409
Germain, Claude
Singing your song, ...893
Gershaw, Fred William
The Blackfeet Confederacy, ... 1903
Highlights of Medicine Hat and district, ... 3025
Medicine Hat, ... 3026
Political history of Alberta, ... 2410
Sammis, the Medicine Hat, ... 3027
The short grass area, ... 3028
Gest, Lillian
History of Moraine Lake in the Canadian Rockies,
east of Lake Louise, Alberta,. 3029
History of Mount Assiniboine in the Canadian Rockies, ... 3030
Getty, Ian Allison Ludlow
The Church Missionary Society among the Blackfoot Indians
of southern Alberta, 1880-1895, ... 200
One century later, ... 1967
Getty, Ronald M.
Historical archaeology in northwestern North America, ... 2037
The Many Snakes Burial (DgOv-12), ... 2033
Getty, Wayne Edwin Allen
Perception as an agent of sociocultural change for the
Stoney Indians of Alberta, ... 1904
Gibson, Jean
The old house, ... 3031
Giesinger, Paul
History of the Giesinger (Gisinger) kinship, ... 2704
Giles, Thomas Edward
Educational administration in Canada,. 1489
Gilham, Dwayne Milton
The consumer spatial behavior of Edmonton's inner
city residents, 1977,. 2192
Gilkes, Margaret
Calgary's finest, ... 2503
Gill, Alison Margaret
Off-farm employment and mobility in the Goodfare district,
Alberta,. 2539
Gill, Dhara S.
A bibliography of socio-economic studies on rural Alberta, Canada, . . . 9
Gillese, John Patrick
Chinook arch, ...563
Kirby's gander,. 664
Gilpin, John Frederick
The city of Strathcona, 1891-1912, ... 3032
Gilt Edge Ladies Booster Club
Buffalo trails and tales, ... 3100

Ginn, David
Magic that moves me,. 1289
Girard, Arthur J.
Plamondon homecoming 73, ... 3033
Girl Guides of Canada. Calgary area
Camp Mockingbird,. 3034
Giroux, Alice (Soeur Marie Flore d'Auvergne)
Les Soeurs de Sainte-Croix dans l'ouest Canadien, ...201
Gladys Women's Institute
Gladys and Dinton through the years, ... 2972
Glenbow Foundation
A preliminary bibliography of the archaeology of Western Canada, . . .7
Western landscape as history, ... 1192
Glenbow-Alberta Institute
AC Leighton, ... 1233
Archibald Thorburn Paintings from the collection of Glenbow-Alberta Institute, Calgary, and Riveredge Foundation, Calgary, . . . 1244
Art in Alberta, Paul Kane to the present, ... 1166
Birds of prey, ... 1193
Contemporary Indian artists, ... 1194
Eskimo prints, Cape Dorset, ... 1195
Ethnic furniture, ... 1158
Focus, ... 1190
The frontier art of RB Nevitt, surgeon, North-West Mounted Police, 1874-78, ... 1222
Glenbow, ... 1196
Glenbow art circuit, 1971-1972, ... 1197
Glenbow collects An exhibition,. 1234
Glenbow past and present, ... 1198
Graphics by Walter J Phillips and Canadian art in three dimensions,. 1199
Historical watercolours by William Armstrong, ... 1145
Janet Mitchell,. 1221
Jim Nicoll, paintings and poetry, ... 1223
John Will, Marvin Jones, ... 1250
Marion Nicoll, ... 1224
The mountains and the sky, ... 1235
National ceramics exhibition, Calgary, October 29 - December 12, 1976,. 1143
New paintings by Otto Rogers, ... 1236
Open studio, ... 1200
Portraits of the Indians, ... 1201
Prairie images, ... 1212
Ranjan Sen Tommie Gallie, ... 1240
Selections, ... 1140
Silversmithing in Canadian history, ... 1242
Through Canadian eyes, ... 1251
Various art media and techniques, ... 1202
Western untitled, ... 1203
William Perehudoff, ... 1228
WJ Phillips views Western Canada, ... 1204

Glenbow-Alberta Institute. Archives
Arnold Lupson photographic collection, Calgary, Alberta, 1926-1947, 1905
George Gibson Coote papers, 1907-1956,. 2411
Lomen Brothers photographic collection, Nome, Alaska, c1900-1935, 2540
Royal Canadian Mounted Police, ... 5
Western Stock Growers' Association papers, 1896-1963, ... 3407
Glendale Women's Institute
Taming the prairie wool,. 3035
Glenn, John Elmer
The role of government legislation, policy and agency activity in irrigation development, ... 3408
Glick, Isaac N.
An analysis of the Human Resources Development Authority in Alberta, ... 1789
Glyde, H.G.
The Alberta golden jubilee anthology, ... 553
Godfrey, Denis
The bridge of fire, ... 665
No Englishman need apply, ... 666
Godsell, Philip Henry
Ethnological notes on Blackfoot and Blood Indians, ... 2065
Pilots of the purple twilight, ... 2335
Goertzen, Peter
Goertzen, ... 2705
Golden Years Club of Bezanson
Smoky River to Grande Prairie, ... 3190
Goldenberg, Helen
Once upon a chinook, ... 2457
Goldstein, Vincent-Marie
Paschal meal, ... 82
Gom, Leona
The singletree, ... 894
Goode, Chrissie
This is thine,. 83
Goodine, Barry Keith
The Alberta Fine Option Program, ... 2476
Goodwin, Lou
Fall madness, ... 1660
Gordon Donaldson Missionary Foundation
Every Christian's ministry,. 156
Gordon, Ernest Barron
A book of Protestant saints, ... 202
Gordon, Stanley Bruce
RB Bennett, MLA, 1897-1905,. 2366
Gore, Lily Grace (Graham)
MD of Kneehill, 1904-1967, ... 3038
Gorosh, Esther
Calgary's 'temple of knowledge', ... 21
Goss, Geoffrey W.
Children in the sun,. 722

Gossage, S.M.
Address by SM Gossage Chairman, Metric Commission to the Canadian Gas Association, Calgary, 18 October, 1973,. 2193
Gottlieb, Adolph
Adolph Gottlieb acrylics on paper, ... 1205
Gottselig, Cheryl
Wills and probate procedure, Alberta, ... 2477
Gould, Ed
Ranching, ... 3409
Gouldie, Helen Norma (Schielke)
Schielke family tree, ... 2706
The Willing family,. 2707
Govier, George W.
Alberta's oil sands in the energy supply picture,. 2270
Govier, Kathleen
Random descent A novel, .667
Gowland, John Stafford
Return to Canada, ... 2609
Sikanaska trail, ...668
Smoke over Sikanaska, ... 3317
Graham, Donna
Prairie silhouettes, ...943
Graham, Frank Neil
Theme and form in the novels of Edward A McCourt, ...527
Graham, Lily Grace *see* Gore, Lily Grace (Graham)
MD of Kneehill, 1904-1967, ... 3038
Grahn, Laurie
Village of Hay Lakes 50th anniversary, 1928-1978, ... 3039
Gran, Kenneth
Atomic feelings, ...895
Grande Prairie and District Old Timers' Association
Pioneers of the Peace,. 2916
Grande Prairie Chamber of Commerce
Grande Prairie today!,. 2680
Grande Prairie trade dollars, ... 2194
Transactions of the first Resources Conference of the Northwest Region, ... 2146
Grande Prairie Women's Institute
History of the Grande Prairie Women's Institute, ... 3410
Grandin, Vital Justin
Monseigneur Grandin vous parle, ...203
Grant, Gene
Phantini's lost book of mental secrets, ... 1290
Grant, John W.
Vignettes of old south Calgary, ... 3040
Grant, Ted
Men of the saddle, ... 3448
Granum History Committee
Leavings by trail,. 3041

Graspointer, Andreas
Some aspects and problems of the archaeology along the Milk River in southeast Alberta, ... 2034
Grassland Pioneers Historical Society
Echoes along the Ribstone,. 2851
Gratz, Humphrey.
Footprints on Mi-Chig-Wun, ... 3042
Gravel, Francine
Et le verbe s'est fait chair, ... 885
Graves, Warren
Chief Shaking Spear rides again, ... 1058
The hand that cradles the rock,. 1059
The Mumberley inheritance, ... 1060
The proper perspective and Who's looking after the Atlantic?, . . . 1061
Scrooge,. 1062
Three plays, ... 1063
Yes, dear, ... 1064
Gravistin, Phyllis Maureen *see* Alcorn, Phyllis Maureen (Gravistin)
In the bend of the Battle, ... 2848
Gray, James Henry
Boomtime,. 2783
Booze, ... 1790
The boy from Winnipeg,. 2784
Men against the desert, ... 3411
The roar of the twenties,. 2785
Troublemaker!,. 2786
The winter years,. 2787
Great Canadian Oil Sands Ltd.
Miracle on the Athabasca, ... 2272
Great Divide Trail Association
The Great Divide Trail, Banff to Waterton It's concept and future, . 1661
Green, Gladys Hope
The Hope family & neighbors of Red Deer Lake, SD No28, ... 2708
Green, Margaret V.
The 49ers,. 3043
Greene, Gordon Kay
Daniel Kent Greene, his life & times, 1858-1921, ... 2709
Greene, Stephen
Stephen Greene, ... 1206
Greenlawn Centennial Committee
In retrospect, 1967, ... 3044
Greenwood, Irene
First lust, ... 896
Greer, Dennis
Edmonton is burning, ... 730
The Hutterite ways,. 1988
A place for everyone, ... 790
Teamwork, ... 791
Whatever you do,. 792

Greer, D.J. *see* Greer, Dennis
The Hutterite ways,. 1988
Gregoret, Gene Roy
Narrative for the film, 'The Trout Lake Cree', ... 1906
Grier, Faye
How about me?, ... 1445
Griffin, John Peter
These are they,. 363
Griffith, Donald
Notes on the Goodridge area, ... 3045
Griffiths, Deidre
Island forest year, ... 3318
Groh, Dennis Gregory
The political thought of Ernest Manning, ... 2412
Grondin, Conde R.
The development of political cynicism among a selected sample of adolescents in Alberta, ... 2367
Groves, Cyril
The growth and development of the English Council of the Alberta Teachers' Association, ... 1545
Groves, Edythe Muriel (McNeill)
Funnybones, ... 897
Poetic reflections,. 898
The prairie hub, ... 3143
Westward bound,. 2797
Yarns for spinning thoughts, ... 899
Grubb, Herbert W.
The economic benefits and costs of irrigation in the eastern irrigation district of Alberta, ... 3444
Grywalski, Stanley
A history of technical-vocational education in the secondary schools of Alberta, 1900-1969, ... 1546
Gudlaugson, Elma Pearl *see* Helgason, Elma Pearl (Gudlaugson)
In the land where the Peace River flows,. 903
Gudlaugson, Magnus Gudmundur
Three times a pioneer,. 3477
Gue, Leslie Robb
A comparative study of value orientations in an Alberta Indian community, ... 1907
Guest, Leslie P.
Lecture domaine,. 1291
Guest, Robert C.
Pioneers of the Peace,. 2916
Guest, Wilfred
Poetic fancies, ... 900
Guillet, Glenn
Glen Guillet,. 1207
Guiltner, James Carl
The Peace River country and McKenzie highway to Yellowknife (John Hart Highway and Alaska Highway, 1867-1967), ... 2681

Gulley, Ruth M. *see* McDonald, Ruth M. (Gulley)
Prairie silhouettes, ...943
Gulutsan, Lena (Hyrhor)
Deedo's children, ... 3478
Gulutson, Metro
Second Banff Conference on Central and East European Studies, Banff Springs Hotel, Banff, Alberta, March 2-5, 1978, . . . 1865
Guy, Pierre
Pierre Guy, ... 1208
Gwagnin, Aleksandr
Khronika zemli Rus'koi (Ukrains'koi), de opysano vsi mista, zamky v provintsiiakh do ykh prynalezhnykh, ... 2738
Gwynne Historical Society
Treasured memories, Gwynne and district, ... 3192
Hacker, Carlotta
Crowfoot, ... 2827
Hackett, John
A historical sketch, Lamont United Church, 1892-1956, ...364
Hackler, James C.
To have or to let go, ... 1757
Hades, Brian M.
Practical contact mind reading, ... 1357
Hades, Michael P.
Bang!, ... 1292
Chandu's magic variations, ... 1281
Double double magic with cards, ... 1298
The dove worker's handbook, ... 1302
Exclusive magic, ... 1353
Genillusions, ... 1288
Handle with care, ... 1355
How to make flashes, bangs and puffs of smoke, ... 1293
The magic of Allan Lambie, ... 1369
The magic shelf, ... 1309
Magic the way I *see* it, ... 1294
The make-up of magic, ... 1295
The master index to magic in print, covering books and magazines in English language published up to and including December, 1964, . . 1351
Mentalistic encore, ... 1265
New concepts in magic, ... 1261
The new make-up of magic, ... 1296
Novel concepts with cards, ... 1262
Sensational mentalism, ... 1340
Stage illusions for the 1, 2 or 3 performer show, ... 1301
Tan Choon Tee on mentalism, ... 1367
Windows to the mind, ... 1364
Hadikin, Wesley Fred
Landscape perception in the Crowsnest Pass area, Alberta, ... 2610
Hagan, John
Criminal justice in a Canadian province, ... 2478

Hagell, Edward Frederic
When the grass was free, .669
Hagman, Mary Wilkinson
Mary and the Holy Thorn,. 1065
Haigh, Richard James
Resident characteristics of six urban fringe communities
in the Edmonton region, ... 2541
Hakluyt, Richard
According to Hakluyt,. 2747
Hall, Cecil T.
The golden years of Redcliff,. 3046
Hall, Gordon Langley
Peter at the Stampede, .670
Peter Jumping Horse, ...671
Hall, Jean *see* Chubb, Jean (Hall)
Leaves of yesteryear, ... 2939
Hall, John
Its the real thing - Hall, ... 1209
Hall, John A.
The great chief, Maskepetoon, warrior of the Crees, ... 2843
The road across Canada, ... 2625
Hall, Tom W.
Rocky Mountain wildlife, ... 3313
Halmrast, Leonard C.
The shepherd politician, ... 2413
Hambly, J.R. Stan
The Battle River country, ... 3047
Saddlebags to stained glass, ...365
Hameed, Syed M.A.
Three or four day work week, ... 2242
Work and leisure in Canada, ... 2156
Hamilton, Jacques
Our Alberta heritage, ... 2828
Hamilton Junior High School, Lethbridge
1874 trek souvenir publication, ... 2504
Hamilton, Sally Anne
An historical geography of coal mining in the Edmonton area, . . . 2542
Hammond, Arthur
The valley of the vanishing birds, ...619
Hampshire, Michael Allen
Down the wild river north, ... 2611
Hampson, Cy
Into the woods beyond, ... 3319
Hancock, Al E.
The road to monetary reform, ... 2115
Social Credit, ... 2116
Hancock, Maxine Louise
Living on less and liking it more, ... 1747
Love, honor and be free,. 1748
People in process,. 1749

Hancock, Ronald Lee
The man sitting in Place Pigalle and other short short stories, ...672
Hand, Fred J.
Bow River Lodge, no1, Calgary, Alta, ... 1837
Hand Hills Book Committee
Hand Hills heritage, ... 3048
Handford, Ellen A.
History of St Mark's Church, ...366
Handicapped Housing Society of Alberta
Access - housing, ... 1721
Handy, C.K.
Research paper on the Alberta Provincial Police, ... 2512
Haney, Harry Damon
Feeder cattle marketing in southern Alberta, ... 2195
Hanks, Jane (Richardson)
Tribe under trust, ... 1908
Hanks, Lucien Mason
Tribe under trust, ... 1908
Hanna Jubilee Committee
Pioneer days of Hanna and district 50th anniversary ed,
Aug 7, 1962,. 3049
Hanna, Nell
Thistle creek, ...673
Hanna North Book Club
Hanna North, ... 3086
Hansen, Evelyn M.
Brick's Hill, Berwyn and beyond, ... 3050
Where go the boats,. 2336
Hansen, Hans
The Dickson story, ... 2971
Hansen, Harry Benjamin
The Hansens, ... 2710
Hansen, Margaret *see* Dragland, Margaret (Hansen)
Conquerville, a growing community,. 2951
Hansen, Myrtle
The Dickson story, ... 2971
Hanson, Eric
Trader Eric and other stories, .674
Hanson, Eric John
Dynamic decade, ... 2273
A financial history of Alberta, 1905-1950, ... 2117
Financing education in Alberta,. 1490
Local government in Alberta,. 2459
The post-Leduc growth of the Edmonton economy, ... 2118
The potential unification of the Edmonton Metropolitan area,. 2119
Some basic concepts in regional income analysis, ... 2120
Hanson, Joan
Frames,. 901
Hantiuk, J.
Impressions de voyage et histoire de St Joseph de Végreville, ... 3269

Hanus, Frantisek
Economic analysis of demand and supply of water in Alberta municipalities, ... 2121
Harburn, Norman Alan
Interpretive unit plan, Peace-Athabasca delta, ... 1663
Harder, J.D.
Proceedings of the Alberta Chamber of Commerce Manpower Conference held in Jasper, October 6-8, 1974, ... 2088
Hardin, Samuel H.
History of greater Vegreville,. . . . 3051
Hardman, Norma Pauline *see* Sluman, Norma Pauline (Hardman)
Poundmaker,. . . . 786
Hardwick, Evelyn
The science, the art and the spirit, ... 3375
Hardy, William George
Alberta, a natural history, ... 3320
The Alberta golden jubilee anthology, ... 553
The bloodied toga, ... 675
The city of libertines, ... 676
Education in Alberta, ... 1491
From sea unto sea, ... 2739
The Greek and Roman world, ... 2740
Origins and ordeals of the western world, ... 2741
Our heritage from the past, ... 2742
The scarlet mantle, ... 677
Harker, Herbert
Goldenrod, ... 678
Turn again home,. . . . 679
Harker, Herbert B.
Daniel Kent Greene, his life & times, 1858-1921, ... 2709
Harker, Randal
Adrift, ... 680
Harlow, Robert G.
A gift of echoes, ... 681
Harmon, Byron
Great days in the Rockies,. . . . 1121
Harmon, Carole
Great days in the Rockies, ... 1121
Harper, Donald Calvin
Secularization and religion in Alberta,. . . . 84
Harris, Joseph Edwin
The Baptist Union of Western Canada, ... 205
Harris, Sam
Bow River Lodge, no1, Calgary, Alta, ... 1837
Harrison, Dick
Alberta in fiction, ... 522
Best Mounted Police stories, ... 562
Crossing frontiers, ... 523
The unnamed country, ... 528

Harrison, Eugene Myers
Giants of the missionary trail, . . . 206
Harrison, Irene
Lure of the homestead, . . . 3052
Hart, Edward John
Diamond hitch,. . . . 3053
The history of the french-speaking community of Edmonton, 1795-1935, . . . 3054
Hart, John Edward
William Irvine and radical politics in Canada, . . . 2368
Harty, Lynn
Beiseker's golden heritage, . . . 3232
Harvey, John Michael
A community development model illustrated with Hinton, Alberta, . 1722
Harvey, Myrna
A nickel's worth of wishing, . . . 556
Harvey, Richard H.
70 years of miracles, . . . 85
Harvey, R.N.
Report on certain industrial and other factors related to the economy of the central Peace River district, Alberta, . . . 2138
Report on the land, industries and related factors in the Peace River Country, Alberta, . . . 2139
Harvison, Clifford W
The Horsemen,. . . . 682
Haslam, I.R.
A perceived needs assessment of amateur sport administrators in Alberta, . . . 1664
Hassbring, Lena Margareta
A geographic analysis of land use in Edmonton's rural-urban fringe zone, . . . 2543
Hatcher, Colin Kirk
Stampede city streetcars, . . . 2337
Hatt, Fred Kenneth
Ninety nine years from tomorrow, . . . 1909
The response to directed social change on an Alberta Metis colony, . 1910
Hatt, Judy
Ninety nine years from tomorrow, . . . 1909
Hattersley, Vera
Gran on Social Credit, . . . 2414
Haughen, Marjorie
Cowley, . . . 2905
Hawgood, Wendy
The valley of the vanishing birds, . . . 619
Hawker, P.
Fort Edmonton, . . . 2031
Hawkey, Frank
A brief history of the Christian faith in Alberta and in the Airdrie pastoral charge of the United Church of Canada,. . . . 438

Hawrysh, Wasyl
My Canada and I, ... 1911
Hay, William A.
RB Bennett and the charge of one-man government,. 2369
Haydn, L.
Spices and beauty, ... 902
Hayes, John Francis
Bugles in the hills, ... 683
Hayhurst, William
A brief history of the Rocky Mountains, ... 3056
Hays 25th Book Committee
From sod to silver, ... 3057
Hayter, Jacqueline Green
Residential mobility and the function of seven selected high rises in central Edmonton, ... 1791
Hayter, Our Savior's Lutheran Church
60th anniversary, ... 367
Haythorne, Donald Francis
The characteristics of Edmonton welfare recipients in relation to employability and labour force classification, ... 2196
Healy, Mary Darina
Comparative factorial ecology of large Alberta cities, 1961-1971, . . 2544
Heard, Ray
Yesteryears of the Hays Municipality,. 3206
Heath, Terrence
Western untitled,. 1203
Heaton Moor and Brookland Book Committee
Seventy years gone by, ... 3058
Heaward, Jeanette
Wo de hombre,. 2640
Heckbert, Douglas Robert
Day parole in Alberta, ... 1792
Hedley, Ralph
East of Beaver Hills, ... 3059
Heffren, Henry Charles
Voices of the pioneers,. 207
Heggie, Grant Barton
A descriptive analysis of vocational rehabilitation programs for the mentally retarded in Alberta, ... 1793
Heibert, Garry
Around you, ... 561
Heidebrecht, Herbert V.
Values of Mennonite youth in Alberta, ... 1912
Heidmeier, Boniface
Pioneering in the west, ... 208
Heinen, Gerty
Iron Springs Christian Reformed Church, 1949-1974, twenty-fifth anniversary,. 368
Heinsen, Annie
Grub-axe to grain, ... 3060

Helenius, Alice Cummings
It's good to remember, ... 3479
Helgason, Elma Pearl (Gudlaugson)
In the land where the Peace River flows,. 903
Helmer, J.W.
Problems in the prehistory of the North American subarctic, ... 2051
Helmericks, Constance
Down the wild river north,. 2611
Helmers, Donna Mary
A study of the developmental program of the Woman's Overnight Shelter, Edmonton, January 23, 1970-May 23, 1973, . . . 1794
Heming, Eileen
Ted of the Mounties, ... 684
Henderson, Elmes
A Medonte pioneer and his famous son, ... 2510
Henderson, Joseph Frank
Passover celebration, ... 86
Hendricks, Larry John
The Edmonton Public Library Government Information Division, an element in community development, ... 22
Hendrickson, Magda
This land is our land, ... 685
Henry, Alexander
Travels and adventures in Canada and the Indian territories, between the years 1760 and 1776,. 2788
Henry, Julianne
Interlude of love, ... 904
Henry, Lorena Ann
The adventure of Cynthia and her friends, ... 686
Herscovitich, Gail
Industrial water use in Edmonton, ... 2122
Hesketh Pope Lease Historical Committee
Memories, yours and mine, ... 3061
Hess, E. Laraine
Osteology and odontology of the Sharphead burial site,. 2035
Hetherington, Arthur J.
Our Lady of Peace, ... 369
Hetland, Gary Dennis Layne
Socio-economic change in the Grande Cache region of Alberta, . . . 1795
Hewitt, Adlyn Miskew
Family laws for Albertans,. 2479
Hewitt, Dorcas Alma
The Fort Pitt trail Mostly tales of pioneer days,. 3062
Hicken, John Orvin
Events leading to the settlement of the communities of Cardston, Magrath, Stirling and Raymond, Alberta, ... 3063
Raymond, 1901-1967, ... 3064
Hickling-Johnston Limited
Alberta growth, ... 2123
Economic study, town of Fort Saskatchewan, Alberta, ... 2124

Hickman, Zina Woolf
Founding of Cardston and vicinity, ... 2872
Hiebert, Henry
Evolution, ... 87
High Prairie Farm Women's Union Centennial Book Committee
Pioneers who blazed the trail, ... 3065
High River Pioneers' and Old Timers' Association
Leaves from the medicine tree, ... 3066
Higinbotham, David
When the west was young, ... 3067
Hilda Town and Country Ladies Club
Hilda's golden heritage, ... 3068
Hill, Agnes Isabel Aston
Through the years, ... 905
Hill, Alexander Staveley
From home to home, ... 2612
Hill, Edna *see* Appleby, Edna (Hill)
Canmore, the story of an era, ... 2856
Hill, Robert C.
Social Credit and the press, ... 2415
Hill Spring. Church of Jesus Christ of Latter-Day Saints
50 years Hill Spring Ward, 1910-1960, ... 370
Hill Spring Cultural Society
Hill Spring and its people, ... 3069
Hillborn, James D., ed
Dusters and gushers, ... 2274
Hillcrest Heritage Society
Prairie echoes, Metiskow, Cadogan, Cairns, ... 3249
Hillerud, John M.
The Duffield site and its fossil bison, Alberta, Canada, ... 2036
Hills of Home Historical Committee
The hills of home, ... 3070
Hills of Hope Historical Committee
Hills of Hope, ... 3010
Hincks, A.
A viewpoint on hostels, ... 1665
Hines Creek High school.
History of Hines Creek, 1867-1967, ... 3071
Hirabayashi, G.K.
The Metis in Alberta society, with special reference to social, economic and cultural factors associated with persistently high tuberculosis incidence, ... 1875
Hiscox, Ingeborg
Thomasina and the trout tree, ... 628
Historical Association of Alberta. Whoop-up Country Chapter
Nineteenth century Lethbridge, ... 3194
Historical Society of Alberta
The early west, ... 2776
Hjartarson, Freida Amelia
Survey of child care arrangements in Edmonton, ... 1750

Hladyshevsky, M.
Ukrainian Catholic parish, Calgary, Alberta, ... 371
Hlus, Carolyn D. Redl- *see* Redl-Hlus, Carolyn D.
Earthbound, ... 965
Hoar, Blanche
Crestomere-Sylvan Heights heritage, ... 2858
Hobart, Charles W.
Ninety nine years from tomorrow, ... 1909
Persistence and change, ... 1973
Hochstein, Lucille Agatha
Roman Catholic separate and public schools in Alberta, ... 1547
Hocking, Anthony
Alberta,. 2613
Hocking, Drake
The nature, extent and sources of environmental knowledge and opinions in Edmonton,. 3339
Hodgson, Charles
The nature, extent and sources of environmental knowledge and opinions in Edmonton,. 3339
Hodgson, Ernest Daniel
The nature and purposes of the public school in Northwest Territories (1885-1905) and Alberta (1905-1963),. 1548
Hodgson, John Fraser
Once upon a life time,. 3480
Wanderings of an expert, ... 3481
Hodgson, Michael Conn
The fiscal development of the city of Edmonton since 1946,. 2461
Hoe, Ban Seng
Structural changes in two Chinese communities in Alberta, Canada, . 1913
Hogg, Archie L.
Tails and trails, 1900-1972, ... 3073
Hohensee, Richard
Seventy five years by the grace of God, ... 372
Hohn, Hubert
The Banff purchase, ... 1122
Byzantine churches of Alberta, ... 1133
Hubert Hohn documentary photographs, ... 1210
Holden, W.N.
The development of transportation in early Calgary, researched by Margaret E Longair, ... 2344
Hollinshead, Michael J.
The cost of confederation, ... 2360
Holloway, J. H.
A history of the Alberta Land Surveyors Association, ... 3412
Holmes, George S.
The Provost story, ... 3204
Holmes, Owen Gordon
Come hell or high water, ... 1597
Holmes, Rex
The last summer,. 2614

Holmes, Robert James
Social work staff turnover in the Alberta Department of Public Welfare, . . . 1796
Holmgren, Eric Joseph
Isaac M Barr and the Britannia Colony, . . . 3074
2,000 place names of Alberta, . . . 2658
Holmgren, Patricia M.
2,000 place names of Alberta, . . . 2658
Holt, Helen Elizabeth *see* Fowlie, Helen Elizabeth (Holt)
Social Plains School District golden jubilee booklet, 1913-1963, . . . 3016
Holt, Stephen
Stormy, . . . 687
Holtslander, Dale
School districts of Alberta, . . . 1492
Honcharenko, Ahapius
Memoirs, . . . 529
Honeyman, Gertrude Evelyn (Dixon)
Poems for old and young, . . . 906
Hooke, Alfred John
A tribute to Hon EC Manning on the occasion of his 50th birthday party, September 30th, 1958, . . . 907
30 + 5, . . . 2416
Hoole, Arthur Herbert
The development of a family agency, . . . 1751
Hoover, Walter B.
Eschata, . . . 908
The Holy City, . . . 909
Hope, Adrian
The story of Chief Medicine Hat, . . . 2829
Hope, Richard Joseph
The Hope family & neighbors of Red Deer Lake, SD No28, . . . 2708
Hopkins, Evan H.
Broken bread, . . . 88
Horn, George M.
Toward a more adequate definition of the notion of transformation, . . . 450
Horna, Jarmila L.A.
Alberta's pioneers from Eastern Europe, . . . 1914
Hornby, Richard
The kidnappers, by Richard Hornby, Two pollution sketches, by Nina F Klaiman, . . . 1066
Horne, Natalie Ruth
If I call, will someone answer?, . . . 910
Horner, Donald George
Income distribution in Alberta agriculture, . . . 3413
Horsch, John
The Hutterian Brethren, 1582-1931, . . . 1915
Horsefield, R.B.
A Cree Bible dictionary, . . . 89
Horvat, Joseph
In the land of the free, . . . 3482

Hoskin, Katharine E.E.
I remember Peace River, Alberta and adjacent districts, ... 3081
Hostetler, John Andrew
The Hutterians in perspective, ... 1916
Houghton, John Reginald
The Calgary public school system, 1939-1969, ... 1549
House, John Douglas
The last of the free enterprisers, ... 2275
Houston, John Richard
Numbering the survivors, ... 2711
Howard, Alice Bell
Memories of Verdant Valley, Cassel Hill, Livingston, Rainbow, . . . 2986
Howard, Jeff
A house for Harry, ... 1723
Howard, Joseph Kinsey
Strange empire, ... 2789
Howe, Helen D.
Seventy-five years along the Red Deer River,. 3075
Howg, Carl Magnus
Our Haugs in America, ... 2712
Hraska, John
Hills of Hope, ... 3010
Huddlestun, Frederick Molden
A history of the settlement and building up of the area in
SW Alberta bordering Waterton Park on the north, from 1889, . . . 3077
Hudson, Arland James
Charles Ora Card, pioneer and colonizer, ... 209
Hughenden Women's Institute
The lantern years, ... 3109
Hughes, John
A history of Athabina, ... 3078
Hughes, Monica
Beyond the dark river,. 688
Crisis on Conshelf Ten, ... 689
Earthdark,. 690
The ghost dance caper, ... 691
Gold-fever trail, ... 692
The tomorrow city, ... 693
Hughes, Stuart
The Frog Lake massacre, ... 1917
Hugo, Pauline
Memoirs of the Ghost Pine homesteaders, ... 3079
Hull, Burling
The amazing world of mentalism,. 1297
Double double magic with cards, ... 1298
Gold medal showmanship for magicians and mentalists, ... 1299
The master mentalist, ... 1354
The new encyclopedic dictionary of mentalism, ... 1300
Stage illusions for the 1, 2 or 3 performer show,. 1301

Hull, Doreen P. *see* McKay, Doreen P. (Hull)
Forty years on, ... 1563
Hull, Raymond
Tales of a pioneer surveyor, ... 2638
Hull, Virginia Lee
A geographical study of the impact of two ethnic groups on the landscape in central Alberta, ... 2545
Hulmes, Frederick George
The senior executive and the fifteenth Alberta legislature, ... 2417
Hummena, Dokiia
Eternal flames of Alberta, ... 2615
Humphreys, David Llewellyn
Joe Clark, ... 2370
Humphreys, James Trowe
Record in stone, ... 2038
Humphreys, Ramona Cecil Marguerite
Legally blind youth of Alberta, ... 1493
Hungry Wolf, Adolf
Blackfoot craftworker's book, ... 1918
Blackfoot people, ... 1919
The Blood people, a division of the Blackfoot confederacy, ... 1920
Charlo's People, ... 1921
Good medicine, ... 2076
The good medicine book, ... 2077
Good medicine companion issue, ... 1922
Good medicine in Glacier National Park, ... 2078
Good medicine thoughts, ... 90
Good medicine Traditional dress issue, ... 1923
Indian summer, ... 1924
Legends told by the old people, ... 2079
Rails in the Canadian Rockies, ... 2338
Siksiká, ... 1869
The spirit at Hidden Valley, ... 2080
Teachings of nature, ... 1925
Tipi life, ... 1926
Hungry Wolf, Beverly
Blackfoot craftworker's book, ... 1918
Siksiká, ... 1869
Hunt, Elnora B.
Twenty-five years proud, ... 1797
Hunter, Emily
How to learn to read syllabics, ... 499
Hurko, T.
10th anniversary first Ukrainian Catholic Church, Smoky Lake, 1964-1974, ... 373
Huse, Peter
Prairie poems, ... 911
Hussar United Church Ladies' Aid
The Hussar heritage, ... 2879

Hustak, Allan
Peter Lougheed A biography, ... 2418
Huston, Mary Louise
The rise of the Social Credit movement in Alberta, 1932-1935, ... 2419
Huston, Mervyn J.
The great Canadian lover and other commentaries and conceits,. . . . 1107
Great golf humor, ... 1106
Hutchinson, Gerald M.
Memorial booklet written on the occasion of the 100th anniversary celebrations honoring the arrival of the Reverend Thomas Woolsey and the Reverend Henry Bird Steinhauer in September, 1855, ... 210
The Rundle journals, 1840-1848, ... 241
Hutchinson, Robert Alexander
Scenic assessment and landscape protection, ... 2546
Hutterite Brethren
Gesang-Buchlein,. 1446
Handbook for sermons on Bible, ... 91
The Hutterian Brethren of America, ... 1927
Hutton, Darryl J.P.
The dove worker's handbook,. 1302
Hyndman, Louis D.
The Edmonton Club, ... 1835
Hyrhor, Lena *see* Gulutsan, Lena (Hyrhor)
Deedo's children, ... 3478
Hyrnchuk, Audrey
Memories, Redwater and district, ... 3080
Hythe Pioneer History Society *see* Pioneer History Society of Hythe and Area
Pioneer round-up,. 3110
Iaremenko, Serhil
Saskachevanka, ... 1447
Ignatius, Ruth Johanna *see* Collins, Ruth Johanna (Ignatius)
Winnifred,. 2946
Imperial Oil Ltd.
A visit to the Leduc oilfield and gas conservation project,. 2276
Wildcat one thirty four, ... 2277
Inamasu, Mary
Anecdotal history of Calgary Separate Schools, ... 1520
Independent Alberta Association
The cost of confederation, ... 2360
The juridicial nature of Canadian federalism,. 2374
Independent Task Force on the Development of Canada's Petroleum and Mineral Resources
Canada's resources and the national interest, ... 2279
Canada's resources and the national interest, ... 2278
Indian Association of Alberta
Address by Harold Cardinal, President, Indian Association of Alberta, during presentation by the Indian Chiefs of Alberta to the Prime Minister and the Government of Canada, June 4, 1970, ... 1877
Alberta Indian Education Center,. 1494
Conference minutes and papers, ... 1890

Indian hunting, fishing and trapping rights today, ... 1928
Indian treaties and the law, ... 2480
A proposal concerning the economic and human resources development of the Indian peoples of Alberta,. 1929

Indian Chiefs of Alberta
Citizens plus, ... 1930

Indians and Metis Historical Club
Red paper vs white paper, ... 1946

Inman, Lester
Beautiful Red Deer One step, ... 1448
Calgary stampede chuckwagon roundup, ... 1449

Innes, Duncan R.
Strathcona High School, 1907-1967 in retrospect, ... 1550

Innisfail and District Historical Society
Candelight years,. 2933
Innisfail, 75 years a town, 1903-1978, ... 3083

Inter-Church Consultants
Like a Chinook, ...219

International Brotherhood of Teamsters, Chauffeurs, Warehousemen and Helpers of America. Local 987 Struggles and progress of Teamsters Local 987, Calgary, Alberta, 1910-1955, ... 2197

International Geographical Union. Commission on Population Geography
Applied population geography, ... 2589

Irma. Sharon Lutheran Church
Golden anniversary, 1910-1960,. 374

Irma. United Church
A history of Irma United Church Published on the occasion of the golden anniversary, ...375

Ironside, Jetske
Pernilla in the perilous forest, ...815

Irvine, William
The farmers in politics, ... 2371
Live or die with Russia, ... 2372
The twain shall meet, by Wm. Irvine and others, ... 2373

Irving, Harold A.
Regional impact of an Alberta steel plant, ... 2198

Irving, John Allan
The Social Credit movement in Alberta, ... 2420

Irving, Will
Hymns for piano accordion, ... 1450

Isaacs Gallery, Toronto
William Kurelek,. 1216

Isaiv, Ivan
Ukrainian Catholic unity, 1906-1966, ...255

Ives, John W.
A spatial analysis of artifact distribution on a boreal forest archaeological site, ... 2039

Ivory, John
Effect of increased wellhead petroleum prices on some Alberta industries, ... 2199

Jablonski-Jones, Martha
Mr Brown and his magic mustache, ... 798
Jackel, David
Figures in a ground, ... 567
Jackknife, Albina
Elizabeth Metis Settlement, ... 3084
Jackson, Frank
A candle in the grub box, ... 3483
Jam in the bedroll, ... 3484
Jackson, Joyce
Luscar come back, ... 3085
Jackson, Norman
Staff perceptions of rehabilitation in the Drumheller Institution, ... 1798
Jackson, Wayne Harry
Ethnicity and areal organization among French Canadians in the Peace River district, Alberta, ... 1931
Jacob, Edmond
Modern Israel in biblical perspective, ... 92
Jacobson, J. Robert
Modern Israel in biblical perspective, ... 92
Jacobson, Jerome
Archaeological reconnaissance north of the Brooks range in northeastern Alaska, ... 2058
Jacoby, A.P.
Persistence and change, ... 1973
Jacques, Barbara E.
A study of social assistance in Alberta, ... 1799
Jakober, Marie
The mind gods, ... 694
James, Donna
Emily Murphy, ... 1752
James, Edward Llewellyn
An historical survey of education in the Strathmore area of Alberta, 1900-1958, ... 1551
James, Ferguson
Tales of the pioneer days, ... 912
James, Jean
Hanna North, ... 3086
St. Peter's Lutheran Church, Scapa, Alberta, 1921-1971, ... 376
This was Endiang, ... 3087
James, John
Fight that ticket, ... 2481
Incorporation and business guide for Alberta, ... 2482
Jameson, Eileen
The science, the art and the spirit, ... 3375
Jameson, George Irwin
The trail riders song, ... 1451
Jameson, Sheilagh S.
Chautauga in Canada, ... 1257

Janis, Joana
History of the Ukrainian Women's Association of Canada, St. John's Cathedral Branch, 1926-1976,. 1838
Janke, John William
Environmental economic issues in the sour gas processing industry in Alberta,. 2280
Jankunis, Frank J.
Southern Alberta A regional perspective,. 3088
Janus Museum Consultants Limited
A responsive environment for the growth of cultural resources in the city of Calgary, October, 1969, ... 1123
Janvier, Alex
Alex Janvier, Edmonton Art Gallery, June 3-July 3, 1973, ... 1211
Janz, Leo
The Janz team story, ... 93
Jasperse, Frank R.
Seasonal variations in employment, ... 2200
Jendyk, Margaret Faulkes
The creative process of drama and its application to drama in education, ... 1258
Jenkins, Betty-Rose
The Rosebud trail, ... 3144
Jenkins, David Danner
Realism and Alberta's secondary aims, ... 1495
Jenkins, J. George
Prairie images, ... 1212
Jensen, Ethel
Tributaries of the Blindman, ... 3089
Jenson, Bodil Jelhof
The county of Mountain View, Alberta, ... 3090
John Howard Society of Alberta
The alcoholic offender - whose responsibility?, ... 1800
Corrections and penology Where are we going?,. 1806
Corrections needs to be corrected,. 1815
John Wilson Elementary School, Innisfail
A look at yesterday,. 3091
Johnson, Alice Margaret
Saskatchewan journals and correspondence Edmonton House, 1795-1800, Chesterfield House, 1800-1802,. 2830
Johnson, Denis Bruce
The Edmonton-Calgary corridor, ... 2579
A functional comparison of the central retail district with two regional shopping centres in Calgary, Alberta, 1963,. 2201
A study of commercial blight and the function of Whyte Avenue, Edmonton,. 2202
Johnson, E. Harper
Younger brother, ...774
Johnson, Elaine
Alberta, the emerging giant, ... 2608

Johnson, G. Rudolph
The Northfield settlement, 1913-1969,. 3092
Johnson, James Foster
The story of a maverick,. 3485
Johnson, Keith
Indian Association of Alberta, ... 1496
Johnson, Leroy Peter Vernon
Aberhart of Alberta, ... 2421
Strictly for posterity, ... 3093
Johnson, Louise C.
First fifty years, Edmonton YWCA, 1907-1957, ... 1839
Johnson, Mary *see* Scriven, Mary (Johnson)
Homesteading in the Consul district, ... 3234
Johnson, Myron
The failure of the CCF in Alberta, ... 2422
Johnston, Alexander
The battle at Belly River, ... 2831
Boats and barges on the Belly, ... 2340
Cowboy politics, ... 3414
The CP Rail High Level Bridge at Lethbridge, ... 2341
1969, ... 1123
Johnston, Cheryl Lynn
Perceptions of the medical social worker's functions in the
Calgary General Hospital, ... 1801
Johnstone Walker Ltd.
The story of JW, 1886-1961,. 2203
Joint International Symposium of Elders and Scholars, Edmonton, 1977
Native religious traditions,. 94
Jones, Brian K.
Something to think about, ... 95
Jones, David
The Crowsnest Pass, a coal mining valley, ... 2547
Jones, David C.
Shaping the schools of the Canadian West,. 1552
Jones, John Yardley- *see* Yardley-Jones, John
All our own work, ... 1103
Jones, Leanne M.
The book about nothing,. .695
Hanok, ...696
Jones, Martha Jablonski- *see* Jablonski-Jones, Martha
Mr. Brown and his magic mustache, ...798
Jones, Marvin
John Will, Marvin Jones, ... 1250
Jones, Ormond
Please put the music back,. 1452
Jones, Owen Douglas
The historical geography of Edmonton, Alberta,. 2548
Jones, Robert L.
Edmonton Senior Residents' Survey report,. 1786

Jones, Sandra
Ready steady go, ... 1067
Jones, William Griffith
Ceiriog capers, ... 913
Over the years at Zion, ... 377
Jordon, Mabel E.
The McDougall Memorial United Church, Morley, Alberta, ... 378
Jorgenson, Robert D.
The squatters, ... 3094
Jouan, Marion L.
A lily bloomed,. 2713
Tomahawk trails,. 3095
Jowett, John Henry
The school of Calvary, ... 96
Junor-Moore, Sheila
The suicide meet,. 1038
Kaasa, Walter H.
Adventures in acting, ... 1034
Kachur, Braj B.
Current trends in stylistics,. 451
Kalbach, W.E.
Persistence and change, ... 1973
Kallen, Urs
A climbing guide to Yamnuska, ... 1666
Kalman, Harold
Medalta, ... 2161
Kampen, Vlasta van
Great Canadian adventure stories, ... 570
Great Canadian animal stories, ... 571
Kamra, Ardis Daphne
An evaluation of the fiction collections in the elementary school libraries of an Alberta school district, ... 23
Kania, Jack
Banff's Christmas wish, ... 658
Karas, Frank Paul
Labour and coal in the Crowsnest Pass, 1925-1935, ... 2204
Karklins, Karlis
Nottingham House,. 2832
Kasa, Gaylerde
Trails and trials, ... 3097
Katyi, Andre
Angels on Devil's Island, ... 1932
Kaufman, Carolyn Reesor
Historic churches of Alberta and the Canadian North West, ... 1124
Kawamura, Leslie
Religion and ethnicity, ... 160
Keats, John
Selected poems, ... 997
Keith, Ronald A.
Bush pilot with a brief case, ... 2342

Kelland, Clarence Budington
The case of the nameless corpse, ...697
Keller, Weldon Phillip
Charles Bowen, ...211
Expendable!, ...212
Kellow, Richard Lawrence
A study of residential water use in Calgary, ... 2126
Kelly, Leroy Victor
North with Peace River Jim, ... 2616
The range men, ... 3415
Kelsey, John Graham Thornton
Communications in a growing organization, ... 1802
Kemp, Gerald
The legal status of volunteer workers and voluntary organizations, . . 2483
Kendal, Wallis
Just Gin, ...698
Kennard, J.K.
The politics of Canadian urban development, ... 2450
Kennedy, Albert Edward
Bargaining unit determination in Alberta, ... 2205
Kennedy, D.M.
The story of our church, St Paul's United, Fairview, ...380
Kennedy, Fred
Alberta was my beat, ... 52
Calgary Stampede, ...1667
Kennedy, Orvis A.
Principles and policies of Social Credit, ... 2423
Kenney, John
The business career of R B Bennett, 1897-1927, ... 2206
Kense, François J.
Papers from Conference on Canadian Archaeology Abroad, held at the University of Calgary, November 23, 24, 25, 1973, ... 2022
Problems in the prehistory of the North American subarctic, ... 2051
Kent, Jennifer
Peter at the Stampede, .670
Peter Jumping Horse, ...671
Kenward, John Kenneth
Political manipulation and rewards in the Crowsnest Pass, southern Alberta, ... 2462
Kenworthy, Mary
Falling leaves Poems, ...914
Gleanings of the years, .915
Kerr, Illingworth
Willowdale, ...832
Kerr, James Stolee
As grace is given, ...213
Kerr, M.
Calahoo trails, ... 2908
Kerri, James Ngoziem Nwannukwu
Fort McMurray, ... 2549

Two studies on Fort McMurray, ... 2588
Keys, Charles L.
Spatial reorganization in a central place system, ... 2127
Kezar, J.
Inkwells and school bells, ... 1553
Khattab, Abdelmoneim M.
The assimilation of Arab Muslims in Alberta, ... 1933
Khehra, Gurnam Singh
Structural changes in the Alberta broiler industry, ... 2207
K.I.K. Historical Committee
KIK country, ... 3096
Kilgour, Betty
As the years go by, ... 3098
Kinette Club of Didsbury
Echoes of an era, ... 3099
King, Donald Robert
Alberta archaeology, ... 2040
Spitzee Anota, ...699
King, Mona F.
Some aspects of post-war migration to Edmonton, Alberta, ... 2550
Kinsella, Norman George
The vowel system of Blackfoot, .500
Kinsella, W.P.
Dance me outside, ...700
Scars, ...701
Kipling, Rudyard
Rudyard Kipling's (Medicine) Hat trick, ... 1108
Kiriak, Illia
Sons of the soil, ...702
Kirman, Joseph M.
Alberta, ... 2617
Saga of Canada, ...916
Kisserbeth, Charles W.
Studies in generative phonology, ...464
Kitchen, Melba
Buffalo trails and tales, ... 3100
Kitsco, John Phillip
Canadian poetry, ...917
Looking back, ...918
Kiyooka, Henry
Harry Kiyooka, paintings and prints, ... 1213
Henry Kiyooka paintings & prints, ... 1214
Kjellberg, Sten Oscar
The Canadian petroleum industry, achievements and prospects, . . . 2281
Klaiman, Nina F.
The kidnappers, by Richard Hornby, Two pollution sketches, by Nina F Klaiman, ... 1066
Klapstein, Elsie Louise
A native community counselling team, ... 1803

Klassen, Henry C.
The Canadian West, ... 1716
Frontier Calgary, town, city and region, 1875-1914, ... 3022
Prairie perspectives, 2, ... 2804
Klein, Mary
Ten dollars and a dream, ... 3101
Klippernstein, David Henry
Recreational enterprises for farmers in Alberta, ... 1668
Klufas, Jean
Memories, Redwater and district, ... 3080
Kluge, Einhard
The green butterfly and other poems, ...919
Knadel, Gladys
Saga of Schuler stalwarts, ... 3298
Knafla, Louis Antone
Law and society in Canada in historical perspective, ... 2470
Science, technology and culture in historical perspective, ... 2746
Knapp, John L.
The economics of industrial water use in Alberta, ... 2128
Knelson, Helen *see* Penner, Helen (Knelson)
Happiness and other poems, ...959
Knill, William Douglas
A classification of theses in education completed at the University of Alberta, 1929-1966, ... 6
Cultural transmission in a closed society, ... 1934
Hutterian education, ... 1497
Know Your Neighbour Project
The history of Drayton Valley, ... 2982
A history of Stony Plain, Alberta, ... 3184
Knowles, Dorothy
Dorothy Knowles, ... 1215
Knowlton, Faye (Pringle)
These were the early days, ... 2714
Koch, Agnes Bernice
The interorganizational bases of community power, ... 1724
Koch, Edward Leo
Home Oil Calgary, ... 2282
Koester, Charles B.
A bibliography of selected theses on (sic) the Library of the University of Alberta relating to Western Canada, 1915-1965, ... 10
Kohut, Irena
Contribution of Donald H Cameron to adult education, ... 1598
Kostash, Myrna
All of Baba's children, ... 1935
Koszec, Paul Caesar
An economic evaluation of the Alberta Estate Tax Rebate Act, . . . 2129
Kozak, Kathryn
Education and the Blackfoot, 1870-1900, ... 1554
Kraulis, J.A.
Alpine Canada, ... 3326

Kreisel, Henry
The betrayal, ...703
Klanak islands,. 704
The rich man, ...705
Kroetsch, Robert
Alberta,. 2618
Badlands, ...706
But we are exiles,. .707
Creation, ...564
Gone Indian,. 708
The ledger, ...920
The sad Phoenician,. .921
Seed catalogue Poems, ...922
The stone hammer poems, 1960-1975, ...923
The studhorse man,. .709
What the crow said, .710
The words of my roaring, ...711
Kubota, Carol
Sirens and cinders, ... 3102
Kumar, S.K. Vasantha
Illusionseseme, ... 1303
Kunelius, Rick
Ski trails in the Canadian Rockies, ... 1669
Kunz, Anita
The lady of the strawberries, ...625
Kurelek, William
Fields, ... 1125
Fox Mykyta,. 655
Jewish life in Canada,. 1936
Kurelek country, ... 1126
Kurelek's Canada, ... 1127
The last of the Arctic,. 1128
Lumberjack, ...712
A northern nativity,. 1129
O Toronto, ... 1130
The passion of Christ according to St Matthew,. 1131
A prairie boy's summer, ...713
A prairie boy's winter, ...714
Someone with me, ... 1132
Who has seen the wind, ...742
William Kurelek,. 1216
William Kurelek,. 1217
Kwofie, Emmanuel N.
Teaching a foreigh (sic) language to the West African student, ...452
Laberge, Myriam
They came, they saw, they lived, ... 3119
LaBissoniere, Jean Placidus
Providence trail blazers, ...214
LaBorde Simat Ltd.
A perspective on the energy resources of Western Canada, ... 2283

Lac La Biche Chamber of Commerce
Lac La Biche pow wow and fish derby, ... 2683
Lac La Biche Heritage Society
Lac La Biche yesterday and today, ... 3103
Lac La Biche. St. Catherine's Catholic Church
Fiftieth anniversary of St Catherine Parish, Lac La Biche, Alberta, 1914-1964,. 381
Lac Ste. Anne Historical Society. Archives Committee
West of the fifth,. 3104
Lacombe and District Board of Trade
The Lacombe story, our heritage,. 3105
Lacombe Rural History Club
Wagon trails to hard top, ... 3106
LaFleur, Phyllis Maria Elena
Three Alberta teachers, ... 1555
Lahren, Larry A.
Northwestern plains archaeology, ... 2041
Lai, Hermia Kwok-Lee
Evolution of the railway network of Edmonton and its land use effects, ... 2343
Lai, Rosita Pek Fong
Community leagues as a community development nuclei, ... 1725
Laing, Lory Mair
Population growth patterns among Alberta Hutterites, ... 1937
Lake, David Wayne
The historical geography of the Coal Branch,. 2551
Lake, Owen Hayden
Autobiography and people I have met along the highways and byways,. 3486
Lambo, Don
Thorny's hideaway, ...734
Lamerton Historical Society
Land of the lakes, ... 3107
Lamont and District Historian
Along the Victoria trail, ... 3254
Lamont, Glenda Rae
Migrants and migration in part of the southwest Peace River region, Alberta,. 2552
Lander, Tim
Except that you're here, ...924
The romantic manifesto for the last ditch, ...925
Lane, P.
Calgary city jail, ...926
Langdon Women's Institute
The Langdon legend, ... 3108
LaPointe, Louis Henry
Children's participation in the marketplace in selected jurisdictions of Alberta, ... 2130
Larden, Robert A.
Our apostolic heritage, ...215

Larner, John W.
The Kootenay Plains (Alberta) land question and Canadian Indian policy, 1799-1947, ... 1938
LaRoque, Emma
Defeathering the Indian,. 1939
Larsen, William W.
Conjuring for children, ... 1304
Genillusions,. 1288
The L W card mysteries, ... 1377
Mental mysteries with cards,. 1312
Puppetrix,. 1305
Twelve illusionettes,. 1306
Larson, Lena
Pioneer round-up,. 3110
LaRue, Garry
The boy in buckskins, ... 596
Ernest C Manning, ... 2403
Last, Edward
Handgathered fruit,. 97
Latham, Ernest
History of District 37-E, part of Multiple District 37, ... 1840
Latta, William
Drifting into grey, ... 927
Summer's bright blood, ... 928
Laughlin, J.E.
Pathfinding on plain and prairie, ... 224
Laurence, Margaret Christine
US expatriates in Calgary and their problems, ... 1940
Lavender, David
The Rockies,. 2553
Law, D.B.
History of the Glenwood District, ... 3111
Lawrence, Edith J. *see* Clark, Edith J. (Lawrence)
Trails of Tail Creek country, ... 2941
Lawrence, Julia
Sheridan Lawrence, Emperor of the Peace,. 3487
Lawrence, Karen A.
Nekuia, ... 929
Lawrence, Sheridan
Sheridan Lawrence, Emperor of the Peace,. 3487
Laxer, James
The big tough expensive job, ... 2284
Laycock, Mae
Bridges of friendship, ... 1941
Lazare, Jerry
The bold heart,. 764
Lazarenko, Joseph M.
The Ukrainian pioneers in Alberta, Canada, ... 2001
LeBlanc, Darrell Robert
A measure of understanding of certain aspects of Alberta industry, . 2208

LeBlanc, Victoria
From preacher to prophet, ... 530
LeButt, Paul
The Calgary Stampede, ... 1670
Leduc. First Baptist Church
75th anniversary, First Baptist Church, Leduc, Alberta, 1894-1969, . . 382
Leduc. Grace Lutheran Church
Grace Lutheran Church (Gnadenthal), Leduc, Alberta Seventy-fifth anniversary, ... 383
Leduc. St. Peter's Lutheran Church
75th anniversary, June 8, 1900-1975, ... 384
Lee, Beatrice
"Destiny", ... 930
Lee, Terence Richard
A manufacturing geography of Edmonton, Alberta, ... 2209
Leeder, Terry
Daughter of the old pioneer, ... 1753
White Forehead of the Cypress Hills, ... 715
Lees, Robert B.
Studies presented to Robert B Lees by his students, ... 459
Leeson, Muriel
I escaped the holocaust, ... 258
Lefsrud, Patricia
History of Our Lady of Victory Church, Thorsby, ... 385
LeGal, Louis
Changing visions - the Canadian landscape, ... 1171
Leggett, Viola (Shanks)
Gem golden jubilee, 1914-1964, ... 3112
Lehmann, Hildegard
Tizz at the Stampede, ... 616
Tizz in the Canadian Rockies, ... 617
Lehner, Cass
The bride & groom waltz, ... 1453
Lehner, Lily
The bride & groom waltz, ... 1453
Lehr, John Campbell
Mormon settlements in southern Alberta, ... 1942
Leinweber, Robert George
A descriptive study of current and future roles of social service personnel in the province of Alberta, ... 1804
LeMay, Bonnie
Boy who has a horse, ... 1068
Roundhouse, ... 1069
Lemieux, Giles
The Crowsnest Pass, a coal mining valley, ... 2547
Lenti, Paul
The amazing world of mentalism, ... 1297
Creation of a magical madman,, ... 1315
Mind and matter,. 1317
S'komplimentary mentalism, ... 1365

Twelve illusionettes,. 1306
Lester, Geoffrey Austin
The distribution of religious groups in Alberta, 1961, ... 98
The land of Peter Pond, ... 2527
On the edge of the shield, ... 2566
Lethbridge Booklet Committee
Lethbridge Alberta's Golden Jubilee, ... 3291
Lethbridge Chamber of Commerce
Fingertip facts about Lethbridge and district,. 2684
Lethbridge, the big little city, ... 2685
Lethbridge Herald
Alberta's golden jubilee,. 3113
Alberta's golden jubilee edition, 1905-1955, ... 3114
Alberta's golden jubilee edition, 1905-1955, ... 3115
Cardston 75th anniversary, 1887-1962, ... 3116
Golden anniversary and progress edition, 1907-1957,. 3117
Lethbridge. Immanuel Lutheran Church
Immanuel Lutheran Church, 60th anniversary, November 2, 1969, . . 386
Lethbridge Junior College
Past, present, and future of the Lethbridge Junior College, ... 1556
Lethbridge Municipal Hospital
Night and day,. 3365
Lethbridge. St. Augustine's Anglican Church
In His service, St Augustine's, Lethbridge, 1886-1976,. 387
Lethbridge. St. Patrick's Catholic Parish
St. Patrick's, Lethbridge, ... 388
Levesque, Gerard R.
The North, ... 2686
Survey of Fairview, located in the heart of the inland empire, ... 2687
Lewis, Oscar
The effects of white contact upon Blackfoot culture, with special reference to the role of the fur trade, ... 1943
Lewis, Richard W.
Devil Red,. 659
Library Association of Alberta
Education for librarianship, ... 34
Library management, ... 24
Liddell, Kenneth Eric
Alberta revisited, ... 2619
I'll take the train,. 2620
Roamin' empire of southern Alberta, ... 2621
This is Alberta, ... 2622
Liebertz, Arnold
Marvelous mysteries of Marvillo, ... 1307
L.I.F.E. History Committee
Ten dollars and a dream, ... 3101
Light, Douglas W.
Tattooing practices of the Cree Indians, ... 2042
Lightner, Theodore M.
Problems in the theory of phonology, ... 454

Liknes, Marina
A treasury of memories, ... 3228
Lillicoe, Jessie
Land of the Spirit, ... 278
Lincoln, Neville J.
Phonology of the Metis French dialect of Saint-Paul, Alberta, ... 455
Linder, A. Dorothy
Ethnic strategies of three minority groups in the city of Calgary, . . 1944
Linder, George
Proceedings, ... 2103
Lindoe, Luke
Lindoe, ACA Gallery, Jan 25-Feb 5, 1971, ... 1218
Lindsay, James F.
Western reunion, ... 971
Lindsay, Nicholas Vachel
Moon songs, ... 1408
Lingas, Helen (Fotos)
My centennial torch for world peace, ... 99
Lister, Phil
Enjoying the Rockies, ... 2623
Lister, Reginald Charles
My forty-five years on the campus, ... 1599
Lister, Robert
The birds and birders of Beaverhills Lake, ... 3321
Livermore, Ronald P.
Bibliography of primary sources for classroom study of the history of Alberta, ... 11
Livesay, Dorothy
Gold sun, ... 1396
Green rain, ... 1397
My hands, ... 1409
Plainsong, ... 1412
Lloydminster Quota Club
Homestead memories, ... 3153
Lockhart, William James
Alberta hog market, conduct and performance, ... 2211
Lodge, Tom
Beyond the Great Slave Lake, ... 3488
Loggie, Margaret
One man in his time, ... 716
Loiselle, Lorraine
They came, they saw, they lived, ... 3119
Lomond Book Committee
History of Lomond and district, ... 3120
Lone Butte Book Club
Lone Butte north, ... 3286
Long, Harold G.
Fort Macleod, ... 2505
Long, John Clifford
An historical study of the establishment of college systems

in Ontario and Alberta in the 1960's, ... 1600
Long, Philip Sheridan
Dreams, dust and depression,. 3489
The great Canadian range,. 3417
Jerry Potts, scout, frontiersman and hero, ... 2833
Your historical Canadian border route no 3, ... 2624
70 years a cowboy (a biography), ... 3490
Long, T.B.
70 years a cowboy (a biography), ... 3490
Longair, Margaret Eleanor (Ritchie)
The development of transportation in early Calgary, researched by Margaret E. Longair,. 2344
Longstreth, Thomas Morris
The Calgary Challengers, ...717
Lore, Mary S.
Historical summary of the Skyline Hikers of the Canadian Rockies, 1933-1970, ... 1671
Lorrain, Edith
Histoire de Girouxville, ... 3250
Lorraine, Sid
Encyclopedia of suspensions and levitations, ... 1269
Losey, Timothy Campbell
Archaeology of the Cormie Ranch Site, an interim report, ... 2043
The Beaver Creek site, ... 2061
The prehistoric cultural ecology of the western prairie-forest transition zone, Alberta, Canada, ... 2044
Lougheed, Don
"Popguns" Don Lougheed, ... 1219
Lougheed Women's Institute.
Verdant valleys in and around Lougheed, ... 3121
Lounsbury, John Patton
The Canadian petroleum industry, ... 2285
The Canadian petroleum industry, achievements and prospects, . . 2281
Love, Britten Innis
Veterinarians of the North-West Territories and Alberta,. 3418
Love, Florence A. (McDonald)
The Lamont Public Hospital School of Nursing, 1912-1914, ... 3366
Love, Harold Clyde
Crop production risk in Alberta, ... 3419
Income variation in beef production,. 2212
Loverso, Caterina Edwards
Vases, ...718
Loveseth, B.
Primitive art and technology,. 2054
Lowenthal, Myra
The boy from Winnipeg,. 2784
Lubeck Merrymakers Society
Our bend in the Peace, ... 3186
Lucas, Daisy
Siding 16, ... 3215

Luckhurst, Margaret
North West Mounted Police, ... 2506
Luckyj, George
The Vaplite collection, ... 586
Lukoms'ka, Ol'ha
Nashym naymenshum, ... 2081
Lund, Jacquiee
Early rangemen, ... 3471
Lundin, Lloyd
Magazine magicana, ... 1308
Lundstrom, Florence
Memoirs of the Edberg pioneers, ... 2997
Lupul, Manoly Robert
Relations in education between the state and the Roman Catholic Church in the Canadian Northwest, with special reference to the provisional district of Alberta, from 1880 to 1905, ... 1557
The Roman Catholic Church and the north-west school question, . . 1558
Ukrainian Canadians, multiculturalism and separatism, ... 2000
Lussier, Philippe
History of St Paul, Alberta, 1909-1959, ... 2985
Lusty, Terrance W.J.
Louis Riel, humanitarian, ... 2790
Metis social-political movement, ... 1945
Red paper vs white paper, ... 1946
Luxton, Eleanor Georgina
Banff, Canada's first national park, ... 3122
The golden link, ... 2834
Lyalta, Ardenode, Dalroy Historical Society
Along the fireguard trail, ... 3123
Lynch-Staunton, Betty (Frankish)
A short history of the Church of St John the Evangelist, Pincher Creek, Alta, ... 389
Lynes, Edith M.
Brief history of Foremost, 1913-1963, ... 3124
Lynn, Esther
Derbytown echoes, ... 3125
Lyon, Louise C.
Culture change and education, ... 1947
Lyseng, Mary J.
The history of educational radio in Alberta, ... 1559
Lysne, David Edgar
Welfare in Alberta, 1905-1936, ... 1805
M & M Systems Research Ltd
A realistic perspective of Canadian confederation, ... 2361
MacCrimmon, Iain
Music for the great highland bagpipe, ... 1454
Macdonald, Cathy
The Edmonton Grads, Canada's most most successful team, ... 1672
MacDonald, D.S.
Corrections and penology Where are we going?, ... 1806

Macdonald, Elizabeth
Japanese Canadians in Edmonton, 1969, ... 1948
MacDonald, George Heath
Edmonton, fort - house - factory, ... 3127
Fort Augustus-Edmonton, ... 3128
Macdonald, John
The history of the University of Alberta, 1908-1958, ... 1601
MacDonald, Marjorie *see* Chapman, Marjorie (MacDonald)
Golden jubilee, 1910-1960, ... 3363
Macdonald, P.
An abbreviated history of the Ponoka United Church of Canada, . . . 409
Macdonald, R.H.
Grant MacEwan, ... 2835
MacDonald, Robert
The romance of Canadian history, ... 2743
MacDougall, Alexander Joseph
Alberta alcoholism treatment programs, community development and citizen involvement, ... 1807
MacEoin, Gary
Man to Man, ... 143
MacEwan, Grant *see* MacEwan, John Walter Grant
Grant MacEwan, ... 2835
MacEwan, John Walter Grant
And mighty women too, ... 2715
The battle for the Bay, ... 2345
Between the Red and the Rockies, ... 3420
Blazing the old cattle trail, ... 3421
Calgary cavalcade from fort to fortune, ... 3129
Cornerstone colony, ... 2791
Entrusted to my care, ... 3343
Eye Opener Bob, ... 53
Fifty mighty men, ... 2716
Harvest of bread, ... 3422
Hoofprints and hitching posts, ... 3423
John Ware's cow country, ... 3424
Memory meadows, ... 3425
Pat Burns, cattle king, ... 2213
Poking into politics, ... 2424
Portraits from the plains, ... 1949
Power for prairie plows, ... 3426
The rhyming horseman of the Qu'Appelle, ... 3427
A short history of Western Canada, ... 2792
Sitting Bull The years in Canada, ... 2836
Tatanga Mani, Walking Buffalo of the Stonies, ... 2837
West to the sea, ... 2793
MacGregor, James Grierson
The Battle River Valley, ... 3130
Behold the shining mountains, ... 2554
Edmonton A history, ... 3131
Edmonton trader, ... 2214

Father Lacombe, ... 216
A history of Alberta, ... 2838
John Rowand, czar of the prairies, ... 2839
The Klondike rush through Edmonton, 1897-1898, ... 3132
North-West of 16, ... 3491
Overland by the Yellowhead, ... 2794
Pack saddles to Tete Jaune Cache, ... 3133
Paddle wheels to bucket-wheels on the Athabasca, ... 3134
Peter Fidler, ... 2795
Senator Hardisty's prairies, 1849-1889, ... 2796
Vilni zemli (free lands), ... 1950
MacIver, Ian
The land and water resources of the Spring Creek basin, ... 2555
Mackay, Donald Stewart
The cultural ecology of the Chipewyan, ... 1951
MacKay, Sheila *see* Russell, Sheila (MacKay)
The living earth, ... 776
Mackenzie, John
Country editor, ... 54
Mackie, Marlene Marie
The accuracy of folk knowledge concerning Alberta Indians, Hutterites, and Ukrainians, ... 1952
The defector from the Hutterite Colony, ... 1953
MacKinnon, Frank
The Crown in Canada, ... 2375
Macklin, Irvin Victor
Life is more than meat, ... 1498
They've turned their back to the Bible, ... 2840
Maclagan, David
Adventures into unknowns, ... 719
Little Cree Badger and the Fire Spirit, ... 2071
Riel's people, ... 1872
MacLean, Hec
Waterhole and the land north of the Peace, ... 3135
Maclean, Raymond Angus
The history of the Roman Catholic Church in Edmonton, ... 217
MacLellan, James Alexander
My years in Lionism, 1931-1975, ... 1841
Sermons, addresses, editorial and other writings, ... 100
MacLeod, H.L.
Properties, investors and taxes, ... 2131
Macleod, R.C.
The North West Mounted Police, 1873-1919, ... 2507
The NWMP and law enforcement, 1873-1905, ... 2508
Macleod Sketch Club, Fort Macleod
Story of Macleod, ... 3136
MacLock, Robert Bruce
The geography of the forest products industries of northern Alberta, . 2215
MacNeil, Harold A.
Report, ... 1615

MacNutt, Ola J.
Aberhart of Alberta, ... 2421
Macpherson, Crawford Brough
Democracy in Alberta, ... 2425
MacRury, Katherine Anne
The occupational adjustment of Vietnamese refugees in Edmonton, Canada,. 1954
Maerz, Leslie R.
Religious education in Alberta public schools,. 1499
Magee, Willis
Peach preserves, ... 3193
Magic Wand Club
The centennial magic book, ... 1310
Magill, Katherine
Back o' Baffuf,. 3492
Magrath and District History Association
Irrigation builders, ... 3137
Magus, Jim
Sex and the single magician, ... 1311
Mahé, Yvette T.M.
I remember Peace River, Alberta and adjacent districts, ... 3081
Mainprize, R.B.
The roll of honour and nominal roll, Princess Patricias' (sic) Canadian Light Infantry, 1939-1945, ... 2754
Maitland, Hugh
Brad Forrest's Calgary adventure,. 720
Majeau, Kevin
Chinook Ridge, 1880-1914, ... 605
Majestic-Farrell Lake Women's Institute
Harvest of memories, ... 3055
Mallett, Robin Barrie
Settlement process and land use change, ... 2556
Malliah, Holavanahally Lingappa
A socio-historical study of the legislators of Alberta, 1905-1967,. . . 2426
Mallory, James Russell
Social Credit and the federal power in Canada, ... 2427
Malmo Women's Institute
Lewisville pioneers, ... 3118
Maloff, Greta
Recollections of the homestead trails, 1900-1978, ... 3138
Malsbary, Dwight R.
An hour at the piano with well-loved hymns, ... 1455
Practical music course in elementary theory and sight-singing, . . . 1383
Malsbary, Pauline
Practical music course in elementary theory and sight-singing, . . . 1383
Manarey, Richard Barrie
The Canadian bayonet, ... 2755
Mandel, Eli
An idiot joy, ... 931
Stony Plain, ... 932

Mandel, Miriam
Lions at her face,. 933
Station 14, ...934
Manly, Morse
Oasis,. 935
Mann, George
Alberta normal schools, ... 1602
Mann, George Adolf
Functional autonomy among English school teachers in the Hutterite colonies of southern Alberta,. 1955
Mann, William Edward
Sect, cult and church in Alberta, .218
Manning, Ernest Charles
Choosing the battleground,. 2428
Political realignment, ... 2376
The problem and the price of survival,. 2429
The Social Credit yardstick, ... 2430
Manning. St. James' Catholic Church
Memories,. 390
Manning, Travis Warren
Country livestock auctions and market performance,. 2216
The economic benefits and costs of irrigation in the eastern irrigation district of Alberta, ... 3444
Performance of the hog marketing system in Alberta, ... 2217
Manning, William George
Toward a breakthrough in education, ... 1500
Mannville and District Old Timers' Association
Trails to Mannville,. 3139
Mannville Old Timers' Association
History of Mannville and district,. 3006
Mansell, Erica
Wheels to Woodville, ... 3140
Manvers, Betty
Love among the pines,. 721
ManWoman
Forever together, ...936
Manzie, Alan Andrew
Evaluations of planning conceptions,. 2557
Mardiros, Anthony
William Irvine,. 2431
Mardon, Ernest G.
Community names of Alberta, ... 2660
The founding faculty, ... 1603
The history of place names in southern Alberta,. 2661
Who's who in federal politics from Alberta, ... 2377
Marie Flore d'Auvergne *see* Giroux, Alice
Les Soeurs de Sainte-Croix dans l'ouest Canadien, ...201
Markle, Alexander George
Genesis of the Lethbridge Public Junior College, ... 1604

Marko, Ieromonakh
The Studit monks, ...163
Marriott, Peter John
Migration of people to and within the county of Grande Prairie, Alberta, 1956 to 1967, ... 2558
Marsan, Jean
La paroisse de Saint Jean-Baptiste Cinquantenaire, ...392
Marsh, John Stewart
The students' guide to Calgary,. 2688
Marsh, John Stuart
Recreation trails in Canada, ... 1673
Marshall, A.M.
Native education in Canada and the United States, ... 1
Marteinson, J.K
The Gate, ... 2756
Martin, Anne
The big tough expensive job, ... 2284
Martin, Hugh
The abiding presence, ...101
Martin, Isabel
Forests to grainfields, ... 3141
Martin, John
Geographic inequalities in property tax levels, ... 2132
Martin, John Julius
The Dinosaur Valley, Drumheller, Alberta,. 3142
The history of Severn Creek School No852 established June 9th, 1903,1560
The prairie hub, ... 3143
The Rosebud trail, ... 3144
Westward bound,. 2797
Martin, Millicent Mary
Garden of remembrance Poems, ...937
Martin, Stephen Paul
Selected aspects of the functional relationship between consumers and commercial ribbons,. 2218
Marty, Sid
Headwaters, ...938
Men for the mountains, ... 3322
Marunchak, Michael Hryhor
Among Ukrainian pioneers of Alberta,. 1956
Maruschak, Pauline
A glimpse into the past, ... 3145
Marvillo *see* Liebertz, Arnold
Marvelous mysteries of Marvillo, ... 1307
Marwayne Chamber of Commerce
Our golden years, Marwayne, Alberta, 1926-1976, ... 3146
Marwayne Farm Women's Union
Pioneering the parklands, ... 3147
Mary, H.W.
The influence of aircraft noise annoyance on single-family house prices,. 2133

Marzolf, Archie Durward
Alexander Cameron Rutherford and his influence on Alberta's educational program, ... 1605
Massey, D.L.
An oil well near Edmonton, ... 2286
Masson, Jack K.
The demise of alphabet parties,. 2463
Edmonton,. 2464
Emerging party politics in urban Canada, ... 2465
Masters, Kathy
Beautiful fields, ... 3148
Masyk, William James
The snowmobile, a recreational technology in Banff National Park, environmental impact and decision making,. 1674
Matejko, Joanna
Polish settlers in Alberta, ... 1957
Mathers, Beatrice
Children in the sun,. 722
Matheson, Sara Evangeline *see* Warren, Sara Evangeline (Matheson)
Andy the milkman, ... 807
Mathews, Robin Daniel Middleton
The plink savoir, ... 939
Plus ça change,. 940
Mathewson, Pamela Ann
The geographical impact of outsiders on the community of Fort Chipewyan, Alberta, ... 1726
Matthiasson, John S.
Two studies on Fort McMurray, ... 2588
Maw, Margaret
Meet southern Alberta, ... 3149
Maxwell, Grant
Like a Chinook, ... 219
Maxwell, Judith
Developing new energy sources,. 2287
Maxwell, Leslie Earl
Abandoned to Christ, ... 102
Crowded to Christ, ... 103
The Holy Spirit in missions, ... 104
The Pentecostal baptism, ... 105
Prairie pillars, ... 106
World missions total war, ... 107
Mays, Victor
Wild winter, ... 831
Mazepa, Bohdan
Flaming accords, ... 941
Starlit horizons, ... 942
Mazurok, Osyp
Al'bom Ukrain'skoi molochars'kö Kooperatsii "Maslosoiuz", 1902-1942, ... 3428

Khronika zemli Rus'koi (Ukrains'koi), de opysano vsi mista, zamky v provintsiiakh do ykh prynalezhnykh, ... 2738
McAlpine, Jennie
Pamela of Echo Glen, ... 723
McBean, Jean
Marriage and family law in Alberta, ... 2484
McCall, Ralph Lewis
The Acme story, 1910-1960, ... 3150
A history of the rural high school in Alberta, ... 1561
McCallum, D. Hall
The golden anniversary of the Alberta Dairymen's Association, . . . 3429
McCallum, Joe
CKUA and 40 wondrous years of radio, ... 2346
McCallum, William Symington
A Scot in Canada, ... 3493
McCartney, Samuel Trevor
Communications in the county of Camrose,. 2347
McCarty, Richard Frances
Fort Assiniboine, Alberta, 1823-1914, ... 3151
McCarty, Tom
As we remember Big Valley, ... 3152
McCawley, James D.
Studies out in left field, ... 465
McClung, Nellie Letitia
Clearing in the West, ... 724
In times like these, ... 1754
McColl, Keith
Outdoors unlimited,. 1675
McConnell, Alice
Klanak islands,. 704
McConnell, William C.
Klanak islands,. 704
McCormick, Peter
Alternatives, ... 2363
McCourt, Edward
Buckskin brigadier, ... 725
The Canadian West in fiction, ... 532
Fasting friar, ... 726
Music at the close, ... 727
Remember Butler, ... 2798
Revolt in the west, ... 2799
The road across Canada, ... 2625
Saskatchewan, ... 2626
Walk through the valley, ... 728
The wooden sword, ... 729
The Yukon and the Northwest Territories, ... 2627
McCracken, Kevin William John
Patterns of intra-urban migration in Edmonton and the residential relocation process,. 2559

McCraw, Louise Harrison
James H McConkey, a man of God,. 220
McCrossan, T.J.
Speaking with other tongues,. 108
McCrum, Elizabeth M.
A register of service, ...221
McCulloch, Dora
On the future of the extension function, ... 1612
McCullough, Edward J.
Historical resources impact assessment, western portion of
Syncrude lease no17, Alberta, ... 2045
Prehistoric cultural dynamics of the Lac La Biche region, ... 2046
McCullough, Karen Margrethe
Modified deer phalanges at the Draper site, ... 2047
McDaniel, R.
Alberta's role in meeting Canada's energy requirements, ... 2137
McDonald, Florence A. *see* Love, Florence A. (McDonald)
The Lamont Public Hospital School of Nursing, 1912-1914, ... 3366
McDonald, Ruth M. (Gulley)
Prairie silhouettes, ...943
McDougall, John
Opening the great West,. 222
Parsons on the plains, ...223
Pathfinding on plain and prairie, ...224
McDougall, Robert
The Cochrane Ranch, 1881-1894,. 3430
McDougall, William Dewar
The first forty years of the Education Society of Edmonton,
1927-1967, ... 1562
McEachern, A.
History of local government, Lac St Anne area,. 2460
McEwen, Alice Maude
The industrial reuse of Alberta's deactivated military bases, ... 2219
McFadden, Isobel
The indomitable Savage,. 3367
McFayden, Hector J.
Field pricing of natural gas in Alberta, 1955-1971, ... 2288
McGeachy, David Alan
The role of selected Edmonton professionals in the business
formation process, ... 2220
McGechie, David Henry
Economic approaches to environmental management of the
Alberta tar sands, ... 2289
McGibbon, Grace D. Bradford
Glimpses of the life and work of the Reverend Richard Bradford,
as scholar, school principal, chaplain, priest of the
Church of England and SPG missionary,. 225
McGugan, Angus Cecil
The first fifty years, ... 3368

McGusty, H.A.
Life in a prairie shack, ... 1405
McHugh, Drake
Edmonton is burning, ...730
McHugh, Sheila Jane (Haire)
Once a mission, ...391
McIlveen, Esther
For love of life,. 944
McInnes, Ron W.
Alberta landlord-tenant relations (residential tenancies), ... 2485
McIntosh, Curtis Emmanuel
A statistical analysis of cattle prices on terminal and auction markets in Alberta, ... 2221
McIntosh, William Andrew
The United Farmers of Alberta, 1909-1920, ... 2432
McKay, Doreen P. (Hull)
Forty years on, ... 1563
McKechnie, Christine
Homestead memories, ... 3153
McKee, Sandra Lynn
Gabriel Dumont, Indian fighter, ... 2800
McKenzie, Leroy R.
The opening line of Paradise Lost, ...533
McKillop, Donalda Murray *see* Copeland, Donalda Murray (McKillop)
Remember, nurse, ... 3357
McKim, Audrey
Andy and the gopher, ...731
Children in the sun,. 722
Lexy for short, ...732
That summer with Lexy, ...733
Thorny's hideaway, ...734
McKinnon, Claire Schuler
Nisku, ...735
McKinnon, John Angus
The Bow River Range, 1898-1974, JY, ... 3494
McKinnon, Lachlin
Lachlin McKinnon, pioneer, 1865-1948, ... 3495
McLaurin, Colin Campbell
Without reservations, ... 2628
McLean, Robert Irwin
A most effectual remedy, ... 1808
McLennan. Saint John the Baptist Parish
La paroisse de Saint Jean-Baptiste Cinquantenaire, ...392
McLeod, Norman Leslie
Calgary College, 1912-1915, ... 1606
McLeod, Scott H.
Nova Scotia farm boy to Alberta MD,. 3369
McLeod, Wilson A.
Pincher Creek United Church, ...408

McMillan, Charles Joseph
Trade unionism in District 18, 1900-1925, ... 2222
McNally, George Frederick
G Fred, ... 1564
McNamara, Eugene
In transit, ... 945
McNamee, James
My uncle Joe, ... 736
Them damn Canadians hanged Louis Riel! A novel, ... 737
McNeil, Harold A.
The problem of quotas, ... 1614
McNeil, W.R.
Wanderlust Poems, ... 946
McNeill, Edythe Muriel *see* Groves, Edythe Muriel (McNeill)
Funnybones, ... 897
McNeill, Leishman
The Calgary Herald's tales of the old town, ... 3154
McOuat, James Earl
Bible history & prophecies, ... 109
McQuaid, Jennifer Ann
Trail conditions and management in the Rocky Mountains, Alberta, . 1676
McRoberts, Mrs. Dick
The times of Irma, ... 3155
Mecca Glen Centennial Committee
Mecca Glen memories, ... 3156
Medicine Hat. Christ the King Catholic Parish
Christ the King Parish, Medicine Hat, 1954-1979, ... 393
Medicine Hat. Fifth Avenue United Church
The ever rolling stream, ... 394
Medicine Hat. Grace Lutheran Church
25 years of Grace, 1953-1978, ... 395
Medicine Hat Historical and Museum Foundation
90 years at Elkwater Lake, Cypress Hills, Alberta, ... 3160
Medicine Hat Historical Society
Early history of Medicine Hat country, ... 3167
Medicine Hat. Westminster United Church
Fortieth anniversary, 1914-1954, ... 396
History of Westminster United Church, Medicine Hat, ... 397
Meekison, Patti
Allison Procter, OBE, LLD 1880-1964, ... 1834
Meeres, E.L.
The homesteads that nurtured a city, ... 3157
Meilen, Bill
Anagramatix, ... 558
Melberg, Karin
Yesterday's children, ... 2718
Mellor, Ian Kenneth
An evaluation of the multiplier effect at Slave Lake and
in its tributory area since the establishment of the
Lesser Slave Lake Special Incentives Area,. 2134

Melnyk, Bohdan
Fox Mykyta, ... 655
Melnyk, George
Of the spirit, ... 1876
Memorial University Art Gallery
13 Calgary painters, ... 1220
Men and Women Unlimited
Pioneer women of Western Canada, ... 2727
Mennonite Church. Alberta-Saskatchewan Conference
History of the Alberta-Saskatchewan Mennonite Conference, ... 245
Menon, V.N.K.
Illusionseseme, ... 1303
Menzies, A.F.
Two dollars per year, ... 55
Menzies, Malcolm A.
The Big Horn School District, ... 3231
Merrett, R.J.
Literature, language and culture, ... 531
Merriken, Ellenor (Ranghild)
The Nose Hills country, ... 3159
Metis Association of Alberta
Many laws, ... 2473
Metis study tour report, December, 1968, ... 1958
Origins of the Alberta Metis, ... 1959
A proposal for progress, ... 1960
Michael, Esther Augusta *see* Fraser, Esther Augusta (Michael)
The Canadian Rockies Early travels and explorations, ... 2825
Wheeler, ... 2536
Michael, Hope Hargrave
History of St John's Presbyterian Church, Medicine Hat, Alberta, 1883-1973, ... 320
90 years at Elkwater Lake, Cypress Hills, Alberta, ... 3160
Michichi Book Committee
A history of the people of Michichi, ... 3225
Middleton, Samuel Henry
Kainai chieftainship, ... 1961
Kootenai Brown, adventurer, pioneer, plainsman, park warden, and Waterton Lakes National Park, ... 1677
Miles, Walter K.
My genealogy, ... 2719
Milk River Old Timers Association
Milk River country, ... 2914
Millar, Gerald Wesley
The measurement of melody, ... 1384
Millar, Will
Tales to warm your mind, ... 947
Millarville Historical Society
Foothills echoes, ... 3161
Millarville, Kew, Priddis and Bragg Creek Historical Society
Our foothills Sarcee Indian Reserve, Bow-Crow Forest, Sheep Run, ... 3162

Miller, H.J.
The story of Sarcee Butte United Church, ... 398
Miller, James A.
The Alberta press and the conscription issue in the First World War, 1914-1918, ... 2378
Miller, Kenneth Frank
Economic efficiency in the utilization and improvement of the publicly owned pastureland of Alberta, ... 3431
Miller, Marjorie
The printed word, ... 1501
Millet and District Historical Society
Tales and trails of Millet, ... 3163
Millet. School
Pioneer days, ... 3273
Milligan, Hilda
Leaves of yesteryear, ... 2939
Milloy, John Sheridan
The Plains Cree, ... 1962
Mills, Eric
Help for husbands (and wives), ... 110
Preachers, priests and critters and other unusual accounts, ... 111
Millward, Peter
A very small rebellion, ... 800
Milo and District Historical Society
Snake Valley, ... 3164
Minch, Stephen
The amazing world of mentalism, ... 1297
Any second now, ... 1313
The book of Thoth, ... 1314
Creation of a magical madman,, ... 1315
Ever so sleightly, ... 1316
Marvelous mysteries of Marvillo, ... 1307
Mind and matter,. 1317
Sleight unseen,. 1318
Minchin, D. Howard
Cost reduction programs of a natural gas distribution firm, ... 2290
Miner, A.
Inkwells and school bells, ... 1553
Minuk, Honour
50 golden years, 1924-1974, ... 1842
Minuk, Syd
50 golden years, 1924-1974, ... 1842
M.I.P. History Book Committee
Spurs and shovels along the Royal Line, ... 3126
Mishell, Ed
Lecture domaine,. 1291
Mishimura, Art
Leaving,. 1013
Miska, John A.
The sound of time, ... 582

Mitchell, Frank E.
A history of pioneering in the Pakan district, ... 3496
Mitchell, Harold
The spice of life, ... 2223
Mitchell, Janet
Janet Mitchell,. 1221
Mitchell, Ken
Davin, the politician, ... 1070
Mitchell, William Ormond
The black bonspiel of Wullie MacCrimmon, ...738
The devil's instrument, ... 1071
Jake and the kid, ...739
The kite, ...740
The vanishing point, ...741
Who has seen the wind, ...742
Mitchner, Ernest Alyn
Chinook Ridge, 1880-1914, ...605
From the ground up, ... 3470
William Pearce and federal government activity in Western Canada, 1882-1904,. 2379
William Pearce, father of Alberta irrigation, ... 3432
Mogen, R. Pat
Alberta,. 2600
Mohan, Elizabeth Marilyn
Aspects of intra-urban mobility, Calgary, 1963-68, ... 2348
Moher, Frank
Pause, ... 1072
Mohr, Hilda (Berg)
The great pioneers who cleared and broke the virgin land of Josephburg, 1867-1967, ... 1963
Mohylianka, Daria *see* Yanda, Doris Elizabeth
My thoughts fly to Ukraine, ... 1031
Molière, Jean Baptiste Paquelin
Sganarelle, ... 1417
Monarch History Book Club *see* Nobleford, Monarch History Book Club
Sons of wind and soil,. 3177
Monckton, Jean A.
All Saints' Anglican Cathedral, 1875-1975, ...399
Moncrieff, Patrick Merlin
Alternative land uses in southwestern Alberta, ... 2560
Monsma, Georgia Ellen
Information analysis of the Alberta criminal justice system,. 2486
Montgomery, Jason
Family crisis as process, ... 1755
Montizambert, Nancy
Canada,. 2801
Moodie, Donald Wayne
The St Albert settlement, ... 2561
Moon, Bryan R.
Fourling, ...743

Moore, E. Barry
Crisis at 9:25, ... 112
Moore, E.J.
Super prediction tricks, ... 1342
Moore, Evelyn
Alberta foothills, ... 3474
The Crowsnest Pass, a coal mining valley, ... 2547
Moore, Linda Ida
Community development and community education, ... 1727
Moore, Winnie
Across the Smoky, ... 3165
Morah, Benson Chukwuma
The assimilation of Ugandan Asians in Calgary, ... 1964
Morasch, Loyde Hudson
Disaggregate modal split model for Calgary, ... 2562
Morgan, Marjorie C.
Packy, the little elephant who came to the cold, ... 744
Morley, Frank Selkirk
Marriage can be beautiful, ... 1756
Personal peace and power, ... 113
A way of life, ... 114
Why a Presbyterian Church, ... 115
Morrin and District History Book Committee
Blooming prairie, ... 3166
Morris, Anne Elizabeth (Peyton)
Alberta school districts in pioneer days, ... 1565
Jacques Lodges, Calgary, Alberta, ... 2720
Morris. John Joseph Harrold
The Presbyterian Church in Edmonton, northern Alberta, and the Klondike, 1881-1925, largely according to official documents, ... 226
Morris, Wildah
Storm, ... 1424
Morrison, Don
The terror of the tar sands, ... 633
Morrison, J. Charles
A study of environmental press at the University of Calgary, ... 56
Morrison Museum Association
There'll always be an Islay, ... 3222
Morrison, R.H.
The conquerors of Prairies, ... 991
Morrissette, George
Prairie howl, ... 948
Morrow, James William
Early history of Medicine Hat country, ... 3167
Morse, Randy
The mountains of Canada, ... 2629
Morton, Colin T.
Standing in the street, ... 745
Motherwell, Elizabeth
No small plans, ... 1607

Motor Car Supply Company of Canada Limited
 50th anniversary, 1912-1962,. 2224
Motyl, J.
 Insights into cultural differences, ... 1989
Mould, Vernon
 The boy who ran away, ...765
 Buckskin brigadier, ...725
 Land of the Chinook, ...823
Mountain Horse, Mike
 My people the Bloods,. 1965
Mouré, Erin
 Empire, York Street, ...949
Moynham, Gordon John
 Natural gas exploration and development in Alberta, ... 2291
Mueller, Walter R.
 Reminiscing with Walt, ... 3497
Mukasa, James M.
 Rural residential subdivision, Parkland County, Alberta, ... 2135
Mullany, J.S.
 Au pays des Peaux-de-Lièvres, ...172
 Blacksmith of God, ...174
Mullins, Gary Edward
 The spatial behaviour of Alberta's electricity industry, 1888-1965, . . 2225
Munroe, Scott William
 Warriors of the rock, ... 1966
Munson, J. West
 Development control vs zoning, ... 2563
Munson Women's Institute
 Munson and district, ... 3168
Murchie, R.W.
 The settlement of the Peace River Country, ... 2965
Murdoch, Olive K.
 They builded better than they knew,. 3169
Murphy, Emily (Ferguson)
 The black candle, by Emily Murphy (Janey Canuck), ... 1809
 Janey Canuck in the West,. .746
Murray, Andrew
 Abide in Christ, ...116
 Like Christ, ...117
 Working for God, ...118
Murray, Kristin
 Kidmonton, ... 2682
Murray, Tom
 Yesteryears of the Hays Municipality,. 3206
Murrell, John
 Uncle Vanya, ... 1047
Murynka, Dan
 Sorrow and wrath Ukrainian poems,. 950
Musson, Clettis V.
 Forty-four foolers, ... 1319

Myers, C. Vernon
Through hell to Alaska A novel, ... 747
Myles, Eugenie Louise (Butler)
Airborne from Edmonton, ... 2349
The Emperor of Peace River,. 748
Remember, nurse, ... 3357
Myrehaug, Donald Melker
ME Lazerte,. 1566
Namao. United Church
Namao United Church 80th anniversary, May 12, 1963, ... 400
Namao United Farm Women
A cameo of the west, ... 3248
Nandt, Frank R.
An evaluation of relocation in urban renewal,. 2564
Nanooch, Henry
Medicine Boy and other Cree tales, ... 2070
Nanton and District Historical Society
Mosquito Creek roundup, ... 3170
Narvaez, Armado
With deck in hand, ... 1320
Nash, Martin A.
Any second now, ... 1313
Ever so sleightly, ... 1316
Sleight unseen,. 1318
National and Provincial Parks Association of Canada.
Calgary-Banff Chapter
Recreation trails in Canada, ... 1673
National Conference on Urban Renewal as it affects Chinatown, Calgary,. . 1969
National Conference sponsored by the Sien Lok Society of Calgary, ... 1728
National Indian Brotherhood
Address by Harold Cardinal, President, Indian Association of Alberta, during presentation by the Indian Chiefs of Alberta to the Prime Minister and the Government of Canada, June 4, 1970,. 1877
National Northern Development Conference
Proceedings, ... 2136
National Spiritual Assembly of the Baha'is of Canada
Oki! Nitsitapee A message to the Blackfoot Indians,. 119
National Technical Conference, 2d, Calgary, ... 1973
Alberta's role in meeting Canada's energy requirements, ... 2137
Native Council of Canada
Declaration of Metis and Indian rights, ... 1885
The forgotten people, ... 1899
Native Women's Society
Report, ... 1855
Naughton, Patrick William
The reaction of homeowners along the North Saskatchewan Valley in Edmonton to the erosional hazard, ... 2565
Nelles, Freda
Community history,. 2863

Nelson, Alice E.
From my heart, . . . 951
Nelson, Ethel
Wild flowers and buffalo bones, . . . 3171
Nelson, James Gordon
The Canadian national parks, today and tomorrow, . . . 2524
Canadian national parks, today and tomorrow, conference 2, . . . 2525
Canadian parks in perspective, . . . 2526
The last refuge, . . . 3344
Nelson, Marie
The history book handbook, . . . 2744
Saddles, sleighs and sadirons,. . . . 3172
They gathered at the river,. . . . 401
Nelson, Mervin James
The Nelson family, . . . 2721
Nelson, Minnie Hope
The Hope family & neighbors of Red Deer Lake, SD No28, . . . 2708
Nelson, Robert A.
The art of cold reading, . . . 1321
Club and party mentalism,. . . . 1322
Comedy mentalism,. . . . 1323
A complete course in stage hypnotism,. . . . 1324
Effective answers to questions, . . . 1325
The ghost book of dark secrets,. . . . 1326
Hellstromism, . . . 1327
How to book your attraction,. . . . 1328
How to read sealed messages, . . . 1329
Manual of publicity and exploitation for the mentalist,. . . . 1330
Mentalism and its presentation,. . . . 1331
The mentalist's manual, . . . 1332
Miracles in mentalism and psychic experimentation, . . . 1333
More effective answers to questions,. . . . 1334
The Nelson master course of hypnotism, . . . 1335
Projected answers, . . . 1336
Secret methods of private readers, . . . 1337
Sensational answers, . . . 1338
Sensational effects, . . . 1339
Sensational mentalism, . . . 1340
A sequel to The art of cold reading,. . . . 1341
Super prediction tricks, . . . 1342
Super-mentality, . . . 1343
Technique of the private reader, . . . 1344
TV mentalism, . . . 1345
Nelson, Tom
Our Alberta heritage, . . . 2828
Nesbitt, Leonard D.
Tides in the West, . . . 3433
Nevitt, Richard Barrington
The frontier art of RB Nevitt, surgeon, North-West Mounted Police, 1874-78, . . . 1222

A winter at Fort Macleod, ... 2509
New Brigden Community Club
The last best west, ... 2975
New Cessford School, Cessford
This is our land, ... 2891
New Dawn Seniors Club
Lengthening shadows of the Neutrals, ... 3173
New Norway Community Club
Memory opens the door, ... 3174
Newsom, Harry E.
Guidelines for the development of public library services in Manitoba, . 25
Library service in Alberta, ... 26
Recommended guidelines for the development of the Parkland Regional Library,. 27
Newton, Elise
Elizabeth McDougall, madonna of the Plains,. 227
Newton, Gary
Quiet winds, ... 970
Niagara Falls Art Gallery and Museum
The passion of Christ according to St Matthew,. 1131
Nichols, Herbert Edward
Alberta's fight for freedom, ... 2433
A handbook of Social Credit,. 2434
Nicholson, Harold
Heart of gold, ... 3175
Nickle, Carl Oloff
A man, a company and an industry in Western Canada, ... 2292
Nicks, Gertrude Cecilia
The archaeology of two Hudson's Bay Company posts, ... 2048
Nicks, John Stewart
The Pine Island posts, 1786-1794,. 2802
Nicoll, Jim
Jim Nicoll, paintings and poetry, ... 1223
Nicoll, Marion
Marion Nicoll, ... 1224
Niedzwiecki, Stella
Ukrainian Rite Catholic Church, ... 228
Nielsen, Dorothy
Bowness Golden Jubilee, 1911-1961,. 3176
Nielsen, William Adam
The potential for wilderness recreation in a sand dune environment in northeast Alberta,. 1678
Nielson, G.E.
The line that joins, ... 2380
Nightingale Women's Institute
The English colony Nightingale and District, ... 2978
Nimchuk, Ivan
Nove slovo, ... 57
Niven, Michael Bryan
Matrimonial property and the conflict of laws in Alberta, ... 2487

Nix, James Ernest
Hillhurst's first sixty years, 1907-1967, ...402
John Maclean's mission to the Blood Indians, 1880-1889,. 229
Missions among the buffalo, ...230
Noble, Charles
Haywire rainbow Poems, ...952
Three 3,. 1018
Noble, Iris (Davis)
Megan, ...749
Noble, Lyle Barry
Man and grizzly bear in Banff National Park, Alberta, ... 3324
Nobleford, Monarch History Book Club
Sons of wind and soil,. 3177
Noel, Oliver
A pictorial history of St Paul and district, ... 3178
Nolan, Michael
Joe Clark, the emerging leader,. 2381
Noland, Kenneth
Kenneth Noland March 6 - April 21, 1975, ... 1225
Norbeck, Carl Sterling
Planning study for a national nature preserve along the South Saskatchewan River, Suffield area, Alberta, ... 1679
Nordegg, Martin
Pioneering in Canada, 1906-1924,. 2226
The possibilities of Canada are truly great,. 2227
Norman Mackenzie Art Gallery, Regina
Adolph Gottlieb acrylics on paper, ... 1205
Diversity, Canada East, ... 1226
Norrie, D.H.
WesCan/INFORM, ... 28
North Lone Pine Women's Institute.
Bucking poles and butter churns, ... 3179
Northern Alberta Development Council
Addresses,. 2100
Report on certain industrial and other factors related to the economy of the central Peace River district, Alberta, ... 2138
Report on the land, industries and related factors in the Peace River Country, Alberta, ... 2139
Northern Alberta Library Development Services
Northern Alberta Library Development Services, 1977-1979, ... 29
Norton, Deryk George
Provincial grants to Alberta municipalities,. 2140
Novak, John A.
The art of escape, ... 1346
Nowicki, Julian Joseph
Recreational capability and use of some north-central Alberta lakes, . 1681
Nussbaumer, Margaret
The Worth Report and developments in Alberta's post-secondary policies and structures, 1968 to 1976, ... 1567

Nychka, Methodius
Mundare, yesterday and today, ... 403
O'Brien, Allison Douglas
A retail sales tax for Alberta, ... 2141
O'Brien, Julia V.
50 years in the Barrhead United Church, ... 404
O'Donoghue, Denise
The challenge of life, ... 2722
O'Dwyer, A.
Fluid filosofies of future fools, ... 568
Oeming, Al
A visit to Al Oeming's Alberta Game Farm, ... 3325
O'Hagan, Howard
The school-marm tree, ... 750
Tay John, a novel, ... 751
Wilderness men, ... 2723
The woman who got on at Jasper Station, and other stories, ... 752
Ohaton Community Book Club
Lure of the homestead, ... 3052
Ohler, Vilda
Echoes of Willow Creek,. 2979
Ohlsson, Ib
Just Gin, ... 698
Ola, Timothy
Agricultural policy in Alberta, ... 3434
Olds Old Timers Association
See Olds first, ... 3180
Olds School of Agriculture
Golden echoes, 1913-1963,. 3435
The ladies present, ... 3416
O'Leary, Timothy J.
A preliminary bibliography of the archaeology of Western Canada, . . . 7
Olecko, Doreen
Sagitawah saga, ... 3181
Oliver, Thelma Isabel
Aspects of alienation in Alberta, ... 2382
Olson, Allan
Hills of Hope, ... 3010
Olson, Merribeth
Criminal forever!,. 161
Olson, Patricia Lee
A scenic resource and recreational analysis of the Milk River Canyon, southeast Alberta,. 1682
Olson, Raymond C.
Sacred solos for accordion,. 1456
Oltmann, Charlotte Ruth
The Kananaskis Valley hikers' and x-c skiers' guide,. 1683
The valley of rumours, ... 3182
O'Malley, Denis Anthony
Regional considerations in pulp, ... 2228

Oman, Mary M.
Canadian cornography, ... 1109
Ondrik, Alice
Etzikom, 1915-1975, ... 3183
One Prairie Province Conference, Lethbridge, ... 1970
Proceedings, ... 2142
O'Neil, Bruce
Bruce O'Neil, ... 1227
O'Neil, Dollie Gray
Pot-pourri,. 953
Onoway and District Historical Society
The pathfinders, ... 3279
Onoway Women's Institute
The pathfinders, ... 3279
Oppel, Audrey Young
The book about nothing,. 695
Hanok, ...696
Opportunities for Youth Project
A history of Stony Plain, Alberta,. 3184
Opryshko, George S.
A history of the schools of the county of Athabasca, ... 1516
Options for Women
Maternity leave in Alberta, ... 1746
Orchard, G.E.
Nineteenth century Lethbridge,. 3194
O'Reilly, Paul J.
Keep them in Thy name, ...120
Orillia Historical Society
A Medonte pioneer and his famous son, ... 2510
Orsel, Edith *see* Eichner, Edith (Orsel)
Golden dreams, story and drawings, ...645
Osborne, Carolyn
Three French-Canadian folk songs for mixed chorus, ... 1431
Osborne, James
The attic, ... 1073
By the sea, ... 1074
Otter, Andy Albert den
Irrigation in southern Alberta, 1882-1901, ... 3436
Sir Alexander T Galt and the northwest,. 2143
A social history of the Alberta Coal Branch, ... 3185
Ousmane, Silla
Ecole bilingue ou unilingue pour les franco-albertains, ... 1484
Oviatt, Barrie Connolly
The papers of William Aberhart as Minister of Education, 1935-1943, 1568
Oviatt, Patricia Elaine
The educational contributions of HC Newland, ... 1569
Owram, Douglas R.
The formation of Alberta, ... 2824
Paley, David Thomas
Person perception skills and the helping relationship,. 1810

Palmer, Asael E.
A history of the Mormon Church in Canada, ... 184
When the winds came, ... 3437
Palmer, Howard
History of minority groups in southern Alberta since 1940, ... 1968
Land of the second chance, ... 1969
Nativism and ethnic tolerance in Alberta, 1920-1972, ... 1970
Responses to foreign immigration,. 1971
Panczuk, Hyrhorij
Conversational Ukrainian, ... 511
Papen, Jean
Georges Bugnet, homme de lettres canadiennes,. 534
Paperny, Myra
The wooden people,. 753
Paproski, Dennis M.
The demand for coal by the electrical generation industry in Alberta, 2229
Paquette, Mary Elizabeth
The environment of language, ... 1570
Paradis, Norma L.(Thomson)
The clan McRae,. 2724
Parel, Anthony
Calgary Aquinas studies, ... 65
Pariseau, Guy
Envers des jours, ... 954
Pariseau, Jean
Albertaines images et autres griffonnages, ... 955
Park Grove Community Centre
Park Grove echoes, ... 2989
Parker, Fred
The first fifty years of Perfection Lodge no 9 (GR Alta) Calgary, 1895-1945, ... 1843
Parker, H. Margaret
Grandma's visit to England & Scotland, ... 2630
Roses of love, ... 956
Parker, James McPherson
The fur trade of Fort Chipewyan on Lake Athabaska, 1778-1835, . . 3187
Parker, Lawrence Lee
An examination of pricing practices and procedures in a local house building industry,. 2230
Parker, Lewis
The bear who stole the chinook and other stories, ... 2073
My uncle Joe, ... 736
The wind along the River, ... 2074
Parker, Peter
The face of yesterday,. 2774
Parker, William
William Parker, mounted policeman, ... 2511
Parker, William Wilder McKinley
Belle Anne of Pine Point, ... 754
Bush homestead girl, ... 755

Canada's 100 birthday verse, ... 957
Flowing gold, ... 756
Greener prairie, ... 757
Lake la Nonne Trail, ... 758
North Star, ... 759
Pansy pie and other poems, ... 958
Roses of love, ... 956
Silver Forks, ... 760
Young Canada A song, ... 1457

Parker,Lewis
Red River adventure, ... 2772

Parlane, Brian
Tell us a missionary story, ... 622

Parlby, Beatrice Georgina
Parish notes, ... 405
Pioneers and progress, ... 3188

Parnell, Missy
Rape of the block, ... 1811

Parnell, Ted
Alternatives to poverty and welfare in Alberta, ... 1812
Disposable native, ... 1972

Parton, Alfred
The story of my life, ... 3498

Pashak, Leonard Barry
The populist characteristics of the early Social Credit movement in Alberta, ... 2435

Pasternak, Carol
Pioneer women of Western Canada, ... 2727

Patching, Edwin Arthur
Students story of wheat, ... 3438

Paterson, John G.
To have or to let go, ... 1757

Paterson, Lynda Elizabeth
Estimation of extra-market benefits associated with the recreational use of the Clearwater-Rocky Forest in Alberta, ... 1684

Patten, Dennis
Sex and the single magician, ... 1311

Patterson, Arthur B.
Smoky River to Grande Prairie, ... 3190

Patterson, E.R.
The early history of the town of Claresholm, ... 3191

Patterson, George William
A comparative study of aspects of the vocalic systems of standard French and the French dialect spoken at Falher, Alberta, ... 457

Patterson, Marney
Alive and free, ... 121
Dare to share, ... 122

Patterson, Muriel Beaton
Messenger of the Great Spirit, ... 231

Patterson, Raymond Murray
The Buffalo Head, ... 3499
Far pastures,. 3500
Patterson, Robert Steven
The establishment of progressive education in Alberta, ... 1571
FWG Haultain and education in the early west,. 1572
Pattison, William Stanley
Hunter guiding activity in northern Alberta, ... 1686
Moose hunting activity in northern Alberta, ... 1685
Patton, Brian
The Canadian Rockies trail guide, ... 2689
Parkways of the Canadian Rockies, ... 2690
Paul, G.S.
Three or four day work week, ... 2242
Paul, John
Banff panorama, a symphonic suite,. 1444
Pawlowske, Kathy
Treasured memories, Gwynne and district, ... 3192
Payne, Edith
The pathfinders, ... 3279
Payne, Hilda Hope
The Hope family & neighbors of Red Deer Lake, SD No28, ... 2708
Payne, Robert John
Children's urban landscapes in Huntington Hills, Calgary, ... 2567
Peace River Centennial Museum
Where go the boats,. 2336
Peace River Chamber of Commerce
Addresses,. 2100
Peace River. St. Paul's United Church
50th anniversary, 1914-1964,. 406
Peace River Women's Institute
I remember Peace River, Alberta and adjacent districts, ... 3081
Peach, Jack
Peach preserves, ... 3193
Sara of the Tenth, ... 1844
Peacock, Gordon
Adventures in acting, ... 1034
Peacock, Patricia
Gold-fever trail, ... 692
Peacock, Ruth
In the bend of the Battle, ... 2848
Peake, Frank Alexander
Anglican beginnings in and about Edmonton, ... 232
Peat, Annie Laurie Stafford
Nineteenth century Lethbridge,. 3194
Peddie, Richard
Urban parks and planning in Calgary, Alberta, ... 2568
Peel, Bruce Braden
A bibliography of the Prairie Provinces to 1953, ... 12
Early printing in the Red River Settlement, 1859-1870 and

its effect on the Riel Rebellion, ... 58
History of the Library, ... 30
The history of the University of Alberta Library, 1909-1979, ... 31
Librarianship in Canada, 1946 to 1967, ... 32
Rossville Mission Press, ... 59
Steamboats on the Saskatchewan, ... 2350
Survey of Canadian academic libraries conducted between January 29 and May 1, 1967, ... 33

Peers, Jeremy James Louden
An analysis of tourist travel to the province of Alberta, ... 2231

Pendant d'Oreille Lutheran Church Women
Prairie footprints, ... 3007

Penelhum, Terence
Mystics and scholars, ... 69

Pengelly, John R.
Mirror, 1913-1966, ... 1573

Pengilly, Gordon D.
Songs of believers, ... 1075

Penner, Helen (Knelson)
Happiness and other poems, ... 959
Night music and other poems, ... 960
Poetry Lane, ... 961
Teardrops and flowers, and other poems, ... 962
Your heart and mine, ... 963

Penton, M. James
Jehovah's Witnesses in Canada, ... 233

Percy, Douglas Cecil
Beyond the tangled mountain, ... 761
Man with the heart of a Viking, ... 123

Perehudoff, William W.
Blazing the old cattle trail, ... 3421
Fifty mighty men, ... 2716
Hoofprints and hitching posts, ... 3423
Tides in the West, ... 3433
William Perehudoff, ... 1229
William Perehudoff, ... 1228

Pérreault, Jacinthe
Political validity of Franco-Albertains 2437

Peter Whyte Gallery, Banff
Beyond exceptional pass, ... 1230
The Group of Seven in the Rockies, ... 1177

Peterson, Dale Douglas
Wholesale trade between Edmonton and selected northern communities, ... 2232

Peterson, Ed
Wetaskiwin Co-op, ... 3439

Peterson, Flora (Culp)
Life and she, ... 3501

Peterson, Leonard
Almighty Voice, ... 1076

Petrigo, Walter
Focus on Calgary, ... 2631
Petrigo's Alberta,. 2632
Petrigo's Calgary, ... 2633
Petroleum Resource Communication Foundation
Our petroleum challenge, ... 2293
Pettinger, David William
A prairie letter, ... 3502
Pettinger, William
A prairie letter, ... 3502
Peyton, Amy
One body in Christ,. 407
Peyton, Anne Elizabeth *see* Morris, Anne Elizabeth (Peyton)
Alberta school districts in pioneer days, ... 1565
Pfeifer, Lillian E
The wolfers, ... 762
Pharis, Gwendolyn Margaret *see* Ringwood, Gwendolyn Margaret (Pharis)
Younger brother, ... 774
Pharis, Robert L.
The golden feather, ... 763
Phelan, Josephine
The bold heart,. 764
The boy who ran away, ... 765
Philip, Catherine Rose
The Crosses of Alberta, ... 2725
The women of Calgary and district, 1875-1914, ... 2726
Philipps, Walter
Johnny Chinook, ... 2075
Phillips, Douglas
Girl of the Rockies, ... 626
Phillips, Grace A.
Tales of Tofield, ... 3195
Phillips, Walter J.
Graphics by Walter J Phillips and Canadian art in three dimensions,. 1199
WJ Phillips views Western Canada, ... 1204
Phillips, W.F.
The smoke horse, ... 650
Phillips, William E.
Hunter guiding activity in northern Alberta, ... 1686
Pich, George
Agriculture innovations, county of St Paul, Alberta, ... 3440
Pidruchney, Anna
From old lands to new, ... 1974
Pierce, R.J.
Reverend John Gough Brick, ... 234
Pierson, Arthur Tappan
Godly self-control, ... 124
Pieuk, Clare L.
Development costs of Alberta crude oil, 1972-1972, ... 2294

Pigeon, D.H.
Research paper on the Alberta Provincial Police, ... 2512
Pike, Graham
The west in action, ... 1656
Pike, Wentworth E.
Eskimos in Alaska, ... 1975
Pincher Creek and District Historical Society
Pincher Papers, 1, ... 3196
Pincher Creek Historical Society
Prairie grass to mountain pass, ... 3197
Pincher Creek Old Timers Association
Pincher Creek Old Timers souvenir album, 1878-1958,. 3198
Pinkman, Francis Edward
Educational upgrading of prisoners in an Alberta correctional institution, 1969-74,. 1813
Pioneer History Society of Hythe and Area
Pioneer round-up,. 3110
Pipestone Community Club
Roads to Pipestone, ... 2977
Plamondon, Arvine *see* Ulliac, Arvine (Plamondon)
Cinquantenaire de l'arrivée des pionniers à Gourin, 11 avril, 1914,. . 3281
Plamondon, Delamen *see* Ché, Delamen (Plamondon)
Jubilé d'or, ... 2932
Plast Association
15th anniversary of the Plast Association in Edmonton, ... 1845
Playle, Marguerite
The hills of home Drumheller Valley, ... 3200
Plett, Jake
Valley of shadows, ...235
Plunkett, Richard Ernest
Central business district employment in Edmonton, 1961-1967, . . . 2233
Poetschke, Donna Marie Brown
Social class and attitudes in Alberta, 1971,. 1730
Poetschke, Thomas R.
Reasons for immigration and ethnic identity, ... 1976
Polish Alliance of Calgary
30th anniversary of Polish Alliance in Calgary, 1931-1961, ... 1977
Pollock, Sharon
The Komagata Maru incident, ... 1077
Walsh, ... 1078
The wreck of the national line, ... 1079
Pollution Workshop, Banff, ... 1970
Proceedings, ... 3345
Pomahac, Gertrude
Education for librarianship, ... 34
Library management, ... 24
Publishing in Canada,. 60
Pomeroy, John D.
Basic make-up for magicians, ... 1348

Dove, silk and flower magic, ... 1349
Mentology, ... 1350
Pong, Raymond
The nature, extent and sources of environmental knowledge and opinions in Edmonton,. 3339
Ponoka and District Historical Society
Ponoka panorama, ... 3201
Ponoka. United Church
An abbreviated history of the Ponoka United Church of Canada, ...409
Pool, Robert
From the ground up, ... 3470
Poons, Larry
Larry Poons recent paintings,. 1231
Popovych, I. Damaskyn *see* Popowich, John Damascene D.
Grammar of Church Slavonic language in Ukrainian reduction, ...507
Popowich, John Damascene D.
Child of God, ...125
Grammar of Church Slavonic language in Ukrainian reduction, ...507
Porter, Eugene Oliver
Lord Beresford and Lady Flo, ... 3441
Potrebenko, Helen
A flight of average persons, ...766
No streets of gold, ... 1978
Taxi!,. 767
Pottage, Bessie Fern
As the wheel turns, ... 3203
Potter, Bruce
Through the bubble, ...535
Potter, Jack
The master index to magic in print, covering books and magazines in English language published up to and including December, 1964, . . 1351
Potvin, Annette
The Sun Dance liturgy of the Blackfoot Indian,. 2050
Powell, Alan Thomas Rees- *see* Rees-Powell, Alan Thomas
Differentials in the integration process of Dutch and Italian immigrants in Edmonton, ... 1983
Prairie Bible Institute
Behold your God,. 126
Bread enough, ...127
Christian harmony Cheerful co-operation in the work of the Gospel, . . .128
Energized to evangelize,. 129
Feed my lambs, ...130
Full faith, ...131
Love's letter,. 132
New Testament survey series, ...133
Practical accordion course,. 1385
Prairie hymns that live, ... 1458
Sound doctrine, ...134
Spirit-filled saints, ...135
Suffering saints, ...136

Transcripts for the accordion, ... 1459
Unclouded communion, ... 137
With God on the Prairies, ... 236
Prather, Robert Allan
Alternative methods of estimating benefits, ... 1687
Pratt, Larry *see* Pratt, Lawrence
The tar sands, ... 2295
Pratt, Lawrence
Prairie capitalism, ... 2299
The state and province building, ... 2144
The tar sands, ... 2295
Presber, Wayne Orlyn
The economics of conventional crude oil enhanced recovery schemes, province of Alberta,. 2296
Prevey, Patricia
A study of the holdings of Canadian award-winning novels in Alberta high school media centres, ... 35
Price, Danny
The Calgary Stampede, ... 1670
Price, Monty
How Grandfather Burleson saved Christmas for the children of Calgary,. 768
Price, Richard
Indian land claims in Alberta, ... 1979
Indian treaties and the law, ... 2480
The spirit of the Alberta Indian treaties, ... 1980
Price, Roy
Ye men of Calgary,. 1460
Priestley, Norman F
Furrows, faith and fellowship, ... 3442
Priestly, Tom M.S.
Proceedings, ... 1864
Prime, Michael George Ray
The maximand of the hospital, ... 3370
Primeau, Marguerite
Dans le muskeg, ... 769
Primrose, Tom
The Cypress Hills, ... 2691
The Lost Lemon Mine, ... 2236
Pringle, Faye *see* Knowlton, Faye (Pringle)
These were the early days,. 2714
Prior, Kenneth H.
The reminiscences of thirty years service in Africa, 1926-1956, ... 237
Prithipaul, K. Dad
Native religious traditions, ... 94
Prokopiw, Orysia Love Olia (Ferbey)
An introduction to Lesya Ukrainka, ... 536
The Ukrainians, ... 1981
Proudfoot, Alexander J.
Intercultural education, ... 1502

Proudfoot, James Alexander
Some aspects of the recreational geography of the North Saskatchewan river valley, Edmonton, ... 1688
Provost Chamber of Commerce
The Provost story, ... 3204
Provost Promotions and Publications Ltd
Calgary 100,. 3205
Prud'homme, Essie
Yesteryears of the Hays Municipality,. 3206
Pryima, Osyp
Ukrainian Catholic unity, 1906-1966, ...255
Puffer, Frances Anita
Friendship and commitment in a volunteer association, the University Women's Club of Edmonton, ... 1846
Puffer, Gordon Percival
A giant among pioneers,. 2728
Putnam, William Lowell
A climber's guide to the Rocky Mountains of Canada, ... 1701
Pyne, Garry H.
The pre-reserve Blackfoot, cultural persistence and change, ... 1982
Quicin, George David
Growth of the Alberta petroleum producing industry 1947-1952, . . 2297
Quigg, J. Michael
The Belly River, ... 2052
Raby, Stewart
Water supplies and watershed management in the Oldman River basin, Alberta, ... 2569
Race, Cecil L.
Compulsory schooling in Alberta, 1888-1942,. 1575
Radford, Tom
Alberta, a celebration,. 2652
Radke, Claude Douglas
Administrative decentralization, ... 3443
Ragan, H.S.
The Commonwealth Games management financial feasibility study, . 1704
Rainier-Bow City History Book Club
Settlers along the Bow, ... 3236
Raisen, Sandra Kalef
Elmwood Drive A case study of municipal decision-making,. 2466
Ramage, Maud
Echoes of Willow Creek,. 2979
RaMayne, Korda
The private medium's secret guide, ... 1352
Ramsay, Edward A.
Apprenticeship discontinuance in three trade areas in the province of Alberta,. 2234
Ranchmen's Club
A short history of the Ranchmen's Club,. 1847
Ranghild, Ellenor *see* Merriken, Ellenor (Ranghild)
The Nose Hills country, ... 3159

Raskevich, Madelana *see* Eggleston, Magdelana (Raskevich)
Mountain shadows, ...642
Rasporich, Anthony W.
Frontier Calgary, town, city and region, 1875-1914, ... 3022
Prairie perspectives, 2, ... 2804
Ratner, Rochelle
The tightrope walker, ...964
Rausch, Paul A.
Sacred solos for clarinet and piano, ... 1461
Rauschenburg, Robert
Robert Rauschenburg - Glass handle, ... 1232
Raymond, J. Scott
Cumancaya, ... 2053
Primitive art and technology,. 2054
Readymade Historical Society
Readymade and district,. 3207
Readymade Women of Unifarm
Readymade and district,. 3207
Ream, Peter Tennant
The Fort on the Saskatchewan,. 3208
Reardon, G.
Primitive art and technology,. 2054
Rechner, Robert Douglas
A regional study of personnel turnover in the Alberta
Department of Public Welfare, ... 1814
Red Deer East Historical Society.
Mingling memories,. 3209
Red Deer. Mount Calvary Lutheran Church
25th anniversary, 1946-1971, Mount Calvary Lutheran Church,
Red Deer, Alberta, 1971, .410
Redd, Kay B.
Raymond, 1901-1967,. 3064
Redekopp, Helen
History of Alberta Mennonite Women in Mission, 1947-1977,. 238
Redfern, Jean
The last summer,. 2614
Redl-Hlus, Carolyn D.
Earthbound, ...965
Redmond, Gerald
Edmonton '78, ... 1649
Soccer practice, ... 1689
Soccer!, ... 1690
Redwater Pioneers Club
Memories, Redwater and district, ... 3080
Reed, Gene
Aunt Gene's ramblings, ...966
Reed, Job
Job Reed's letters, ... 3503
Reeder, Joseph
Koo-Koo-sint, ...999

Reese, Will
The money tree, ... 967
Rees-Powell, Alan Thomas
Differentials in the integration process of Dutch and Italian immigrants in Edmonton, ... 1983
Reeves, Brian O.K.
An archaeological resource inventory of Waterton Lakes National Park and preliminary archaeological report for 1971, . . . 2055
Culture changes on the northern plains, 1000 BC to 1000 AD, . . . 2056
Historical resources impact assessment, western portion of Syncrude lease no17, Alberta, ... 2045
The Kenney Site,. 2057
Reghr, T.D.
The possibilities of Canada are truly great,. 2227
Rehwinkel, Bessie Lee (Efner)
Dr Bessie,. 3371
Reid, Bradford Guy
Aircraft noise and residential property values, ... 2145
Reid, Crowther & Partners Limited
Report on the impact of a proposed synthetic crude oil project on Fort McMurray for Syncrude Canada Ltd, ... 2298
Reid, Douglas Craig Somers
Corrections needs to be corrected,. 1815
Reid, Gordon
Around the Lower Peace, ... 3210
Frontier notes, ... 3211
Notes of the north, ... 3212
Reid, Helen Audrey
An investigation of the role of the school librarian in Alberta,. 36
Reid, John Edmund
Sports and games in Alberta before 1900, ... 1691
Reid, Monty Garson
Book of definition, ... 968
Karst means stone, ... 969
Reilly, Helen
Compartment K, ... 770
Reilly, Pat
Alberta,. 2634
Rendall, Harold A.
The trade areas of Camrose, Wetaskiwin and Ponoka, ... 2235
Rendall, Ted Seator
In God's school, ... 138
Jeremiah, prophet of crisis,. 139
Living the abundant life, ... 140
Nehemiah, ... 141
Render, Lorne Edgar
AC Leighton, ... 1233
Archibald Thorburn Paintings from the collection of Glenbow-Alberta Institute, Calgary, and Riveredge Foundation, Calgary, . . . 1244
Glenbow collects An exhibition,. 1234

The mountains and the sky, ... 1235
Prairie images, ... 1212

Renshaw, Ted
Prairie profiles, ... 866

Repka, William
Howard Lowrie, MD, physician, humanitarian, ... 3372

Repp, Isobel
Bowtell tales to 1976, ... 3214

Resources Conference of the Northwest Region, 1st, Grande Prairie, ... 1960
Transactions of the first Resources Conference of the Northwest Region, ... 2146

Rexboro. St. Aidan and St. Hilda Anglican Church
St. Aidan & St. Hilda, 1911-1971, ... 411

Reynolds, A. Bert
Siding 16, ... 3215

Rice, Harold R.
Exclusive magic, ... 1353

Richards, John
Prairie capitalism, ... 2299

Richards, Leonard
Community development in Alberta, ... 1731

Richardson, George H.W.
The Conservative Party in the provisional district of Alberta, 1887-1905, ... 2383

Richardson, Jane *see* Hanks, Jane (Richardson)
Tribe under trust, ... 1908

Richeson, Meg
Publishing in Canada, ... 60

Richman, Sharon Lea
The faces, ... 1080
Quiet winds, ... 970

Ricinus-Caroline History Committee
In the shade of the mountains, ... 3216

Ricker, Harold Byron
Frontiers and reflections, ... 239

Rickey, Catherine Jessie
Jeannie, ... 1462

Riddle, Helen
Echoes of a bell, ... 412

Ridgewood Women's Institute
Ridgewood community, Red Deer, Alberta, 1889-1967, ... 2884

Riediger, Alfred Jacob
Transient men in Edmonton, ... 1816

Riel, Louis
The diaries of Louis Riel, ... 2805

Rigby, Douglas William
Recreation travel patterns of Edmontonians, ... 1692

Rightmire, Richard
The master mentalist, ... 1354

Riis, Sharon
The true story of Ida Johnson, ... 771
Riley, Daniel Edward
The Lost Lemon Mine, ... 2236
Riley, Louise
The mystery horse, ... 772
Train for Tiger Lily, ... 773
Rimmer, Harry
The last of the giants, ... 240
Ringrose, Christopher Xerxes
Western reunion, ... 971
Ringwood, Gwendolyn Margaret (Pharis)
Look behind you neighbour, ... 1081
The rainmaker, ... 1082
The sleeping beauty, ... 1083
Widger's way, ... 1084
Younger brother, ... 774
Rinkoff, Sharon
Alberta, ... 2600
Rippington, Dennis J.
Let swords slash for freedom!, ... 972
Ritchie, Margaret Eleanor *see* Longair, Margaret Eleanor (Ritchie)
The development of transportation in early Calgary,
researched by Margaret E. Longair, ... 2344
Ritchie, Ronald Stuart
A hard look ahead, ... 1732
Ritter, W.
Grace Lutheran Church 50th anniversary, 1928-1978, ... 439
Rivercourse Sewing Circle
Rivercourse centennial, ... 3217
Riveredge Foundation
Archibald Thorburn Paintings from the collection of Glenbow-
Alberta Institute, Calgary, and Riveredge Foundation, Calgary, . . . 1244
Rivière Qui Barre Book Committee
The wheels of time, ... 3008
Robb, R.J.
Trinity United Church golden jubilee anniversary, ... 413
Robbins, Sidney
The Providence Child Development Centre, ... 1817
Robert, George Rene
Political orientations of Calgary children from grade four to eight, . . 2436
Roberts, Lathrop E.
Of us and the oxen, ... 3504
Roberts, Richard Henry
Factors involved in the selection of outdoor recreation locations
by residents of the municipal district of Foothills, ... 1693
Roberts, Sarah Ellen
Of us and the oxen, ... 3504
Roberts, Spencer
Smoke over Sikanaska, ... 3317

Roberts, Stanley C.
A summary report on the proceedings of Alternatives Canada, a Canada West Conference on Confederation, held at Banff, March 27-29, 1978,. 2384
Roberts, T. Dale
Heart of gold, ... 3175
Robertson, John H.
Papers from Conference on Canadian Archaeology Abroad, held at the University of Calgary, November 23, 24, 25, 1973, . . . 2022
Robertson, Robin
Handle with care, ... 1355
Robinson, Bart
Banff Springs, ... 3218
The Canadian Rockies trail guide, ... 2689
Great days in the Rockies, ... 1121
Robinson, Darrell
Canadian cornography, ... 1109
Robinson, Robert Thomas
The Temporary Absence Program in Alberta,. 1818
Roche, Douglas J.
The Catholic revolution, ... 142
The human side of politics,. 2385
It's a new world, ... 61
Justice not charity, ... 2386
Man to Man, ... 143
What development is all about, ... 2387
Rocky Mountain House Jubilee Committee
Stories of the pioneers of the west country, ... 2882
Rocky Mountain House Reunion Historical Society
The days before yesterday,. 3219
Rodney, James B.
Small Claims Court guide for Alberta,. 2488
Rodney, William
Kootenai Brown, his life and times, 1839-1916, ... 2841
Roe, Peter G.
Cumancaya, ... 2053
Roen, Hazel Bessie
The grass roots of Dorothy, 1895-1970, ... 3220
Roenisch, Rich
Spitzee days,. 3240
Rogers, Edith Blanche (Cox)
History made in Edmonton, ... 3221
Rogers, Otto
New paintings by Otto Rogers, ... 1236
Rogers, Walter Bob
Changing rural attitudes, ... 1714
The economic benefits and costs of irrigation in the eastern irrigation district of Alberta, ... 3444
Effects of farm technology and consequent problems of adjustment, effects of industrialization on agricultural production, ... 3445

The role of religion in social and economic development, ... 144
The rural church, the farm family, ... 3446
Stimulants to social development in slow growing regions, ... 1734
World population and distribution of food, ... 2147
Rolly View. St. Paul's Lutheran Church
History of St Paul's Lutheran Church, Rolly View, formerly
Rosenthal East, Leduc, ... 414
Romaine, Edward
This is Alberta in 1963, ... 2636
Ronaghan, Allen
All the way over, ... 2729
Earnest-minded men, ... 2467
A history of St Saviour's Parish, Vermilion, Alberta, and
associated parishes, 1907-1967, ... 415
The hospital on the hill, 1912-1962, ... 3373
Morrison, SD No 1639, ... 1576
There'll always be an Islay, ... 3222
Ronal *see* Allesi, Ron
The magic of Ronal, ... 1264
Ronning, Chester
A memoir of China in revolution from the Boxer Rebellion
to the People's Republic,. 2745
Rosemary Historical Society
Rosemary, land of promise, ... 3223
Rosenthal, Joseph
The Queen's cowboy, ... 829
Ross, Carlyle Bonston Albert
A case study of the success of settlement in a southern Peace River
district, ... 2571
Ross, David Philips
The causes of labour disputes in Alberta, 1955-1962, ... 2237
Ross, Leonard W.
Educational television,. 1503
Ross, Mary Francis (Antoniuk)
Oh! The Coal Branch,. 3224
Ross, Toni, *see* Ross, Mary Frances (Antoniuk)
Oh! The Coal Branch,. 3224
Ross, W.E.
Meet southern Alberta, ... 3149
Rosyth Farm Women's Union
Rosyth memoirs, 1906-1965, ... 2889
Rothwell, Alfred
Love and good sense, ... 3374
Round, W.E.
Trail blazer of the Canadian Rockies, ... 2653
Rout, James D.
Execution against land in Alberta, ... 2489
Routledge, Penelope Dawn
The North-West Mounted Police and their influence on the
sporting and social life of the North-West Territories, 1870-1904, . . 2513

Rowe, Jean I.
A history of the people of Michichi, ... 3225
Royal Bank of Canada
The Royal Bank of Canada, 8th Avenue & Centre Street, Calgary, Alberta, ... 3447
Royal Candian Legion no. 192. Ryley Branch. Ladies Auxiliary
Beavertales, ... 2900
Royer, Lucien
Political validity of Franco-Albertains, ... 2437
Royick, Alexander
Lexical borrowings in Alberta Ukrainian, ... 508
Rude, Selmer J.
Life experiences, ... 3505
Ruder, Anemone
Westward ho! 1903, ... 632
Rump, Paul Charles
The recreational land use of the Bow, Kananaskis, and Spray Lakes Valleys, ... 1694
Rumsey Centennial Book Committee
Pioneer days, ... 3226
Rundle, Robert Terrill
The Rundle journals, 1840-1848, ... 241
Running, Arnold
Stay but till tomorrow, ... 775
Rusak, Stephen Thaddeus
Relations in education between Bishop Legal and the Alberta Liberal government, 1905-1920, ... 1577
Rush Centre Women's Institute
Esther community history, ... 3227
Russell, Andy
Alpine Canada, ... 3326
Andy Russell's adventures with wild animals, ... 3327
Grizzly country, ... 3328
The high west, ... 3312
Horns in the high country, ... 3329
Men of the saddle, ... 3448
The Rockies, ... 2637
Trails of a wilderness wanderer, ... 3506
Trails of a wilderness wanderer, ... 3330
Russell, Charles M.
Charles M Russell, 1864-1926, ... 1237
Whoop-up country, ... 2842
Russell, Sheila (MacKay)
The living earth, ... 776
Rust, Ronald Stuart
An analysis and evaluation of land use in the special areas of Alberta, 2572
Rustland, Mary Randine
Treasures, ... 973
Rutledge, Elaine
A treasury of memories, ... 3228

Ryan, Joan
Wall of words, ... 1985
Rycroft, Jean Fraser
The Teepee Creek terror, ... 3270
Ryga, George
Ballad of a stone picker,. 777
Captives of the faceless drummer,. 1085
The ecstasy of Rita Joe, ... 1086
The ecstasy of Rita Joe and other plays, ... 1087
The hungry hills, ...778
Night desk, ...779
Ploughmen of the glacier, ... 1088
Seven hours to sundown,. 1089
Sunrise on Sarah,. 1090
Sabine, Robert Douglas
Pigeon Lake summer cottage shoreland use, ... 2573
Sadler, Barry
Conflicts of perception and use in Banff National Park, ... 2574
Sadock, Jerrold M.
Studies presented to Robert B Lees by his students, ...459
Sager, David
The golden feather, ...763
Salt, Jim R.
The birds of Alberta, ... 3331
Salt, Walter Ray
The birds of Alberta, ... 3331
Salwen, Bert Bennett
Archaeological reconnaissance north of the Brooks range
in northeastern Alaska, ... 2058
Sanderson, George P.
Right under their noses, ... 1356
Sanderson, James Francis
Indian tales of the Canadian prairies, ... 2082
Sanderson, Mary M.
Historical panorama of Alix and district,. 3229
Sandilands, John
Western Canadian dictionary and phrase book, ...460
Sanford Evans Services Ltd.
Alberta place guide (and) Alberta population maps, ... 2662
Saskatoon Gallery and Conservatory
8 Calgary artists,. 1238
Savage, Candace
Our Nell, ... 1758
Savage, Harry
Alberta, a celebration,. 265
Andy Russell's adventures with wild animals,. 332
Multimonster in paradise, ...98
Packy, the little elephant who came to the cold,. 74
Station 14, ...93
8 cents worth of Canada and a few sense more, ... 123

Savaryn, Petro
Ukrainian Catholic unity, 1906-1966, ... 255
Sawatzky, Aron
The Mennonites of Alberta and their assimilation,. 1986
Sawchuk, William
Let us learn Ukrainian Book I, ... 509
Scace, Robert Chaston
Banff,. 2575
The Canadian national parks, today and tomorrow, ... 2524
Canadian parks in perspective, ... 2526
The management and use of a Canadian plains oasis, ... 2576
Scandia Historical Committee
Scandia since seventeen,. 3230
Scarfe, Neville V.
Alberta, where the mountains meet the plains, ... 2586
Scenic Heights Farmers' Union
The Big Horn School District, ... 3231
Schaeffer, Claude E.
Blackfoot shaking tent, ... 145
Schalkwyk, Helene M.E.
Mushrooms of the Edmonton area, edible and poisonous,. 3332
Scharff, Robert
Canada's mountain national parks, ... 2692
Glacier National Park and Waterton Lakes National Park,. 2693
Scharschmidt, Gunter Herbert
A manual in contrastive linguistics, ... 461
Schatz, Edward R.
Practical contact mind reading,. 1357
Schcherbak, Mykola
The burning wood, ... 537
Schick-Swanson Library and Information Consultants
Pollution in Alberta A bibliography,. 13
Schielke, Helen Norma *see* Gouldie, Helen Norma (Schielke)
Schielke family tree, ... 2706
Schissel, Wendy
Beiseker's golden heritage, ... 3232
Schleich, David John
No sweet land, ... 780
Schofield, Fred H.
Pincher Papers, 1, ... 3196
Scholefield, Billy
No rocking chair for me!, ... 146
Schultz, Harold John
William Aberhart and the Social Credit party, ... 2438
Schultz, Wolfgang Martin
The people and resources of northeastern Alberta,. 2148
Schulze, Eric J.
The story of New Sarepta Moravians, ... 416
Schutz, Fred
Pas-ka-poo, ... 3233

Schwartz, Arthur Mark
Patterns of influence in the collective bargaining system of Alberta Teachers' Association, ... 1504
Schwermann, Albert Henry
The beginnings of Lutheran Church, Canada, covering the years 1941 to 1964, ... 242
Scobie, Stephen
Air loom, ... 974
Airwaves, sealevel, landlock, ... 975
Babylondromat, ... 976
The birken tree, ... 977
In the silence of the year, ... 978
Leonard Cohen, ... 538
One word poems, ... 979
The rooms we are, ... 980
Stone poems,. 981
Scott, John William
The history of the Faculty of Medicine of the University of Alberta, 1913-1963, ... 3376
Scott, Margaret
Bowtell tales to 1976, ... 3214
Scott, R.
Struggles and progress of Teamsters Local 987, Calgary, Alberta, 1910-1955, ... 2197
Scott, Rose
Allison Procter, OBE, LLD 1880-1964, ... 1834
Scott, William Guy
Urban growth management, ... 2577
Scott, Winfield
Golden memories, Warburg and district, ... 2923
Scott-Brown, Joan M.
Stoney ethnobotany, ... 1987
Scotton, Carol Myers
Choosing a lingua franca in an African capital, ... 462
Scown, Dennis R.
A history and analysis of the 1971 Alberta general election, ... 2388
Scratch, John Ronald
The editorial reaction of the Alberta press to the Bennett government, 1930-1935, ... 2389
Scriven, Mary (Johnson)
Homesteading in the Consul district, ... 3234
Scriven, Ralph
Homesteading in the Consul district, ... 3234
Scrymgeour, J.A.
Impressionist paintings from the collection of Mr. and Mrs. J.A. Scrymgeour and Westbourne International Industries, ... 1178
Seagel, Erica Jill
Some aspects of the distribution of snowmobiles in southern Alberta,. 169
Seale, Ronald Gordon
Some geographical aspects of the coal industry in Alberta, ... 223

Seastone, Don
Proceedings, ... 2103
Seidel, Rolf Christian
The Hutterite ways,. 1988
Seminar on Cultural Differences, University of Alberta, 1963.
Insights into cultural differences, ... 1989
Semischen, Orest
Byzantine churches of Alberta, ... 1133
Sen, Ranjan
Ranjan Sen Tommie Gallie, ... 1240
Senior Citizen's Club of Provost
Early furrows, ... 3235
Serafy, Meir
Structure and organization of political parties in Alberta,. 2439
Service, G.T.
The Gate, ... 2756
Setterington, Arthur
Off-beat (sic) mental effects,. 1358
Straight line mysteries, ... 1359
Stranger mysteries, ... 1360
Shankovs'kyj, Ihor
Korotke lito, ...982
Shanks, Viola *see* Leggett, Viola (Shanks)
Gem golden jubilee, 1914-1964, ... 3112
Shanley, Albin
Golden dreams, story and drawings, ...645
Shapiro, David
Three aspects of the economics of education in Alberta, ... 1505
Sharma, Hari Dutt
Income contribution of the petroleum industry to the province of Alberta for the period 1964-1976, and public policy,. 2300
Sharp, Henry Stephen
The kinship system of the Black Lake Chipewyan,. 1990
Sharp, Paul Frederick
Whoop-up country, ... 2842
Shaw, Charles Aeneas
Tales of a pioneer surveyor, ... 2638
Shaw, David
The wit and wisdom of Bob Edwards, ... 49
Shaw, Hazel
Echoes of a bell, ...412
Shaw, J.W.
The hospital on the hill, 1912-1962, ... 3373
Shaw, Keith
Chief Mountain country, ... 3237
Sheehan, Elizabeth A.
And we came after, ...417
Sheehan, Nancy M.
Shaping the schools of the Canadian West, ... 1552

Sheehan, Patricia
Social change in the Alberta foothills, ... 1733
Sheep River Historical Society
In the light of the flares,. 3238
Shell Oil Company of Canada Ltd
The Jumping Pound story, ... 2301
Shelton, Francis Drake
A survey of library facilities in Alberta schools, ... 37
Shepherd, George
West of yesterday, ... 3239
Sheppard, Art
We proved God, ... 147
Sheppard, Bert
Spitzee days,. 3240
Sheppard, Greta
We proved God, ... 147
Sheppard, June
Report on academic women, ... 1613
Sheremeta, James
A survey of professional entertainment and theatre in Edmonton, Alberta, before 1914, ... 1259
Sherman, Roger
With deck in hand, ... 1320
Sherwood, John C.
The conjurer's calculator, ... 1361
Sherwood Park. Sherwood Heights Junior High
Fluid filosofies of future fools, ... 568
Shevchenko Scientific Society in Canada. Western Canada Branch
Collected papers on Ukrainian settlers in Western Canada, ... 1992
Shevchenko, Taras Hryhorovych
Haydamaky,. 983
Shevolov, George Y.
A historical phonology of the Ukrainian language,. 510
Shiels, Bob
Calgary,. 3241
Shingadia, Ashwin
Edmonton Centre, ... 2390
Shinnie, P.L.
Papers from Conference on Canadian Archaeology Abroad, held at the University of Calgary, November 23, 24, 25, 1973, . . . 2022
Shone, Margaret Ann
Confluence of mental health and legal systems in the process for compulsory civil commitment in Alberta,. 1819
Shope, Gladys Cynthia Rebecca *see* Diesel, Gladys Cynthia Rebecca (Shope)
The legend of Owl Hoot Hill, ... 638
Short Grass Historical Society
Long shadows, ... 3242
Shortall, Leonard
The in-betweener, ... 649

Shrier, Clarence
I don't know what your God can do, but my God can do anything,. . . . 148
Shute, Allan
Double feature,. 781
Forever together, ...936
Kidmonton, ... 2682
Multimonster in paradise, ...984
The rain-orb, ...782
Sandman's land, ...888
39 below, ...592
Sibbald Women's Institute
Sibbald community history, 1910-1962, ... 3243
Sicks' Lethbridge Brewery Ltd.
Brands and how to read them, ... 3449
Siddall, Annie Louise *see* Gaetz, Annie Louise (Siddall)
Footprints of the Gaetz family, ... 2703
Siegel, Paul J.
Doorway to delusion, ... 1362
Mentalism a la mode, ... 1363
Windows to the mind,. 1364
Siemens, William J.
Wo de hombre,. 2640
Siermanchewsky, Gregory
Mundare, yesterday and today, ...403
Sievwright, Eric Colville
The effect of petroleum development on the Alberta economy, 1947-1957, ... 2302
Sikabonyi, Laszlo A.
Billion barrel oil swindle, ...783
Silver, Phillip
Counsellor extraordinary, ... 1039
Simon, Frank
History of the Alberta Provincial Institute of Technology and Art,. . 1578
Simon, Maurice
Bridgeland Riverside memories,. 1579
Simon, Olaf Emil Hugo
Curse of the gods, ...784
To hell with Canada, ... 2391
Simpkins, Bill
Chinook country, ... 2641
Simpkins, James Nathaniel
Jasper, ... 1110
Simpson, Ian Stewart
Memoirs of a soldier, ... 2759
Sims, Cort
The Beaver Creek site, ... 2061
Sinclair, Robert
Robert Sinclair, ... 1241
Sinclair, Virginia
Golden memories of Taber Central School, Taber, Alberta, 1910-1971,1580

Sinclare, Colin
My sister, ... 1463
Singh, Jaswant
Land use changes in the Eastern Irrigation District of Alberta, ... 2578
Siska, George Edward
A survey of centralized library services in Alberta schools
and library utilization in senior high schools, ... 38
Sisters of Charity of Our Lady of Evron
60th anniversary, St Louis Hospital, Bonnyville, Alberta,. 3377
Sisters of Charity of St. Vincent de Paul of Halifax
50th anniversary, Immaculata Hospital, Westlock, Alberta,. 3378
Skeels, Lydia Lowndes Maury
Location of the Indian tribes at first white contact in Alberta, Canada,1991
Skinner, Murray
Proceedings of the Alberta Chamber of Commerce Manpower
Conference held in Jasper, October 6-8, 1974, ... 2088
Skolnik, William
Hoarse music, ... 1045
Skomp, Stephen
S'komplimentary mentalism, ... 1365
Skorupskyj, Volodymyr
Along the way,. 985
Asters still blooming, .986
The homeless, ...987
My home, ...988
Skuba, Michael
Population density and pupil transportation costs in Alberta, ... 2351
Skwarok, Josephat
The Eastern Catholic Churches, ...149
Slatter, E.J.
Eric Lafferty Harvie, ... 2303
Slavutych, Yar
Along the Zarorozhian places, ...989
Collected papers on Ukrainian settlers in Western Canada, ... 1992
Collected works, 1938-1978, ...990
The conquerors of Prairies,. 991
Conversational Ukrainian, ...511
Greatness of Taras Shevchenko, ...539
An introduction to Ukrainian, ...512
L'oiseau de feu, ...992
Majesty (Ukrainian poems), ...993
Mudroschi mandriv, ...994
The muse in prison,. 540
Northern lights, ...995
Oasis,. 935
Rozstriliana muza, ...996
Selected poems, ...997
Shevchenko's celebration, ...541
Shevchenko's greatness, ...542
T Shevchenko's craftsmanship, ...543

Trophies, ...998
Ukrainian Christian names A dictionary,. 506
Ukrainian for beginners,. .513
Ukrainian for children, ...514
Ukrainian in pictures, ...515
Ukrainian literature in Canada,. 544
Ukrains'ka mova za zorovo-slukhovoiu metodoiu, ...516
Ukrains'ka poeziia v Kanadi,. 545
Sluman, Norma Pauline (Hardman)
Blackfoot Crossing, ...785
Poundmaker,. 786
Smeeton, Miles
Moose magic, ... 3333
Smiley, Charles W.
The art of communication,. 1091
Smith, Benjamin George
An activity systems impact analysis of the Edmonton Transit System strike, 1973-1974, ... 2352
Smith, Donald B.
One century later, ... 1967
Smith, Frank Allan
Corpse in handcuffs, ...787
Defectors are dead men,. .788
The traitor mask,. 789
Smith, Graham
Boycott against Alberta,. 2149
Smith, Ivy
A second language as a communication skill, ...463
Smith, John Merle
The marching call, ...793
The mystery horse, ...772
Smith, J.W.
Early man and environments in northwest North America, ... 2027
Smith, Margot
Pioneer women of Western Canada,. 2727
Smith, Marion Roberta
Koo-Koo-sint, ...999
Prairie child,. 1000
The rubbing rock, ... 1001
Smith, Mary Irene (Doherty)
Songs of the Athabasca,. 1002
Smith, Mary Marcia
The ideological relationship between the United Farmers and the Cooperative Commonwealth Federation, ... 2440
Smith, Mary *see* Yorath, Mary (Smith)
West,. 1033
Smith, Patricia Ruth
Dawn to dusk, ... 2730
Smith, Peter Douglas
The United Farmers of Alberta and the Ginger Group, ... 2441

Smith, Peter John
Edmonton, the emerging metropolitan pattern, ... 2531
The Edmonton-Calgary corridor, ... 2579
Smith, Philip
The treasure-seekers, ... 2304
Smith, Rachel A.
Aboriginal man and environments on the plateau of northwest America, ... 2008
Early man and environments in northwest North America, ... 2027
Smith, Sidney Bailey
Through the years with Sidney B Smith,. 3507
Smith, Starr
A place for everyone, ...790
Teamwork, ...791
Whatever you do,. 792
Smithson, Ken
Tributaries of the Blindman, ... 3089
Smyth, Donald Ross
A storage and retrieval system for the abstracts of theses in education completed at the University of Alberta, ... 39
Smyth, John M.
New trends in high school administration, ... 1506
Sneyd, Doug
John Rowand, fur trader, ...597
Snider, Howard
Namus, ... 1003
Snider, Howard Mervin
Variables affecting immigrant adjustment, ... 1993
Snipe, James Holloway
The ecological and economic impact of water resource development in southern Alberta, ... 3346
Snow, John
These mountains are our sacred places, ... 1994
Snow, John Vance
Beginnings, ... 1004
Count illusions,. 1005
Snyder, Juanita Carroll
No rocking chair for me!, ...146
Raise up the foundations, ...244
Snyder, Robert Carl
Gospel duets for the trumpet, with piano accompaniment, ... 1464
Gospel songs for the trumpet trio, with piano accompaniment,. . . . 1465
Specials for brass, with piano accompaniment, ... 1466
Snyder, William
The battle hymn of the Dominion and other poems, ... 1006
Waitress! there's an eye in my soup!, ... 1007
Soby, Karen
Quiet winds, ...970
Soby, Trudy
Be it ever so humble, ... 3244

A walk through old Calgary, ... 3245
Social Credit Co-ordinating Centre, Mexborough, Eng.
Alberta's progress, ... 2442
Social Plains Women's Institute
Social Plains School District golden jubilee booklet, 1913-1963, . . . 3016
Soderstrom, Roger William
An analysis of the Edmonton Social Planning Council, ... 1820
Solbert, Rommi
Andy and the gopher, ...731
Solecki, Ralph S.
Archaeological reconnaissance north of the Brooks range
in northeastern Alaska, ... 2058
Somerset, Bertram
Years of wonder, ... 1581
Sommerville, Iris Constance *see* Allan, Iris Constance (Somerville)
Wop May, bush pilot, ...599
Soop, Everett
Soop takes a bow, ... 1111
Sorgard, Marie
Coyote Flats, ... 3247
Sorrells, Harley R.
Northwestern plains archaeology, ... 2041
Southern Alberta Institute of Technology
Sixty years, '16 - '76, ... 1582
Southern Alberta Pioneer and Old Timers Association
The golden link, ... 2834
Meet southern Alberta, ... 3149
Southern Alberta Tourist Council
Visit southern Alberta, land of green acres,. 2694
Southesk, James Carnegie,
Earl of Saskatchewan and the Rocky Mountains, ... 2642
Spalding, Jeffrey J.
Silversmithing in Canadian history, ... 1242
Sparby, Harry Theodore
A history of the Alberta school system to 1925, ... 1583
Speers, Bertha M.
A cameo of the west, ... 3248
Speight, Anne
Prairie echoes, Metiskow, Cadogan, Cairns, ... 3249
Spence, Anthony John
Legal aid, ... 2490
Spencer, J.A.
Crystal Spring Indian camp site, ... 2059
Spencer, Keith Robinson
Fond memories, ... 1134
Spencer, Richard Bruce
A study of the wildlife on four selected Edmonton ravines and of
the recreation uses and preferences of city ravines, ... 3334
Spicer, John
Christ today,. 150

God's people today, ...151
Spiller, Edward Vincent
The early history of scouting in Calgary, Alberta, ... 1849
Spiteri, Ed
Hutterites,. 1995
Images of a city, ... 1135
Spohr, Gregory
Selected climbs in the Canmore area, ... 1696
Sponchia, Carl Raymond
Public accounting in Lethbridge, ... 2150
Sprague, Marshall
The great gates, ... 2643
Spratt, Wendy
The nature of things, ... 3323
Sproule, Albert Frederick
The role of Patrick Burns in the development of Western Canada, . . 2239
Spruce Grove. St. Andrew's United Church
An historical sketch of St Andrew's United Church, Spruce Grove, Alberta, 1920-1970,. 418
Spruce View School Area Historical Society
Grub-axe to grain, ... 3060
Spurrell, William
Adventures in two worlds, ... 3508
Srebrnik, Leokadia
Economic evaluation of ethylene production in Alberta, ... 2305
St. Albert Historical Society
St Albert, a pictorial history,. 2895
St. André, Lucie
Histoire de Girouxville, ... 3250
St. Isidore. Parish Historical Committee
Album souvenir St Isidore, 1953-78,. 419
St. Joseph's General Hospital, Vegreville
Memories,. 3379
St. Joseph's Seminary, Edmonton
St. Joseph's Seminary 50th anniversary, 1927-1977, ...420
St. Lina History Book Committee
St. Lina and surrounding area, ... 3251
St. Lina. St. Helene's Catholic Church
Cinquantenaire, Ste Hélène de Ste-Lina,. 421
St. Mary's Hospital, Camrose
St. Mary's Hospital, Camrose, Alberta, 50th anniversary, 1924-1974, 3380
St. Paul. Ecole Racette
Projet centenaire, Grade 10, ... 3252
St. Vincent. Catholic Church
Cinquantenaire de la paroisse Saint-Vincent, Alberta, 1905-1956, . . .422
Stacey, Earl Clifford
Beaverlodge to the Rockies, ... 3253
The Monkman Pass Highway, ... 2353
Peace Country heritage, ... 3450
WD Albright, ... 3451

Stahlke, Herbert F.W.
Current trends in stylistics,. 451
Stainton, Irene Hackett
Along the Victoria trail, ... 3254
Staite, M.J.
Flood plain management in the Drumheller Valley, ... 2580
Stamp, Robert Miles
School days, ... 1584
Shaping the schools of the Canadian West,. 1552
Stampnick, Ken
The wooden people, ...753
Standard Community
Golden jubilee celebration, June 19th, 1960, ... 3255
Standard Historical Book Society
From Danaview to Standard,. 3256
Standell, Albert
Anecdotal history of Calgary Separate Schools, ... 1520
Standera, O.
WesCan/INFORM, ... 28
Starchuk, Orest
A survey of Russian literature of the xviii and xlx centuries, ...546
The Ukrainian language, ...517
The Ukrainian language questionnaire, ...518
Stauffer, Ezra
History of the Alberta-Saskatchewan Mennonite Conference, ...245
Staum, Martin S.
Science, technology and culture in historical perspective, ... 2746
Stavely Historical Book Society
The butte stands guard, ... 3257
Stechishin, Julius William
Istoriia poselennia ukraintsiv u Kanadi, ... 1996
Steele, Charles Frank
Prairie editor, ... 62
Steele, Harwood Elmes Robert
The marching call, ...793
Steiner, Michael
Alberta '73, ... 1164
Steinig, Serafina
Cos' ci oddam Panie, ...246
Stelfox, Henry
Poems, ... 1008
Rambling thoughts of a wandering fellow, 1903-1968, ... 3509
When the sawflies mate in summer and other Alberta poems, ... 1009
When the sawfly flies and other poems, ... 1010
Stelfox, John G.
Rambling thoughts of a wandering fellow, 1903-1968, ... 3509
Stenson, Fred
Lonesome hero, ...794
Stephens, Douglas
Chuckwagon of the Circle B,. 654

Steur, Elizabeth *see* de Steur, Elizabeth
Once upon a chinook, ... 2457
Stevens, George Roy
A city goes to war, ... 2757
Princess Patricia's Canadian Light Infantry, 1919-1957, ... 2758
Stevens, Grey Philip
A residential subdivision for Calgary, Alberta, ... 2581
Stevenson, Scotty
Alberta,. 1467
Stewart, David
Planning the use of available resources in upgrading the health of registered Indians in Alberta, ... 3381
Stewart, George C.
Alberta real estate buying/selling guide, ... 2491
Stewart, Irene
These were our yesterdays,. 3382
Stewart, John Smith
Memoirs of a soldier, ... 2759
Stewart, Kenneth Fenwick
RB Bennett as MP, 1910-1917,. 2392
Stewart, Norman
Children of the pioneers,. 3510
Stibbe, Hugo L.P.
The distribution of ethnic groups in Alberta, according to the 1961 census, ... 1997
Stickel, Lorna J.
A study of depreciative behavior in three underdeveloped highway campgrounds in Jasper National Park, Alberta, ... 1697
Stiles, Kirk
Thimbles with a light touch, ... 1366
Stocken, Harry William Gibbon
Among the Blackfoot and Sarcee,. 247
Stokes, Ernest B.
The development and evaluation of an urban growth model for Calgary,. 2582
Stone, Bertha
Medicine Hat and other verses,. 1011
Stone, Donald Norman George
The process of rural settlement in the Athabasca area, Alberta, ... 2583
Stone, Pearl R.
Dog Pound, 1880-1920, ... 2913
People and places by Pearl, ... 3258
Stony Plain Golden Age Club
Anniversary in gold, ... 2731
Stony Plain. St. Matthew's Evangelical Lutheran Church
St. Matthew's Evangelical Lutheran Church, ... 423
Stony Plain. United Church
50 years 1925-1975, ... 424
Stooshnoff, Paul William
Quiet winds, ... 970

Storey, H.C.
A review of the work of the Health of Animals Branch in Alberta,. . 3452
Stout, Clarence Howard
Backtrack on old trails, ... 63
From frontier days in Leduc and District, ... 3021
Strathcona Historical Group
Strathcona, the asset of heritage, ... 3260
Strathcona Writing Group
Strathcona harvest, ... 584
Street, Arthur George
Cooper's crossing, ... 795
Stremecki, Edward J.
How to read and run a river, ... 1698
Stretch, Dianne Kathryn
From prohibition to government control, ... 1821
Stringer, Arthur John Arbuthnott
The mud lark, ... 796
Stringham, Bryant L.
The School Act, 1970,. 1507
Stryd, Arnoud H.
Aboriginal man and environments on the plateau of northwest America, ... 2008
Stubbs, Hugh
The early devisers, ... 3261
Stump, Sarain
American Indian graphic symbols and their adaptation in art,. . . . 2060
There is my people sleeping, ... 1012
Sturm, Ingrid
Golden memoirs, 1912-1963, ... 2968
Sugden, Thomas Curtis
The consolidated school movement in Alberta, 1913-1963, ... 1585
Sugino, Shan
The Rockies,. 2644
Suknaski, Andrew
Leaving,. 1013
Sullivan, Brian E.
Recreation travel in the Cypress Hills,. 1699
Sullivan, R.D. Barry
Alberta incorporation guide, ... 2492
Summer Institute of Linguistics, Santa Cruz, Calif.
The Blackfoot alphabet, with exercises, ... 501
Summers, Merna
The skating party, ... 797
Sundbo, Beatrice
Treasures in heaven, ... 152
Sunshine Women's Institute.
The history of the border country of Coutts, ... 3262
Suski, Julien
Edmonton,. 2468

Susko, Rudolf
Economics of size on Alberta grain farms, ... 3453
Sutherland, Ronald H.
Readings on language in Canada, ...458
Sveen, Evelyn
The golden years, ... 3263
Svidzins'kyi, Volodymyr
Selected poems, ... 1014
Swann, Francis Richard
Progressive Social Credit in Alberta,1935-1940, ... 2444
Swanson, Cecil
The days of my sojourning A reminiscence, ...248
The harvest of the years, ...425
Swindlehurst, Edward B.
Furrows, faith and fellowship, ... 3442
4-H in Alberta, 1917-1967, ... 3454
Swinton, George
Inuit games and contests, ... 1247
Switlick, Lillian
An exploratory study of factors affecting responses of
Cree students to literary selections, ... 1508
Switzer, H.A.
Edson United Church history, ...353
Switzer, Phil
The money tree, ...967
Swyripa. Frances
Ukrainian Canadians, ... 1998
Symons, Margaret
Calgary's finest, ... 2503
Symposium on Stimulants to Social and Economic Development in
Slow Growing Regions
The role of religion in social and economic development, ...144
Stimulants to social development in slow growing regions, ... 1734
Syncrude Canada Ltd
The Beaver Creek site, ... 2061
Syncrude Lease no 17, ... 2062
The Syncrude story, ... 2306
Szwedek, A. J.
Word order, sentence stress and reference in English and Polish, ...466
Taber Booklet Committee.
Golden jubilee, commemorating fifty years of picture history
of Taber, Alberta, 1905-1955, ... 3264
Taber Historical Committee
From tank 77 to Taber today, ... 3265
Tailfeathers, Gerald
The white calf, ...652
The white peril, ...653
Tait, Douglas
People of the buffalo, ... 1871

Takla, Emile Fawzy
Changes in land use patterns in downtown Calgary, 1953-1969, . . . 2584
Tan, Choon Tee
Tan Choon Tee on mentalism, ... 1367
25 experiments in mentalism,. 1368
Tanaka, Hiroshi
Asian landscapes, as seen by a Japanese pilgrim, ... 2645
Tansem, Wallace
The legend of the mighty Peace, ... 1015
Tap, Monica
Mr Brown and his magic mustache, ... 798
Taraska, Elizabeth Ann
The Calgary craft union movement, 1900-1920,. 2240
Tardif, Emile
Centenaire de Saint-Albert, ... 3266
Saint Albert,. 3267
Targett, Reginald Bryan
The education of exceptional children in the Calgary public school system, 1965, ... 1509
Task Force on Social Development
Report from the Task Force on Social Development, an independent citizens study committee, ... 1735
Taylor, Anthony James Charles
The magic of Allan Lambie, ... 1369
Taylor, Ernest Fraser
Archaeology of the Peace Hills area of central Alberta, Canada, . . 2063
Taylor, Jim
The suicide meet,. 1038
Taylor, John Benjamin
JB Taylor landscapes,. 1243
Taylor, Larry
The politics of Canadian urban development, ... 2450
Taylor, William
The ghost ship,. 834
The hand of Robin Squires, ... 627
Teal, Greg
Urban anthropology and the problems of the formation of social classes, ... 1999
Teather, Audrey
The boy and the buffalo, ... 825
The medicine man, ... 827
Mickey the beaver, and other stories, ... 828
Samson's long ride, ... 830
Teepee Creek Stampede Historical Society
The Teepee Creek terror, ... 3270
Teilfer, Beatrice
Poems of country living, ... 1016
Telmer, Frederick Harold
An analysis of the iron and steel industry in Alberta, ... 2241

Tessler, Ronnie
Crackin' out,. 1700
Tetz, Gerry
Please put the music back,. 1452
Teviotdale, Agnes Kathleen (Wilson)
Vast prospects and splendid songs, ... 3268
Théroux, Théodore
Impressions de voyage et histoire de St Joseph de Végreville, ... 3269
Theatre Passe Muraille
Far as the eye can see, ... 1097
Thibault, Margaret Fraser
The Teepee Creek terror, ... 3270
Thibault, Pierrette
Le français parle,. 449
Thibodeau, Ruth
The Moyerton story, "cradled 'twixt hills", ... 3271
Thierfelder, Vivian
The telephone man,. 2330
Thierman, Lois Mary
Student reflections, ... 1510
Thirnbeck, Alan Roger
An analysis of a group of prairie settlements north east of Calgary, . 2585
Thomas, Clara
Janey Canuck in the West,. 746
Thomas, Garnet
Soaring with Yawstring,. 1112
Thomas, Harriet Hartley
From barnacle to Banff,. 2695
Thomas, Jack
Silver sage, ... 3272
Thomas, Lewis Gwynne
Essays on Western history In honour of Lewis Gwynne Thomas,. . . 2778
The Liberal Party in Alberta, ... 2445
Thomas, Lewis Herbert
Essays on Western history In honour of Lewis Gwynne Thomas,. . . 2778
The struggle for responsible government in the North-West
Territories, 1870-97, ... 2393
Thomas, Pearl
Brooks, ... 2967
Thomasville Community Club
The 49ers,. 3043
Thompson, Brian
Many laws, ... 2473
Thompson, Harlan *see* Holt, Stephen
Stormy, ... 687
Thompson, Henry
Buffalo days and nights,. 2777
Thompson, Jean
Pioneer days, ... 3273

Thompson, J.O.
Three 3,. 1018
Thompson, Margaret Ellis
The Baptist story in Western Canada, ...250
Thompson, Ray
The Queen's story, 1906-1967, ... 1586
Thompson, Raymond
Pioneers of Athabasca, ... 3274
Wilderness adventures, ... 2646
Thompson, Ruby G. Lea (Trench)
Pioneers of Athabasca, ... 3274
Thompson, Stella Margery
Prorationing of oil in Alberta and some economic implications, . . . 2307
Thomson, Dorothy J.
Vine of His planting, ...251
Thomson, Georgina Helen
Crocus and meadowlark country, ... 3511
Thomson, Hugh Ross
An introduction to the prehistory of the Peace River country, ... 2064
Thomson, John H.R.
Fourteen generations in North America, ... 2732
Thomson, Norma L. *see* Paradis, Norma L. (Thomson)
The clan McRae,. 2724
Thorburn, Archibald
Archibald Thorburn Paintings from the collection of Glenbow-Alberta Institute, Calgary, and Riveredge Foundation, Calgary, . . . 1244
Thorington, James Munroe
A climber's guide to the Rocky Mountains of Canada, ... 1701
Thorner, Thomas
The not so peaceable kingdom, ... 1823
Thornton, Spencer
Thornton's secrets of mental magic, ... 1370
Thorsell, James W.
Recreational use in Waterton Lakes National Park, ... 1702
Thorseth, Jessie Braisher
Thoughts of a passer-by,. 1017
Ticehurst, Judith E.
The matter of perception in the fiction of WO Mitchell, ...547
Tilgen, Jean
Crestomere-Sylvan Heights heritage,. 2858
Tillenius, Clarence
Kirby's gander,. 664
Tilley. Bethany Lutheran Church
Bethany Lutheran Church twenty-fifth anniversary, 1930-1955, ...426
Tillim, Sidney
Sidney Tillim, ... 1245
Tjart, David
An inquiry into the religious value orientations of public and private school students at the grade eight level, ...153

Toews, David Waltner- *see* Waltner-Toews, David
The earth is one body,. 1022
Tofield Historical Society
Tales of Tofield, ... 3195
Tofield Jubilee Committee
A concise history of Tofield and district, ... 3275
Toma, Darrell Michael
Alberta Grazing Associations, ... 3455
Tomahawk Trail Book Club
Tomahawk trails,. 3095
Tombs, Thomas Poole
Social problems of Edmonton, 1963 survey,. 1824
Trends in sucidal behavior,. 1825
Tomkins, Doreen Margaret
Alberta, where the mountains meet the plains, ... 2586
Tomkins, George S.
Alberta, where the mountains meet the plains, ... 2586
Tomyn, William
Alberta, bastion of freedom, ... 2151
Toogood, J.A.
For the record, ... 3456
Tookey, Olive
Below the flight path, ... 3360
Torhjelm, Gary Douglas
The urban hierarchy in Alberta, ... 1736
Toth, Nancy
Pattern without end, ... 1019
Touchings, Dawne
Nature trails in Edmonton, ... 1703
Toverud, Mrs. Alf
Let us not forget,. 3276
Townsend, Arthur Herbert
Cariboo country saints and shenanigans, ... 252
Tall tales that are true, ... 154
Tozer, Aiden Wilson
That incredible Christian, ... 155
Trace, Harry Douglas
An examination of some factors associated with the decline of the coal industry in Alberta, ... 2243
Tracie, Carl Joseph
Agricultural settlement in the south Peace River area, ... 3457
An analysis of three variables affecting farm location in the process of agricultural settlement,. 3458
Travers, T.H.E.
Science, technology and culture in historical perspective, ... 2746
Travis, John
The Rundle adventure story, ... 253
Travis, L.D.
History of local government, Lac St. Anne area, ... 2460

Treacy, Robert M.
Sandstone brick and wood, ... 3278
Tregillus, Eleanor
The science, the art and the spirit, ... 3375
Trench, Ruby G. Lea *see* Thompson, Ruby G. Lea (Trench)
Pioneers of Athabasca, ... 3274
Trnavskis, Boris
Internal accessibility in the Peace River area, Alberta, ... 2587
Passenger demand for a 1976 Q S T O L aircraft system in the Calgary-Edmonton corridor, ... 2354
Trochu History Book Committee
Remember when, ... 2973
Trochu. St. John's Lutheran Church
Our journey, ... 427
Trofimenkoff, Susan Mann
The twenties in western Canada, ... 2807
Trogen, George Gary
Budget reform in Alberta, ... 2446
Trost, Nick
Cardman's secrets, easy to perform, hard to detect, ... 1371
ESP session with Nick Trost, ... 1372
Nick Trost's card problems, ... 1373
Nick's routine with the cups and balls, ... 1374
Nick's table trix, ... 1375
Truscott, Graham
Every Christian's ministry, ... 156
Truss, Jan
Bird at the window, ... 799
The judgement of Clifford Sifton, ... 1092
Ooomerahgi Oh, and A very small rebellion, ... 1093
A very small rebellion, ... 800
Trussler, Norma Erdine
Educational programs for Indian adults in southern Alberta, ... 1511
Tsiapera, Maria
Generative studies in historical linguistics, ... 467
Tunney, Evelyn
Sisters of Service, Edson, Alberta, 1926-1976, ... 3383
Turnbull, Elizabeth
The pathfinders, ... 3279
Turner, Joan Iris
Edmonton and vicinity rural and urban youth, ... 1737
Turner, John Davenall
The artful codger, ... 1113
JD Turner, ... 1246
Tuttle, George M.
The story of St Stephen's, Edmonton, ... 254
Twa, Jeanne
Let's play northern pole, ... 1020
Twaits, William Osborn
Energy taxation, ... 2308

Twofeathers, Shannon
People of the buffalo, ... 1871
Tymchuk, Lee
Early Calgary friends,. 3280
Tyre, Robert
Lethbridge, the action city, ... 2152
Tyson, Basil
UFOs, ... 157
Udo, Reuben K.
Applied population geography, ... 2589
Uher, Lorna
Crow's black joy, ... 1021
Uhler, Russell S.
Oil and gas finding costs, ... 2309
Uhryn, Michael
Interest groups and the Alberta Labour Act, ... 2244
Ukrainian Canadian Research Foundation
Persistence and change, ... 1973
Ukrainian Pioneers' Association of Alberta
Ukrainians in Alberta, ... 2002
Ukrainian Women's Association of Canada
Ukrainian Canadiana,. 1136
Ukrainian Womens' Association of Canada. Olha Bassarab Branch
An introduction to Lesya Ukrainka, ... 536
Ulliac, Arvine (Plamondon)
Cinquantenaire de l'arrivée des pionniers à Gourin, 11 avril, 1914,. . 3281
Ume, Theo Azuka
Human rights awareness among certain socio-economic groups in Edmonton with implications for community development work, . . 1738
United Church of Canada. Westlock and District Pastoral Charge
The first fifty years, ... 428
University of Alberta
Inuit games and contests, ... 1247
A pictorial history of golden jubilee week, Edmonton and Calgary, October 26-November 1, 1958, ... 1608
University of Alberta. Archives
A guide to the Chancellor's papers, ... 1609
A guide to the papers of Louis Auguste Romanet, 1890's, 1900,. . . 2647
A guide to the President's papers,. 1610
A guide to the William Pearce papers, series 5, settlement, 1880-1927, 1611
A guide to the William Pearce papers, series 6, surveys, 1878-1928, . 2808
A guide to the William Pearce papers, series 7, irrigation, 1890-1927, 3459
University of Alberta. Committee for Social Research
The Metis in Alberta society, with special reference to social, economic and cultural factors associated with persistently high tuberculosis incidence, ... 1875
University of Alberta Conference on Literacy, October 22-23, 1976
Literature, language and culture, ... 531
University of Alberta. Department of Art and Design
JB Taylor landscapes,. 1243

University of Alberta. Department of English
Mag pil, ...576
University of Alberta. Department of Extension
Anagramatix, ...558
A study of commercial blight and the function of
Whyte Avenue, Edmonton,. 2202
University of Alberta. Department of Extension.
Advisory Committee on Learning Resources
The development of a Learning Resources Centre as a base
for the expansion of continuing education in Alberta, ... 40
University of Alberta. Department of Geography
Atlas of Alberta, ... 2655
Junior atlas of Alberta, ... 2659
University of Alberta. Faculty of Library Science
Education for librarianship, ... 34
University of Alberta. Faculty of Library Science. Class of 1972.
Frog 'n all, ... 41
University of Alberta. Practicum in Rapid Transit
An immediate alternative to the McKinnon Ravine Freeway, ... 2355
Light rapid transit, ... 2356
University of Alberta. Senate. Task Force on the Future of the Extension Function
On the future of the extension function, ... 1612
University of Alberta. Senate. Task Force on the State of Women
Report on academic women, ... 1613
University of Alberta. Senate. Task Force on University Entrance Requirements
The problem of quotas, ... 1614
Report, ... 1615
University of Calgary Archaeological Association
Aboriginal man and environments on the plateau of northwest
America, ... 2008
Diffusion and migration, their roles in cultural development, ... 2026
Early man and environments in northwest North America, ... 2027
Historical archaeology in northwestern North America, ... 2037
Papers from Conference on Canadian Archaeology Abroad, held at the
University of Calgary, November 23, 24, 25, 1973,. 2022
Post-pleistocene man and his environment on the northern plains, . . 2049
Primitive art and technology,. 2054
Problems in the prehistory of the North American subarctic, ... 2051
University of Lethbridge Art Gallery
John Will, Marvin Jones, ... 1250
Urchak, Stephen
The history of Two Hills, including the Lanuke District, ... 2904
Van Camp, Jack
Planning for urban wildlife, ... 3347
Van Der Mark, Christine
Honey in the rock, ...801
In due season, ...802
Van Deurzen, Anthony
An analysis of Alberta's beef cattle industry problems, ... 2245

Van Dyke, S.
Problems in the prehistory of the North American subarctic, ... 2051
Van Herk, Aritha
Judith A novel,. 803
When pigs fly, ... 804
Van Kirk, Sylvia Marian
The development of national park policy in Canada's national parks, 1885 to 1930, ... 2590
Van Pelt, Nancy L.
Parent education guide, ... 1759
Vandersteene, Roger
Wabasca, ... 2648
Vanek, Anthony L.
Aspects of subject-verb agreement, ... 519
A Doukhobor Russian lexical & dialectological questionnaire,. 520
Studies presented to Robert B Lees by his students, ... 459
Vassarely, Victor de
Vassarely, ... 1248
Vaughan, Louisa
The work of faith with power, ... 256
Vauxhall and Districts Book Committee
Where waters flow, ... 3282
Vegreville. St. Martin's School
50th Anniversary, 1907-1957, ... 1587
Verhagen, Matthew A.
Teachers' evaluation of religious education in the elementary schools of the Calgary Roman Catholic Separate Schools District, No 1, . . . 1512
Verkruysse, Patricia Louise
Small legacy of truth,. 548
Vermilion Oldtimers' Association
Vermilion memories, ... 3283
Veteran Historical Society
Pictorial album of Veteran, Loyalist and Hemaruka,. 2852
Veteran Jubilee Publicity Committee
Memoirs of Veteran, ... 3284
Veteran Regional History
Where the prairie meets the hills,. 2853
Vetter, Shirley
Where the prairie meets the hills,. 2853
Viking Historical Society
Let us not forget,. 3276
Villy, Barbara *see* Cormack, Barbara (Villy)
The house,. 631
Vimy. Our Lady of Victory Catholic Church
Cinquantenaire, golden jubilee, 1920-1970,. 429
Vitt, Kurt H.
Bruderfeld Moravian Church 75th anniversary, 1895-1970,. 430
Clement Hoyler, God's pacemaker for Moravians in Canada, ... 257
Heimtal Moravian Church, ... 431

Voitkiv, Mykhailyna
Ukrainian Catholic Women's League of Canada, ... 1850
Voyer, Sylvain
Edmonton had a beautiful river valley,. 1137
Vulcan and District Historical Society
Wheat country, ... 3285
Wade, Bryan
This side of the Rockies,. 1094
Wagland, Keith
Medalta, ... 2161
Wagner, Neil
Summer's bright blood, ...928
Wainwright. Gilt Edge Ladies Booster Club *see* Gilt Edge Ladies Booster Club
Buffalo trails and tales, ... 3100
Wainwright. Grace Lutheran Church
Commemorating fifty years of Christian service to Wainwright and District by Grace Church, 1908-1958, ...432
Walker, Bernal Ernest
G Fred, ... 1564
Public secondary education in Alberta,. 1588
Walker, Donovan R.
The Commonwealth Games management financial feasibility study, . 1704
Walker, Ella May
Fortress north, ...805
Walker, Ian
Some effects of continuing to provide subsidies for low income families Study, ... 1826
Walker, Margaret (Macleod)
Come down from yonder mountain, ...806
Walker, Marion Ruth
John Walker Barnett, first general secretary of the Alberta Teachers' Association,. 1589
Waltner-Toews, David
The earth is one body,. 1022
Walton, Robert N.
Lone Butte north, ... 3286
Wandering River Women's Institute.
Wandering River history book, 1968, ... 3287
Warburg and District Historical Society
Golden memories, Warburg and district, ... 2923
Ward, Edward Neville
Residential water use in the Hardisty district, Edmonton, Alberta,. . 2246
Ward, Roland Gerald
Country residential development in the Edmonton area to 1973, . . . 2591
Ward, Tom
Cowtown, ... 3288
Warner, Neil Morgan
Shoplifters in Bigstore, ... 1827
Warner Old Timers' Association
Warner pioneers, ... 3289

Warren, Ernest Herbert Falkland
Seventy south Alberta years, ... 3512
Warren, R.E.
The church in the valley, ... 433
Warren, Sara Evangeline (Matheson)
Andy the milkman, ... 807
Echoes from my song tree, ... 1023
Prairie panels, ... 1024
Songs of the island, ... 1025
Waskahegan Trail Association
The Waskahegan trail guide book, ... 1705
Waskatenau School
Waskatenau, 1867-1967, ... 3290
Wasylynchuk, Mary Ann
The development of women's field hockey in Alberta, 1962-1973, . . . 1706
Waterhole Old Timers Association
Waterhole and the land north of the Peace, ... 3135
Watson, George
Lethbridge Alberta's Golden Jubilee, ... 3291
Through the looking glass, ... 3292
Watson, Kenneth Frank
Landbanking in Red Deer, ... 2592
Watson, Sheila
The double hook, ... 808
Four stories, ... 809
Sheila Watson, a collection, ... 587
Watson, Wilfred
Friday's child, ... 1026
I begin with counting, ... 1027
The sorrowful Canadians and other poems, ... 1028
Watt, Carol Luanne
The role of a change agent as a factor in resource development in a reserve community, ... 2003
Waugh, Earle D.
Native religious traditions, ... 94
Wear, Robert Dalattin
Nomads versus cultivators, ... 2004
Webber, Frank
Code of the rangeland, ... 810
The curse of the wolf, ... 811
Grudge, ... 812
The northwest quarter of thirty-six, ... 3513
The publish it yourself author, ... 64
Twenty pebbles, and other stories, ... 813
Was it all a dream?, ... 2394
Webber, Franklyn Millard *see* Webber, Frank
Code of the rangeland, ... 810
Weber, Manasseh
Such was life, ... 3293

Webster, Douglas Richard
The incidence impact of a regional development program based on employment creation,. 2153
Weidenhamer, T. C.
The Alberta School Trustees' Association, ... 1590
Weih, G.P.
Golden dreams, story and drawings,. 645
Weikum, Edward
Don't call on me,. 1468
On the hill, ... 1469
Weinberger, A.M.
I escaped the holocaust, ... 258
Weinrich, John E.
Economic impact of the Canadian gas industry, local, provincial and regional, ... 2310
Weir, Joan
Career girl, ... 814
Wensel, Joan
The Alberta Women's Bureau, ... 1739
Werner, B.
Fort Edmonton, ... 2031
West of the 4th Historians Book Committee
West of the fourth, ... 3294
Westbourne International Industries
Impressionist paintings from the collection of Mr. and Mrs. J.A. Scrymgeour and Westbourne International Industries, ... 1178
Westbury, Marilyn Louise
The financing and implementation of community development programs by the Alberta government, ... 1740
Westerdale Willing Workers History Committee.
A trail grows dim, ... 3295
Western Association of Sociology and Anthropology
Canadian confrontations, ... 1873
Perspectives on regions and regionalism and other papers, ... 1729
Western Canada Research Project
A bibliography of selected theses on (sic) the Library of the University of Alberta relating to Western Canada, 1915-1965, ... 10
Western Canadian Studies Conference,. 1976
The Canadian West, ... 1716
Western Canadian Studies Conference, ... 1977
One century later, ... 1967
Western Canadian Studies Conference,. 1969
Prairie perspectives,. 2803
Western Canadian Studies Conference,. 1970
Prairie perspectives, 2, ... 2804
Western Canadian Studies Conference,. 1972
The twenties in western Canada, ... 2807
Western Canadian Studies Conference,. 1973
Western perspectives 1, ... 2809

Western Catholic Reporter(newspaper)
It's a new world, ... 61
Western Economics Opportunities Conference,. 1973
Follow-up on the Western Economic Opportunities Conference, ... 2095
A report on the Western Economic Opportunities Conference,. 2098
Western Economics Opportunity Conference, ... 1978
Federal expenditures in the Western Region, ... 2094
Western Library Associations Regional Conference, 1st, Calgary, 1964.
Proceedings, ... 42
Western Retail Lumbermen's Association
75 years, ... 2247
Westervelt, Anne Carol Forrester
Farmers' markets, ... 2248
Wetaskiwin. Bethel Lutheran Church
Bethel Lutheran Church, Wetaskiwin, Alberta, 1908-1973, ...434
Wetaskiwin. Calvary Lutheran Church
Calvary Lutheran Church, 1898-1973, 75th anniversary, ...435
Wetaskiwin. Clear Vista School
Clear Vista, ... 1532
Wetaskiwin. First United Church
Anniversary church history, 1893-1973, ...436
Wetaskiwin R.C.M.P. Centennial Committee
Siding 16, ... 3215
Wetton, Cecilia
The promised land, ... 3296
Wheatley, Sheila Kathleen
The effect of an alcoholic treatment program on certain
alienation and personality dimensions, ... 1828
Wheatsheaf Women's Institute
Pioneer heritage of Kirriemuir, Altario and Compeer, ... 3199
Wheeler, William
The Calgary Challengers, ...717
The map-maker, ...826
Wop May, bush pilot, ...599
Whillans, James William
First in the West,. 2649
Whishaw, Laura
As far as you'll take me,. 2650
Whitaker, Muriel
Children's literature, ...549
Great Canadian adventure stories, ...570
Great Canadian animal stories, ...571
Pernilla in the perilous forest, ...815
White, Helene R.
A time for fun,. 1710
White, Joseph M.
5 micro-mental programs, ... 1376
Whitehead, Jimmy Carl
Country residential growth in the Calgary region, ... 2593

Whitely, Opal Stanley
Opal, ... 2651
Whitesell, Faris Daniel
Great personal workers, ...158
The Proverbs, ...159
Whiting, Peter Gouinlock
An economic evaluation of recreation in Alberta provincial parks in the South Saskatchewan River basin, ... 1707
Whitla Community Clubs
Tribute to Whitla pioneers, ... 3297
Whitlock, An
An Whitlock, ... 1249
Whitney, G.
Fluid filosofies of future fools, ...568
Whittle, F.H.
St. James United Church, Edmonton, Alberta, 1854 to 1979, ...437
Whyte, Jon
The Rockies,. 2644
Three 3,. 1018
Weathered wood,. 2899
Whyte, Thomas
Dismissal leading to lustfulness, ... 1095
Free beer, ... 1096
Wiebe, Rudy
Alberta, a celebration,. 2652
The blue mountains of China, ...816
Far as the eye can see, ... 1097
First and vital candle,. 817
Getting here,. 569
Peace shall destroy many, ...818
The scorched wood people,. 819
Stories from Western Canada A selection, ...583
The temptation of Big Bear, ...820
Where is the voice coming from?,. 821
Wiedeman, Joyce
Saga of Schuler stalwarts, ... 3298
Wiedrick, Laurence George
Student use of school libraries in Edmonton open area elementary schools, ... 43
Wiggins, F.
History of local government, Lac St Anne area,. 2460
Wiggins, Frank W.
The immigrant, an autobiography, ... 2733
Wilcer, Armin
A study of the degree of implementation of recommendations pertaining to the control of education made by the Royal Commisssion on Education in Alberta, 1959, ... 1513
Wilk, Stephen William
A brief history of the Christian faith in Alberta and in the Airdrie pastoral charge of the United Church of Canada,. 438

One day's journey, ... 3299
Wilkie, David Robert
Fitness and Amateur Sport Act in Alberta,. 1708
Wilkin, Karen
Art in Alberta, Paul Kane to the present, ... 1166
Modern painting in Canada, ... 1189
Wilkinson, Florence Gertrude
The Indians of Alberta hear the Gospel, ... 260
Will, John
John Will, Marvin Jones, ... 1250
Williams, Allan Geoffrey
Commuter expenditure patterns in the Edmonton region, ... 2154
Williams, C.D.
Sabretache, ... 2751
Williams, Frances Jane *see* Fraser, Frances Jane (Williams)
The bear who stole the chinook and other stories, ... 2073
Williams, Fred C.
The fifth horseman,. 822
Williams, James Davies
A history of the Edmonton, Dunvegan and British Columbia
railway, 1907-1929,. 2357
Williams, Jeffery
Princess Patricia's Canadian Light Infantry, ... 2760
Williams, Mabel Berta
The Banff-Jasper highway descriptive guide, ... 2696
Williams, Vicky
Calgary, then and now, ... 3300
Williamson, Hector
Interface, ... 574
Interface tu, ... 575
Williamson, Moncrieff
Robert Harris, 1849-1919,. 1138
Through Canadian eyes,. 1251
Willihnganz, R.C.
The 16 hour counselor(!), ... 1829
Willing, Will
Grace Lutheran Church 50th anniversary, 1928-1978, ... 439
Willis, Geoffrey Allan
Development of transportation in the Peace River region of
Alberta and British Columbia, with an evaluation of present day
rail and road commodity flow patterns, ... 2358
Willison, Gladys A.
Land of the Chinook, ... 823
Stars in time, ... 2448
Willms, Arthur Henry
Public utility regulation in Alberta, ... 2311
Willow Creek Historical Society
Echoes of Willow Creek,. 2979
Willsie, Merle
White Creek echoes, ... 3301

Wilson, Agnes Kathleen *see* Teviotdale, Agnes Kathleen (Wilson)
Vast prospects and splendid songs, ... 3268
Wilson, Betty
To teach this art,. 3384
Wilson, Dora
Cherished memories, ... 3302
Wilson, F.N.
The spirit at Hidden Valley, ... 2080
Wilson, Leonard Samuel
Some factors relating to the attraction of manufacturing
industries to the province of Alberta, ... 2155
Wilson, LeRoy John
The education of the farmer,. 3460
Perren Baker and the United Farmers of Alberta,. 1514
Wilson, M.E.
A Medonte pioneer and his famous son, ... 2510
Wilson, Robert Nathaniel
Ethnological notes on Blackfoot and Blood Indians, ... 2065
Wilson, Thomas Edmund
Trail blazer of the Canadian Rockies, ... 2653
Windsor, Robert Francis
The campus fringe of University of Alberta, ... 2594
Winfield Conroy Club *see* Conroy Club
Trail blazers, ... 3277
Winnipeg Art Gallery
William Kurelek,. 1217
Winspear, Frances George
Out of my mind, ... 2734
Winter, G.R.
Stimulants to social development in slow growing regions, ... 1734
Winterburn Women's Institute.
Memory trails to Winterburn, ... 3303
Wipf, J.B.
Handbook for sermons on Bible, ... 91
Wolfart, Hans Christoph
Meet Cree, ...502
An outline of Plains Cree morphology,. 503
Women of Unifarm
Family laws for Albertans,. 2479
Women's Christian Temperance Union, *see* Alberta Women's
Christian Temperance Union
The story of the years, ... 1763
Wong, Robert Allan Gerald
Conflict between cross-country skiers and snowmobilers in Alberta, . 1709
Wong, William Ho-Ching
Migration patterns in west-central Alberta,. 2595
Woo, Helen Mun-Ying
Population-store relationships over time in north-west Calgary,
1949-1968, ... 2249

Wood, Cornelia R.
The story of the Alberta Women's Institutes, 1909-1955, ... 1851
Wood, George
The journey goes on , ... 1252
Wood, Kerry
Bessie the coo, ...824
The boy and the buffalo, ...825
A corner of Canada, ... 3304
The creek, ... 3335
The great chief, Maskepetoon, warrior of the Crees, ... 2843
The Icelandic-Canadian poet, Stephan Gudmundsson Stephansson, 1853-1927, ...550
A letter from Red Deer, ... 3305
A lifetime of service George Moon, ... 2250
The map-maker, ...826
The medicine man, ...827
Mickey the beaver, and other stories, ...828
The Queen's cowboy, .829
Red Deer, ... 3306
Samson's long ride, .830
A time for fun, ... 1710
Wild winter, ...831
Willowdale, ...832
Wood, Marjorie M.
Bessie the coo, ...824
The creek, ... 3335
Woodward, Kenny
Phantini's lost book of mental secrets, ... 1290
Words Unlimited Writers Group
Alberta writers speak, .557
Wordsworth, William
The daffodils, ... 1389
Workshop on religion and ethnicity, University of Calgary, ... 1977
Religion and ethnicity, .160
Wormington, Hannah Marie
An introduction to the archaeology of Alberta, Canada, ... 2066
Worth, Walter H.
Before six, ... 1515
Woychuk, John Kenneth
Tax-exempt property, ... 2157
Wright, Bruce William
A proxemic analysis of the Iroquoian settlement pattern, ... 2067
Wright, Helen Kerr
Images, ... 1029
Nellie McClung and women's rights, ... 1760
Wright, John G.
Recommended guidelines for the development of the Parkland Regional Library, ... 27
Wright, Laurali Rose (Bunny)
Neighbours, ...833

Wright, P.F.
Moose magic, ... 3333
Wright, Robert W.
An analysis of the liquified petroleum gas industry in Alberta, . . . 2312
Wright, T. Page
The L W card mysteries, ... 1377
Writing for Pleasure Group.
Settling matters, ...581
Wuttunee, William I.C.
Ruffled feathers, ... 2005
Yakymyshyn, Severian
Mundare, yesterday and today, ...403
Yanda, Doris Elizabeth
Canadian tapestry, ... 1030
My thoughts fly to Ukraine, ... 1031
The songs of my heart, ... 1032
Yardley-Jones, John
All our own work, ... 1103
Second offence, ... 1104
Up for the third time, ... 1105
Yates, Norman
Norman Yates,. 1253
Yeager, John
Dots Magic, ... 1378
Yedlin, Tova
Alberta's pioneers from Eastern Europe, ... 2006
Yeoford Ladies Club
Trail blazers, ... 3277
Yorath, Mary (Smith)
West, ... 1033
Young, Delbert A.
According to Hakluyt,. 2747
The ghost ship,. 834
The mounties, ...835
Young, G.S.
Southern Alberta A regional perspective,. 3088
Young, J.
A short history of Westminster Prebyterian Church,. 440
Young, Robert
Indian treaties and the law, ... 2480
Youngstown Women's Institute.
Youngstown and district pioneers,. 3307
Yuen, Abraham Chick-To
Generating citizen involvement,. 1830
Yuen, Kildy Wing-Han
Preventive social services as community development, ... 1831
Yurko, William John
On being a Conservative, ... 2395
Zarn, George
Prairie boys afloat, ... 2761

Zaslow, Morris
Alberta's story,. 2844
Zella Women's Institute.
Zella remembers from oil lamps to oil wells, ... 3308
Zentner, Henry
The Indian identity crisis, ... 2007
Prelude to administrative theory, ... 1741
Zieber, George Henry
Inter- and intra-city location patterns of oil offices for
Calgary and Edmonton, 1950-1970, ... 2313
Ziehl, Gary
Criminal forever!,. 161
Zilynsky, Orest
An anthology of Ukrainian lyric poetry, ... 559
Zirkie, Larry E.
The creative world of puppetry,. 1260
Zwicky, Arnold M.
Studies out in left field, ... 465
Zyla, Wolodymyr T.
The burning wood, ... 537
The poetry of Yar Slavutych,. 551

TITLE INDEX

TITLE INDEX

The A B C of sculpture. 1139
Abandoned to Christ. 102
Abbé Quirion. 162
An abbreviated history of the Ponoka United Church of Canada.. 409
Aberhart of Alberta. 2421
Abide in Christ.. 116
The abiding presence. 101
Aboriginal man and environments on the plateau of northwest America. . . . 2008
Abraham Cristall. 1880
A.C. Leighton. 1233
Access - housing. 1721
Accessions, 1972-1974. 1160
According to Hakluyt. 2747
The accuracy of folk knowledge concerning Alberta Indians, Hutterites, and Ukrainians. 1952
Acme memories. 2846
The Acme story, 1910-1960. 3150
Across the Smoky. 3165
An activity systems impact analysis of the Edmonton Transit System strike, 1973-1974. 2352
The Adamson saga, 1536-1936. 2697
Address by S.M. Gossage. Chairman, Metric Commission to the Canadian Gas Association, Calgary, 18 October, 1973. 2193
Addresses. 2100
Administrative decentralization. 3443
Adolph Gottlieb acrylics on paper. 1205
Adrift.. 680
The adventure of Cynthia and her friends. 686
Adventures in acting. 1034
Adventures in two worlds. 3508
Adventures into unknowns. 719
Adventures of the midnight janitor. 864
Adventuring for Christ. 196
The affair at Timber Lake. 603
Afterpiece. 636
The agrarian frontier near Red Deer and Lacombe, Alberta, 1884-1914. . . 2871
Agricultural policy in Alberta. 3434
Agricultural settlement in the south Peace River area. 3457
Agriculture innovations, county of St. Paul, Alberta. 3440
Air loom. 974
Air Museum of Canada, Calgary, Canada. 2314
Airborne from Edmonton. 2349
Aircraft noise and residential property values. 2145
Airwaves, sealevel, landlock. 975
Alberta. 2617
Alberta, a celebration. 2652
Alberta, a natural history. 3320
Alberta, Aberhart and Social Credit. 2401

Alberta album of curling. 1654
Alberta alcoholism treatment programs, community development
and citizen involvement. 1807
Alberta archaeology. 2040
Alberta, bastion of freedom. 2151
The Alberta butter industry. 2162
The Alberta Child Welfare client system and the decision-making process. . 1778
The Alberta community health self-study outline. 3359
Alberta contemporary drawings. 1161
Alberta days. 872
Alberta diamond jubilee anthology. 552
Alberta divorce guide. 2475
The Alberta Fine Option Program. 2476
Alberta foothills. 3474
The Alberta golden jubilee anthology. 553
Alberta Grazing Associations. 3455
Alberta growth. 2123
Alberta hail research a major agricultural disaster. 3397
Alberta hog market, conduct and performance. 2211
Alberta Improvement District 124. 1874
Alberta in fiction. 522
Alberta incorporation guide. 2492
Alberta Indian Education Center. 1494
The Alberta Indian, his past, his present, his future. 1900
Alberta Indian youth. 1882
Alberta labour. 2174
Alberta, land of freedom and opportunity. 2815
Alberta landlord-tenant relations (residential tenancies). 2485
The Alberta Motor Association. 2326
Alberta normal schools. 1602
Alberta place guide (and) Alberta population maps. 2662
The Alberta press and the conscription issue in the
First World War, 1914-1918. 2378
Alberta, profile of development. 2099
Alberta, province of opportunity. 2108
Alberta real estate buying/selling guide. 2491
Alberta revisited. 2619
Alberta school districts in pioneer days. 1565
The Alberta School Trustees' Association. 1590
Alberta short run crude oil supply, 1972. 2265
The Alberta Social Credit Party. 2397
The Alberta Society of Artists, 1975. 1162
Alberta, the emerging giant. 2608
Alberta, the pioneer years. 2826
Alberta was my beat. 52
Alberta, western treasure chest. 2603
Alberta, where the mountains meet the plains. 2586
Alberta women in the 1920's. 1745
The Alberta Women's Bureau. 1739
Alberta Women's Institutes, 1909-1954. 3391

Alberta world reflections. 1163
Alberta writers speak. 557
Alberta '73. 1164
Albertaines images et autres griffonnages. 955
Alberta's coal industry, 1919. 2158
Alberta's County of Mountain View. 2847
Alberta's Department of Neglected Children, 1909-1929.
A case study in child saving. 1782
Alberta's fight for freedom. 2433
Alberta's golden jubilee. 3113
Alberta's golden jubilee edition, 1905-1955. 3115
Alberta's oil sands in the energy supply picture. 2270
Alberta's petroleum paternity. 2251
Alberta's pioneers from Eastern Europe. 2006
Alberta's progress. 2442
Alberta's role in meeting Canada's energy requirements. 2137
Alberta's story. 2844
Al'bom Ukrain'skoi molochars'kö Kooperatsii. "Maslosoiuz", 1902-1942. . . 3428
Album souvenir. 336
Album souvenir St. Isidore, 1953-78.. 419
Album souvenir, 1928-1978. 2948
The alcoholic offender - whose responsibility? 1800
Alex Janvier, Edmonton Art Gallery, June 3-July 3, 1973. 1211
Alexander Cameron Rutherford and his influence on
Alberta's educational program. 1605
Alive and free. 121
All Alberta '69. 1165
All of Baba's children. 1935
All our own work. 1103
All Saints' Anglican Cathedral, 1875-1975. 399
All the way over. 2729
Allison Procter, O.B.E., LL.D. 1880-1964. 1834
Almighty Voice. 1076
Along the Burnt Lake Trail. 2906
Along the fireguard trail. 3123
Along the Victoria trail. 3254
Along the way. 985
Along the Zarorozhian places.. 989
Alpine Canada. 3326
Alternative land uses in southwestern Alberta. 2560
Alternative methods of estimating benefits. 1687
Alternatives. 2363
Alternatives to poverty and welfare in Alberta. 1812
Always a Strathcona. 2753
The amazing world of mentalism. 1297
American Indian graphic symbols and their adaptation in art. 2060
Among the Blackfoot and Sarcee. 247
Among Ukrainian pioneers of Alberta. 1956
Anagramatix.. 558
An analysis and evaluation of land use in the special areas of Alberta. . . . 2572

An analysis of a group of prairie settlements north east of Calgary. 2585
An analysis of Alberta's beef cattle industry problems. 2245
An analysis of the Edmonton Social Planning Council. 1820
An analysis of the Human Resources Development Authority in Alberta. . . . 1789
An analysis of the iron and steel industry in Alberta. 2241
An analysis of the liquified petroleum gas industry in Alberta. 2312
An analysis of the Public Assistance Appeal System in Alberta. 1773
An analysis of the relationship between sale values of public grazing leases and sale values of comparable private range lands in southern Alberta. 3403
An analysis of the sulphur industry in Alberta. 2166
An analysis of three variables affecting farm location in the process of agricultural settlement. 3458
An analysis of tourist travel to the province of Alberta. 2231
Ancient Hispanic inscriptions. 2009
And mighty women too. 2715
And we came after. 417
Andy and the gopher. 731
Andy Russell's adventures with wild animals. 3327
Andy the milkman. 807
Anecdotal history of Calgary Separate Schools. 1520
Angels on Devil's Island. 1932
Anglican beginnings in and about Edmonton. 232
The Anglican Church in Calgary. 180
The animals of the wilds.. 468
Annexation and amalgamation in the territorial expansion of Edmonton and Calgary. 2455
Anniversary. 337
Anniversary church history, 1893-1973. 436
Anniversary in gold. 2731
Answers to questions. 1284
The ante-room. 637
An anthology of Ukrainian lyric poetry. 559
An anthology of Ukrainian poetry in Canada, 1898-1973.. 560
Any second now. 1313
Aperçu historique de l'A.C.F.A. 1859
Apparitions, animations, and aces. 1287
Applied population geography. 2589
Apprenticeship discontinuance in three trade areas in the province of Alberta. 2234
An approach to planning river valley trails. 1647
April weather. 1386
Archaeological reconnaissance north of the Brooks range in northeastern Alaska. 2058
An archaeological resource inventory of Waterton Lakes National Park and preliminary archaeological report for 1971. 2055
The archaeology and prehistory of southern Alberta as reflected by ceramics. Late prehistoric and protohistoric cultural developments. . . 2019
Archaeology in Alberta. 2010
Archaeology of the Cormie Ranch Site, an interim report. 2043

Archaeology of the Peace Hills area of central Alberta, Canada. 2063
The archaeology of two Hudson's Bay Company posts. 2048
Archibald Thorburn. Paintings from the collection of Glenbow-Alberta Institute, Calgary, and Riveredge Foundation, Calgary. 1244
Armando Brasini. 1149
Arnold Lupson photographic collection, Calgary, Alberta, 1926-1947. . . . 1905
Around the Lower Peace. 3210
Around you. 561
Arrangements of alphabet Cree and syllabic symbols.. 469
Arrangment (sic) of oral Cree for beginners. 470
The Arrowwood story (Mistsa-Katpiskoo). 2857
Art in Alberta, Paul Kane to the present. 1166
The art of cold reading. 1321
The art of communication. 1091
The art of escape. 1346
The artful codger. 1113
An arts council in your community? 1116
As far as you'll take me. 2650
As grace is given. 213
As it happened. 1832
As long as the sun shines, the rivers flow and the grass grows. 1853
As the wheel turns. 3203
As the years go by. 3098
As we remember Big Valley. 3152
Asian landscapes, as seen by a Japanese pilgrim. 2645
Aspects de l'histoire et de l'éconmie de Falher. 2515
Aspects of alienation in Alberta. 2382
Aspects of intra-urban mobility, Calgary, 1963-68. 2348
Aspects of subject-verb agreement.. 519
The assimilation of Arab Muslims in Alberta. 1933
The assimilation of Ugandan Asians in Calgary. 1964
Asters still blooming. 986
At the end of the road.. 868
At the seventy-fifth milestone. 267
At your service, part one. 2859
At your service, part two. 2860
The Athabasca Landing Trail. 2969
Atlas of Alberta. 2655
Atomic feelings.. 895
The attic. 1073
Attitudes of clients and counsellors toward the Edmonton Family Court Conciliation Project. 1742
Attitudes of selected students at the University of Alberta toward physical activity. 1624
Attitudes toward identity in a Ukrainian parish. 1891
Au pays des Peaux-de-Lièvres. 172
Aunt Gene's ramblings. 966
Autobiography and people I have met along the highways and byways. . . . 3486
Autosegmental account of phonological emphasis. 447
Awasis book. 471

BA welcomes you to the new Pincher Creek Gas processing and sulphur plant, October 15th, 1958. 2253
Babylondromat. 976
Back o' Baffuf. 3492
Background papers and proceedings. 2091
Backtrack on old trails. 63
The badge and the blotter. 2496
Badlands. 706
Baker Lake prints/estampes. 1167
Ballachey, Besant, Bienvenue, Clark, Crockett, Gallie, Graff, Hohn, Mable, Roberts, Robertson, Van Wyk on paper. 1141
Ballad of a stone picker. 777
Bands by the Bow. 1381
Banff. 2575
Banff, Canada, proposed site for 1968 Winter Olympic Games. 2667
Banff, Canada, requests. 2599
Banff, Canada's first national park. 3122
Banff National Park. 2597
Banff panorama, a symphonic suite. 1444
Banff prehistory. 2021
The Banff purchase. 1122
Banff Springs. 3218
The Banff-Jasper highway descriptive guide. 2696
Banff's Christmas wish. 658
Bang! 1292
The Baptist story in Western Canada. 250
The Baptist Union of Western Canada.. 205
Barbara Ballachey. 1147
Barefoot days. 3469
Bargaining unit determination in Alberta. 2205
Basic make-up for magicians. 1348
Basilian Brothers. 166
The Basilian priest. 167
The battle at Belly River. 2831
Battle Bend pioneers. 2873
The battle for the Bay. 2345
The battle hymn of the Dominion and other poems. 1006
The Battle River country. 3047
The Battle River Valley. 3130
Bawlf Lutheran, 1902-1972. 271
Be it ever so humble. 3244
The bear who stole the chinook and other stories. 2073
The beast in the bag and Wild West circus. 1052
Beautiful fields. 3148
Beautiful Red Deer. One step. 1448
The Beaver Creek site. 2061
Beaverlodge Artists. 1115
Beaverlodge to the Rockies. 3253
Beavertales. 2900
Beef procurement by Edmonton restaurants. 2188

Before six. 1515
Beginnings. 1004
The beginnings of Lutheran Church, Canada, covering the years 1941 to 1964. 242
Behold the shining mountains. 2554
Behold your God. 126
Beiseker's golden heritage. 3232
Belle Anne of Pine Point.. 754
The Belly River. 2052
Below the flight path. 3360
Bénédiction des cloches de la paroisse-cathédrale de Saint Paul, Alberta, Dimanche, le 26 juin 1960. 321
Les Bérubés de Beaumont. 2699
Bert Borch. 1148
The Bessarabian German dialect in Medicine Hat, Alberta. 448
Bessie the coo. 824
The best Edmonton stories. 2926
Best in the west by a damsite, 1900-1940. 2870
Best Mounted Police stories. 562
The best of Bob Edwards. 48
Bethany Lutheran Church twenty-fifth anniversary, 1930-1955. 426
Bethel Lutheran Church, Wetaskiwin, Alberta, 1908-1973. 434
The betrayal. 703
Between the Red and the Rockies. 3420
Beyond exceptional pass. 1230
Beyond the dark river. 688
Beyond the Great Slave Lake. 3488
Beyond the tangled mountain.. 761
Bible history & prophecies. 109
A bibliography of African linguistics. 3
Bibliography of material relating to southern Alberta published to 1970. 8
Bibliography of primary sources for classroom study of the history of Alberta. . 11
A bibliography of selected theses on (sic) the Library of the University of Alberta relating to Western Canada, 1915-1965. 10
A bibliography of socio-economic studies on rural Alberta, Canada. 9
A bibliography of the Prairie Provinces to 1953. 12
Big Bear, Indian patriot. 2781
Big Hill country. 2945
The Big Horn School District. 3231
The big tough expensive job. 2284
The Big Valley story. 3015
Biggest sellout in history. 2268
Bilingualism, biculturalism & education. 1476
Bill Miner, train robber. 1764
Billion barrel oil swindle. 783
Bird at the window. 799
The birds and birders of Beaverhills Lake. 3321
The birds of Alberta. 3331
Birds of prey. 1193
The birken tree.. 977

Bishop Vital Grandin, Oblate of Mary Immaculate, first bishop of St. Albert (Alberta), Canada. 173
The black bonspiel of Wullie MacCrimmon.. 738
The black candle, by Emily Murphy (Janey Canuck). 1809
Black gold with grit. 2266
The Blackburn story. 2700
The Blackfeet Confederacy. 1903
The Blackfoot alphabet, with exercises.. 501
Blackfoot craftworker's book. 1918
Blackfoot Crossing. 785
Blackfoot ghost dance. 72
Blackfoot people. 1919
Blackfoot shaking tent.. 145
A Blackfoot winter count. 73
Blacksmith of God. 174
Blazing the old cattle trail. 3421
The Blood people, a division of the Blackfoot confederacy. 1920
Blood red the sun. 2817
The bloodied toga.. 675
Blooming prairie. 3166
The blue and gold. 1439
Blue flame in the foothills. 187
The blue mountains of China.. 816
Blue Pete in the badlands. 601
Blueberry Mountain history. 2942
The blue-eyed sheiks. 2267
Boats and barges on the Belly. 2340
Bob Blair's pipline. 2252
The bold heart. 764
Bonnie McSmithers is at it again! 593
Bonnie McSmithers you're driving me dithers.. 594
Bonnyville in question, 1975. 1861
The book about nothing. 695
The book of Catullus of Verona done into English verse by William Hardy Alexander. 840
Book of definition.. 968
A book of Protestant saints.. 202
The book of Thoth. 1314
Boomtime. 2783
Booze. 1790
Born again.. 67
Bow Island, 1912-1962, 50th anniversary. 2881
Bow River Lodge, no.1, Calgary, Alta.. 1837
The Bow River Range, 1898-1974, JY. 3494
Bowness Golden Jubilee, 1911-1961. 3176
Bowtell tales to 1976. 3214
The box beyond. 1040
The boy and the buffalo. 825
The boy from Winnipeg. 2784
The boy in buckskins. 596

Boy who has a horse. . . . 1068
The boy who ran away. . . . 765
Boycott against Alberta. . . . 2149
Brad Forrest's Calgary adventure. . . . 720
Brands and how to read them. . . . 3449
Bread enough. . . . 127
Breakaway.. . . . 657
Brick's Hill, Berwyn and beyond. . . . 3050
The bride & groom waltz. . . . 1453
Bride of the gorilla. . . . 1035
The bridge of fire.. . . . 665
Bridgeland Riverside memories. . . . 1579
Bridges of friendship. . . . 1941
Bridging the years, Carmangay and district. . . . 2922
A brief history of Delburne United Church, 1903 to 1958. . . . 304
Brief history of Emmaus Lutheran Congregation, Brightview, Alberta, and Zion Lutheran Congregation, Peace Hill, Alberta. . . . 276
Brief history of Foremost, 1913-1963. . . . 3124
A brief history of the Christian faith in Alberta and in the Airdrie pastoral charge of the United Church of Canada. . . . 438
A brief history of the petroleum industry in Canada. . . . 2254
A brief history of the Rocky Mountains. . . . 3056
Broken bread. . . . 88
Brooks. . . . 2967
Bruce O'Neil. . . . 1227
Bruderfeld Moravian Church 75th anniversary, 1895-1970. . . . 430
Buckboard to brotherhood. . . . 169
Bucking poles and butter churns. . . . 3179
Buckskin brigadier. . . . 725
Budget reform in Alberta. . . . 2446
Buffalo Coulee progress (1902-1967). . . . 2902
Buffalo days and nights. . . . 2777
The Buffalo Head. . . . 3499
Buffalo trails and tales. . . . 3100
Bugles in the hills.. . . . 683
Bummy peepee in the toto. . . . 1051
Buried treasures. . . . 2936
The burning wood. . . . 537
Bush homestead girl. . . . 755
Bush pilot with a brief case. . . . 2342
The business career of R. B. Bennett, 1897-1927. . . . 2206
But we are exiles. . . . 707
The butte stands guard. . . . 3257
By canoe from Toronto to Fort Edmonton in 1872 among the Iroquois and Ojibways, with a chapter on winter in Canada, by An anonymous traveler. . . . 2605
By the sea. . . . 1074
Byzantine churches of Alberta. . . . 1133
The Cactus Flower site and the McKean complex in Alberta. . . . 2016
Calahoo trails. . . . 2908

Calgary. 3241
Calgary - in sandstone. 2959
Calgary. A poem. 836
Calgary, Alberta, Canada. Her industries and resources. 2168
Calgary. An illustrated history. 3011
Calgary, an urban study. 2516
The Calgary and Edmonton Railway and the 'Edmonton Bulletin'. 2331
Calgary applies for the X Olympic Winter Games, 1978. 2606
Calgary Aquinas studies. 65
Calgary Branch, Alberta Northwest Territories Division, The Canadian
Red Cross Society. 3352
Calgary carriage collection. 2324
Calgary cavalcade from fort to fortune. 3129
The Calgary Challengers. 717
Calgary city jail. 926
Calgary College, 1912-1915. 1606
The Calgary craft union movement, 1900-1920. 2240
Calgary General Hospital, 1890-1955. 3350
Calgary Golf and Country Club 75 anniversary. 1633
The Calgary Herald's tales of the old town. 3154
Calgary, metropolitan structure and influence. 2169
Calgary printmakers. 1168
The Calgary public school system, 1939-1969. 1549
Calgary Stampede. 1667
Calgary stampede chuckwagon roundup. 1449
Calgary, then and now. 3300
The Calgary Town Council, 1884-1895. 2456
Calgary 100. 3205
The Calgary-Edmonton, Edmonton-Calgary trail. 2321
Calgary's Anglican cathedral. 309
Calgary's finest. 2503
Calgary's great stampede show. A poem. 837
Calgary's stone frigate, H.M.C.S. Tecumseh, 1923-1973. 2748
Calgary's 'temple of knowledge'.. 21
Calvary Lutheran Church, 1898-1973, 75th anniversary. 435
A cameo of the west. 3248
The Cameron Commission - two years after. 1472
The Cameron Commission ten years after. 1483
Camp Mockingbird. 3034
Camping perception and camping satisfaction in Alberta Provincial Parks. . 1657
The campus fringe of University of Alberta. 2594
Campus in the clouds. 1591
Canada. 2801
Canada West Foundation. 2402
Canada x ten. 1169
Canada's mountain national parks. 2692
Canada's resources and the national interest. 2279
Canada's worst mine disaster. 2811
Canada's 100 birthday verse. 957
The Canadian bayonet. 2755

Canadian confrontations. . . . 1873
Canadian cornography. . . . 1109
Canadian languages in their social context. . . . 445
The Canadian national parks, today and tomorrow. . . . 2524
Canadian national parks, today and tomorrow, conference 2. . . . 2525
Canadian Pacific in the Rockies. . . . 2317
Canadian parks in perspective. . . . 2526
The Canadian petroleum industry. . . . 2285
The Canadian petroleum industry, achievements and prospects. . . . 2281
Canadian poetry. . . . 917
The Canadian Prairie Provinces from 1870 to 1950. . . . 1717
The Canadian Rockies. Early travels and explorations. . . . 2825
The Canadian Rockies trail guide. . . . 2689
Canadian tapestry. . . . 1030
The Canadian West. . . . 1716
The Canadian West in fiction. . . . 532
Canadian Western Natural Gas Company Limited, 1912-1972. . . . 2257
Les canadiens français de la région de Saint-Paul. . . . 2892
Candelight years. . . . 2933
A candle in the grub box. . . . 3483
Canmore, the story of an era. . . . 2856
Cantata sacra. . . . 1387
Captives of the faceless drummer. . . . 1085
The Carbon murders mystery. . . . 1765
Cardman's secrets, easy to perform, hard to detect. . . . 1371
Cardston diamond jubilee, 1887-1962, jubilee souvenir. . . . 2921
Cardston 75th anniversary, 1887-1962. . . . 3116
Career girl.. . . . 814
Cariboo country saints and shenanigans. . . . 252
The Carstairs United Church, 1906-1956. . . . 308
The case history of Alberta's oil. . . . 2269
The case of the nameless corpse.. . . . 697
A case study in economic development. . . . 2093
A case study of the success of settlement in a southern Peace River district. . 2571
Catch them all from Calgary. . . . 1635
The Catholic revolution. . . . 142
The cattle compact. . . . 3464
The causes of labour disputes in Alberta, 1955-1962. . . . 2237
Ceiriog capers. . . . 913
Celebrate with Castor, 1910-1960. . . . 2929
Centenaire de Saint-Albert. . . . 3266
The centennial magic book. . . . 1310
Central business district employment in Edmonton, 1961-1967. . . . 2233
Certain traditions. . . . 1170
The challenge of life. . . . 2722
Chandu's magic variations. . . . 1281
Change in a central place system. . . . 2159
Changes in land use patterns in downtown Calgary, 1953-1969. . . . 2584
Changing rural attitudes. . . . 1714
The changing scene. . . . 2937

Changing visions - the Canadian landscape. . . . 1171
Chaps and chinooks. . . . 2901
The characteristics of Edmonton welfare recipients in relation to employability and labour force classification. . . . 2196
Charcoal's world. . . . 1886
Charles Bowen. . . . 211
Charles M. Russell, 1864-1926. . . . 1237
Charles Ora Card, pioneer and colonizer. . . . 209
Charlo's People. . . . 1921
Chatter chips from Beaver Dam Creek. . . . 2917
Chautauga in Canada. . . . 1257
Cherished memories. . . . 3302
Chester and Bentham. . . . 1155
Chesterfield House and the Bow River Expedition. . . . 2779
Chief Mountain. . . . 198
Chief Mountain country. . . . 3237
Chief Shaking Spear rides again. . . . 1058
Child of God.. . . . 125
Child of the morning. . . . 662
Children in the sun. . . . 722
Children of the pioneers. . . . 3510
Children's literature.. . . . 549
Children's participation in the marketplace in selected jurisdictions of Alberta. . . . 2130
Children's urban landscapes in Huntington Hills, Calgary. . . . 2567
Chinese urban communities in southern Alberta, 1885-1925. . . . 1884
Chinook. . . . 1044
Chinook arch. . . . 563
Chinook country. . . . 2641
Chinook Ridge, 1880-1914. . . . 605
Chipewyan semantics. . . . 497
Choosing a lingua franca in an African capital. . . . 462
Choosing the battleground. . . . 2428
Christ the King Parish, Medicine Hat, 1954-1979. . . . 393
Christ today. . . . 150
Christian harmony. Cheerful co-operation in the work of the Gospel. . . . 128
Christmas. . . . 1388
A chronicle of the Canadian West. . . . 2497
Chuckwagon of the Circle B. . . . 654
The church in the valley. . . . 433
The Church Missionary Society among the Blackfoot Indians of southern Alberta, 1880-1895. . . . 200
Church of the Good Shepherd 65th anniversary. . . . 326
Cinquantenaire de la paroisse Saint-Vincent, Alberta, 1905-1956. . . . 422
Cinquantenaire de l'arrivée des pionniers à Gourin, 11 avril, 1914. . . . 3281
Cinquantenaire, golden jubilee, 1920-1970. . . . 429
Cinquantenaire, Ste. Hélène de Ste-Lina. . . . 421
Citizen participation - Fact or fiction. . . . 1776
Citizens plus. . . . 1930
Citizens' resource catalogue. . . . 1720

The city and the subcommunity. 1866
A city goes to war. 2757
The city of libertines. 676
The city of Strathcona, 1891-1912. 3032
CKUA and 40 wondrous years of radio. 2346
The clan McRae. 2724
A classification of theses in education completed at the University
of Alberta, 1929-1966. 6
Clear Vista. 1532
Clearing in the West. 724
Clement Hoyler, God's pacemaker for Moravians in Canada. 257
Cleverville, Champion, 1905 to 1970. 2943
A climber's guide to the Rocky Mountains of Canada. 1701
A climbing guide to Yamnuska. 1666
Club and party mentalism. 1322
Cluny, an ancient fortified village in Alberta. 2030
Coaching goaltenders. 1644
Coaldale, the gem of the West. 2944
The Cochrane Ranch, 1881-1894. 3430
Code of the rangeland. 810 anniversaire, 1911-1961. 1595
Collected papers on Ukrainian settlers in Western Canada. 1992
Collected works, 1938-1978. 990
The collective unconscious. 1172
Collège Saint-Jean cinquantième
Come down from yonder mountain. 806
Come hell or high water. 1597
Comedy magic. 1271
Comedy mentalism. 1323
Commemorating fifty years of Christian service to Wainwright and
District by Grace Church, 1908-1958. 432
Commercial card magic. 1272
The Commonwealth Games management financial feasibility study. 1704
Communications in a growing organization. 1802
Communications in the county of Camrose. 2347
Communities of Calgary. 2949
Communities six. 2950
Community development and community education. 1727
Community development experiences in the Chipewyan community
of Cold Lake, Alberta. 1712
Community development in Alberta. 1731
A community development model illustrated with Hinton, Alberta. 1722
Community development programs in Alberta. 1713
Community history. 2863
Community leagues as a community development nuclei. 1725
Community names of Alberta. 2660
The community school, a focus on living. 1485
Commuter expenditure patterns in the Edmonton region. 2154
Comparative factorial ecology of large Alberta cities, 1961-1971. 2544
A comparative study of aspects of the vocalic systems of standard
French and the French dialect spoken at Falher, Alberta. 457

A comparative study of value orientations in an Alberta Indian community. . 1907
Compartment K. . . . 770
A complete course in stage hypnotism. . . . 1324
Compulsory schooling in Alberta, 1888-1942. . . . 1575
A concise history of capital punishment in Canada. . . . 1766
A concise history of Tofield and district. . . . 3275
Conference minutes and papers. . . . 1890
Conflict between cross-country skiers and snowmobilers in Alberta. . . . 1709
Conflicts of perception and use in Banff National Park. . . . 2574
Confluence of mental health and legal systems in the process for compulsory civil commitment in Alberta. . . . 1819
Conformity and deviance. . . . 1867
The conjurer's calculator. . . . 1361
Conjuring for children. . . . 1304
The conquerors of Prairies. . . . 991
Conquerville, a growing community. . . . 2951
The Conservative Party in the provisional district of Alberta, 1887-1905. . . 2383
The consolidated school movement in Alberta, 1913-1963. . . . 1585
The consumer spatial behavior of Edmonton's inner city residents, 1977. . . 2192
Contemporary Indian artists. . . . 1194
Contribution of Donald H. Cameron to adult education. . . . 1598
Conversational Ukrainian. . . . 511
The Co-operative Commonwealth Federation of Canada. . . . 2365
Cooper's crossing. . . . 795
A corner of Canada. . . . 3304
Cornerstone colony. . . . 2791
Coronation. . . . 2952
Corpse in handcuffs.. . . . 787
Corrections and penology. Where are we going? . . . 1806
Corrections needs to be corrected. . . . 1815
Cos' ci oddam Panie. . . . 246
The cost of confederation. . . . 2360
Cost reduction programs of a natural gas distribution firm. . . . 2290
Counsellor extraordinary. . . . 1039
Count illusions. . . . 1005
Country editor. . . . 54
Country livestock auctions and market performance. . . . 2216
Country residential development in the Edmonton area to 1973. 2591
Country residential growth in the Calgary region. . . . 2593
The county of Mountain View, Alberta. . . . 3090
Coversational Cree. . . . 472
Cowboy politics. . . . 3414
A cowboy's memoirs. . . . 3463
Cowley. . . . 2905
Cowtown. . . . 3288
Coyote Flats. . . . 3247
The CP Rail High Level Bridge at Lethbridge. . . . 2341
Crackin' out. . . . 1700
Creation.. . . . 564
Creation of a magical madman, . . . 1315

The creative process of drama and its application to drama in education. . . . 1258
The creative world of puppetry. 1260
Cree. 473
A Cree Bible dictionary. 89
Cree. Nehiyawewin. 475
Cree picture dictionary. 476
Cree reader. 477
Cree tenses and explanation. 478
Cree. Twelve basic lesons. 479
Cree vocabulary. 480
Cree vocabulary for little beginners. 481
Cree vocabulary, 2nd level. 482
Cree. What they do book. 483
The creek. 3335
Crescent Heights United Church. 315
Crestomere-Sylvan Heights heritage. 2858
Criminal forever!. 161
Criminal justice in a Canadian province. 2478
Crisis at 9:25. 112
Crisis on Conshelf Ten. 689
Croation Catholic Parish Our Lady of Mercy, 1967-1977.. 290
Crocus and meadowlark country. 3511
Crop production risk in Alberta. 3419
The Crosses of Alberta. 2725
Crossing frontiers.. 523
Crowded to Christ. 103
Crowfoot. 2827
Crowfoot, Chief of the Blackfeet. 2821
The Crown in Canada. 2375
Crow's black joy. 1021
The Crow's Nest Pass agreement in review. 2318
Crowsnest and its people. 2957
The Crowsnest Pass, a coal mining valley. 2547
Crystal Spring Indian camp site. 2059
The cultural ecology of the Chipewyan. 1951
Cultural transmission in a closed society. 1934
Culture change and education. 1947
Culture changes on the northern plains, 1000 B.C. to 1000 A.D. 2056
Cumancaya. 2053
Cumberland memories. 2958
Current trends in stylistics. 451
The curried chicken apocalypse. 877
Curse of the gods.. 784
The curse of the wolf. 811
The Cypress Hills. 2691
The daffodils. 1389
Dance me outside.. 700
Daniel Kent Greene, his life & times, 1858-1921. 2709
Dans le muskeg. 769
Dare to share. 122

The dark strangler. 1767
Das nordliche Peace River Country, Alberta, Kanada. 2532
Daughter of the old pioneer. 1753
Davin, the politician. 1070
Dawn to dusk. 2730
The day after tomorrow. 646
Day parole in Alberta. 1792
The days before yesterday. 3219
The days of my sojourning. A reminiscence.. 248
The days of our years. 266
Dear old golden rule days, 1898-1967. 1519
The death of Albert Johnson. 1768
The death's head knight. 1153
Declaration of Metis and Indian rights. 1885
The declension of nouns in Ukrainian. 504
Dedication of Brentview Baptist Church. 281
Dedicatory services for the reconstructed organ and the renovated sanctuary. Sunday, May 29, 1966. 284
Deedo's children. 3478
Defeathering the Indian. 1939
The defector from the Hutterite Colony. 1953
Defectors are dead men. 788
The Delia Craigmyle saga. 2874
The demand for coal by the electrical generation industry in Alberta. . . . 2229
The demise of alphabet parties. 2463
Democracy in Alberta. 2425
Derbytown echoes. 3125
Descendants of Benjamin Bullock III. 2702
A descriptive analysis of vocational rehabilitation programs for the mentally retarded in Alberta. 1793
A descriptive study of current and future roles of social service personnel in the province of Alberta. 1804
Desperado deals. 1280
"Destiny." 930
Developing new energy sources. 2287
The development and evaluation of an urban growth model for Calgary. . . 2582
Development control vs. zoning. 2563
Development costs of Alberta crude oil, 1972-1972. 2294
The development of a family agency. 1751
The development of a Learning Resources Centre as a base for the expansion of continuing education in Alberta. 40
The development of national park policy in Canada's national parks, 1885 to 1930. 2590
The development of political cynicism among a selected sample of adolescents in Alberta. 2367
The development of sports in Alberta, 1900-1918. 1629
The development of the Lethbridge School District No. 51 to 1960. 1518
The development of the Red Deer community in relation to the development of western Canada. 2963

The development of transportation in early Calgary, researched by Margaret E. Longair. 2344
Development of transportation in the Peace River region of Alberta and British Columbia, with an evaluation of present day rail and road commodity flow patterns. 2358
The development of women's field hockey in Alberta, 1962-1973. 1706
Development proposal for the eastern slopes of the Canadian Rockies, Alberta, Canada. 1620
Devil Red. 659
The devil's instrument. 1071
The devil's lighter, a novel. 606
Diamond hitch. 3053
The diaries of Louis Riel. 2805
The Dickson story. 2971
Differentials in the integration process of Dutch and Italian immigrants in Edmonton. 1983
Diffusion and migration, their roles in cultural development.. 2026
The Dinosaur Valley, Drumheller, Alberta. 3142
Direction for education. 1480
The dirty scenario, a novel. 607
Disaggregate modal split model for Calgary. 2562
Discovering music. 1379
Discussion notes for a seminar on the management of public parks and recreation services. 1630
Dismissal leading to lustfulness. 1095
The dispensational theology and political ideology of William Aberhart. . . 2406
The dispersal of Hutterite colonies in Alberta, 1918-1971. 1893
Disposable native. 1972
The disposition of crown petroleum and natural gas rights in Alberta. . . . 2261
The distribution of ethnic groups in Alberta, according to the 1961 census. . 1997
The distribution of religious groups in Alberta, 1961. 98
Diversions. 565
Diversity, Canada East. 1226
Divertimento for brass quintet. 1390
Divertimento for orchestra. 1391
Divorce guide for Alberta. 2474
Do you believe in television? 1151
Do you know? 2396
Docile à l'Esprit-Saint.. 189
Dog Pound, 1880-1920. 2913
Dominion Cartridge Company-Canadian Industries Limited shotshells, 1886-1954. 2184
Don't call on me. 1468
Doorway to delusion. 1362
Dorothy Knowles. 1215
Dots Magic. 1378
Double double magic with cards. 1298
Double feature. 781
The double hook. 808
A Doukhobor Russian lexical & dialectological questionnaire. 520

Dove, silk and flower magic. 1349
The dove worker's handbook. 1302
Down a wet highway. 2596
Down Cereal's memory trails, 1910-1967. 2931
Down the trail of memories. 884
Down the wild river north. 2611
Down timberland trail.. 621
Dr. Bessie. 3371
A dream of sky people. 1053
Dreams, dust and depression. 3489
Drifting into grey.. 927
Drug report. 1785
Drybelt pioneers of Sundial, Enchant (and) Retlaw. 2987
The Duffield site and its fossil bison, Alberta, Canada. 2036
Dusters and gushers. 2274
The duties of the provincial government toward the aging homeowner. . . . 1787
Dynamic decade. 2273
The dynasty. 2399
The eagle and the raven. A novel. 663
The Eagle calls. 2976
Early Calgary friends. 3280
The early devisers. 3261
Early furrows. 3235
Early history and growth in Edmonton Diocese. 186
Early history of Calder School and district. 2909
Early history of Medicine Hat country. 3167
The early history of scouting in Calgary, Alberta. 1849
The early history of the town of Claresholm. 3191
Early man and environments in northwest North America. 2027
Early man in America. 2028
Early printing in the Red River Settlement, 1859-1870 and its effect on the Riel Rebellion. 58
Early rangemen. 3471
Early settlers of the Shady Nook district and the close surrounding area. . . . 2897
The early west. 2776
Earnest-minded men. 2467
The earth is one body. 1022
Earthbound. 965
Earthdark. 690
East of Beaver Hills. 3059
East prairie metis, 1939-1979. 2991
Eastburg. 2992
The Eastern Catholic Churches. 149
Echoes along the Ribstone. 2851
Echoes from my song tree. 1023
Echoes of a bell. 412
Echoes of an era. 3099
Echoes of silence. 3354
Echoes of Willow Creek. 2979
Echos argentins au Diocèse de Saint-Paul-en-Alberta, 1948-1973. 190

Ecole bilingue ou unilingue pour les franco-albertains. 1484
The ecological and economic impact of water resource development
in southern Alberta. 3346
Economic analysis of demand and supply of water in Alberta municipalities. 2121
An economic analysis of institutional buying patterns for meats in
Edmonton and surroundings. 2189
Economic approaches to environmental management of the Alberta tar sands. 2289
The economic base of Camrose. 2109
The economic benefits and costs of irrigation in the eastern irrigation district of
Alberta. 3444
Economic change in the Grande Cache region of Alberta. 2085
Economic efficiency in the utilization and improvement of the publicly
owned pastureland of Alberta. 3431
Economic evaluation of ethylene production in Alberta. 2305
An economic evaluation of recreation in Alberta provincial parks
in the South Saskatchewan River basin. 1707
An economic evaluation of the Alberta Estate Tax Rebate Act. 2129
Economic impact of the Canadian gas industry, local, provincial and regional. 2310
An economic output and pricing policy for service co-operatives. 3385
Economic study, town of Fort Saskatchewan, Alberta. 2124
An economic system for Canada. 2107
The economics of conventional crude oil enhanced recovery schemes,
province of Alberta. 2296
The economics of industrial water use in Alberta. 2128
Economics of size on Alberta grain farms. 3453
The ecstasy of Rita Joe. 1086
The ecstasy of Rita Joe and other plays. 1087
The editorial reaction of the Alberta press to the Bennett government,
1930-1935. 2389
Edmonton. 2468
Edmonton. A history. 3131
The Edmonton aldermanic election of 1962. 2452
Edmonton and vicinity rural and urban youth. 1737
Edmonton Centre. 2390
The Edmonton Club. 1835
Edmonton collects. 1173
Edmonton Exhibition, the first hundred years. 2175
Edmonton, fort - house - factory. 3127
The Edmonton Grads, Canada's most most successful team. 1672
Edmonton had a beautiful river valley. 1137
Edmonton is burning. 730
The Edmonton Moravian Church 50th anniversary celebration. 334
The Edmonton Public Library Government Information Division,
an element in community development. 22
Edmonton Senior Residents' Survey report. 1786
The Edmonton story. 2927
Edmonton Symphony Orchestra comes of age. 1382
Edmonton, the emerging metropolitan pattern. 2531
Edmonton, the way it was. 3012
Edmonton trader. 2214

Edmonton trails. . . . 2666
Edmonton Transit System story, 1903-1978. . . . 2325
Edmonton '78. . . . 1649
The Edmonton-Calgary corridor. . . . 2579
Edmonton's Catholic schools. . . . 1526
Edmonton's impact on surrounding urban centers. . . . 2533
Edson flashback. . . . 2996
Edson United Church history. . . . 353
Education and government. . . . 1481
Education and the Blackfoot, 1870-1900. . . . 1554
Education behind the buckskin curtain. . . . 1527
Education for librarianship. . . . 34
Education in Alberta. . . . 1491
The education of exceptional children in the Calgary public school system, 1965. . . . 1509
The education of the farmer. . . . 3460
Education through television. . . . 1470
Educational administration in Canada. . . . 1489
The educational contributions of H.C. Newland. . . . 1569
Educational programs for Indian adults in southern Alberta. . . . 1511
Educational television. . . . 1503
Educational upgrading of prisoners in an Alberta correctional institution, 1969-74. . . . 1813
Educational values in Alberta. . . . 1478
The effect of an alcoholic treatment program on certain alienation and personality dimensions. . . . 1828
Effect of increased wellhead petroleum prices on some Alberta industries. . . . 2199
The effect of petroleum development on the Alberta economy, 1947-1957. . . . 2302
The effect of rising energy costs on Canadian industries. . . . 2187
Effective answers to questions. . . . 1325
Effects of farm technology and consequent problems of adjustment, effects of industrialization on agricultural production. . . . 3445
The effects of white contact upon Blackfoot culture, with special reference to the role of the fur trade. . . . 1943
The eightieth anniversary. . . . 288
The Elbow-Sheep headwaters, a recreational wilderness. . . . 1616
Electoral perception of federalism. . . . 2364
The elixir. . . . 1048
Elizabeth McDougall, madonna of the Plains. . . . 227
Elizabeth Metis Settlement. . . . 3084
Elmwood Drive. A case study of municipal decision-making. . . . 2466
Emerging party politics in urban Canada. . . . 2465
Emily Murphy. . . . 1752
The Emperor of Peace River. . . . 748
Empire, York Street. . . . 949
Employer/employee rights in Alberta. . . . 2472
En mission dans l'ouest canadien. . . . 199
Encyclopedia of suspensions and levitations. . . . 1269
Energized to evangelize. . . . 129
Energy taxation. . . . 2308

Energy use in Canada in comparison with other countries. 2111
The English colony. Nightingale and District. 2978
Enjoying the Rockies. 2623
Enns, Evans & Ulrich. 1186
Entrusted to my care. 3343
Envers des jours. 954
The environment of language. 1570
An environmental bibliography for reference sources of information and films. . 4
Environmental economic issues in the sour gas processing industry in Alberta. 2280
Environmental impact assessment of a sour gas processing development
in the Brazeau region of Alberta. 3337
Equalization of assessments in Alberta. 2090
Eric Lafferty Harvie. 2303
Ernest C. Manning. 2403
Eschata. 908
Eskimo prints, Cape Dorset. 1195
Eskimos in Alaska. 1975
ESP session with Nick Trost. 1372
Especially Babe. 604
Essays on Western history. In honour of Lewis Gwynne Thomas. 2778
The establishment of progressive education in Alberta. 1571
Esther community history. 3227
Estimation of extra-market benefits associated with the recreational
use of the Clearwater-Rocky Forest in Alberta. 1684
Et le verbe s'est fait chair. 885
Eternal flames of Alberta. 2615
Eternal pathways. 78
Ethnic furniture. 1158
Ethnic strategies of three minority groups in the city of Calgary. 1944
Ethnicity and areal organization among French Canadians in the
Peace River district, Alberta. 1931
Ethnological notes on Blackfoot and Blood Indians. 2065
Etzikom, 1915-1975. 3183
An evaluation of relocation in urban renewal. 2564
An evaluation of the fiction collections in the elementary school libraries
of an Alberta school district.. 23
An evaluation of the multiplier effect at Slave Lake and in its
tributory area since the establishment of the Lesser Slave
Lake Special Incentives Area. 2134
Evaluations of planning conceptions. 2557
Events leading to the settlement of the communities of Cardston,
Magrath, Stirling and Raymond, Alberta. 3063
The ever rolling stream. 394
Ever so sleightly. 1316
Every Christian's ministry. 156
Evolution. 87
Evolution démographique de la population canadienne-française
de la region de Rivière la Paix. 2520
The evolution of the central area of Edmonton, Alberta, 1946-1966. . . . 2518
Evolution of the railway network of Edmonton and its land use effects. . . . 2343

An examination of economic factors affecting the location and operation of the beef packing industry in Canada, with particular reference to Alberta. 2167
An examination of pricing practices and procedures in a local house building industry. 2230
An examination of some factors associated with the decline of the coal industry in Alberta. 2243
Examination of the petroleum industry in Alberta. 2259
Except that you're here. 924
Exclusive magic. 1353
Execution against land in Alberta. 2489
An exhibition of five recent works by Larry Bell, John McCracken, DeWain Valentine, Ron Cooper, Peter Alexander. 1174
The expanding relation. 1718
Expendable! 212
Exploration du langage des enfants francophones albertains de cinq ans.. . . . 443
An explorative study of factors affecting outdoor recreation demand of the Edmonton adult population, Alberta, Canada. 1642
An exploratory study of factors affecting responses of Cree students to literary selections. 1508
Exploring Paul's Epistles.. 80
Eye Opener Bob. 53
The face of yesterday. 2774
The faces. 1080
Factors involved in the selection of outdoor recreation locations by residents of the municipal district of Foothills. 1693
Facts about funerals. 1762
The failure of the CCF in Alberta. 2422
Fall madness. 1660
Falling leaves. Poems. 914
Family crisis as process. 1755
Family laws for Albertans. 2479
Fanfare and passacaglia. 1392
Far as the eye can see. 1097
Far pastures. 3500
Far-away flags. 854
Farm land tenure in Alberta. 3398
Farm stored grain on the Prairies, a cost study. 3405
The farmers in politics. 2371
Farmers' markets. 2248
Fasting friar. 726
Father Lacombe. 216
Favorite Gospel hymns in all major keys, transcribed for the piano. 1440
Federal expenditures in the Western Region. 2094
Feed my lambs.. 130
Feeder cattle marketing in southern Alberta. 2195
Feist, A.C.A. Gallery, Jan. 25-Feb. 5, 1971. 1188
Fellfield. 566
Fencelines and Furrows. 3003
Fêtes du 60ième anniversaire, Paroisse de l'Immaculée-Conception.. 329

Fibber's fables. 618
Field pricing of natural gas in Alberta, 1955-1971. 2288
Fields. 1125
The fifth horseman. 822
Fiftieth anniversary of St. Catherine Parish, Lac La Biche, Alberta, 1914-1964. 381
Fiftieth anniversary, 1910-1960. 324
Fiftieth anniversary, 1916-1966. 342
Fifty dollar bride. 3467
Fifty golden years, 1914-1964. 165
Fifty mighty men. 2716
Fifty years on the coulee rim. 2974
Fight that ticket. 2481
Figures in a ground. 567
A financial history of Alberta, 1905-1950. 2117
The financial implications of international trade participation by Alberta secondary industries. 2106
The financing and implementation of community development programs by the Alberta government. 1740
Financing education in Alberta. 1490
Fingertip facts about Lethbridge and district. 2684
Fire canoe. 2320
First and vital candle. 817
First Baptist Church 75th anniversary, March 7, 1976. 263
The first fifty years. 3368
First fifty years, Edmonton Y.W.C.A., 1907-1957. 1839
The first fifty years of Perfection Lodge no. 9 (G.R. Alta.) Calgary, 1895-1945. 1843
The first forty years of the Education Society of Edmonton, 1927-1967. 1562
First in the West. 2649
First lust. 896
First Spiritualist Church. 313
The first ten years, 1967-1977. 282
The first 25 years, 1954-1979. 345
The fiscal development of the city of Edmonton since 1946. 2461
Fitness and Amateur Sport Act in Alberta. 1708
Five natural areas in the city of Calgary. 1628
Five short plays. 1041
Flaming accords. 941
A flight of average persons. 766
Flood plain management in the Drumheller Valley. 2580
Flowing gold. 756
Fluid filosofies of future fools. 568
Focus. 1190
Focus on Calgary. 2631
Folk art of Pakistan. 1175
Follow-up on the Western Economic Opportunities Conference. 2095
Fond memories. 1134
Fools and masters. 1049
Fools and wise men. 2164

Foothills echoes. 3161
Foothills U.C.W., 1903-1978. 314
Footprints of the Gaetz family. 2703
Footprints on Mi-Chig-Wun. 3042
For love of life. 944
For the record. 3456
The forest. 620
Forests to grainfields. 3141
Forever together. 936
Forgotten magic. 1273
The forgotten people. 1899
The formation of Alberta. 2824
Fort Assiniboine, Alberta, 1823-1914. 3151
Fort Augustus-Edmonton. 3128
Fort Edmonton. 2031
Fort Macleod. 2505
Fort Macleod - Our colourful past. 3013
Fort McMurray. 2549
The Fort on the Saskatchewan. 3208
The Fort Pitt trail. Mostly tales of pioneer days. 3062
Fortieth anniversary, 1914-1954. 396
Fortress north. 805
Forty years on. 1563
Forty-four foolers. 1319
The founding faculty. 1603
Founding of Cardston and vicinity. 2872
Four bagatelles. Piano solo. 1393
Four Canadian folk-songs. 1394
Four development proposals for the eastern slopes of the Canadian Rockies, northern portion only. 1621
Four little studies for piano. 1395
Four stories. 809
Fourling.. 743
Fourteen generations in North America. 2732
Fox Mykyta. 655
Frames. 901
Le français parle. 449
La France contemporaine, 1900-1976. 2736
The Franciscans in Edmonton. 50 years, 1901-1959. 195
The Frank Slide story. 2854
Freckled blue and other poems. 857
Free beer. 1096
Freedom of the air. 2332
Freeway west. 3019
Friday's child. 1026
A friend in need. 3349
Friendship and commitment in a volunteer association, the University Women's Club of Edmonton. 1846
The Frog Lake massacre. 1917
Frog 'n all.. 41

From barnacle to Banff. 2695
From Danaview to Standard. 3256
From drums to drums. Souvenir program.. 331
From frontier days in Leduc and District. 3021
From home to home. 2612
From hymnbook to keyboard. 1441
From my heart.. 951
From old lands to new. 1974
From prairie to park. 1625
From preacher to prophet. 530
From prohibition to government control. 1821
From sea unto sea. 2739
From slate pencil to instant ink. 1543
From sod to silver. 3057
From tank 77 to Taber today. 3265
From the Bigknife to the Battle, Gadsby and area. 3005
From the buffalo to the Cross. 178
From the ground up. 3470
The frontier art of R.B. Nevitt, surgeon, North-West Mounted Police, 1874-78. 1222
Frontier Calgary, town, city and region, 1875-1914. 3022
Frontier days. 3023
A frontier guide to Calgary to Medicine Hat. 2671
A frontier guide to Calgary-Banff highway. 2672
Frontier guide to enchanted Banff and Lake Louise. 2673
A frontier guide to mystic Jasper and the Yellowhead Pass. 2663
A frontier guide to outlaws of Manitoba. 1769
A frontier guide to the Dewdney Trail. 2664
A frontier guide to the dynamic Crow's Nest Pass. 2665
Frontier guide to the Fraser Canyon 'Valley of death'. 2674
Frontier guide to the incredible Rogers Pass. 2675
Frontier guide to the romantic Crow's Nest Pass. 2676
Frontier guide to Waterton, land of leisure. 2677
Frontier notes. 3211
Frontiers and reflections. 239
Full faith. 131
Functional autonomy among English school teachers in the Hutterite colonies of southern Alberta. 1955
A functional comparison of the central retail district with two regional shopping centres in Calgary, Alberta, 1963. 2201
Funnybones. 897
The fur trade at Lesser Slave Lake, 1815-1831. 2862
Fur trade governor. 2771
The fur trade of Fort Chipewyan on Lake Athabaska, 1778-1835. 3187
Furrows, faith and fellowship. 3442
F.W.G. Haultain and education in the early west. 1572
G. Fred. 1564
Gabriel Dumont, Indian fighter. 2800
Garden of remembrance. Poems. 937
Garrington Post Office, 1907. 2896

The Gate. . . . 2756
Gem golden jubilee, 1914-1964.. . . . 3112
Generating citizen involvement. . . . 1830
Generative studies in historical linguistics. . . . 467
The genesis and early growth of the Alberta Human Resources Research Council. . . . 1780
Genesis of the Lethbridge Public Junior College. . . . 1604
Genillusions. . . . 1288
A geographic analysis of land use in Edmonton's rural-urban fringe zone. . . . 2543
Geographic inequalities in property tax levels. . . . 2132
A geographic study of the distribution of population change in Alberta, 1931-1961. . . . 2528
The geographical impact of outsiders on the community of Fort Chipewyan, Alberta. . . . 1726
A geographical study of the impact of two ethnic groups on the landscape in central Alberta. . . . 2545
The geography of the forest products industries of northern Alberta. . . . 2215
George Gibson Coote papers, 1907-1956. . . . 2411
Georges Bugnet, homme de lettres canadiennes. . . . 534
Gesang-Buchlein. . . . 1446
Gethsemani, a dramatic poem. . . . 886
Getting here. . . . 569
Getting the games. . . . 1640
The ghost book of dark secrets. . . . 1326
The ghost dance caper.. . . . 691
The ghost ship. . . . 834
Ghost towns journal. . . . 2855
Ghost towns of Alberta. . . . 2678
A giant among pioneers. . . . 2728
Giants of the missionary trail.. . . . 206
A gift of echoes. . . . 681
Girl of the Rockies. . . . 626
Glacier National Park and Waterton Lakes National Park. . . . 2693
Gladly would he teach. . . . 1528
Gladys and Dinton through the years. . . . 2972
Gleanings of the years.. . . . 915
The Gleichen call. . . . 2893
Glen Guillet. . . . 1207
Glenbow. . . . 1196
Glenbow art circuit, 1971-1972. . . . 1197
Glenbow collects. An exhibition. . . . 1234
Glenbow past and present. . . . 1198
Glengarry golden anniversary, 1920-1970. . . . 1522
A glimpse into the past. . . . 3145
Glimpses of the life and work of the Reverend Richard Bradford, as scholar, school principal, chaplain, priest of the Church of England and S.P.G. missionary. . . . 225
The goat in the boat, by Uncle Gary. . . . 1438
Godly self-control.. . . . 124
God's people today. . . . 151

Goertzen. 2705
Gold medal showmanship for magicians and mentalists. 1299
Gold rush. 2888
Gold sun. 1396
Golden anniversary and progress edition, 1907-1957. 3117
The golden anniversary of the Alberta Dairymen's Association. 3429
The golden anniversary of the Alberta Pharmaceutical Association, 1911-1961. 3348
Golden anniversary, 1910-1960. 374
Golden anniversary, 1915-1965. 274
Golden dreams, story and drawings. 645
Golden echoes, 1913-1963. 3435
The golden feather. 763
Golden jubilee. 338
Golden jubilee celebration, June 19th, 1960. 3255
Golden jubilee, commemorating fifty years of picture history of Taber, Alberta, 1905-1955. 3264
Golden jubilee, Empress, 1914-1964. 2998
Golden jubilee, Round Hill, Alberta, 1905-1955. 3036
Golden jubilee souvenir of the foundation of the Order of Our Lady of Charity. 194
Golden jubilee, 1906-1956. 301
Golden jubilee, 1910-1960. 3363
Golden kernels of Granum. 2980
The golden link. 2834
Golden memoirs, 1912-1963. 2968
Golden memories of Taber Central School, Taber, Alberta, 1910-1971. 1580
Golden memories, Warburg and district. 2923
Golden memories, 1912-1963. 2885
The golden trail. 2920
The golden years. 3263
The golden years of Redcliff. 3046
Goldenrod. 678
Gold-fever trail. 692
Gone Indian. 708
The good land of Alberta. 3037
Good medicine. 2076
The good medicine book. 2077
Good medicine companion issue. 1922
Good medicine in Glacier National Park. 2078
Good medicine thoughts. 90
Good medicine. Traditional dress issue. 1923
Good morning, Your worship. 2458
Gospel duets for the trumpet, with piano accompaniment. 1464
Gospel songs for the trumpet trio, with piano accompaniment. 1465
Grace Baptist Church, 1912-1972. 286
Grace for 25 years, 1950-1975. 287
Grace Lutheran Church (Gnadenthal), Leduc, Alberta. Seventy-fifth anniversary. 383
Grace Lutheran Church 50th anniversary, 1928-1978. 439

Grain and chaff. 867
Grain varieties in Alberta, summarized by Alberta Wheat Pool for Alberta's School students. 3388
Grammar of Church Slavonic language in Ukrainian reduction. 507
Gran on Social Credit. 2414
Le grand chef des prairies. 175
Grande Prairie, capitol (sic) of the Peace. 2915
Grande Prairie today! 2680
Grande Prairie trade dollars. 2194
Grandma's visit to England & Scotland. 2630
Grant MacEwan. 2835
Graphics by Walter J. Phillips and Canadian art in three dimensions. 1199
The grass roots of Dorothy, 1895-1970. 3220
Grassy Lake and Suitor sites. 2011
Great Canadian adventure stories. 570
Great Canadian animal stories. 571
The great Canadian lover and other commentaries and conceits. 1107
The great Canadian oil patch. 2271
The great Canadian range. 3417
The great Canadian super show of Canadian ideas. 1176
The great chief, Maskepetoon, warrior of the Crees. 2843
Great days in the Rockies. 1121
The Great Divide Trail, Banff to Waterton. It's concept and future. 1661
The great gates. 2643
Great golf humor. 1106
The great lone land. 2955
Great moments of the X1 Commonwealth Games. 1662
Great personal workers. 158
The great pioneers who cleared and broke the virgin land of Josephburg, 1867-1967. 1963
The Great Plains Project looks at new modes of transportation. 2316
Greatness of Taras Shevchenko. 539
The Greek and Roman world. 2740
The green butterfly and other poems. 919
Green rain. 1397
Greener prairie. 757
Greg Arnold. 1146
Grizzly country. 3328
The Group of Seven in the Rockies. 1177
Growing old effectively. 1761
Growth. 204
The growth and development of the English Council of the Alberta Teachers' Association. 1545
Growth of the Alberta petroleum producing industry. 1947-1952. 2297
The growth of the metal industries in Edmonton. 2181
Grub-axe to grain. 3060
Grudge. 812
A guide to publishing in education. 2
A guide to the Chancellor's papers. 1609
A guide to the historic sites of the Gull Lake region of Alberta. 2023

A guide to the papers of Louis Auguste Romanet, 1890's, 1900. 2647
A guide to the President's papers. 1610
A guide to the William Pearce papers, series 5, settlement, 1880-1927. . . . 1611
A guide to the William Pearce papers, series 6, surveys, 1878-1928. 2808
A guide to the William Pearce papers, series 7, irrigation, 1890-1927. . . . 3459
Guidelines for the development of public library services in Manitoba. 25
The gulls. 1398
Habitat St. Paul, 1976-1980. 2984
Half a century of Service, 1912-1962. 2258
A half mile of hell. 1626
Halfbreed. 1870
Hand Hills heritage. 3048
The hand of Robin Squires.. 627
The hand that cradles the rock. 1059
Handbook for sermons on Bible.. 91
A handbook of Social Credit. 2434
Handgathered fruit. 97
Handle with care. 1355
Hanna First United Church golden anniversary, 1912-1962. 310
Hanna North. 3086
Hanok. 696
The Hansens. 2710
The happen stance. 79
Happiness and other poems. 959
Harbinger. 572
A hard look ahead. 1732
Harriot! 1042
Harry Kiyooka, paintings and prints. 1213
Harvest of bread. 3422
Harvest of memories. 3055
The harvest of the years. 425
Haydamaky. 983
Haywire rainbow. Poems.. 952
He & she &. 846
Headwaters. 938
Heart of gold. 3175
Heaven via Little New York. 168
Heimtal Moravian Church. 431
Hellstromism. 1327
Help for husbands (and wives). 110
Hendrik Bres, Ann Clarke Darrah, Eva Deiner. 1150
Henry Kiyooka paintings & prints. 1214
Henry Marshall Tory. 1596
The Hereford in Canada, 1860-1968. 3393
The heritage of Bancroft. 2864
Heritage of service. 3353
Heritage Park memories. 2912
Les héritiers de lord Durham. 1860
The high plains.. 643
The high west. 3312

Highlands United Church, Edmonton, Alberta, 50th anniversary, 1912-1962. 327
Highlights of Medicine Hat and district. 3025
Hilda's golden heritage. 3068
Hill Spring and its people. 3069
Hillhurst's first sixty years, 1907-1967. 402
The hills of home. 3070
The hills of home. Drumheller Valley. 3200
Hills of Hope. 3010
Hinton, Alberta, 1811-1957. 2535
Histoire de Girouxville. 3250
Historic churches of Alberta and the Canadian North West. 1124
Historical archaeology in northwestern North America. 2037
An historical geography of coal mining in the Edmonton area. 2542
The historical geography of Edmonton, Alberta. 2548
An historical geography of settlement in the North Saskatchewan
River Valley, Edmonton. 2519
The historical geography of the Coal Branch. 2551
Historical panorama of Alix and district. 3229
A historical phonology of the Ukrainian language. 510
A historical publication, Spruce Ave. School, 1918-1978. 1541
Historical resources impact assessment, western portion of
Syncrude lease no.17, Alberta. 2045
A historical sketch, Lamont United Church, 1892-1956. 364
An historical sketch of St. Andrew's United Church, Spruce Grove,
Alberta, 1920-1970. 418
An historical study of the establishment of college systems in Ontario
and Alberta in the 1960's. 1600
Historical summary of the Skyline Hikers of the Canadian Rockies,
1933-1970. 1671
A historical survey of education in early Blackfoot Indian culture
and its implication for Indian schools. 1525
An historical survey of education in the Strathmore area of Alberta,
1900-1958. 1551
Historical watercolours by William Armstrong. 1145
History. 2876
A history and analysis of the 1971 Alberta general election. 2388
The history book handbook. 2744
History made in Edmonton. 3221
A history of Alberta. 2838
History of Alberta Mennonite Women in Mission, 1947-1977. 238
A history of Athabina. 3078
A history of Avonmore United Church from 1908. 319
History of Bindloss School District 3603, 1919-1969. 1542
History of Canadian Martyrs Church. 283
A history of Claresholm United Church, 1904-1969. 311
History of Coaldale United Church, 1904-1975. 312
The history of Cravath Corners, 1910-1926. 2878
The history of Dalum, commemorating its 50th anniversary, May 5, 1968. . 2962
History of District 37-E, part of Multiple District 37. 1840
The history of Drayton Valley. 2982

The history of education in Calgary. 1537
A history of educational institutions in Mormon communities of southern Alberta, 1954. 1533
The history of educational radio in Alberta. 1559
The history of Filipinos in Alberta. 1895
History of greater Vegreville. 3051
History of Hines Creek, 1867-1967. 3071
A history of Irma United Church. Published on the occasion of the golden anniversary.. 375
History of local government, Lac St. Anne area. 2460
History of Lomond and district. 3072
History of Mannville and district. 3006
History of minority groups in southern Alberta since 1940. 1968
History of Moraine Lake in the Canadian Rockies, east of Lake Louise, Alberta. 3029
A history of motoring in Alberta. 2327
History of Mount Assiniboine in the Canadian Rockies. 3030
The history of organized farm women of Alberta. 3468
History of Our Lady of Victory Church, Thorsby. 385
A history of pioneering in the Pakan district. 3496
The history of place names in southern Alberta. 2661
History of Red Deer, Alberta. 2964
The history of Severn Creek School No.852 established June 9th, 1903. . . . 1560
History of St. Agnes Parish. 318
History of St. Anthony's Parish.. 358
History of St. John's Presbyterian Church, Medicine Hat, Alberta, 1883-1973. 320
History of St. Mark's Church. 366
History of St. Paul, Alberta, 1909-1959. 2985
History of St. Paul's Lutheran Church, Rolly View, formerly Rosenthal East, Leduc. 414
A history of St. Paul's United Church, Coleman, Alberta.. 356
A history of St. Saviour's Parish, Vermilion, Alberta, and associated parishes, 1907-1967. 415
A history of Stony Plain, Alberta. 3184
A history of technical-vocational education in the secondary schools of Alberta, 1900-1969. 1546
History of the Alberta community college system, 1957-1969. 1594
A history of the Alberta Land Surveyors Association. 3412
History of the Alberta Provincial Institute of Technology and Art. 1578
A history of the Alberta school system to 1925. 1583
History of the Alberta-Saskatchewan Mennonite Conference. 245
A history of the Anglican Diocese of Calgary. 181
The history of the border country of Coutts. 3262
The history of the Calgary Highlanders, 1921-1954. 2752
History of the churches of the Acme area. 261
A history of the City of Edmonton Police Department. 2499
The history of the Eastern Irrigation District. 3400
A history of the Edmonton, Dunvegan and British Columbia railway, 1907-1929. 2357

The history of the Faculty of Medicine of the University of Alberta, 1913-1963. 3376
History of the Fort Kent parish. 262
The history of the Freedom and Naples communities. 3018
The history of the french-speaking community of Edmonton, 1795-1935. 3054
History of the Giesinger (Gisinger) kinship. 2704
History of the Glenwood District. 3111
History of the Grande Prairie Women's Institute. 3410
A history of the Huxley area. 2845
History of the Library. 30
A history of the Mormon Church in Canada. 184
A history of the people of Michichi. 3225
History of the Ranfurly United Church and its congregation. 355
The history of the Roman Catholic Church in Edmonton. 217
A history of the rural high school in Alberta. 1561
A history of the schools of the county of Athabasca. 1516
A history of the settlement and building up of the area in S.W. Alberta bordering Waterton Park on the north, from 1889. 3077
History of the Ukrainian Women's Association of Canada, St. John's Cathedral Branch, 1926-1976. 1838
The history of the University of Alberta Library, 1909-1979. 31
The history of the University of Alberta, 1908-1958. 1601
The history of the world, A.D. 1960 to A.D. 2000. 2735
A history of Trinity Lutheran Church, the Evangelical Lutheran Church of Canada. 302
The history of Two Hills, including the Lanuke District. 2904
The history of Walterdale. 2970
History of Westminster United Church, Medicine Hat. 397
The history of Willingdon, 1928-1978. 2934
A history of Writing-On-Stone. 2025
History, ownership & government of Alberta Wheat Pool. 3389
Hivernant archaeology in the Cypress Hills. 2029
Hoarse music. 1045
Hobbema, une florissante mission indienne de l'ouest. 176
The Holy City. 909
The Holy Spirit in missions. 104
Holy Trinity church ... 75th anniversary. 328
Home Oil Calgary. 2282
The homeless. 987
Homestead memories. 3153
Homesteading in the Consul district. 3234
Homesteads and happiness. 2994
The homesteads that nurtured a city. 3157
Honey in the rock. 801
Hoofprints and hitching posts. 3423
The Hope family & neighbors of Red Deer Lake, S.D. No.28. 2708
The Hope slide story. 2762
Horns in the high country. 3329
A horse for Running Buffalo. 656
A horse named Joe. 660

Horseman in scarlet. 624
The Horsemen. 682
The hospital on the hill, 1912-1962. 3373
An hour at the piano with well-loved hymns. 1455
The house. 631
A house for Harry. 1723
The house of words. 47
Housing designs for the Alberta Metis Association, 1973. 1711
How about me? 1445
How can a song be blue. 554
How Grandfather Burleson saved Christmas for the children of Calgary. . . . 768
How to book your attraction. 1328
How to learn to read syllabics. 499
How to make flashes, bangs and puffs of smoke. 1293
How to prepare a local history. 2737
How to read and run a river. 1698
How to read sealed messages. 1329
Howard Lowrie, M.D., physician, humanitarian. 3372
Hub of three hamlets. 3076
Hubert Hohn documentary photographs. 1210
Human rights awareness among certain socio-economic groups in Edmonton with implications for community development work. . . . 1738
The human side of politics. 2385
The hungry hills. 778
Hunter guiding activity in northern Alberta. 1686
Hunter-land owner relations in east central Alberta. 1652
The hunting hand and other poems. 879
Hurry up, Bonnie. 595
The Hussar heritage. 2879
The Hutterian Brethren of America. 1927
The Hutterian Brethren, 1582-1931. 1915
Hutterian education. 1497
The Hutterians in perspective. 1916
The Hutterite ways. 1988
The Hutterites. 1898
Hymn styling for alert adults. 1442
Hymns for piano accordion. 1450
I begin with counting. 1027
I don't care what it looks like, as long as it's warm. 1054
I don't know what your God can do, but my God can do anything. 148
I escaped the holocaust. 258
I remember Peace River, Alberta and adjacent districts. 3081
I will lift mine eyes. 1399
I would do it again. 2919
An icecream cone feeling in the dark of December. 555
The Icelandic-Canadian poet, Stephan Gudmundsson Stephansson, 1853-1927. 550
Identification of social needs in the inner city, Emonton and Calgary. . . . 1781
The ideological relationship between the United Farmers and the Cooperative Commonwealth Federation. 2440

An idiot joy. 931
If I call, will someone answer? 910
Ihur Dmystruck. 1159
I'll take the train. 2620
Illusionseseme. 1303
An illustrated guide to projectile points for the Alberta region. 2032
An illustrated history of Western Canada. 2768
Images. 1029
Images of a city. 1135
Images of Banff and Canmore and the use of Banff National Park
by motel visitors. 1637
Immanuel Lutheran Church, 60th anniversary, November 2, 1969. 386
An immediate alternative to the McKinnon Ravine Freeway. 2355
The immigrant, an autobiography. 2733
The immorality of the motor car. 2339
The impact of foreign investment on Canadian society. 2125
The impact of the Great Slave Lake Railway on agricultural land use
in the North Peace, Alberta. 2522
The impossible dream. 1592
Impressionist paintings from the collection of Mr. and Mrs. J.A. Scrymgeour
and Westbourne International Industries. 1178
Impressions de voyage et histoire de St. Joseph de Végreville. 3269
In due season. 802
In God's school. 138
In His service, St. Augustine's, Lethbridge, 1886-1976. 387
In jeopardy. 573
In just spring. 1400
In retrospect, 1967. 3044
In the beginning. 2953
In the bend of the Battle. 2848
In the land of the free. 3482
In the land where the Peace River flows. 903
In the light of the flares. 3238
In the shade of the mountains. 3216
In the silence of the year. 978
In times like these. 1754
In transit. 945
In tribute to the Basilian pioneers, 1902-1963. 268
In tribute to the Basilian pioneers, 1902-1977. 269
The in-betweener. 649
The incidence impact of a regional development program based on
employment creation. 2153
Income contribution of the petroleum industry to the province of Alberta
for the period 1964-1976, and public policy. 2300
Income distribution in Alberta agriculture. 3413
Income variation in beef production. 2212
Incorporation and business guide for Alberta. 2482
Indian Association of Alberta. 1496
Indian hunting, fishing and trapping rights today. 1928
The Indian identity crisis. 2007

Indian land claims in Alberta. 1979
Indian names for Alberta communities. 2657
Indian summer. 1924
Indian tales of the Canadian prairies. 2082
Indian treaties and the law. 2480
Indian tribes of Alberta. 1887
The Indians of Alberta hear the Gospel. 260
The indomitable Savage. 3367
The industrial reuse of Alberta's deactivated military bases. 2219
Industrial water use in Edmonton. 2122
The influence of aircraft noise annoyance on single-family house prices. . . 2133
The influence of irrigation and the railroad on the settlement of southern Alberta. 2812
The influence of professional, institutional and biographical factors on the attitudes of forest resource managers in Alberta. 3336
Information analysis of the Alberta criminal justice system. 2486
Inglewood and Ramsay. 3082
Inkwells and school bells. 1553
Innisfail, 75 years a town, 1903-1978. 3083
An inquiry into the religious value orientations of public and private school students at the grade eight level. 153
Inside magic. 1270
The inside story. 44
Insights into cultural differences. 1989
The integration of southern Alberta with Canada, 1700-1885. 2529
Inter- and intra-city location patterns of oil offices for Calgary and Edmonton, 1950-1970. 2313
Intercultural education. 1502
Interest groups and the Alberta Labour Act. 2244
Interface. 574
Interface tu. 575
Interlude of love. 904
Internal accessibility in the Peace River area, Alberta. 2587
The interorganizational bases of community power. 1724
Interpretive unit plan, Peace-Athabasca delta. 1663
Into all the world. 77
Into the woods beyond. 3319
An introduction to Lesya Ukrainka. 536
An introduction to the archaeology of Alberta, Canada. 2066
An introduction to the prehistory of the Peace River country. 2064
An introduction to Ukrainian.. 512
Introit and choral prayer. 1401
Inuit games and contests. 1247
An investigation of the role of the school librarian in Alberta. 36
Iron Springs Christian Reformed Church, 1949-1974, twenty-fifth anniversary. 368
Irradiations, No.18. 1402
Irrigation builders. 3137
Irrigation in southern Alberta, 1882-1901. 3436
Is there anything wrong?. 71

Isaac M. Barr and the Britannia Colony. 3074
Island forest year. 3318
Istoriia poselennia ukraintsiv u Kanadi. 1996
It's a new world. 61
It's good to remember. 3479
Its the real thing - Hall. 1209
Jack Bush, works on paper. 1152
Jacques Lodges, Calgary, Alberta. 2720
Jake and the kid. 739
Jam in the bedroll. 3484
James H. McConkey, a man of God.. 220
Janet Mitchell. 1221
Janey Canuck in the West. 746
The Janz team story. 93
Japanese Canadians in Edmonton, 1969. 1948
Jasper. 1110
Jasper National Park. 2598
J.B. Taylor landscapes. 1243
J.D. Turner. 1246
Jean-Côté, histoire et généalogie d'une paroisse du nord albertain. 2988
Jeannie. 1462
Jehovah's Witnesses in Canada. 233
Jeremiah, prophet of crisis. 139
Jerry Potts, plainsman. 2822
Jerry Potts, scout, frontiersman and hero. 2833
Jewish life in Canada. 1936
Jim Nicoll, paintings and poetry. 1223
Joanie's magic boots. 611
Job Reed's letters. 3503
Joe Clark. 2370
Joe Clark, the emerging leader. 2381
Joe Fafard. 1187
John Chalke. 1154
John Maclean's mission to the Blood Indians, 1880-1889. 229
John Rowand, czar of the prairies. 2839
John Rowand, fur trader.. 597
John Walker Barnett, first general secretary of the
Alberta Teachers' Association. 1589
John Ware's cow country. 3424
John Will, Marvin Jones. 1250
Johnny Chinook. 2075
The journey goes on 1252
Journeys to the far west. 2769
Joyau dans la plaine. 191
Jubilé d'argent. 379
Jubilé de Falher. 3001
Jubilé d'or. 2932
Jubilee brochure. 3387
The Judas conspiracy. 608
The judgement of Clifford Sifton. 1092

Judith. A novel. . . . 803
The Jumping Pound story. . . . 2301
Junior atlas of Alberta. . . . 2659
Junkyard. . . . 1055
The juridicial nature of Canadian federalism. . . . 2374
Just Gin. . . . 698
Justice not charity. . . . 2386
Kainai chieftainship. . . . 1961
The Kananaskis Valley hikers' and x-c skiers' guide. . . . 1683
Karst means stone. . . . 969
Keep them in Thy name. . . . 120
Kenneth Noland. March 6 - April 21, 1975. . . . 1225
The Kenney Site. . . . 2057
Khronika zemli Rus'koi (Ukrains'koi), de opysano vsi mista, zamky v provintsiiakh do ykh prynalezhnykh. . . . 2738
Kidmonton. . . . 2682
The kidnappers, by Richard Hornby, Two pollution sketches, by Nina F. Klaiman. . . . 1066
Kids! Honey fun with Berta bee. . . . 3386
K.I.K. country. . . . 3096
Kinship and migration among Calgarian residents of Indian origin. . . . 1862
The kinship system of the Black Lake Chipewyan. . . . 1990
Kirby's gander. . . . 664
Kit Coleman, Queen of Hearts. . . . 51
The kite. . . . 740
Klanak islands. . . . 704
The Klondike rush through Edmonton, 1897-1898. . . . 3132
Knox United Church, south Edmonton, diamond jubilee of present building, 1907-1967. . . . 330
The Komagata Maru incident. . . . 1077
Koo-Koo-sint. . . . 999
Kootenai Brown, adventurer, pioneer, plainsman, park warden, and Waterton Lakes National Park. . . . 1677
Kootenai Brown, his life and times, 1839-1916. . . . 2841
The Kootenay Plains (Alberta) land question and Canadian Indian policy, 1799-1947. . . . 1938
Korotke lito. . . . 982
Kroetsch's tragicomic romance. . . . 521
Kurelek country. . . . 1126
Kurelek's Canada. . . . 1127
The L. W. card mysteries. . . . 1377
A la claire fontaine. . . . 1403
Labor unrest in Edmonton and district and its coverage by the Edmonton press, 1918-1919. . . . 2160
Labour and coal in the Crowsnest Pass, 1925-1935. . . . 2204
Lac La Biche pow wow and fish derby. . . . 2683
Lac La Biche yesterday and today. . . . 3103
Lac Ste.-Anne. Sakahigan. . . . 192
Lachlin McKinnon, pioneer, 1865-1948. . . . 3495
The Lacombe story, our heritage. . . . 3105

The ladies present. 3416
Lady Godiva on a plaster horse. 858
The lady of the strawberries. 625
Lake la Nonne Trail. 758
Lakes of the Lac La Biche District. 2669
The Lamont Public Hospital School of Nursing, 1912-1914. 3366
Lamoureux. 2861
Lamoureux, ses débuts, ses pionniers. 3014
The land and water resources of the Spring Creek basin. 2555
The land of open doors. 2602
The land of Peter Pond. 2527
Land of promise. 2886
Land of red and white. 3020
Land of the Chinook. 823
Land of the lakes. 3107
Land of the second chance. 1969
Land of the Spirit. 278
Land use changes in the Eastern Irrigation District of Alberta. 2578
Landbanking in Red Deer. 2592
Landfall. 847
Landmarks. 1833
The landscape of southwestern Alberta. 2514
Landscape perception in the Crowsnest Pass area, Alberta. 2610
Landscapes. 1404
The Langdon legend. 3108
Language use in Canada. 453
The lantern years. 3109
Larry Poons recent paintings. 1231
The last best west. 2975
The last of the Arctic. 1128
The last of the free enterprisers. 2275
The last of the giants. 240
The last refuge. 3344
The last summer. 2614
The latchkey kid. 612
Law and society in Canada in historical perspective. 2470
Learning Cree. 484
Leaves from the medicine tree. 3066
Leaves of yesteryear. 2939
Leaving. 1013
Leavings by trail. 3041
Lecture domaine. 1291
The ledger. 920
Legal aid. 2490
The legal status of volunteer workers and voluntary organizations. 2483
Legally blind youth of Alberta. 1493
The legend of Daniel Williams. 2501
The legend of Owl Hoot Hill. 638
The legend of the mighty Peace. 1015
Legends of Wesakecha. 2068

Legends told by the old people. 2079
Lengthening shadows of the Neutrals. 3173
Leonard Cohen.. 538
Lesser Slave Lake study. 2089
Let swords slash for freedom! 972
Let the chaps fall where they may. 1099
Let us learn Ukrainian. Book I. 509
Let us not forget. 3276
Lethbridge. Alberta's Golden Jubilee. 3291
Lethbridge, city of the year. 2210
Lethbridge, the action city. 2152
Lethbridge, the big little city. 2685
Let's learn Cree. Namoya ayiman.. 485
Let's play northern pole. 1020
A letter from Red Deer. 3305
Leurs rêves, nos mémoires. 2875
Lewisville pioneers. 3118
Lexical borrowings in Alberta Ukrainian.. 508
Lexy for short. 732
The Liberal Party in Alberta. 2398
Librarianship in Canada, 1946 to 1967. 32
Library management. 24
Library service in Alberta. 26
Life and she. 3501
Life experiences. 3505
Life in a prairie shack. 1405
Life is more than meat. 1498
A lifetime of service. George Moon. 2250
Light and other poems. 869
Light rapid transit. 2356
Like a Chinook.. 219
Like Christ. 117
A lily bloomed. 2713
Lin Chien-Shih. 1156
Lindoe, A.C.A. Gallery, Jan. 25-Feb. 5, 1971. 1218
The line that joins. 2380
Linguistic diversity in Canadian society. 456
Lions at her face. 933
Literature associated with ranching in southern Alberta. 526
Literature, language and culture. 531
Little Cree Badger and the Fire Spirit. 2071
Little Cree dictionary. Cree to English.. 486
Little hunter book. Machesis. 487
The little white schoolhouse. 1531
Live or die with Russia. 2372
Liverpool Daisy. 613
The living earth. 776
Living on less and liking it more. 1747
Living the abundant life. 140

Local government financing in Alberta, including an appraisal of provincial-municipal financial relationships. 2101
Local government in Alberta. 2459
Local migration in east central Alberta. 2534
A location analysis for hog assembly centres in Alberta. 2182
Location of the Indian tribes at first white contact in Alberta, Canada. 1991
L'oiseau de feu.. 992
Lomen Brothers photographic collection, Nome, Alaska, c.1900-1935. 2540
Lone Butte north. 3286
The loneliness of the poet/housewife.. 844
Lonesome hero. 794
Long Lance. 1868
Long live the king. 1523
Long shadows. 3242
Look and play. 1380
A look at yesterday. 3091
Look behind you neighbour. 1081
Looking back. 918
Loopy loop. 1274
Lord Beresford and Lady Flo. 3441
The lore of the wilds. 2069
The Lost Lemon Mine. 2236
Louis 'David' Riel. 2780
Louis Riel. 2773
Louis Riel, humanitarian. 2790
Louis Riel, 1844-1885. 2775
Love among the pines. 721
Love and good sense. 3374
Love, honor and be free. 1748
Love's letter. 132
Lu Brent's best magic tricks. 1279
Lucifer and Lucinda. 640
Lumberjack. 712
Lure of the homestead. 3052
Luscar come back. 3085
Mag pil.. 576
Magazine magicana. 1308
Magic in store. 1268
The magic of Allan Lambie. 1369
The magic of Ronal. 1264
The magic shelf. 1309
Magic that moves me. 1289
Magic the way I see it. 1294
Magic with a marked deck. 1282
Magnetrix. 1286
Majesty (Ukrainian poems). 993
Major magic. 1275
The Majorville cairn and medicine wheel site, Alberta. 2020
The make-up of magic. 1295
A man, a company and an industry in Western Canada. 2292

Man and grizzly bear in Banff National Park, Alberta. 3324
The man sitting in Place Pigalle and other short short stories. 672
Man to Man. 143
Man with the heart of a Viking. 123
Management alternatives in residential water supply. 2113
The management and use of a Canadian plains oasis. 2576
Manpower requirements in the food service industry with implications for vocational education in Alberta. 2177
A manual in contrastive linguistics. 461
Manual of publicity and exploitation for the mentalist. 1330
A manufacturing geography of Edmonton, Alberta. 2209
Many laws. 2473
The Many Snakes Burial (DgOv-12). 2033
The map-maker. 826
The marching call. 793
Marion Nicoll. 1224
Marketing of wood chips from Alberta sawmills. 2191
Marriage and family law in Alberta. 2484
Marriage can be beautiful. 1756
The Martin family, Pine Hill-Ridgewood, 1889- 2717
Marvelous mysteries of Marvillo. 1307
Mary and the Holy Thorn. 1065
The Mary Shelley play. 1036
The master index to magic in print, covering books and magazines in English language published up to and including December, 1964. 1351
Master magic. 1276
The master mentalist. 1354
Masters of the sixties. 1179
The Mater Admirabilis Chapel. 1406
Maternity leave in Alberta. 1746
Matrimonial property and the conflict of laws in Alberta. 2487
The matter of perception in the fiction of W.O. Mitchell. 547
The maximand of the hospital. 3370
Mayerthorpe Pastoral Charge history. 362
The McDougall Memorial United Church, Morley, Alberta.. 378
M.D. of Kneehill, 1904-1967. 3038
M.E. Lazerte. 1566
A measure of understanding of certain aspects of Alberta industry. 2208
Measurement of a forest's contribution to the economy of Alberta. 2176
The measurement of melody. 1384
Mecca Glen memories. 3156
Medalta. 2161
Medicine Boy and other Cree tales. 2070
Medicine Hat. 3026
Medicine Hat and other verses. 1011
The medicine man. 827
A Medonte pioneer and his famous son. 2510
Meet Cree.. 502
Meet southern Alberta. 3149
Meeting place of many waters. 2947

Megan. . . . 749
A memoir of China in revolution from the Boxer Rebellion to the People's Republic. . . . 2745
Memoirs. . . . 529
Memoirs of a soldier. . . . 2759
Memoirs of life in Alberta. . . . 3002
Memoirs of the Edberg pioneers. . . . 2997
Memoirs of the Ghost Pine homesteaders. . . . 3079
Memoirs of Veteran. . . . 3284
Memories. . . . 390
Memories of a pioneer schoolteacher. . . . 1535
Memories of central Alberta. . . . 3462
Memories of Fairgrove district. . . . 3158
Memories of Verdant Valley, Cassel Hill, Livingston, Rainbow. . . . 2986
Memories of yesterday. . . . 3465
Memories of yesteryear, with Beth Campbell. . . . 305
Memories, Redwater and district. . . . 3080
Memories, yours and mine. . . . 3061
Memory meadows. . . . 3425
Memory opens the door. . . . 3174
Memory trails to Winterburn. . . . 3303
Men against the desert. . . . 3411
Men for the mountains. . . . 3322
Men in scarlet. . . . 2498
Men of the saddle. . . . 3448
The Mennonites of Alberta and their assimilation. . . . 1986
Mental mysteries with cards. . . . 1312
Mentalism a la mode. . . . 1363
Mentalism and its presentation. . . . 1331
Mentalistic encore. . . . 1265
The mentalist's manual. . . . 1332
Mentology. . . . 1350
Messenger of the Great Spirit. . . . 231
Messiah Lutheran through seventy years, 1901-1971. . . . 306
The Metis in Alberta society, with special reference to social, economic and cultural factors associated with persistently high tuberculosis incidence. 1875
The Metis people of Canada. . . . 1857
Metis social-political movement. . . . 1945
Metis study tour report, December, 1968. . . . 1958
Mickey the beaver, and other stories. . . . 828
Migrants and migration in part of the southwest Peace River region, Alberta. 2552
Migration of people to and within the county of Grande Prairie, Alberta, 1956 to 1967. . . . 2558
Migration patterns in west-central Alberta. . . . 2595
Milk River country. . . . 2914
The Milo-Queenstown U.F.W.A. and F.W.U.A. . . . 3404
Mind and matter. . . . 1317
The mind gods. . . . 694
Minerva's stepchild. . . . 614
Mingling memories. . . . 3209

Mini-parks for Edmonton. . . . 1648
Minute music for small hands. For piano. . . . 1407
Miracle on the Athabasca. . . . 2272
Miracles in mentalism and psychic experimentation. . . . 1333
Mirror of life. . . . 882
A mirror of our dreams. . . . 1256
Mirror, 1913-1966. . . . 1573
Missions among the buffalo. . . . 230
Modern Israel in biblical perspective.. . . . 92
Modern painting in Canada. . . . 1189
Modified deer phalanges at the Draper site. . . . 2047
The money tree.. . . . 967
The Monkman Pass Highway. . . . 2353
Monseigneur Grandin vous parle. . . . 203
The moon pool. . . . 609
Moon songs. . . . 1408
Moose hunting activity in northern Alberta. . . . 1685
Moose magic. . . . 3333
More Edmonton stories. . . . 2928
More effective answers to questions. . . . 1334
More master magic. . . . 1277
Mormon settlements in southern Alberta. . . . 1942
Morrison, S.D. No. 1639. . . . 1576
Mosquito Creek roundup. . . . 3170
A most diversified character. . . . 2983
A most effectual remedy. . . . 1808
Mother and her family. . . . 2698
The mountain heights, and other poems. . . . 889
Mountain shadows. . . . 642
The mountaineers. . . . 1643
The mountains and the sky. . . . 1235
The mountains of Canada. . . . 2629
The mounties. . . . 835
A moving story. . . . 2328
The Moyerton story, "cradled 'twixt hills." . . . 3271
Mr. Brown and his magic mustache. . . . 798
The mud lark. . . . 796
Mudroschi mandriv. . . . 994
Multimonster in paradise. . . . 984
The Mumberley inheritance. . . . 1060
Mundare, yesterday and today. . . . 403
Munson and district. . . . 3168
Murder on the plains. . . . 1770
The muse in prison. . . . 540
Mushrooms of the Edmonton area, edible and poisonous. . . . 3332
Music at the close. . . . 727
Music for the great highland bagpipe. . . . 1454
My Canada and I. . . . 1911
My centennial torch for world peace.. . . . 99
My Cree people. . . . 1896

My fifteen years with 4-H clubs. 3395
My forty-five years on the campus. 1599
My genealogy. 2719
My hands. 1409
My heritage from the builders of Canada. 1902
My home. 988
My life on the range. 3472
My people the Bloods. 1965
My sister. 1463
My thoughts fly to Ukraine. 1031
My tribe the Crees. 1888
My uncle Joe. 736
My years in Lionism, 1931-1975. 1841
The mystery horse. 772
Mystics and scholars. 69
Namao United Church 80th anniversary, May 12, 1963. 400
Namus. 1003
Narrative for the film, 'The Trout Lake Cree'. 1906
The Narrows site in Waterton Lakes National Park, Alberta. 2018
Nashym naymenshum. 2081
National ceramics exhibition, Calgary, October 29 - December 12, 1976. . . . 1143
National Conference sponsored by the Sien Lok Society of Calgary. 1728
The National Policy as seen by the editors of the Medicine Hat newspapers. 2362
A native community counselling team. 1803
Native education in Canada and the United States. 1
Native religious traditions. 94
Nativism and ethnic tolerance in Alberta, 1920-1972. 1970
Natural and recreational features of Sandy Beach. 1641
Natural gas exploration and development in Alberta. 2291
The nature and purposes of the public school in Northwest Territories (1885-1905) and Alberta (1905-1963). 1548
The nature and role of Regional Offices of Education in the Province of Alberta. 1482
The nature, extent and sources of environmental knowledge and opinions in Edmonton. 3339
The nature of things. 3323
Nature trails in Edmonton. 1703
Nehemiah. 141
Neighbours. 833
Nekuia. 929
Nellie McClung. 1743
Nellie McClung and women's rights. 1760
The Nelson family. 2721
The Nelson master course of hypnotism. 1335
Never had a chance. 647
New concepts in magic. 1261
The new encyclopedic dictionary of mentalism. 1300
The new land. 577
The new make-up of magic. 1296
New paintings by Otto Rogers. 1236

New Testament survey series. . . 133
New trends in high school administration. . . 1506
Next-year country. . . 1715
Nick Trost's card problems. . . 1373
A nickel's worth of wishing. . . 556
Nick's routine with the cups and balls. . . 1374
Nick's table trix. . . 1375
Night and day. . . 3365
Night desk.. . . 779
Night music and other poems.. . . 960
Nineteenth century Lethbridge. . . 3194
Ninetieth anniversary of McDougall United Church, Edmonton, Alberta, Sunday, October 22, Monday, October 23. Anniversary speaker, Rev. J.E. Nix. . . 332
Ninety nine years from tomorrow. . . 1909
Nisku.. . . 735
No Englishman need apply.. . . 666
No rocking chair for me! . . 146
No small plans. . . 1607
No streets of gold. . . 1978
No sweet land. . . 780
Nomads versus cultivators. . . 2004
Norman Yates. . . 1253
A normative study of track and field events for the Alberta Special Games. . 1631
The North. . . 2686
The North Saskatchewan River book. . . 2601
North Star. . . 759
North West Mounted Police. . . 2506
The North West Mounted Police, 1873-1919. . . 2507
North with Peace River Jim. . . 2616
Northern Alberta Library Development Services, 1977-1979. . . 29
The northern approaches. . . 2750
Northern lights.. . . 995
A northern nativity. . . 1129
The Northfield settlement, 1913-1969. . . 3092
Northland Utilities Limited. . . 2185
The North-West Mounted Police and their influence on the sporting and social life of the North-West Territories, 1870-1904. . . 2513
North-West of 16. . . 3491
The northwest quarter of thirty-six. . . 3513
Northwestern plains archaeology. . . 2041
The Norwegian settlers, Eagle Hill and Bergen. . . 1892
The Nose Creek story from 1792. . . 2877
The Nose Hills country. . . 3159
The not so peaceable kingdom. . . 1823
Notes of the north. . . 3212
Notes on the Goodridge area. . . 3045
Nottingham House. . . 2832
Nova Scotia farm boy to Alberta M.D. . . 3369
Nove slovo.. . . 57

Novel concepts with cards. 1262
Now there was an athlete. 1680
Numbering the survivors. 2711
The numeral in Ukrainian, its forms and uses.. 505
The NWMP and law enforcement, 1873-1905. 2508
O Lord, Thou hast searched me and known me. 1410
O send out Thy light and Thy truth. The prayer and cornerstone of
twenty-five years of Christian instruction, 1932-1957. 179
O sing unto the Lord. 1411
O Toronto. 1130
Oasis. 935
Oatmeal porridge and green poplar poles. 3466
Oblate Fathers in Calgary. 164
Observations on the development of schism in an Alberta Indian
revitalization movement. 1881
The occupational adjustment of Vietnamese refugees in Edmonton, Canada. 1954
Occupational mobility of farm people in the Bonnyville district,
a low-income agricultural area. 2523
Occupational organization in real estate. 2186
Of the spirit. 1876
Of us and the oxen. 3504
Off-beat (sic) mental effects. 1358
Off-farm employment and mobility in the Goodfare district, Alberta. . . . 2539
Ogden whistle. 2894
Oh! The Coal Branch. 3224
Oil and gas finding costs. 2309
Oil and gas in Alberta. 2256
The oil and gas lease in Canada. 2469
Oil in Canada West, the early years. 2263
An oil well near Edmonton. 2286
Oki! Nitsitapee. A message to the Blackfoot Indians. 119
Okotoks. 50th anniversary celebrations, 6 Sept. 54. 3009
The old house. 3031
Old man's garden. 3315
On being a Conservative. 2395
On the edge of the shield. 2566
On the future of the extension function. 1612
On the hill. 1469
Once a mission.. 391
Once upon a childhood. 629
Once upon a chinook. 2457
Once upon a life time. 3480
Once upon a little town. 630
One body in Christ. 407
One century later. 1967
One day's journey. 3299
One hundred years of dentistry. 3361
One man in his time. 716
One of many.. 270
One word poems. 979

One-armed star from the east. 193
A one-party dominant system. 2409
Ooomerahgi Oh, and A very small rebellion. 1093
Opal. 2651
Open studio. 1200
The opening line of Paradise Lost. 533
Opening the great West. 222
Operation of Program 5 in Alberta. 2165
Origins and ordeals of the western world. 2741
The origins of oil and gas. 2255
Origins of the Alberta Metis. 1959
Osteology and odontology of the Sharphead burial site. 2035
Ouest canadien, historique et index. 46
Our Alberta heritage. 2828
Our apostolic heritage. 215
Our bend in the Peace. 3186
Our foothills. Sarcee Indian Reserve, Bow-Crow Forest, Sheep Run. 3162
Our golden years, Marwayne, Alberta, 1926-1976. 3146
Our Haugs in America. 2712
Our heritage. 2823
Our heritage from the past. 2742
Our journey. 427
Our Lady of Peace. 369
Our local industry in Fort Macleod. 2190
Our Nell. 1758
Our petroleum challenge. 2293
Out of my mind. 2734
Outdoor recreation planning in Alberta. 1632
Outdoors unlimited. 1675
An outline of Plains Cree morphology. 503
Over the years at Zion. 377
Overland by the Yellowhead. 2794
Le père Albert Lacombe. Arsous-kitsi-parpi. 170
Pack horse in the Rockies. 1100
Pack saddles to Tete Jaune Cache. 3133
Packy, the little elephant who came to the cold. 744
Paddle wheels to bucket-wheels on the Athabasca. 3134
Pages from a medium's notebook. 1347
Pages from the past. 2814
Pamela of Echo Glen. 723
Panorama. 578
Pansy pie and other poems. 958
Paper bag magic. 1266
Papers. 2770
Papers from Conference on Canadian Archaeology Abroad, held at the University of Calgary, November 23, 24, 25, 1973. 2022
The papers of William Aberhart as Minister of Education, 1935-1943. 1568
Pardon my therapy. 1771
Parent education guide. 1759
Parish means people. 296

Parish notes. 405
The park country. 3024
Park Grove echoes. 2989
The Parkland Regional Library. 15
Parkways of the Canadian Rockies. 2690
La paroisse de Saint Jean-Baptiste. Cinquantenaire. 392
Parsons on the plains. 223
A partial study of the resource potential of the Stony Indian reservation. . . 2112
Paschal meal. 82
Pas-ka-poo. 3233
Pass the McMurray salt please! 2178
Passenger demand for a 1976 Q S T O L aircraft system in the Calgary-Edmonton corridor. 2354
The passion of Christ according to St. Matthew. 1131
Passover celebration. 86
Past and present. 3189
Past, present, and future of the Lethbridge Junior College. 1556
Pat Burns, cattle king. 2213
Patchwork pictures. 76
The pathfinders. 3279
Pathfinding on plain and prairie. 224
Pattern without end. 1019
Patterns of influence in the collective bargaining system of Alberta Teachers' Association. 1504
Patterns of intra-urban migration in Edmonton and the residential relocation process. 2559
Pause. 1072
Peace Country heritage. 3450
Peace River country. 602
The Peace River country and McKenzie highway to Yellowknife. (John Hart Highway and Alaska Highway, 1867-1967). 2681
Peace shall destroy many. 818
Peach preserves. 3193
Peckertracks. 639
Pen and plow. 50
The Pentecostal baptism. 105
People and places by Pearl. 3258
The people and resources of northeastern Alberta. 2148
People, culture and learning. 1901
People in process. 1749
People of the buffalo. 1871
Perambulance and Pipe dream. 1043
A perceived needs assessment of amateur sport administrators in Alberta. . . 1664
Perception as an agent of sociocultural change for the Stoney Indians of Alberta. 1904
The perception of instrumental values among the young Blood Indians of Alberta. 1897
Perceptions of co-therapy. 1777
Perceptions of the medical social worker's functions in the Calgary General Hospital. 1801

Perceptual variations of retailing in Edmonton. 2179
Perennials and politics. 2405
Performance linguistique.. 444
Performance measurement indicators. 16
Performance of the hog marketing system in Alberta. 2217
Periodicals in Alberta high schools. 19
Pernilla in the perilous forest.. 815
Perren Baker and the United Farmers of Alberta. 1514
Persistence and change. 1973
Person perception skills and the helping relationship. 1810
Personal contact affecting city children's knowledge of and
attitudes to Alberta Indians. 1858
Personal peace and power. 113
A perspective on the energy resources of Western Canada. 2283
Perspectives on regions and regionalism and other papers. 1729
Peter at the Stampede.. 670
Peter Deacon Drawings, Nov. 6- 26. 1157
Peter Fidler. 2795
Peter Jumping Horse. 671
Peter Lougheed. A biography. 2418
Petrigo's Alberta. 2632
Petrigo's Calgary. 2633
Petrographic studies of north western plains ceramics. 2015
Phantini's lost book of mental secrets. 1290
Phone book magic. 1267
Phonology of the Galician German dialect of Stony Plain, Alberta. 446
Phonology of the Metis French dialect of Saint-Paul, Alberta. 455
Phonology of the Volhynian German dialect of the Edmonton area.. 442
The photographic moment. 1037
Pictorial album of Veteran, Loyalist and Hemaruka. 2852
A pictorial history of golden jubilee week, Edmonton and Calgary,
October 26-November 1, 1958. 1608
A pictorial history of St. Paul and district. 3178
A picture history of Alberta. 2818
The Piegan country. 2981
Pierre Guy. 1208
Pigeon Lake summer cottage shoreland use. 2573
Pilots of the purple twilight. 2335
Pincher Creek Old Timers souvenir album, 1878-1958. 3198
Pincher Creek United Church. 408
Pincher Papers, 1. 3196
The Pine Island posts, 1786-1794. 2802
Pioneer days. 3273
The pioneer days of Barrhead. 2867
Pioneer days of Hanna and district. 50th anniversary ed., Aug. 7, 1962. . . 3049
Pioneer heritage of Kirriemuir, Altario and Compeer. 3199
Pioneer reflections. 2903
Pioneer round-up. 3110
Pioneer women of Western Canada. 2727
Pioneering in Canada, 1906-1924. 2226

Pioneering in the west. 208
Pioneering the parklands. 3147
The Pioneers. 333
Pioneers and progress. 3188
Pioneers of Athabasca. 3274
Pioneers of the Peace. 2916
Pioneers who blazed the trail. 3065
A place for everyone. 790
Place-names of Alberta. 2656
The Plains Cree. 1962
Plains Cree dictionary in the "Y" dialect. 489
Plains Indian. 1185
Plainsong. 1412
Plamondon homecoming 73. 3033
Planning for urban wildlife. 3347
The planning of new residential areas in Edmonton, 1950-1976. 2538
Planning study for a national nature preserve along the South Saskatchewan River, Suffield area, Alberta. 1679
Planning the use of available resources in upgrading the health of registered Indians in Alberta. 3381
Play objects. 1180
Playboy illustration. 1142
Please put the music back. 1452
The plink savoir. 939
Ploughmen of the glacier. 1088
Plus ça change. 940
Poèmes. 863
A poem as long as the highway. 848
Poems. 1008
Poems for children. 870
Poems for old and young. 906
Poems for people over 25. 871
Poems of country living. 1016
The poems of Ray Bagley. 843
Poems of the Peace River Country and others. 862
Poems of W.D. Albright, 1881-1946. 839
Poetic fancies. 900
Poetic reflections. 898
Poetry Lane. 961
The poetry of Yar Slavutych. 551
Poking into politics. 2424
Police Coulee. 2012
Polish settlers in Alberta. 1957
A political analysis of public participation in educational policy in Alberta. . 1486
The political geography of a border settlement. 2530
Political history of Alberta. 2410
A political history of Seba Beach. 2454
Political manipulation and rewards in the Crowsnest Pass, southern Alberta. 2462
Political orientations of Calgary children from grade four to eight. 2436
Political realignment. 2376

The political thought of Ernest Manning. 2412
Political validity of Franco-Albertains. 2437
The politics of Canadian urban development. 2450
Pollution in Alberta. A bibliography.. 13
The Ponoka book. 3202
Ponoka panorama. 3201
"Popguns" Don Lougheed. 1219
Population density and pupil transportation costs in Alberta. 2351
Population growth patterns among Alberta Hutterites. 1937
Population-store relationships over time in north-west Calgary, 1949-1968. . 2249
The populist characteristics of the early Social Credit movement in Alberta. 2435
Portrait of a pioneer. 2999
Portraits from the plains. 1949
Portraits of the Indians. 1201
The possibilities of Canada are truly great. 2227
The post-Leduc growth of the Edmonton economy. 2118
Post-pleistocene man and his environment on the northern plains. 2049
The potential for wilderness recreation in a sand dune environment
in northeast Alberta. 1678
The potential unification of the Edmonton Metropolitan area. 2119
Pot-pourri. 953
Pottery in Alberta. 1114
Poundmaker. 2813
Power for prairie plows. 3426
Power for progress, thermal and hydro plants. 2170
Practical accordion course. 1385
Practical contact mind reading. 1357
A practical guide to ventriloquism. 1254
Practical music course in elementary theory and sight-singing. 1383
Prairie boys afloat. 2761
A prairie boy's summer. 713
A prairie boy's winter. 714
Prairie capitalism. 2299
Prairie child. 1000
Prairie echoes, Metiskow, Cadogan, Cairns. 3249
Prairie editor.. 62
Prairie footprints. 3007
Prairie grass to mountain pass. 3197
Prairie howl. 948
The prairie hub. 3143
Prairie hymn originals from our piano studios. Varied ideas of twelve pianists. 1443
Prairie hymns that live. 1458
Prairie images. 1212
A prairie letter. 3502
Prairie panels. 1024
Prairie Park School District No.1582. 1574
Prairie perspectives. 2803
Prairie perspectives, 2. 2804
Prairie pillars. 106
Prairie poems. 911

Prairie profiles. 866
Prairie silhouettes.. 943
Prairie sod and goldenrod. 2956
Prairie symphony.. 644
Prairie trails. 2925
A preacher's poems. 892
Preachers, priests and critters and other unusual accounts. 111
Prehistoric cultural dynamics of the Lac La Biche region. 2046
The prehistoric cultural ecology of the western prairie-forest
transition zone, Alberta, Canada. 2044
A preliminary bibliography of the archaeology of Western Canada. 7
Prelude and allegro for violin and piano. 1413
Prelude to administrative theory. 1741
The pre-reserve Blackfoot, cultural persistence and change. 1982
The Presbyterian Church in Edmonton, northern Alberta, and
the Klondike, 1881-1925, largely according to official documents. 226
Preventive social services as community development. 1831
Primitive art and technology. 2054
Princess Patricia's Canadian Light Infantry. 2760
Princess Patricia's Canadian Light Infantry, 1919-1957. 2758
Principles and policies of Social Credit. 2423
The printed word. 1501
Printmaking. 1119
The private medium's secret guide. 1352
The problem and the price of survival. 2429
The problem of quotas. 1614
The problem of resource development of the Blackfoot Reserve
of southern Alberta. 2105
Problems affecting Canadian participation in the development of the
oil and gas resources of Canada. 2260
Problems in the prehistory of the North American subarctic. 2051
Problems in the theory of phonology.. 454
Proceedings. 2102
Proceedings of the Alberta Chamber of Commerce Manpower
Conference held in Jasper, October 6-8, 1974. 2088
The process of rural settlement in the Athabasca area, Alberta. 2583
Production efficiency in Alberta beef feedlots. 2183
Productivity relationships in Alberta Government Telephones. 2322
Progress report no. 2 on actions resulting from resolutions. 2087
Progressive Social Credit in Alberta,1935-1940. 2444
Project 72. 1784
Projected answers. 1336
Projet centenaire, Grade 10. 3252
Prometheus rebound. 859
The promised land. 3296
The proper perspective and Who's looking after the Atlantic? 1061
Properties, investors and taxes. 2131
A proposal concerning the economic and human resources development
of the Indian peoples of Alberta. 1929
A proposal for a trail planning methodology, a case study. 1639

A proposal for progress. 1960
Proposed school for Calgary's retarded children. 1479
Prorationing of oil in Alberta and some economic implications. 2307
Proudly Western. 2766
The Proverbs.. 159
The Providence Child Development Centre. 1817
Providence trail blazers. 214
Provincial grants to Alberta municipalities. 2140
The Provost story. 3204
A proxemic analysis of the Iroquoian settlement pattern. 2067
Psalm 150. 1414
Public accounting in Lethbridge. 2150
The public health policies of the United Farmers of Alberta government, 1921-1935. 3356
Public secondary education in Alberta. 1588
Public utility regulation in Alberta. 2311
The publish it yourself author. 64
Publishing in Canada. 60
Pupil transportation in Alberta. 2319
Puppetrix. 1305
Quality education - what price? 1474
The Queen's cowboy. 829
The Queen's story, 1906-1967. 1586
The quest of the Golden Gannet. 610
Quiet winds. 970
Rails in the Canadian Rockies. 2338
Railways in southern Alberta. 2323
The rainmaker. 1082
The rain-orb. 782
Raise up the foundations.. 244
Rambling thoughts of a wandering fellow, 1903-1968. 3509
Ranching. 3409
Random descent. A novel. 667
The range men. 3415
Ranjan Sen. Tommie Gallie. 1240
Rape of the block. 1811
Raymond, 1901-1967. 3064
R.B. Bennett and the charge of one-man government. 2369
R.B. Bennett as M.P., 1910-1917. 2392
R.B. Bennett, M.L.A., 1897-1905. 2366
The reaction of homeowners along the North Saskatchewan Valley in Edmonton to the erosional hazard. 2565
Read and write. The Cree language. 490
The Readiness Centre. 1775
Readings on language in Canada. 458
Ready steady go. 1067
Readymade and district. 3207
Realism and Alberta's secondary aims. 1495
A realistic perspective of Canadian confederation. 2361
Reasons for immigration and ethnic identity. 1976

The rebirth of Canada's Indians. 1878
Recollections of the homestead trails, 1900-1978. 3138
Recommended guidelines for the development of the Parkland
Regional Library. 27
Record in stone. 2038
Recreation trails in Canada. 1673
Recreation travel in the Cypress Hills. 1699
Recreation travel patterns of Edmontonians. 1692
Recreational activities and perception in the Kananaskis region, Alberta. . . 1651
Recreational capability and use of some north-central Alberta lakes. 1681
The recreational capability and use of Wabamun Lake and the
eastern half of Lesser Slave Lake. 1622
Recreational enterprises for farmers in Alberta. 1668
The recreational land use of the Bow, Kananaskis, and Spray Lakes Valleys. 1694
Recreational use in Waterton Lakes National Park. 1702
The recreational use of the hydro-electric power reservoirs of Alberta. . . . 1627
The Red Cross Lady (Mary H. Conquest M.B.E.) 3358
Red Deer. 3306
Red Deer irrigation development. 3399
The Red Deer region. 2517
Red paper vs white paper. 1946
Red River adventure. 2772
Red serge wives. 2500
Reflections. 2880
Regina's terrible tornado. 2763
Regional considerations in pulp. 2228
Regional impact of an Alberta steel plant. 2198
A regional study of personnel turnover in the Alberta Department of
Public Welfare. 1814
A register of service.. 221
Relations in education between Bishop Legal and the Alberta Liberal
government, 1905-1920. 1577
Religion and ethnicity. 160
Religion for people. 81
Religious education in Alberta public schools. 1499
Remember Butler. 2798
Remember, nurse. 3357
Remember when. 2973
Reminiscences. 3213
The reminiscences of thirty years service in Africa, 1926-1956. 237
Reminiscing in Ferguson Flats, 1900-1974. 3004
Reminiscing with Walt. 3497
Report. 1855
Report and proceedings. 2104
Report from the Task Force on Social Development, an independent
citizens study committee. 1735
Report on academic women. 1613
A report on Blood Indian chief tipi circle and the Stevens Rock at Foremost,
Alberta. 2013

Report on certain industrial and other factors related to the economy of the central Peace River district, Alberta. 2138
A report on exports and imports through British Columbia, 1972, with special reference to the Pacific Rim countries of Asia and Oceania. . . 2096
Report on the impact of a proposed synthetic crude oil project on Fort McMurray for Syncrude Canada Ltd. 2298
Report on the land, industries and related factors in the Peace River Country, Alberta. 2139
A report on the National Energy Conference, Ottawa, January 22-23, 1974. 2097
A report on the Western Economic Opportunities Conférence. 2098
Reports on the last Indian battle and the Lindy campsite, the Sundial Butte cairn site, the Gergel campsite, the Burmis Boulder paving site. . . . 2014
Requiem and other poems. 873
Rerun.. 634
Research paper on the Alberta Provincial Police. 2512
Research studies by Western Canadian geographers. 2570
Resident characteristics of six urban fringe communities in the Edmonton region. 2541
Resident participation in rural development. 2521
Residential mobility and the function of seven selected high rises in central Edmonton. 1791
A residential subdivision for Calgary, Alberta. 2581
Residential water use in the Hardisty district, Edmonton, Alberta. . . . 2246
A resource planning study of the wildlife of Cypress Hills Provincial Park, Alberta. 3341
Resources inventory and guide to environmental studies. 3340
The response of public school supporters to a proposed bilingual elementary school in the city of Calgary. 1487
The response to directed social change on an Alberta Metis colony. 1910
Responses to foreign immigration. 1971
A responsive environment for the growth of cultural resources in the city of Calgary, October, 1969. 1123
A retail sales tax for Alberta. 2141
The return and other poems. 841
Return to Canada. 2609
A reunion, 1957-1978. 1539
Reverend John Gough Brick. 234
A review of legislation pertaining to petroleum resources. 2471
A review of the work of the Health of Animals Branch in Alberta. 3452
Revolt in the west. 2799
Rhymes from the foothills. 890
Rhymes of a prairie Scot. 887
Rhymes of an old timer. 891
Rhymes of reason and dis-reason. 881
The rhyming horseman of the Qu'Appelle. 3427
The rich man. 705
Ridgewood community, Red Deer, Alberta, 1889-1967. 2884
Riel's Manitoba uprising. 2764
Riel's people. 1872
Right under their noses. 1356

The rise of the Social Credit movement in Alberta, 1932-1935. 2419
The rise of the United Farmers of Alberta. 2407
Rivercourse centennial. 3217
The road across Canada. 2625
A road map study based on the 1974 official Alberta road map. 2654
The road to monetary reform. 2115
The road to Ya Ha Tinda. 3000
Road to yesterday. 579
Roads to Pipestone. 2977
Roamin' empire of southern Alberta. 2621
The roar of the twenties. 2785
Robert Harris, 1849-1919. 1138
Robert Rauschenburg - Glass handle. 1232
Robert Sinclair. 1241
Robertson United Church, golden anniversary, 1969. 335
The Rockies. 2644
Rocky Mountain skylines. 2635
Rocky Mountain wildlife. 3313
The role of a change agent as a factor in resource development
in a reserve community. 2003
The role of government and business in Alberta's export trade. 2086
The role of government legislation, policy and agency activity
in irrigation development. 3408
The role of Patrick Burns in the development of Western Canada. 2239
The role of religion in social and economic development. 144
The role of selected Edmonton professionals in the business
formation process. 2220
The role of successive town and city councils in the evolution
of Edmonton, Alberta, 1892 to 1966. 2453
The roll of honour and nominal roll, Princess Patricias' (sic) Canadian Light
Infantry, 1939-1945. 2754
Rollicking rhymes. 874
The Roman Catholic Church and the north-west school question. 1558
Roman Catholic separate and public schools in Alberta. 1547
The romance of beef. 3402
The romance of Canadian history. 2743
The romantic manifesto for the last ditch. 925
Rondo. 1415
The rooms we are.. 980
Roots. 1984
Ropes with a different twist. 1283
The Rosebud trail. 3144
Rosemary, land of promise. 3223
Roses of love.. 956
Rossville Mission Press. 59
Rosyth memoirs, 1906-1965. 2889
Roughingly yours. 1263
Roundhouse. 1069
The Royal Bank of Canada, 8th Avenue & Centre Street, Calgary, Alberta. 3447
Royal Canadian Mounted Police. 5

Rozstriliana muza. 996
The rubbing rock. 1001
Rudy Wiebe as storyteller. 525
Rudyard Kipling's (Medicine) Hat trick. 1108
Ruffled feathers. 2005
The rum runners. 1772
The Rundle adventure story. 253
The Rundle journals, 1840-1848. 241
The rural church, the farm family. 3446
Rural municipal government in Alberta, taxation and finance. 2084
Rural residential subdivision, Parkland County, Alberta. 2135
Rutherford school, 1910-1967, centennial open house. 1540
Sabretache. 2751
Sacred Heart Parish, 1912-1972. 352
The sacred scrolls of the southern Ojibway. 74
Sacred solos for accordion. 1456
Sacred solos for clarinet and piano. 1461
The sad Phoenician. 921
Saddlebags to stained glass.. 365
Saddles, sleighs and sadirons. 3172
Saga of Canada. 916
Saga of Schuler stalwarts. 3298
Sagitawah saga. 3181
Saint Agnes Parish, Edmonton, Alberta, silver anniversary, 1953-1978. . . . 317
Saint Albert. 3267
A salute to the Arab pioneers of northern Alberta. 1863
Salute to the past. 3475
Sam Steele. 2502
Sammis, the Medicine Hat. 3027
Samson's long ride. 830
Samuel Trivett, missionary with the Blood Indians.. 182
Sandman's land. 888
Sandstone brick and wood. 3278
Sara of the Tenth. 1844
Saskachevanka. 1447
Saskatchewan. 2626
Saskatchewan and the Rocky Mountains. 2642
Saskatchewan journals and correspondence. Edmonton House,
1795-1800, Chesterfield House, 1800-1802. 2830
Saskatchewan's provincial police. 2493
Say hi to Owsley. 1056
Scandia since seventeen. 3230
The scarlet mantle. 677
Scarlet, rifle green, and khaki. 2749
Scars. 701
Scenic assessment and landscape protection. 2546
A scenic resource and recreational analysis of the Milk River Canyon,
southeast Alberta. 1682
Schielke family tree. 2706
The School Act, 1970. 1507

School days. 1584
School districts of Alberta. 1492
The school of Calvary. 96
The school-marm tree. 750
Schools of the Foothills Province. 1529
Schools of the parkland, N.W.T. 1886 - Alberta, 1967. 1517
Science, technology and culture in historical perspective. 2746
The science, the art and the spirit. 3375
The scorched wood people. 819
A Scot in Canada. 3493
Scotty's mare. 661
Scouting in Calgary. 1848
Scrooge. 1062
Sculpture in steel. 1181
The sea. 875
The seagull. 1046
The search.. 648
The search for souls.. 243
Seasonal variations in employment. 2200
Seasons. 3309
Seasons. Fall. 3310
Seasons. Summer. 3311
Second Banff Conference on Central and East European Studies, Banff Springs Hotel, Banff, Alberta, March 2-5, 1978. 1865
A second language as a communication skill. 463
Second offence. 1104
Secret methods of private readers. 1337
Sect, cult and church in Alberta. 218
The secular in the sacred. 171
Secularization and religion in Alberta. 84
See Olds first. 3180
Seed catalogue. Poems. 922
The seed-pod book of joy. 865
Selected aspects of the functional relationship between consumers and commercial ribbons. 2218
Selected climbs in the Canmore area. 1696
Selected poems. 1014
Selections. 1140
Senator Hardisty's prairies, 1849-1889. 2796
The senior executive and the fifteenth Alberta legislature. 2417
Sensational answers. 1338
Sensational effects. 1339
Sensational mentalism. 1340
A sense of place. 580
Separation. 1416
A sequel to The art of cold reading. 1341
Sergeant Harry Morren, Royal North West Mounted Police. 2494
Sermons, addresses, editorial and other writings. 100
Service for the seventies. 1473

Service of dedication by the Right Rev. G.R. Calvert, D.D., Bishop of Calgary, St. Martin's Day, November 11, 1960, 3.00 p.m. 297
The settlement of the Peace River Country. 2965
The settlement of the West. 2806
Settlement process and land use change. 2556
Settlers along the Bow. 3236
Settling matters. 581
Seven hours to sundown. 1089
Seventy Bible lessons. 75
Seventy five years by the grace of God.. 372
Seventy south Alberta years. 3512
Seventy years gone by. 3058
Seventy years under God, for God.. 277
Seventy-fifth anniversary. 285
Seventy-fifth anniversary, 1901-1976. 265
Seventy-five years along the Red Deer River. 3075
Sex and the single magician. 1311
Sganarelle. 1417
Shadows of the Neutrals. 2954
Shaman. 1057
Shangri La. 2607
Shaping the schools of the Canadian West. 1552
She has done what she could (Mark 14, 8 NASV).. 188
She who knows the truth of Big Bear. 2767
Sheila Watson, a collection.. 587
The shepherd politician. 2413
Sheridan Lawrence, Emperor of the Peace. 3487
Sheriffs and outlaws of Western Canada. 2495
Sherwood Park. 2537
Shevchenko's celebration.. 541
Shevchenko's greatness. 542
Shining mountains. 2639
Shoplifters in Bigstore. 1827
Shorelines. 849
The short grass area. 3028
A short history of the Church of St. John the Evangelist, Pincher Creek, Alta. . 389
A short history of the Ranchmen's Club. 1847
A short history of Western Canada. 2792
A short history of Westminster Prebyterian Church. 440
Shortgrass country. 2907
Shout with joy. 1418
Sibbald community history, 1910-1962. 3243
Siding 16. 3215
Sidney Tillim. 1245
Sikanaska trail. 668
Siksiká. 1869
Silver Forks. 760
Silver jubilee.. 292
Silver sage. 3272
Silversmithing in Canadian history. 1242

Singing rails and tales. 2935
Singing wires. 2329
Singing your song.. 893
The singletree. 894
Sir Alexander T. Galt and the northwest. 2143
Sirens and cinders. 3102
Sister Roxy. 641
Sisters of Service, Edson, Alberta, 1926-1976. 3383
Sitting Bull. The years in Canada. 2836
Sixty years of service, 1917-18 to 1977-78. 3396
Sixty years, '16 - '76. 1582
The skating party.. 797
Sketches of women pioneer educators of Edmonton. 1538
Ski trails in the Canadian Rockies. 1669
S'komplimentary mentalism. 1365
The sleeping beauty. 1083
Sleight unseen. 1318
Slide-images. 845
Small Claims Court guide for Alberta. 2488
The small high school in Alberta. 1488
Small legacy of truth. 548
The smoke horse. 650
Smoke over Sikanaska. 3317
Smoky River to Grande Prairie. 3190
Snake Valley. 3164
The snowbird decades. 2333
The snowmobile, a recreational technology in Banff National Park, environmental impact and decision making. 1674
Soaring with Yawstring. 1112
Soccer practice. 1689
Soccer! 1690
The social agency. 1788
Social change in the Alberta foothills. 1733
Social class and attitudes in Alberta, 1971. 1730
Social Credit. 2116
Social Credit and the federal power in Canada. 2427
Social Credit and the press. 2415
The Social Credit movement in Alberta. 2420
The Social Credit yardstick. 2430
A social history of the Alberta Coal Branch. 3185
Social Plains School District golden jubilee booklet, 1913-1963. 3016
Social problems of Edmonton, 1963 survey. 1824
Social work staff turnover in the Alberta Department of Public Welfare. . . 1796
Society and politics in Alberta. 2443
Socio-economic change in the Grande Cache region of Alberta. 1795
A socio-historical study of the legislators of Alberta, 1905-1967. . . . 2426
Sodbusters invade the Peace. 2883
Sodbusting to subdivision. 2966
Les Soeurs de Sainte-Croix dans l'ouest Canadien. 201

Some aspects and problems of the archaeology along the Milk River in southeast Alberta. 2034
Some aspects of business education in Canada with particular reference to Alberta. 2163
Some aspects of industrial linkages in Edmonton's oil industry, with special reference to the tertiary sector. 2262
Some aspects of post-war migration to Edmonton, Alberta. 2550
Some aspects of the distribution of snowmobiles in southern Alberta. 1695
Some aspects of the recreational geography of the North Saskatchewan river valley, Edmonton. 1688
Some aspects of wilderness perception in Alberta. 1650
Some basic concepts in regional income analysis. 2120
Some did, some didn't win their $10.00 bet with the government. 3246
Some effects of continuing to provide subsidies for low income families. Study. 1826
Some factors relating to the attraction of manufacturing industries to the province of Alberta. 2155
Some facts about Calgary Power Ltd. 2171
Some geographical aspects of the coal industry in Alberta. 2238
Some we have met and stories they have told. 2701
Someone. 1419
Someone with me. 1132
Something to think about. 95
Sonata. 1420
Sonata for alto saxophone and piano. 1421
Sonatina for organ. 1422
Sonatina no.3. Piano solo. 1423
Songbook. 850
Songs for my owl. 878
Songs of believers. 1075
The songs of my heart. 1032
Songs of the Athabasca. 1002
Songs of the island. 1025
Sonnets of the space age. 876
Sons of the soil. 702
Sons of wind and soil. 3177
Soop takes a bow. 1111
Sorrow and wrath. Ukrainian poems. 950
The sorrowful Canadians and other poems. 1028
Sound doctrine. 134
The sound of time. 582
Sounding. 855
Southern Alberta. A regional perspective. 3088
Souvenir du cinquantenaire des Filles de Jésus au Canada. Province de l'ouest canadien (Alberta et Montana). 197
Souvenir of the consecration of St. Mary's Cathedral, Calgary, Alberta, December 11th, 1957. 298
Souvenir of the dedication and official opening. 307
Souvenir of the golden jubilee, 1908-1958. 272
Souvenirs. 2820

A spatial analysis of artifact distribution on a boreal forest archaeological site. 2039
The spatial and economic impact of recreational expenditures and sales in the Pigeon Lake area of Alberta. 2092
The spatial behaviour of Alberta's electricity industry, 1888-1965. 2225
Spatial reorganization in a central place system. 2127
Speaking with other tongues. 108
The special breed. 883
Specials for brass, with piano accompaniment. 1466
The spice of life. 2223
Spices and beauty. 902
The spirit at Hidden Valley. 2080
The spirit of Alberta. 2819
The spirit of the Alberta Indian treaties. 1980
Spirit-filled saints. 135
Spitzee Anota. 699
Spitzee days. 3240
The splendid pauper. 3461
Sports and games in Alberta before 1900. 1691
Spurs and shovels along the Royal Line. 3126
The squatters. 3094
St. Aidan & St. Hilda, 1911-1971. 411
St. Albert, a pictorial history. 2895
The St. Albert settlement. 2561
St. Andrew's Parish 50. 339
St. Barnabas Church. 340
St. Barnabas Church, Medicine Hat, 1884-1974. 279
St. Benoit Parish 50th anniversary. 360
St. Bonifatius Kirche, 1960-1970, Calgary, Alberta. 295
St. James United Church, Edmonton, Alberta, 1854 to 1979. 437
St. John's Evangelical Lutheran Church, Western Canadian Synod, organized 1903, dedicated May 28, 1972. 343
St. John's of Alberta. 1544
St. Joseph's Seminary 50th anniversary, 1927-1977. 420
St. Lina and surrounding area. 3251
St. Mary the Virgin, 1914-1974, 60th anniversary. 354
St. Mary's Hospital, Camrose, Alberta, 50th anniversary, 1924-1974. 3380
St Mary's of the Assumption in the Canadian Rockies Banff, Alberta. 280
St. Matthew's Evangelical Lutheran Church. 423
St. Matthew's Evangelical Lutheran Church, Spruce Grove, Alberta, seventy-fifth anniversary. 357
St. Michael and All Angels' Anglican Church, Calgary, anniversary, June 3rd, 1959. 299
St. Patrick's, Lethbridge. 388
St. Peter's Lutheran Church, Scapa, Alberta, 1921-1971. 376
Staff perceptions of rehabilitation in the Drumheller Institution. 1798
Stage illusions for the 1, 2 or 3 performer show. 1301
Stampede city streetcars. 2337
Standing in the street. 745
Stanley Jones School anniversary, 1913-1973. 1524

Starlit horizons. . . 942
Stars in time. . . 2448
The state and province building. . . 2144
Station 14. . . 934
A statistical analysis of cattle prices on terminal and auction markets in Alberta. . . 2221
The status and anticipated manpower requirements by selected sectors of the agricultural industry in Alberta. . . 3406
Stay but till tomorrow. . . 775
Steamboats on the Saskatchewan. . . 2350
Stephen Greene. . . 1206
Still God's country. . . 2918
Stimulants to social development in slow growing regions. . . 1734
The stone hammer poems, 1960-1975. . . 923
Stone poems. . . 981
Stoney ethnobotany. . . 1987
Stony Plain. . . 932
Stops of interest in Alberta. . . 2679
A storage and retrieval system for the abstracts of theses in education completed at the University of Alberta. . . 39
Stories from Western Canada. A selection. . . 583
Stories of old St. Albert. . . 3259
Stories of the pioneers of the west country. . . 2882
Storm. . . 1424
Stormy. . . 687
The story of a maverick. . . 3485
The story of Alberta Division, Canadian Weekly Newspapers Association. . . 45
The story of Blairmore, Alberta, 1911-1961. . . 2887
The story of Chief Medicine Hat. . . 2829
The story of Johnny Doogit. . . 635
The story of J.W., 1886-1961. . . 2203
Story of Macleod. . . 3136
The story of my life. . . 3498
The story of New Sarepta Moravians. . . 416
The story of our church, St. Paul's United, Fairview. . . 380
Story of rural municipal government in Alberta, 1909-1969. . . 2449
The story of Sarcee Butte United Church. . . 398
The story of St. Stephen's, Edmonton. . . 254
The story of the Alberta Women's Institutes, 1909-1955. . . 1851
The story of the Lethbridge Municipal Railway, 1912-1947. . . 2334
The story of the years. . . 1763
The story so far, 5. . . 851
Straight line mysteries. . . 1359
Strange empire. . . 2789
Strange trafficking and curious merchandise. . . 524
Stranger mysteries. . . 1360
Strathcona Baptist Church story. . . 347
Strathcona harvest. . . 584
Strathcona High School, 1907-1967 in retrospect. . . 1550
Strathcona, the asset of heritage. . . 3260

Strathearn United Church, Edmonton, Alberta, 1951-1961. 348
Streaking. 860
Strictly for posterity. 3093
Structural changes in the Alberta broiler industry. 2207
Structural changes in two Chinese communities in Alberta, Canada. 1913
Structure and organization of political parties in Alberta. 2439
The struggle for responsible government in the North-West
Territories, 1870-97. 2393
Struggles and progress of Teamsters Local 987, Calgary, Alberta, 1910-1955. 2197
Student reflections. 1510
Student use of school libraries in Edmonton open area elementary schools.. . . 43
The students' guide to Calgary. 2688
Students' story of co-operation. 3390
Students story of wheat. 3438
The studhorse man. 709
Studies in generative phonology.. 464
Studies in Stoney morphology and phonology. 496
Studies out in left field. 465
Studies presented to Robert B. Lees by his students. 459
The Studit monks.. 163
Study guide for the Commission of Educational Planning report
entitled "A choice of futures". 1471
A study of broiler marketing in Alberta. 2180
A study of commercial blight and the function of Whyte Avenue, Edmonton. 2202
A study of depreciative behavior in three underdeveloped highway
campgrounds in Jasper National Park, Alberta. 1697
A study of educational finance in Alberta, 1958-1971. 1477
A study of environmental press at the University of Calgary. 56
A study of leisure-time interests and activities of first year women
at the University of Alberta. 1623
A study of residential water use in Calgary. 2126
A study of social assistance in Alberta. 1799
A study of the degree of implementation of recommendations
pertaining to the control of education made by the Royal
Commisssion on Education in Alberta, 1959. 1513
A study of the developmental program of the Woman's Overnight Shelter,
Edmonton, January 23, 1970-May 23, 1973. 1794
A study of the holdings of Canadian award-winning novels in
Alberta high school media centres. 35
A study of the incidence, nature and cause of football injuries in the
city of Edmonton during 1969. 1645
A study of the incidence of juvenile delinquency and its treatment
in Edmonton in 1944. 1774
A study of the wildlife on four selected Edmonton ravines and of
the recreation uses and preferences of city ravines. 3334
Study on pollution. 3338
Such was life. 3293
Suffering saints.. 136
Suffield archaeological project, 1972. Preliminary report. 2017
The suicide meet. 1038

Suite for solo flute. 1425
Summary of salary survey of the professional staff in twenty-six Canadian public and university libraries, June, 1962. 17
A summary report on the proceedings of Alternatives Canada, a Canada West Conference on Confederation, held at Banff, March 27-29, 1978. 2384
Summer of childhood. 3473
Summer's bright blood. 928
The Sun Dance liturgy of the Blackfoot Indian. 2050
Sunrise on Sarah. 1090
Super prediction tricks. 1342
Super-mentality. 1343
Supply of natural gas in Alberta. 2264
Survey of Canadian academic libraries conducted between January 29 and May 1, 1967. 33
A survey of centralized library services in Alberta schools and library utilization in senior high schools. 38
Survey of child care arrangements in Edmonton. 1750
A survey of educational media services of Calgary public schools, conducted on behalf of the Calgary School Board. 20
Survey of Fairview, located in the heart of the inland empire. 2687
A survey of leisure reading in the junior high schools of Alberta. 1655
A survey of leisure reading in the senior high schools of Alberta. 1636
A survey of library facilities in Alberta schools. 37
A survey of professional entertainment and theatre in Edmonton, Alberta, before 1914. 1259
A survey of recreation components operating in selected areas of Alberta. . . 1658
A survey of Russian literature of the xviii and xlx centuries. 546
A survey of seven recently constructed public library buildings in the United States and Canada. 14
Sweet Jesu, King of bliss. 1426
Symposium. Perception and alcoholism. 1822
Syncrude Lease no. 17. 2062
The Syncrude story. 2306
T. Shevchenko's craftsmanship. 543
Tailfeathers, Indian artist. 1118
Tails and trails, 1900-1972. 3073
Take a note. 1278
Take away the names. 856
Take me where the water's warm. 1050
Taking possession.. 842
Tales and trails of Millet. 3163
Tales from two townships. 2961
Tales of a pioneer surveyor. 2638
Tales of the pioneer days. 912
Tales of the tarsands. 2960
Tales of Tofield. 3195
Tales tall and true. 2083
Tales to warm your mind. 947
Tall tales that are true. 154
The taming of Molly. 68

Taming the prairie wool. . . . 3035
Tan Choon Tee on mentalism. . . . 1367
The tar sands. . . . 2295
Tatanga Mani, Walking Buffalo of the Stonies. . . . 2837
Tattooing practices of the Cree Indians. . . . 2042
Tax-exempt property. . . . 2157
Taxi! . . . 767
Tay John, a novel. . . . 751
Teachers' evaluation of religious education in the elementary schools of the Calgary Roman Catholic Separate Schools District, No. 1. . . . 1512
Teachers of the Foothills Province. . . . 1530
Teaching a foreigh (sic) language to the West African student. . . . 452
Teaching of the Cree language. Basic simplified method. . . . 491
Teachings of nature. . . . 1925
Teamwork. . . . 791
Teardrops and flowers, and other poems. . . . 962
Technique of the private reader. . . . 1344
Ted of the Mounties. . . . 684
The Teepee Creek terror. . . . 3270
The telephone man. . . . 2330
Tell us a missionary story. . . . 622
Tell us a story. . . . 623
The Temporary Absence Program in Alberta. . . . 1818
The temptation of Big Bear. . . . 820
The ten dollar bets. . . . 2938
Ten dollars and a dream. . . . 3101
Ten folk songs for four hands, for players young and old. . . . 1427
Ten Washington artists. . . . 1182
Tenth anniversary of St. Basil's Villa, Pigeon Lake, Alberta 1950-1960. . . . 249
The terror of the tar sands. . . . 633
That incredible Christian. . . . 155
That summer with Lexy. . . . 733
The theatre of protest in America. . . . 1255
Them damn Canadians hanged Louis Riel! A novel. . . . 737
Theme and form in the novels of Edward A. McCourt. . . . 527
Theme and variations for piano. . . . 1428
There is my people sleeping. . . . 1012
There'll always be an Islay. . . . 3222
These are they. . . . 363
These mountains are our sacred places. . . . 1994
These were our yesterdays. . . . 3382
These were the early days. . . . 2714
They builded better than they knew. . . . 3169
They came, they saw, they lived. . . . 3119
They came west. . . . 2898
They gathered at the river. . . . 401
They've turned their back to the Bible. . . . 2840
Thimbles with a light touch. . . . 1366
Third anniversary exhibition, April 5 - May 7, 1972. . . . 1183
This is Alberta. . . . 2622

This is Alberta in 1963. 2636
This is Calgary. 2668
This is our land. 2891
This is thine. 83
This land is our land. 685
This side of the Rockies. 1094
This was Endiang. 3087
Thistle creek. 673
Thomasina and the trout tree. 628
Thornton's secrets of mental magic. 1370
Thorny's hideaway. 734
Those tumultuous years. 1593
Thoughts of a passer-by. 1017
Three Alberta teachers. 1555
Three aspects of the economics of education in Alberta. 1505
Three duets, for two violins. 1429
Three folk songs of old Manitoba. 1430
Three French-Canadian folk songs for mixed chorus. 1431
Three German dialects in Barrhead, Alberta. Phonology and interference. . . . 441
Three little hills of home. 861
Three miniatures for piano. 1432
Three or four day work week. 2242
Three plays. 1063
Three sketches for orchestra. 1433
Three times a pioneer. 3477
Three. 3. 1018
Through Canadian eyes. 1251
Through cloud and sunshine. 1534
Through hell to Alaska. A novel. 747
Through the bubble. 535
Through the looking glass. 3292
Through the years. 905
Through the years with Sidney B. Smith. 3507
Tides in the West. 3433
The tightrope walker. 964
Tim and his friends. 492
Tim goes to the farm. 493
Timberline tales. 2072
A time for fun. 1710
The times of Irma. 3155
Tipi life. 1926
Tizz at the Stampede. 616
Tizz in the Canadian Rockies. 617
To be poor in Canada. 1783
To have or to let go. 1757
To hell with Canada. 2391
To mothers with love. 1744
To teach this art. 3384
To the future, your heritage, Ripley. 1883, 1903-1963. 2869
Tomahawk trails. 3095

Tommie Gallie, '75. 1191
The tomorrow city. 693
A touch of gas. 3342
Toward a breakthrough in education. 1500
Toward a generative grammar of Blackfoot (with particular attention
to selected stem formation processes). 498
Toward a more adequate definition of the notion of transformation. 450
Towards a new compass. 880
Town of Devon, Alberta. 2670
The trade areas of Camrose, Wetaskiwin and Ponoka. 2235
Trade unionism in District 18, 1900-1925. 2222
Trader Eric and other stories. .674
Tradition and transition. 3401
Trail blazer of the Canadian Rockies. 2653
Trail blazers. 3277
Trail conditions and management in the Rocky Mountains, Alberta. 1676
A trail grows dim. 3295
The trail riders song. 1451
The trail through the Pembina Valley, 1790-1912. 2849
Trails and trials. 3097
Trails grown over. 3394
Trails Northwest. 2866
Trails of a wilderness wanderer. 3506
Trails of Tail Creek country. 2941
Trails to highways. 2993
Trails to Mannville. 3139
Trails to the Bow. 2924
Train for Tiger Lily. 773
The traitor mask. 789
Transactions of the first Resources Conference of the Northwest Region. . . 2146
Transcripts for the accordion. 1459
Transient men in Edmonton. 1816
Transitions. 585
Travels and adventures in Canada and the Indian territories,
between the years 1760 and 1776. 2788
Treasured memories, Gwynne and district. 3192
Treasures. 973
Treasures in heaven. 152
The treasure-seekers. 2304
A treasury of memories. 3228
Trends and change in Canadian society. 1719
Trends in sucidal behavior. 1825
Tribe under trust. 1908
Tributaries of the Blindman. 3089
A tribute to Hon. E.C. Manning on the occasion of his 50th birthday
party, September 30th, 1958. .907
Tribute to Whitla pioneers. 3297
Trinity United Church golden jubilee anniversary. 413
Trio no. 2, for piano, violin and cello. 1434
Trophies. 998

Troublemaker!. 2786
The true story of Ida Johnson. 771
Turn again home. 679
Turn him loose! Herman Linder, Canada's Mr. Rodeo. 1653
T.V. mentalism. 1345
The twain shall meet, by Wm. Irvine and others. 2373
Twelve illusionettes. 1306
The twenties in western Canada. 2807
Twenty pebbles, and other stories. 813
Twenty-fifth anniversary.. 275
Twenty-five years proud. 1797
The twenty-third Psalm, for medium voice and piano. 1435
Two chorale preludes for organ, with Hammond organ registration. 1436
Two dollars per year. 55
Two songs. 1437
Two studies on Fort McMurray. 2588
Two wheelchairs and a family of three.. 66
Twopence to cross the Mersey. 615
U.F.O.s. 157
Ukrainian Canadiana. 1136
Ukrainian Canadians. 1998
Ukrainian Canadians, multiculturalism and separatism. 2000
Ukrainian Catholic parish, Calgary, Alberta. 371
Ukrainian Catholic unity, 1906-1966. 255
Ukrainian Catholic Women's League of Canada. 1850
Ukrainian Christian names. A dictionary.. 506
Ukrainian for beginners. 513
Ukrainian for children.. 514
Ukrainian in pictures. 515
The Ukrainian language. 517
The Ukrainian language questionnaire. 518
Ukrainian literature in Canada. 544
The Ukrainian pioneers in Alberta, Canada. 2001
Ukrainian Rite Catholic Church. 228
The Ukrainians. 1981
Ukrainians in Alberta. 2002
Ukrains'ka mova za zorovo-slukhovoiu metodoiu.. 516
Ukrains'ka poeziia v Kanadi. 545
Unchaga = Peace. 359
Uncle Vanya. 1047
Unclouded communion. 137
Under the Chinook Arch. 2930
Understanding children's art. 1120
The unfinished revolt. 2359
United Church in Calgary. 185
The United Farmers of Alberta and the Ginger Group. 2441
The United Farmers of Alberta, 1909-1920. 2432
The United Farmers of Alberta, 1921-1935. 2400
A university collects. 1117
The unjust society. 1879

The unnamed country. 528
Up for the third time. 1105
Urban affairs in Alberta. 2451
Urban anthropology and the problems of the formation of social classes. . . . 1999
Urban growth management. 2577
The urban hierarchy in Alberta. 1736
Urban parks and planning in Calgary, Alberta. 2568
U.S. expatriates in Calgary and their problems. 1940
User survey. 18
The valley of rumours. 3182
Valley of shadows. 235
The valley of the vanishing birds. 619
Values of Mennonite youth in Alberta. 1912
The vanishing point. 741
The Vaplite collection. 586
Variables affecting immigrant adjustment. 1993
Various art media and techniques. 1202
Vases. 718
Vassarely. 1248
Vast prospects and splendid songs. 3268
Verdant valleys in and around Lougheed. 3121
Vermilion Lakes, Banff National Park. 3314
Vermilion memories. 3283
A very small rebellion. 800
Veterinarians of the North-West Territories and Alberta. 3418
The vice-regal cowboy. 2404
Victoria Park. 2850
A viewpoint on hostels. 1665
Vignettes of old south Calgary. 3040
Village of Hay Lakes 50th anniversary, 1928-1978. 3039
Vilni zemli (free lands). 1950
Vine of His planting. 251
Visions of my grandfather. 852
Visions of tomorrow. 1285
Visit southern Alberta, land of green acres. 2694
A visit to Al Oeming's Alberta Game Farm. 3325
A visit to the Leduc oilfield and gas conservation project. 2276
Vital Grandin, o.m.i.. 177
Voices of the pioneers. 207
The vowel system of Blackfoot. 500
Wabasca. 2648
Wages and salaries in the public sector. 2114
Wagon trails plowed under. 2990
Wagon trails to hard top. 3106
Waitress! there's an eye in my soup! 1007
A walk through old Calgary. 3245
Walk through the valley. 728
Wall of words. 1985
Walsh. 1078
Wandering River history book, 1968. 3287

Wanderings of an expert. . . . 3481
Wanderlust. Poems. . . . 946
Wapi. . . . 494
Warner pioneers. . . . 3289
Warriors of the rock. . . . 1966
Was it all a dream? . . . 2394
The Waskahegan trail guide book. . . . 1705
Waskatenau, 1867-1967. . . . 3290
Water supplies and watershed management in the Oldman River basin, Alberta. . . . 2569
A water use projection model for the North Saskatchewan River Basin, Alberta, 1980-1985. . . . 2110
Waterhole and the land north of the Peace. . . . 3135
A way of life.. . . . 114
W.D. Albright. . . . 3451
We are Metis. . . . 1889
We are the new nation. . . . 1883
We have with us tonight. . . . 1536
We print and we read. Grade 1. . . . 495
We proved God. . . . 147
We remember . . . Pete Knight. . . . 1638
We take pleasure in introducing you to Alberta Women's Institutes. . . . 3392
We thy servants, 1939-1967. . . . 3364
Weathered wood. . . . 2899
Weep for the Cowboy. . . . 1101
Welfare in Alberta, 1905-1936. . . . 1805
WesCan/INFORM. . . . 28
Wesley United Church, Calgary, Alberta, fiftieth anniversary, 1906-1956. . . . 303
Wesley's 60 years, 1907-1967. . . . 350
West. . . . 1033
The west in action. . . . 1656
West of the fifth. . . . 3104
West of the fourth. . . . 3294
West of yesterday. . . . 3239
West to the cattle country. . . . 651
West to the sea. . . . 2793
West 71. . . . 1184
Western Canada. Location of operating mines, processing plants and metallurgical works, 1974. . . . 2172
Western Canada. Location of processing of materials of agricultural origin. . . . 2173
Western Canadian dictionary and phrase book. . . . 460
Western landscape as history. . . . 1192
Western moods. . . . 588
Western perspectives 1. . . . 2809
Western profiles. . . . 589
Western reunion. . . . 971
Western Stock Growers' Association papers, 1896-1963. . . . 3407
The western Swan Hills. . . . 1617
Western untitled. . . . 1203
Westward bound. . . . 2797

Westward ho! 1903. 632
Wetaskiwin Co-op. 3439
What about the Grey Nuns? 259
What development is all about. 2387
What I saw at the Stampede. 1102
What the crow said. 710
Whatever you do. 792
Wheat country. 3285
Wheat heart of the West. 2865
Wheeler. 2536
The wheels of time. 3008
Wheels to Woodville. 3140
When pigs fly. 804
When the arrow flies. 70
When the grass was free. 669
When the sawflies mate in summer and other Alberta poems. 1009
When the sawfly flies and other poems. 1010
When the west was young. 3067
When the winds came. 3437
Where do we go from here? 1856
Where go the boats. 2336
Where is the voice coming from? 821
Where the prairie meets the hills. 2853
Where the wheatlands meet the range. 2940
Where the wind blows. 183
Where waters flow. 3282
While I still remember. 3476
While rivers flow. 3355
White. 853
The white calf. 652
White Creek echoes. 3301
White Forehead of the Cypress Hills. 715
A white man's country. 1894
The white peril. 653
White Sioux. 598
An Whitlock. 1249
Who has seen the wind. 742
Who owns the earth? 590
Wholesale trade between Edmonton and selected northern communities. . . 2232
Whoop-up country. 2842
Who's who in federal politics from Alberta. 2377
Why a Presbyterian Church. 115
Why bilingual education? 1475
Widger's way. 1084
Wild flowers and buffalo bones. 3171
Wild flowers of Alberta. 3316
Wild rose country. 591
Wild winter. 831
Wildcat one thirty four. 2277
A wilderness. 1098

Wilderness adventures. 2646
Wilderness men. 2723
Wildlands for recreation. 1618
William Aberhart and Social Credit in Alberta. 2447
William Aberhart and the Social Credit party. 2438
William Irvine. 2431
William Irvine and radical politics in Canada. 2368
William Kurelek. 1217
William Parker, mounted policeman. 2511
William Pearce and federal government activity in Western Canada, 1882-1904. 2379
William Pearce, father of Alberta irrigation. 3432
William Perehudoff. 1229
The Willing family. 2707
The Willmore Wilderness Park. 1619
Willowdale. 832
Wills and probate procedure, Alberta. 2477
The wind along the River. 2074
Wind, willows and prairie-wool. A centennial project. 2890
Windows to the mind. 1364
Winds of change. 2995
Winnifred. 2946
A winter at Fort Macleod. 2509
The winter years. 2787
The Wiser-Stephens 1 site - 40CF81. 2024
The wit and wisdom of Bob Edwards. 49
With deck in hand. 1320
With God on the Prairies. 236
Without reservations. 2628
W.J. Phillips views Western Canada. 1204
Wo de hombre. 2640
The wolfers. 762
The woman who got on at Jasper Station, and other stories. 752
The women of Calgary and district, 1875-1914. 2726
The wooden people. 753
The wooden sword. 729
Wop May, bush pilot. 599
Word order, sentence stress and reference in English and Polish. 466
The words of my roaring.. 711
Work and leisure in Canada. 2156
The work of faith with power.. 256
Working for God. 118
World missions total war. 107
World population and distribution of food. 2147
The Worth Report and developments in Alberta's post-secondary policies and structures, 1968 to 1976. 1567
The wreck of the national line. 1079
Yarns for spinning thoughts. 899
Ye men of Calgary. 1460
A year to remember. 2910

Years of wonder. 1581
Yes, dear. 1064
Yes, father. 3362
Yesterday's children. 2718
Yesteryears of the Hays Municipality. 3206
Young Canada. A song. 1457
Young contemporary Calgary artists exhibition. 1144
Young fur trader. 600
Young people of all ages. 1852
Younger brother. 774
Youngstown and district pioneers. 3307
Your heart and mine. 963
Your historical Canadian border route no. 3. 2624
Zella remembers from oil lamps to oil wells. 3308
4-H in Alberta, 1917-1967. 3454
5 micro-mental programs. 1376
The Yukon and the Northwest Territories. 2627
8 Calgary artists. 1238
8 cents worth of Canada and a few sense more. 1239
10th anniversary first Ukrainian Catholic Church, Smoky Lake, 1964-1974. . . 373
13 Calgary painters. 1220
15th anniversary of the Plast Association in Edmonton. 1845
The 16 hour counselor(!). 1829
25 experiments in mentalism. 1368
25 years, First Christian Reformed Church, Red Deer. 273
25 years of alumnae life. 3351
25 years of basketball championships, 1915-1940. 1646
25 years of Grace, 1953-1978. 395
25th anniversary of St. Pius the Tenth Parish, Calgary. 300
25th anniversary, 1946-1971, Mount Calvary Lutheran Church,
Red Deer, Alberta, 1971. 410
30 + 5. 2416
30th anniversary of Polish Alliance in Calgary, 1931-1961. 1977
39 below. 592
40th anniversary of the St. John's Institute, 1959. 1836
The 49ers. 3043
50 golden years, 1924-1974. 1842
50 years at the foot of the hill, 1925-1975. 291
50 years. Hill Spring Ward, 1910-1960. 370
50 years in the Barrhead United Church. 404
50 years of Grace, 1919-1969. 289
50 years. 1925-1975.. 424
50th anniversary. 1634
50th anniversary, Crescent Heights High School, 1915-1965. 1521
50th anniversary, Division 583, Amalgamated Transit Union. 2315
50th anniversary, Immaculata Hospital, Westlock, Alberta. 3378
50th Anniversary, 1907-1957. 1587
50th anniversary, 1912-1962. 351
50th anniversary, 1914-1964. 406
50th anniversary, 1917-1967. 323

60th anniversary. 367
60th anniversary, St. Louis Hospital, Bonnyville, Alberta. 3377
60th anniversary, Trinity Evangelical Lutheran Church, 1902-1962. 349
70 years a cowboy (a biography). 3490
70 years of miracles.. 85
75 years. 2247
75 years of grace, 1894-1969. 361
75th anniversary, Bethany Lutheran Congregation, Dickson, Alberta. 316
75th anniversary, First Baptist Church, Leduc, Alberta, 1894-1969. 382
75th anniversary, June 8, 1900-1975.. .384
75th anniversary, Ukrainian Catholic Parish of St. Nicholas, St. Michael. . . .344
75th anniversary, 1883-1958. 2911
1874 trek souvenir publication. 2504
1885. The Riel Rebellion. 2765
The 1921 Alberta provincial election. 2408
1952-1977, Paroisse Ste-Anne. 346
2,000 place names of Alberta. 2658
90 years at Elkwater Lake, Cypress Hills, Alberta. 3160

SUBJECT INDEX

SUBJECT INDEX

Aberhart, William 1568, 2401, 2406, 2421, 2438, 2447
Academic libraries 33
Accordion (Music) - Instruction 1385
Accountants - Alberta - Correspondence, reminiscences, etc 2734
Accounting 2150
Acculturation 1944, 1947, 1953, 1989
Acculturation, *see also* names of individual ethnic groups
Accurate News and Information Act (Alberta) 2415
Acme - History 2846, 3150
Acme. United Church 261
Adamson family 2697
Aden - History 3070
Adolescents - Business attitudes 2208
Adolescents - Political attitudes 2367, 2436
Adult education - Alberta 1511, 1592, 1598, 1612
Adult education - History 1536
Aeronautics 2333, 2349
Aeronautics - Canada 2314
Aesop - Adaptations 618
Africa - Description 237
Africa - Fiction 761
African languages - Bibliography 3
Aged - Housing 1786, 1787
Aging 1761
Agricultural cooperatives 3385, 3428
Agricultural cooperatives *see also* Albert Wheat Pool
Agricultural education 3401, 3460
Agricultural industries 2173
Agricultural produce - Marketing 2248
Agriculture - Alberta 2572, 3434, 3442
Agriculture - Economics 3406, 3413, 3431, 3453
Agriculture - Juvenile literature 3470
Agriculture - Peace River (district) 2522, 3457, 3458
Agriculture - Prairie Provinces 3420, 3422
Agriculture - St. Paul 3440
Agrologists 3456
Air Museum of Canada 2314
Aircraft noise 2133, 2145
Airdrie - History 3299
Airdrie. United Church 438
Alaska - Artifacts 2027
Alaska - Description 2650
Alaska - Pictorial views 2540
Alberta - Artifacts 2010, 2066
Alberta Association of Municipal Districts and Counties 2449
Alberta - Atlases 2655, 2659
Alberta - Biography 1745, 2377, 2701, 2715, 2716, 2816
Alberta Board of Industrial Relations 2205

Alberta, central - Description 2602
Alberta, central - Economic conditions 2127
Alberta, central - Social conditions 1733
Alberta. Child Welfare Dept 1778
Alberta College 1439
Alberta - Commerce 2086
Alberta Commission on Educational Planning 1471, 1567
Alberta Dairymen's Association 3429
Alberta. Department of Agriculture 3434, 3443
Alberta. Department of Education 1478, 1482
Alberta. Department of Neglected Children 1782
Alberta. Department of Public Welfare 1796, 1814
Alberta - Description 52, 2586, 2600, 2613, 2615, 2618, 2619, 2622, 2634, 2636, 2650, 2652, 2679
Alberta, east central - Migration 2534
Alberta - Ecology 2544
Alberta - Economic conditions 1733, 2086, 2099, 2104, 2108, 2114, 2123, 2144, 2148, 2149, 2151, 2176, 2300, 2302, 2360, 2446
Alberta - Economic history 2117
Alberta - Fiction 522, 605, 631, 639, 648, 657, 673, 688, 708, 709, 711, 721, 736, 771, 776, 796, 801, 831, 832
Alberta Fine Option Program 2476
Alberta - French language 444
Alberta Game Farm 3325, 744
Alberta Government Telephones 2322, 2330
Alberta Grazing Associations 3455
Alberta Hereford Association 3387
Alberta - Historic buildings 1124, 1133
Alberta - History 209, 2815, 2816, 2818, 2819, 2823, 2824, 2826, 2828, 2834, 2838, 2840, 2844
Alberta - History - Bibliography 11
Alberta - History - Juvenile literature 2814
Alberta - Hospitals 3370
Alberta Human Resources Development Authority 1789
Alberta Human Resources Research Council 1780, 1802
Alberta Indian Development System 1929
Alberta Indian Education Center 1494, 1930
Alberta - Industries 2106, 2108, 2155, 2199, 2208, 2219
Alberta Institute of Agrologists 3456
Albérta - Juvenile literature . 625, 659, 660, 661, 687, 749, 2753, 759, 2603, 2617
Alberta Land Surveyors Association 3412
Alberta - Land zoning 2563
Alberta Legal Aid Plan 2490
Alberta - Local finance 2101, 2140
Alberta - Local government 2084, 2101, 2140, 2449, 2459, 2463
Alberta - Maps 2654
Alberta Mennonite Women in Mission 238
Alberta Motor Association 2326
Alberta NewStart 1803
Alberta, northeastern - Recreation 1678

Alberta, northeastern - Social conditions 2148
Alberta, northern - Commerce 2232
Alberta, northern - Fiction 619
Alberta, northern - History 3133
Alberta, northern - Juvenile literature 633
Alberta Pharmaceutical Association 3348
Alberta - Photographic collections 2608
Alberta - Pictorial views 2604, 2632
Alberta - Politics . . 1103, 1104, 1105, 2364, 2379, 2383, 2388, 2390, 2408, 2409, 2410, 2413, 2416, 2417, 2424, 2425, 2426, 2427, 2437, 2439, 2443, 2446, 3442
Alberta - Politics - Fiction 608, 730
Alberta - Population 1997, 2528
Alberta Provincial Institute of Technology and Art *see* Southern Alberta Institute of Technology
Alberta Provincial Police 2512
Alberta Real Estate Association 2186
Alberta Royal Commission on Education, 1959 . . . . 1472, 1483, 1513
Alberta - Rural development 2521
Alberta Salt Company 2178
Alberta School Trustees' Association 1515, 1590
Alberta, southern - Artifacts 2013, 2019
Alberta, southern - Bibliography 8
Alberta, southern - Crime 1823
Alberta, southern - Description 2621, 2671, 2694, 3483, 3507
Alberta, southern - Economic conditions 2143
Alberta, southern - Environmental studies 3346
Alberta, southern - Fiction . . . 526, 601, 643, 644, 681, 699, 706, 762, 775, 795
Alberta, southern - Geography 3088
Alberta, southern - Historical geography 2529
Alberta, southern - History 2143, 2812, 2842, 2855, 3028, 3088, 3149
Alberta, southern - Juvenile literature 823
Alberta, southern - Pictorial views 2641
Alberta, southern - Population 1968, 1969
Alberta, southwestern - Geography 2514
Alberta, southwestern - Land use 2560
Alberta Special Games 1631
Alberta Teachers' Alliance *see* Alberta Teachers' Association
Alberta Teachers' Association 1473, 1504
Alberta Teachers' Association. English Council 1545
Alberta Teachers' Association - History 1530, 1589
Alberta. University *see* University of Alberta
Alberta Veterinary Medical Association 3418
Alberta, west central - Settlement 2595
Alberta Wheat Pool 3389, 3390, 3394, 3433, 3438
Alberta Women's Bureau 1739
Alberta Women's Christian Temperance Union 1763
Alberta Women's Institutes 1851, 3391, 3392
Albright, William Donald 3450, 3451
Alcohol and alcohol related problems *see* Alcoholism
Alcoholism 1800, 1807, 1822, 1828

Alder Flats - History . . . 3277
Alienation *see* Separatism
Alix - History . . . 3188, 3229
Alix. St. Pancras Anglican Church . . . 405
Alix. United Church . . . 264
All Saints Anglican Cathedral, Edmonton . . . 399
Alliance - History . . . 2848
Almighty Voice (Cree chief) . . . 2723, 2810
Almighty Voice (Cree chief) - Drama . . . 1076
Altona - History . . . 3199
Americans in Calgary . . . 1940
Amist - History . . . 3109
Amusements - Management . . . 1328
Anglican Church in Alberta . . . 225
Anglican church in Alberta, southern . . . 247
Anglican Church in Alix . . . 405
Anglican Church in Athabasca . . . 221
Anglican Church in Bashaw . . . 405
Anglican Church in Calgary . . 180, 181, 183, 248, 293, 294, 297, 2299, 301, 425
Anglican Church in Edmonton . . . 165, 232, 325, 328, 340, 341, 342, 2399
Anglican Church in Edson . . . 354
Anglican Church in Fort Vermilion . . . 359
Anglican Church in Innisfail . . . 366
Anglican Church in Lamerton . . . 405
Anglican Church in Lethbridge . . . 387
Anglican Church in Mirror . . . 405
Anglican Church in Pincher Creek . . . 389
Anglican Church in Rexboro . . . 411
Anglican Church in Vermilion . . . 415
Anglo-American Exploration Ltd . . . 2292
Angus Ridge - History . . . 2863
Animals - Alberta . . . 3319, 3327, 3509
Animals - Calgary . . . 3347
Animals - Cypress Hills . . . 3341
Animals - Edmonton . . . 3334
Animals in art - Exhibitions . . . 1193
Animals - Legends and stories . . . 571, 664, 744, 824, 828
Animals - Rocky Mountains . . . 3312, 3313
Animals *see also* Birds
Annexation . . . 2119
Anthrop-geography - Pacific Northwest . . . 2008
Apostolic Church of Pentecost . . . 215
Apprenticeship . . . 2234
Aquinas, Thomas, St . . . 65
Arabs in Alberta . . . 1863, 1933
Archaeology - Bibliography . . . 7
Archaeology - Conferences . . . 2022
Archaeology - Exhibitions . . . 2010
Archaeology - North America . . . 2037
Archer Memorial Hospital of Lamont School of Nursing, Lamont . . . 3366

Architecture - Rome 1149
Architecture *see also* subdivision Historic buildings under names of places, e.g. Calgary - Historic buildings
Ardenode - History 3123
Ardrossan - History 3302
Armena - History 1519
Armena. Scandia Lutheran Church 265
Armena - Schools 1519
Arrow-heads 2032, 2038
Arrowwood - History 2857
Art, Children's *see* Children's art
Art - Conferences 2054
Art, Eskimo *see* Inuit art
Art - Exhibitions 1140, 1142, 1153, 1154, 1155, 1159, 1160, 1162, 1165, 1170, 1171, 1172, 1182, 1183, 1184, 1186, 1189, 1193, 1197, 1199, 1200, 1202, 1203, 1204, 1205, 1206, 1207, 1208, 1211, 1213, 1214, 1215, 1218, 1219, 1221, 1226, 1230, 1238, 1240, 1241
Art, Indian *see* Indian art
Art, Pakistani *see* Pakistani art
Art *see also* Drawings, Paintings, Portraits
Art societies - Alberta 1116
Arts, Ukrainian *see* Ukrainian arts
Asia in art 2645
Assiniboine language *see* Stoney language
Assiniboine Mountain - History 3030
Association canadienne-française de l'Alberta 2437
Athabasca - Antiquities 2062
Athabasca - Description 2646
Athabasca - Fiction 751
Athabasca - History 221, 2527, 2832, 3134
Athabasca Landing Trail 2969
Athabasca - Schools 1516
Athabasca - Settlement 2583
Athabina - History 3078
Athapascan language *see* Chipewyan language
Austrians in Alberta 1963
Automobile industry and trade 2224
Automobiles 2327
Avonmore United Church, Edmonton 319
Bacon, Francis - Plays 1039
Baker, Perren 1514
Bancroft - History 2864
Bands (Music) - Calgary 1381
Bands (Music) - Instruction 1380
Banff Centre School of Fine Arts 1591, 1592, 1598, 1607
Banff - Description 2599, 2606, 2667, 2673
Banff - Fiction - Juvenile literature 658
Banff - History 2695, 2898, 2899, 3053, 3122
Banff National Park 3324
Banff National Park - Artifacts 2021

Banff National Park - Description 2639
Banff National Park - Environmental aspects 1674
Banff National Park - Geology 2597
Banff National Park - Land use 2574, 2575
Banff National Park - Recreation 1637
Banff. Peter Whyte Gallery *see* Peter Whyte Gallery, Banff
Banff - Recreation 1637
Banff School of Fine Arts *see* Banff Centre School of Fine Arts
Banff - Social conditions 1724
Banff Springs Hotel 3218
Banff. St. Mary's of the Assumption Catholic Church 280
Banff-Jasper Highway 2696
Baptist Church in Calgary 169, 267, 281, 284, 286
Baptist Church in Edmonton 347, 372
Baptist Church in Leduc 382
Baptist Church in Lethbridge 263
Baptist Church in Western Canada 205, 250
Bardo - Fiction 685
Barnett, John Walker 1589
Barons - History 2865
Barr Colonists 3074, 3296
Barr Colonists - Juvenile literature 632
Barr, Isaac M. 3074
Barrhead - German language 441
Barrhead - History 2866, 2867, 2868, 2992, 3058, 3094, 3263
Barrhead. United Church 404
Bashaw - History 3148
Bashaw. St. Peter's Anglican Church 405
Basilian Fathers 166, 167, 268, 269, 403
Basketball 1646, 1672
Bassano - History 2870
Battle Bend - History 2873
Battle River Valley - History 3130
Bawlf. Lutheran Church 271
Bayonets 2755
Bearberry Valley - History 3138
Bears *see* Grizzly bears
Bearspaw - History 3035
Beaumont - Geography 2545
Beaver Creek (site) - Artifacts 2061
Beaver Mines - History 2876
Beaverhills Lake - Biography 3321
Beaverlodge Agricultural Research Station 3450
Beaverlodge - History 3253
Beddington - History 2877
Bees - Juvenile literature 3386
Beiseker - History 3232
Beiseker. Our Lady of Assumption Catholic Parish 272
Bellevue. St. Cyril's Church 274
Belly River 2831

Belly River - Archaeology 2014, 2052
Belly River - Navigation 2340
Bennett, Richard Bedford Bennett, 1st viscount 2206, 2366, 2369, 2392
Beresford, Delayal James De La Poer, Lord 3441
Bergen - History 1892
Berrymoor - History 3141
Bérubé family 2699
Berwyn. Bissell Memorial Church 275
Berwyn - History 3050
Bethany Lutheran Church, Dickson 316
Bethel Lutheran Church, Wetaskiwin 434
Bethlehem Lutheran Church, Bruderheim 277
Bezanson - History 3190
Biatecka, Maria Kolumbia 246
Bible - Dictionaries 89
Bible in the schools *see* Religion in the public schools
Bible - Studies 75, 76, 80, 105, 109, 126, 127, 128, 129, 130, 131, 132, 133, 134, 135, 136, 137, 138, 139, 140, 141, 159, 2735
Big Bear (Cree chief) 2767, 2781, 2817
Big Bear (Cree chief) - Fiction 820
Big Horn (school district) - History 3231
Big Valley - History 3015, 3152
Bighorn Plains 1938
Bilingualism 1475, 1476, 1484, 1487
Bindloss - History 1542, 2885, 3016, 3075
Bindloss - Schools 1542
Birch Mountains - Artifacts 2039
Birds - Alberta 3331
Birds - Beaverhills Lake 3321
Bishop, Acenith A 2730
Bissell Memorial United Church, Berwyn 275
Blackburn family 2700
Blackburn, Robert Patterson 2700
Blackfeet Confederacy *see* Blackfoot Indians
Blackfoot Crossing - Fiction 785
Blackfoot Indians 1908
Blackfoot Indians - Calendar 73
Blackfoot Indians - Costumes 1918
Blackfoot Indians - Culture 1919, 1982
Blackfoot Indians - Economic conditions 2105
Blackfoot Indians - Education 1525, 1554
Blackfoot Indians - History 1554, 1869, 1903
Blackfoot Indians - Juvenile literature 653, 656, 763
Blackfoot Indians - Kinship 2065
Blackfoot Indians - Legends 2073, 2074, 2077, 2078
Blackfoot Indians - Missions 200, 247
Blackfoot Indians - Religion 72, 73, 119, 145, 2050
Blackfoot Indians - Social change 1943
Blackfoot language 500, 501
Blackfoot language - Grammar 498

Blackie - History 3003
Blair, Bob 2252
Blairmore - History 2887
Blind - Education 1493
Blood Indians - Archaeology 2013
Blood Indians - Culture 1965
Blood Indians - Culture conflict 1882
Blood Indians - Customs 1920
Blood Indians - History 1868, 1961
Blood Indians - Kinship 2065
Blood Indians - Missions 198, 229
Blood Indians - Psychological aspects 1897
Blueberry Mountain - History 2942
Bluffton - History 3089
Boating 1698
Boer War 2759
Bon Accord - History 2939
Bonnyville - Economic conditions 2093
Bonnyville - Employment 2523
Bonnyville - French language 1861
Bonnyville - History 3023
Bonnyville - Hospitals 3377
Borradaile - History 3214
Botany *see* Plants
Botha - History 3462
Boudicca - Fiction 663
Bow City - History 3236
Bow Island - History 2881, 2946, 3272
Bow River Range 3494
Bow River Valley - Description 3469
Bow Valley - Recreation 1694
Bowen, Charles 211
Bowlen, John James 2404
Bowness - History 3176
Bowtell - History 3214
Boy Scouts 1844, 1848, 1849, 1852
Boyne Lake - Description 3513
Bradford, Richard 225
Bragg Creek - History 3162
Brant - History 3003
Brentview Baptist Church, Calgary 281
Breton - History 3141
Brick, John Gough 234
Brightview. Emmaus Lutheran Church 276
Brisebois, Ephrem A. - Juvenile literature 3280
Britannia Colony *see* Barr Colonists
British Columbia - Commerce 2096
British Commonwealth Games 1640, 1704
British Commonwealth Games - Photographic collections 1649, 1662
Britton, James 1570

Broadcasting . . . 2332
Brookland (school district) - History . . . 3058
Brooks - Description . . . 3501
Brooks - Fiction . . . 757
Brooks - History . . . 2967
Brooks Range, Alaska - Antiquities . . . 2058
Brown, John George *see* Brown, Kootenai
Brown, Kootenai . . . 1677, 2677, 2841
Brownfield - History . . . 2954
Brownvale - History . . . 3050
Bruderfield Moravian Church, Edmonton . . . 430
Bruderheim. Bethlehem Lutheran Church . . . 277
Buchanan, William Asbury . . . 62
Buck Lake - History . . . 3277
Buckingham House - Archaeology . . . 2048
Buffalo Child Long Lance (Blood Indian) . . . 1868
Buffalo Coulee (school district) - History . . . 2902
Buffalo - History . . . 3075
Buffalo Lake - History . . . 2941
Buford - History . . . 2903
Bugnet, Georges . . . 534
Building *see* Construction industry
Bullock family . . . 2702
Bull's Head - Juvenile literature . . . 3280
Burns, Patrick . . . 2213, 2239
Burnt Lake - History . . . 2906
Bush pilots . . . 2335, 2342
Bush pilots - Juvenile literature . . . 599
Business education . . . 2163
Businesses, small *see* Small businesses
Butler, Sir William . . . 2798
Butter industry - Alberta . . . 2162
Buxton, Earl W . . . 1555
Byemoor - History . . . 2918
Cactus Flower (site) - Artifacts . . . 2016
Calahoo - History . . . 2908
Calder School, Edmonton . . . 2909
Calgary and Edmonton Railway . . . 2331
Calgary - Biography . . . 2720, 2726, 3278
Calgary. Brentview Baptist Church . . . 281
Calgary - Buildings . . . 2959
Calgary. Canadian Martyrs Catholic Church . . . 282, 283
Calgary. Cathedral Church of the Redeemer . . . 309
Calgary. Central United Church . . . 401
Calgary - Chinatown . . . 1728
Calgary. Christ Church . . . 425
Calgary College . . . 1606
Calgary. Crescent Heights High School . . . 1521
Calgary. Crescent Heights United Church . . . 315
Calgary - Description . . . 2668, 2688, 3493

Calgary - Economic conditions 2131, 2169
Calgary - Environmental studies 3338
Calgary - Expansion 2455, 2582, 2593
Calgary Family Bureau 1751
Calgary. Fire Department 3102
Calgary. First Baptist Church 267, 284
Calgary. First Lutheran Church 285
Calgary. First Spiritualist Church 313
Calgary General Hospital 1801
Calgary - Geography 2562
Calgary. Glengarry Elementary School 1522
Calgary Golf and Country Club 1633
Calgary. Grace Baptist Church 286
Calgary. Grace Lutheran Church 287
Calgary Herald (newspaper) 44
Calgary. Heritage Park 2912
Calgary Highlanders *see* Canada. Army. Calgary Highlanders
Calgary. Hillhurst United Church 402
Calgary - Historic buildings 3244, 3245, 3278
Calgary - History 2719, 2850, 2859, 2860, 2894, 2910, 2911, 2912, 2949, 2950, 3011, 3017, 3022, 3034, 3040, 3076, 3082, 3129, 3154, 3176, 3189, 3193, 3205, 3213, 3241, 3288, 3300
Calgary - History, military 2749
Calgary - Hospitals 3350, 3351, 3374, 3375
Calgary - Industries 2168, 2169
Calgary Inter-Faith Community Action Committee 219
Calgary - Juvenile literature 717, 720, 768
Calgary. King Edward School 1523
Calgary. Knox United Church 288
Calgary - Land use 2584
Calgary - Mayors 2458
Calgary. Mount Calvary Lutheran Church 289
Calgary Municipal Railway 2337
Calgary - Museums 1123
Calgary. Our Lady of Mercy Croation Catholic Parish 290
Calgary. Our Lady of Perpetual Help Catholic Parish 291
Calgary - Parks 1625, 1628, 1630, 2568
Calgary - Pictorial views 1135, 2631, 2633, 2912, 3300
Calgary - Police 2503
Calgary - Politics 2456, 2457, 2458, 2466
Calgary Power Ltd 2171
Calgary Public Library 21
Calgary Real Estate Board 2186
Calgary - Recreation 1635
Calgary. Sacred Heart Catholic Church 369
Calgary - Schools 1487, 1520, 1543, 1549, 1579, 1584
Calgary - Social conditions 1735, 1781, 1944
Calgary - Sports 1680
Calgary. St. Anthony's Catholic Parish 292
Calgary. St. Barnabas' Anglican Church 293, 294

Calgary. St. Boniface Catholic Church . . . 295
Calgary. St. Joseph's Catholic Church . . . 296
Calgary. St. Martin's Anglican Church . . . 297
Calgary. St. Mary's Cathedral . . . 298
Calgary. St. Michael and All Angels' Anglican Church . . . 299
Calgary. St. Pius the Tenth Catholic Parish . . . 300
Calgary. St. Stephen's Anglican Church . . . 301
Calgary. St. Stephen's Ukrainian Church . . . 371
Calgary Stampede . . . 1634, 1667
Calgary Stampede - Caricatures and cartoons . . . 1102
Calgary Stampede - Juvenile literature . . . 616, 654, 670, 671, 1670
Calgary Stampede - Music . . . 1449
Calgary Stampeder Football Club . . . 1660
Calgary. Stanley Jones School . . . 1524
Calgary - Subdivisions . . . 2581
Calgary - Transportation . . . 2337, 2344, 2348, 2354
Calgary. Trinity Evangelical Lutheran Church . . . 302
Calgary. Trinity United Church . . . 413
Calgary - Urban planning . . . 1728, 2516, 2567
Calgary Urban Treaty Indian Alliance . . . 1985
Calgary. Wesley United Church . . . 303
Calgary (district) - Settlement patterns . . . 2585
Calgary-Banff highway . . . 2672
Calvary Lutheran Church, Wetaskiwin . . . 435
Cameron Commission *see* Alberta Royal Commission on Education
Cameron, Donald . . . 1592, 1598, 1607
Campbell, Alexander Maxwell . . . 2713
Campbell family . . . 2713
Campgrounds . . . 1697
Camping . . . 1657
Camrose - Commerce . . . 2235
Camrose - Communication . . . 2347
Camrose - Description . . . 3505
Camrose - Economic conditions . . . 2109
Camrose. Grace Lutheran Church . . . 439
Camrose - History . . . 2920
Camrose - Hospitals . . . 3380
Camrose Lutheran College . . . 213
Camrose. Messiah Lutheran Church . . . 306
Camrose. St. Francis Xavier Catholic Church . . . 307
Camrose. United Church . . . 365
Canada. Army. Calgary Highlanders . . . 2752
Canada. Army. Fort Garry Horse . . . 2756
Canada. Army. Lord Strathcona's Horse . . . 2753
Canada. Army. Loyal Edmonton Regiment. (3rd Battalion, Princess Patricia's Light Infantry) . . . 2754, 2757, 2758, 2760
Canada. Army. 8th Canadian Reconnaissance Regiment (14th Canadian Hussars) . . . 2751
Canada - Constitutional history . . . 2375, 2427
Canada - Defenses . . . 2750

Canada. Dept. of Agriculture. Experimental Station,
Beaverlodge, *see* Beaverlodge Agricultural Research Station
Canada - Description 2605, 2609, 2612, 2625
Canada - Economic conditions 2091, 2103, 2107, 2125
Canada - Federal-provincial relations *see* Federalism
Canada - Foreign aid 2386, 2387
Canada - Foreign relations - U.S.A 2380
Canada - Foreign relations - U.S.S.R 2372
Canada - History 2739, 2743
Canada. Navy 2761
Canada - Politics 2362, 2377, 2385, 2388, 2390, 2391, 2394
Canada. Royal Canadian Mounted Police, *see* Royal Canadian Mounted Police
Canada - Social conditions 1719
Canada West Foundation 2402
Canadian literature 524
Canadian literature - Collections 556, 561, 562, 563, 564, 567, 570, 582
Canadian Lutheran Bible Institute 179
Canadian Martyrs Catholic Church, Calgary 282
Canadian Martyrs Church, Calgary 283
Canadian Nazarene College, Red Deer 251
Canadian Northern Railway 2227
Canadian Pacific Railway 2317
Canadian Red Cross Society. Alberta-Northwest Territories Division.
Calgary Branch 3352
Canadian Weekly Newspapers Association. Alberta Division 45
Canadian Western Natural Gas Co. Ltd 2257, 2258
Canmore - History 2856
Canmore - Recreation 1637, 1696
Capital punishment 1766
Carbon - History 3037
Card, Charles Ora 209
Card tricks 1262, 1263, 1272, 1277, 1280, 1282, 1287, 1298, 1312, 1313,
1314, 1316, 1318, 1320, 1355, 1371, 1372, 1373, 1375, 1377, 1378
Cardogan - History 3249
Cardston - Fiction 679
Cardston - History 2872, 2921, 3063, 3116, 3237
Caricatures and cartoons - Alberta 1098, 1101, 1102, 1103, 1104, 1105
Caricatures and cartoons - Rocky Mountains 1100
Carmangay - History 2922
Carnwood - History 3141
Caroline - History 3216
Carriages 2324
Carseland - History 2924
Carstairs - History 2925
Carstairs. United Church 308, 412
Castor - History 2917, 2929
Cathedral Church of the Redeemer, Calgary 309
Catholic Church 142, 143
Catholic Church in Alberta 100, 3266, 3267
Catholic Church in Battle River 390

Catholic Church in Beiseker . . . 272
Catholic Church in Bellevue . . . 274
Catholic Church in Calgary . . . 164, 178, 282, 283, 290, 291, 292, 295, 296, 298, 300, 309, 369
Catholic Church in Camrose . . . 307
Catholic Church in Coalhurst . . . 391
Catholic Church in Drumheller . . . 323
Catholic Church in Edmonton . . . 186, 217, 317, 318, 329, 336, 338, 339, 345, 346, 358
Catholic Church in Edson . . . 352
Catholic Church in Fort Kent . . . 262
Catholic Church in Lac La Biche . . . 381
Catholic Church in Lac Ste. Anne . . . 192
Catholic Church in Lamoureux . . . 199
Catholic Church in Lethbridge . . . 388
Catholic Church in Mallaig . . . 379
Catholic Church in McLennan . . . 392
Catholic Church in Medicine Hat . . . 393
Catholic Church in Pickardville . . . 360
Catholic Church in St. Isidore . . . 419
Catholic Church in St. Lina . . . 421
Catholic Church in St. Paul . . . 190, 191, 321
Catholic Church in St. Vincent . . . 422
Catholic Church in Thorsby . . . 385
Catholic Church in Vegreville . . . 199, 3269
Catholic Church in Vimy . . . 429
Catholic Church *see also* Eastern Catholic Churches
Catholic schools *see* Separate schools
Catholic Women's League, Edmonton . . . 186
Cattle brands . . . 3447, 3449
Cayley - History . . . 2930
C.C.F. *see* Co-operative Commonwealth Federation
Central Alberta *see* Alberta, central
Central Baptist Church, Edmonton . . . 372
Central Lutheran Church, Edmonton . . . 324
Central United Church, Calgary . . . 401
Ceramics *see* Pottery
Cereal - History . . . 2931
Cereal - Schools . . . 1565
Cessford - History . . . 2891
Champion - History . . . 2943
Charcoal (Kainah Indian) . . . 1886
Charismatic movement . . . 108
Chautauga . . . 1257
Chauvin - History . . . 2935
Chauvin. Westminster Presbyterian Church . . . 440
Cheadle - History . . . 2924
Chesterfield House . . . 2779, 2830
Chestermere Lake - History . . . 2937, 3172
Chickens *see* Poultry

Child care 1749, 1750, 1759, 1778, 1782, 1817
Children - Alberta 1858
Children as consumers 2130
Children's art 1120
Children's literature *see* Juvenile literature
Children's theatre 1256
China - Description 2373, 256
China - History 2745
Chinese in Alberta 1884
Chinese in Alberta - Social change 1913
Chinese in Calgary 1728, 1866
Chinook - Schools 1565
Chipewyan Indians - Artifacts 2051
Chipewyan Indians - Culture 1951, 2051
Chipewyan Indians - Kinship 1990
Chipewyan Indians - Social change 1726
Chipewyan Indians - Social conditions 1712
Chipewyan language 497
Christ Church, Calgary 425
Christ Church, Edmonton 325
Christian converts *see* Converts
Christian life 79, 83, 96, 97, 101, 102, 110, 111, 113, 114, 116, 117, 118, 124, 148, 150, 151, 152, 154, 155, 235, 1744, 1747, 1748, 1756
Christian Reformed Church in Iron Springs 368
Christianity 81
Chuckwagon racing 1626
Church and education 1557, 1558, 1577
Church and social problems 1941
Church architecture 1124, 1133
Church Missionary Society 200
Church of God - History 207
Church of Jesus Christ of Latter-Day Saints in Canada see Mormons
Church of St. John the Evangelist, Pincher Creek 389
Church of the Good Shepherd, Edmonton 326
Church Slavonic language 507
Churches, rural 3446
Citizens' associations - Edmonton 1720
Clairmont - History 3190
Claresholm - History 2940, 3191
Claresholm. United Church 311
Clark, Charles Joseph *see* Clark, Joe
Clark, Joe 2370, 2381
Class distinction *see* Social classes
Clearwater-Rocky Forest - Recreational capability 1684
Cleverville - History 2943
Clifford E. Lee Collection 1247
Clive - History 3188
Clive. United Church 433
Cluny - Artifacts 2030
Coal Branch - Historical geography 2551

Coal Branch - History 3185, 3224
Coal mining - Alberta 2158, 2229, 2238, 2243
Coal mining - Crowsnest Pass 2204, 2547
Coal mining - Edmonton 2542
Coal mining - Hinton 2535
Coal mining - Labour unions 2222
Coal mining - Luscar 2223
Coal mining - Nordegg 2226, 2227
Coaldale - History 2944
Coaldale. United Church 312
Coalhurst. St. Joseph's Catholic Parish 391
Cochrane Game Farm 3333
Cochrane - History 2945
Cochrane Ranch 3430
Cohen, Leonard 538
Cold Lake - Social conditions 1712
Cole, Andrew F 2730
Coleman, Kit 51
Coleman. St. Paul's United Church 356
Collective bargaining 2237
Collège Universitaire Saint Jean 1595
Commerce *see* Retail trade
Commonwealth Games, *see* British Commonwealth Games
Community and school - Edmonton 1485
Community colleges - Alberta 1594, 1600
Community colleges - Ontario 1600
Community development - Alberta 1713, 1731, 1739, 1740
Community development - Cold Lake 1712
Community development - Edmonton 1725, 1738, 1830, 1831
Community development - Hinton 1722
Community development - Red Deer 1727
Community leagues 1725
Community schools 1485
Compeer - History 3199
Confederation 2360, 2361, 2374, 2910
Conjuring 1261, 1264, 1265, 1266, 1267, 1268, 1270, 1271, 1273, 1274, 1275, 1276, 1277, 1278, 1279, 1281, 1283, 1286, 1288, 1289, 1290, 1291, 1292, 1293, 1294, 1297, 1299, 1300, 1301, 1302, 1303, 1306, 1307, 1309, 1310, 1311, 1315, 1317, 1319, 1322, 1323, 1326
Conjuring - Apparatus and supplies 1295, 1296
Conjuring - Bibliography 1308
Conjuring Creek - Description 63
Conjuring - Dictionaries 1269
Conjuring - Juvenile literature 1304
Conquerville - History 2951
Conquest, Mary Hagen (Owen) 3358
Conrich - History 2937, 3172
Conscription, military *see* Military conscription
Conservation of wildlife *see* Wildlife - Conservation
Consort - History 2955

Construction industry - Edmonton 2230
Consul - History 3234
Converts - Biography 67, 68, 161, 258
Conveyancing - Alberta 2491
Co-operative Commonwealth Federation 2365, 2422, 2440
Cooperatives, agricultural *see* Agricultural cooperatives
Coote, George Gibson 2411
Cormie Ranch (site) - Artifacts 2043
Cornwall, James Kennedy 2616
Coronation - History 2952, 2953, 2954, 3173
Countess - History 2870
Coutts - History 3262
Cowboys 3448
Cowley - History 2905
Cowley. United Church 314
Coyote Flats - History 3247
Craigmyle - History 2874
Cravath Corners - History 2878
Cree Indians 1881, 1962
Cree Indians - Culture 1888, 1896, 1906, 1907
Cree Indians - Culture conflict 1882
Cree Indians - Customs 2648
Cree Indians - Education 1508
Cree Indians - Fiction 786, 827
Cree Indians - Juvenile literature 735, 825
Cree Indians - Legends 2068, 2069, 2070, 2071
Cree Indians - Social change 2003
Cree Indians - Tattooing 2042
Cree language 59, 503
Cree language - Alphabet 469
Cree language - Dictionaries 89, 476, 486, 489
Cree language - Grammar 473, 478
Cree language - Study and teaching 491
Cree language - Text-books . . . 468, 470, 471, 472, 474, 475, 477, 479, 480, 481, 482, 483, 484, 485, 487, 488, 490, 492, 493, 494, 495, 499, 502
Cremona - History 3258
Crescent Heights School, Calgary 1521
Crescent Heights United Church, Calgary 315
Creśtomere (School District) - History 2858
Crime 1823
Criminal justice - Administration 2486
Criminal law 2478
Criminals - Manitoba 1769
Cristall, Abraham 1880
Cross family 2725
Crossfield - History 2956
Crowfoot (Blackfoot chief) 2821, 2827
Crown petroleum rights 2261
Crowsnest Pass Agreement 2318

Crowsnest Pass - Description 2610, 2676
Crowsnest Pass - History 2665, 2957
Crowsnest Pass - Juvenile literature 2547
Crowsnest Pass - Labour 2204
Crowsnest Pass - Politics 2462
Crystal Spring (site) - Artifacts 2059
Culture conflict 1873, 1917, 1989, 2004
Cumberland (school district) - History 2958
Cunningham, Catherine Yule 188
Curling 1654
CUTIA *see* Calgary Urban Treaty Alliance
Cypress Hills - Archaeology 2029
Cypress Hills - Description 2691
Cypress Hills - History 3160, 3239, 3344, 3408
Cypress Hills Provincial Park 2576, 3341
Cypress Hills - Recreation 1699
Czar - History 2851, 3109
Dairy farming 3429
Dairy farming *see also* Butter industry
Dalemead - History 2961
Dalroy - History 3123
Dalum - History 2962
Davin, Nicholas Flood 1070
Day care *see* Child care
Day parole 1792
Daysland. Knox United Church 266
De Winton - History 2966
Deaf - Education 1501
Debolt - History 3165
Delacour - History 2937, 3172
Delburne - History 3206
Delburne. United Church 304
Delia - History 2874
Demons 157
Dentistry - Alberta 3361
Depression 2787, 3411, 3489
Depression - Fiction 822
Derbytown - History 3125
Devil *see* Demons
Devon - Description 2670
Dewberry - History 3044
Dewdney Trail - History 2664
Dickson. Bethany Lutheran Congregation 316
Dickson - History 2971
Didsbury - History 2847, 3099, 3258, 3293
Dinton - History 2972
Divorce - Alberta 2474, 2475
Dixonville - History 3101
Doctors *see* Physicians
Dogpound - History 2913

Dogpound Valley - History . . . 3295
Domestic relations - Alberta . . . 2479, 2484
Dominican Sisters . . . 246
Dominion Cartridge Co . . . 2184
Donalda - History . . . 2974
Donnelly - History . . . 2875
Dorothy - History . . . 3220
Doucet, Joseph - Juvenile literature . . . 3280
Draper (site)- Archaeology . . . 2047
Drawings - Exhibitions . . . 1157, 1161
Drayton Valley - History . . . 2982
Drug abusers, Rehabilitation programs *see* Rehabilitation programs for drug abusers
Drugs *see* Narcotics . . . 1785
Drumheller East - History . . . 2986
Drumheller - History . . . 3061, 3142, 3200
Drumheller Institution . . . 1798
Drumheller. Knox United Church . . . 322
Drumheller - Land use . . . 2580
Drumheller. St. Anthony's Catholic Parish . . . 323
Duchess - Description . . . 3486
Duffield (site)- Archaeology . . . 2036
Duhamel - History . . . 3047
Dumont, Gabriel . . . 2800
Dumont, Gabriel - Fiction . . . 819
Dutch in Edmonton . . . 1983
D'Youville, Marie Marguerite *see* Youville, Marie Marguerite d'
Eagle Creek - Description . . . 3502
Eagle Hill - History . . . 1892, 2976
Eagle Valley - History . . . 2990
Eaglenest Portage (site) - Artifacts . . . 2039
Early childhood education . . . 443, 1515
East Central Alberta *see* Alberta, east central
East Europeans . . . 1864
East Europeans in Alberta . . . 1914, 2006
East Europeans in Canada . . . 1865
East Indians in Canada . . . 1894
East Prairie - History . . . 2991
Eastburg - Description . . . 3491
Eastburg - History . . . 2992
Eastern Catholic Churches . . . 149
Eastern Irrigation District . . . 3400, 3444
Eastern Irrigation District - Land use . . . 2578
Eckville - History . . . 2994
Ecology - Bibliography . . . 4
Edberg - History . . . 2997
Edgerton - History . . . 2995
Edmonton . All Saints' Anglican Cathedral . . . 399
Edmonton . Avonmore United Church . . . 319
Edmonton - Biography . . . 1538

Edmonton . Bruderfield Moravian Church 430
Edmonton Bulletin (newspaper) 2331
Edmonton . Calder School 2909
Edmonton . Central Baptist Church 372
Edmonton . Central Lutheran Church 324
Edmonton . Christ Church 325
Edmonton . Church of the Good Shepherd 326
Edmonton Club 1835
Edmonton . Collège Universitaire Saint Jean 1595
Edmonton - Commerce 2232
Edmonton Commercial Graduates Basketball Club 1646, 1672
Edmonton Dental Nurses and Assistants Association 3361
Edmonton - Description 1902, 2607, 2733, 2734, 2983
Edmonton - Description - Juvenile literature 2682
Edmonton Dunvegan and British Columbia railway 2357
Edmonton - Economic conditions 2118, 2119, 2132, 2145, 2154, 2192
Edmonton Education Society *see* Education Society of Edmonton
Edmonton - Environmental studies 3340
Edmonton Exhibition 2175
Edmonton - Expansion 2455, 2531, 2533, 2577, 2591
Edmonton Family Court Conciliation Project 1742, 1757
Edmonton Federation of Community Leagues 1725
Edmonton - Fiction 730, 779, 805
Edmonton - Geography 2543, 2565
Edmonton - German language 442
Edmonton Grads, *see* Edmonton Commercial Graduates Basketball Club
Edmonton . Heimtal Moravian Church 431, 432
Edmonton . Highlands United Church 327
Edmonton - Historic buildings 3260
Edmonton - Historical geography 2518, 2519, 2542, 2548
Edmonton - History 1984, 2331, 2518, 2888, 2909, 2926, 2927,
2928, 2970, 3032, 3054, 3127, 3128, 3131, 3221, 3268
Edmonton . Holy Trinity Church 328
Edmonton - Hospitals 3360, 3368
Edmonton House 2830
Edmonton House - Archaeology 2048
Edmonton . Immaculate Conception Catholic Church 329
Edmonton Industrial Airport 2133
Edmonton . Knox-Metropolitan United Church 330
Edmonton - Labour disputes 2160
Edmonton - Manufactures 2209
Edmonton . McDougall United Church 331, 332, 333
Edmonton . Moravian Church 334
Edmonton - Parks 1647, 1648, 2557
Edmonton - Pictorial views 1134, 1137
Edmonton - Police 2499
Edmonton - Politics 2452, 2453, 2461, 2464, 2468
Edmonton Public Library 16, 18, 22
Edmonton . Queen Alexandra School 1586
Edmonton - Recreation 1642, 1688

Edmonton - Residential mobility 1791
Edmonton . Robertson-Wesley United Church 335, 407
Edmonton . Ross Sheppard Composite High School 1539
Edmonton . Royal Alexandra Hospital 3360
Edmonton . Rutherford School 1540
Edmonton . Saint Joachim Church 336
Edmonton . Saints Constantine and Helen Romanian Othodox Parish . . . 337
Edmonton - Satellite communities 2537, 2541
Edmonton - Schools 1526, 3221
Edmonton - Settlement 2550, 2559
Edmonton - Social conditions 1781, 1824, 1831
Edmonton Social Planning Council 1820
Edmonton . Spruce Avenue School 1541
Edmonton . St. Agnes Catholic Church 317, 318
Edmonton . St. Alphonsus Catholic Parish 338
Edmonton . St. Andrew's Catholic Parish 339
Edmonton . St. Anthony's Catholic Parish 358
Edmonton . St. Barnabas Anglican Church 340
Edmonton . St. Faith's Anglican Church 341
Edmonton . St. James United Church 437
Edmonton . St. John the Evangelist Anglican Church 342
Edmonton . St. John's Evangelical Lutheran Church 343
Edmonton . St. John's Institute 1836
Edmonton . St. Joseph's Seminary 420
Edmonton . St. Nicholas, St. Michael Ukrainian Catholic Church 344
Edmonton . St. Pius X Catholic Parish 345
Edmonton . St. Stephen's College 254
Edmonton . Ste. Anne Catholic Parish 346
Edmonton . Strathcona Baptist Church 347
Edmonton . Strathcona High School 1550
Edmonton . Strathearn United Church 348
Edmonton - Subdivisions 2538, 2594
Edmonton Symphony Orchestra 1382
Edmonton Transit System 2325, 2352
Edmonton - Transportation 2325, 2339, 2343, 2352, 2354, 2355, 2356
Edmonton . Trinity Evangelical Lutheran Church 349
Edmonton - Urban planning 2119
Edmonton . Wesley United Church 350
Edmonton . Westminster United Church 351
Edmonton Women's Shelter 1794
Edmonton-Calgary corridor 2579
Edmonton-Calgary Trail 2321
Edmonton-Devon Restricted Development Area 2546
Edson - Drama 1081
Edson - History 2996, 3274
Edson - Hospitals 3383
Edson . Sacred Heart Catholic Parish 352
Edson . United Church 353
Edson-Grande Prairie Trail - History 3274
Education, adult *see* Adult education

Education - Alberta 1478, 1482, 1486, 1491, 1533, 1568, 1571, 1572, 1575
Education - Alberta - Finance 1474, 1477, 1490, 1505
Education and church *see* Church and education
Education, Business *see* Business education
Education - Calgary 1480, 1537
Education - Canada 1489
Education - Curricula 1570
Education, early childhood *see* Early childhood education
Education - Finance 1500
Education - Lethbridge 1518
Education - Periodicals - Bibliography 2
Education, secondary *see* Secondary education
Education Society of Edmonton 1562
Education - Theses 39
Education - Theses - Bibliography 6
Educational radio *see* Radio in education
Edwards, Bob 53
Elbow-Sheep Wilderness 1616
Electric power 2170, 2225, 2229
Elizabeth Metis Settlement 3084
Elk Island National Park - Description 3318
Elk Point - History 2880, 3004
Elkwater - History 3160
Elnora - History 2936
Emmaus Lutheran Church, Brightview 276
Employment 2200
Employment- Edmonton 2196, 2233
Empress - History 2998
Empress. St. Mary the Virgin Anglican Church 354
Enchant - History 2987
Endiang - History 3087
Energy consumption 2111
Energy policy 2284
Energy resources - Alberta 2137
Energy resources - Canada 2097
Energy resources - Costs 2187, 2199
Energy resources - Western Canadia 2283
Energy resources *see also* Petroleum industry, Natural Gas industry
England - Description 2630
English language 461, 466
English language - Pronunciation 447
English language - Slang 460
Enoch Band 2003
Erasmus, Peter 2777
Eskimo art *see* Inuit art
Eskimos *see* Inuit
Estate Tax Rebate Act (Alberta) 2129
Esther - History 3227
Ethnic groups 1968, 1969, 1970, 1971, 1984, 1997
Ethnic groups - Religion 160

Ethnic groups *see also* names of specific ethnic groups
Ethylene 2305
Etzikom - History 3183
Evangelistic work 106, 121, 122, 147, 156, 158, 171
Evangelistic work *see also* Missions
Evangelists - Biography 85, 146
Evolution 87
Exceptional children 1788
Exceptional children - Education 1509, 1775
Eye Opener (newspaper) 48, 49, 53
Fairgrove - History 3158
Fairview - Description 2687
Fairview - History 3135, 3175
Fairview. St. Paul's United Church 380
Falher - French language 457
Falher - Geography 2515
Falher - History 2875, 3001, 3119
Family 1755
Farm life 3446, 3466, 3469, 3473, 3475, 3476, 3477, 3478, 3479, 3480, 3481, 3482, 3483, 3484, 3485, 3486, 3487, 3496, 3497, 3498, 3501, 3503, 3504, 3505, 3508, 3510, 3511, 3513
Farm mechanization 3426, 3445
Farm tenancy 3398
Farm Women's Union of Alberta 3468
Farmers' markets *see* Agricultural produce - Marketing
Farming *see* Agriculture
Farrell Lake - History 3055
Fawcett *see* Athabina
Federal - History 2953
Federal Technical and Vocational Training Act (1961) 2165
Federalism 2363, 2364, 2384
Ferguson, Emily *see* Murphy, Emily (Ferguson)
Ferguson Flats - History 3004
Fidler, Peter 2795
Field hockey 1706
Filipinos in Alberta 1895
Filles de Jésus 197
First Baptist Church, Calgary 267, 284
First Baptist Church, Leduc 382
First Baptist Church, Lethbridge 263
First Christian Reformed Church, Red Deer 273
First Lutheran Church, Calgary 285
First Spiritualist Church, Calgary 313
First United Church, Hanna 310
First United Church, Wetaskiwin 436
Fish Creek Provincial Park 3347
Fishing 1635, 1675
Fitness and Amateur Sport Act (Canada) 1708
Flatbush *see* Athabina
Flathead Indians 1921

Fleet - History 2953
Flying saucers *see* Unidentified flying objects
Folk tales 2075, 2083
Food - Distribution 2147
Food services - Labour 2177
Food services *see also* Restaurants
Football 1660
Football - Injuries 1645
Foothills (municipal district) - History 2901, 3162
Foothills (municipal district) - Recreation 1693
Forbes, Alexander 417
Foreign ownership of natural resources *see* Natural resources - Foreign ownership
Foremost - History 2907, 3124
Forest industries - Alberta 2176, 3336
Forest industries - Alberta, northern 2215
Forest industries *see also* Lumber industry, Pulp and paper
Forestburg - Description 3465
Forestburg - History 3261
Fort Assiniboine - History 3151
Fort Augustus 3128
Fort Chipewyan - Geography 2566
Fort Chipewyan - History 3187
Fort Chipewyan - Social conditions 1726
Fort Edmonton 2605, 3127, 3128
Fort Edmonton - Fiction 765
Fort Edmonton - History 3012
Fort Edmonton - Pictorial views 3012
Fort Edmonton - Reconstruction 2031
Fort Garry Horse *see* Canada. Army. Fort Garry Horse
Fort Kent. Catholic Church 262
Fort Macleod - Fiction 723
Fort Macleod - History 2505, 2509, 3013, 3067, 3136
Fort Macleod - Industries 2190
Fort Macleod. Trinity United Church 363
Fort McMurray - Geography 2549
Fort McMurray - History 2947, 2960
Fort McMurray - Industries 2178
Fort McMurray - Settlement 2588
Fort Saskatchewan - Economic conditions 2124
Fort Saskatchewan - History 2861, 3208
Fort Vermilion. St. Luke's Mission 359
Fortune-telling 1284, 1285, 1321, 1325, 1334, 1336, 1337, 1338, 1341, 1344, 1347, 1352
Four-day week 2242
France 2736
Franciscans 195
Franciscans - Missions - Alberta 208
Frank - History 2854
Franke, Erich 2755

Fraser Canyon - Description . . . 2674
Freedom - History . . . 3018
Freemasons . . . 1837, 1843
Freight rates . . . 2318
French Canadians in Alberta . . . 1859, 1860, 2437, 2545
French Canadians in Bonnyville . . . 1861
French Canadians in Edmonton . . . 3054
French Canadians in Peace River (district) . . . 1931, 2520, 620
French Canadians in St. Paul . . . 2892
French language . . . 449
French language - Alberta . . . 443, 444, 1861
French language - Falher . . . 457
French language - Pronunciation . . . 452, 455, 457
French language - St. Paul . . . 455
French language - Teaching . . . 463
Frewen, Moreton . . . 3461
Frog Lake - History . . . 3020
Frog Lake Massacre . . . 1917, 2782, 2817
Funerals . . . 1762
Fur trade . . . 1943, 2048, 2779, 2788, 2802, 2830, 2839, 2849, 2862, 3187
Fur trade - Juvenile literature . . . 597, 600, 765
Furniture - Exhibitions . . . 1158
Gadsby - History . . . 3005
Gaetz family . . . 2703
Gallie, Tommie . . . 1191
Galt School of Nursing, Lethbridge . . . 3363
Galt, Sir Alexander Tilloch . . . 2143
Game Farms *see* Alberta Game Farm, Camrose Game Farm
Garnier, Henri . . . 199
Garrington - History . . . 2896
Gem - History . . . 3112
Genesee. St. John's School of Alberta . . . 1544
Geographical names - Alberta . . . 2656, 2657, 2658, 2660, 2662
Geographical names - Southern Alberta . . . 2661
Geography - Essays . . . 2570
Gergel (campsite) - Artifacts . . . 2014
German language - Barrhead . . . 441
German language - Medicine Hat . . . 448
German language - Phonology . . . 442
German language - Pronunciation . . . 446
German language - Stony Plain . . . 446
Germans in Alberta . . . 2545
Germans in Edmonton . . . 1976
G.H. Dawe Community Centre, Red Deer . . . 1727
Ghost dance . . . 72
Ghost Pine - History . . . 3079
Ghost towns - Alberta . . . 2678
Ghost towns - Southern Alberta . . . 2855
Gibson, R.B . . . 168
Giesinger family . . . 2704

Girl Guides . . . 1833, 1852
Girouxville - History . . . 2948, 3250
Gisinger family *see* Giesinger family
Glacier National Park - Description . . . 2693
Gladys Ridge - History . . . 2972
Gleichen - History . . . 2893, 3143
Glenbow-Alberta Institute - Pictorial views . . . 1196, 1198
Glengarry Elementary School, Calgary . . . 1522
Glenwood - History . . . 3111
Goertzen family . . . 2705
Gold mining - Alberta . . . 2236
Golden Hind (ship) - Juvenile literature . . . 834
Goodfare - Employment . . . 2539
Goodridge - History . . . 3045
Gourin - History . . . 3281
Grace Baptist Church, Calgary . . . 286
Grace Lutheran Church, Calgary . . . 287
Grace Lutheran Church, Camrose . . . 439
Grace Lutheran Church, Leduc . . . 383
Grace Lutheran Church, Wainwright . . . 432
Grain - Economics . . . 3405, 3419
Grain - Juvenile literature . . . 3388
Grain *see also* Wheat
Grammar . . . 450
Grande Cache - Economic conditions . . . 1795, 2085
Grande Cache - Social conditions . . . 1795
Grande Prairie - Commerce . . . 2194
Grande Prairie - Description . . . 2680
Grande Prairie - History . . . 244, 2915, 2916
Grande Prairie - Natural resources . . . 2146
Grande Prairie - Settlement . . . 2558
Grande Prairie. St. Paul's United Church . . . 417
Grandin, Vital Justin . . . 173, 177, 203
Granum - History . . . 2979, 2980, 3041
Grassy Lake - Artifacts . . . 2011
Gray, James Henry . . . 2784
Grazing land . . . 3431, 3455
Great Depression *see* Depression
Great Divide Trail . . . 1639, 1661, 1673
Great Plains Project . . . 2316
Great Slave Lake - Description . . . 3488
Great Slave Lake Railway . . . 2522
Greece - History . . . 2740
Greene, Daniel Kent . . . 2709
Greene family . . . 2709
Greenlawn - History . . . 3044
Grey Nuns . . . 189, 259
Grizzly bears . . . 3324, 3328
Group of Seven - Exhibitions . . . 1177
Guaranteed annual income . . . 1812

Guest farms . . . 1668
Guest, Robert . . . 1115
Gull Lake - Antiquities . . . 2023
Gull Lake - Description . . . 2023
Gwynne - History . . . 3192
Hail control . . . 3397
Hand Hills - History . . . 3048
Handicapped children - Education . . . 1479
Handicapped persons - Agencies . . . 1797
Handicapped persons - Housing . . . 1721
Handicapped persons *see also* specific handicaps, e.g. Blind
Handicrafts . . . 1710
Hanna - Description . . . 912
Hanna. First United Church . . . 310
Hanna - History . . . 3049, 3086, 3286
Hanna - Schools . . . 1534
Hanna - Social conditions . . . 1715
Hansen family . . . 2710
Hardisty - History . . . 2889
Hardisty, Richard . . . 2796
Harris, Robert . . . 1138
Harrison, Stanley . . . 3427
Harvey, James Shand *see* Shand-Harvey, James
Harvie, Eric Lafferty . . . 2303
Hat-shepsut, Queen of Egypt - Fiction . . . 662
Haug family . . . 2712
Haultain, Frederick William Gordon . . . 1572
Hay Lakes - History . . . 3039, 3145
Haynes. United Church . . . 264
Hays - History . . . 3057, 3206
Hayter. Our Savior's Lutheran Church . . . 367
Heaton Moor - History . . . 3058
Heimtal Moravian Church, Edmonton . . . 431, 432
Hemaruka - History . . . 2852, 2853
Hemaruka - Pictorial views . . . 2852
Henday, Anthony . . . 2554
Hereford cattle . . . 3387, 3393, 3402
Heritage Park, Calgary . . . 2912
Hesketh - History . . . 3061
High Level - History . . . 3210, 3211, 3212
High Prairie - History . . . 3065
High River - History . . . 3066, 3240, 3424
High schools . . . 1488, 1561
High schools - Administration . . . 1506
Highlands United Church, Edmonton . . . 327
Hiking . . . 1671
Hilda - History . . . 3068
Hill Spring. Church of Jesus Christ of Latter-Day Saints . . . 370
Hill Spring - History . . . 3069
Hillcrest - History . . . 3249

Hillcrest - Mine disaster 2811
Hillhurst United Church, Calgary 402
Hines Creek - History 3071, 3186
Hinton - Geography 2535
Hinton - History 2535
Hinton - Social conditions 1722
History, ancient 2741, 2742
Hoadley - History 3089
Hobbema - History 176
Hockey coaching 1644
Hodgson, John Fraser 3480
Hogs - Marketing 2182, 2211, 2217
Hohn, Hubert 1122
Holden. United Church 305
Hollingshead, Archie 2330
Holy Spirit 104, 105
Holy Trinity Church, Edmonton 328
Home Oil Company Limited 2282, 2304
Homesteading *see* Farm life
Hope Evangelical and Reformed Church, Stony Plain 270
Hope family 2708
Hope slide 2762
Horseman's Hall of Fame 2324
Horses 3423, 3425
House building *see* Construction industry
Housing 1711, 1786, 1787
Howg family 2712
Howse, Jane Mary *see* Livingston, Jane Mary (Howse)
Hoyler, Clement 257
Hudson Bay Railway 2345
Hudson's Bay Company 2830, 2832, 3128
Hudson's Bay Company *see also* names of forts, e.g. Fort Edmonton
Hughenden - History 2851, 3109
Human rights 1738
Hungarians in Alberta 1932
Hungarians in Canada - Literature 582
Hunink, Majorie 1115
Hunting - Alberta 1685, 1686
Hunting - Cartoons 1098
Hunting - Economics 1652, 1685, 1687
Huntington Hills, Calgary 2567
Hussar - History 2879
Hutterites 1952, 1995
Hutterites - Assimilation 1867, 1934
Hutterites - Culture 1927
Hutterites - Discrimination 1898
Hutterites - Drama 1071
Hutterites - Education 1497, 1901, 1955
Hutterites - History 1915, 1916
Hutterites - Hymns 1446

Hutterites - Juvenile literature . . . 1988
Hutterites - Population . . . 1937
Hutterites - Sermons . . . 91
Hutterites - Settlement patterns . . . 1893
Hutterites - Social change . . . 1953
Huxley - History . . . 2845, 2936
Hypnotism . . . 1324, 1335
Hyrhor, John . . . 3478
Hythe - History . . . 3110
Iddesleigh - History . . . 3126
Immaculata Hospital, Westlock . . . 3378
Immaculate Conception Catholic Parish, Edmonton . . . 329
Immanuel Lutheran Church, Lethbridge . . . 386
Imperial Oil Ltd . . . 2284
Incorporation - Alberta . . . 2482, 2492
Independence movement *see* Separatism
Indian art - Exhibitions . . . 1185, 1194
Indian Association of Alberta . . . 1496
Indian Battle Coulee - Archaeology . . . 2013
Indians - Alaska - Antiquities . . . 2058
Indians - Alberta . . . 1900, 1952, 3415
Indians - Archaeology . . . 2044, 2046, 2049
Indians - Artifacts . . . 2040, 2041, 2043, 2045, 2062
Indians - Canada . . . 1873
Indians - Costumes . . . 1923
Indians - Culture . . . 1876, 1924, 1939, 2007
Indians - Discrimination . . . 1858, 1972
Indians - Dwellings . . . 1926
Indians - Economic conditions . . . 1890
Indians - Education . . . 1494, 1496, 1502, 1511, 1527, 1901, 1947
Indians - Education - Bibliography . . . 1
Indians - Fiction . . . 821
Indians - Food . . . 1925
Indians - Geographical names . . . 2657
Indians - Government relations . . . 1877, 1878, 1879, 1929, 1930, 1938, 1946, 1967, 1979, 1980, 2005
Indians - Health . . . 3381
Indians - History . . . 1967, 1991
Indians - Housing . . . 1723
Indians - Kinship . . . 1862
Indians - Land claims . . . 1899, 1979, 2005
Indians - Legal status . . . 1853, 1885, 1928, 1980, 2473, 2480
Indians - Legends . . . 2076, 2079, 2080
Indians - Medicine . . . 1925
Indians - Migration patterns . . . 1862
Indians - Missions . . . 260
Indians - North America . . . 2028
Indians - Pacific Northwest . . . 2008
Indians - Photographic collections . . . 1905
Indians - Portraits . . . 1201

Indians - Pottery 2015, 2019, 2066
Indians - Religion 1922, 90, 94
Indians - Social agencies 1803
Indians - Social change 1929, 1947
Indians - Social conditions 1713, 1854, 1855, 1856, 1878, 1985
Indians - Treaties 2480
Indians - Tribes 1887
Indians - Wars 2831
Indians *see also* Plains Indians and names of specific tribes, e.g. Blackfoot Indians
Indus - History 2961
Industry *see* Manufacturing and names of industries, e.g. Lumber industry, Meat industry
Innisfail - Historic buildings 3031
Innisfail - History 2933, 3083, 3091
Innisfail. St. Mark's Anglican Church 366
Inscriptions - Portugal 2009
Inscriptions - Spain 2009
Intercultural education 1901
Inter-faith Community Action Committee, Calgary 219
Inuit - Alaska 1975
Inuit - Antiquities 2058
Inuit art - Exhibitions 1167, 1195, 1247
Irma - History 3155
Irma. Sharon Lutheran Church 374
Irma. United Church 375
Iron industry - Alberta 2241
Iron Springs. Christian Reformed Church 368
Iroquois Indians - Settlement 2067
Irricana - History 3096
Irrigation 2812, 3399, 3400, 3408, 3432, 3436, 3444, 3459
Irvine, William 2368, 2431
Islay - History 3222
Islay - Hospitals 3373
Islay - Schools 1576
Italians in Edmonton 1983, 1993
Japanese in Edmonton 1948
Jasper - Fiction 750
Jasper - History 3053
Jasper National Park 1676
Jasper National Park - Geology 2598
Jasper National Park - History 2663
Jasper National Park - Tourist facilities 1697
Jasper Park Lodge 2607
Jean Côté 2988
Jehovah's Witnesses in Canada 233
Jenner - Fiction 604
Jews in Canada 1936
Jews in Edmonton 1880
Johns, Walter H 1593

Johnson, Albert 1768, 2723
Johnstone Walker Ltd 2203
Josephburg - History 1963
Journalism 50, 51, 52, 55, 63, 2160, 2389, 2415
Judaism 82, 86, 92
Jughandle Ranch 3467
Julius Caesar - Fiction 675, 677
Juvenile delinquency 1774
Juvenile delinquents, Rehabilitation programs *see* Rehabilitation programs for juvenile delinquents
Juvenile literature 549
Juvenile literature - Collections 568, 570, 571
Juvenile literature *see also* subdivision Juvenile literature under specific subjects, e.g. Cree Indians - Juvenile literature
Kananaskis Valley 1683
Kananaskis Valley - History 3182
Kananaskis Valley - Recreation 1651, 1694
Kathryn. High School 1563
Kathyrn - History 3096
Kearney, Joseph Marie Patrick 172
Keith - History 3035
Kelsey, Henry 2649
Kenney (site)- Archaeology 2057
Keoma - History 3096
Kew - History 3161
Killam - History 2938
Killam - Schools 1574
King Edward School, Calgary 1523
Kinsmen Club of Calgary 1842
Kipp - History 3177
Kirk, Maria (Marshall) 244
Kirriemuir - History 3199
Kitscoty - History 3043
Klondike gold rush 2888, 3132
Klondike gold rush - Juvenile literature 692
Kneehill (municipal district) - History 3038
Knight, Pete 1638
Knox United Church, Calgary 288
Knox United Church, Daysland 266
Knox United Church, Drumheller 322
Knox-Metropolitan United Church, Edmonton 330
Komagata Maru (ship) 1894
Komagata Maru (ship) - Drama 1077
Kootenay Plains 1938
Koreans in Edmonton 1999
Kowalczyk, Antoine 174, 193
Kroetsch, Robert 521
Labour Act (Alberta) 2244
Labour disputes 2160, 2237
Labour laws - Alberta 2472

Labour - Politics . . . 2244
Labour *see also* Apprenticeship, Collective bargaining, Employment
Labour unions . . . 2164
Labour unions - Alberta . . . 2174, 2205
Labour unions - Calgary . . . 2197, 2240
Labour unions - Crowsnest Pass . . . 2204
Labour unions - Western Canada . . . 2222
Lac La Biche - Archaeology . . . 2046
Lac La Biche - Description . . . 2683
Lac La Biche - History . . . 2669, 3103
Lac La Biche Pow Wow and Fish Derby . . . 2683
Lac La Biche. St. Catherine's Catholic Church . . . 381
Lac Ste. Anne - Fiction . . . 755, 758
Lac Ste. Anne - History . . . 192, 3104
Lac Ste. Anne - Politics . . . 2460
Lacombe, Albert . . . 175, 216
Lacombe, Albert - Juvenile literature . . . 170, 764
Lacombe - History . . . 2871, 3002, 3105, 3106
LaGlace (district) - History . . . 3092, 3231
Lake Louise - Description . . . 2673
Lake Louise - History . . . 3029
Lake McGregor *see* McGregor Lake
Lakes - Recreation . . . 1627, 1681
Lambie, Allan . . . 1369
Lamerton. Anglican Church . . . 405
Lamerton - History . . . 3107
Lamont - History . . . 3059, 3254
Lamont - Hospitals . . . 3366
Lamont. United Church . . . 364
Lamoureux - History . . . 199, 2861, 3014
Land seizure for payment of debts . . . 2489
Landlord and tenant relations - Alberta . . . 2485
Landscape paintings - Exhibitions . . . 1192, 1235
Langdon - History . . . 3108
Languages - Canada . . . 458
Languages - Social aspects *see* Sociolinguistics
Languages - Teaching . . . 452
Languages - Uganda . . . 462
Law - Canada . . . 2470
Lawrence, Sheridan - Fiction . . . 748
LaZerte, Milton Ezra . . . 1528, 1566
Leduc. First Baptist Church . . . 382
Leduc. Grace Lutheran Church . . . 383
Leduc - History . . . 3021
Leduc. St. Peter's Lutheran Church . . . 384
Legal aid - Alberta . . . 2490
Legal, Emile Joseph . . . 1577
Leighton, Alfred Crocker . . . 1233
Leisure . . . 2156
Lemon Mine . . . 2236

Lesser Slave Lake - Economic conditions 2089, 2134, 2153
Lesser Slave Lake - History 2862
Lesser Slave Lake - Recreation 1622
Lesser Slave Lake - Social conditions 1874
Lesser Slave Lake Special Area Program 2134
Lethbridge - Bridges 2341
Lethbridge Community College 1556, 1604
Lethbridge - Description 2684, 2685, 3481, 3512
Lethbridge - Economic conditions 2150, 2152
Lethbridge . First Baptist Church 263
Lethbridge . Galt School of Nursing 3363
Lethbridge - Geography 2556
Lethbridge - History 2143, 3067, 3113, 3114, 3115, 3117, 3194, 3291, 3292, 3503
Lethbridge - Hospitals 3365
Lethbridge . Immanuel Lutheran Church 386
Lethbridge - Industries 2210
Lethbridge Junior College *see* Lethbridge Community College
Lethbridge Municipal Railway 2334
Lethbridge - Pictorial views 3113
Lethbridge - Police 2496
Lethbridge Public Junior College *see* Lethbridge Community College
Lethbridge - Schools 1518
Lethbridge . St. Augustine's Anglican Church 387
Lethbridge . St. Patrick's Catholic Parish 388
Lethbridge - Transportation 2334
Lethbridge . University *see* University of Lethbridge
Lethbridge - Urban renewal 2564
Lewisville - History 3118
Liberal Party 2398, 2445
Libraries 32
Libraries - Canada 32
Libraries - Edmonton 40
Libraries - Management 24
Libraries - Salaries 17
Libraries *see also* Academic libraries, School libraries, etc.
Library conferences 42
Life styles 1747
Lindbergh - History 3004
Linder, Herman 1653
Lindy (campsite) - Artifacts 2014
Linguistics 459, 467
Linguistics - Humour 465
Linguistics - Social aspects, *see* Sociolinguistics
Lions International 1840, 1841
Liquor traffic 1772, 1790, 1821
Lister, Reginald Charles 1599
Literacy 531
Lithuanians in Alberta - Fiction 642
Livestock associations 3414
Livingston, Jane Mary (Howse) 2719

Livingston, Samuel Henry Harkwood 2719
Livingston, Samuel Henry Harkwood - Juvenile literature 3280
Lloydminster - Description 3493
Lloydminster - Geography 2530
Lloydminster - History 3062, 3074, 3153, 3294, 3296
Lloydminster - Juvenile literature 632
Lloydminster - Politics 2530
Local history - Historiography 2737, 2744, 3299
Lomen Brothers Photographic Collection 2540
Lomond - History 3072, 3120
Lone Pine - History 3179
Longview - History 3073
Lord Strathcona's Horse *see* Canada. Army. Lord Strathcona's Horse
Lost Lemon Mine 2236
Lougheed - History 3121
Lougheed, Peter 2418
Lowrie, Howard 3372
Loyal Edmonton Regiment *see* Canada. Army. Loyal Edmonton Regiment. (3rd Battalion, Princess Patricia's Light Infantry)
Loyalist - History 2852, 2853
Loyalist - Pictorial views 2852
Lubeck - History 3186
Lucerne (school district) - History 3171
Lumber industry - Alberta 2191, 2247
Lupson, Arnold 1905
Luscar - History 2223, 3085
Lutheran Church in Bawlf 271
Lutheran Church in Brightview 276
Lutheran Church in Bruderheim 277
Lutheran Church in Calgary 285, 287, 302
Lutheran Church in Camrose 306, 439
Lutheran Church in Canada 196, 242
Lutheran Church in Dickson 316
Lutheran Church in Edmonton 324, 343, 349
Lutheran Church in Hayter 367
Lutheran Church in Irma 374
Lutheran Church in Leduc 383, 384
Lutheran Church in Lethbridge 386
Lutheran Church in Medicine Hat 395
Lutheran Church in Peace Hill 276
Lutheran Church in Red Deer 410
Lutheran Church in Rolly View 414
Lutheran Church in Scapa 376
Lutheran Church in Spruce Grove 357
Lutheran Church in Stony Plain 361, 423
Lutheran Church in Tilley 426
Lutheran Church in Trochu 427
Lutheran Church in Wainwright 432
Lutheran Church in Wetaskiwin 434, 435
Lyalta - History 3123

Lynass, Agnes 1555
MacEwan, John Walter Grant 2835
MacGregor, James Grierson 3491
Maclean, John 229
Macleod, James Alexander Farquharson - Juvenile literature 829
MacNaught, Euphemia 1115
Mad Trapper of Rat River *see* Johnson, Albert
Magic *see* Conjuring
Magrath - History 3063, 3137
Mainprize, William Graham 3354
Majorville (site) - Artifacts 2020
Make-up, Theatrical 1348
Mallaig. St. John of Brebeuf Catholic Parish 379
Malmo - History 3118
Manitoba - History 2774
Manitou Lake - Description 3469
Manning, Ernest Charles 207, 2403, 2412
Manning. St. James' Catholic Church 390
Mannville - History 3006, 3139
Manpower 2087, 2088
Manpower *see also* Work, Leisure, Productivity
Manufacturing 2209
Many Snakes (burial site)- Artifacts 2033
Marital conciliation *see* Edmonton Family Court Conciliation Project
Marriage 1748, 1756
Marriage counselling 1742, 1757
Marryat, Mary Irene *see* Parlby, Mary Irene (Marryat)
Martin family 2717
Marwayne - History 3146, 3147
Maskepetoon (Cree chief)- Juvenile literature 2843
Maternity leave 1746
Mathematical recreations 1361
Matrimonial property - Alberta 2487
May, Wop - Juvenile literature 599
Mayerthorpe - Schools 1553
Mayerthorpe. United Church 362
McClung, Nellie Letitia 548, 724, 1743, 1758, 1760
McClung, Nellie Letitia - Juvenile literature 1753
McConachie, Grant 2342
McConkey, James H 220
McCourt, Edward 527
McDougall, Elizabeth 227
McDougall, George Millward 230
McDougall, John 222, 230, 596
McDougall, John A 2214
McDougall Memorial United Church, Morley 378
McDougall United Church, Edmonton 331, 332, 333
McGregor Lake - History 3164
McKenzie Highway - Description 2681
McLennan - History 3119

McLennan. St. John the Baptist Catholic Parish 392
McLeod, Scott H 3369
McNally, George Frederick 1564
McRae family 2724
Meat industry - Alberta 2167, 2182, 2195, 2212, 2213, 2216, 2217, 2221, 2239, 2245
Meat industry - Economics 2183, 2212
Meat industry - Edmonton 2188, 2189
Mecca Glen - History 3156
Medalta Potteries 2161
Medicine - Calgary - History 3375
Medicine Hat. Christ the King Catholic Parish 393
Medicine Hat - Description 1108
Medicine Hat. Fifth Avenue United Church 394
Medicine Hat - Geography 2556
Medicine Hat - German language 448
Medicine Hat. Grace Lutheran Church 395
Medicine Hat - History 2968, 3025, 3026, 3027, 3167
Medicine Hat. John's Presbyterian Church 320
Medicine Hat - Juvenile literature 731
Medicine Hat - Politics 2362
Medicine Hat. St. Barnabas Anglican Church 279
Medicine Hat. Westminster United Church 396, 397
Medicine Hat (Cree chief) 2829
Meeting Creek - History 3097
Mennonite Women in Mission - Alberta 238
Mennonites 245
Mennonites - Assimilation 1986
Mennonites - Education 1901
Mennonites - Fiction 818
Mennonites - Psychology 1912
Mental illness - Legal aspects 1819
Mentally handicapped - Recreation 1631
Mentally handicapped, Rehabilitation programs *see* Rehabilitation programs for the mentally handicapped
Merna - History 3203
Messiah Lutheran Church, Camrose 306
Metal industries - Edmonton 2181
Methodist Church - Missions 222, 223, 224, 227, 230, 231, 241, 253, 2797
Metis - Economic conditions 2085
Metis - Fiction 819
Metis - French language 455
Metis - Government relations 1883, 1910
Metis - History 191, 2991, 3084, 3178
Metis - Housing 1711
Metis - Juvenile literature 1857, 1872
Metis - Kinship 1959
Metis - Land claims 1899
Metis - Legal status 1885, 2473
Metis - Social change 1795, 1889, 1909, 1910, 1945, 1960

Metis - Social conditions 1870, 1874, 1875, 1958
Metiskow - History 3249
Metric system 2193
Mexico Ranch 3441
Michichi - Description 3485
Michichi - History 3225
Middleton, Samuel Henry 198
Migration 2026
Military conscription 2378
Military Music - History 1381
Milk River - Archaeology 2034
Milk River - History 2914, 3070, 3242
Milk River - Recreation 1682
Millarville - History 3161, 3162
Millet - History 3163, 3273
Millicent - History 3126
Milo and Queenstown Farm Women's Union of Alberta 3404
Milo - History 3164
Milton, John 533
Mind reading 1327, 1357
Miner, William A 1764
Mining industries 2172, 2278, 2279
Mirror - History 2869, 3107
Mirror - Schools 1573
Mirror . St. Monica's Anglican Church 405
Missionaries 77, 123
Missionaries - Biography 70, 93, 206, 237, 256
Missions 104, 107
Missions - Juvenile literature 622
Mitchell, William Ormond 535, 547
Mnemonics 1343
Monarch - History 3177, 884
Monetary policy - Alberta 2115, 2116
Monitor - History 3228
Monkman Pass Highway 2353
Moon, George 2250
Moose 3333
Moraine Lake - History 3029
Moravian Church in Canada 257
Moravian Church in Edmonton 334, 430, 431, 432
Moravian Church in New Sarepta 416
Moravian Church in Wainwright 432
Morinville - Description 3498
Morkin (site)- Artifacts 2015
Morley. McDougall Memorial United Church 378
Morley - Social conditions 1966
Mormons in Alberta 209, 1942, 2702, 2872, 3063, 3507
Mormons in Alberta - Education 1533
Mormons in Alberta - Fiction 679
Mormons in Canada 184

Mormons in Hill Spring . . . 370
Morren, Harry Fuller . . . 2494
Morrin - History . . . 3166
Morrison (school district) - History . . . 1576
Motherhood . . . 1744
Motor Car Supply Company of Canada Limited . . . 2224
Mount Assiniboine *see* Assiniboine Mountain
Mount Calvary Lutheran Church, Calgary . . . 289
Mountain sheep . . . 3329
Mountain View (county) - History . . . 2847, 3090
Mountaineering . . . 1666, 1696, 1701
Mountaineers - Biography . . . 1643
Moyerton - History . . . 3271
Multiculturalism . . . 1864, 1865, 2000
Mundare. St. Peter's and St. Paul's Ukrainian Catholic Church . . 268, 269, 403
Munson - History . . . 3168
Murder . . . 1765, 1770
Murphy, Emily (Ferguson) . . . 1752
Mushrooms - Alberta . . . 3332
Music - Children's literature . . . 1379
Mysticism . . . 69
Namao - History . . . 3248
Namao . United Church . . . 400
Names, geographical *see* Geographical names
Nanton - Description . . . 3511
Nanton - History . . . 3170
Naples - History . . . 3018
Narcotics . . . 1785, 1809
Narrows (site) - Artifacts . . . 2018
National Energy Conference, 1974 . . . 2097
National parks - Description . . . 2692
National parks - Land use . . . 2524, 2525, 2526
National parks - Pictorial views . . . 2635
National parks - Policy . . . 2590
Natural gas industry . . . 2252, 2253, 2255, 2256, 2264, 2268, 2290, 2291, 2301, 2309, 2311
Natural gas industry - Economic aspects . . . 2280, 2288, 2310
Natural gas industry - Environmental impact . . . 2280, 3337
Natural history - Alberta . . . 3320, 3330
Natural history - Cypress Hills . . . 3344
Natural history - Elk Island . . . 3318
Natural history - Juvenile literature . . . 3309, 3310, 3311, 3323, 3335
Natural history - Rocky Mountains . . . 3326
Natural history - Vermilion Lakes . . . 3314
Natural resources . . . 2136
Natural resources - Alberta . . . 2089, 2148
Natural resources - Conservation . . . 3343
Natural resources - Foreign ownership . . . 2268, 2269
Nature trails . . . 1647
Nature trails - Calgary . . . 1628

Nature trails - Edmonton . . . 1703, 2666
Nature trails - Rocky Mountains . . . 1673, 1676, 2689
Nature trails *see also* names of specific trails, e.g. Great Divide Trail, Waskahegan Trail
Nelson, Eric Leonard . . . 1767
Nelson family . . . 2721
Nemiskam - History . . . 2907
Neutral Hills - History . . . 3173
New Brigden - Description . . . 3502
New Brigden - History . . . 2975
New Norway - History . . . 3047, 3174
New Sarepta. Moravian Church . . . 416
Newland, Hubert Charles . . . 1569
Newspapers . . . 45, 54, 56, 57, 2362, 2378
Newspapers *see also* Journalism
Newton, William . . . 232
Nickle, Samuel Clarence . . . 2292
Nicoll, Jim . . . 1223
Nightingale - History . . . 2978
Nobleford - History . . . 3177
Nordegg, Martin . . . 2226, 2227
Normal schools *see* Teachers' colleges
North Saskatchewan River - Description . . . 2601
North Saskatchewan River - Erosion . . . 2565
North Star. St. Elizabeth's Catholic Church . . . 390
North West Pulp & Power Ltd . . . 2535
Northeastern Alberta *see* Alberta, northeastern
Northern Alberta Library Development Services . . . 29
Northern Alberta Pioneers' and Oldtimers' Association . . . 3169
Northern Alberta *see* Alberta, northern
Northern development . . . 2136
Northfield - History . . . 3092
Northland Utilities Ltd . . . 2185
North-West Mounted Police *see* Royal Canadian Mounted Police
North-West Territories - Description . . . 2627, 2686
North-West Territories - Politics . . . 2393
North-West Territories - Social conditions . . . 2513
Norwegians in Alberta . . . 1892
Norwegians in Alberta - Fiction . . . 685
Norwood Readiness Centre, Edmonton . . . 1775
Nose Hills - History . . . 3159
Notikewin. Sacred Heart Catholic Church . . . 390
Nursing - Alberta . . . 3353, 3355, 3362, 3382
Nursing - Arctic . . . 3357
Nursing - Edmonton . . . 3360, 3384
Nursing - Lamont . . . 3366
Nursing - Lethbridge . . . 3363
Oblates of Mary Immaculate - Missions - Calgary . . . 164
Ohaton - History . . . 3052
Oil and gas leases - Alberta . . . 2469

Oil sands 2266, 2270, 2272, 2287, 2289, 2295, 2298
Ojibway Indians - Religion 74
Okotoks - History 3009
Oldman River 2569
Olds Agricultural and Vocational College 3416, 3435
Olds College Alumni Association 3396
Olds - History 2847, 3180
One Big Union 2164
O'Neil, Bruce 1227
Onoway - History 3279
Oregon - Description 2651
Ornithology *see* Birds
Ouest canadien (newspaper) 46
Our Lady of Assumption Catholic Parish, Beiseker 272
Our Lady of Mercy Croatian Catholic Church, Calgary 290
Our Lady of Perpetual Help Parish, Calgary 291
Our Lady of Victory Catholic Church, Vimy 429
Our Savior's Lutheran Church, Hayter 367
Outdoor recreation . . . 1625, 1627, 1630, 1641, 1642, 1682, 1693, 1699, 1702
Outdoor recreation - Edmonton 3334
Outdoor recreation - Planning 1632
Oxley Ranch 2612
Paintings - Exhibitions 1141, 1144, 1150, 1152, 1156, 1164, 1166, 1169, 1173, 1178, 1179, 1209, 1212, 1216, 1217, 1220, 1222, 1224, 1225, 1228, 1229, 1234, 1236, 1237, 1243, 1244, 1245, 1248, 1249, 1251, 1252, 1253
Pakan - History 3496
Pakistani art - Exhibitions 1175
Paper industry *see* Pulp and paper
Paradise Valley - History 3271
Park Grove - History 2989
Park rangers - Biography 1677, 3317, 3322
Parker, William 2511
Parkland Regional Library 15, 27
Parkland (county) - Urban expansion 2135
Parlby, Mary Irene (Marryat) 2405
Parry - History 3233
Patricia - History 3126
Peace Hill. Zion Lutheran Church 276
Peace Hills - Archaeology 2063
Peace River Jim *see* Cornwall, James Kennedy
Peace River - Navigation 2336
Peace River (district) - Archaeology 2064
Peace River (district) - Biography 2718, 3451
Peace River (district) - Communications 2587
Peace River (district) - Description 239, 2611, 2614, 2616, 2646, 2681, 3473, 3483, 3484, 3487, 3497, 3500
Peace River (district) - Economic conditions 2100, 2138, 2139
Peace River (district) - Fiction 602, 620, 716, 748, 760, 769, 802
Peace River (district) - Geography 2532
Peace River (district) - History 201, 2883, 2916, 2965, 3081, 3210, 3477

Peace River (district) - Poems . . . 903
Peace River (district) - Population . . . 2520
Peace River (district) - Settlement 1931, 2522, 2552, 2555, 2571, 3458
Peace River (district) - Transportation . . . 2358
Peace River (town). St. Paul's United Church . . . 406
Pearce, William . . . 1611, 2379, 2808, 3432, 3459
Pembina Valley - History . . . 2849
Pemuka - History . . . 3228
Pendant d'Oreille - History . . . 3007
Penology . . . 1806, 1815
Peru - Antiquities . . . 2053
Petroleum industry . . . 2254, 2255, 2256, 2259, 2260, 2262, 2263, 2265, 2267, 2268, 2269, 2273, 2274, 2275, 2276, 2277, 2278, 2279, 2281, 2285, 2286, 2293, 2294, 2303, 2309, 2312, 2313, 2471
Petroleum industry - Biography . . . 2251
Petroleum industry - Economic aspects . . . 2296, 2297, 2299, 2300, 2302, 2305, 2307, 2308
Petroleum industry - Fiction . . . 606, 607, 697, 747, 783
Petroleum industry - History . . . 2271
Petroleum rights *see* Crown petroleum rights
Pettinger, William . . . 3502
Peyton - Schools . . . 1565
Phonology . . . 464
Photography - Exhibitions . . . 1190, 1210
Physical education - Injuries . . . 1659
Pickardville. St. Benoit Catholic Church . . . 360
Piegan Coulee - History . . . 2981
Piegan Indians - Juvenile literature . . . 650, 652
Pigeon Lake - Economic conditions . . . 2092
Pigeon Lake - History . . . 2977
Pigeon Lake - Settlement . . . 2573
Pigeon Lake. St. Basil's Villa . . . 249
Pilots *see* Bush pilots
Pincher Creek. Church of St. John the Evangelist . . . 389
Pincher Creek - History . . . 3196, 3197, 3198
Pincher Creek - Social conditions . . . 1898
Pincher Creek. United Church . . . 408
Pine Lake - History . . . 2936
Pine Point - Fiction . . . 754
Pipestone - History . . . 2977
Place names *see* Geographical names
Plains Indians - Archaeology . . . 2056
Plains Indians - Biography . . . 1949
Plains Indians - Juvenile literature . . . 598, 1871
Plains Indians - Legends . . . 2082
Plains Indians - Writing . . . 2060
Plamondon - History . . . 2932, 3033
Plants - Alberta . . . 3315
Plast Association, Edmonton . . . 1845
Poles in Alberta . . . 1957

Poles in Calgary 1977
Police Coulee - Artifacts 2012
Polish language 466
Polish language - Pronunciation 447
Political parties - Canada 2465
Political parties, *see also* names of specific parties, e.g. Liberal Party
Pollution 3342, 3345
Pollution - Alberta - Bibliography 13
Pollution - Calgary 3338
Pollution - Edmonton 3339
Pond, Peter 2527
Ponoka - Commerce 2235
Ponoka - History 3156, 3201, 3202
Ponoka. United Church 409
Ponoka. Zion United Church 377
Poons, Larry 1231
Population studies 2589
Portraits - Exhibitions 1201
Pottery- Alberta 1114
Pottery - Canada - Exhibitions 1143
Pottery, Indian *see* Indians - Pottery
Pottery - Peru 2053
Potts, Jerry 2822, 2833
Poultry industry - Alberta 2180, 2207
Poundmaker (Cree chief) 2813
Poundmaker (Cree chief) - Fiction 786
Poverty 1779, 1783, 1812, 2192
Powder River Cattle Company 3461
Prairie Bible Institute 77, 188, 212, 236
Prairie Park (school district) - History 1574
Prairie Provinces - Bibliography 12
Prairie Provinces - Biography 2727
Prairie Provinces - Economic conditions 2142
Prairie Provinces - Fiction 528, 532
Prairie Provinces - History 2783, 2785, 2786, 2801, 2804, 2806
Prairie Provinces - Politics 2142
Prairie Provinces - Social conditions 1717
Presbyterian Church 115
Presbyterian Church in Alberta 204, 226, 417
Presbyterian Church in Calgary 187
Presbyterian Church in Chauvin 440
Presbyterian Church in Medicine Hat 320
Preschool education *see* Early childhood education
Preservation of wildlife *see* Wildlife - Conservation
Preventive Social Services Program 1831
Priddis - History 3162
Prince Edward Island - Fiction 807
Princess Patricia's Light Infantry *see* Canada. Army. Loyal Edmonton
Regiment. (3rd Battalion, Princess Patricia's Light Infantry) 2754
Printing - History - Red River Settlement 58

Printing - History - Rupert's Land 59
Printmaking 1119, 1168
Prints, Eskimo *see* Inuit art
Prisoners 1800
Prisoners, Rehabilitation programs *see* Rehabilitation programs for prisoners
Private companies - Alberta 2482, 2492
Procter, Allison 1834
Program 5, Federal Technical and Vocational Training Act (1961) 2165
Progressive Conservative Party 2376, 2383, 2389, 2395
Prohibition 1772, 1808, 1821
Project Pandora 554
Prophets 139
Protestants - Biography 202
Providence Child Development Centre 1817
Provincial parks - Alberta 1657
Provincial parks - Economics 1707
Provost - Description 3204
Provost - History 3235
Psychic games 1322, 1367, 1368
Public health - Alberta 3356, 3359
Public libraries 14
Public libraries - Alberta 26
Public libraries - Manitoba 25
Public schools and religion *see* Religion in the public schools
Public welfare *see* Social assistance
Publishers and publishing - Canada 60, 64
Publishers and publishing - Great Britain 47
Puffer, William Franklin 2728
Pulp and paper 2228
Puppets and puppet-plays 1260, 1305
Quirion, l'Abbé 162
Quotations, English 1334
Race relations 1970
Radio and education - History 1559
Radio stations 2346
Railroads 2338, 2358, 2620
Railroads - Alberta, southern 2323, 2812
Railroads - Edmonton 2343
Railroads - History 2638
Railroads *see also* names of specific railways, e.g. Edmonton and
Calgary Railway
Railways *see* Railroads
Rainier - History 3236
Rainy Hills - History 3246
Rainy Hills, *see* Iddlesleigh
Ranch life 3467, 3499, 3506
Ranching 526, 3403, 3409, 3415, 3417, 3421, 3424, 3430, 3441, 3463,
3464, 3467, 3471, 3472, 3488, 3490, 3493, 3494, 3495, 3500, 3512
Ranching - Fiction 669, 810
Ranching - Juvenile literature 651, 734, 772, 3474

Ranchmen's Club 1847
Ranfurly. United Church 355
Rangers *see* Park rangers
Raymond - History 3063, 3064
R.C.M.P. *see* Royal Canadian Mounted Police
Reading for leisure 1636, 1655
Readymade - History 3207
Real estate *see* Real property
Real property 2133, 2145, 2186
Real property - Alberta 2491
Real property taxation 2090, 2131, 2132, 2157
Recreation - Administration 1658, 1664, 1708
Recreation *see also* Sports and also names of specific sporting activities
Recreational travel 1692
Red Cross 3352, 3358, 3364
Red Deer. Canadian Nazarene College *see* Canadian Nazarene
College, Red Deer
Red Deer - Economic conditions 2127
Red Deer. First Christian Reformed Church 273
Red Deer. G.H. Dawe Community Centre 1727
Red Deer - History 2963, 2964, 3024, 3157, 3304, 3305, 3306
Red Deer. Mount Calvary Lutheran Church 410
Red Deer - Music 1448
Red Deer River - Irrigation 3399
Red Deer - Schools 1517
Red Deer - Urban design 2592
Red Deer (district) - Description 3510
Red Deer (district) - Economic conditions 2093
Red Deer (district) - Geography 2517
Red Deer (district) - History 2871, 2906, 3209
Red River Rebellion *see* Riel Rebellion, 1869
Red River settlement 2791
Red River settlement - Juvenile literature 2772
Redcliff - History 3046
Redemption *see* Salvation
Redwater - History 3080
Regina - Tornado 2763
Regional economics 2120
Regional planning - Bibliography 9
Regionalism 1729
Rehabiliation Society of Calgary for the Handicapped 1797
Rehabilitation programs for drug abusers 1784
Rehabilitation programs for juvenile delinquents 1774
Rehabilitation programs for prisoners 1776, 1792, 1798, 1813, 1818
Rehabilitation programs for the mentally handicapped 1793
Rehwinkel, Bessie Lee (Efner) 3371
Religion and education *see* Church and education
Religion in the public schools 153, 1498, 1499, 1512
Religious denominations *see* Sects
Restaurants - Edmonton 2188

Retail trade - Calgary . . . 2201, 2249
Retail trade - Central Alberta . . . 2159
Retail trade - Edmonton . . . 2179, 2202, 2218
Retlaw - History . . . 2987
Rexboro. St. Aidan and St. Hilda Anglican Church . . . 411
Ribstone - History . . . 2851
Ricinus - History . . . 3216
Ridgewood - History . . . 2884
Rieger, Thomas F . . . 1555
Riel, Louis . . . 2773, 2775, 2780, 2789, 2790, 2805
Riel, Louis - Fiction . . . 737, 819
Riel, Louis - Juvenile literature . . . 800
Riel Rebellion, 1869 . . . 58, 2764
Riel Rebellion, 1869 - Fiction . . . 819
Riel Rebellion, 1885 . . . 2765, 2799, 2800
Riel Rebellion, 1885 - Fiction . . . 725, 736, 737, 786, 819
Rimbey - History . . . 3233
Ripley - History . . . 2869
Rivercourse - History . . . 3217
Rivers - Recreational use . . . 1698
Riviére Qui Barre - History . . . 3008
Robertson-Wesley United Church, Edmonton . . . 335, 407
Roche, Douglas J . . . 2385
Rocky Mountain House - Description . . . 3509
Rocky Mountain House - History . . . 2882, 3219, 3479
Rocky Mountains - Description . 2536, 2637, 2640, 2643, 2653, 2689, 2690, 2825, 3317, 3322, 3326, 3499
Rocky Mountains - Fiction . . . 647, 668, 741, 752, 770
Rocky Mountains - Geography . . . 2553
Rocky Mountains - History . . . 2825, 2919, 3053, 3056
Rocky Mountains - Juvenile literature . . . 617, 626, 650, 2623
Rocky Mountains - Legends . . . 2072
Rocky Mountains - Pictorial views . . . 1121, 2629, 2635, 2644
Rocky Mountains - Recreation . . . 1618, 1620, 1621, 1669, 1683, 1701
Rodeos . . . 1638, 1653, 1656, 1700, 3270
Rodeos - Fiction . . . 678
Rogers Pass - Description . . . 2675
Rolly View. St. Paul's Lutheran Church . . . 414
Romanet, Louis Auguste . . . 2647
Romanian Orthodox Church in Edmonton . . . 337
Rome - Architecture . . . 1149
Rome - Fiction . . . 676
Rome - History . . . 2740
Ronaghan family . . . 2729
Rosebud - History . . . 3144
Rosebud - Schools . . . 1560
Rosemary - History . . . 3223
Ross Sheppard Composite High School, Edmonton . . . 1539
Rossville Mission Press . . . 59
Rosyth - History . . . 2889

Round Hill - History . . . 3036
Rowand, John . . . 2839
Rowand, John - Juvenile literature . . . 597, 600
Rowley - History . . . 3226
Royal Alexandra Hospital, Edmonton . . . 3360
Royal Canadian Mounted Police . . . 1222, 2497, 2498, 2500, 2504, 2505, 2506, 2507, 2508, 2509, 2513, 2797, 3067
Royal Canadian Mounted Police - Bibliography . . . 5
Royal Canadian Mounted Police - Fiction . . . 562, 682, 683
Royal Canadian Mounted Police - Juvenile literature 598, 624, 684, 715, 829, 835
Royce - History . . . 3186
Rumsey - History . . . 3226
Rundle, Robert Terrill . . . 231, 241, 253
Running Horse Movement . . . 1881
Rural development . . . 1668
Rural development - Bibliography . . . 9
Rural schools . . . 1531
Russian language . . . 461, 520
Russian language - Pronunciation . . . 454
Russian literature . . . 546
Rutherford, Alexander Cameron . . . 1605, 1609
Rutherford School, Edmonton . . . 1540
Ryley - History . . . 2900
Sacred Heart Catholic Church, Calgary . . . 369
Sacred Heart Catholic Church, Notikewin . . . 390
Sacred Heart Catholic Parish, Edson . . . 352
Saint Joachim Church, Edmonton . . . 336
Saints Constantine and Helen Romanian Orthodox Parish, Edmonton . . . 337
Sales tax . . . 2141
Salvation . . . 103, 112, 121, 127
Salvation Army Grace Hospital, Calgary . . . 3374
Sandy Beach . . . 1641
Sangro - History . . . 2990
Sara, Frederic Leslie . . . 1844
Sarcee Butte. United Church . . . 398
Sarci Indians - Missions . . . 247
Saskatchewan - Description . . . 2626
Saskatchewan Grain Growers' Association . . . 3460
Saskatchewan Provincial Police - History . . . 2493
Saskatchewan River - Navigation . . . 2350
Saskatchewan River *see also* North Saskatchewan River, South Saskatchewan River Savage, Margaret . . . 3367
Sawmills *see* Lumber industry
Scandia - History . . . 3230
Scandia Lutheran Church, Armena . . . 265
Scapa. St. Peter's Lutheran Church . . . 376
Schielke family . . . 2706
School Act (Alberta) . . . 1507
School busing . . . 2319, 2351
School libraries - Alberta . . . 19, 20, 23, 35, 36, 37, 38

School libraries - Edmonton 43
Schools - Alberta 1492, 1529, 1547, 1548, 1561, 1581, 1583, 1585
Schools - Western Canada 1552
Schools *see also* Rural schools, Separate schools
Schuler - History 3298
Science and civilization 2746
Scollard - History 3226
Sculptures - Exhibitions 1139, 1174, 1181
Seba Beach - Politics 2454
Secondary education 1495
Secondary education - Alberta 1588
Sects - Alberta 84, 98, 218
Sedalia - History 2890
Sedgewick - History 3158
Sedgewick - Schools 1574
Seed cleaning - Economics 3385
Separate schools - Alberta 1547
Separate schools - Calgary 1512, 1520, 1659
Separate schools - Edmonton 1526
Separatism 608, 2000, 2359, 2360, 2374, 2382, 2384
Sermons 71, 95, 100
Service industries - Labour 2200
Service industries *see also* Retail trade, Restaurants
Severn Creek. School 1560
Shady Nook (school district) - History 2897
Shaking tent ceremony 145
Shand-Harvey, James 3133
Sharon Lutheran Church, Irma 374
Sharphead (burial site) 2035
Shepard - History 2961
Sherwood Park 2537
Shevchenko, Taras Hryhorovych 539, 541, 542, 543
Shoplifting 1827
Sibbald - History 3243
Sien Lok Society of Calgary 1728
Sifton, Clifford - Drama 1092
Siksika Indians *see* Blackfoot Indians
Silversmithing - Exhibitions 1242
Simpson, Sir George 2771
Siovan languages *see* Stoney language
Sisters of Charity of Our Lady of Evron 3377
Sisters of Charity of Providence 214
Sisters of Our Lady of Charity of Refuge 194
Sisters of Providence of St. Vincent de Paul 3380
Sisters of Service 3383
Sisters of the Holy Cross 201
Sitting Bull (Dakota chief) 2836
Sitting Bull (Dakota chief) - Drama 1068
Sitting Bull (Dakota chief) - Juvenile literature 715
Sketches *see* Drawings

Ski trails 1669, 1683
Skiing 1709
Skyline Hikers of the Canadian Rockies 1671
Slavic Languages - Grammar 519
Slavutych, Yar 537, 551
Slezina, Anthony 1914
Small businesses 2220
Small Claims Court - Alberta 2488
Small Legs, Nelson Jr 1985
Smith, Charley 3467
Smith, Marie Rose 3467
Smith, Sidney Bailey 3507
Smoky Lake - History 3290
Smoky Lake. Sts. Volodymyr and Olga Ukrainian Catholic Church - History 373
Snowmobiles 1674, 1695, 1709
Soccer 1689, 1690
Social assistance - Alberta 1773, 1799
Social assistance - Calgary 1826
Social assistance - Edmonton 2196
Social assistance - History 1805
Social classes 1730, 1736
Social Credit Party 2115, 2116, 2396, 2397, 2399, 2401, 2403, 2414, 2415, 2416, 2419, 2420, 2423, 2427, 2428, 2429, 2430, 2433, 2434, 2435, 2438, 2442, 2444, 2447, 2448
Social development 1734
Social Plains (school district) - History 3016
Social workers 1771, 1777, 1796, 1801, 1804, 1810, 1814
Sociolinguistics 462
Sociolinguistics - Canada 445, 453, 456
Sociological jurisprudence 2470
Sociology 1718, 1741
Sociology, christian 84, 144
Sociology - Congresses 1873
Sociology, rural 1714
Soil conservation 3437
Soil scientists *see* Agrologists
Sommerville family 2698
Sour gas processing industry 2280, 3337, 3342
South Saskatchewan River basin - Recreation 1707
South Saskatchewan River - Description 2596
Southern Alberta Institute of Technology 1578, 1582
Southern Alberta Institute of Technology *see also* Alberta College of Art
Southern Alberta *see* Alberta, southern
Southwestern Alberta *see* Alberta, southwestern
Speaking in tongues *see* Charismatic movement
Special Areas Act (Alberta) 2572
Spending patterns of consumers 2154
Spirit River - Description 3497
Spirit River. United Church 278
Spiritualism 3501

Spiritualist Church in Calgary . . . 313
Sports - Alberta . . . 1624, 1629, 1691
Sports - Calgary . . . 1852
Spray Lakes Valley - Recreation . . . 1694
Spruce Avenue Church, Edmonton . . . 1541
Spruce Grove. St. Andrew's United Church . . . 418
Spruce Grove. St. Matthew's Evangelican Lutheran Church . . . 357
Spruce View - History . . . 3060
Spruces (stopping house) . . . 3031
St. Agnes Catholic Church, Edmonton . . . 317, 318
St. Albert - Historical geography . . . 2561
St. Albert - History . . . 2895, 3259, 3266, 3267
St. Albert - Pictorial views . . . 2895
St. Alphonsus Catholic Parish, Edmonton . . . 338
St. Andrew's Catholic Parish, Edmonton . . . 339
St. Andrew's United Church, Spruce Grove . . . 418
St. Anthony's Catholic Parish, Calgary . . . 292
St. Anthony's Catholic Parish, Drumheller . . . 323
St. Anthony's Catholic Parish, Edmonton . . . 358
St. Augustine's Anglican Church, Lethbridge . . . 387
St. Barnabas' Anglican Church, Calgary . . . 293, 294
St. Barnabas Anglican Church, Edmonton . . . 340
St. Barnabas Church, Medicine Hat . . . 279
St. Basil's Villa, Piegeon Lake . . . 249
St. Benoit Catholic Church, Pickardville . . . 360
St. Boniface Catholic Church, Calgary . . . 295
St. Bonifatius Kirche, Calgary . . . 295
St. Catherine's Catholic Church, Lac La Biche . . . 381
St. Cyril's Catholic Church, Bellevue . . . 274
St. Elizabeth's Catholic Church, North Star . . . 390
St. Faith's Anglican Church, Edmonton . . . 341
St. Francis Xavier Catholic Church . . . 307
St. Isidore. Catholic Parish . . . 419
St. James' Catholic Church, Manning . . . 390
St. James United Church, Edmonton . . . 437
St. John Ambulance Association . . . 3349
St. John of Brebeuf Catholic Parish, Mallaig . . . 379
St. John the Evangelist Anglican Church, Edmonton . . . 342
St. John's Evangelical Lutheran Church, Edmonton . . . 343
St. John's Hospital, Edson . . . 3383
St. John's Institute, Edmonton . . . 1836
St. John's Lutheran Church, Trochu . . . 427
St. John's School of Alberta, Genesee . . . 1544
St. Joseph's Catholic Church, Calgary . . . 296
St. Joseph's Catholic Parish, Coalhurst . . . 391
St. Joseph's Church, Vegreville . . . 3269
St. Joseph's General Hospital, Vegreville . . . 3379
St. Joseph's Seminary, Edmonton . . . 420
St. Lina - History . . . 3251
St. Lina. St. Helene's Catholic Church . . . 421

St. Louis Hospital, Bonnyville 3377
St. Luke's Anglican Mission, Fort Vermilion 359
St. Mark's Anglican Church, Innisfail 366
St. Martin of Tours Catholic Parish, Vegreville 199
St. Martin's Anglican Church, Calgary 297
St. Martin's School, Vegreville 1587
St. Mary's Cathedral, Calgary 298
St. Mary's Hospital, Camrose 3380
St. Mary's of the Assumption Catholic Church, Banff 280
St. Matthew's Evangelical Lutheran Church, Spruce Grove 357
St. Matthew's Evangelical Lutheran Church, Stony Plain 361
St. Michael and All Angels' Church, Calgary 299
St. Monica's Anglican Church, Mirror 405
St. Nicholas, St. Michael Ukrainian Catholic Church, Edmonton 344
St. Pancras Anglican Church, Alix 405
St. Patrick's Catholic Parish, Lethbridge 388
St. Paul - Agriculture 3440
St. Paul - French language 455
St. Paul - History 190, 191, 2892, 2984, 2985, 3178, 3252
St. Paul - Social conditions 2984
St. Paul. St. Paul's Catholic Cathedral 321
St. Paul's United Church, Coleman 356
St. Paul's United Church, Fairview 380
St. Paul's United Church, Grande Prairie 417
St. Paul's United Church, Peace River 406
St. Peter's and St. Paul's Ukrainain Catholic Church, Mundare 403
St. Peter's and St. Paul's Ukrainian Catholic Church, Mundare 268, 269
St. Peter's Anglican Church, Bashaw 405
St. Peter's Lutheran Church, Leduc 384
St. Pius the Tenth Catholic Parish, Calgary 300
St. Pius X Catholic Parish, Edmonton 345
St. Saviour's Parish, Vermilion 415
St. Stephen's Anglican Church, Calgary 301
St. Stephen's College, Edmonton 254
St. Stephen's Ukrainian Church, Calgary 371
St. Vincent. Catholic Church 422
Stampedes *see* Rodeos
Standard - History 3255, 3256
Standish family 2711
Stanley Jones School, Calgary 1524
Starland - Description 3508
Stavely - History 3093, 3257
Ste. Anne Catholic Parish, Edmonton 346
Steamboats 2320, 2340, 2350
Steel industry - Alberta 2198, 2241
Steele, Sir Samuel Benfield 2502, 2510
Steele, Sir Samuel Benfield - Fiction 793
Steele, Sir Samuel Benfield - Juvenile literature 624
Steinhauer, Henry Bird 210
Stephansson, Stephan Gudmundsson 550

Stettler - History 2941, 3462
Stevens Rock 2013
Stirling - History 3063
Stoney Indians - Archaeology 2035
Stoney Indians - Culture 1994
Stoney Indians - Culture change 1904
Stoney Indians - Customs 2640
Stoney Indians - History 1994
Stoney Indians - Juvenile literature 830
Stoney Indians - Land claims 1938
Stoney Indians - Social change 1987
Stoney Indians - Tribal structure 1966
Stoney language 496
Stony Indian Reservation - Natural resources 2112
Stony Plain - Biography 2731
Stony Plain - Geography 2545
Stony Plain - German language 446
Stony Plain - History 3184
Stony Plain. Hope Evangelical and Reformed Church 270
Stony Plain. St. Matthew's Evangelical Lutheran Church 361, 423
Stony Plain. United Church 424
Strange, Thomas Bland - Fiction 725
Strathcona Baptist Church, Edmonton 347
Strathcona High School, Edmonton 1550
Strathcona - Historic buildings 3260
Strathcona - History 3032
Strathcona's Horse *see* Canada. Army. Lord Strathcona's Horse
Strathearn United Church, Edmonton 348
Strathmore - Description 54
Strathmore - Schools 1551
Studit monks 163
Stylistics 451
Suffield - Artifacts 2017
Suffield - Land use 1679
Suicide 1825
Suitor (site) - Artifacts 2011
Sulphur 2253, 2301
Sulphur industry 2166
Sun Dance 1961, 2050
Sunberry Valley - History 3138
Sundial Butte (cairn) - Artifacts 2014
Sundial - History 2987
Sundre - History 2847, 2896, 2990, 2999, 3000, 3125, 3138
Sunnynook - History 2891
Sunnyslope - History 3042
Sunwapta Pass - Description 2696
Surveying 3412
Swan Hills 1617
Swanson, Cecil 248
Swift Current - Description 3480

Sylvan Heights (school district) - History . . . 2858
Syncrude Canada Ltd . . . 2287, 2295, 2298, 2306
Syncrude lease no. 17 - Artifacts . . . 2045, 2062
Syncrude lease no. 22 - Artifacts . . . 2061
Taber. Central School . . . 1580
Taber - History . . . 3264, 3265
Tail Creek - History . . . 2941
Tailfeathers, Gerald . . . 1118
Talbot - Description . . . 3504
Talbot - History . . . 2954
Tarot . . . 1314
Tatanga Mani (Stoney Indian) . . . 2837
Tattooing . . . 2042
Taxation . . . 2084
Taxation of estate . . . 2129
Teachers - Alberta . . . 1530, 1566
Teachers' assistants - Alberta . . . 1502
Teachers colleges - Alberta . . . 1602
Teachers - Edmonton . . . 1538
Technology and civilization . . . 2746
Tecumseh (H.M.C.S.) . . . 2748
Teepee Creek - History . . . 3270
Tees - Schools . . . 1573
Tees. United Church . . . 264
Telephones . . . 2329
Television in education . . . 1470, 1503
Temperance . . . 1763
Temporary Absence Program in Alberta . . . 1818
Theatre . . . 1255, 1258
Theatre - Edmonton . . . 1259
Thompson, David - Juvenile literature . . . 826
Thompson, David - Poetry . . . 999
Thomson family . . . 2732
Thorsby. Our Lady of Victory Catholic Church . . . 385
Three Hills - History . . . 3038, 3079, 3098
Throne - History . . . 2953
Tiger Lily - Juvenile literature . . . 773
Tilley. Bethany Lutheran Church . . . 426
Tofield - History . . . 2886, 3195, 3275
Tomahawk - History . . . 3095
Tongues, gift of *see* Charismatic movement
Tory, Henry Marshall . . . 1596
Tourist industry - Alberta . . . 2231
Toys - Exhibitions . . . 1180
Trade dollars . . . 2194
Trade unions *see* Labour unions
Traffic courts - Alberta . . . 2481
Training programs for the unemployed . . . 2165
Transients . . . 1816
Transit workers - Calgary . . . 2197, 2315

Trapping . . . 3506
Trapping *see* Fur trade
Tricks . . . 1268, 1276, 1277, 1290, 1360, 1364
Trinity Evangelical Lutheran Church, Calgary . . . 302
Trinity Evangelical Lutheran Church, Edmonton . . . 349
Trinity United Church, Calgary . . . 413
Trinity United Church, Fort Macleod . . . 363
Trivett, Samuel . . . 182
Trochu - History . . . 2973, 3038
Trochu. St. John's Lutheran Church . . . 427
Trout Lake - Description . . . 1906, 2648
Tuberculosis among Metis . . . 1875
Turkish language - Pronunciation . . . 454
Turner, John Davenall . . . 1246
Turner Valley - Description . . . 168
Turner Valley - History . . . 3238
Twin Butte - History . . . 3077
Two Hills - History . . . 2904
Uganda - Languages . . . 462
Ugandan Asians in Calgary . . . 1964
Ukraine - Description . . . 1902
Ukraine - History . . . 2738
Ukrainian arts . . . 1136
Ukrainian Catholic Church - History . . . 255
Ukrainian Catholic Church in Calgary . . . 228, 371
Ukrainian Catholic Church in Edmonton . . . 344
Ukrainian Catholic Church in Mundare . . . 268, 269, 403
Ukrainian Catholic Church in Smoky Lake . . . 373
Ukrainian Catholic Women's Leagues . . . 1850
Ukrainian language . . . 504, 505, 517, 518
Ukrainian language - Dictionaries . . . 506
Ukrainian language - Pronunciation . . . 510
Ukrainian language - Text-books . . . 509, 511, 512, 513, 514, 515, 516
Ukrainian language - Vocabulary . . . 508
Ukrainian literature . . . 544
Ukrainian literature - Collections . . . 586
Ukrainian poetry . . . 540, 545
Ukrainian poetry - Collections . . . 559, 560
Ukrainian poets . . . 540
Ukrainian Women's Association of Canada. Saint John's Cathedral Branch . 1838
Ukrainian Youth Association, Edmonton . . . 1845
Ukrainians - Culture . . . 1902
Ukrainians - Folk tales . . . 2081
Ukrainians - History . . . 1981
Ukrainians in Alberta 702, 1941, 1950, 1952, 1956, 1973, 1974, 1978, 2001, 2002
Ukrainians in Canada . . . 1836, 1996, 1998, 2000
Ukrainians in Canada - History . . . 1838
Ukrainians in Edmonton . . . 1891, 1911
Ukrainians in Western Canada . . . 1935, 1992
Ukrainians - Juvenile literature . . . 2081

Ukrainka, Lesya 536
Ulliac, Joseph 3281
Undentified flying objects 157
Union of Alberta Municipalities 2101
Unions *see* Labour unions
United Church in Acme 261
United Church in Airdrie 438
United Church in Alix 264
United Church in Barrhead 404
United Church in Berwyn 275
United Church in Calgary 185, 288, 289, 303, 315, 401, 402, 413
United Church in Camrose 365
United Church in Carstairs 308, 412
United Church in Central Alberta 239
United Church in Claresholm 311
United Church in Clive 433
United Church in Coaldale 312
United Church in Coleman 356
United Church in Cowley 314
United Church in Daysland 266
United Church in Delburne 304
United Church in Drumheller 322
United Church in Edmonton 319, 327, 330, 331, 332, 333, 335, 348, 350, 351, 407, 437
United Church in Edson 353
United Church in Fairview 380
United Church in Fort Macleod 363
United Church in Fort Saskatchewan 3208
United Church in Grande Prairie 417
United Church in Hanna 310
United Church in Haynes 264
United Church in Irma 375
United Church in Lamont 364
United Church in Mayerthorpe 362
United Church in Medicine Hat 397
United Church in MedicineHat 394, 396
United Church in Morley 378
United Church in Namao 400
United Church in Peace River 239, 406
United Church in Pincher Creek 408
United Church in Ponoka 377, 409
United Church in Ranfurly 355
United Church in Sarcee Butte 398
United Church in Spirit River 278
United Church in Spruce Grove 418
United Church in Stony Plain 424
United Church in Tees 264
United Church in Turner Valley 168
United Church in Westlock 428
United Church in Wetaskiwin 436

United Farm Women of Alberta *see* Farm Women's Union of Alberta
United Farmers Association 2408, 2411
United Farmers of Alberta . . . 1514, 2400, 2407, 2432, 2440, 2441, 3356, 3460
United Farmers of Canada 2371
Universities - Entrance requirements 1614, 1615
Universities - Fiction 666, 745
University of Alberta - Collections 1117
University of Alberta - Description 2594
University of Alberta. Faculty of Extension 1592
University of Alberta. Faculty of Medicine - History 3376
University of Alberta. Faculty of Nursing - History 3384
University of Alberta - History 1593, 1599, 1601, 1608
University of Alberta. Hospital - History 3368
University of Alberta. Library 30, 31
University of Alberta. St. Stephen's College *see* St. Stephen's College
University of Calgary 56
University of Calgary. Student Counselling Services 1829
University of Lethbridge - History 1597, 1603
University Women's Club of Edmonton 1832, 1846
Urbanization - Alberta 2451
Urbanization - Canada 2450
U.S.A. - Foreign relations - Canada 2380
U.S.S.R. - Foreign relations - Canada 2372
Vanguard - Fiction 629, 630
Vauxhall - History 3282
Vegreville - History 2886, 2989, 3051, 3269
Vegreville - Hospitals 3379
Vegreville. St. Joseph's Church 3269
Vegreville. St. Martin of Tours Catholic Parish 199
Vegreville. St Martin's School 1587
Ventriloquism 1254
Vermilion Lakes - Description 3314
Vermilion River (County) - Politics 2467
Vermilion (district) - Description 3492
Vermilion (district) - History 2902, 3283
Vermilion (district) - Schools 1576
Vermilion (town). St. Saviour's Anglican Parish 415
Veteran - History 2852, 2853, 3284
Veteran - Pictorial views 2852
Veterinary medicine 3418, 3452
Vietnamese in Edmonton 1954
Viking - History 3276
Vilna - History 3290
Vimy. Our Lady of Victory Catholic Church 429
Vocational education - Alberta 1546
Volunteer agencies 1732
Volunteer workers 2483
Volunteers in correctional institutions 1776
Voyages and travels 2628
Voyages and travels - Juvenile literature 2747

Vulcan - History 2993, 3285
Wabamun Lake - History 3010
Wabamun Lake - Recreation 1622
Wabasca - Description 2648
Wainwright. Grace Lutheran Church 432
Wainwright - History 2902, 3100
Wallace, Robert Charles 1610
Walsh, James Morrow - Drama 1078
Walsh, James Morrow - Juvenile literature 598, 715
Walter, John 2970
Wandering River - History 3287
Warburg - History 2923
Wardens, park *see* Park rangers
Ware, John 3424
Warner - History 3289
Waskahegan Trail 1705
Waskatenau - Fiction 756
Waskatenau - History 3290
Water resources 2110, 2113, 2121, 2122, 2126, 2128, 2246, 2569, 3346
Waterhole - History 3135
Waterton Lakes National Park - Artifacts 2018, 2055
Waterton Lakes National Park - Description 2677, 2693
Waterton Lakes National Park - History 1677
Waterton Lakes National Park - Recreation 1702
Watson Lake - Fiction 811
Watson, Sheila 567, 587
Welfare, public *see* Social assistance
Wesley United Church, Calgary 303
Wesley United Church, Edmonton 350
West central Alberta *see* Alberta, west central
Westerdale - History 3295
Western alienation *see* Separatism
Western Canada Bibliographic Information Centre 28
Western Canada - Bibliography 10
Western Canada - Description 2642
Western Canada - Economic conditions 1716, 2094, 2095, 2098, 2102
Western Canada - Folk tales 2083
Western Canada - History 2766, 2768, 2769, 2770, 2776, 2778, 2792, 2793, 2797, 2803, 2807, 2809
Western Canada - Social conditions 1716, 2102
Western Canadian literature 523
Western Canadian literature - Collections 552, 553, 554, 555, 557, 558, 565, 566, 572, 573, 576, 577, 578, 579, 580, 581, 583, 584, 585, 588, 589, 590, 591
Western Canadian poetry - Collections 574, 575, 592
Western Cartage & Storage Company 2328
Western Retail Lumbermen's Association 2247
Western separatism *see* Separatism
Western Stock Growers' Association 3407, 3414
Westlock - History 3094

Westlock - Hospitals . . . 3378
Westlock. United Church . . . 428
Westminster Presbyterian Church, Chauvin . . . 440
Westminster United Church, Edmonton . . . 351
Wetaskiwin. Bethel Lutheran Church . . . 434
Wetaskiwin. Calvary Lutheran Church . . . 435
Wetaskiwin - Commerce . . . 2235
Wetaskiwin Co-operative Association . . . 3439
Wetaskiwin. First United Church . . . 436
Wetaskiwin - History . . . 2863, 3019, 3215
Wetaskiwin - Schools . . . 1532
Wheat . . . 3438
Wheeler, Arthur Oliver . . . 2536
White Creek - History . . . 3301
Whitecourt - History . . . 3181
Whitla - History . . . 3297
Whyte Gallery *see* Peter Whyte Gallery, Banff
Wiebe, Rudy . . . 525, 530
Wild flowers - Alberta . . . 3316
Wilderness areas . . . 1616, 1617, 1618, 1619, 1650, 1678, 1679
Wildlife - Conservation . . . 3343
Wildlife - Conservation - Alberta . . . 1686, 3346
Wildlife - Conservation - Cypress Hills . . . 3344
Wildlife - Conservation - Fish Creek Provincial Park . . . 3347
Wildlife *see also* Animals, Birds
Wildwood - Description . . . 3482
William Roper Hull Home, Calgary . . . 1788
Williams, Daniel . . . 2501
Willing family . . . 2707
Willingdon - History . . . 2934
Willmore Wilderness Park . . . 1619
Willow Creek Historical Society . . . 2979
Willow Creek - History . . . 2979
Wills - Alberta . . . 2477
Wilson, Harry . . . 3268
Wilson, Thomas Edmund . . . 2653
Winfield - History . . . 3277
Winnifred - History . . . 2946
Winnipeg - History . . . 2784
Winterburn - History . . . 3303
Wiser-Stephens 1 (site) - Artifacts . . . 2024
Wolf Creek Indian Reserve - Archaeology . . . 2035
Women - Biography . . . 1745, 2715, 2726, 2727
Women - Education . . . 1613
Women - Employment . . . 1613
Women's Christian Temperance Union, *see* Alberta Women's Christian Temperance Union
Women's Institutes of Alberta *see* Alberta Women's Institutes, and also names of individual institutes
Women's rights . . . 1754, 1758, 1760

Women's sports 1623, 1706
Wood Buffalo National Park 1663
Woodville (school district) - History 3140
Woolsey, Thomas 210
Work 2156
World War I 2759
World War II 2761
World War II - Fiction 646, 665
Worth Commission *see* Alberta Report on Educational Planning
Writing-On-Stone - History 2025
Yamnuska Mountain 1666
Yeoford - History 3277
Young family 2714
Young Women's Christian Association, Edmonton 1839
Youngstown - History 3307
Youth - Attitudes 1737
Youth - Drug abuse 1785
Youth hostels 1620, 1621, 1665
Youville, Marie Marguerite d' 189
Yukon Territory - Description 2627, 2686
Zella - History 3308
Zion Lutheran Church, Peace Hill 276
Zion United Church, Ponoka 377
Zoology *see* Animals
4-H clubs 3395, 3454

SERIES INDEX

SERIES INDEX

A.C.A. Comix, 1. 1153
Alberta library in Ukrainian-Canadian Studies. 1998, 2000
Alberta Teachers' Association. Research monograph, 8. 1490
Alberta Teachers' Association. Research monograph, 16. 1474
Alberta Teachers' Association. Series on problems in education, 40. 1472
American Ethnological Society. Monographs, 6. 1943
Amethyst library. 721
Archaeological Society of Alberta. Newsletter, 28. 2043
Archaeological Society of Alberta. Lethbridge Centre. Project, 8, 13-16. 2014
Archaeological Society of Alberta. Lethbridge Centre. Project, 9-10. 2013
Archaeological Society of Alberta. Lethbridge Centre. Project, 11. 2012
Archaeological Society of Alberta. Lethbridge Centre. Project, 17-18. 2011
B.C. geographical series, 24. Occasional papers in geography. 2570
A Beaverbook for young Canadians. 1670
Bibliothèque ecclésie, 58. 177
A Bodima Book. 3300
Boreal Institute for Northern Studies. Occasional publications, 7. 2566
Boreal Institute for Northern Studies. Occasional publications, 12. 2527
Brad Forrest adventure series, 4. 720
Buckbooks. 847
Buckskin books, 9. 825
Cahiers de géographie, 1. 2515
Caledonia writing series. 911
Canada in transition series. 2299
Canada series. 2613
Canada West Foundation. Publication, 73-74/03. 2097
Canada West Foundation. Publication, 76-77/01. 2361
Canadian centennial series. 1963
Canadian Church Historical Society. Off-print, 7. 232
Canadian Church Historical Society. Offprint, 10. 234
Canadian composers facsimile series. 1417
Canadian crime classics. 1767, 1765
Canadian Energy Research Institute. Study, 3. 2187
Canadian Energy Research Institute. Study, 7. 2309
Canadian Energy Research Institute. Study, 8. 2111
Canadian Heritage Library. 1127, 2888
Canadian Historical Association. Historical booklet, 310. 2507
Canadian history series, v4. 2739
Canadian history through the press series. 2401
Canadian library in Ukrainian studies. 586
Canadian Masonic Research Association. Papers, 28 & 29. 1837
Canadian Masonic Research Association. Papers, 72. 1843
Canadian Plains Studies. Occasional paper, 1. 1718
Canadian playwrights series. 1064
Canadian pocket book. 705
Canadian theses on microfiche, 3009. 1663
Canadian theses on microfiche, 8455. 2112
Canadian theses on microfiche, 10119. 2432
Canadian theses on microfiche, 16974. 1893

Canadian theses on microfiche, 16990. 1912
Canadian theses on microfiche, 17045. 2052
Canadian theses on microfiche, 17068. 2582
Canadian theses on microfiche, 17136. 1970
Canadian theses on microfiche, 17460. 443
Canadian theses on microfiche, 17471. 522
Canadian theses on microfiche, 17501. 448
Canadian theses on microfiche, 17542. 1791
Canadian theses on microfiche, 17562. 2199
Canadian theses on microfiche, 17576. 2128
Canadian theses on microfiche, 17589. 1725
Canadian theses on microfiche, 17598. 718
Canadian theses on microfiche, 17646. 1073
Canadian theses on microfiche, 17697. 2490
Canadian theses on microfiche, 17709. 2064
Canadian theses on microfiche, 17710. 1738
Canadian theses on microfiche, 17713. 2245
Canadian theses on microfiche, 17722. 2003
Canadian theses on microfiche, 17745. 1830
Canadian theses on microfiche, 19197. 1477
Canadian theses on microfiche, 19676. 2592
Canadian theses on microfiche, 19737. 2369
Canadian theses on microfiche, 19763. 2264
Canadian theses on microfiche, 19768. 2265
Canadian theses on microfiche, 19777. 2409
Canadian theses on microfiche, 19778. 1904
Canadian theses on microfiche, 19795. 1724
Canadian theses on microfiche, 19805. 1499
Canadian theses on microfiche, 19810. 1964
Canadian theses on microfiche, 19814. 2294
Canadian theses on microfiche, 19824. 2388
Canadian theses on microfiche, 20970. 1629
Canadian theses on microfiche, 20973. 1631
Canadian theses on microfiche, 21022. 2478
Canadian theses on microfiche, 21024. 2121
Canadian theses on microfiche, 21059. 1807
Canadian theses on microfiche, 21068. 2378
Canadian theses on microfiche, 21280. 1545
Canadian theses on microfiche, 21348. 2576
Canadian theses on microfiche, 21364. 1512
Canadian theses on microfiche, 21514. 1508
Canadian theses on microfiche, 21560. 2382
Canadian theses on microfiche, 21728. 547
Canadian theses on microfiche, 21747. 1712
Canadian theses on microfiche, 21758. 1742
Canadian theses on microfiche, 21792. 2180
Canadian theses on microfiche, 21804. 525
Canadian theses on microfiche, 21830. 2195
Canadian theses on microfiche, 21854. 2280
Canadian theses on microfiche, 21861. 2422

Canadian theses on microfiche, 21894. 2218
Canadian theses on microfiche, 21907. 1726
Canadian theses on microfiche, 21940. 1687
Canadian theses on microfiche, 21986. 1507
Canadian theses on microfiche, 22275. 2354
Canadian theses on microfiche, 22500. 3370
Canadian theses on microfiche, 23359. 444
Canadian theses on microfiche, 23365. 2234
Canadian theses on microfiche, 23669. 226
Canadian theses on microfiche, 23729. 3341
Canadian theses on microfiche, 23790. 2240
Canadian theses on microfiche, 23990. 2092
Canadian theses on microfiche, 24010. 2455
Canadian theses on microfiche, 24040. 2367
Canadian theses on microfiche, 24056. 3413
Canadian theses on microfiche, 24073. 2127
Canadian theses on microfiche, 24079. 1937
Canadian theses on microfiche, 24097. 2134
Canadian theses on microfiche, 24107. 3434
Canadian theses on microfiche, 24132. 2352
Canadian theses on microfiche, 24970. 496
Canadian theses on microfiche, 24978. 2016
Canadian theses on microfiche, 24983. 2020
Canadian theses on microfiche, 25001. 2406
Canadian theses on microfiche, 25012. 2366
Canadian theses on microfiche, 25042. 56
Canadian theses on microfiche, 25048. 2726
Canadian theses on microfiche, 25049. 2296
Canadian theses on microfiche, 25078. 2446
Canadian theses on microfiche, 25449. 2084
Canadian theses on microfiche, 26094. 521
Canadian theses on microfiche, 26693. 441
Canadian theses on microfiche, 26696. 2654
Canadian theses on microfiche, 26708. 1627
Canadian theses on microfiche, 26752. 1891
Canadian theses on microfiche, 26864. 2802
Canadian theses on microfiche, 26921. 1820
Canadian theses on microfiche, 26948. 1706
Canadian theses on microfiche, 26956. 3460
Canadian theses on microfiche, 27455. 548
Canadian theses on microfiche, 27509. 1731
Canadian theses on microfiche, 27628. 2177
Canadian theses on microfiche, 27638. 1884
Canadian theses on microfiche, 27643. 1652
Canadian theses on microfiche, 27695. 2289
Canadian theses on microfiche, 27757. 1828
Canadian theses on microfiche, 27766. 1831
Canadian theses on microfiche, 28495. 2024
Canadian theses on microfiche, 28536. 1944
Canadian theses on microfiche, 28539. 2219

Canadian theses on microfiche, 28806. 2577
Canadian theses on microfiche, 30502. 2773
Canadian theses on microfiche, 30507. 1639
Canadian theses on microfiche, 30525. 2544
Canadian theses on microfiche, 30563. 1682
Canadian theses on microfiche, 30582. 1813
Canadian theses on microfiche, 30588. 3347
Canadian theses on microfiche, 30613. 2519
Canadian theses on microfiche, 30626. 3398
Canadian theses on microfiche, 30664. 1784
Canadian theses on microfiche, 30676. 2113
Canadian theses on microfiche, 30689. 2564
Canadian theses on microfiche, 30752. 3151
Canadian theses on microfiche, 30774. 2135
Canadian theses on microfiche, 30790. 1684
Canadian theses on microfiche, 30797. 1730
Canadian theses on microfiche, 30810. 2489
Canadian theses on microfiche, 30834. 3334
Canadian theses on microfiche, 30852. 153
Canadian theses on microfiche, 31933. 2812
Canadian theses on microfiche, 31970. 2188
Canadian theses on microfiche, 31977. 3359
Canadian theses on microfiche, 31980. 22
Canadian theses on microfiche, 32003. 2207
Canadian theses on microfiche, 32012. 929
Canadian theses on microfiche, 32056. 2383
Canadian theses on microfiche, 32178. 2439
Canadian theses on microfiche, 32832. 1819
Canadian theses on microfiche, 32833. 1739
Canadian theses on microfiche, 33092. 2548
Canadian theses on microfiche, 33206. 1672
Canadian theses on microfiche, 34034. 19
Canadian theses on microfiche, 34043. 2198
Canadian theses on microfiche, 34051. 2130
Canadian theses on microfiche, 34054. 2131
Canadian theses on microfiche, 34081. 1987
Canadian theses on microfiche, 34088. 1823
Canadian theses on microfiche, 34141. 2086
Canadian theses on microfiche, 34160. 2529
Canadian theses on microfiche, 34166. 2186
Canadian theses on microfiche, 34167. 3342
Canadian theses on microfiche, 34204. 1598
Canadian theses on microfiche, 34220. 2563
Canadian theses on microfiche, 34229. 2567
Canadian theses on microfiche, 34230. 535
Canadian theses on microfiche, 34321. 1782
Canadian theses on microfiche, 34341. 1657
Canadian theses on microfiche, 34365. 2415
Canadian theses on microfiche, 34373. 2039
Canadian theses on microfiche, 34379. 2200

Canadian theses on microfiche, 34384. 1496
Canadian theses on microfiche, 34402. 1555
Canadian theses on microfiche, 34449. 2487
Canadian theses on microfiche, 34450. 1567
Canadian theses on microfiche, 34457. 2145
Canadian theses on microfiche, 34463. 1818
Canadian theses on microfiche, 35808. 2305
Canadian theses on microfiche, 35828. 3337
Canadian theses on microfiche, 36341. 3385
Canadian theses on microfiche, 36372. 2533
Canadian theses on microfiche, 36384. 3032
Canadian theses on microfiche, 36405. 2546
Canadian theses on microfiche, 36411. 2205
Canadian theses on microfiche, 36422. 2044
Canadian theses on microfiche, 36426. 1559
Canadian theses on microfiche, 36438. 2557
Canadian theses on microfiche, 36443. 743
Canadian theses on microfiche, 36448. 1678
Canadian theses on microfiche, 36455. 1075
Canadian theses on microfiche, 36456. 2232
Canadian theses on microfiche, 36460. 1976
Canadian theses on microfiche, 36466. 2513
Canadian theses on microfiche, 36493. 1740
Canadian theses on microfiche, 36494. 2248
Canadian theses on microfiche, 37260. 1637
Canadian theses on microfiche, 37273. 1651
Canadian theses on microfiche, 37297. 2046
Canadian theses on microfiche, 37298. 2047
Canadian theses on microfiche, 37316. 35
Canadian theses on microfiche, 37509. 2408
Canadian theses on microfiche, 38083. 2206
Canadian theses on microfiche, 38310. 229
Canadian theses on microfiche, 38424. 2871
Canadian theses on microfiche, 38452. 1951
Canadian theses on microfiche, 38575. 530
Canadian theses on microfiche, 40141. 2189
Canadian theses on microfiche, 40157. 1659
Canadian theses on microfiche, 40159. 2191
Canadian theses on microfiche, 40170. 2541
Canadian theses on microfiche, 40179. 2035
Canadian theses on microfiche, 40254. 1727
Canadian theses on microfiche, 40286. 1575
Canadian theses on microfiche, 40291. 968
Canadian theses on microfiche, 40342. 804
Canadian theses on microfiche, 40352. 2154
Canadian theses on microfiche, 40495. 2300
Canadian theses on microfiche, 40506. 1821
Canadian theses on microfiche, 40511. 1999
Canadian theses on microfiche, 40530. 1827
Canadian theses on microfiche, 40536. 2595

Canadian theses on microfilm, 1110. 2397
Canadian theses on microfilm, 1423. 2440
Canadian theses on microfilm, 1705. 1694
Canadian theses on microfilm, 2772. 2568
Canadian theses on microfilm, 2778. 1693
Canadian theses on microfilm, 2779. 1991
Canadian theses on microfilm, 3872. 2453
Canadian theses on microfilm, 4021. 3408
Canadian theses on microfilm, 4037. 1966
Canadian theses on microfilm, 4051. 1699
Canadian theses on microfilm, 4603. 1862
Canadian theses on microfilm, 4614. 1778
Canadian theses on microfilm, 4644. 1796
Canadian theses on microfilm, 4710. 2249
Canadian theses on microfilm, 4937. 1910
Canadian theses on microfilm, 5309. 3356
Canadian theses on microfilm, 6105. 1799
Canadian theses on microfilm, 6138. 1814
Canadian theses on microfilm, 6243. 3458
Canadian theses on microfilm, 6263. 2426
Canadian theses on microfilm, 6715. 2417
Canadian theses on microfilm, 6808. 2549
Canadian theses on microfilm, 6862. 2056
Canadian theses on microfilm, 7676. 2412
Canadian theses on microfilm, 7706. 1606
Canadian theses on microfilm, 7750. 2311
Canadian theses on microfilm, 8101. 1592
Canadian theses on microfilm, 8388. 3443
Canadian theses on microfilm, 8433. 1953
Canadian theses on microfilm, 8435. 2057
Canadian theses on microfilm, 8443. 3464
Canadian theses on microfilm, 8492. 1509
Canadian theses on microfilm, 8648. 2201
Canadian theses on microfilm, 8765. 2462
Canadian theses on microfilm, 8841. 2018
Canadian theses on microfilm, 8852. 200
Canadian theses on microfilm, 8898. 37
Canadian theses on microfilm, 8904. 2587
Canadian theses on microfilm, 8956. 1801
Canadian theses on microfilm, 9171. 2029
Canadian theses on microfilm, 9662. 2313
Canadian theses on microfilm, 10037. 1866
Canadian theses on microfilm, 10039. 1775
Canadian theses on microfilm, 10040. 171
Canadian theses on microfilm, 10042. 1776
Canadian theses on microfilm, 10045. 1777
Canadian theses on microfilm, 10062. 1487
Canadian theses on microfilm, 10090. 1549
Canadian theses on microfilm, 10136. 2348
Canadian theses on microfilm, 10152. 2435

Canadian theses on microfilm, 10162. 1695
Canadian theses on microfilm, 10177. 2584
Canadian theses on microfilm, 10180. 2585
Canadian theses on microfilm, 10183. 1511
Canadian theses on microfilm, 10194. 11
Canadian theses on microfilm, 10555. 2569
Canadian theses on microfilm, 10630. 2392
Canadian theses on microfilm, 11078. 2368
Canadian theses on microfilm, 11127. 1882
Canadian theses on microfilm, 11288. 2398
Canadian theses on microfilm, 11297. 2021
Canadian theses on microfilm, 11298. 1881
Canadian theses on microfilm, 11320. 1493
Canadian theses on microfilm, 11323. 1798
Canadian theses on microfilm, 11336. 1940
Canadian theses on microfilm, 11383. 1736
Canadian theses on microfilm, 13190. 1789
Canadian theses on microfilm, 13299. 1713
Canadian theses on microfilm, 13318. 2167
Canadian theses on microfilm, 13327. 1482
Canadian theses on microfilm, 13334. 2179
Canadian theses on microfilm, 13361. 2534
Canadian theses on microfilm, 13394. 1722
Canadian theses on microfilm, 13487. 2560
Canadian theses on microfilm, 13498. 1566
Canadian theses on microfilm, 13513. 1810
Canadian theses on microfilm, 13609. 2244
Canadian theses on microfilm, 13627. 1707
Canadian theses on microfilm, 13633. 2157
Canadian theses on microfilm, 13837. 1594
Canadian theses on microfilm, 13857. 2114
Canadian theses on microfilm, 13885. 2204
Canadian theses on microfilm, 13891. 500
Canadian theses on microfilm, 13898. 1600
Canadian theses on microfilm, 13903. 2288
Canadian theses on microfilm, 13933. 3324
Canadian theses on microfilm, 14021. 1570
Canadian theses on microfilm, 15178. 3336
Canadian theses on microfilm, 15180. 2160
Canadian theses on microfilm, 15217. 2364
Canadian theses on microfilm, 15244. 2610
Canadian theses on microfilm, 15257. 1668
Canadian theses on microfilm, 15272. 2559
Canadian theses on microfilm, 15276. 1676
Canadian theses on microfilm, 15336. 780
Canadian theses on microfilm, 15353. 2441
Canadian theses on microfilm, 15358. 1697
Canadian theses on microfilm, 15538. 1773
Canadian theses on microfilm, 15599. 2562
Canadian theses on microfilm, 28499. 1486

The Canadians. 1743, 1752, 2502, 2813
Canplay series. 1045
Carleton library, 97. 1917
Carleton library, 114. 2371
Carleton library, 122. 2275
Catholic action library, 16. 57
Catholic action library, 19. 163
Central and East European Ethno-Cultural Groups in Alberta
Study Project. Monographs, papers and reports, 1. 2006
Century Calgary historical series, v.1. 3189
Century Calgary historical series, v.2. 2949
Century Calgary historical series, v.3. 1852
Century Calgary historical series, v.4. 243
Century Calgary historical series, v.5. 2859
Century Calgary historical series, v.6. 2860
Chinook books, 1. 738
Coles Canadian collection. 224, 1809
Collection 'La gerbe d'or'. 769
Collection joie de lire. 170
Corgi books, T145. 1868
Cotman color series. 2634
Coulton, R.L. Miscellaneous memoirs, 4. 2023
Council of Planning Librarians. Exchange bibliography, 1260, 1261, 1262. . . . 9
Current inquiry into language and linguistics, 2. 467
Current inquiry into language and linguistics, 4. 465
Current inquiry into language and linguistics, 6. Slavic linguistics, 1. 454
Current inquiry into language and linguistics, 7. 3
Current inquiry into language and linguistics, 7. Sociolinguistics series, 3. . . 445
Current inquiry into language and linguistics, 12. Sociolinguistic series, 4. . . 453
Current inquiry into language and linguistics, 20. 452
Current inquiry into language and linguistics, 23. Slavic linguistics, 5. . . . 519
Current inquiry into language and linguistics, 24. 450
Current inquiry into language and linguistics, 25. Slavic linguistics, 7. . . . 447
Current inquiry into language and linguistics, 30. 449
Curriculum series, 32. 2727
A Dell book. 603
Denver Museum of Natural History. Proceedings, no. 11. 2066
Documentaire oblat. 203
Dome Petroleum Teaching Fellowship, 1968. 463
Dome Petroleum Teaching Fellowship, 1969. 1506
Drama at Calgary, playscript no.1. 1066
Edmonton social studies enterprise series, 4. 600
Environment series. 3344
Ethno-cultural Groups in Alberta Study Project. Monographs,
papers and reports, 3. 1914
An Exposition-Banner Book. 783
Famous regiments. 2760
Festival Singers choral series, E.I. 1014. 1388
Festival Singers choral series, E.I. 1015. 1406
Fiddlehead poetry books. 853

Fiddlehead poetry books, 244. 844
Focus on energy, 1. 2254
Focus on energy, 2. 2255
French writers of Canada series. 620
Frontier books, 1. . . . . 624, 2854
Frontier books, 2. 1770
Frontier books, 3. 2765
Frontier books, 4. . . . . 231, 597, 2236
Frontier books, 5. . . . . 2665, 2676
Frontier books, 6. 2621
Frontier books, 7. 1764
Frontier books, 8. 2675
Frontier books, 9. 2763
Frontier books, 10. 2673
Frontier books, 11. 1772
Frontier books, 12. 2762
Frontier books, 13. 2674
Frontier books, 14. 2800
Frontier books, 15. 2677
Frontier books, 16. 1768
Frontier books, 17. 2672
Frontier books, 18. 2811
Frontier books, 19-20, 27. 2664
Frontier books, 21. 2494
Frontier books, 22. 2691
Frontier books, 23. 1626
Frontier books, 24. 2671
Frontier books, 25. 2810
Frontier books, 26. 1769
Frontier books, 28. 2493
Frontier books, 29. 2321
Frontier books, 30. 2663
Frontier books, 31. 2764
Frontier books, 32. 2782
Frontier books, 33-34. 2679
Frontier books, 35. 227
Frontier books, 39-40. 2855
A frontier publication. 2495
Frontiers and pioneers. 715, 1753
Ginn Studies in Canadian History. Teacher's manual. 2286
Glenbow archives series, 1. 3407
Glenbow archives series, 2. 2737
Glenbow archives series, 3. 2540
Glenbow archives series, 4. 2411
Glenbow archives series, 5. 5
Glenbow archives series, 6. 1905
Glenbow-Art Gallery Catalogue, 2-1968. 1202
Glenbow Foundation. Occasional paper, 1. 73
Glenbow-Alberta Institute. Art Gallery. Catalogue, 3. 1199
Glenbow-Alberta Institute. Art series, 1. 1234

Glenbow-Alberta Institute. Art series, 2. 1118
Glenbow-Alberta Institute. Art series, 3. 1233
Glenbow-Alberta Institute. Art Series, 4. 1190
Glenbow-Alberta Institute. Historical paper, 1. 222
Glenbow-Alberta Institute. Historical paper, 2. 2616
Glenbow-Alberta Institute. Historical paper, 3. 2653
Glenbow-Alberta Institute. Occasional paper, 2. 2822
Glenbow-Alberta Institute. Occasional paper, 3. 72
Glenbow-Alberta Institute. Occasional paper, 4. 2657
Glenbow-Alberta Institute. Occasional paper, 5. 145
Glenbow-Alberta Institute. Occasional paper, 6. 2042
Good medicine books, 1. 2076
Good medicine books, 2. 1922
Good medicine books, 3. 1923
Good medicine books, 4. 2078
Good medicine books, 5. 1926
Good medicine books, 6. 90
Good medicine books, 7. 2079
Good medicine books, 8. 2080
Good medicine books, 9. 1896
Good medicine books, 10. 1921
Good medicine books, 12. 1919
Good medicine books, 13. 1924
Good medicine books, 14. 1925
Good medicine books, 15. 1918
Great stories of Canada. 725
Great stories of Canada, 7. 826
Great stories of Canada, 10. 764
Great stories of Canada, 12. 2772
Great stories of Canada, 14. 2843
Great stories of Canada, 17. 2799
Great stories of Canada, 22. 829
Gronk, series 4, 8. 979
Haydn booklet, 1. 902
Hearthstone books. 1902
Heritage books, 2. 746
Historical heritage series. 2194
Historical phonology of the Slavic languages, 4. 510
Historical Society of Alberta, v.1 241
Historical Society of Alberta, v.2 2158
Historical Society of Alberta, v.3 2824
Historical Society of Alberta. Whoop-up Country Chapter.
Occasional paper, 4. 2323
Historical Society of Alberta. Whoop-up Country Chapter.
Occasional paper, 5. 3436
Historical Society of Alberta. Whoop-up Country Chapter.
Occasional paper, 8. 3194
Historical Society of Alberta. Whoop-up Country Chapter.
Occasional paper, 9. 3503

Historical Society of Alberta.Whoop-Up County Chapter.
Occasional paper, 7 2341
History of Canadian cities. 3011
Horizon books. 68, 93, 235, 618
House of Anansi poetry series, 38. 949
How they lived in Canada. 1872
HRI observation series, 10. 2287
Hudson's Bay Record Society. Publication, v.26. 2830
Iroquois Press sacred series, 6. 1426
Issues in Canadian history. 2447
Laurentian library, 14. 742
Library Association of Alberta. Occasional papers, 1. 24
Mercury series. History series. Paper, no. 1. 2807
A Micky Hades lecture book. 1291
The New Canadian Geography Project, regional pattern series. 1733
New drama, 1. 1087
Newcommen address. 2292
Nineteenth century American literature. 2117
Oeuvre des tracts, 412. 162
Onomastica, 43. 2661
Open letter, 3rd ser, no. 1. 587
A Panther book, 999. 646
Papers in linguistics. Monograph series, 1. 459
Papers in linguistics. Monograph series, 2. 451
Papers in linguistics. Monograph series, 3. 464
People and places in Canada. 2282, 2547, 3474
A poetry north publication. 940
Portraits of Canadians in struggle series. 3372
Prairie books. 2620, 3421
Prairie play series, 2. 1070
A Provost publication. 3205
A Railfare book. 2337
A region of America book. 2553
Regional studies of Canada. 2586
Ryerson paperbacks, 34. 532
Ryerson travel library. 2622
S R supplements, 8. 94
Scholarly reprint series. 1908
The secret circle mysteries, 8. 619
Selected academic readings. 1947
Self-counsel series. . 2472, 2474, 2475, 2477, 2481, 2482, 2484, 2488, 2491, 2492
Slavic linguistics, 3. 466
Social credit in Alberta, its background and development, 3. 1715
Social credit in Alberta, its background and development, 4. 2425
Social credit in Alberta, its background and development, 5. 2427
Social credit in Alberta, its background and development, 6. 218
Social credit in Alberta, its background and development, 8. 2445
Social credit in Alberta, its background and development, 10. 2420
The social history of Canada. 1754
The Social history of Canada, 29. 2602

Sociolinguistics series, 1. 456
Sociolinguistics series, 2. 462
Southwestern studies. Monograph, 25. 3441
Story of Canada series. 2801
Studies in Canadian literature. 538
Studies in land use history and landscape change, 7. 2525
Studies in land use history and landscape change. National park series, 2. . 2575
Studies in land use history and landscape change. National park series, 3. . 2524
Studies in land use history and landscape change. National park series, 5. . 1674
A studio book. 3312
A Swallow paperback, 53. 752
Syncrude Canada. Environmental research monograph, 1973-4. 2062
Syncrude Canada. Environmental research monograph, 1974-2. 2061
Syncrude Canada. Environmental research monograph, 1978-2. 2045
Talonplays. 1085, 1090
Theatre for young people. 1256
To the builders of the Peace series. 2553, 3451
Traveller's Canada. 2618, 2626, 2627
Tubinger Geographische Studien, 18. 2532
Turnstone Press. Poetry series 1, no.7. 922
Ukrains'ka vil'na akademiia nauk. Literatura, 7. 542
University of Alberta studies in geography. 2579
University of Alberta. Archives. Manuscript group, 2. 1609
University of Alberta. Archives. Manuscript group, 3/2. 1610
University of Alberta. Archives. Manuscript group, 7. 2647
University of Alberta. Archives. Manuscript group, 9/2. . . . . 1611, 2808, 3459
University of Alberta. Department of Agricultural Economics and
Rural Sociology. Applied Research Bulletin, 14. 1686
University of Alberta. Department of Agricultural Economics and
Rural Sociology. Research bulletin, 1. 2212
University of Alberta. Department of Agricultural Economics.
Research bulletin, 2. 2148
University of Alberta. Department of Agricultural Economics.
Research bulletin, 4. 2217
University of Alberta. Department of Agricultural Economics and
Rural Sociology. Research bulletin, 3. 3444
University of Alberta. Department of Agricultural Economics and
Rural Sociology. Research bulletin, 5. 3419
University of Alberta. Department of Agricultural Economics and
Rural Sociology. Special report, 4. 144
University of Alberta. Department of Agricultural Economics and
Rural Sociology. Special report, 5. 2147
University of Alberta. Department of Agricultural Economics and
Rural Sociology. Special report, 6. 3445
University of Alberta. Department of Agricultural Economics and
Rural Sociology. Special report, 7. 3446
University of Alberta. Department of Agricultural Economics and
Rural Sociology. Special report, 8. 1714
University of Alberta. Department of Anthropology. Occasional paper, 1. . . 2028

University of Alberta. Department of Extension. Agricultural Economics.
Technical Bulletin, 1. 2216
University of Alberta. Department of Political Science. Occasional papers, 4. 2463
University of Alberta. Department of Political Science. Occasional papers, 5. 2144
University of Calgary studies in history, 1. 2746
University of Calgary studies in history, 2. 2470
University of Calgary. Department of Archaeology. Occasional papers, 1. . . 2058
University of Calgary. Department of Archaeology. Occasional papers, 2. . . 2053
University of Calgary. Department of Archaeology. Occasional papers, 3. . . 2009
University of Calgary. Department of Archaeology. Occasional papers, 4. . . 2030
University of Manitoba. Center for Settlement Studies. Series 2.
Research reports, no.6. 2588
Urban studies series. 2516
Waterloo sacred choral library. 1399, 1410, 1411, 1414
Waterloo secular choral library. 1404
We built Canada. 1760
Western Canadian literature for youth. 565, 573, 578, 579,
580, 585, 588, 589, 590, 2083
Western geographical series, 11. 2169
Western geographical series, 15. 2531
Working papers in linguistic series, 1. 520
World discovery program, 1. 2617
You're unique. 790, 791, 792